Lemberg, Lwów, L'viv, 1914–1947:
Violence and Ethnicity in a Contested City

Central European Studies

Charles Ingrao, founding editor
Gary B. Cohen, editor
Howard Louthan, editor
Franz A. J. Szabo, editor
Daniel L. Unowsky, editor

Lemberg, Lwów, L'viv, 1914–1947:
Violence and Ethnicity in a Contested City

Christoph Mick

Purdue University Press
West Lafayette, Indiana

Copyright 2016 by Purdue University. All rights reserved.

Printed in the United States of America.

Licensed edition with permission from Otto Harrassowitz publishing company, Wiesbaden © Otto Harrassowitz GmbH & Co. KG, Wiesbaden, 2011.

The translation of this work was funded by Geisteswissenschaften International—Translation Funding for Humanities and Social Sciences from Germany, a joint initiative of the Fritz Thyssen Foundation, the German Federal Foreign Office, the collecting society VG WORT and the Börsenverein des Deutschen Buchhandels (German Publishers & Booksellers Association).

Cataloging-in-Publication data on file at the Library of Congress.

Mick, Christoph, author.
 [Kriegserfahrungen in einer multiethnischen Stadt. English]
 Lemberg, Lwów, L'viv, 1914-1947: Violence and Ethnicity in a Contested City / by Christoph Mick.
    pages cm.—(Central European studies)
 Includes bibliographical references and index.
        ISBN 978-1-55753-671-6 (pbk.: alk. paper)
        ISBN 978-1-61249-391-6 (epdf)
        ISBN 978-1-61249-392-3 (epub)
        1. L'viv (Ukraine)—History—20th century.
        2. World War, 1914-1918—Ukraine—L'viv.
        3. World War, 1939-1945—Ukraine—L'viv.
        4. Jews—Ukraine—L'viv.
        5. L'viv (Ukraine)—Ethnic relations.
I. Title.
 DK508.95.L86M53513 2016
 947.7'9—dc23
                                    2015027352

Cover image: Austrian postcard from 1915, commemorating the reconquest of L'viv, June 22, 1915.

To Helen

Contents

Foreword	ix
Preface	xi
Chapter 1: Introduction	1
Chapter 2: World War I	17
Chapter 3: The Fight for the City	137
Chapter 4: Reconstruction and Remembrance, 1920–1939	209
Chapter 5: World War II	259
Chapter 6: Conclusion	373
Appendix: Maps	379
Acronyms	383
Bibliography	387
Index	427

Foreword

The territories of today's Baltic states, western Belarus, and western Ukraine have had a particularly complex and, at times, troubled history over the last one hundred years. They belonged to the Tsarist and Habsburg empires before 1914 and saw much fighting and repeated changes in political control during and just after World War I. During the 1920s and 1930s they were governed by the independent Baltic and Polish republics, and then after autumn 1939 experienced new devastating warfare and shifted back and forth between Nazi and Soviet control. After 1945 they all fell under the rule of the Soviet Union, which imposed on them its political, economic, and social systems.

Christoph Mick's book tells a compelling story of how the inhabitants—Catholic Poles, Catholic and Orthodox Ukrainians, Jews, and others—in the old capital of Austrian Galicia experienced the traumas of the two world wars and the successive sweeping political changes. This book originated as a *Habilitation* thesis for the University of Tübingen and was initially published by Otto Harrasowitz Verlag in 2010 as *Kriegserfahrungen in einer Multiethnischen Stadt: Lemberg, 1914-1947 [War Experiences in a Multiethnic City: Lemberg/Lwów/L'viv, 1914-1947]*. This English version represents a revised and shortened version of the German volume. It is a study of great originality based on a large body of archival research in L'viv, Kiev, Warsaw, and Moscow as well as a wealth of contemporary printed sources and scholarly studies. In Mick's accounting, political control over the city changed hands some seven times between 1914 and 1947. Before World War I, there were serious political and social tensions among Poles, Ukrainians/Ruthenians, and Jews in Lemberg/Lwów/L'viv, but only limited and infrequent violence. The changes of control over the city during the war led to new power relations, increased inter-group frictions, and episodes of shocking violence. After a brief period of Ukrainian rule, incorporation into an independent Polish Republic in late November 1918 led to intensified civil conflict and new large-scale attacks on Jews. Over the next two decades, the Polish government tried to suppress Ukrainian nationalism in the city and the surrounding region and persecuted

Ukrainian nationalist leaders. Antisemitism increased sharply during the 1930s. After the outbreak of World War II, the city experienced first Soviet occupation, then Nazi occupation, and finally Soviet conquest. The Nazis deported and murdered nearly all of the large Jewish population, and at the end of the war the Soviet forces expelled the Poles who had not already been deported or murdered.

Mick offers a vivid analysis of how the city's inhabitants experienced the changes in political control and government policies toward the various national and religious groups. He argues persuasively for focusing on just how individuals and groups experienced the events that transpired and how they perceived their meaning if we are to understand the impacts and legacies. Mick demonstrates persuasively how the longer term ethnic and national politics and ideology of the inhabitants themselves shaped their experiences and understandings of war and peace and how they were prepared to deal with each other. The wide scope of Mick's study and his compelling account of the successive changes in relations among the different language and religious groups who once lived as neighbors in Lemberg/Lwów/L'viv adds fascinating new dimensions to our knowledge of the travails of Central and East-Central Europe during the bloody twentieth century. The book is a most welcome addition indeed to the series, Central European Studies.

Gary B. Cohen
Series editor

Preface

This is the revised and shortened English edition of my book *Kriegserfahrungen in einer multiethnischen Stadt: Lemberg 1914-1947* published in 2010 in the series of the German Historical Institute in Warsaw by Harrassowitz. I cut those parts of the book which did not deal explicitly with war and war remembrance and added some material which had become available since the German edition was published. Some of the ideas I fleshed out in certain chapters of this book I had discussed previously in other publications, journals and edited volumes, but all were revised and updated for this publication.

The translation of the book was funded by the program *Geisteswissenschaften International*, jointly financed by the Fritz Thyssen Stiftung, VG Wort, Börsenverein des Deutschen Buchhandels and the German Foreign Office. I am very grateful to these institutions.

The research for the book was supported by a three month grant of the German Historical Institute in Warsaw. The Alexander von Humboldt Foundation awarded me a Feodor Lynen grant which gave me the opportunity to spend 1998 in Warsaw. Special Research Area (*Sonderforschungsbereich*) 437 of the German Research Foundation on "War experiences, war and society in modern times" at the University of Tübingen made this project possible. I am grateful to the chairmen of the *Sonderforschungsbereich* Anton Schindling and Dieter Langewiesche for their support. The Institute for Eastern European History and Area Studies at the University of Tübingen was my academic home for 20 years. The directors of the Institute, Dietrich Geyer and Dietrich Beyrau, always encouraged me. I would also like to thank the many colleagues who gave me the opportunity to present my research at conferences and workshops or who commented on papers and chapters: Omer Bartov, Ray Brandon, John-Paul Himka, Jaroslav Hrytsak, Andreas Kappeler, and Timothy Snyder. I am deeply grateful for the good company of friends and colleagues, whether in Tübingen, L'viv, Warsaw, Moscow, Kiev/Kyiv, Berlin, Vienna, Paris or Kenilworth, in particular Vasyl' Rasevych, Andrej Doronin, Włodzimierz Borodziej, Robert Traba, Ralph Schattkowsky,

Christian Harde, Ingrid Schierle, Klaus Gestwa, Benno Ennker, Bianka Pietrow-Ennker, Gerd Braitmaier, Katrin Steffen, Rainer Horn and Roberta Bivins. A special thank-you goes to the archivists. Myroslava Djadjuk and Tanja Semenova of the Central Historical State Archive of Ukraine in L'viv were particularly helpful.

The History Department of the University of Warwick—my new academic home—gave me the opportunity to finish the project.

I would like to thank my translator Helen Schoop for her work.

My special thanks go to Gary B. Cohen for recommending and accepting the book for this series and to Charles T. Watkinson and Katherine M. Purple, the former director and current managing editor of Purdue University Press. I know that I tested their patience but they always remained supportive. I am also grateful to Dianna Gilroy, who helped with preparing the book for publication.

Concerning the spelling and transliteration of names and places, over the last 100 years L'viv and East Galicia experienced many regime changes and belonged to several different states. Consequently every place has several different names. If there was a well-established English name (according to Merriam Webster dictionary), I used this name: therefore L'viv (the English transcription of the Ukrainian Львів) and not Lviv or Lvov (deriving from Russian Львов) but Kiev (deriving from Russian Киев) and not Kyiv or Kyïv (from Ukrainian Київ). In all other cases I used the names which were most common in contemporary sources and administration.

Christoph Mick
July 2015, Leamington Spa

CHAPTER 1

Introduction

In the twentieth century, L'viv (Ukrainian: Львів, Polish: Lwów, German: Lemberg, Russian Львов), now a city in Ukraine, experienced war not just once but many times. Between 1914 and 1947, the city went through seven regime changes and was shelled by Russian, Ukrainian, German, and Soviet artillery and bombed by German and Soviet planes. In November 1918, Poles and Ukrainians fought one another for control of the city. Twenty-five years later, both sides were prepared to battle it out again. During the same period, the city's Jewish population lived through several pogroms and experienced repeated bouts of anti-Semitic violence up until the time when almost all the Jews of L'viv were murdered by Nazi Germany. After World War II, the Soviet government forced the Polish population to leave the city. A quick look at the ethnic and religious composition of the population shows how catastrophically the city was affected by two world wars. In 1914 half of the city's population was Roman Catholic (mostly Poles), 28 percent were Jewish, and 18 percent were Greek Catholic (about two-thirds of them Ruthenians/Ukrainians[1]).[2] By 1947, L'viv had become an almost homogeneously Ukrainian city. The overwhelming majority of the population was Ukrainian, with Russians as the city's largest ethnic minority. Approximately 80 percent of the city's inhabitants had arrived during or after the war.

This book is about the connections between war, nation-building, and the increasing brutality of ethnic conflicts in L'viv. Before the Great War, the city was a center of both Ukrainian and Polish national movements and home to a large and vibrant Jewish community. The decades before the Great War were mostly peaceful, but there was one big problem. Imperial and national projects intersected in the city. Neither Polish nor Ukrainian nationalists could imagine their future nation-states without L'viv. The Russian Empire wanted the city, and Austria-Hungary did not want to relinquish it. Analyzing the history of L'viv means studying imperial projects, ethnic and national conflicts, successful and failed attempts at state-building, different occupation regimes, "ethnic cleansing," nationally motivated mass murder, and national socialist genocide. But this presents only one side of the picture. L'viv was also a melting pot of cultures; in the words of the Austrian author Joseph Roth, it was a "city of blurred boundaries."[3]

This book follows an approach based on what is termed *Erfahrungsgeschichte*, or the history of experience. The German words *Erlebnis* and *Erfahrung* both translate as "experience," but their meaning is subtly different. *Erlebnis* means an event together with the emotions experienced during the event, while *Erfahrung* is the result of a successful interpretation of an event, whereby the event is given a meaning. This differentiation mirrors the findings of the sociology of knowledge.[4] Peter Berger and Thomas Luckmann noted that human reality is a social construct. Languages, institutions, and traditions are part of a framework that shapes how people perceive reality.[5] The German historian Reinhart Koselleck introduced this approach in historiography. He defines *Erfahrung* (experience) as a process in which perception, interpretation, and actions are continuously adjusting to one another. Expectations of the future together with people's previous conditioning affect this continual process of adjusting experiences. Expectations and conditioning function as the filters through which events are perceived and provide models with the help of which reality is interpreted. With events mediated by expectations and conditioning, the selfsame events can result in completely different experiences. This is the sense in which I use the term *experience*—in other words, in the sense of *Erfahrung* rather than *Erlebnis*.[6] I am not looking for the *one* historical "truth." I accept that there are many different "constructions of reality" and that there are many subjective "truths" that may contradict one another. I assume (unless I have evidence of the contrary) that historical subjects really believe what they are saying.

I start with four assumptions: (1) ethnicity and religion were the most important identity markers in L'viv and deeply influenced individual war experiences; (2) ethnic, social, and political relations developed within the frameworks set by the respective state or occupying power; (3) different war experiences resulted in postwar conflicts about the meaning of the respective war, and these conflicts about the meaning of events played an important role in marking the boundaries between ethnic groups; and (4) the experiences of World War I, the Polish-Ukrainian War of 1918–19, and the Polish-Soviet War of 1920 shaped the perceptions and actions of L'viv Poles, Ukrainians, and Jews in World War II.

This book focuses on the period of the two world wars and draws on a multitude of local histories.[7] Books on the German occupation of Eastern Europe during World War II fill whole libraries. While Warsaw and many cities of west and central Poland are well researched, L'viv and East Galicia have not received the attention they deserve. In communist Poland and Soviet Ukraine, many war-related topics were taboo. Authors were obliged to adhere strictly to Soviet interpretations.[8] This only changed after 1989. Polish and Ukrainian historians have since been making up for lost time and have begun to research the Polish-Ukrainian War of 1918–19, the Soviet and German occupations, "ethnic cleansing," the Nazi genocide of Jews, and the Polish-Ukrainian conflict in World War II.[9]

The "myth of Galicia" (understood as the imagined peaceful coexistence of many cultures and ethnicities prior to World War I) has interested historians and the public even outside Poland and Ukraine.[10] A number of books and articles on L'viv during the two world wars have recently been published. Polish historian Henryka Kramarz analyzed the work of the city administration in World War I, while Russian historian Aleksandra Bakhturina studied the Russian occupation policy. German historian Torsten Wehrhahn wrote a history of the West Ukrainian People's Republic. The fate of the Polish population in L'viv during World War II and in the immediate postwar period has been researched by Grzegorz Hryciuk, Tarik Amar, and William Risch.[11]

In most cases, Jewish historians concentrate on the Jewish, Ukrainian historians on the Ukrainian, and Polish historians on the Polish history of L'viv. "The others" are only interesting insofar as they are relevant for the "own." In this approach, the multiethnic character of L'viv merely plays out as a backdrop to the respective national histories. The sufferings of the "own" and the crimes of the "others" take center stage. I chose to take another road and analyzed the interactions between Poles, Ukrainians, and Jews without arguing for any specific national point of view.

My research is based on three types of sources. The first type consists of "ego documents," or diaries, letters, memoirs, and autobiographies. I used sources that had been produced as close to the events recounted as possible. There is, however, one caveat. It was difficult to catch the perspectives of workers, peasants, clerks, craftsmen, and petty tradesmen. Most autobiographical texts that survived the war were written by members of the elite. In some cases, I was lucky and found documents where the voices of nonelite members of the community could be heard. Immediately after the pogrom of November 1918, members of the Jewish community interviewed pogrom victims, many of them petty tradesmen, and collected written accounts of the events.[12] In the interwar period, the Polish Society for the Study of the Defense of Lwów and Little Eastern Poland encouraged people to write about their experiences of the Polish-Ukrainian War of 1918–19. The Society also collected the memoirs and diaries of eyewitnesses.[13] Essays written by Polish children after their evacuation to Iran in 1942–43 offer an unusual perspective of the Soviet occupation of 1939–41.[14] The *Archiwum Wschodni* (Eastern Archive) of the Polish journal *Karta* holds copies of eyewitness accounts by Polish officials, policemen, and railway men who were deported to the Soviet Union between 1939 and 1941.[15]

Karta has also organized several essay competitions on life in the Polish eastern territories and holds private collections of accounts by former inhabitants of the *Kresy*. Eyewitness accounts of Jewish life in the Jewish Historical Institute in Warsaw under Soviet and German occupation were consulted.[16]

The second type of source is official documents, or reports and other documents from regional and local administrative bodies (Austria-Hungary, the Second Polish Republic, and the Soviet Union), the regional administrations of the various occupying powers (Russia for the period of 1914–15, the Soviet Union for 1939–41, and Germany for 1941–44), political organizations, and many other institutions. The most important collections are held in various archives in L'viv. To reconstruct the perspectives of the respective central governments, I also worked in archives in Vienna, Moscow, Berlin, Warsaw, and Kiev (Kyiv).

The third type is published sources: published memoirs and diaries; local, regional, and national newspapers; journals; and also monuments, cemeteries, buildings, rituals, symbols, and celebrations.

Before plunging into World War I, the account starts with a brief sketch of the city and the state of interethnic relations in L'viv in 1914.

L'viv was the capital of the Austrian Crown land known as the Kingdom of Galicia and Lodomeria (often referred to simply as Galicia). It had become a part of Austria after the first partition of Poland in 1772. For the following one hundred years, German was the language of the administration, and the city of L'viv was governed by appointed mayors and officials, many of them from Bohemia or the German-speaking provinces of the Austrian Empire.[17] This changed in 1867 when Austria's defeat in the Austro-Prussian War spurred a period of reforms. In the years that followed, the Crown land was given more and more rights, and the Polish elites used them to strengthen their political and cultural hold on the region.

Galicia, however, was not exclusively inhabited by Poles. In 1869 the Crown land had a population (excluding the army) of 5,481,000. Within the space of less than fifty years, the population had almost doubled, and by 1910 it numbered 7,966,527. In the western part of Galicia (west of the river San), more than 88 percent of the population were Roman Catholics, almost all of them Poles. In East Galicia (east of the river San), only about 25 percent of the population were Roman Catholic; more than 60 percent of the population were Greek Catholic, most of them Ruthenians/Ukrainians. And 8 percent of the population in West Galicia and 12 percent in East Galicia were Jewish (see table 1.1).

All East Galician districts had substantial resident populations of Jews and Poles. Three-quarters of the agrarian population were Ukrainian, while in the towns and cities Jews and Poles were the majority population. Urbanization was slow, but this did not prevent the capital L'viv from expanding with impressive speed. The city's population rose from 87,000 in 1869 to 212,000 in 1914.

	West Galicia	%	East Galicia	%	Galicia, total	%
Roman Catholic	2,381,940	88.6	1,349,630	25.3	3,731,570	46.5
Greek Catholic	86,585	3.2	3,294,420	61.7	3,381,005	42.1
Jewish	213,173	7.9	658,722	12.4	871,895	10.9
Protestant	7953	0.3	30,371	0.6	28,324	0.5
Orthodox	165	0.0	2680	0.0	2845	0.0

Table 1.1. Population in the Crown land Galicia and Lodomeria according to denomination/religion (1910).[18]

Year	Total	RC	%	GC	%	Jewish	%	Other	%
1869	87,100	46,300	53.2	12,400	14.2	26,300	30.2	2100	2.4
1890	127,900	67,300	52.6	21,900	17.2	36,100	28.1	2600	2.1
1910	206,100	105,500	51.2	39,300	19.2	57,400	27.8	3900	1.8

Note. RC = Roman Catholic; GC = Greek Catholic.

Table 1.2. Population of L'viv (which in 1910 included 11,000 soldiers), according to religion/denomination (rounded to the next hundred).

In 1910 (see table 1.2) 51.2 percent of L'viv inhabitants were Roman Catholics (almost all of them Poles), 27.8 percent were Jewish and 19.2 percent Greek Catholics. A considerable number of Greek Catholics living in L'viv cannot be easily categorized as either Polish or Ukrainian. This also applies to a small percentage of the Jewish population. Some had mixed loyalties, and others identified with the Polish nation. In addition to Ruthenians, Poles, and Jews, there were also around three hundred Armenians living in the city. They had their own Armenian Catholic archbishop, and over the centuries they had become ardent Polish patriots. The city's population also included Catholic Germans, Protestants, and a small Russian Orthodox community.[19]

The legal and political framework of the Austrian Empire changed dramatically in the last third of the nineteenth century. The previously powerless Galician Diet was reformed and given more rights, particularly with regard to culture, education, welfare, and agriculture. It also oversaw the local and regional administration. It was elected by four curiae, which privileged the nobility and the wealthier Polish population. Between 1848 and 1915, Vienna always appointed a Polish politician as governor of Galicia, and the "Polish Club"—the name given to the Polish deputies of the Imperial Parliament in Vienna—became an influential force, often supporting the government. Many Poles held ministerial positions. Galician regional and local administrations were dominated by Poles, but a few Ukrainians also held positions in the administration and the judicial system.[20] In the 1870s and 1880s, the Polish elites thoroughly Polonized schools and university education. Polish replaced German as the dominant language of higher education and the administration. This had negative consequences for the Ukrainian language, but Ukrainian protests and interventions by the imperial center forced the Polish elites to make concessions. Some chairs at L'viv University were Ukrainized, and several secondary and many primary schools were opened where children were taught in Ukrainian.[21]

The imperial reforms aimed to modernize the country, settle the conflicts between ethnic nationalities, and liberalize society. Newspapers and journals mushroomed, and a number of modern political parties were founded.[22] Several electoral reforms increased the number of people with the right to vote for the parliament in Vienna. Universal male suffrage (above the age of twenty-four) was introduced in 1907. The Polish Club in parliament persistently pressured for more autonomy rights for Galicia, while the Ukrainian deputies were opposed to more autonomy as long as Galicia continued to be dominated by Polish elites. Ukrainian deputies demanded that the Crown land be divided at some unspecified future time into a Polish part and a Ukrainian part.[23]

In the 1870s L'viv was granted a high degree of local self-administration; the city was administered by a municipal council whose members were elected by the wealthier and educated section of the population. In 1913 just 15,800 of the city's inhabitants had the right to vote.[24] The city council and administration were dominated by Poles. Before 1914, no Ukrainian was a member of the city council, although the number of Jewish councilors rose to fifteen (out of a total of one hundred members).[25]

In the last third of the nineteenth century, L'viv developed into a modern city with a competent administration and a modern infrastructure that included gas lighting, trams, and electricity. Liberalization made it possible for Poles, Ukrainians, and Jews to articulate and propagate their ideas about the future of their respective nations and of the city and region. The Polish elite found it difficult to decide where to draw the boundaries of the Polish nation. The Polish nation was potentially open, as was the territory of the future Polish state. According to the broadest, "Jagiellonian" definition, anyone whose ancestors had lived within the borders of the former Polish-Lithuanian Commonwealth could become a member of the nation.[26] A modern Polish nation might thus extend far beyond the old "noble nation" (the multiethnic nobility) of the Commonwealth and could also embrace Jews, Lithuanians, Ukrainians, and Belarusians. But by 1900, this was no longer an option, as nation-building had also taken off among the other ethnic groups. In the twentieth century, the concept of who or what constituted the Polish nation became increasingly narrow until it comprised mainly Catholic Poles who demonstrated their affinity to the Polish nation by their Roman Catholic faith, by speaking Polish, participating in national celebrations, and identifying with Polish culture and history (*Polak-Katolik*). The door was kept ajar for Belarusians and Ukrainians. A considerable part of the Polish elite viewed them as "ethnic raw material" without much in the way of historical traditions and with far inferior cultures. They could be merged into the Polish nation. The situation was rather different for Jews. Some members of the Jewish elite became ardent Polish patriots, but politicians from the influential Polish National Democratic Party considered them to be an alien element whose "race" prevented them from becoming truly Polish.[27]

Religious and social conflicts became nationally charged. The overwhelming majority of East Galician peasants were Ukrainians, while the majority of estate owners were Polish as were hundreds of thousands of peasants. After the failed Galician Uprising of 1846, the Polish national movement had begun to reach out to the peasantry. Over the next sixty or seventy years, it made great progress in transforming Roman Catholic, Polish-speaking peasants into Polish patriots but failed to convince the Ukrainian-speaking, Greek Catholic peasantry.[28] The different denomination, language, and script (Ukrainian uses the Cyrillic script) and the concurrence of ethnic difference and social antagonisms made it much harder to win the support of Ruthenian peasants. Some of the Greek Catholic elite, however, considered themselves part of the Polish nation: *gente Ruthenus, natione Polonus*. A Ruthenian national movement (partly inspired by the Ukrainian movement in Russian Ukraine) developed, which insisted on the distinction between Ruthenians and Poles. Once the Polish option was defeated, there would be three directions in which the Ruthenian national movement could develop.[29]

First, they could define themselves as Ruthenians, that is, different from Poles, Russians, and the Ukrainian-speaking population in the Russian Empire. This option was very strong in some regions such as the Carpathian Mountains but did not convince the majority of the Greek Catholic population. The second option was to identify with the Russian nation. The Russophile movement, which viewed Ruthenians/Ukrainians as a branch of the Russian nation/people, was especially influential in the 1870s and 1880s. It established education societies and later even set up its own party. It received some support from the most conservative elements of the Polish establishment in an attempt to divide the Ukrainian national movement but faced opposition from the Austrian authorities, who tried to prevent a strong pro-Russian movement in a region so close to the Russian border. The Russophile party received support from the Russian Empire, both directly from the Russian Orthodox Church and nationalist organizations and secretly from the Russian government. The attraction of the Russian cultural sphere was, in part, because of the similarities between the Greek Catholic and the Russian Orthodox Church, with both Churches sharing the same rites and Slavic liturgical language (Church Slavonic) as well as the Julian calendar. Unlike Roman Catholic priests, but like Russian Orthodox ones, Greek Catholic priests are permitted to marry and have families. Some Greek Catholic clergymen supported the Russophiles.

However, an affinity to Russian culture and religion did not necessarily indicate political allegiance to Russia. Some Greek Catholic clergy were Old Ruthenians who regarded Ruthenians as firmly rooted in the East Slavic Orthodox world but remained loyal to the Austrian emperor. Their cultural Russophilism did not translate into political Russophilism, and they believed that the future of East Galicia lay with Austria-Hungary and not with the Russian Empire.[30]

By 1900, the Ukrainian national movement had changed. In the wake of modernization, a new secular intelligentsia (students and professors, lawyers and advocates, functionaries of the cooperative sector, civil servants and teachers, journalists, secondary school teachers, politicians, and authors) had emerged. Many were the children of Greek Catholic priests; others came from peasant families and had profited from the proliferation of Ukrainian-language primary and secondary education facilities.[31] John-Paul Himka estimated that their number rose from one thousand in 1850 to more than ten thousand in 1900.[32] This new intelligentsia also provided leaders for the Ukrainian national movement that tried to reach out to the peasantry.

In the 1890s the Ukrainophiles overtook the Russophiles to become the dominant national movement within the Greek Catholic population. The Ukrainophiles created a network of organizations that left similar Russophile attempts far behind. They published newspapers and books in Ukrainian and founded cooperatives, reading clubs, sport clubs, and branches of the education society Prosvita, established in 1868. In the villages, teachers, priests, and cantors functioned as intermediaries between the urban intelligentsia and the peasantry.[33] Ukrainophiles were originally critical of the Greek Catholic Church, but after Andrij Sheptyts'kyj was appointed archbishop and began to support the Ukrainian option, the Greek Catholic Church and the Ukrainian national movement were reconciled. The Ukrainophiles viewed Russophiles and Poles as the most important impediments to Ukrainian nation-building in East Galicia.[34] By 1908, Prosvita had 2048 reading clubs, each with an average of fifty members: "by joining reading clubs, peasants joined the nation."[35] The many and varied activities of Ukrainian organizations were linked and publicized by Ukrainian newspapers. A Ukrainian public sphere started to develop in Galicia.[36] While in cities and towns Greek Catholics were exposed to the assimilationist power of Polish culture, in villages Roman Catholic peasants often assimilated to their Ukrainian-speaking environment.[37] One of the high points in the political mobilization of the Ukrainian peasantry was a gathering of forty thousand Ukrainians on January 20, 1906, on the Vysoky Zamok in L'viv in support of a reform of the electoral laws governing elections to the imperial parliament.[38] Ukrainian patriots fought against the dominance of Poles in public life, in the school system, and at L'viv University. Many parents preferred to send their children to German-language schools if the only other option was a Polish school.

The Jewish population had no uniform national affiliation. Poles became a minority among the Jewish elite (sometimes with, sometimes without, converting to Roman Catholicism), and another larger group joined the Jewish national movement and supported Zionism, but the majority did not join any national project.[39] Jews were overrepresented in both the wealthiest and the poorest strata of society. Before the war, 63 percent of lawyers and 67 percent of traders and merchants in L'viv were Jewish. The outward appearance and behavior of the assimilated group were no different from that of their Polish and Ukrainian neighbors. Their language was Polish, and they visited Polish theaters and worshipped in the progressive synagogue, the temple. The majority of the Jewish population, however, clung to the traditions of Eastern European Jewry, dressing in kaftans and sporting beards and side curls. Many were among the poorest of the city's residents.[40] Anti-Semitism was a recurrent problem in the region. Peasants attacked Jews in the context of the election campaign of 1898 and the agrarian strikes after 1900,[41] but there were no anti-Jewish excesses in L'viv.

I write of "Poles," "Ukrainians," and "Jews," but boundaries were blurred. There were Greek Catholics who identified with the Polish nation, Roman Catholic peasants whose daily language was Ukrainian, Polish nationalists who worshiped in synagogues, and so forth. Some did not identify with any nation. A peasant woman might respond to a question about her nationality by saying that she was a peasant or by giving her religious affiliation, or she might just say that she was "from here." Many Greek Catholics were married to Roman Catholics, although marriages between Christians and Jews were rare.[42]

As a result of the conscious separation into different nations or ethnicities, the number of all-Galician organizations decreased, with "cross-ethnic" institutions being replaced or complemented by organizations whose membership was either Polish, Ukrainian, or Jewish. Consequently, the number of sport clubs, cultural institutions, professional organizations, cooperatives, and political parties tripled. Instead of a single all-Galician institution, organizations were often Polish, Ukrainian, or Jewish.[43]

From the 1880s onward, the Polish-Ukrainian conflict dominated ethnic relations, although moderate Polish and Ukrainian politicians repeatedly tried to reach a compromise.[44] In this context, alliances continued to cross ethnic or religious boundaries. In 1908 the reactionary Polish estate owners (Podolians) allied with Ukrainian Russophiles during elections to the parliament in Vienna. As a result, the number of Ukrainophile deputies decreased. Governor Andrzej Potocki had supported this alliance, and in an act of revenge Governor Potocki was shot dead by the Ukrainian student Myroslav Sichyns'kyj. Sichyns'kyj became a Ukrainian hero, but Potocki's murder led to retaliatory attacks on Ukrainian institutions by Polish students.[45] Other violent clashes occurred in connection with the issue of a setting up a Ukrainian university in L'viv or increasing the Ukrainian influence in the existing university. The most violent clashes occurred on July 1, 1910, when one Ukrainian student was killed and 130 students were arrested by the police.[46]

Michał Bobrzyński, the new governor of Galicia, pursued a different policy to that of his murdered predecessor, Potocki. He fought the Russophile movement, cooperated with moderate Ukrainian politicians, and tried to broker a Polish-Ukrainian agreement.[47] The agreement was strongly opposed by the Podolians, the Polish National Democrats, and the Russophiles.[48] In 1914, in the teeth of fierce resistance by the opposition, Bobrzyński managed to reach an agreement with the Ukrainian national movement. The agreement included: (1) the establishment of a Ukrainian university in L'viv within the next ten years; (2) increasing the number of Ukrainian deputies in the Diet; (3) support for Ukrainian education societies; and (4) the creation of more Ukrainian schools.[49] Five Roman Catholic bishops protested against this attack on established Polish rights, forcing Bobrzynski to step down. The important parts of the agreement were approved by the Diet, but the agreement was never enacted. The war put a halt to all attempts at reform.[50]

Vienna supported the Ukrainophiles as a counterweight to Russian and Polish aspirations but left the administration of the Crown land in Polish hands. The nationalist Russian press and the Russian government regarded East Galicia as a potential target for expansion. In their view, there were no Ukrainians—only "Little Russians" who were simply another branch of the Russian people.[51] In 1913 the Russophiles in the region began to intensify their activities. The Austro-Hungarian authorities put some of them on trial for treason. One of these trials, held in L'viv, ended with the acquittal of the accused.[52] Ukrainophile politicians objected the verdict and called several protest meetings. One meeting proclaimed "that there are no Russians in Austria-Hungary at all and that the Ukrainian nation, which is conscious of its national characteristics and independence, lives in Galicia, the Bukovina and Hungary."[53]

Ethnic conflicts during and after the war originated in prewar conflicts, but this does not explain why they became so violent and, at times, brutal. The next chapter aims to explain why previously blurred boundaries became fixed and ethnic conflicts dominated the public space. Before 1914, ethnic conflicts were contained. The periodic violent clashes between Polish and Ukrainian students cost one Ukrainian his life and, in 1908 Polish governor Potocki was killed by a Ukrainian student. But before the war, all groups ultimately had good reasons to believe that they could improve their position through peaceful means. A tradition of peaceful resolution of civil conflicts had developed in the last decades of Austria-Hungary. The administration and police in Galicia were dominated by Poles, but they were kept in check by the central authorities and acted (mostly) in the interests of the state to keep the peace and maintain public order. The war ended this—*cum grano salis*—peaceful coexistence.

Notes

1. *Ruthenian* was the official term used to refer to the Ukrainian-speaking population of the Habsburg Empire. Ruthenian is a translation of the terms *rusyn* (nomen: the Ruthenian) and *rus'kyj* (adjective: Ruthenian). In the 1890s the Ruthenian national movement started to use the term *Ukrainian*, initially in the composite form "Ruthenian-Ukrainian" and later as a stand-alone term. The new name emphasized the commonality of the Ruthenians with the Ukrainian-speaking population in the western provinces of the Russian Empire.
2. These are only approximate numbers. The censuses of the Habsburg Empire did not inquire into nationality, only asking respondents about their everyday language and religious affiliation. That is why statistics on nationality can only be compiled based on specific indications. Roman Catholics in L'viv were almost exclusively Poles, while Greek Catholics were, for the most part, Ruthenians. But about one-third of the Greek Catholic population in L'viv listed Polish as their everyday vernacular and thus cannot simply be classified as part of the Ruthenian-Ukrainian group. Many of them viewed themselves as Poles of Ruthenian extraction. Among the Jewish population, there was a small group of people who regarded themselves as Jewish Poles. The overwhelming majority viewed themselves as part of a religious community ethnically very distinct from Ruthenians and Poles.
3. Joseph Roth, "Lemberg: Die Stadt," *Frankfurter Zeitung*, November 11, 1924 (printed in Joseph Roth, *Werke*, vol. 2 [Cologne: Kiepenheuer & Witsch, 1990], 285).
4. Peter Berger and Thomas Luckmann, *The Social Construction of Reality: A Treatise in the Sociology of Knowledge* (Garden City, NY: Anchor Books, 1966). On the use of "Erfahrung" in historical research, see Reinhart Koselleck, "'Erfahrungsraum' und 'Erwartungshorizont'—zwei historische Kategorien," in *Vergangene Zukunft: Zur Semantik geschichtlicher Zeiten*, ed. Reinhart Kosellek (Frankfurt am Main: Suhrkamp, 1989), 349–72. Reinhart Koselleck, "Erfahrungswandel und Methodenwechsel: Eine historisch-anthropologische Skizze," in *Historische Methode*, ed. Christian Meier and Jörn Rüsen (Munich: dtv, 1988), 13–61. On war experience, see Klaus Latzel, "Vom Kriegserlebnis zur Kriegserfahrung: Theoretische und methodische Überlegungen zur erfahrungsgeschichtlichen Untersuchung von Feldpostbriefen," *Militärgeschichtliche Mitteilungen* 56 (1997), 1–30. Reinhart Koselleck, "Der Einfluß der beiden Weltkriege auf das soziale Bewusstsein," in *Der Krieg des kleinen Mannes: Eine Militärgeschichte von unten*, second ed., ed. Wolfram Wette (Munich: Piper, 1995), 324–43.
5. Latzel, "Vom Kriegserlebnis," 15–16.
6. This approach was used in the Sonderforschungsbereich (Special Research Area) 437 on "The Experience of War—War and Society in Modern History" at the University of Tübingen, funded by the Deutsche Forschungsgemeinschaft. Nikolaus Buschmann and Horst Carl, "Zugänge zur Erfahrungsgeschichte des Krieges: Forschung, Theorie, Fragestellung," in *Die Erfahrung des Krieges: Erfahrungsgeschichtliche Perspektiven von der französischen Revolution bis zum Zweiten Weltkrieg*, ed. Nikolaus Buschmann and Horst Carl (Paderborn: Ferdinand Schöningh, 2001), 11–26. Nikolaus Buschmann and Aribert Reimann, "Die Konstruktion historischer Erfahrung: Neue Wege zu einer Erfahrungsgeschichte des Krieges," in *Die Erfahrung des Krieges*, 261–71. Matthias Asche and Anton Schindling, eds., *Das Strafgericht Gottes: Kriegserfahrungen und Religion im Heiligen Römischen Reich Deutscher Nation im Zeitalter des Dreißigjährigen Krieges* (Münster: Aschendorffsche Verlagsbuchhandlung, 2001).
7. Some examples are: *Tomasz Szarota, Warschau unter dem Hakenkreuz: Leben und Alltag im besetzten Warschau 1.10.1939 bis 31.7.1944* (Paderborn: Schöningh, 1985).

Wanda Lewandowska, *Życie codzienne Wilna w latach II wojny światowej* (Warsaw: Neriton, 1997). Jan Gross, *Polish Society under German Occupation: The Generalgouvernement 1939–1944* (Princeton, NJ: Princeton University Press, 1979). Gabriele Lesser, *Leben als ob: Die Untergrunduniversität Krakau im Zweiten Weltkrieg* (Freiburg: Treffpunkt, 1988).

8. There were some exceptions: Ryszard Torzecki, *Kwestia ukraińska w Polsce w latach 1923–1929* (Cracow: Wydawnictwo Literackie, 1989); Jan Gruchała, *Rząd austriacki i polskie stronnictwa polityczne w Galicji wobec kwestii ukraińskiej 1890–1914* (Katowice: Uniwersytet Śląski, 1988); Mirosława Papierzyńska-Turek, *Sprawa ukraińska w Drugiej Rzeczypospolitej 1922–1926* (Cracow: Wydawnictwo Literackie, 1979); and Henryk Wereszycki, *Pod berłem Habsburgów: Zagadnienia narodowościowe* (Cracow: Wydawnictwo Literackie, 1975).

9. The most important are: Alexander Victor Prus, *Nationalizing a Borderland: War, Ethnicity, and Anti-Jewish Violence in East Galicia, 1914–1920* (Tuscaloosa: University of Alabama Press, 2005); Jan Gross, *Revolution from Abroad: The Soviet Conquest of Poland's Western Ukraine and Western Belorussia*, expanded ed. (Princeton, NJ: Princeton University Press, 2002); Marek Figura, *Konflikt polsko-ukraiński w prasie Polski Zachodniej w latach 1918–1923* (Poznań: Wydawnictwo Poznańskie, 2001); Michał Klimecki, *Polsko-ukraińska wojna o Lwów i Galicję Wschodnią 1918–1919* (Warsaw: Volumen, 2000); Eliyahu Jones, *Żydzi Lwowa w okresie okupacji 1939–1945* (Łódź: Oficyna Bibliofilów, 1999); Ludwik Mroczka, *Spór o Galicję Wschodnią 1914–1923* (Cracow: Wydawnictwo Naukowe WSP, 1998); Vasyl' Veryha, *Vyzvol'ni zmahannja v Ukraïni 1914–1923 rr.*, 2 vols. (L'viv: Misioner, 1998); Stepan A. Makarchuk, *Ukraïns'ka Respublika Halychan* (L'viv: Svit, 1997); Dieter Pohl, *Nationalsozialistische Judenverfolgung in Ostgalizien 1941–1944: Organisation und Durchführung eines staatlichen Massenverbrechens*, second ed. (Munich: Oldenbourg, 1997); Thomas Sandkühler, *"Endlösung" in Galizien: Der Judenmord in Ostpolen und die Rettungsinitiativen von Berthold Beitz 1941–1944* (Bonn: Dietz, 1996); Adam Sudoł, *Początki sowietyzacji kresów wschodnich: Jesień 1939 roku* (Bydgoszcz: Wyższa Szkoła Pedagogiczna w Bydgoszczy, 1997); Keith Sword, *Deportation and Exile: Poles in the Soviet Union, 1939–48*, new rev. ed. (Houndsmills: Macmillan, 1996); Eugeniusz Misiło, ed., *Repatriacja czy deportacja: przesiedlenie Ukraińców z Polski do USRR 1944–1946*, 2 vols. (Warsaw: Archiwum Ukraińskie, 1996, 1999); Grzegorz Łukomski, Czesław Partacz and Bogusław Polak, *Wojna Polsko-Ukraińska 1918–1919* (Koszalin: Wydawnictwo Uczelniane Wyższej Szkoły Inżynierskiej w Koszalinie, 1994); Vladimir Melamed, *Evrei vo L'vove (XII–pervaja polovina XX veka): Sobytija, obshchestvo, ljudi* (L'viv: Tekop, 1994); Jerzy Węgierski, *Lwów pod okupacją sowiecką, 1939–1941* (Warsaw: Editions Spotkania, 1991); Maciej Kozłowski, *Między Sanem a Zbruczem: Walki o Lwów i Galicję Wschodnią 1918–1919* (Cracow: Znak, 1990) and *Zapomniana wojna: Walki o Lwów i Galicję Wschodnią 1918–1919*, second ed. (Bydgoszcz: Instytut Wydawniczy Świadectwo, 1999); Torzecki, *Kwestia ukraińska w Polsce w latach 1923–1929*.

10. On the "myth of Galicia," see Kerstin S. Jobst, *Der Mythos des Miteinander: Galizien in Literatur und Geschichte* (Hamburg: Deutsche Gesellschaft für Osteuropakunde, Zweigstelle Hamburg, 1998); Anna Veronika Wendland, "Galizien: Westen des Ostens, Osten des Westens: Annäherung an eine ukrainische Grenzlandschaft," *Österreichische Osthefte* 42, no. 3/4 (2000): 389–421; Andreas Kappeler, "Die Ukraine in der deutschsprachigen Historiographie," *Österreichische Osthefte* 42, no. 3/4 (2000): 161–77.

11. Henryka Kramarz, *Samorząd Lwowa w czasie pierwszej wojny światowej i jego rola w życiu miasta* (Cracow: Wydawnictwo Naukowe WSP, 1994); Aleksandra Ju. Bakhtu-

rina, *Politika Rossijskoj Imperii v Vostochnoj Galitsii v gody Pervoj Mirovoj Vojny* (Moscow: Assotsiatsija Issledovatelej Rossijskogo Obshchestva 20 veka, 2000); Grzegorz Hryciuk, *Polacy we Lwowie, 1939–1944*: Życie codzienne (Warsaw: Książka i Wiedza, 2000); Grzegorz Hryciuk, *"Kumytet": Polski Komitet Opiekuńczy Lwów Miasto w latach 1941–1944* (Toruń: Adam Marszałek, 2000); Grzegorz Hryciuk, *"Gazeta Lwowska" 1941–1944*, second rev. ed. (Wrocław: Wydawnictwo Uniwersytetu Wrocławskiego, 1996); Grzegorz Hryciuk, "Prasa ukraińska i ukraińskojezyczna w Galicji Wschodniej w latach 1939–1944," *Dzieje Najnowsze* 27 (1997): 47–66; Grzegorz Hryciuk, "'Nowy Kurs?' Ewolucja polityki radzieckiej wobec Polaków we Lwowie (Czerwiec 1940–Czerwiec 1941)," *Wrocławskie Studia z Historii Najnowszej* 6 (1998): 47–66; Tarik Amar, *The Making of Soviet Lviv, 1939–1963* (Princeton: Princeton University, 2006).
12. Tsentral'nyj Derzhavnyj Istorychnyj Arkhiv Ukraïny, m. L'viv (TsDIAL), f. 837, op. 1, spr. 71.
13. Derzhavnyj Arkhiv L'vovskoï Oblasti (DALO), f. 257. See also the collection of Polish memoirs and casualty lists: *Obrona Lwowa: Źródła do dziejów walk o Lwów i województwa południowo-wschodnie 1918–1920*, vols. 1–2: *Relacje Uczestników* (L'viv: 1933, 1936 [reprint: Warsaw: Volumen, 1991, 1993]); vol. 3: *Organizacja listopadowej obrony Lwowa, ewidencja uczestników walk, lista strat* (L'viv: Volumen, 1938 [reprint: Warsaw, 1994]).
14. A selection of these letters have been published in Irena Grudzinska-Gross and Jan Gross, eds., *War through Children's Eyes: The Soviet Occupation of Poland and the Deportations 1939–1941* (Stanford: Hoover Institution Press, 1981).
15. Archiwum Wschodni Ośrodku Karta (AW), sygn. MINF 135, Lwów Relacje.
16. Żydowski Institut Historyczny (ŻIH), Archiwum Ringelbluma (Ring). ŻIH, Teka Lwowska. ŻIH, Relacje. Some sources have been published in Michał Grynberg and Maria Kotowska, eds., *Życie i zagłada Żydów polskich 1939–1945: Relacje świadków* (Warsaw: Oficyna Naukowa, 2003); and Andrzej Żbikowski, ed., *Archiwum Ringelbluma: Konspiracyjne Archiwum Getta Warszawy*, vol. 3: *Relacje z Kresów* (Warsaw: ANTA, 2000).
17. Aleksander Czołowski, *Pogląd na organizacje i działalność dawnych władz miejskich do 1848 r.* (L'viv: Gmina Królestwa Stołecznego Miasta Lwowa 1896); and Rudolf A. Mark, "'Polnische Bastion und ukrainisches Piemont': Lemberg 1772–1921," in *Lemberg—Lwów—Lviv: eine Stadt im Schnittpunkt europäischer Kulturen*, ed. Peter Fäßler, Thomas Held, and Dirk Sawitzky (Cologne: Böhlau, 1998), 46–74 especially 47. On the history of L'viv in the years before World War I, see Christoph Mick, "Nationalismus und Modernisierung in Lemberg," in *Städte im östlichen Europa: zur Problematik von Modernisierung und Raum vom Spätmittelalter bis zum 20. Jahrhundert*, ed. Carsten Goehrke and Bianka Pietrow-Ennker (Zurich: Chronos, 2006), 171–213.
18. Antoni Podraza, "Problem pograniczy w Europie Środkowo-Wschodniej (na przykładzie pogranicza polsko-ukraińskiego)," in *Prace Komisji Środkowoeuropejskiej Polskiej Akademii Umiejętności*, vol. 4 (Cracow: Polska Akademia Umiejętności, 1996), 106. Rudolf A. Mark, *Galizien unter österreichischer Herrschaft: Verwaltung—Kirche—Bevölkerung* (Marburg: Herder-Institut, 1994), 80–85.
19. On the Galician Germans, see Isabel Röskau-Rydel, *Deutsche Geschichte im Osten Europas: Galizien, Bukowina, Moldau* (Munich: Siedler, 2002).
20. Since 1873 the House of Deputies of the Imperial Council in Vienna was elected through the curia system (landowners elected 85 deputies, chambers of commerce 21, cities 118, rural communities 128). The election reform in 1896–99 added a fifth, general curia, which brought some representatives of the Ruthenian peasantry into the

parliament. The election reform of 1906 abolished the curia system for elections to the Imperial Council and introduced universal male suffrage. Harald Binder, "Die Wahlreform von 1907 und der polnisch-ruthenische Konflikt in Ostgalizien," Österreichische Osthefte 38 (1996): 293–320; Olena Arkusha, *Halyts'kyj Sejm. Vyborchi kampaniï 1889 i 1895 rr.* (L'viv: Natsional'na Akademija nauk Ukraïny Instytut Ukraïnoznavstva im. I. Kryp'jakevycha, 1996), 9–14; Christoph Freiherr Marschall von Bieberstein, *Freiheit in der Unfreiheit: Die nationale Autonomie der Polen in Galizien nach dem österreichisch-ungarischen Ausgleich von 1867: Ein konservativer Aufbruch im mitteleuropäischen Vergleich* (Wiesbaden: Harrassowitz, 1993), 221–24.

21. Svjatoslav Pacholkiv, *Emanzipation durch Bildung: Entwicklung und gesellschaftliche Rolle der ukrainischen Intelligenz im habsburgischen Galizien (1890–1914)* (Vienna: Verlag für Geschichte und Politik, 2002), especially 85–90; and Kazimierz Bartoszewicz, *Dzieje Galicji: Jej stan przed wojną i "wyodrębnienie"* (Warsaw: Gebethner i Wolff, 1917), 179.

22. Georg Stourzh, "Die Gleichberechtigung der Volksstämme als Verfassungsprinzip 1848–1867," in *Die Habsburgermonarchie 1848–1918*, vol. 3, part 2: *Die Völker des Reiches*, ed. Adam Wandruszka and Peter Urbanitsch (Vienna: Österreichische Akademie der Wissenschaften, 1980), 1081.

23. Józef Buszko, *Polacy w Parlamencie Wiedeńskim 1848–1918* (Warsaw: Wydawnictwo Sejmowe, 1996). Mark, "'Polnische Bastion und ukrainisches Piemont,'" 57. Wolfdieter Bihl, "Die Ruthenen," in *Die Habsburger Monarchie*, vol. 3: *Die Völker des Reiches*, ed. Adam Wandruszka and Peter Urbanitsch (Vienna: Verlag der Österreichischen Akademie der Wissenschaften, 1980), 555–84. On Galician politicians in Vienna, see Harald Binder, *Galizien in Wien: Parteien, Fraktionen und Abgeordnete im Übergang zur Massenpolitik* (Vienna: Verlag der Österreichische Akademie der Wissenschaften, 2005).

24. Józef Buszko, "Die Stellung der Polen und Ukrainer zur jüdischen Frage im autonomen Galizien," Österreichische Osthefte 38, no. 3 (1996): 275–91, especially 278–79. Melamed, *Evrei vo L'vove*, 108–12.

25. *Wiadomości statystyczne o mieście Lwowie*, vol. 15: *1912–1922* (L'viv: Gmina Królewskiego Stołecznego miasta Lwowa, 1926), 87.

26. On these different options, see Norman Davies, *God's Playground: A History of Poland*, vol. 2, rev. second ed. (New York: Columbia University Press, 2005), 3–11.

27. Olaf Bergmann, *Narodowa Demokracja wobec problematyki żydowskiej w latach 1918–1929* (Poznań: Wydawnictwo Poznańskie, 1998), 11–20.

28. Anna Veronika Wendland, *Die Russophilen in Galizien: Ukrainische Konservative zwischen Österreich und Russland 1848–1915* (Vienna: Verlag der Österreichische Akademie der Wissenschaften, 2001), 49–97. John-Paul Himka, *Galician Villagers and the Ukrainian National Movement in the Nineteenth Century* (Houndmills: Palgrave Macmillan 1988), 3–10; John-Paul Himka, "The Transformation and Formation of Social Strata and their Place in the Ukrainian National Movement in Nineteenth-Century Galicia," *Journal of Ukrainian Studies* 23 (Winter 1993): 3–22, especially 5–7; John-Paul Himka, "The Greek Catholic Church and Nation-Building in Galicia, 1772–1918," *Harvard Ukrainian Studies* 8 (December 1984): 426–52; John-Paul Himka, "German Culture and the National Awakening in Western Ukraine before the Revolution of 1848," in *German Ukrainian Relations in Historical Perspective*, ed. John-Paul Himka and Hans-Joachim Torke (Edmonton: Canadian Institute of Ukrainian Studies Press, 1994), 29–44, especially 30–34; Jan Kozik, *Ukraiński ruch narodowy w Galicji w latach 1830–1848* (Cracow: Wydawnictwo Literackie, 1973); Bartoszewicz, *Dzieje Galicji*, 1–22.

29. John-Paul Himka, "Construction of Nationality in Galician Rus': Icarian Flights in Almost all Directions," in *Intellectuals and the Articulation of the Nation*, ed. Michael D. Kennedy and Ronald G. Suny (Ann Arbor: University of Michigan Press, 1999), 109–64.
30. On the Russophile movement, see Wendland, *Die Russophilen in Galizien*.
31. Mychajlo Shvahuljak, "Shtrykhy do politychnoho portreta L'vova (druha polovyna XIX–pochatok XX st.)," in Lwów: *Miasto—społeczeństwo—kultura*, vol. 1, ed. Henryk W. Żaliński and Kazimierz Karolczak (Cracow: Wydawnictwo Naukowe WSP, 1995), 183–94; Dariusz Maciak, *Próba porozumienia polsko-ukraińskiego w Galicji w latach 1888–1895* (Warsaw: Wydawnictwo Uniwersytetu Warszawskiego, 2006), 61–62.
32. Himka, "The Transformation," 13. Filipp Swistun, writing in 1896, counted 1,100 members of the secular intelligentsia, 23,000 educated clerics, and 1,700 primary school teachers. Fedor Swistun, *Prikarpatskaja Rus' pod władeniem Austrii*, 2 vols. (L'viv, unknown publisher, 1896–1897; reprint: Trumbull: Hardy, 1970), 346–47.
33. Himka, *Galician Villagers*, 133–42.
34. Shvahuljak, "Shtrykhy do politychnoho portreta L'vova," 183–94, especially 183–87. See also Orest Subtelny, *Ukraine: A History*, third ed. (Toronto: University of Toronto Press, 2000), 243–51.
35. John-Paul Himka, "Priests and Peasants: The Greek Catholic Pastor and the Ukrainian National Movement in Austria, 1867–1900," *Canadian Slavonic Papers* 21 (1979): 8.
36. Ibid., 6. Maciak, *Próba porozumienia polsko-ukraińskiego w Galicji*, 58.
37. Czesław Partacz, *Od Badeniego do Potockiego: Stosunki Polsko-Ukraińskie w Galicji w latach 1888–1908* (Toruń: Wydawnictwo Adam Marszałek, 1996), 172–85. Olena Arkusha, "Pol's'ki politychni seredobyshcha L'vova ta Krakova na zlami XIX–XX stolit': sproba poruvnjannja," in *L'viv: Misto—suspil'stvo—kul'tura*, vol. 3, ed. Mar'jan Mudryj (L'viv: L'vivs'kyj Derzhavnyj Universytet imeni Ivana Franka, 1999), 374.
38. Stepan Makarchuk, "Hromads'ko-politychnyj tsentr Zakhidnoukraïns'koho kraju," in *L'viv: Istorychni narysy* (L'viv: Ivan Krypiakevych Institute of Ukrainian Studies of the National Academy of Sciences of Ukraine, 1996), 267–90, especially 278.
39. Leila P. Everett, "The Rise of Jewish National Politics in Galicia, 1905–1907," in *Nationbuilding and the Politics of Nationalism: Essays on Austrian Galicia*, ed. Andrei S. Markovits and Frank E. Sysyn (Cambridge, MA: Harvard University Press, 1982), 149–77; Israel Bartal, ed., *Focusing on Galicia: Jews, Poles, and Ukrainians, 1772–1918* (London: Littmann Library of Jewish Civilization, 1999); Miroslav Hroch, "Zionism as a European National Movement," *Jewish Studies* 38 (1998): 73–81; Adolf Gaisbauer, *Davidstern und Doppeladler: Zionismus und jüdischer Nationalismus in Österreich* (Vienna: Böhlau, 1988), 63–66; Melamed, *Evrei vo L'vove*, 107–33; Urszula Jakubowska, "Życie polityczne we Lwowie na przełomie XIX I XX wieku," in *Galicja i jej dziedzictwo*, vol. 1: *Historia i Polityka*, ed. Kazimierz Bonusiak and Józef Buszko (Rzeszów: Wydawnictwo Wyższej Szkoły Pedagogicznej, 1994), 92–93; Michał Bobrzyński, *Z moich pamiętników* (Wrocław: Wydawnictwo Zakładu Narodowego im. Ossolińskich, 1957), 317–18.
40. Ewa Rutkowska, *Wyznania i narodowości we Lwowie w latach 1857–1939 na tle ogólnej struktury demograficznej miasta*. Unpublished master's thesis, Uniwersytet Jagielloński, Cracow, 1993.
41. Wilhelm Feldman, *Stronnictwa i programy polityczne w Galicyi 1846–1906*, vol. 2 (Cracow: Książka, 1907), 121, 247; Buszko, "Die Stellung der Polen und Ukrainer," 283; Józef Hampel, "Lwowskie środowiska ukraińskie wobec narodzin ruchu ludowego v Galicji," in *Lwów: Miasto—społeczeństwo—kultura*, vol. 1, ed. Henryk W. Żaliński and Kazimierz Karolczak (Cracow: Wydawnictwo Naukowe WSP, 1995), 110–18; Ts-

DIAL, f. 146, op. 8, spr. 1580, ark. 11–13: the chief of the police in L'viv, Reinlender, to the governor's office, February 18, 1914.
42. Klaus Bachmann, *Ein Herd der Feindschaft gegen Russland: Galizien als Krisenherd in den Beziehungen der Donaumonarchie mit Russland (1907–1914)* (Vienna: Oldenbourg, 2001), 30–35.
43. Stefan Zabrowarny, "Institucionalny rozwój ukrainskiego ruchu narodowego we Galicji w latach 1864–1914," *Warszawskie Zeszyty Ukrainoznawcze* 2 (1994): 74–75. On Sokół, see Jan Snopko, *Polskie towarzystwo gimnastyczne "Sokół" w Galicji 1867–1914* (Białystok: Wydawnictwo Uniwersytetu w Białymstoku, 1997). On the Shevchenko Society, see Mykoła Muszynka, "Towarzystwo Naukowe im. Szewczenki i jego rola w narodowym odrodzeniu Ukraińców na terenie Galicji," in *Galicja i jej dziedzictwo*, vol. 3: *Nauka i oświata*, ed. Andrzej Meissner and Jerzy Wyrozumski (Rzeszów: Wydawnictwo Wyższej Szkoły Pedagogicznej, 1995), 69–78; and Wilhelm Feldman, *Stronnictwa i programy polityczne w Galicyi 1846–1906*, vol. 1 (Cracow: Książka 1907), 107–12.
44. Partacz, *Od Badeniego do Potockiego*, 48; Czesław Partacz, "Przyczyny i przebieg konfliktu Ukraińsko-Polskiego," *Przegląd Wschodni* 2 (1992/93): 841–49. Maciak, *Próba porozumienia polsko-ukraińskiego w Galicji*.
45. Jakubowska, "Życie polityczne we Lwowie," 84–85, 88; Jurij Mykhal's'kyj, *Pol's'ka suspil'nist' ta ukraïns'ke pytannja v Halychyni v period sejmovykh vyboriv 1908 r.* (L'viv: Kamenjar, 1997); Partacz, *Od Badeniego do Potockiego*, 227–35; Józef Buszko, "Zur politischen Krise von 1908: Slawen der Donaumonarchie. Das tragische Ende des Grafen Andrzej Potocki als Statthalter von Galizien," Österreichische Osthefte 11 (1968): 321–28. Bachmann, *Ein Herd der Feindschaft gegen Russland,* S. 132–37.
46. Jakubowska, "Życie polityczne we Lwowie," 87. Politisches Archiv des Auswärtigen Amtes (Political Archive of the German Foreign Office, PA), R-8969: report of the German consulate in L'viv, July 2, 1910. Vasyl' Mudryj, *Zmahannja za ukraïns'ki universytety v Halychyni* (L'viv: Naukove tovarystvo im. Shevchenka, 1999), 48–51.
47. Urszula Jakubowska, "Życie polityczne we Lwowie," 85.
48. For more on the governors, see Mar'jan Mudryj, "Halyts'ki Namisnyky v systemi Ukraïns'ko-pol's'kych vzajemyn (1849–1914)," *Visnyk L'vivs'koho Universytetu: Serija Istorychna* 33 (1999): 91–101.
49. Bobrzyński, *Z moich pamiętników*, 314–17.
50. Partacz, "Przyczyny i przebieg konfliktu Ukraińsko-Polskiego," 849.
51. Wendland, *Die Russophilen in Galizien*, 427–39; Bachmann, *Ein Herd der Feindschaft gegen Russland*, 227–30.
52. Bachmann, *Ein Herd der Feindschaft gegen Russland*, 234–50.
53. *Dilo*, May 4, 1914: L'viv proty rosyjskoï invazyï.

CHAPTER 2

World War I

O godzinie ósmej rano	Around the eighth hour of the morning
Białe fany wywieszano.	White flags are hung outside.
Każdy pyta, co się stało	Everyone asks what has happened.
Miasto Lwów się już poddało.	The city of Lwów has just surrendered.
Od Zielonej, Łyczakowa,	From Zielona Street, from Łyczaków,
Moskal wkracza już do Lwowa.	the Muscovite is already marching into Lwów
Pierwsza patrol już przybyła,	The first patrol has just arrived,
Na rynku się ustawiła.	It has lined up on Market Square.
Ludzie im się przypatrują,	The people look at them,
Wódką, jadłem ich częstują.	They regale them with vodka and food.
Moskal bierze, nic nie pyta,	The Muscovite takes and asks nothing,
Byle była okowita.	as long as it is hard liquor.
Moskal chytry, Moskal zuch	The Muscovite is cunning, the Muscovite is intrepid,
Za Warszawę zabrał Lwów.	Instead of Warsaw he took Lwów.
Lecz w Karpatach góry śliski (sic!),	But in the Carpathians the mountains are tricky,
Tam Moskale łami pyski.[1]	That's where the Muscovite will get his face smashed.

Summer 1914

The assassination in Sarajevo cast L'viv into a state of tense expectancy. The city was abuzz with wild rumors. In the city squares, in cafés, and in their homes, residents argued about possible consequences and discussed the policies of the great powers. Enthusiasm for the expected war was most pronounced among the Polish population. But their expectations of the August events were not because of a patriotic upsurge of support for the Habsburg Empire but were, rather, a manifestation of Polish nationalism. The first demonstrations already included a number of red and white flags and patriotic Polish songs. Polish patriots hoped that a European war would reinvigorate the Polish question. Some Galician National Democrats anticipated a Russian victory—as did their party leader, Roman Dmowski—and sought to cooperate with the tsarist empire. But the majority of Polish politicians in Galicia backed Vienna. On August 16, 1914, members of the Diet and various party leaders met in Cracow to set up a Supreme National Committee (Naczelny Komitet Narodowy), which would be responsible for the military affairs of the Galician Poles. On the day of its inception, the committee called on the members of the association of Polish riflemen to form a Western Legion (Legion Zachodni) in Cracow and an Eastern Legion (Legion Wschodni) in L'viv.[2] Many young men took the opportunity to join Polish military units. The imperial-royal army leadership watched these developments with mixed feelings. Although they provided the imperial-royal army with highly motivated units, it was obvious that Polish patriotism rather than loyalty to the Austrian emperor had attracted these volunteers to the colors. The legions marched into battle with the strong support of the population. The general mood was optimistic, anticipating a quick victory over Russia.[3]

Attempts to form an independent Ukrainian unit within the imperial-royal army were less successful. The General Ukrainian National Council, the political representation of Ukrainians in Austria-Hungary, appealed for volunteers.[4] The imperial-royal army had only recently begun supporting the organization of Ukrainian riflemen, although they been supporting Polish clubs for many years. Governor Bobrzyński only approved the statute at the beginning of 1913; a short time later, the first association of Sich riflemen was founded.[5] Although recruitment for the Ukrainian legions started late, by the end of August 1914 about ten thousand volunteers had come forward.[6] However, the government in Vienna only approved the successive formation of eight battalions with a mere eight hundred soldiers per unit. The newly formed battalions were not placed under a single command but were incorporated into other units of the imperial-royal army. In the first phase of the war, the number of Ukrainian Sich riflemen was limited to two thousand men.[7]

Loyalties among the Ruthenians were divided. The Russophiles backed Russia; the Ukrainophile movement supported Austria-Hungary. On August 1, the three most important parties (Radicals, National Democrats, and Social Democrats) formed a Supreme Ukrainian Council,[8] which sided uncompromisingly with Austria in its battle against Russia, the "historical enemy of the Ukraine."[9] The peasants were generally loyal, although in some areas they were prepared to give credence to the myth of the good tsar who had freed the peasants and who would chase away "the masters and the Jews."[10]

The head of the Greek Catholic Church, Archbishop Andrij Sheptyts'kyj, took care to ensure that there could be no doubt about which side he supported. In a pastoral letter, he admonished the faithful to remain loyal to the emperor and warned his people against those who would wish to incite them to treason, a coded reference to the Russophiles: "This war is being fought on our account because the Muscovite tsar could not bear that in the Austrian Empire we are free in national matters and questions of faith; he wants to ensure that we lose this liberty, to put us in chains."[11]

The Jewish population lived in mortal fear of the Russian troops and was resolutely pro-Austrian. News of the pogroms in the Russian Empire had spread across East Galicia. Rabbi Bernard Hauser called on young Jewish men to volunteer and join Jewish combat units, but his appeal had little effect.[12]

Their close association as brothers in arms in the imperial-royal army did not curb the conflict between Poles and Ukrainians. The municipal authorities of L'viv donated 1.5 million krone to the Polish legions. Mayor Józef Neumann justified the donation by pointing out that L'viv was a Polish city.[13] The Ukrainian Main Council protested this ascription, laying claim to the city and demanding that Ukrainian units should also receive municipal monies but to no avail.[14]

The war did not go well for Austria-Hungary. By the middle of August, the Eighth Russian Army under General Aleksej A. Brusilov had broken through the Austrian lines and was advancing rapidly toward L'viv. The civil and military authorities sought to explain the defeat by hinting at treason. Most Russophile organizations had already been closed at the beginning of the war and their facilities handed over to the municipal and district authorities.[15] The army high command had ordered that lists of suspicious persons be drawn up and used the lists as the basis for subsequent arrests. The military command in Sokal reported that the [local] Greek Catholic priest, a supporter of the Russophiles, had communicated with Russian troops using a system of flags.[16] Such individual stories, whatever their truth, created the basis for generalized assumptions that shaped the perceptions and interpretations of the Austrian military units, who were unfamiliar with East Galicia's complex ethnic structures. Ruthenians were held in general suspicion. The civil authorities and the military commanders suspected them of Russophilia and accused them of treason. These suspicions affected not only supporters of the Russophile movement but also Old Ruthenians and Ukrainophiles. Several thousand Ruthenians were summarily hanged on suspicion alone or were sentenced to death by military courts and executed.[17] Others were arrested and detained in camps. In November 1915 some 5,700 Ruthenians were interned under terrible conditions at Camp Talerhof near Graz.[18] After the war, the Ukrainian Civil Committee in L'viv estimated the number of Ukrainian civilians who had been executed or died in Austrian camps to be close to twenty-five thousand.[19]

Polish elites used the opportunity to weaken the inconvenient Ukrainophile movement by excessively exaggerating the influence of the Russophile party on the Ruthenian population. Governor Witold Korytowski was not entirely blameless for this turn of events. He reported to Vienna that the Ukrainian movement had practically no influence over the population and that Ruthenians were generally pro-Russian.[20]

Looking back, the Austrian diplomat and Ukraine expert Baron Leopold von Andrian[21] declared in July 1915, "Unfortunately, the personal motives and above all the rancor of influential local Polish elements against the hated Ukrainians [*Ukrainertum*] appears to have resulted, especially given the haste precipitated by the events of war, in many completely loyal priests with Ukrainophile tendencies but who were very well disposed toward Austria being exiled from Galicia, which of course increased the number of abandoned parishes even more."[22]

Polish civil servants were the natural points of contact for Austrian military authorities who wished to understand the situation in the province. The reports of Baron von Giesl, the representative of the Austrian foreign ministry at the army high command (AOK) in Przemyśl, cemented the myth of "Ruthenian betrayal."[23] Just how successful this stigmatization of Ukrainians was is borne out by the reactions outside military circles. In 1916 the German Maria von Gember, writing about her personal experiences, stated that "most Ruthenians leaned towards Russia." The "appalling betrayal" by this "duped and bewitched people" had cost thousands of Austrians their lives.[24]

Ukrainian politicians defended themselves hotly against such accusations of betrayal. They penned countless memoranda in support of interned Ukrainians. The Ukrainophiles, who also had participated in the denunciations of Russophiles, accused the regional authorities of persecuting not the Russophiles but the supporters of the Ukrainian national movement: "The Polish administration of Galicia seized the opportunity provided by the war to politically compromise the entire Ukrainian nation and destroy it physically and morally."[25]

Not all members of the state apparatus were affected by this psychosis of betrayal. One civil servant in the administration of the Crown land recommended complying with Ukrainian demands on the use of the Ukrainian language and the creation of a Ukrainian university to secure the loyalty of the Ruthenians, pointing out that this would additionally appeal to Ukrainians within the Russian Empire.[26] At the end of August 1914, the Austrian high command informed the military and army commands that "strengthening the patriotic feelings amongst the loyal Ukrainian population in East Galicia is of central military importance and the arrest of such persons should therefore only be undertaken after a conscientious examination of the grounds for suspicion." The danger that "persons patriotically disposed might also be affected by the measures taken against the Russophile elements" had been recognized. But these orders did not result in any improvements. Two months later, the Ministry of the Interior ordered an examination into whether Polish civil servants were "in fact behaving with due objectivity towards the Ukrainian population" and directed Governor Korytowski to take the necessary steps to ensure that they behaved correctly.[27]

Soldiers of the imperial-royal army found it difficult to differentiate between Ruthenians and Russians. Ukrainian notices and newspapers written in Cyrillic were believed to be written in Russian.[28] In January 1915 the supreme commander Archduke Friedrich was still having to explain to the soldiers of this multiethnic empire that Ruthenians and Russians were different peoples. Every soldier should know that not all Ruthenians were traitors and that not every denunciation should be believed. The Ruthenian population loyal to the state should be treated in a friendly manner; otherwise, there was the danger that they would "view our soldiers as the enemy and the Cossacks, whose language and lineage is similar [to their own], as their savior."[29]

The "Representation of the Ukrainian Catholic Clergy"[30] in Vienna complained that "our Ukrainian people who have already suffered from Muscovite violence have also had to endure the scandalous injustice whereby they and their faithful clergy stand accused of treasonable disloyalty to our state and the Catholic Church by enemies of the Ukrainian people." These enemies had attempted through calumnies to "destroy the Ukrainian people at one stroke, not merely in the opinion of our state but in that of the entire civilized world."[31]

The consequence was that in the early weeks of the war, the Ukrainian population suffered traumatic experiences. Their traditional Austrophilia was put to a severe test. Instead of trusting in their loyalty, the military leadership relied on the opinions of Polish politicians and provincial civil servants. Settlements and farms were burned down as alleged centers of espionage, and numerous peasants were executed. But Ukrainian hatred was directed in the first instance not against the state and the army but against Poles and Jews, who were blamed for the repression.[32]

One Ukrainian memorandum cited the economic rivalry between Ukrainian cooperative societies and rural Jews as the motive for denunciations. Violent attacks on Ukrainians were generally imputed to Poles, but there were also scattered reports of Jewish attacks.[33] The Greek Catholic clergyman Jaroslav Levyts'kyj witnessed Jews beating Ukrainians who had been arrested at L'viv train station. Neither the police nor the army intervened.[34] The "All-Polish" (National Democratic) press encouraged this tacit persecution of Ukrainians. Ukrainians and "even Greek Catholics were reviled on the streets as Moskalophiles and traitors." Speaking Ukrainian in public was not advisable and was considered "truly heroic." "'The Ruthenians are all the same, all of them traitors'—screamed the readers of Słowo Polskie in the streets, the streetcars, the coffeehouses and the restaurants."[35] According to Levyts'kyj, women and children lived in terror, with many of them too afraid to attend Mass in Greek Catholic churches.[36]

This widespread mistrust of the Ruthenian population did not prevent the imperial and royal military authorities from launching a propaganda campaign in the Ukraïna, promising national—Ukrainian—self-determination.[37] In August, emigrants from the Ukraïna in L'viv set up the League for the Liberation of Ukraine with the avowed aim of creating an independent state and becoming a center for the organization of anti-Russian propaganda. The league threw itself into printing publications in Austria-Hungary and in neutral countries abroad and issued numerous pamphlets for the Ukraïna. The foreign ministry supported such activities in the hope of fomenting disturbances behind the Russian front lines. But by August 1914, the Austro-Hungarian armies were already in retreat. As the occupation of L'viv appeared imminent, the center of Ukrainian politics shifted to Vienna.[38]

Bad tidings about the severe reverses suffered by the imperial and royal armies began flooding back to L'viv. News of the advancing Russian army kept the city on tenterhooks. What the people saw with their own eyes belied the official exhortations to stick it out and the reports of victories.[39] Eyewitnesses described the nervous mood of the population.[40] The inhabitants watched as "an endless row of little peasant carts [passed] carrying wounded soldiers, heavily laden carts piled high with refugees, most of them Jews, their eyes staring with fear and horror, scattered troop units, defenders of the fatherland who had only sad stories to tell."[41] The imperial and royal armies lost the battle for L'viv, one of the greatest struggles in the eastern theater of war. The city filled with one hundred thousand refugees. In addition to more than forty thousand Jews,[42] many landowners, civil servants, and Ukrainophile clergymen also sought shelter in the capital. The mood was almost unbearably tense.[43]

The tension exploded on the evening of August 27 in a general panic. A rumor that Russian troops were shortly going to enter the city spread like wildfire. "Those terrible words 'The Cossacks are coming' almost drove everyone out of their minds."[44]

Several thousand people fled from the eastern parts of the city to the city center; carriages, carts and other vehicles clogged Łyczaków Street. Many sought refuge in the churches. The rumor was not confirmed, and the mood became calmer, but the tide of refugees began to swell again. When the state authorities and the state banks were evacuated during the night of August 30, it became obvious that the fall of the city was imminent. At the last moment tens of thousands of citizens attempted to flee, by train, in carriages, on horse-drawn carts or even pushing wheelbarrows. People jostled one another on the station platforms. Thousands spent the night in the station and rushed to the carriages as soon as any train appeared. But the major part of the transport was reserved for the army and for the evacuation of the authorities, and not all those wishing to leave the city were able to do so.[45] The station was littered with items of luggage that had not found room in the compartments and had been abandoned by fleeing citizens. Families were separated. The young Polish count Russocki heard that eight persons had suffocated and that three hundred had fallen unconscious during the panic.[46]

The majority of the Jewish elite left but about forty thousand out of a total of 56,751 Jewish inhabitants remained in the city.⁴⁷ Nevertheless, at the beginning of the Russian occupation more Jews were living in the city than before the war as many refugees were left stranded in L'viv. And, above all, "the poor without distinction of religion" had remained. The poor had no reserves to finance their flight or any lengthy exile. Many civil servants for whom L'viv already constituted a place of refuge and others who had not found room in the trains and horse-drawn carts also remained in the city. Russophile Poles and Ruthenians remained voluntarily as did, according to council member Marceli Chlamtacz, a few who stayed out of a sense of duty.⁴⁸ In the end, almost fifty thousand people, most of them well-to-do citizens, fled the city.⁴⁹

Chlamtacz explained the flight of the educated classes as the result of the conflict between the Western European and Eastern European worldview, suggesting that the latter was characterized by despotism and belief in the Orthodox Church.⁵⁰ This cliché is typical of the apprehensions with which the middle classes received the Russian soldiers. There was an almost atavistic fear of "the Russians." The thunder of cannons could be heard from afar, and burning houses and farms were visible from the surrounding hills. The Russian troops, particularly the Cossacks, were preceded by their terrible reputation. Rumors of unspeakable atrocities reached the city. The population was almost insane with fear, and those who had been forced to remain were deeply depressed. Until the very end, rumors continued to circulate, prophesying a speedy Russian defeat in the near future, and the Jewish population, in particular, pinned their hopes on these rumors.⁵¹

The populace had every reason to hope for a miraculous turning of the war. Jews had been among the most prominent victims of violence in the province. About one hundred thousand of the eight hundred thousand Galician Jews had fled to the western part of Austria-Hungary, most of them to Vienna. In L'viv, the Jewish population trembled as more and more tidings of pogroms reached the city.⁵² Uncertainty and fear led members of all religious denominations to flock to churches and synagogues. In the evenings, Roman Catholics and Greek Catholics thronged around statues of the Virgin, praying for help and salvation.⁵³

First Regime Change: The Russian Occupation

Invasion

After the police and the army had left the city on August 31, the L'viv municipal council set up a citizens' militia, which was entrusted with the task of keeping the public peace during the transition period. The militia included a few police but consisted mainly of older members of the intelligentsia and the middle classes who had not been considered fit for military service.⁵⁴ But the militia was not enough to compensate for the withdrawal of the police force. Members of the city's underclass, often joined by respectable citizens, took the opportunity to plunder the supplies of the army and the railway and to loot abandoned apartments and shops. Because many of the Jewish elite had left the city and about two-thirds of all shops belonged to Jews, the Jewish population was particularly hard hit by these predatory attacks.[55] The three-and-a-half days prior to the entry of the Russian troops were "truly days of terror," and not only for the Jews.[56]

News of attacks and looting reached the city from neighboring villages.[57] Many different contemporary sources show that ethnic, religious or even national categories played a subordinate role in these attacks. While the rallying cry of the looters in L'viv was that the time of the rule by the Jews and the *Panowie* (Polish: masters) was now at an end, empty Ukrainian apartments and houses were not spared. In his memoirs, one chronicler quotes the words of one looter, who said, "Now Catholics will also own something." The fact that the goods and properties plundered belonged predominantly to Jews and Poles was not, in the first instance, an indication of ethnic hatred but stemmed in the main from the existing distribution of wealth and property. Looting occurred where there was something of value for the taking. Some Christian witnesses reported that many members of the city's proletariat and many peasants were financially dependent on Jewish moneylenders and that their hatred of all Jews was correspondingly great.[58] In the countryside, the few Polish peasants also participated in the attacks and the looting alongside their Ukrainian counterparts. When a Greek Catholic priest left his diocese, he ran a great risk of his parishioners robbing his house and dividing up his land.[59]

The looting declined with the invasion of the Russian troops but did cease entirely because the soldiers themselves participated in the pillage.[60] In L'viv, looters pushing carts loaded with furniture and other goods stolen from shops were still on the streets after the Russians had entered the city. A contemporary Polish witness heard one peasant in one of the villages of L'viv district say, "Our father has come; now our rights apply." Irrespective of the origin of their loot, looters often claimed that the goods had been Jewish property.[61] In the countryside, individual military commanders and Orthodox priests invited the population to help themselves to the estates, to ignore forest and grazing rights, and to divide the arable land among themselves. The local Russian commanders hoped that this would win over the peasants to support the occupying power.[62] These peasants now feared the return of Austrian rule, by which they could expect to be called to account for their misdeeds. However, there are no records that the Russian supreme command or the central authorities condoned this behavior by local commanders. In Stanislau (Stanisławów, Stanyslaviv), peasants appeared in the city with empty carts that they hoped to fill with booty. Only after placards went up threatening to punish looters did order gradually return.[63] The designated military governor for Galicia, Lieutenant General Count Georgij A. Bobrinskij, reported to the chief of staff of the commander in chief General N. N. Janushkevich that all arson attacks on estates and pogroms against Jews had occurred during the period of lawlessness when there was no authority in charge.[64] But this was not strictly true. Eyewitness reports published by the *Jüdische Kriegsarchiv*[65] show that the Jewish fear of the Russian troops was well founded. The Cossacks had a particular predilection for looting properties belonging to or administered by Jews.[66] Atrocities were reported from many different localities. Orthodox Jews were subjected to humiliations such as cutting off their side curls and beards. In many places near the front, all Jews were forced to leave their homes and sent on forced marches to the east. In Rohatyn alone, 570 Jews were evicted. In the Kolomea district, the local occupying authorities imposed contributions on the Jewish community in retaliation for alleged acts of sabotage.[67] In the little town of Husiatyn, Cossacks carried out a bloody pogrom and looted Jewish property. Four hundred of the town's seven hundred houses belonging to Jews were burned to the ground. Jewish neighborhoods in Buczacz and Brody went up in flames; in Tłuste, only 200 of 516 Jewish houses remained intact. In Nadwórna, Cossacks set fire to the houses of Jews in revenge for Jews previously sheltering Polish legionaries. Mass rapes occurred in many places. Izak Bernstein reported from Nadwórna "that on the day before the town was burnt down, the Cossacks rounded up all the women next to the synagogue and raped them." Not even pregnant or ill women were spared. The next day, the Cossacks raped the women fleeing the fire. Similar scenes were repeated in Sołotwino, Delatyn, Dębice, and Tarnów.[68] After Russian rule was established, rapes and looting tended to occur primarily in the outer areas of the city away from the immediate scrutiny of the occupying authorities.[69]

The citizens of L'viv hung Russian flags and white flags from their houses to placate the feared Russians. Catholics placed pictures of saints in their windows, partly out of piety and partly to indicate that the inhabitants of the house were Christians. Although the Russians were perceived as adhering to another denomination, they were still Christians, and it was hoped that they could be mollified by such symbols. The Jews, on the other hand, anticipated that they were likely to suffer most from Russian occupation. Some Jews followed their Christian neighbors' example and placed pictures of saints in their windows.[70] But the windows of most Jewish houses "stood empty as only a few [Jews] decided to borrow pictures from Christians and set them up."[71]

Standing at the head of a delegation of the municipal council, the officiating mayor of L'viv, Tadeusz Rutowski, met the Russian commanding officer General von Rode at the beginning of Łyczaków Street, the city's eastern trunk road, to hand over the keys of the city. The general demanded sixteen hostages as guarantors for the peaceful entry of the troops into the city. Four prominent persons from each group—Poles, Ukrainians, Old Ruthenians, and Jews—agreed to their nomination by the municipal council and were billeted in the Hotel George. This choice also indicated a recognition of the Ukrainians as a separate group to the Old Ruthenians.

The municipal council called on the population to remain calm and to offer no resistance. The streets were completely empty as the city awaited the entry of the troops. With relief the inhabitants found that the Russian soldiers were not the figures of fear they were expecting and the Christian population began to venture out on the streets again. One Polish observer smugly commented that the Jews had outdone everyone else in their cheering of the troops who entered on September 3 and noted that Jews had put up Russian signs on their shops within days of the occupation.[72] But according to other Ukrainian and Polish sources, traditionally dressed Jews remained hidden in their houses for days.[73] The Russian army made an overwhelming impression on the population. Onlookers were particularly impressed by the diversity of nations and ethnicities among the soldiers. The troops entered the city to the accompaniment of music and songs. Bohdan Janusz viewed the multiethnic composition of the army through the lens of traditional anti-Russian stereotypes, referring to them as "Asian hordes" moving westward.[74] But such descriptions are the exception in contemporary sources. Perceptions were guided more by fascination than by fear. Only the songs they sang sounded "fearsome" to Count Russocki.[75] Two Ukrainian eyewitnesses commented that the invasion had occurred "without order" and "without military discipline." A few hours later, the streets through which the troops had passed had looked like a huge pigsty. Some looting had also occurred in one of the streets.[76] But the majority of eyewitnesses gave the Russian army full marks for their behavior that day. Their military commanders had had the foresight to order the closing of all taverns and inns and imposed a strict prohibition on the sale and serving of alcohol.[77] The troops behaved with exemplary discipline, the feared attacks did not occur. The takeover of the city "took place smoothly and flawlessly."[78]

Even before L'viv had fallen, Bobrinskij reported to Janushkevich, who was in charge of the occupation policy, that the residents everywhere were calm. The peasants treated the Russian in a friendly manner, only supporters of "the so-called party of the Ukrainians" were reserved. Because the Austrians had deported most of the Russophile priests, only "Ukrainizing" priests headed by Archbishop Sheptyts'kyj had remained. The Polish and Jewish residents adopted a wait-and-see policy but were not overtly hostile.[79]

The first contact the inhabitants of L'viv had with the new authorities was the Russian military governor Colonel Sergej Sheremetev. His sympathetic behavior toward the city's Polish representatives soon earned him a good reputation with the majority of the city's population.[80] His approach to the Poles was thrown into stark relief by his brusque attitude toward the Ukrainian delegation, making him unpopular with Ukrainians.[81] The new rulers of L'viv largely adhered to the rules of the Hague Conventions of 1899 and 1907. Colonel Sheremetev ordered that soldiers were only permitted to obtain goods from shops in return for payment. All requisition orders had to bear Sheremetev's signature, and requisitioning could only be carried out by patrols commanded by an officer.[82] The Russian military authorities then invited the local population to report any violations.[83] But these strict rules did not prevent soldiers and officers from pillaging abandoned houses and shops.[84]

It was initially far from clear whether Russian rule would be merely temporary. The recapture of the city appeared imminent, fueling the fear of a repeat of the looting. Many Jews from the lower classes collected in front of the city hall seeking protection. When some shots fell, the citizens' militia had difficulty in calming the Russian soldiers. On September 11, Sheremetev threatened draconian measures, including the death penalty, for arson, or for any form of resistance.[85]

The noise of battle was heard in the city center for several days, although the city itself did not come under fire.[86] But the residents of L'viv did experience some of the horrors of war. The hospitals were insufficient to treat the numbers of wounded soldiers, and public buildings were cleared to create makeshift hospitals. Austrian military doctors and nurses had remained in the city to attend to those of the wounded who could not be moved. Together with their Russian colleagues they tended to the victims of war. The stubborn attempts by the imperial-royal troops to recapture the city brought new waves of wounded soldiers to the city. Streetcars resembled hospital trains. Austrian and Russian soldiers were carried to separate hospitals while wounded officers on both sides were tended in the Red Cross hospital.[87] The stream of wounded soldiers into the military hospitals continued for the next months.

Occupation Policies

After the military situation became calmer, Count Georgij A. Bobrinskij[88] was officially appointed the military governor of Galicia on September 18. Right from the start, the new governor made it clear that L'viv, East Galicia, and the Lemko region could expect to become part of the Russian Empire after the war.[89] According to the Russian view, these areas were fulfilling their historical destiny by once again becoming an "original part of Russia" after centuries of foreign rule.[90] The Ruthenian population was considered a branch of the Russian nation but one whose "Russian" nature had been obscured under foreign rule. With the advent of the new order, Ruthenians would soon recognize their affiliation with the Russian people.[91] Russian was declared the official language and the language of education, and Russian governors, district commissioners, district captains, and police were appointed. The local administrative authorities were permitted to continue their work as long as they behaved loyally. The military governor also promised religious tolerance.[92]

The aim of these policies was to strip the Poles of any illusions about the future of East Galicia while still offering them a number of positive incentives. The manifesto issued by the Russian commander in chief, Grand Duke Nikolaj Nikolaevich, in August 1914 promised a unified Poland under tsarist rule. After the final Russian victory, the plan was to unite West Galicia with Russian Poland, while East Galicia would become an "ordinary" province in the Russian Empire.[93]

Military governor Bobrinskij shied away from arresting prominent politicians even if they had previously come out in support of Austria. His pragmatic policy was effective and encouraged Polish dignitaries, even those hostile to the new rulers, to behave correctly; some even changed sides. In August 1914 the university professor and National Democratic politician Stanisław Grabski was still proclaiming his loyalty to Austria-Hungary. But soon after Russian troops had entered the city he was calling on Polish legionaries to leave the Austrian army.[94]

The city council was suspended but the military authorities were happy to draw on the services of the municipal administration headed by a provisional mayoralty. About fifty of the city's one hundred councilors had remained in the city, including three of the fifteen Jewish councilors. The elected mayor, Józef Neumann, was in Cracow, and his deputy, Tadeusz Rutowski, took over his role. Rutowski was assisted by two deputy mayors, the Roman Catholic Leonard Stahl and the Jew Filip Schleicher, who had the responsible task of maintaining food supplies to the city with the help of the municipal Supplies Department.[95] Those who had remained in the city sharply criticized the officials who had left the city "in the lurch."[96]

The occupied territories were divided into three provinces (Czernowitz, Tarnopol, and L'viv) following the Russian model, with each province consisting of fourteen to sixteen districts. The province of Przemyśl was added after its capture. The provinces were ruled by governors, the districts (*uezdy*) and cities by district or town and city captains. Every district captain was assisted by two aides and six civil servants. The Austrian judges were initially left in office and even police—those who had not fled—were kept on.[97] The judges continued to dispense justice using the Austrian codes of law, although politically charged cases were tried in front of military courts. The continued employment of Austrian civil servants was a temporary but expedient solution. The deputy director of the Chancellery of Foreign Affairs, N. A. Bazili, traveled through the occupied territories in the fall of 1914. Bazili criticized the fact that the old municipal council of L'viv had continued in office because of a lack of Russian civil servants and police. Someone, presumably Janushkevich, added the comment "unacceptable" on the margin.[98]

New Russian civil servants and police were sent to the city.[99] But policing in rural areas remained woefully inadequate. Robberies and thefts occurred "on a previously unknown scale."[100] The occupying authorities urged the government to send more Russian police to maintain public order.[101] Bazili also urgently recommended sending Russian civil servants, judges, regular police, and secret police to East Galicia. Without massive support it would be impossible to stamp out hostile elements.[102] The military governor's comprehensive demand for more staff was not complied with. The wholesale blanketing of the country with Russian bureaucracy was postponed until peacetime.[103]

The occupiers also took symbolic possession of L'viv. The Russian flag flew above the city hall, and all accessible Austrian emblems were replaced by the imperial Russian eagle.[104] Under a number of pretexts, Rutowski prevaricated and managed to prevent the Austrian eagle from being removed from the city hall, where it was still on display during the tsar's visit to L'viv.[105] The university administration also delayed removing the symbols of Austrian imperial power.[106] But even these delays could not prevent the Russification of time, money, and public spaces. Petersburg time and the Julian calendar were introduced, and a general curfew was imposed between 10 p.m. and 4 a.m.[107] The ruble was now the main currency, and its exchange rate to the krone was set at one to three.

Russian dominance was cemented and made visible through the deployment of Russian symbols, the performance of Russian rituals, the establishment of Russian festivals, Russian time, and the Russian language. Military governor Bobrinskij ordered that all shops and businesses carry Cyrillic names and signs and that they remove all signs and symbols of Austrian rule. Many shopkeepers had already preempted his order, putting up Cyrillic signs or exchanging Latin letters for Cyrillic ones in German and Polish words. German inscriptions had been removed as a precautionary measure even before the Russian troops entered L'viv. The same happened to black-and-yellow decorations and Austrian eagles in shop windows. Although Polish symbols proved to be somewhat more recalcitrant, Polish signs and inscriptions began to be gradually replaced by Russian ones. Rutowski managed to prevent Russian street signs from being put up for several months.[108] Bobrinskij gave him a last period of grace to comply by March 1, 1915, when Russian street signs were finally fixed above Polish street names.[109] Russian grammars and dictionaries appeared in bookshops, and portraits of Nikolaj II and his family took the place of pictures of Emperor Franz Josef in shop windows.[110]

The populace was ordered to celebrate Russian public holidays such as the birthday of the tsar and to decorate public buildings with Russian flags. But many celebrations met with only a subdued response, and ceremonies remained limited to the governor's office.[111] The Russian police reported that businessmen and bank directors intervened to stop their buildings from being decorated with Russian flags.[112] Yet public celebrations were not always modest, given that the Russian police sometimes went from house to house to lend weight to their demands.[113] And so, on the tsar's name day on December 19, 1914 (December 6 according to the Julian calendar), and to celebrate the capture of Przemyśl all houses, with the exception of the city hall and the palaces of Archbishops Bilczewski and Teodorowicz, flaunted Russian flags.[114] After the three Catholic archbishops categorically refused to replace the traditional prayers for the Austrian emperor during Mass with intercessory prayers for the tsar, the occupiers contented themselves with ensuring that at least the name Franz Josef was not spoken aloud and that the emperor's name not mentioned in the intercessory prayers. Believers and priests were free to silently add the name of their preferred ruler. This issue was so important for the occupiers that they took to monitoring church services to ensure that nobody deviated from this practice.[115]

To prevent any disturbances or attempts at assassination, the authorities took the precaution of arresting several hundred residents of L'viv before the visit by the tsar and Grand Duke Mikhail to L'viv on September 22. Ukrainophiles once again suffered the greatest repressions, with three hundred of them placed under arrest. The official visit took place under tight security, and the program of the tsar's visit was only published at the last minute. After a service in the church of the garrison in Kleparów Street, Nikolaj drove to the governor's palace, where a crowd had gathered to cheer him.[116] Maria von Gember reported that peasants from villages that had converted to Russian Orthodoxy had been brought to the city and that they were the only ones who had welcomed the tsar, waving church flags as he drove past.[117]

For some supporters of Russian annexation, Russification was not happening fast enough, nor was it carried out consistently. In an article published in the Petrograd newspaper *Novoe Vremja*, D. N. Vergun, a member of the Galician-Russian Society, described his impressions a few weeks after the capture of the city. He had wished to examine "whether the native Russian [Ruthenian] population was satisfied and whether the cultural union of Galicia with Russia, which so many Russian generations had been preparing for, was progressing." But he primarily noted what had not changed and declared disappointedly: "There have been almost no changes in the [city] center. The same Jewish shops, the same Polish signs! The black-white-yellow flag salutes from the high tower of the old city hall. Above it, the Galician lion gleams happily." Vergun was particularly irritated by the fact that soldiers addressed passersby in Polish, even though the military governor had declared in his first speech that L'viv was a Russian city. Even in the palace of the military governor, the adjutant spoke to petitioners in Polish. The portraits of the Habsburg emperor were still hanging on the walls. At the train stations, Russian signs were still flanked by Polish ones. "Galicians look at this bilingualism as a violation of their rights as an indigenously Russian people and as an adaptation to the conditions of Austria-Hungary."[118] Subsequently, Polish signs were removed, which led to protests by a delegation of liberal Russian Duma delegates. Such unnecessary provocations could only damage the war effort. The delegates urged caution, preferring to defer fundamental changes until peacetime.[119]

In Petrograd, it was carefully noted that the Polish parties in Galicia had unanimously sided with Austria at the start of the war and had called for the creation of Polish legions to fight against Russia.[120] Bazili reported that the Poles were now behaving correctly but remained hostile. Poles in L'viv were continually emphasizing the city's Polish nature. While the National Democrats, who nursed Russian sympathies, attempted to work against the prevailing anti-Russian mood in the population, the "progressives"—and they predominated among the Galician authorities—were unconditionally Austrophiles.[121] Bazili had judged the mood correctly. During his first visit to Bobrinskij, Rutowski had demonstratively spoken in Polish and referred to L'viv as Polish city, a procedure that boosted his popularity among his compatriots still further.[122] At the New Year's reception, Rutowski again emphasized that "Lwów is and was a Polish city."[123] Polish and Jewish politicians made a point of speaking Polish or French when they met with representatives of the occupiers to indicate their distance from the Russians and to demonstrate their Polish patriotism and abiding loyalty to the Habsburg Empire. Rutowski communicated exclusively in French with the governor, both when talking to him and in his correspondence. Bobrinskij usually replied in Russian, sometimes in French.[124] Bobrinskij spoke only broken Polish; Rutowski could not speak Russian. At the beginning of 1915, the governor informed Rutowski of his order that all correspondence with the municipal council and the city administration must no longer be written in French but had to be written in both Russian and Polish.[125]

Supported by prominent politicians in Russian Poland, Bobrinskij attempted to convince the Polish elites of the benefits of allying themselves with Russia. At the instigation of the military governor, Russian and Polish members of the State Council and delegates of the State Duma visited L'viv in October 1914 to meet with Galician politicians and encourage cooperation with Russia. Grabski and a number of others switched sides, while Chlamtacz and Rutowski, speaking for the majority, continued to declare their loyalty to Austria.[126] Chlamtacz left the National Democratic Party in protest. Although the assembly refused his request, Grabski managed subsequently to win over twenty-four prominent politicians and dignitaries to support a pro-Russian appeal. Most of the signatories were National Democrats (nine) and Podolians (eight). Notwithstanding these differences in opinion, leading Polish dignitaries, among them Archbishops Bilczewski and Teodorowicz, met every Sunday at Rutowski's, Count Badeni's, or Count Piniński's to coordinate their tactics.[127]

Despite these demonstrations of the municipal council's continued loyalty to Austria, the Polish delegation from Russia defended their co-nationals in Galicia. They purported to discover feelings of "passive goodwill" toward Russia among Galician Poles. The delegates requested protection for landowners and the stern punishment of property offenses, pointing out that the aim must be to convince Poles that a better future beckoned to them as part of the Russian Empire.[128] Grabski suggested bringing together one hundred Polish politicians from Russian Poland and Galicia in L'viv to launch an all-Polish pro-Russian movement. He recommended that the occupiers set up a civil administration in Galicia to convince Poles of the honesty of their intentions. It was important to outline the main features of future self-government, which had to include free use of the Polish language, the unimpeded right to follow their own religion, and local autonomy. Bobrinskij supported the initiative but was of the opinion that the announcement should be more limited and should consist of a reminder of the manifesto by the supreme commander regarding the Polish question.[129] Janushkevich was opposed to the idea of convening Polish politicians in L'viv. Once the outcome of the war had been decided, then Warsaw would be the most suitable place for such an assembly.[130] Grabski accepted the deferment, which was made even easier for him as Governor Bobrinskij had begun to place more and more confidence in him. Bobrinskij noted hopefully that the majority of Polish representatives in East Galicia, who had previously been wavering, had now openly gone over to the side of Russia, a change that Bobrinskij ascribed to Grabski's influence. Although Grabski remained a Polish patriot first and foremost, he appeared to be convinced of the benefits of cooperating with Russia. He was hoping for a speedy union of Poznán, the Kingdom of Poland, and West Galicia under Russian rule. After talks with landowners, L'viv residents, and Warsaw politicians, Bobrinskij had come to the conclusion that the Poles were largely resigned to the incorporation of East Galicia in Russia and to the loss of their elite status. But Poles continued to hope that they would be guaranteed the right to speak Polish and open Polish schools and that they would enjoy equal rights in elections and equal access to the civil service. Bobrinskij believed that it would be very useful—provided Janushkevich agreed—if he could give such promises.[131]

Bobrinskij's optimism was premature. The measures implemented by the occupiers were unlikely to win the favor of the Polish population. The Russians began seizing state-owned and municipal properties, showing a special predilection for requisitioning houses and apartments whose owners had fled. Numerous soldiers were billeted in private houses. High-ranking officers and civil servants were accommodated in good hotels or elegant houses.[132] In the countryside, the estates of landowners whose families had remained while the owners had fled were the first to be seized. The occupiers only refrained from seizing estates if the landowner had instructed a legal agent to administer the estate prior to the owner's flight.[133] However, Bobrinskij softened this order, reserving the final decision for himself and limiting the confiscation of estates to cases where their owners had offered armed resistance or had engaged in propaganda directed against Russia.[134]

Bobrinskij tried to come to an arrangement with the regional elites which would accommodate local conditions. This brought him into conflict with the policies of the supreme commander, represented by his chief of staff Janushkevich. The Russian Orthodox Church, nationalist Russian journalists, and representatives of various ministries who visited East Galicia criticized the moderate policies of the military governor. Equipped with the authority provided them by their respective ministers, these newly arrived officials worked at cross-purposes to the military governor.[135] Bobrinskij's cooperative policies are exemplified by his dealings with the L'viv mayoralty. Although Bobrinskij was fully aware of its Polish nationalist stance and loyalty to Habsburg, he nevertheless sought its cooperation. He valued the mayoralty's work and efficiency and had no intention of jeopardizing the smoothly running machinery of municipal administration.[136] Janushkevich, however, was of the opinion that the mayoralty only represented Polish interests to the exclusion of other groups. He doubted that Rutowski was well disposed toward Russians but did not want to act rashly. He therefore suggested appointing two "Russians" from the local population to the city's administration.[137] Rutowski implored the military governor to abandon this plan and to hold new elections for the municipal council instead. Bobrinskij was afraid that the appointment of even a single Russian (by which he meant Russophile) could lead to the resignation of the entire mayoralty. Janushkevich relented, and the whole matter came to nothing.[138]

The schools and universities were another sensitive issue affecting the relationship between the Russian occupiers and the local population. L'viv University and L'viv Polytechnic were shut down immediately. Word soon got around that the Russians intended to transform the university into a Russian university and compensate the Poles by creating a university in Warsaw, which would also offer work to the majority of L'viv professors. After Starzyński, the rector of L'viv University had fled, the university's prorector, Professor Adolf Beck, took charge. Professor Beck was a Polish patriot accepted by the Russian authorities notwithstanding his Jewish faith. The university administration continued to work, research was allowed, and the university was finally permitted to hold final examinations. The Duma member D. N. Chikhachev was sent to the university as the military governor's delegate, where he acted as a sort of unofficial minister for education for the occupied territories. The Russian occupiers dealt fairly with the university. Russian officers and civil servants used the reading room in the university library. In the end, the library only lost seventy-nine volumes, most of them books that had been borrowed and not returned by their Russian readers prior to the precipitous retreat of the Russian troops.[139]

Primary and secondary schools were closed until the end of 1914 to prevent anti-Russian sentiments of "the teaching staff who are still entirely unknown to us" from influencing the pupils.[140] The long-term plan was to set up Russian schools across all of East Galicia. The intention was that the only private Polish schools remaining would be located in L'viv and the curriculum of these schools would include the compulsory teaching of Russian. To recruit staff for the new

Russian language schools, courses were set up in five cities to teach the teachers Russian, to improve their skills, and to vet their reliability.[141] But the courses only attracted a few hundred teachers, most of whom signed up out of poverty.[142]

The Polish population attempted to continue educating their children while sidelining the occupiers. A number of underground schools were set up in L'viv. Teachers taught their pupils, particularly those in the higher grades, in private houses. Wealthy families engaged private tutors to teach their children.[143]

Rutowski made an effort to ensure that schools were opened. He was supported by Polish and liberal Russian members of the Duma who argued that students were hanging around the streets with nothing to occupy them and were disturbing the public order. Opening schools, it was suggested, would also win over parents to the new government.[144] Rutowski pointed out that keeping twenty-four thousand children "undisciplined and unoccupied" served no military purpose.[145] Bobrinskij was amenable to his arguments. A few private Russian and Polish primary and secondary schools opened their doors again at the start of the year. But schools were only permitted to use textbooks that had been printed in Russia or that had previously been examined and passed by the censors. At least five hours of Russian and Russian literature per week were compulsory.[146] In February 1915 Bobrinskij gave his permission to open nine Polish and two Russian schools.[147] The supreme commander of the southwestern front remained suspicious. Before the war, all teaching in German-, Polish-, and Ukrainian-language schools had been deeply hostile to Russia. The proposal was made to set up a supervisory body of six inspectors and a director who would report to the military governor to ensure control of what was being taught.[148]

Rutowski advocated the opening of at least one more Polish secondary school. A Polish school committee was prepared to underwrite the entire costs of maintaining the schools.[149] In the end, ten Polish schools and two Russian schools were allowed to open. Rutowski was still dissatisfied and demanded the opening of two more schools. He argued that with the opening of the two Russian schools, the Ruthenians were relatively better off than the Poles were compared to the prewar era.[150] This was yet another indication of how much Rutowski favored Polish interests. Neither Rutowski nor the Polish delegates were interested in Ukrainian schools, and Rutowski accepted their conversion into Russian-language schools without demur. The occupiers categorically refused to accept any Ukrainian-language schools, and Rutowski made no attempt to get involved on behalf of the Ukrainian residents of the city.[151]

Daily Life

The situation in the city normalized soon after the Russian troops had entered the city. Gas and water supplies were working, the streetcars were operating, and cafés and restaurants were open.¹⁵² Because all clubs, associations, and societies had ceased their activities, social life mostly played out in private residences and taverns.¹⁵³ Cultural life largely came to a stop.¹⁵⁴ Cafés and restaurants were now filled with well-paid Russian civil servants and officers. As time passed, many officers and civil servants sent for their families to come to L'viv and "the coffeehouses and pastry shops . . . hummed with life." Shops for luxury goods also benefitted from this influx of new customers.¹⁵⁵ However, the run on luxury items gradually began to ebb, and satisfying their daily needs became more important for this new segment of the population as well. Russian merchants also entered the town in the wake of the troops so that initially there was no lack of foodstuffs, provided there was enough money to pay for them.¹⁵⁶ The Greek Catholic priest Jaroslav Levyts'kyj reported that food was always available in sufficient quantities. What was lacking was fuel, alcohol, coffee, and occasionally tobacco.¹⁵⁷ However, Bohdan Janusz reported that speculators were exploiting existing food shortages.¹⁵⁸ The arrival of Russian Orthodox priests "with their long hair and shaggy beards . . . caused a general sensation" and was also a new experience for the city's residents.¹⁵⁹

Some residents came to an arrangement with the occupiers and profited from their dealings with their new overlords. Ukrainian newspapers smirked that the "beauties of L'viv" were making up to the Russian soldiers.¹⁶⁰ L'viv had become a "modern Babel." "Within a short time L'viv had become almost entirely Russian in its external appearance; the respectable middle-classes appeared to have disappeared from exterior view as if they had been overwhelmed by foreign elements."¹⁶¹ Janusz criticized the "fashionable ladies" who had either fled or welcomed the soldiers with vodka, grumbling that they were not to be found in the hospitals and that the women from the poor classes were bearing the brunt.¹⁶²

Ukrainian authors repeatedly pointed to the political about-face of the Polish National Democratic camp. Little had remained of many Poles' purported Austrophilia after the Russian troops had entered the city. Now these selfsame Poles were arguing for a pan-Slavic community.¹⁶³ It was important to remain on one's guard even in private conversations, because many persons who had been sworn "devourers of Russians" had suddenly changed into Slavophiles who now waxed lyrical about Russia's greatness and power.¹⁶⁴

Poles, Ukrainians, Jews, and Russian occupiers did not move in isolated circles. This is most obvious when looking at the culture of the coffeehouses. Members of the intelligentsia, irrespective of their national or religious persuasions, tended to meet in Café Szkocka, where assimilated Jews, Ukrainian lawyers, and Polish journalists discussed the latest news. Visitors to the Grand Hotel were predominantly Jewish. Russian officers frequented the Renaissance, the American Café, the Avenue, and the Roma. National Democrats gathered in separate rooms in Szkocka and Café Sztuka while the public in the Wiener Kaffeehaus was mixed.¹⁶⁵

The Russian occupation cut off the city from its old lines of communication. The citizens of L'viv still learned about current events in the Habsburg Empire and at the front from newspapers, but now international politics and the war were described from the Russian point of view. L'viv was almost entirely cut off from western information.¹⁶⁶ Although Polish dailies were still permitted to appear, strict regulations and precensorship ensured that no undesirable news would be published in their pages. The difficult conditions and limited news forced journalists to concentrate on local topics. They were forced to obtain reports on the war from the Russian press or Polish language newspapers published in Russia. Newspapers were banned from referring to Galician Ukrainians as *ruski* (Ruthenians). Instead, they had to use the term *rosyjski* (Russian). At the same time, a cultural offensive was launched. Works of Russian literature were serialized in newspapers and journals. If individual numbers of the *Wiener Freie Presse* or other Austrian newspapers found their way to the city, this was welcomed as a sensation.¹⁶⁷ All sorts of rumors about important German, Austrian, or Russian victories, the heroic deeds of the Polish legions, and Russian barbarities made the rounds.¹⁶⁸ Everyone was attempting to make sense of the many different and contradictory pieces of news.¹⁶⁹

The Wiener Kaffeehaus, a popular L'viv café, functioned as a stock exchange, where information about the situation of the war and international politics was swapped. The information was garnered from legal and illegal newspapers, prisoners' reports, chauffeurs, and officers of the Russian army. When this came to the notice of the authorities, a number of persons in that circle were deported to Russia. The informal meetings in cafés continued up until the end of the Russian occupation but the watchful eyes of the gendarmerie ensured that a free exchange of opinions and information was no longer possible.¹⁷⁰ The gendarmerie believed the Wiener Kaffeehaus to be a center for Mazepists (*mazepincy*), yet another term used to describe Ukrainophiles, which referenced Hetman Mazepa, an ally of Charles XII.¹⁷¹

Unlike the Jews, the Christian population was less afraid of the Russian army than of the Russian police. The police established nine commissariats and recruited informers from the population. The Russian secret police, the Okhrana, set up a system of surveillance and was able to make use of local informers. The Okhrana was constantly looking to recruit spies.¹⁷² The police was quick to note who did not decorate his house with Russian flags despite being prompted to do so, who held anti-Russian speeches in the coffeehouses or criticized the Russophiles. There was even an informer in the circle of dignitaries who met up regularly at Rutowski's to coordinate their approach toward the occupying power. The informer passed on hostile comments made in the run-up to the tsar's visit to the gendarmerie and reported on Rutowski's appeal to make it clear to the tsar that L'viv was an "entirely Polish city." Informers did not come from a single group in the population. One police report, for example, was based on several denunciations, including information from two Roman Catholics, two Greek Catholics, and one Russian Orthodox person.[173]

Denunciations for private or political reasons occurred on a daily basis. Persons could be detained for merely talking German on the street. The population experienced the nightly house searches, arrests and confiscations as despotic and arbitrary acts.[174] Zieliński reported that even some of his Polish compatriots had become "Judases" who denounced refugees and Austrian soldiers in hiding to the occupying power.[175]

The city's Jewish population was subjected to particularly tight surveillance: "In Jewish houses the janitors ruled, who enjoyed the support of the Russian power and harassed the inhabitants in an impossible manner. At that time the janitor was the master of the house and not the Jewish owner."[176] Members of all religious and ethnic groups were arrested and deported to the interior of the Russian Empire, many to Siberia. It was not always evident to the victims or their relatives which criteria determined arrests and deportations.[177] The notorious venality of Russian civil servants meant that even people with an unblemished record were obliged to prove their innocence through financial "donations."[178] This arbitrary rule meant that many men, particularly those of an age where they would be liable for conscription, went into hiding.

The prevailing conditions meant that refugees suffered most, followed by the groups of former imperial-royal civil servants. In their frantic rush to evacuate the city, the Austrian authorities had neglected to pay their civil servants a designated advance amounting to a quarter of their annual salary. Public servants along with the families of civil servants who had fled the city were now cut off from their source of income.[179] Rutowski estimated the number of people affected to be as high as sixteen thousand.[180] Some were evacuated to smaller towns, but there were still about twenty-five thousand people (a figure that included dependents) in the city who had no regular source of income.[181] The municipality proposed the establishment of a syndicate of banks that would provide the necessary resources at the expense of the imperial and royal government. This would allow the payment of an advance to unemployed public servants amounting to between 30 and 50 percent of their monthly salary. The city was prepared to find 600,000 rubles, while the banks were expected to come up with 1,350,000.[182] Bobrinskij tolerated this initiative along with the attempt to remedy the lack of cash resources by the emission of municipal assignats. Admittedly, the Russians considered the proposed sum of one million krone too high. They had no interest in extending the municipal council's influence.[183] Finally, the sum was confirmed, and by February 5, 1915, some 887,000 krone were distributed to about 9,000 beneficiaries. Between thirty and thirty-five thousand people, the equivalent of about 15 percent of the city's population, benefited from these measures.[184]

In L'viv, coins and notes of small denominations were in acute short supply. By the middle of September 1914, it was impossible to buy anything using bills with large denominations, forcing people to sell them for less than their nominal value. The local authorities therefore issued one hundred thousand bills of their own to the value of one krone each and guaranteed that they would later be changed for regular banknotes. The municipality's standing was evident by the fact that these bills were also accepted as legal tender in nearby villages whereas peasants often rejected rubles.[185] City hall was besieged by petitioners. In addition to former public servants, the majority were the families and dependents of soldiers, unemployed artisans, widows, and orphans. In the winter of 1914/1915, the number of weekly petitions for firewood alone stood at ten thousand.[186] The municipal forest was given over to the lower classes. It was easier for university professors, who were allocated supplies from the university's stock of firewood and additionally received financial assistance.[187]

With the evacuation of the imperial and royal authorities and the loss of the Galician hinterland, many of the city's inhabitants had lost their jobs. They eked out a living doing odd jobs and casual work. Even formerly important civil servants now sold newspapers or attempted to get a living as street vendors. Small businesses run from home sprang up everywhere, most of them set up by women. Only the bakeries continued to do a flourishing trade. Conditions were particularly threatening for artisans and small tradesmen who depended on supplies. Out of 590 formerly self-employed craftspeople, only 20 percent did not have to seek additional means of earning a living.[188]

Given the critical social conditions the role of charitable organizations became increasingly important. They organized charity concerts and collected money for invalids at church services.[189] Although some relief organizations did not differentiate between persons in need based on ethnicity or religion, others were careful to discriminate and cared exclusively for members of their respective group. "Never were the distinctions between social classes in L'viv as blurred as during the time of occupation. The common experience of suffering and privation, of hope and longing made us all brothers. High school teachers could be seen hawking, vending and carrying heavy loads; court officials together with teachers and students were in the municipal timber yard chopping wood to earn 2 krone daily with heavy labor."[190]

But the population was not quite as "classless" as Maria von Gember, cited earlier, may have thought. Soup kitchens—primarily sustained by women—were set up. In November 1914 twenty-eight soup kitchens fed twenty thousand people every day.[191] The Polish Praca Kobiet (Women's Work) set up a soup kitchen for Poles, another soup kitchen was operated by Ukrainian women, and Jewish women ran soup kitchens for the children of Jewish refugees.[192] Help for the Jewish population also came from Jewish organizations in America and Russia. With the permission of the military governor, in January 1915, the seventy-five-year-old Jew David Feinberg from St. Petersburg founded a Jewish Relief Committee, which twenty prominent Jews from L'viv joined. The lawyer Jakób Diamand took the chair.[193]

Public soup kitchens were supported by municipal and city-funded social organizations. At the end of January 1915, some 38,160 meals were being served up daily in 33 soup kitchens across the city, of which only 1,282 were paid for. Twenty-one of these soup kitchens were each doling out between 500 and 2,000 meals every day. However, the intelligentsia ate separately from the proletariat.[194] At the beginning of 1915, about 10,543 meals were being served in "intelligentsia kitchens," with 27,617 meals prepared in "people's kitchens." Approximately 25 percent of the population were kept fed by these kitchens.[195] A few weeks later 70 municipal soup kitchens were handing out food, of which 42,672 meals were handed out free of charge and 1,693 were paid for. For many people, these modest midday meals constituted their main meal. Around one hundred tons of provisions were required for these kitchens alone, including seventy tons of flour and bread. The city consumed about 1,680 tons, or 168 wagonloads, of flour; 50 tons of rice; and 1,000 tons of pulses every month. In addition to the soup kitchens, the city also ran eighteen shops in which basic food staples were sold at prices that undercut the going market prices. Ten tons of flour were sold daily. Every family received one kilo of flour, allowing ten thousand families to benefit from these cheaper foodstuffs. This pricing policy was intended to make it more difficult for speculators who were offering foodstuffs at prices that exceeded the stipulated maximum price. Ensuring a sufficient supply of provisions for the city was a difficult logistical task, and Deputy Mayor Schleicher dealt with it brilliantly. During the first months of the war, the city had benefited from extensive stocks of food it had laid in, in July and August. This allowed the municipal council to influence the prices for flour, salt, sugar, and rice and to compensate for shortfalls in supplies. It was impossible to supply the city's need for provisions from the surrounding villages, and the occupation cut off all transportation links to the west. For officials to ensure sufficient supplies in the town, foodstuffs had to be brought in from Russia and transported huge distances, which considerably increased their costs. In February 1915 the city was therefore forced to increase the price for one kilogram of flour by five kopeks, bringing the price to twenty-one kopeks. But sufficient means of transporting provisions were still lacking. Municipal shops were empty, and the price of flour rose to twenty-three rubles for one hundred kilograms. Schleicher requested Bobrinskij's help in securing two hundred railway carriages to transport the ordered supplies from Russia.[196] Overall, the war brought about an "immense increase in prices."[197] By the fall of 1914, the top prices for bread and flour were already 50 percent higher than the prewar prices. Prices on the black market were even higher.[198]

In the wake of the Russian soldiers, a number of infectious diseases such as diphtheria, typhus, and cholera reached the town. Russian authorities and the city's administration worked together to contain the danger of contagion and to isolate cases with disease.[199] The lack of medicines was a problem. The death rate increased dramatically, rising from 22.52 per thousand in 1914 to 36.9 per thousand in 1915. In 1916 the death rate dropped to 22.6 again. The number of deaths from typhus, smallpox, measles, Asian cholera, and German measles increased significantly. The poor diet and general malnutrition manifested themselves in an increase in deaths from gastrointestinal infections (see table 2.1).[200]

	1914	1915	1916
Typhus	29	190	56
Smallpox	—	595	121
Measles	8	3	38
Asiatic cholera	13	782	—
Ordinary cholera	27	49	4
German measles	77	239	31
Other	1	15	8

Table 2.1. Deaths from infectious diseases, 1914–1916.

Discrimination and Anti-Semitism

The occupying forces regarded Jews with suspicion. At the beginning of September, the military governor had already summoned representatives of the Jewish community, including Deputy Mayor Schleicher; the deputy chairman of the Kahal, Jakób Diamand; and Rabbis Bernard Hauser and Leib Braude, and accused L'viv Jews of hiding Jews who had deserted from the Russian army and helping them escape. The delegation had to promise that the Jewish population would not encourage anti-Russian propaganda. In return, Bobrinskij promised tolerance and equal rights.[201] Schleicher was considered suspect by the occupying forces based on nothing more than his Jewish denomination. Bobrinskij imputed hostile intentions to him although there was no proof of such intent.[202] After a visit to the headquarters of the commander in chief, Bobrinskij even returned with the intention of relieving Schleicher of his duties.[203] But Schleicher's commitment to the welfare of the city's population managed to convince Bobrinskij of his utility. The military governor was highly satisfied with his work, and Schleicher remained in office until the end of the Russian occupation.[204]

The Russian troops included many sons of Ukrainian peasants. According to reports by eyewitnesses, they entered the country harboring the notion that Austria was an entirely Jewish state that oppressed the Slavs.[205] Anti-Semitism was particularly rife among the Cossacks. In the early days of the occupation, they roamed the city's streets in search of Jews, whom they beat and robbed. The best protection against such attacks was to wear a cross or a medallion of Jesus or the Virgin Mary.[206]

The Cossacks were also responsible for the pogrom on September 27, 1914, which the Jewish population had long expected. The ostensible reason for the attacks was some shots fired from a house in which Jews lived. Hundreds of Cossacks subsequently rampaged through the Jewish quarter, shooting and plundering indiscriminately. It is not known how many Jews were killed in the attacks. Zieliński, who witnessed the pogrom, mentioned forty-seven dead and the same number of wounded.[207] The Ukrainian Social Democrat Teofil' Melen' spoke of forty-nine victims, only half of whom had been Jewish.[208] In contrast, Janusz knew of only three deaths.[209] The municipal council later reported that thirty-eight persons had been killed during "a shooting by Russian soldiers."[210] The authorities did not carry out any investigations and blamed the attacks on "Jewish provocation." According to one rumor, however, the trigger for the pogrom had not been the shots by a Jew but had been Russian soldiers shooting at their officers.[211] The pogrom had no consequences for the Cossacks. Instead, the three houses from which the supposed shots had emanated were seized. Four Jews were taken as hostages.[212] Jakób Schall ascribed the pogrom to a provocation by an Okhrana officer. On the morning of September 27, rumors had already been circulating about an imminent pogrom. At three o'clock in the afternoon, the following had then probably occurred: someone had attempted to rob a soldier in the market square. When the soldier shouted for help, the unidentified thief escaped into one of the houses shooting into the crowd as he made his escape. The police then surrounded the building and opened fire. Eight Jews were seriously injured in the shooting. At the same time, three hundred Jews were arrested, none of whom were involved in the incident. At this point, the Cossacks arrived and began rampaging through the streets, shooting and roughing up Jews. About forty Jews died either directly or as a consequence of these atrocities. It was only a few days later that the occupation authorities began spreading the story that shots had been fired at Russian soldiers from Jewish buildings. As a result, Jewish representatives were summoned to appear before the town's military administrator, Major General Eikhe, who demanded the alleged Jewish perpetrators be handed over.[213] The Jewish population stopped visiting the synagogues to protest against the arrests and because they feared another pogrom. Bobrinskij attempted to calm matters down and sent for two rabbis, promising them that such incidents would not be repeated. The intervention by an influential Jew from St. Petersburg was able to obtain the release of the Jewish hostages a short time later. After that, with the exception of occasional attacks on individual Jews, the Jewish residential neighborhood remained quiet.[214] The pogrom also unsettled the town's Christian inhabitants.[215]

The occupying forces categorized the Jewish population as Austrophile and considered them an inexhaustible reservoir of potential traitors. Poor Jews were the main victims as the majority of well-to-do Jews had fled.[216] The discrimination experienced by the Jewish population increased their dislike of Russian rule and their attachment to the Austrian monarchy, which in turn confirmed the authorities' opinion of them, leading to renewed discrimination. Galician Jews aided Austrian prisoners of war despite the high personal risk they ran themselves, providing them with food or hiding them. Many Jews were not even put off from offering such assistance by the threat of further punishment and discrimination.[217]

The supreme command of the Russian army pursued a decidedly anti-Jewish line, bringing it into conflict with the Council of Ministers, which had recommended treating the Jewish population gently.[218] The chief of staff of the commander in chief, N. N. Janushkevich, viewed Galician Jews as representing the "Jewish question" in the Russian Empire, in fact, as indicative of an international problem. He hoped to use the war to diminish the economic standing of Jews.[219] The occupying forces carried out an inventory of Jewish-owned property in the Gouvernements L'viv, Tarnopol, and the eastern districts of the Gouvernement Przemyśl. The appraisal listed 7,985 Jewish landholders who owned 305,933 *Morgen* (= 435,060 acres) of land.[220] Janushkevich would have preferred to dispossess all Jewish landowners and accused Bobrinskij of treating the Jewish population too gently.[221]

A the beginning of October 1914, the chairman of the Council of Ministers, I. L. Goremykin already voiced his objections to any further forms of discrimination against the Jewish population. He was not principally opposed to such policies but believed that putting them into action at that moment was premature. As long as the war continued, it was important to treat Jews like any other Austrian subjects.[222] In 1915 the Council of Ministers repeated this recommendation, but initially they were unsuccessful.[223] The Jewish population served as a useful scapegoat for the policy problems of the occupying forces. Chamberlain Bazili commented that the behavior of the Jews was "naturally very hostile." He interpreted economically motivated actions as political statements, believing that Jews removed coins from circulation to create a scarcity of money, speculated with food and concealed food supplies to increase prices.[224]

Contemporary Polish and Ukrainian witnesses also viewed Jewish merchants with distrust. Russian soldiers sold the goods they seized during looting to merchants. Levyts'kyj was of the opinion that Jews profited most from such acts.[225] Although Janusz noted that everyone was involved in some form of trading and dealing, Jews were "particularly prominent."[226] This is unsurprising because in L'viv—as in all of East Galicia—the majority of traders and merchants were Jewish. But this knowledge did not enter into the interpretation of actions.

The occupiers found the rampant anti-Semitism useful as a means of scoring points by implementing anti-Jewish measures. In Stanislau, one Orthodox priest informed his parishioners that the Russians had come "to liberate the Galician population from the Jewish yoke."²²⁷ One Ukrainian chronicler reported from Stryj that mainly the Jews were living in terror. The underclasses of the Christian population adopted the anti-Semitic slogans of the Cossacks, and the threat of a pogrom was repeatedly in the air. Jewish women hid themselves, and many older Jewish men no longer dared to leave their homes.²²⁸

In a telegram sent to the supreme command at the beginning of 1915, Janushkevich stated that the Jews were terrorizing the Russian (in other words, the Ruthenian) and Polish populations. The policies against Jews should not be toned down. He proposed that requisitioning should first target Jews, although thefts and looting should be prevented.²²⁹ As the Russian troops increasingly came under pressure, the Jews were scapegoated. Janushkevich insisted that men of Jewish extraction should no longer be allowed to serve as judges in L'viv. In the name of the commander in chief, he ordered that they must be immediately removed from their positions and replaced for the time being by their deputies. Only judges who were well disposed toward the Russians should remain in office. He ordered Bobrinskij to comb through all the authorities in the entire Generalgouvernement "with this in mind" (i.e., the removal of Jews) and to report to him without delay about the measures he had taken.²³⁰ Bobrinskij consequently dismissed both Jewish judges officiating at the district and appellate courts of L'viv and asked whether Jewish chancellery officials should also be dismissed.²³¹ The commander in chief, Grand Duke Nikolaj Nikolaevich, finally decided that "in view of the hostile relations persons of Jewish origin exhibited towards all things Russian," all Jews should be removed from the Galician judicature.²³²

The religious affiliations of those sent into exile also clearly demonstrate the occupiers' anti-Semitic policies. Until April 16, 1915, 970 Christians were exiled while the number of Jews sent into exile was 1,160. Of these, 726 Christians and 520 Jews were exiled to other parts of the Russian Empire, while 244 Christians and 640 Jews were only sent to the eastern districts of Galicia.²³³ However, Bobrinskij did not wish to seize the property and homes of exiled persons because their relocation had been a preventative measure and their guilt had not been proved. The property of Jewish hostages was only sequestered in Czernowitz. Bobrinskij rejected accusations that his civil servants were behaving recklessly toward the Jewish population. The military governor was opposed to excluding Jewish families in Galicia from all forms of state aid "because of the hostility against Russia and Russian interests which characterizes all Jews." Charitable aid was organized by municipal and rural charitable committees and received only very limited funding from the occupying forces. Moreover, loyal Jews should not be excluded "to prevent a conviction of our national enmity towards all Jews from taking hold among them."²³⁴

Unequal treatment of Jews was the rule rather than the exception. But L'viv was under the spotlight of international public attention. Events occurring there were soon known more generally. The occupiers therefore attempted to play by the rules. Matters in other regions, which attracted less international attention, were a little different. Czernowitz was briefly recaptured by Austrian units. When the Russian troops returned, they found a strongly decreased population. Some Jews, the military governor believed, had fled in fear of being called to account because they had committed atrocities against some of those persons who had helped the Russian troops during the first occupation. The governor took seventeen well-respected Jews as hostages to guard against acts of espionage. At the same time, he demanded the payment of fifty thousand rubles as a pledge of future good conduct.[235]

In Sokal, the Russian troops spared one estate that was administered by a Polish Catholic but looted the estate administered by a Jew. The troops only set fire to four buildings, all of them belonging to Jews.[236] After the fall of Przemyśl, which had been unavailingly besieged for months, the occupiers revenged themselves on the Jewish population. The Russian commanding officer ordered all Jews to leave the city. About seventeen thousand reached L'viv, where they were provisionally housed in makeshift shelters by the authorities.[237] The Ukrainian Social Democrat Mykola Hankevych stated, "The Jews suffered most under the barbarians. The "liberators of Galicia" behaved like Assyrians. The Jewish problem has become the problem of the Ukrainian people, exploited, oppressed and ill-treated by tsarist rule. The Moscow barbarians incite Ukrainian peasants to destroy Jewish shops and Jewish property. The tsarate used the reactionary instincts of the masses to further its own egoistical policies."[238]

In the spring of 1915, the violence escalated, with Jews subjected to constant harassments. Jews were the preferred targets when laborers were recruited to dig trenches. The occupying power also began to remove the Jewish population from areas near the front lines. These forcible evacuations were accompanied by looting and arson. Often, the evicted persons did not know where to go. The army evicted four thousand Jews in Dobromil, who were then forced to camp outside in the suburbs. Dispossessed Jews moved to Sambor and finally to L'viv.[239] Hankevych gave the following description of the events in Śniatyn: "4352 Jews were assembled on the market square, of which 19 were hanged on the spot, allegedly for treason. The assembled persons moved in the direction of Bessarabia. Terrible scenes occurred on the market square of Śniatyn. The weeping of the old, the lamenting and groans of the women, the screams of the children. A truly Dantesque hell. The Jews were robbed of all their possessions and all of the women were raped."[240]

The longer the war continued, and the greater the losses suffered by the Russian troops, the more they directed their aggression against local populations, particularly against the Jews. When after three years of occupation (after the February revolution had occurred) Austrian troops advanced on the little town of Dubkovcy, where Kyryl Levyts'kyj lived, the Russian troops abandoned any last vestiges of discipline. Once it had become clear that the Russian occupation would not last, Russian soldiers began systematically looting gold and valuables from houses and apartments. Jewish women were the most frequent victims of rape, but in a nearby village of Dubkovcy, according to the report by Levyts'kyj, Russian soldiers raped all girls and women between the ages of seven and seventy, irrespective of whether they were Christians or Jews.[241]

Church Policy and Russification

In the eyes of the leaders, Ukrainians were "Little Russians" and thus part of the Russian people. Ukrainian was considered a Russian dialect, a type of garbled Russian debased by borrowings from the Polish, Czech, and German languages, and its literature an artificial product created by the "intelligentsia of the Ukrainian Mazepist party." Minister-President I. L. Goremykin ordered that the same restrictive rules on the use of the Ukrainian language should be used as were the rule in the Russian Empire. All Ukrainian- or Russian-language books that had not been published in Russia had to be removed from all bookshops in L'viv. Newspapers were not permitted to be published in Ukrainian even if they were pro-Russian. Only flyers and handbills directed at the local population were permitted to use "dialect." However, the military authorities declined to forbid the use of Ukrainian as a spoken language. Use of Ukrainian was permitted as the colloquial language of the local population.[242] Russian as the language of instruction was introduced in Ukrainian high schools, with only primary schools permitted the use of the vernacular dialect (i.e., Ukrainian). However, in kindergartens, Ukrainophiles were allowed a free hand. Children were taught in Ukrainian. It was also forbidden to wear yellow and blue ribbons during processions. The children nevertheless continued to do so and to sing songs in Ukrainian.[243]

Ukrainophile institutions, cooperatives, and libraries were closed down. Only the insurance company Dnister and the Agrobank were allowed to continue in business until March 1915. Thereafter, these institutions also ceased operations, and their cash reserves were confiscated. In many Galician villages, the premises of Ukrainian shooting associations, credit unions, and trading companies and of the Prosvita Society were not simply closed down but destroyed or looted. The confiscated buildings were either taken over by the administration of the occupying forces or handed over to the Russophile Kachkovs'kyj Society.[244]

Ukrainophiles viewed the occupation as a direct attack on the Ukrainian nation.[245] Conversely, the occupiers viewed the educational and cooperative activities of the Ukrainophiles as an attempt to detach the Ruthenians from the Russian nation.[246] When he first took office, the military governor also received a Ukrainian delegation in addition to Polish, Russophile, and Jewish delegations, but he showed no sympathy for their concerns and dismissed them ungraciously. The fact that about one million anti-Russian leaflets compiled by the Ukrainian National Council in L'viv and aimed at the Ukrainian population in the Russian Empire lay ready for distribution may have contributed to his hard-line attitude. Only the advance of the Russian troops had prevented the distribution of the leaflets.[247]

The Ukrainian population had only limited means to protest publicly against these policies. The funerals of prominent Ukrainians turned into public manifestations of Ukrainian national feeling. Almost the entire Ukrainian intelligentsia of the city took part in the funeral of the author Mychajlo Pavlyk in January 1915. Half a dozen clergymen read the services and performed the ceremonies. The funeral was accompanied by huge numbers of police. Jaroslav Levyts'kyj joked one might have thought that a captain of the constabulary was being buried.[248] On February 17, 1915, dozens of members of the Ukrainian intelligentsia, politicians and clergymen were arrested in L'viv and other cities and villages of East Galicia and were brought to overcrowded holding cells. A minority was released after nine days.[249] More arrests and numerous house searches were carried out immediately prior to the tsar's second visit to L'viv.[250]

The occupiers relied on the support of Ruthenian Russophiles, selecting the new members of the National Council from among their numbers.[251] In contrast, the authorities mistrusted the protestations of loyalty made by Polish National Democrats, even if they argued in favor of an alliance with the tsar. The government was well aware that it could expect only limited support from the National Democrats.[252] Their partisanship of Russia was purely tactical and would only hold as long as they expected it to offer benefits for the Polish cause. For the Russophiles, however, the annexation of East Galicia into the Russian Empire represented the fulfillment of their political goals. They proffered suggestions on how Russification could best be implemented. Dudykevych recommended that Archbishop Sheptyts'kyj, the Jesuits and the Order of the Basilian monks be expelled and their property handed over to the Russian Orthodox Church (ROC). He wished to lay the groundwork for the unification of the Russian Orthodox and Greek Catholic Churches but intimated that it would be necessary to be patient with the remaining Uniates. He proposed to start by closing the schools and reopening them under Russian supervision. The university should be transformed into a Russian university, and Russian should immediately become the language of instruction in high school. Dudykevych wished to place the judiciary under Russian control, but local employees could be retained in subordinate positions. Lands and estates should be distributed among the "Russian [Ruthenian] peasantry" and the debts they owed to Jews and Polish banks should be canceled. Further recommendations by Dudykevich included shifting the administration of the general governate from "Polish L'viv" to Halych. Jews should not be permitted to become Russian nationals, and it should be made clear to the Poles that Galicia was Russian soil. Their national energies should be diverted to Poznań, Silesia, East Prussia, and Pomerania. The notes on the margins show that Janushkevich read the memorandum and that he entirely approved of the recommendations. The only suggestion he dismissed was relocating the seat of the military governor from L'viv to Halych.[253]

Religious policies were entirely focused on the relationship between the Russian Orthodox and Greek Catholic Churches. The Russian authorities viewed the Greek Catholic Church as an important obstacle to incorporating Ruthenians into the Russian nation. Suppression of the Uniate Church hinged on both aggressive and defensive motives. Minister of the Interior N. A. Maklakov identified three main enemies of Russia and of the Russian Orthodox Church. In addition to the Roman Catholic Order of the Jesuits, these included the Greek Catholic Order of the Basilians and the consistory of the metropolitan bishop of L'viv together with the various establishments of the Order of the Studists. All of them aimed to alienate the population of western Ukraine from Russia and the Orthodox Church. The minister of the interior considered the missionary work of the Studists to be particularly dangerous if East Galicia was to be incorporated into the Russian Empire. It was tantamount to opening the door to Greek Catholic propaganda in the western governorates.[254] The Uniate Church had already attempted to purchase land on the Russian side of the border before the war and to set up settlements of Greek Catholic believers there.[255]

There was no disagreement between the Orthodox Church and the state regarding the ultimate goal of their religious policies, namely, to eliminate the Uniate Church and incorporate the Greek Catholic faithful into the Russian Orthodox Church. In the words of the designated head of the Russian Orthodox Church in Galicia, Archbishop Evlogij, the "national union of Galicia with Russia will only be permanent [*prochno*], when it [Galicia] is also united in our own [*rodnoj*] Orthodox faith."[256] However, the secular authorities and the church leaders were divided with regard to how quickly this should happen and what latitude should be accorded to the Russian Orthodox Church in the meantime. As long as the war continued, it was in the interests of the military administration to proceed cautiously. The Greek Catholic population should not be antagonized and set against the occupying power by rash and hasty measures, and there must be no disturbances to public order near the front.[257]

The Orthodox episcopacy and the Holy Synod under ober-procurator V. K. Sabler had other priorities. Although they were also opposed to forcible conversions, they hoped to start their missionary work while the war was still on. In the opinion of various leaders within the Orthodox Church, the Greek Catholic Church in Galicia was not a true Catholic Church. The "Galician people" had remained Orthodox, and their affiliation to the Union was only formal.[258] After only a few weeks of war, Nikolaj II personally decided to send the Russian Orthodox archbishop of Volhynia to Galicia as administrator for the interests of Orthodox believers. Archbishop Evlogij had proved his worth in his diocese as a keen opponent of the Uniate Church. In the first months, Evlogij was based in the monastery of Pochaev from where he pursued his goals, calling on Greek Catholic priests to return to the faith of their forefathers. The Russian press announced somewhat overhastily that three Orthodox dioceses had been set up in Galicia. Greek Catholic clerics regarded these measures as the start of a campaign of forcible conversions and kept their distance from the Orthodox archbishop.[259]

The nationalist Galician-Russian Society supported the Holy Synod. The Society had been set up before the war and attempted to advance the Russification of Galicia by combating the Greek Catholic Church. Already in September 1914, the society demanded that the Order of the Basilians be banned and that all Greek Catholic bishops who supported a rapprochement between the Roman Catholic and the Greek Catholic Churches be removed from office. The society additionally urged that any form of propaganda directed against the Russian Orthodox Church should be severely punished and that Uniate priests should be expelled from villages in which the peasants had converted to the Russian Orthodox faith. One month later, the society demanded that Russian Orthodox priests familiar with the area be sent out, that Greek Catholic cathedrals where the majority of the congregation professed to be Russian Orthodox be transferred to the Russian Orthodox Church, and that the Order of the Jesuits be banned. Russian nationalists expected that removing Greek Catholic priests, in particular, would have a big impact. They anticipated that the semi-literate population would not know the difference between the Greek Orthodox and the Russian Orthodox Churches and believed that only Greek Catholics priests were preventing congregations from converting to the Russian Orthodox faith. Replacing Uniate priests by Orthodox priests was, in their opinion, a simple and unproblematic measure to achieve mass conversions.[260] According to the Galician-Russian Society, the "wish of the Galicians, in particular of the common people, to join the Orthodox faith" was of an "elemental nature."[261]

Evlogij's aggressive anti-Union policies also disquieted Polish politicians. It awakened memories of events that had taken place only a few years before when the campaign against the Uniate Church in the district of Chełm led to the area's redistricting and its removal from Russian Poland. The general staff similarly took issue with the policies of the Synod and the Russian Orthodox Church and took the matter to the Council of Ministers, which declared that the matter did not fall within its remit and referred the supreme command back to the Holy Synod.[262] Supreme Commander Grand Duke Nikolaj Nikolaevich ordered Janushkevich to make sure that "our spiritual power" did not exert pressure on the Greek Catholic

Church and its believers.²⁶³ The supreme commander complained to Tsar Nikolaj II about Archbishop Evlogij, whose proselytizing zeal exacerbated religious antagonisms in Galicia and was in danger of creating a flashpoint in the rear of the troops. The grand duke suggested placing the control of religious policies in the hands of the occupying administration. The tsar shared the view of the supreme commander and confirmed by telegram that other religious denominations must be tolerated in East Galicia.²⁶⁴

Janushkevich then explained to Bobrinskij that "our spiritual power," that is, the Russian Orthodox Church, could not be allowed to put pressure on Greek Catholics or Greek Catholic clergymen to convert to Russian Orthodoxy. There could be no restrictions on religious freedom. Conversions were only permissible if they were entirely voluntary. The authorities were obliged to uphold the rights and interests of the Galician population.²⁶⁵ In the weeks that followed, Bobrinskij, working closely together with Janushkevich, defined the rules for the future church policies. A Russian Orthodox priest could only be sent to a particular parish if three-quarters of the parishioners had decided to convert to Russian Orthodoxy. Even then, the Greek Catholic cleric would retain control of the village church.²⁶⁶ Some districts even held a plebiscite.²⁶⁷ However, if the Greek Catholic priest had previously fled, it sufficed if the majority of the congregation requested a Russian Orthodox priest. In such cases, the Russian Orthodox priest was permitted to use the local church, but he was initially obliged to celebrate Mass according to the Greek Catholic rites. Many reasons could prompt parishes to request a Russian Orthodox priest. It could be an expression of the parishioners' preference for the Russian Orthodox Church, but it could also be that the peasants preferred having a Russian Orthodox priest to not having any priest at all.²⁶⁸

As Evlogij recognized how difficult it was to win over a substantial number of Greek Catholic clerics to the Russian Orthodox faith, he turned his attention to the Greek Catholic parishioners themselves and tried to obtain changes to the rules. He pleaded in vain that churches should pass to the Russian Orthodox Church against the wishes of the local Greek Catholic priest if there was a two-thirds majority of Russian Orthodox believers in the parish.²⁶⁹ Bobrinskij rejected his proposal as he had no wish to provide the Austrian government with material for an international propaganda campaign targeting Russia's religious policies in the occupied territories.²⁷⁰ However, the military governor was prepared to make some concessions to the bishop and he permitted the Russian Orthodox Church to take over churches in certain cases after a one month period of transition, if it could be shown that the services of the local Greek Catholic priest were not in much demand.²⁷¹

But the confiscation of all Greek Catholic churches and of the palace of the metropolitan bishop, which Evlogij had demanded, was out of the question for Bobrinskij. Nor, as long as the war continued, was he prepared to permit the closure of the monasteries of the Basilian monks. He continued to advocate a policy of gradual and nonviolent acceptance of Russian Orthodoxy and repeated his request to tone down proselytizing activities.[272] The Greek Catholic churches were therefore not simply closed down nor were Greek Catholics forbidden to practice their faith, but attempts were made by various means to expand the influence of the Russian Orthodox Church. If a Greek Catholic priest had left his parish during hostilities, the occupying authorities prevented him from returning. The governor alone decided whether the priest would be permitted to return to his parish or whether he would be replaced by a colleague.[273] Such decisions took several months, and the outcome was often that a Russian Orthodox priest was sent instead.[274] Greek Catholic priests who returned without permission to their parishes were not allowed to use the churches and had to hold masses in secret in their own homes.[275]

The result was a shortage of Greek Catholic priests in the villages. The Russophile priests had been interned by the Austro-Hungarian authorities, the Ukrainophile priests were interned by the Russian occupiers or had fled their villages. Bobrinskij and Evlogij noted with concern that Greek Catholics attended Mass in Roman Catholic churches and Greek Catholic parishes turned to Roman Catholic priests for their religious needs. Bobrinskij therefore proposed that Russian Orthodox priests should hold services in abandoned churches but without forcing the local population to attend and without demanding a formal renunciation of the Union. He correctly noted that the population considered itself to be "Orthodox," so that formal conversion to the Russian Orthodox Church was not necessary. If Russian Orthodox priests held church services without changing the Greek Catholic rite, this could result in a relatively noiseless and conflict-free transference of the population to the Russian Orthodox Church. He additionally proposed allowing Greek Catholic priests to convert to Russian Orthodoxy and permitting Russian Orthodox priests to hold masses according to the models of Greek Catholic Russophile priests. This catalogue of measures approved of by the Supreme Commander did not go far enough for Evlogij, but he accepted them as they weakened the previous restrictions placed on missionary work.[276] The rites commonly used in East Galicia and the ceremonial robes were to be retained; even the "little Russian" variant of Church Slavonic could continue to be used during services unless the parishioners wished for religious services "like in Russia, like in Kiev."[277] The peasants were told that the religion was the same. The guiding theme was not conversion but a "return" to the Orthodox faith. The Russophile press (*Prykarpatskaja Rus'*, *Holos Naroda*) supported the anti-Union campaign. The general ignorance concerning the theological differences between the Greek Catholic and Russian Orthodox Churches meant that voting in the villages was open to abuses and manipulation.[278]

In November 1914 a commission from the Ministry of the Interior visited Galicia, questioned local peasants and studied the files of the military governor. The commission recommended removing Greek Catholic priests from their parishes. If possible, removal should be voluntary in return for material compensation, but the use of additional forms of pressure should also be permitted. Greek Catholic priests should be replaced by Russian Orthodox priests. After talking to peasants, the commission came to the conclusion that asking parishes to vote on their preference was inexpedient. The peasants were afraid of voting for a change of faith or of signing a petition. But if they were assigned a Russian Orthodox priest, they would willingly accept him. The commission viewed the Greek Catholic church hierarchy as the biggest obstacle to a large-scale conversion of the peasantry. If the hierarchy could be removed, it would rob the Greek Catholic clerics of their leaders.[279]

One frequently used method to remove unwanted Ukrainophile clerics was the prohibition of any form of anti-Orthodox propaganda, a prohibition that was strictly enforced. Even emphasizing Greek Catholic autonomy and the theological differences between the two denominations could be construed as a violation of this prohibition and result in the imprisonment and exile of the priest concerned. A denunciation lodged by an informer from among the ranks of parishioners sufficed.[280] The immediate cause for the detention and banishment of Archbishop Sheptyts'kyj were sermons in which he had stressed the advantages of the union with Rome compared to Orthodoxy.[281] However, the Ministry of the Interior had long since been working toward the elimination of Sheptyts'kyj, because they had correctly recognized his enormous influence over the Ruthenian population. Nor could there be any doubt of Sheptyts'kyj's Austrophile attitude and his dedication to the Ukrainian national cause. At first, the occupying authorities had attempted to win over the archbishop to their side or at least persuade him to be neutral. They several times demanded his word of honor not to undertake anything against the Russian Orthodox Church or the Russian state. The foreign ministry and the occupying administration initially baulked at taking severe measures against Archbishop Sheptyts'kyj as they particularly wished to avoid antagonizing the Greek Catholic population and turning them against Russia and had no desire to offer Austria ammunition for anti-Russian propaganda campaigns. But the Ministry of the Interior considered Sheptyts'kyj to be a security risk and prepared his arrest. Imprudent sermons finally offered them the desired pretext. The Russian gendarmerie then additionally discovered a top secret correspondence in the palace of the metropolitan bishop, which indicated that Sheptyts'kyj had been planning a pro-Union campaign in the event of Austrian troops invading Russia. Sheptyts'kyj was first placed under house arrest, then sent to Kursk and finally—to cut off all contacts to East Galicia—brought to a Russian Orthodox monastery near Suzdal'.[282] This was a severe blow to the Greek Catholic Church and the Ukrainian national movement. For the Ukrainian inhabitants of L'viv, the metropolitan bishop had been the last remaining authority from whom they could seek "protection and comfort." His palace had become a center of Ukrainian social life.²⁸³

The occupying authorities continued their attempts to curb the zeal of the Russophiles and of the Russian Orthodox clergy, for whom the practiced religious tolerance had gone too far. Bobrinskij still considered sending Orthodox missionaries to be risky.²⁸⁴ Although he permitted V. F. Dudykevich, the local chairman of the Galician-Russian Society, to encourage conversions to Russian Orthodoxy in private, he warned him against any attempts to coerce Greek Catholics or to interfere in the affairs of the administration. However, Bobrinskij also considered it inappropriate that the Russian Orthodox Church only had a single small church in L'viv at its disposal. He therefore requested Archbishop Evlogij to postpone his journey to L'viv until Bobrinskij could persuade the consistory of the Cathedral of St. George to hand over one of the large Greek Catholic churches to the Russian Orthodox Church. The archbishop's assumption of office must be held in a suitably dignified setting in a prestigious church.²⁸⁵ Bobrinskij's request was also connected to the wish not to put too great a strain on the mood of Poles and Ruthenians by the early arrival of Evlogij.²⁸⁶ But Bobrinskij promised Evlogij that both the Preobrazhens'kyj and the Uspens'kyj cathedrals would become Russian Orthodox, although he had not yet received the consent of either of the consistories. But he did not expect St. George's Cathedral to become Russian Orthodox any time in the near future. Although he did not rule out appropriating the cathedral, he believed the time was not yet ripe for such a move.²⁸⁷

Much to the displeasure of Ukrainophile priests, the consistory of St George's Cathedral, the Greek Catholic church of the metropolitan bishop, allowed the Russian Orthodox Church to use the Uspens'kyj and Preobrazhens'kyj cathedrals for church services on December 6 and 7 (Russian calendar).²⁸⁸ This meant that Evlogij was able to celebrate Masses on the tsar's name day in two of the most important Greek Catholic churches in the city. Evlogij sent out a message to the "Galician-Russian people (*narod*) and its clergy," whose "Russian spirit" had not been destroyed by being educated in the Latinate tradition. He called on the priests of the "Galician Rus" to be the spiritual leaders of the people in the "organic unification with the great Russian nation" and to "establish and consolidate the historical union with the Orthodox Russian Church."²⁸⁹ At the end of his sermon in the Preobrazhens'kyj cathedral, Evlogij declared that despite the two-hundred-year affiliation of the "Galician people" (*narod*) to the Union with Rome, they had always been considered Orthodox (*pravoslavnyj*). "Our common Mother—the great Orthodox Russia and our Holy Orthodox Russian Church opens its arms to you."²⁹⁰

The Russophiles were in raptures, and the representative of the foreign ministry on the general staff reported that the unanimous opinion was that the Greek Catholic Church was now finished. But only a few days later he criticized the sermon. It had not been very tactful of Evlogij and not conducive to the union of the two churches that the archbishop had preached such an aggressive sermon in a cathedral that did not belong to the Russian Orthodox Church. The majority of the Greek Catholic clergy strongly objected to the sermon. A group of Old Ruthenian clergymen wrote to Evlogij that they considered conversion to be a sin. The church rites and traditional culture of the people [*narodnost'*] were all that connected them to the Russian Orthodox Church; they had joined the Roman Catholic Church entirely of their own free will and were subject to the Roman Catholic pope, the successor to Peter, who had been appointed by God.[291]

The consistories of the Preobrazhens'kyj and Uspens'kyj cathedrals had close ties to two organizations that, until the outbreak of the war, had been controlled by Russophiles: the Stauropygian Institute and the Narodnyj Dim. The consistories had not left the Greek Catholic Church; before giving their permission to hold Orthodox Masses in the cathedrals they had sought the approval of Bilets'kyj, the head of the consistory of St. George's Cathedral and the deputy of the metropolitan bishop. Bilets'kyj was an Old Ruthenian who had remained deeply loyal to the Catholic Church and the Habsburg dynasty. He only gave his permission for Orthodox Masses to be held in the two cathedrals on the two specific days. Despite their predilection for Orthodoxy, thereafter the consistories did not dare to allow their churches to be used permanently for Orthodox services. Bilets'kyj finally gave his permission to hold Orthodox services in the Preobrazhens'kyj cathedral also at Christmas—but without the preaching of any sermons. His permission to hold Orthodox services in the churches was conditional on meeting three stipulations: first, any such arrangement should only apply as long as the war continued; second, the sensibilities of Greek Catholic believers must not be offended; and, third, alternating Greek Catholic and Russian Orthodox Church services must be held. Bobrinskij objected to these proposals, as did representatives of the Russian Orthodox Church, who argued that there must be enough churches available for the Russian garrison during the upcoming high holidays. Bobrinskij leaned toward the position of the Russian Orthodox Church but did not dare make a decision without the backing of the chief of staff. He proposed giving Bilets'kyj the choice of either entirely handing over the Preobrazhens'kyj cathedral or allowing Orthodox services to be held in all nine Greek Catholic churches.[292]

The cautious church policies advocated by the military governor were not adequately reflected at a local level, where they tended to be distorted. Thus, the income of Greek Catholic clergymen was reduced because some of their lands were handed over to Orthodox priests.[293] In some areas, Russian officials and Orthodox priests threatened Greek Catholic priests and pressed church communities to convert to Russian Orthodoxy. In the district of Bohorodczany, the military command allowed Greek Catholic priests only to hold masses between six and seven in the morning; during the rest of the day, the church was given over to Orthodox priests. In other districts, Orthodox priests ignored the instructions of the military governor, forcing Greek Catholic priests to hand over the keys of their churches and using the Greek Catholic churches as they pleased. In a number of parishes, Greek Catholic priests were arrested, interned, or deported to Russia.[294]

In other Greek Catholic churches, Orthodox priests prepared to hold masses even without permission. Bobrinskij turned a deaf ear to protests by Bilets'kyj, the head of the consistory of St. George's Cathedral in L'viv, that Orthodox priests had forcibly taken possession of Greek Catholic churches.[295] In some parishes, Greek Catholic parishioners attended Orthodox services out of necessity and made use of the services of Orthodox priests, while in other parishes Russian soldiers forced the parishioners to attend church. But for christenings and funerals Greek Catholic peasants often traveled to neighboring villages where a Greek Catholic priest still officiated.[296] The Austrian authorities noted that while the Greek Catholic Church was subjected to continual discrimination and harassment, they also recognized that the Russians did not want to alienate the Greek Catholic population by excessively severe measures.[297]

Bobrinskij did not deviate from his strategy of caution. In a circular sent to the military governors, he confirmed the following rules: in Greek Catholic parishes abandoned by their priests, a simple majority of believers wishing to convert to Orthodoxy was enough for a Russian Orthodox priest to be sent out. The Russian Orthodox priest would immediately be allowed to use the local church. Although two months earlier Bobrinskij had advocated retaining the Greek Catholic rites for some time to come, he now considered this would only be necessary initially. If the Greek Catholic priest had remained in his parish, 75 percent of parishioners as before would have to request the services of an Orthodox priest. The Orthodox priest could only use the local church with the permission of the Greek Catholic priest. A Greek Catholic church would only be transferred to the Russian Orthodox Church if Greek Catholic services had been sparsely attended over a period of one month. In the months that followed, the Russian Orthodox Church continued to expand its activities in Galicia. Evlogij wrote to Petrograd that by the end of 1914, fifty-three Greek Catholic parishes already wished to convert to Orthodoxy.[298]

Evlogij recognized that the Greek Catholic clergy "in the majority does not side with Russian Orthodoxy" and that there was "little hope of a union with the Orthodox Church." He saw no basis that offered an immediate hope of the "conversion of the entire Russian population of Galicia from the Union (with Rome) to Orthodoxy." A representative of the Interior Ministry thought that gaining the support of some Greek Catholic priests to spread the "all Russian idea" was more likely than persuading them to convert to the Russian Orthodox faith.[299] The Holy Synod would therefore have to accept the coexistence of Orthodoxy and the Uniate Church in Galicia for some time. Evlogij did receive some funds from the treasury for his proselytizing activities. In January 1915 Nikolaj II approved the decision by the Council of Ministers to grant twenty thousand rubles to Orthodox clergymen and their assistants. The Holy Synod decided to distribute Orthodox leaflets and other writings in Galicia listing "Catholic deviations" in Greek Catholic teachings or religious books and offering readers information on the Russian Orthodox Church.[300]

The future of the Greek Catholic Church appeared in danger. The Ukrainian parliamentary representation in the Austrian Imperial Council issued a protest against the "crimes committed against the most important sacred sites of the people."[301] The Catholic clergy were concerned about the pressure to convert put on Greek Catholics by the Russian Orthodox Church. On December 31, 1914, representatives of the Greek Catholic chapter met in the house of the Greek Catholic metropolitan bishop to deliberate in secret with the Roman Catholic archbishop Bilczewski and the Jesuit priest Sopuch on how best to defend the Greek Catholic Church.[302]

But the concerns about the future of the Greek Catholic Church were premature, for the war was turning against the Russian Empire. Russian troops suffered two crushing defeats: on the northeast front at the battle of Tannenberg around the middle of August and at the battle of the Masurian Lakes on September 22 and 23, 1914, forcing them to withdraw from East Prussia. On the southwestern front, the Russian armies were bogged down at the stronghold of Przemyśl, which they only managed to capture in March 1915. The Carpathian offensive had already collapsed in the winter of 1914/1915. The morale of officers and soldiers worsened as military reversals, inadequate military leadership, the lack of ammunition, and the general problems with supplies continued.[303] Tensions in the occupying administration increased, and the authorities began to implement more severe measures. The Ministry of the Interior viewed the Greek Catholic Church now primarily as a stronghold of Ukrainian nationalism standing in the way of a Russification of the conquered territories. The representative of the foreign ministry at the Russian supreme command described the Greek Catholic Church in February 1915 as the most important support of the "Mazepists."[304] Bobrinskij took this into account and began to facilitate the posting of Orthodox clerics to Greek Catholic parishes. While the other regulations remained in place, now if a parish was without a priest, even a minority of parishioners could request that a Russian Orthodox priest be sent to minister to their needs. If a Greek Catholic priest converted to Russian Orthodoxy, he was permitted to remain in his parish. Local officials misunderstood some of the passages of these directives and pressed the local clergy to convert, although bribes could occasionally persuade officials to desist.[305] In subsequent months, the procedures governing the sending of Russian Orthodox clergy were further simplified and eased. But until the end,

Greek Catholic peasants continued to refuse to append their signatures to formal requests to send Orthodox priests. Some parishes preferred to turn to Roman Catholic priests rather than welcome a Russian Orthodox priest in their midst.[306]

The Greek Catholic priest Jaroslav Levyts'kyj was not surprised that parishioners in some villages converted to the "Russian faith." He confirmed that ordinary people did not understand the differences between the Orthodox and the Greek Catholic faith.[307] They were not familiar with the term *Catholic*. One Greek Catholic priest had made many enemies in his parish preaching about the Catholic belief of "Ruthenian Catholics." His parishioners had rejected being described as "Catholics," describing themselves as "Orthodox." Levyts'kyj ascribed this misunderstanding to the fact that the term *orthodox* (*pravoslavnyj*) was used in the prayer books. It had not been possible to explain the meaning the word held in Greek Catholicism to believers. The same applied to the word *rus'kyj* (as opposed to *russkij*). Levyts'kyj accused the conservatives in the Greek Catholic Church of contributing to this confusion by refusing to change the word *pravoslavnyj*. Before the invasion, he himself had been a conservative, but his experiences in rural areas had convinced him of the necessity of changing these terms.[308]

The Ukrainophiles did not differentiate between the policies of the occupying power and the proselytizing activities of the Russian Orthodox Church. For them, the church policies constituted an attack on the existence of their nation. In Ukrainian memoirs, cases in which Greek Catholic peasants converted to Russian Orthodoxy are played down. Konstantina Malyts'ka declared apodictically in 1937: "with very few exceptions our villages have preserved their faith and their nationality."[309] In contrast, one Russian Church newspaper wrote that more than thirty thousand believers had converted to Orthodoxy in the first few months of the occupation. But these figures also include parishioners who attended Orthodox Masses or used the services of an Orthodox priest. This often did not involve breaking with the Greek Catholic Church. According to other reports, between fifty and one hundred Greek Catholic parishes had converted en masse to Orthodoxy. Given the figure of around 3.5 million Greek Catholics, the share of persons converting to Orthodoxy in 1914 would have still been less than 1 percent.[310] Until July 27, 1915, Baron Andrian had heard of only twenty-three priests who had fallen away from Greek Catholicism and fled with the Russian troops; thirteen priests had not converted but had still fled. Forty-three parishes had converted to Orthodoxy, fifteen in the district of Brody, and twelve in the district of Zborów.[311]

In L'viv and other major cities, church policies were implemented more reticently than in the villages where the local military commanders and Orthodox priests could virtually do as they pleased. In L'viv, a few Greek Catholic priests wore Orthodox crosses around their necks. The Ukrainophiles, however, described these incidents as rare and exceptional. Levyts'kyj thought that the Russian occupiers had demonstrated that Catholicism and Russophilia were like fire and water. Maybe the higher levels of education were the reason that in L'viv, many Greek Catholics preferred to attend Roman Catholic churches rather than going to hear the "bearded guests" in Greek Catholic churches.[312] But there may also have been another reason. In L'viv, the percentage of people who were Greek Catholic but considered themselves part of the Polish nation was higher. A few years later, many of them converted to Roman Catholicism, taking the identification of Polishness with Roman Catholicism to its logical conclusion.

Segue

Jewish traders and refugees brought the news of Russian defeats to the city. The exaggerated and sometimes false reports of enormous Russian losses found particularly attentive listeners among those who had suffered most under the Russian occupation and therefore hoped for a speedy return of Austrian rule.[313] Such hopes were fanned by the imperial-royal army which dropped leaflets from airplanes telling of overwhelming victories in France and on the eastern front and reporting—wrongly—that Paris had been captured and—correctly—that Warsaw had fallen and calling on the population to hold out.[314]

The news of the fall of Przemyśl on March 22, 1915, triggered hysterical reactions. The successful defense of the city had become a symbol of the resistance against the Russians and had kept the hope alive that the fortunes of war would turn. The capture of Przemyśl led to a number of nervous breakdowns and suicides. Only Polish National Democrats and Ruthenian Russophiles hailed the news of Russian victories and believed the rumors that the war would soon end.[315] Columns of prisoners from the Austrian-Hungarian army were led through the city, also with the aim of robbing the loyal population of the hope of any return to the old order.[316]

But the conquest of Przemyśl marked the beginning of the end of the Russian advance. On April 19 and 21, 1915, a large-scale German–Austrian advance began at Gorlice and Tarnów; it met an ill-prepared opponent, and the Russian troops were pushed back to behind Brody and Czernowitz. By the middle of June, Russian troops began evacuating L'viv. Hostages were taken along to secure the retreat but also to protect local residents who had supported the Russians from attacks by their neighbors.[317] Two days before the withdrawal from L'viv, Bobrinskij had more than thirty local dignitaries from L'viv deported to Russia,[318] among them the acting mayor, Tadeusz Rutowski; the two deputy mayors, Schleicher and Stahl; and the incumbent vice chancellor of the university, Adolf Beck. Several hundred hostages were taken in Galicia. The hostages were brought to Kiev, placed in "honorable arrest" and kept in—relatively comfortable—accommodation. The Russian authorities separated the groups strictly according to religious affiliations. Despite protests from the other Poles and in contravention of his own request, Adolf Beck, himself a Pole but of Jewish faith, was not housed together with his co-nationals but with his fellow Jews. The Poles received support from the local Polish relief committee while Jews were helped by a Jewish relief committee.[319]

In addition to Jews, the Russian occupiers had a predilection for taking Ukrainophiles with them as hostages to Russia. According to a provisional list drawn up by the Ukrainian newspaper *Dilo*, 173 Ukrainians were deported as hostages between September 1914 and June 1915, among them 45 clergymen and the heads or directors of Ukrainian institutions and schools. Among the hostages were Archbishop Sheptyts'kyj, the vice chancellor and deputy vice chancellor of the Greek Catholic Theological Seminary, several directors and board members of the Dnister insurance company, and the director of the Narodna Torhivlja.[320] While Jaroslav Levyts'kyj was able to hide, Konstantyna Malyts'ka was deported to Siberia and was only able to return after the end of the war.[321] According to the information available to the municipal council, during the Russian occupation a total of 211 persons from L'viv were deported to distant settlements in Russia.[322] On November 7, 1915, there were still 114 hostages from Galicia in the Russian Empire, in addition to 34 persons exiled for administrative reasons, who were still kept under arrest.[323]

As the front line moved closer to the city, the occupiers began recruiting laborers to dig trenches. Men were hunted down on the streets and impressed as laborers. And the authorities did not shrink from subterfuge. A military concert was announced, the audience surrounded, and the men in the audience picked out and put to work. For weeks, many young men did not dare show their faces on the streets.[324] Finally, a huge train of baggage and followers began to move off toward the east. The Russian officials and officers took many valuables and furniture with them. Shops were plundered, but much was also simply destroyed to prevent it falling into the hands of the Austrian troops. As the Russians withdrew, they were accompanied by refugees who had incriminated themselves by cooperating too closely with the Russians, among them Polish National Democrats and Ruthenian Russophiles.[325] The percentage of persons fleeing was particularly high in those communities that had converted to Orthodoxy. The chairmen of parish councils who had cooperated with the Russians often fled with them.[326] The Russian authorities announced that all men between the ages of eighteen and fifty years must leave the city. Some people interpreted this as an order and accompanied the Russian troops—even if they had not previously compromised themselves.[327] However, many refugees returned to their parishes again after only a few months.[328]

The Russian occupation had resulted in substantial material losses for the city and its residents. The city had incurred huge debts to ensure that sufficient supplies of food were available to the inhabitants and to keep the administration functioning. It had succeeded in averting the worst misery. L'viv had escaped heavy war damage. The city administration calculated that the Russian occupation, including damages, requisitions, and unpaid bills, had cost 5,970,207 krone.³²⁹ The situation was much worse in the regions farther to the east where the front lines moved back and forth several times. The destruction caused by the war was immense, and numerous estates had been plundered. After a tour of inspection undertaken in August 1917, the German consul general Heinze could not imagine how Austria would be able to finance the reconstruction.³³⁰

The image left by the Russian occupation was ambivalent. The soldiers of the regular army had not made a bad impression. Von Gember described them as quiet, very fond of children, devout and good-natured to the poor. The Cossacks in contrast were perceived as crude and violent.³³¹ The Russian occupying authorities in L'viv had tried to adhere to the international rules of war, to maintain the peace and uphold law and order in the areas under their control, and to exercise a certain amount of religious tolerance. But in the more rural areas the face shown by the occupying regime had been rather different, with arbitrary exercise of power, blackmail, robbery, and corruption the order of the day.

But the Russian occupiers had not only made enemies. Right from the start Russian politicians and high-ranking officers had done what they could to help the destitute and needy population. It was hoped that this would win over the peasants and the urban lower classes to Russia and would prevent the outbreak of epidemics in the hinterland behind the front lines.³³² Chamberlain Bazili reported that the "Russian [*sic!*] peasantry doubtlessly sympathises with us." To curb the influence of the "Ukrainians" Russia must behave generously to the Galicians who had "waited so long for the unification with Russia." This would be best achieved by large-scale relief efforts. "In the future the Russian [*Ruthenian*] population expects that we will free them from the Jewish yoke." Large Jewish and Polish estates (comprising about 35 percent of the total land) should be redistributed to the peasants, and the debts owed to Jews should be canceled.³³³ The occupying power repeatedly provided substantial food supplies that were then used by the city administration in public soup kitchens or distributed directly to the population.³³⁴ Ukrainophile clergymen reported that the troops had behaved kindly to the population and had occasionally given away food to the poor. For strategic reasons a number of roads had been paved which—according to Kyryl Levyts'kyj—"under Polish rule would not have been built until the end of the world." Day laborers were employed to carry out the roadwork, and the stones were not just requisitioned but also bought so that "the people earned well": "The Russians paid well and stole even better. For three years the soldiers and the peasants too lived quietly; the people had no fear neither by day nor by night; they could earn money."³³⁵

As long as the Russian army had been victorious, it had paid for the goods it needed to supply its troops. Large-scale requisitioning without compensation only started shortly before the troops retreated.³³⁶ Even Austrian civil servants noted that the Russians had treated the general population well and "in a politically very skilful manner had attempted to make their regime as pleasant as possible for the Ruthenian peasants."[337] An imperial and royal gendarmerie inspector observed in December 1915: "The sympathies of the population are in many cases on the side of the Russians because during the invasion they gave victuals, fuel and monetary assistance to the people, imposed no taxes and commandeered no recruits, provided horses, at a price of 5 rubles per horse, for farming and in many cases had the fields tilled themselves, and drafted in Jews to perform the same services as Christians were obliged to undertake (e.g. street cleaning) and putting a stop to their hegemony."[338]

Baron Andrian, the leading expert on Galicia of the Austrian foreign ministry, shared this opinion. After Galicia had been recaptured, he toured the area and drew up a report that had a large impact and was widely read, including by the minister-president and numerous other ministers and high-ranking officers: "The war was fought against the Poles, Jews and Germans and against that part of the Ruthenian intelligentsia which had dared to admit to being Austrian, Ukrainophile and Catholic. A peasant, unless he put on a particularly blatant display of his Ukrainism . . . , was treated mildly, even quite well. Particularly in material terms he did brilliantly."[339]

In times of need, peasants had received large amounts of cheap food. The peasantry had been exhorted to plunder and to exercise the rights of the masters. The hint that the tsar intended to distribute landowners' estates among the peasants had considerably increased the sympathy for Russian rule. Andrian considered this all very understandable. It was strange that the Poles accused the peasants of not completely rejecting the Russians because of their own Ukrainian sympathies ("Ukrainism"): "Of course only the intelligentsia adhere to Ukrainism as a conscious principle; for the peasants it is simply a fact which they do not think much about, that they are Ruthenians and not Russians. The most important consideration for them is the question of material well-being, on which the Russian government based its political work in the most skilful manner."

The Polish peasants in West Galicia had been won over by the same means. "Moreover, one has to consider, if one wishes to acknowledge the impact of the laid-back and benevolent Russian system of government toward the peasants who appear to be nationally indifferent, how little agreeable the rule of their Polish masters was for the Ruthenian peasants . . . Russian rule is just incomparably more pleasant for the peasants than the Polish Schlachta."[340]

Summing up his impressions, Andrian commented that the Ruthenian peasants had "like almost all of peasants been fairly apathetic toward the political vicissitudes which accompanied the war, and primarily considered them insofar as they affected their own pockets": "The only spiritual chord in the psyche of peasants, that of religion, is not tuned to a moskalophile mood, because otherwise, considering the extremely unfavorable conditions, defections to the schism would have been much more numerous. Any potentially existing sympathies for the Russians did not have a nationalist-idealistic base but a material basis entirely. Cases of treason were the work of individual persons, most of them probably seduced by money."[341]

In Przemyśl, the Russian occupiers had also distributed food and money, winning the support of the lower classes. Russian propaganda exploited the social conflicts and existing resentments to drum up support among the population. The rhetoric of liberation played an important role. At every opportunity, it was emphasized "that they were battling against the common hereditary enemies of Russians and Poles and of all Slavs, respectively, i.e. against the Germans and the Jews, to free the population of Galicia from them."[342]

There is not much information available on the relationship between the Ukrainian residents of L'viv and the Ukrainian soldiers serving in the Russian army. Bohdan Janusz summed it up as follows: "All in all, the Russian soldiers, particularly the Ukrainians, behaved kindly to the population, which in turn felt a bond with them, generally treated them well by helping the wounded and the sick, and behaved kindly to them."[343]

The Ukrainophile teacher Konstantina Malyts'ka drew attention to a further issue. Looking back, she wrote that the national consciousness of the Ukrainian soldiers in the Russian army was not very marked, but the "gleam of a national consciousness" had nevertheless led soldiers to look for Ukrainian folk literature and folk art in the bookshops and shops of L'viv.[344]

A bit more can be said about the encounters between Ukrainian soldiers and the local population in provincial towns and rural areas. At the beginning of the Russian occupation, Jevhen Kalytovs'kyj jotted in his diary that the Cossacks viewed Stryj as a Ukrainian city and talked Ukrainian both to the local Ruthenians and to the other inhabitants. If they were addressed in Polish, they replied, "I don't understand." Kalytovs'kyj noted that most of the Jews had also begun to talk Ukrainian. However, when the town was briefly recaptured a few days later by Austrian troops, the rejoicing of the population knew no bounds. Ukrainians, Poles, and Jews welcomed the soldiers with flowers, bread, and cigarettes.[345]

A lively trade in bartered objects developed between Russian soldiers and the population in which not only plundered goods but even items of equipment such as boots and rifle belts changed hands.[346] Corruption was characteristic for the regime. The venality of civil servants was common knowledge. It was possible to obtain the release of arrested relatives from prison by paying a ransom.[347]

In Russia, the Galician occupation policies were controversial. In the fall of 1914, the expert on Galicia in the foreign ministry and former vice-consul in L'viv, Olfer'ev, had sharply criticized the Russian policies implemented so far. The appointed civil servants were unsuitable, and the administration and the army had set the population against the Russian occupation because of their robberies, looting, and acts of violence.[348] Not long after the Russian retreat from L'viv A. Terovskij declared that the Russian occupation policies had been a disaster. He blamed military governor Bobrinskij and the majority of the civil servants appointed to work in Galicia. With the exception of the governor of Czernowitz, the most important persons of the occupation regime had been unfamiliar with the country, had appointed incompetent officials, and had encouraged nepotism. Instead of favoring the "Russian" population, they had allied themselves with the Polish "masters" and the Jews, who suppressed the Galician peasants. This brought the Russian regime into disrepute.[349]

In April 1915 the Russian gendarmerie reported in the run-up to the planned second visit of the tsar that most of the inhabitants of L'viv had not been won over: "On the whole, the disposition towards the Russian ruler and his Majesty amongst the Jews, Poles and Ukrainians with a few negligible exceptions is very hostile and not sympathetic."[350]

Second Regime Change: Nationalism versus Loyalty to the Empire

Liberation and the Settling of Accounts

Two major fears beset the inhabitants of L'viv in the last days of the Russian occupation. They dreaded an outbreak of robbery and looting coupled with the deportation of men liable for conscription. In neighboring villages, Jews were attacked; rapes, arson, and deportations were frequent.[351] The tense atmosphere mirrored the mood of the population during the withdrawal of the Austrian troops in August 1914. Nobody knew whether the city might yet become a theater of war. The inhabitants hid in their houses from where the noise of battle apprised them of the gradual approach of the front. Then the artillery of the Central Powers began shelling the bridges, streets, and army barracks. On May 16, planes began dropping bombs, but they inflicted little damage. All traffic ceased, all shops and other facilities were closed. The Jewish population feared an attack by the Cossacks.[352] Shortly before they withdrew, the Russian troops emptied the military depots or set fire to them. The streets were deserted with only a few Cossacks still patrolling them. This state of uncertainty ended with the entry of the Austro-Hungarian troops into the city on June 22, 1915, at noon. The tensions in the population exploded in scenes of "enthusiastic joy."[353] Maria von Gember noted that the "public mood palpated with inexpressible joy. Total strangers hugged each other in an upsurge of feeling; some of them wept with emotion, other laughed and cheered, others again raised their hands to give thanks to Heaven, yet others kneeled down and kissed the earth, which was Austrian again, which was free once more."[354]

Subsequently, the Poles, Ukrainians, and Jews quarreled about who had rejoiced most about the return of the imperial-royal troops. Jakób Schall thought it logical "that the entering Austrian-Hungarian troops were welcomed most warmly by the Jews, as they had suffered most under the Russian invasion and therefore had the most reason to be overjoyed that the Cossack hordes had finally left the city."[355]

But the spirit of rejoicing was no less strong among Ukrainians. Jaroslav Levyts'kyj commented: "the enthusiasm of the Ukrainian population of L'viv knew no bounds." Many Ukrainians emerged from their hiding places in cellars and barns. The portraits of the tsar disappeared from the shop windows, and the portraits of the German and Austrian emperors returned.[356] On June 23, at a gathering of the General Ukrainian Council, Kost' Levyts'kyj thanked the victorious armies for their "liberation of the ancient capital city of Ukrainian princes."[357]

The new city captain (Stadthauptmann) Colonel Franz Riml never doubted that the enthusiasm was genuine because "it was apparent that our entry was viewed as a liberation from the yoke of slavery of the Russians." The army was welcomed with "tremendous jubilation by the population": "Nevertheless, an attentive observer could not miss the fact that certain classes of the population or persons made an all too pronounced show of their joy (Jews) or expressed this joy with a mingled sweet and sour expression (compromised persons of political persuasion, Okhrana members and others)."[358]

One inspector of the imperial-royal gendarmerie also did not trust the enthusiasm: "The patriotic enthusiasm which had erupted during the entry of our troops in L'viv was quickly followed by disenchantment, which changed to a chastened and insincere mood. People feign loyalty out of fear, believe that the Russians will return and are cautious and reserved towards us."[359]

The Przemyśl military command came to the conclusion that the "Russian troops had been almost uniformly received in a friendly manner and had also been treated that way." The occupiers had not conformed to the terrible picture Austrian propaganda had drawn of them. The Poles, in particular, had been pleasantly surprised by the behavior of the Russian occupiers. However, the Ukrainians—so the military command believed—had suffered much and were genuinely overjoyed by the liberation. Poor Jews also voiced negative opinions about the Russians. While the marauding Russian soldiers had given them a hard time, nevertheless—and here a popular stereotype comes into play—"the moneyed Jews were quite skillful in getting on the right side of the Russians, had rendered them all manner of services required and done good business at the same time." Overall, the military command noted that the invasion had "greatly demoralized" the entire population "politically and morally." The dictum was often heard that it didn't matter who was in charge at the top; the main thing was to live well and cheaply. And that had been the case during the Russian occupation.[360]

Legation councilor (Legationsrat) Leopold Baron von Andrian reported that "now, after almost 50 years' renewed rule by Poles of the Ruthenian territories, one can say that Polishness, despite all the passionate national work, does not possess the assimilatory power to expunge the Ruthenian majority." It was not to be wondered at "that part of a tribe, which neither the Poles nor the Russians wish to permit to act out its nationality, and which received the Austrian concept of the state almost exclusively through a Polish medium, had embraced moskalophile ideals." However, the percentage of lapsed Ruthenians had been much lower than had been originally surmised. He explained, moreover, "that . . . if the true facts were taken into account, there could be no question of Ruthenians having gone over to the Russian camp lock, stock and barrel, as was occasionally insinuated, particularly by the Polish side." The Ukrainian intelligentsia had "by and large, despite the most severe reprisals by the Russians behaved entirely correctly." Mass flights of Ruthenian peasants had only occurred in a few districts already known before the war for their deep-rooted Russophilia. In the districts of Kamionka-Strumilowa, Rawa-Ruska, Złoczów, and Żółkiew, whole village communities had fled with the Russians. In the district of L'viv, which had recorded the greatest exodus of people, about 1,400 people, including children, out of a total of 72,000 Ruthenians, in other words, less than 2 percent of the total Ukrainian population, had left. The refugees included not only Okhrana agents but also many peasants who had participated in the looting and pillaging or who had converted to the Russian Orthodox faith.[361]

Andrian also addressed the issue of the behavior of the political parties and of various social groups. Most of the landholders who had remained had "behaved impeccably." Socializing with Russian officers had been the result more "of weakness than of ill will." But overall, Andrian was disappointed by the behavior of the nobility: "with a few notable exceptions, in which particularly the ladies had given an example of patriotic sacrifice" they had not behaved as one "would expect of the foremost estate of the realm, which had for decades reaped so many honors and material benefits from the state." The nobility had, as yet, not learned anything from the war. Its comments were based on the supposed ignorance of non-Poles about Galician matters as before. Sentences such as "There is only one nation in Galicia and it is the Polish nation," "The Ruthenians are only a variant exaggerated by "Vienna," "Ruthenians all showed themselves to be traitors during the war, the only thing to do now was to abolish the Union, forcibly convert the Greek Orthodox believers to the Latin rites and abolish the use of the Cyrillic script (i.e., to Polonize the Ruthenians by state intervention)," "all the mischief in Galicia was caused by the fact that 'Vienna' meddled too much in Galician affairs"—could be heard daily.

Andrian did not have a single good word to say about the Polish National Democrats. They had behaved "for the most part downright treacherously" and the Podolian nobility had "to put it mildly . . . behaved weakly."[362]

The military authorities confirmed his criticisms of the behavior of the National Democratic Party: "I am personally of the opinion that while the Austrian Poles are in the first instance Poles, the overwhelming majority are also well-disposed towards Austria. The opposite can self-evidently only be said of the National Democratic (Grabski) Party."[363]

The reports sharply criticized the collaboration by members of the Polish elites while the patriotism of the Ukrainian population and their support of the Austrian Empire were praised. In the district of L'viv, the Ukrainian population had behaved "patriotically and loyally to the emperor" and had cared for Austrian prisoners of war and helped them escape despite the great danger this involved. In contrast, the few Poles had behaved as passively as the Jews had initially done out of fear.[364] Colonel Riml therefore considered the Ukrainian population as potential allies who should in future be put to better use for the benefit of the state: "Ukrainians are extremely friendly to Austria and with strong guidance by the ruling elite could be educated to become proper Austrians. As yet, the Ukrainian idea has not gained enough of a foothold, and even less so in Russian Ukraine. Given the low level of culture of the Ukrainian peasant it is not surprising that material benefits are closer to his heart than national advantages."

It was this that had enabled the Russians to get some of the parishes on their side. In the archdiocese of L'viv, only approximately thirty of three thousand priests had converted to Russian Orthodoxy. The majority of the Greek Orthodox clergy, particularly the younger ones, were Ukrainophile and "good Austrians and good Catholics."[365]

Riml and Andrian had nothing but praise for the two archbishops, Bilczewski and Teodorowicz, whose behavior like that of the clergy had been "generally irreproachable." Bilczewski had neither spent time socially with Russians nor had he permitted prayers for the Russian tsar to be said in Catholic churches.[366] In general, the antibloc parties were now more discredited than the old *Statthalterblock* (governor bloc), whose members had remained loyal to Austria.[367]

Andrian was generally satisfied with the behavior of the civil servants in L'viv but noted that collaboration had been extensive in the small provincial towns. In Stanislau, for example, the town's chief of police had immediately begun working under the Russians. According to information given to Andrian, the chief of police had informed on pro-Austrian persons, whereupon they had been deported. The situation was completely different in the capital: "In L'viv the majority of civil servants who had remained behind behaved, despite the terrible material and financial distress in which they had been precipitated . . . , in generally extremely well."[368]

Two thousand railway workers had refused to continue working under Russian occupation. In contrast, "especially among the cultured classes in L'viv, one part had come to terms with the Russian regime surprisingly quickly."[369]

The Polish elite attempted to downplay the extent of collaboration and to lay the blame on strangers and newcomers to the city: "it was the political refugees who broke the national alliance in Galicia at the time of the invasion of L'viv." Only a very small number of National Democrats had sided with the Russians.[370] "Russophilism remained the exception and for every person there were purely individual reasons for it; party membership did not play any important part in it."[371]

The disloyal behavior of many National Democrats and the Podolian nobility's lukewarm support of the Austrian Empire had weakened the Polish position, and the Austrian central authorities drew the consequences. Andrian recommended appointing "an entirely Austrian governor, to be above the country's nations, possibly from among one of the generals." He suggested that Ruthenian and Austrian civil servants from western Austria could be brought in to serve as a counterweight to the "allowedly personally irreproachable but nationally often biased Polish civil servants." Andrian proposed acknowledging the Jews as a nation and placing them on an equal footing to the two *Landesnationen* (recognized regional nations), that is, Ruthenians and Poles.[372] He hoped to turn the 650,000 East Galician Jews into supporters of the government and that Polonization would lose its appeal. He recommended refusing to permit the return of Russophile clergymen to their parishes and pensioning off the 340 teachers who had attended Russian training courses immediately.[373] The government did not follow all of his recommendations but an Austrian general was later appointed governor; the region itself came under military administration.

The new governor, General Hermann von Colard, confirmed Andrian's assessment "wholeheartedly." Polish nationalism weakened the feeling of being an Austrian citizen. "Particular national ambitions and not least purely personal interests dominate the thoughts and emotions to such an extent that only little is left for the state." Colard believed that the positive sympathies of the Jews toward Austria had been strengthened, although there had been many cases of collaboration. Nevertheless, the Galician Jewish community had emerged "from the military campaign as even more staunch supporters of Austria." But Colard ascribed this to "much too pronounced opportunism" and warned against equating the Jewish attitude with unconditional loyalty. He also considered it wrong to accuse all Ruthenians across the board of disloyalty. Despite the strong Russian pressures, the majority had remained loyal to the empire. East Galician peasants were "at heart and in their disposition largely politically indifferent." Like Andrian, Colard came to the conclusion that the "system of Polish hegemony in this part of the country failed completely during the invasion." The nobility should therefore be recompensed for the losses it had suffered, but there should be no amnesty for collaborators. The civil service needed to be purged, and its ethnic composition changed through the systematic promotion of Ukrainians. Unlike Andrian, Colard believed it was too early to take any decision on partitioning the Crown land.

Colard wanted to combat the All-Polish propaganda in schools, increase the numbers of Ruthenian secondary schools and promote Austrian patriotism. Setting up a Ruthenian university—possibly with a German orientation—could win over Ruthenian intellectuals to the Austrian cause. Colard thought it would be better if trade, particularly in the smaller townships and villages, was not exclusively in the hands of Jews. And Colard recommended showing leniency to peasants and only punishing traitors severely.[374]

All Russophiles were removed from public office and positions of importance in the Church.[375] While the governor's office assumed that many Greek Catholic clergymen still supported Russia,[376] most commentators opposed the accusations of collective betrayal aimed at the Ukrainian population. In the last year of the war, the imperial and royal army high command repeated the accusations that led to thousands of Ukrainians losing their lives or liberty, but in the end, the army high command came to a conciliatory conclusion:

> In addition to this movement which had been incited by the intelligentsia, the Orthodox Russification propaganda still exerted an influence which appears to be even more dangerous to this simple peasant people. The superb staging of this movement which can only be described as a direct preparation for war, the attendant circumstances and horrors of the war naturally achieved an important success, which already perniciously manifested itself in August through collusion with the enemy and even open enmity against our troops. It became apparent that the moskalophile intelligentsia, first and foremost the clergy and teachers with their deep-rooted influence, followed by the lawyers and in some instances public officials, were behind this systematic approach, and their tools were the peasants.[377]

Polish rule had "brutalized" the Ukrainian people and had driven them into the arms of the Russophiles. The army high command believed the Ukrainians to be loyal and considered them an "element which contributed to the support of the state"; they offered an effective counterweight to subversive tendencies and formed a "bulwark along the eastern borders of the empire."[378]

The Greek Catholic Church learned from the experiences of the Russian occupation and attempted with the help of certain moderate reforms to weaken the attraction of the Russian Orthodox Church. Khomyshyn, the Greek Catholic bishop of Stanislau temporarily introduced the use of the Gregorian calendar in his diocese and deleted the words *tsar* and *Orthodox* (*pravoslavnyj*) from Church prayers. However, all final decisions on these matters were kept pending until the return of Archbishop Sheptyts'kyj from Russia.[379]

The military authorities took harsh action against real or supposed collaborators. Denunciations were a daily occurrence. The police agent Theodor Ahne found it extremely difficult to ascertain whether genuine political crimes had been committed in view of the flood of mutual recriminations:

> The accusations are generally all lumped together; it doesn't matter whether someone has committed a common felony or a political crime or merely a misdemeanour, everyone is now designated politically suspect and extremely Russophile. The biggest difficulties arose from the endeavor to find out the truth, as old hatreds, personal vindictiveness and attempts to cover up own mistakes or gain an advantage are often the basis of the charges made . . . witnesses often report something they heard but did not experience themselves or something that cannot be proved, always citing others as the chief witnesses, who in turn are unable to positively state something themselves.[380]

Hundreds of arrests were made in L'viv alone. All over the country, cases were brought against Poles and Ukrainians who had violated laws or worked closely with the occupiers.[381] A Polish chronicler reported that the Austrian authorities were horrified by the extent of the looting and had launched inquiries against 32,498 persons by the end of 1915.[382] The government also proceeded against university professors in L'viv. Preliminary investigations were opened against those persons who had fled together with the Russian troops.[383] Many Poles were arrested and accused of treason. For Polish elites who had dominated the Crown land for more than fifty years, this was a new and unexpected experience that poisoned their relationship to the Jews, the Ukrainians, and the Austrian authorities.[384] The wave of denunciations assumed such enormous proportions that the two archbishops Bilczewski and Teodorowicz personally approached the governor to discuss the issue.[385]

In October 1915 the Ukrainian National Council protested to the Ministry of Justice about the large number of proceedings that had been initiated against Ukrainian peasants for having looted estates and Jewish properties. At the trials, Polish landowners confronted Ruthenian peasants. This "revived the old national-political, social and economic antagonisms again." The Ukrainian Council suspected the governor's office of going easy on the Polish peasants in western Galicia while Ruthenian peasants were harshly prosecuted for comparable misdeeds. The council argued that there had been extenuating circumstances. On one hand, the peasants had already been ruined by the war; on the other hand, it would not be advisable to stir up trouble in this area near the front lines by carrying out mass arrests. Moreover, in the trials Ruthenians were often charged with robbery "although it was a matter of appropriating other people's abandoned property."[386] The governor's office rejected the accusation of favoring Polish peasants in western Galicia. All offenses committed were prosecuted, irrespective of the perpetrator's nationality.[387]

With the government blanketing the region with a wave of trials and arrests that, in addition to looters and informers, also affected numerous innocent victims of denunciations, the government gradually forfeited the sympathies of the population. Prominent persons in L'viv also criticized the suspension of municipal self-government. After the withdrawal of the Russian troops, the councilors had chosen a council committee of six, to be headed by Marceli Chlamtacz, to carry out official duties for the time being. But on June 30, 1915, Governor Korytowski informed them, writing from the provisional official seat of the governor's office in Biała (Bielitz) that the right to self-government would remain suspended. Instead, he appointed Kreishauptmann Kazimierz Grabowski as provisional head of the administration. He selected two deputies for the government commissioner out of the group of elected municipal councilors. A provisional advisory board consisting of eighteen members was set up to replace the municipal council, which also included representatives of the Jewish population and for the first time also from the Ukrainian population. This meant that in certain areas, self-government effectively continued. Grabowski relied on committees and representatives of the municipal council.[388]

An anonymous memorandum, classified by the foreign ministry as reliable and authentic, harshly criticized the administration of the city and the Crown land immediately after the recapture of the area. In the first few weeks, Hungarian units had ensured law and order, registered all of the inhabitants and removed those who were residing illegally in the city. During this time, numerous raids and searches had been carried out. Because the Hungarians had difficulties making themselves understood and communicating with the inhabitants, misunderstandings and unjustified arrests were frequent. The Hungarians were finally replaced by Czechs. While understanding each other was no longer an issue, the Czech Stadtkommandant (town or city captain) suspected Russophile tendencies everywhere, even proceeding against Poles loyal to Habsburg rule. He had ordered the closure of all retirement homes, refuges, and hospitals reserved for former members of the Polish legions.[389]

This led to an appreciable cooling of relations between Poles and the Austrian authorities. Government commissioner Grabowski—the memorandum continued—was "a completely incompetent character": "In those circles which support Austria it is said with bitter sarcasm: The military administration of L'viv should be awarded medals by the Russians for it competently managed to alienate the inhabitants of L'viv from Austria." The author of the memorandum demanded the immediate removal of the military administration and the reinstatement of autonomous local councils.[390]

In July 1918 the last Austrian governor, Count Karl von Huyn, confirmed the criticisms directed against the military administration in the immediate aftermath of the recapture of the region. The patriotic enthusiasm of the population had cooled considerably following the repressions. Only the policies of the subsequent military commander who had taken the particular circumstances into account had restored some of the monarchy's popularity with the general population.[391]

Rising Anti-Semitism

Contemporary Polish, Ukrainian and Jewish witnesses played down the willingness of their respective group to collaborate and exaggerated the willingness of the "others." In memoirs, when the topic of denunciation is mentioned, the nationality or religion is only noted when the informer belonged to another group. If he or she is a member of their own group, the authors content themselves with mentioning the name but do not make generalizations.[392] Jaroslav Levyts'kyj only specifies the nationality or religion when Poles or Jews do the informing. At the beginning of the war, a Ukrainian woman had informed against her brother for "defeatist" talk, but Levyts'kyj does not address the issue.[393]

A well-known anti-Semite disseminated libelous publications in which he accused the Jews of having welcomed the Russian troops with flowers. He went on to assert that the Jews had in actual fact been supporters of the tsar. The newspaper *Słowo Polskie* repeated the accusations.[394] Such calumnies were not without effect. They influenced the perceptions of the Christian population, fitting the stereotype of Jews as unprincipled profiteers who managed to turn even emergencies to their own advantage. This provided a pattern of interpretation that was then reconfirmed and buttressed with other stories. The reports about Jewish resistance and Jewish suffering under Russian occupation frustrated these expectations but were not reflected in the interpretative process and thus did not result in any change in experiences. And thus, one of the central war experiences of the Christian inhabitants of L'viv included "Jewish speculators" but not Jewish resistance or Jewish suffering. General Riml accepted these interpretations and incorporated them uncritically in his reports to Vienna. He described the Jews as "patriots out of need but not out of conviction" and accused them of having immediately offered their services to the Russians and conducted business with them. He reported that many Jews had been in the Okhrana and had subsequently fled. Riml stated, "The behavior of the Jews of L'viv during the Russian invasion gave great offense to the rest of the population, generating a previously unknown degree of anti-Semitism."[395]

Such voices cannot simply be written off as "false." They do bear some relation to reality. Like their Christian counterparts, Jewish merchants also did business with the occupiers, some of them did sell their wares at prices that exceeded the officially stipulated maximum prices, and they did put up Russian-language shop signs. But none of the contemporary sources written immediately at the time of the events confirms the story of the enthusiastic welcome offered to the Russian troops or the claim that many Jews who had fled to Russia were agents of the Okhrana. The manifest exaggerations and false statements were disseminated by anti-Semites, and in an atmosphere abuzz with rumors, they fell on fruitful ground. Many of the inhabitants had perforce come to an arrangement with the Russians and now faced the problem of justifying their behavior to the Austrian authorities. As, objectively, the Jewish elites and the Jewish population had compromised themselves least, they were also least affected by the wave of trials and arrests now sweeping the country. Accusations such as the ones described earlier aimed to discredit the Jewish population in the eyes of the authorities.

In the summer of 1915, an anonymous letter was sent to the governor's office and the Ministry of the Interior in Vienna, bearing the signature "the deeply grieved Jewish people." The letter writers begged the central authorities for help because in L'viv, neither the municipal council nor the police authorities attended to the needs of the Jews or protected them from the Polish population. Rioting could easily break out. The authorities had imposed draconian punishments on Jewish merchants for allegedly forcing up prices. "There now exist, in these serious and hard times, imperial and royal officials in Galicia who have adopted the morals and manners of the Russians, and poor fellow citizens who had already been destroyed by the Russians are now also being oppressed by these officials and betrayed to the Russophile population." The anonymous authors accused the district captains (*Bezirkshauptleute*), mayors, and judges of having collaborated with the Russians and now of harassing the Jewish population. In some areas, the authorities tolerated looters retaining Jewish property they had stolen. The authors demanded the reward for the patriotic behavior of the Jews during the Russian occupation.[396]

The accusations were not unfounded. The letter's anonymity reduces its credibility, but the Zionist Executive Committee also appealed to the government because "national chauvinism and racial hatred was interposing itself between the Jews and their rights; many reinstated institutions indulged more than before in arbitrary rule."[397] The Jewish National Association reported to the Ministry of the Interior that after the Russian troops had left, the Jews were again being persecuted: "Many cases have been noted of the most blatant perversion of justice against Jewish citizens and it must be stated that certain Polish classes of the population and categories of officials have apparently made it their business to systematically persecute Jews, ousting them, pauperizing them and humiliating them in front of the authorities and the population. In particular, the cases cited above indicate the tendency to remove Jewish citizens from office and to harass Jewish tradesman gratuitously. All of this is done under the excuse of 'war-induced necessity.'"

Conflicts erupted in many places when Jews who had fled to the west returned and demanded the return of their stolen property or reinstatement into their old positions. In Komarno, the Jewish mayor wanted to take office again, but the authorities chose to leave the acting Polish deputy mayor in office, who had discharged the duty of mayor during the Russian occupation. A particularly bitter pill for Jews to swallow was when they were left at the mercy of the same people who had previously bullied them during the Russian occupation:

In Rymanow the Russians appointed a grocer named Marceli Nadziakiewicz as mayor. He bullied the Jews terribly and encouraged Russian policemen to beat the Jews whom he forced to do heavy manual labor repairing the roads and recovering bodies. He also beat them. Markus Leib Silbermann died from this mistreatment by policemen. The Russians arranged for aid and flour to be distributed to the working population through the offices of the mayor. He gave nothing to Jews. In the presence of the witnesses Jakob Lerner and Israel Schreiber he called out to the policeman: "Give each Hebrew one hundred nahajkas on my responsibility." To the witness Baruch Amster he commented: "Thank God that Austria is no longer here. The Russians are here now and we will settle our accounts with you Jews, it is all over with you now." After the Russians were ousted, the responsible district administration [Bezirkshauptmannschaft] confirmed this man as mayor in Rymanow and deposed the former Jewish mayor. Additional witnesses: Mechel Bodenstein, Nathan Liff, Jakob Rücker, Binem Simon, Leib Keller and Nathan Aron Liff, all in Rymanów.

The Jewish National Society (Jüdischer Nationalverein) accused the civil and military authorities in Borysław of preferentially arresting Jews. There were similar tales from other parishes in the district of Drohobycz. In Żydaczów—the report continued—only Jews were selected to dig trenches or do similar heavy manual labor. The Jewish National Society also complained about the Bezirkshauptmann in Dolina, who was biased and hostile to the Jewish population. "The damages and losses reported by Jewish citizens were completed ignored by the k.k. district administration in Dolina; however when they inquired into these matters the Jews were given the truly Russian reply: 'Why did you come back? We don't need you here. We were glad to be rid of you.'" City captain (Stadthauptmann) Glazewski also wrote in the official gazette that "quite a number of conscripts for the Landsturm, **in particular those of Mosaic denomination**" had attempted to evade military service using all sorts of tricks and deceits.[398]

The governor's office responded by requesting information on Jewish-Polish relations from the district authorities. Based on their reports, the governor's office came to the conclusion that the accusations were "completely unjustified." The examples were "partly fraudulent, partly twisted, in general however pure invention." The governor adopted the arguments and reasoning of its regional administrative authorities.[399] Governor Colard was quick to defend his administration following the logic of all administrative authorities, but the problem was also that the persons accused of misdemeanors were the self-same people who, as regional chiefs of administration, had been asked to assess the validity of the accusations. The district captains did not merely repudiate the accusations; some of them took the opportunity in their turn to levy accusations against the Jewish population. The district captain of Przemyśl emphasized that all sections of the population, irrespective of their religion or nationality, had been obliged to labor on public works. Persons who had participated in acts of theft or plunder had been brought to justice.[400] The authorities in Tarnów praised the good coexistence between the Jewish and the Christian communities, and this was confirmed by eminent Jewish citizens. Disagreements between the mayor and Jewish inhabitants were considered to be of a purely personal nature.[401] The district captain of Sanok reported that Poles and Jews had lived together entirely amicably during the Russian occupation, and the authorities in Żółkiew also had no negative incidents to report.[402] In Rzeszów, the district authorities asked Chief Rabbi Lewin to confirm that there had been no local Polish pogroms against Jews.[403]

The district captain of Sambor combined his defense of the local Polish population with an attack against the Jews. "The slurs against Poles I consider to be slanders of the most vicious sort and outrageous lies. It is not a characteristic of Poles nor does it run in their blood to denounce someone, to take revenge or betray someone." In his account, the Poles had behaved with the utmost benevolence toward the Jews; there had only been a few individual and isolated cases of assault. The district captain then proceeded to belie his own words and denounced Jewish citizens himself. Although the Jews were loyal, the district captain continued, and detested the Russians, and almost all the Jews had fled, those who had remained had been the first to hang up Russian-language signs and then, when the imperial-royal army had returned they had even kissed the horses. The district captain alleged that the merchant Finsterbusch, whom he considered "guilty of high treason," owed his acquittal "to an outstanding extent to his professed creed." The district captain went on to state that he had heard that a Jew had led Cossacks to a room where nine Catholic girls had taken refuge. And he knew of a case in which Jews had looted and plundered alongside the Cossacks.[404]

Police director Reinlender also condemned Jewish accusations as "malicious defamation dictated by their hatred of Poles and civil servants of Polish nationality": "As regards the city of L'viv, there can be no question of organized anti-Semitism among the Polish population. The only party, the National Democratic Party, which might possibly be accused of having anti-Semitic tendencies, did not cultivate this tendency in practice and only opposed Zionism, although admittedly its opposition to Zionism was sharp."[405]

Moreover, Jews had benefited from state humanitarian aid just as much as the Christian population had. A ritual soup kitchen had even been set up for Orthodox Jews. And in the person of Filip Schleicher, a Jew was even head of municipal supplies. "Up to now not a single case could be ascertained in which the Poles of L'viv displayed a hostile attitude towards the Jewish population during the invasion or, for instance, informed on Jews to the Russian authorities."[406]

Anti-Semitism had increased in Polish society in the first year of the war. But at the same time, exploratory talks were held between Polish politicians and representatives of the Jewish population in which Jewish support of Polish national demands were discussed. Biliński, the chairman of the Polish Club, met with five rabbis from East Galicia. Biliński purportedly demanded that the rabbis declare on behalf of all Galician Jews that "the Jews will henceforth stick together with the Poles and pursue a common policy." According to the anonymous author, the Poles wished to strengthen their position that had been weakened by the "treacherous actions of the All-Polish party." But the anonymous author believed that the "real mood of the huge majority of all of the Jewish population" was quite different because "the monstrous sufferings which the Jews were subjected to during the war in Galicia by the Russians" were mainly "owing to the All-Poles." He followed this up by recounting cases in which Polish civil servants in the East Galician province had betrayed Jews to the Russians or had refused to help them: "The bitterness of the Jews against the Poles is very great, so that the rabbis will be forced to stand by the Jews and proceed against the Poles. . . . In L'viv, the treacherous actions of 'Słowo Polskie,' 'Gazeta Narodowa' and 'Wiek Nowy' which were the cause of so much suffering are still very fresh in the minds of local Jews, so that a close association with the Poles is inconceivable."

The author felt that the Jews were completely on the side of the Austrian government.[407] This impression was also confirmed by Baron von Andrian. The attachment of the Jewish population to the Austrian monarchy had increased even more after their oppression by the Russians. While individual Jews had prospered "exceedingly well in their business," the majority had fared badly. "The most terrible destitution" now prevailed among the Jewish population. Andrian had also noted that the Polish proclivities of the Jews had begun to waver and that Jews were "endeavoring with a certain tenacity to parade their German affiliations towards the Poles."[408]

But this did not apply to all Galician Jews. Prominent Jewish supporters of assimilation to the Polish nation issued a joint statement in which they opposed the accusations directed against the Poles: "The fate of Poland is our fate, the suffering of Poland is our suffering, the felicity of Poland will be our felicity also." Since the province had obtained its autonomy, the "cultural and political development of the Jews had made enormous progress." This was due both to the Austrian administration and to the actions of the Polish population. Even the anti-Semitic party in the Kingdom of Poland had not attempted to incite the mob against Jews. "We Jews in the Austrian part of Poland consider the liberation of Poland from Russian rule as the sole means to achieve a just and sensible solution for the Jewish question in Poland . . . The Jewish question is a part of the Polish question. Poland's freedom is the freedom of the Polish Jews." The signatories included the president of the Chamber of Lawyers and former deputy mayor of L'viv Tobiasz Askenaze, the Social Democratic member of the Imperial Council Herman Diamand, and the leaders of the Jewish communities of L'viv, Cracow, and Przemyśl, Szymon Schaff, Samuel Tilles and Jakób Glanz, respectively.[409] In March 1917 Dr. Emil Parnas and Herman Feldstein, writing in Yiddish, called on the mercantile community to donate money in aid of ill and injured Polish legionnaires.[410]

But all of this did not prevent the continued rise of anti-Semitism. The crucial factors were economic. Many Poles and Ukrainians blamed Jewish tradespeople for the rises in prices and the problems with supplies. The Przemyśl military command reported in November 1916: "The fact that many rich Jewish merchants buy goods, hide them and push up prices has recently caused much bitterness among the poorer mass of the population, and agitation has fomented this bitterness into hatred and provocation."[411]

Police agent Theodor Ahne shared this opinion. "Jews in Galicia achieve everything, truly everything with money, right or wrong", he wrote, adding that they always had enough to eat and after only a few years everyone owned their own house.[412]

Polish–Ukrainian Rivalry

The Russian occupation temporarily paralyzed the Ukrainophile movement, but the movement was not fundamentally weakened. Shortly after the Russian troops left, a Committee of Ukrainians of the City of L'viv was formed that called for the "rebuilding of Ukrainian life in the capital city of Galician Ukraine."[413] Not long afterward, the first Ukrainian newspaper, *Nove Slovo*, appeared and Ukrainian societies and institutions recommenced their activities.[414] The governor appointed Ukrainophile persons to the administration of the National House and the Stauropygian Institute before placing both institutions together with the property belonging to the Kachkovs'kyj Society entirely under Ukrainian administration in February 1916.[415] West Ukrainian politicians continued to back Austria as their best hope of achieving their national political aims. Kost' Levyts'kyj stated on December 28, 1915, that the "Ukrainian nation anticipated that the Austrian monarchy would bring their hope of national freedom [*volja*] to fruition" and expected that Ukrainians would be permitted to govern their territories themselves under Habsburg rule.[416]

Ukrainian national leaders endeavored to combine their forces. On April 5, 1916, the Ukrainian National Committee set up a permanent Committee of the General Ukrainian Council with six departments.[417] The council was headed by an executive committee composed of National Democrats, Radicals, and Social Democrats.[418]

The Ukrainian–Polish conflict had remained quiescent under Russian occupation. The Russian occupying forces had paralyzed the Ukrainian movement as a political force. Once the imperial-royal army returned, the Polish–Ukrainian struggle entered a new phase. The Austrian government played off the groups against one another, but the government also prevented the conflict from spilling over into violence that would have been destabilizing and could have jeopardized military efforts. This became apparent in the spring of 1916 when a heated quarrel sprang up between the Ukrainian daily newspaper *Dilo* and the Polish press. Initially, the quarrel turned on the issue of which group had collaborated more with the Russians. The Ukrainian press accused Poles of having informed against Ukrainians. The Polish daily newspaper *Kurier Lwowski*, in its turn, issued a sweeping recrimination, accusing all Greek Catholics of collaboration.[419]

The press also quarreled about the occupied territory of Chełm. The General Ukrainian National Council had espoused the setting up of Ukrainian schools and proposed sending Greek Catholic priests to the area.[420] The Greek Catholic Church even attempted to reinstate their former diocese of Chełm, which the Russian government had dissolved in the nineteenth century.[421] These proselytizing activities angered the Polish press. The Ukrainian newspaper *Dilo* in its turn accused Polish civil servants of suppressing the "Ukrainian character" of the territory. As the exchanges of polemical arguments escalated, the Kriegsüberwachungsamt (War Monitoring Office) asked the governor's office to put pressure on the editors and increase censorship. Polish and Ukrainian editors were summoned to the police headquarters, and it was represented to them that the press must not foment hatred between nationalities.[422]

Ukrainian politicians continued to demand that the regional authorities use the ethnonym "Ukrainians" instead of "Ruthenians" in all official correspondence. They also complained of other slights: in Przemyśl, official notices had only been issued in Polish and German but not in Ukrainian; in Winniki, no representative of the Ukrainian population had been appointed to the advisory board of the office of the district captain (Bezirkshauptmannschaft).[423] But the new names were only implemented very slowly. The presidium of the Ukrainian Parliamentary Representation requested the government again in December 1917 to ensure that the authorities only used the ethnonyms "Ukrainian" and "Ukrainians."[424]

L'viv continued to be both the site and the object of contention between Poles and Ukrainians. In January 1916 *Dilo* once again raised the issue of a Ukrainian university and protested against an account by a Polish newspaper according to which the Ukrainians had agreed to Czernowitz as the venue for a Ukrainian university. No Ukrainian would be willing to accept any other site than L'viv, the "age-old Ukrainian city." A Ukrainian university could only be set up here "in the center of cultural activity for the entire Ukrainian country."[425] When governor Freiherr Erich von Diller visited L'viv on April 23, 1916, on the occasion of his assumption of office, several Ukrainian delegations used the occasion to present their standpoint. The delegation of the Ukrainian National Committee[426] welcomed the new governor "to our country, to the former capital city of Ukrainian princes." They expressed the hope that Diller would assist them to achieve Ukrainian demands: the appointment of Ukrainian civil servants, the placing of Ukrainian language on an equal footing, the establishment of a Ukrainian university, and, finally, after the end of the war at the very latest, national self-government. At the same time, the delegation emphasized the loyalty of Ukrainians, who remained staunchly true to the throne and the Habsburg dynasty.[427]

This vaunted Ukrainian loyalty was sorely tried in November 1916. The proclamation of the Kingdom of Poland on November 5 by both emperors, the letter sent by the Austrian emperor to the Austrian Council of Ministers on November 4 announcing the separation of Galicia and the proclamation of Galicia's special status within the Habsburg monarchy on December 11, 1916, was welcomed enthusiastically by Polish society. The Poles of L'viv responded with "unabated enthusiasm" and with celebratory mass demonstrations. Police director Reinlender reported no increase in irredentism, but the Poles expected that Galicia and the Kingdom of Poland would be united in the not too distant future.[428] The resurgence of Poland was solemnly invoked during mass rallies: the time in which the dreams of their fathers would come true was approaching.[429]

On November 5, Polish residents took to the streets waving white-and-red flags and decorated their houses. On the same evening, a mass rally with several thousand persons was held at the Mickiewicz monument. Enthusiastic speeches were held and national songs were intoned. Then one thousand Polish youths marched through the town.[430] On November 11, white-and-red flags and banners with the white Polish eagle flew throughout the city. Polish institutions and schools were decorated and many citizens wore patriotic badges. Polish shops were closed, celebrations were held in schools, and celebratory Masses held in the churches. The play *Kościuszko at Racławice* was performed in the municipal theater, a play that glorifies the victory of the Polish insurgency against Russian troops in 1794. When the play showed the return of the victorious troops to Cracow, the applause continued unabated for quite some time. Prominent representatives from the army and the authorities, including General Böhm-Ermoli, the military commander (Stadtkommandant) of L'viv General Riml, police director Reinlender, government commissioner Grabowski, and the rector of the university, Kazimierz Twardowski, also attended the main gala event. At the start of the ceremony the anthem "Jeszcze Polska nie zginęła" ("Poland has not yet perished") was intoned. A gathering of Polish students which met up at the same time declared that the proclamation was tantamount to the establishment of a Polish state. At the end of the celebration, the 150 participants cheered for a free and independent Poland and sang the national anthem.[431] After the special status of Galicia had been proclaimed, the mood of the population was enthusiastic.[432]

The Jewish community in L'viv joined in the Polish jubilation. Already on November 7, they invited the advisory council of the city, the rabbis, civil servants, teachers of faith schools, the administrations of the synagogues, the council of the Jewish hospital, and representatives from all institutions of the Jewish community to a celebration in the large hall of the Jewish community. The deputy government commissioner for L'viv and acting head of the Jewish community Ozyasz Wasser assured the Poles of Jewish solidarity. His remarks were typical of the identity concept of Jewish Poles and conformed to the attitude Polish society expected of all Jews. Finally, after many efforts and bloody sacrifices the liberation of the Polish nation was approaching. "We, Jews and Poles, who are linked to the Polish nation with its traditions by an eight hundred year history, are deeply and sincerely conscious of this historical period." According to Ozyasz Wasser, the Jews were happy that Poland would finally become a free and independent state. The Jews, who throughout their history had suffered so much and still continued to suffer, understood what the Poles had suffered during the last 120 years far better than anyone else. "That is why the joy of the Polish nation is our joy, and its happiness is our happiness." Speaking in the name of the Jews assembled there, he wished free Poland a brilliant development and good fortune to all its citizens. At the end, he called for the assembled listeners to give a cheer for "a free and independent Poland."[433]

The Ukrainian reaction was entirely different. The press criticized the proclamation of the Kingdom of Poland. The emperor's announcement that Galicia's autonomy would be expanded was greeted with fierce protests. The Ukrainian press viewed it as an attack on the Ukrainian people who were being handed over to the mercy of Polish rule. Only censorship prevented the publication of leading editorials on November 7, 1916, criticizing the government. The clubs of the National Democrats and the Radicals in the House of Deputies (Abgeordnetenhaus) opposed the separation of Galicia from the Habsburg Empire and declared that the Ukrainian people would continue to strive for national autonomy in a Crown land of their own. Kost' Levyts'kyj even asked the German ambassador in Vienna whether the German Reich could intercede with the Austrian government on behalf of the Ukrainians.[434] On November 5, 1916, Ukrainian members of parliament protested to the new minister-president, Ernest von Koerber, about the expansion of Galician autonomy and demanded the partition of the Crown land. Territories that were ethnographically Ukrainian should be allowed to govern themselves.[435]

The threat of Galician unification with the Kingdom of Poland and the expansion of Galician autonomy united the different Ukrainian political groups. On November 8, the Radical and the National Democratic clubs of the House of Deputies united to form a Ukrainian Parliamentary Representation, which became a focal point for Ukrainian politics in subsequent months. It was headed by Julijan Romanchuk, with Lev Bachyns'kyj und Jevhen Petrushevych acting as deputy chairmen. Even the Social Democrat Semen Vityk wanted to join the club. The different Ukrainian representations and the press bombarded the government with protests and demands.[436] The Radicals demanded that the National Democrats distance themselves from the government. A further meeting was held on November 8, during which, according to information obtained by the Ministry of the Interior, the Radicals emerged stronger than before.⁴³⁷

Galvanized by the impending threat of the unification of Galicia with the Kingdom of Poland, officers of the Ukrainian Sich riflemen set up a secret military organization that established contacts to the Ukrainian Parliamentary Representation and leaders of the Ukrainian National Democratic Party. But the parliamentary members feared that if information about this conspiracy were to leak out, their position in Vienna, which was based on loyalty to the government, would be much diminished. Petrushevych and Kost' Levyts'kyj induced the officers to dissolve their secret military organization.⁴³⁸

On February 1 and 2, 1917, the expanded Ukrainian National Committee and trusted representatives of the National Democratic Party held a meeting the hall of the Lysenko Musical Society. Almost all of its 150 participants were members of the intelligentsia and included numerous members of the Imperial Council (Herrenhaus and Abgeordnetenhaus) and the Diet. Kost' Levyts'kyj gave a report on the activities of the General Ukrainian Council, which included Social Democrats, Radicals, and National Democrats. Levyts'kyj fiercely attacked the Poles, referring to them as the "eternal enemies of the Ukrainian people" who did not hesitate to traduce Ukrainians as traitors and spies. But the General Ukrainian Council had managed to convince the government of the loyalty of the Ukrainian nation. The demission of Governor Korytowski and the appointment of an Austrian general were welcomed. The council intervened in Vienna on the Chełm issue, supported the recruitment of Ukrainian riflemen, and attempted to exert some influence on the reconstruction of the Galician administration. But overall, the political situation for the Ukrainians had deteriorated. The thorny issue of a Ukrainian university still remained unresolved, and in the summer of 1916, the districts of Chełm, Hrubieszów, and Tomaszów were incorporated in the Generalgouvernement Lublin. The council viewed the planned exceptional status of Galicia as the most serious threat. Although Ukrainian politicians were prepared to be positive about Stürgkh's government, they were highly critical of Ernest von Koerber, because the hated imperial decrees and letters had been issued during the latter's brief term of office as minister-president. Ukrainian politicians welcomed the accession of Emperor Charles to the throne as a favorable sign that they thought might lessen the threat of a planned special status for Galicia. In the subsequent debates, Longin Tsehel's'kyj accused the General Ukrainian Council and its chairman Kost' Levyts'kyj of not having sufficiently pushed the national interests. The resolution protested against the special status of Galicia, the incorporation of the Chełm region and other Ukrainian territories in the Generalgouvernement or a future Polish state.⁴³⁹ In a second resolution, the assembly called on Ukrainian district organizations and their delegates to set up a national organization with subsidiaries in all parishes. Finally, after a hotly contended debate, the powers and responsibilities of the General Ukrainian Council and those of the Ukrainian Parliamentary Representation were differentiated from each other, although the boundaries remained unclear. The function of the General Ukrainian Council would be to represent the general interests of all Ukrainians while the Parliamentary Representation would be the sole representative of the political interests of the Ukrainian people. And thus, according to the police agent present at the discussions, the planned ousting of Levyts'kyj failed.[440]

Once the first flush of euphoria had died down, the Polish population became more skeptical about the likelihood of an immediate unification of Galicia with the Kingdom of Poland. The uncompromisingly hostile reaction of the Ukrainian parties contributed to this sobering disillusionment. The difficulties in obtaining enough supplies and the daily problems caused by the war further depressed the general mood.[441] The Polish population increasingly began to turn away from Austria, which had neither consistently supported Polish national and political demands nor appeared to be capable of ensuring sufficient supplies of foodstuffs and other necessities.

The Russian February revolution and the overthrow of the tsar had sweeping and cataclysmic consequences for Eastern Europe. The new provisional government of Russia promptly recognized Poland's right to exist, changing the political starting point in Galicia. The Entente and the United States, which had just entered the war, now no longer needed to make allowance for the interests of its Russian ally in the matter of the Polish question. Poland's independence was now on the agenda of international politics. This devalued the Austro-Polish option, and Austria-Hungary and Germany were forced on the defensive as they could not keep pace with the promises of the Entente. Nevertheless, Galician Poles still felt some loyalty toward the Austrian monarchy, not least because they needed Vienna's support to fend off Ukrainian claims. A further by-product of the February revolution was the release of the hostages taken by the Russian troops during their retreat from Galicia.

Tadeusz Rutowski had already returned from Russia in November 1916. In Cracow, he got a foretaste of what he could expect in L'viv. The Cracow City Council gave him a hero's welcome, granting him honorary citizenship of the city. In L'viv, the reception hosted by the mayor was the last action undertaken by the "Rutowski Committee," which had been set up in his support and had collected thousands of signatures demanding his release. Rutowski's portrait was displayed in stationery shops and bookshops; busts of Rutowski went on sale. The Ulica Teatralna was renamed Ulica Rutowskiego, and his name was given to a cultural endowment. During the celebration, Rutowski held a key speech in which he evoked the achievements and sacrifices of those who had gone before and praised the commitment and efforts of the current generation: "Lwów has always been the bastion against which the barbarian waves broke during their attacks on Poland." Anyone who looked on the walls and monuments of the past knew that this past was linked to the lives of every new generation. Rutowski also found warm words for the recently deceased Austrian emperor but followed them up by opining that it was now no longer a question of autonomy but of a Polish state.[442] His speech deeply upset the Ukrainian press, particularly because Rutowski had only talked of "Poles without distinction of creed or nationality." *Dilo* claimed that Rutowski had no right to speak in the name of Ukrainians as they had no wish to live under this "common roof."[443]

Rutowski annoyed Ukrainian leaders anew by his refusal to establish a section in the planned municipal orphanage in which Greek Catholic orphans would be looked after by Ukrainian teachers and staff. A Ukrainian delegation had justified their demand by contending that Polish teachers and staff would educate Ukrainian children in a "spirit of Polish nationalism." However, Rutowski did make the concession that parents were entitled to demand that their children be educated "in Ukrainian." He promised that the children's religious needs would be catered to by a Greek Catholic priest.[444]

On September 10, 1917, Archbishop Sheptyts'kyj also returned to L'viv from his Russian exile, which had been followed by a lengthy stay abroad. The Ukrainians had prepared a similarly rapturous reception for him as the Poles had given Tadeusz Rutowski some nine months earlier. An immense crowd gathered at the station. A guard of honor from the Forty-First Infantry Regiment stood awaiting him accompanied by a band. Archduke Wilhelm had traveled to L'viv in person to welcome the returning archbishop. Archbishop Bilczewski; the chairman of the consistory of St. George's Cathedral, Bilets'kyj; the German Consul, Heinze; and representatives from the university, the town, various Ukrainian societies, and the governor's office had come to the station. The Jewish community was represented by Ozyasz Wasser, the Orthodox rabbi Leib Braude, and the rabbi of the progressive community, Guttmann. The chairman of the reception committee, Stepan Fedak; police director Józef Reinlender; and a member of the Imperial Council, Kost' Levyts'kyj, all gave speeches. The spectators lined the streets from the train station to the archiepiscopal palace. A thanksgiving service was subsequently held in St. George's Cathedral. The same evening the metropolitan bishop received 120 specially invited guests; with the exception of Heinze, Reinlender, and Archduke Wilhelm, the guests consisted only of Ukrainian dignitaries and politicians. In talks, Sheptyts'kyj expressed the hope that the ecclesiastical connection between eastern Ukraine and Russia would be dissolved and replaced by a closer connection to the Vatican, either in the form of a union or in the form of an autocephalous church.[445]

Anti-German protests broke out in L'viv after the Polish legions had been disbanded, in parallel to the eruption of student protests in Warsaw. With almost all Polish territories controlled by the Central Powers, communications between

Posen, Warsaw, Cracow, Vilnius, and L'viv had become much easier, and reactions were swifter. On May 15, 1917, a meeting was held in the student dormitories in L'viv, during which students protested sharply against the German government. To demonstrate their solidarity with the students of Warsaw, the meeting voted to go on strike the following day. Several hundred students assembled at the approach to the university to prevent students of other nationalities from entering the university. To prevent excesses, the rector's office decided without further ado to cancel all lectures.[446]

Although conservative Ukrainian and Polish parties were irreconcilably opposed to each other, not all bridges had been burned between the social democratic parties. A public meeting held on May 1, 1918, in Borysław was attended by about six thousand citizens, and the audience was addressed by a Polish, a Ukrainian, and a Jewish Social Democrat. All the speakers criticized the conduct of the war and the existing social order. Shouts of "long live the revolution" were heard from the ranks of the spectators.[447] The Polish Social Democratic party called a meeting in the Polish National House, scheduling it to coincide with the celebrations on May 1, 1917. About one thousand people, many of them elderly workmen, small traders, clerical workers, and railroad workers, attended. The list of speakers also included Herman Diamand and Mykola Han'kevych. While Diamand spoke as a Polish Social Democrat, Han'kevych appeared as the representative of Ukrainian social democracy. Diamand emphasized that the war, despite the enormous suffering, had brought about the liberation of Poland and the downfall of tsarism. After Diamand had finished speaking, Han'kevych acclaimed the Russian proletarians who had done away with tsarism, the "oppressor and enemy of both Poles and Ukrainians." He stressed, just as Diamand had done before him, the necessity of achieving a reconciliation between Poles and Ruthenians. At the end of the meeting, the organizers appealed to the persons assembled there to disperse quietly. Only four hundred of them, most of them women, refused to follow suit. Together with a few youths, they crossed the Ringplatz to stand in front of the city hall loudly protesting the lack of food supplies. The police dispersed the crowd and arrested three women. On the same day, there were a few incidents when tools were downed and workers briefly walked out.[448]

L'viv councilors were dissatisfied with the provisional administration of the city and again urged the governor to either schedule new elections or to create a provisional council made up of previously elected councilors and dignitaries. They criticized that the government commissioner was not familiar with the local conditions and had not sufficiently consulted with representatives of the local population. Only the most acute problems were being tackled and there was a complete absence of more far-sighted policies.[449] Their demands were repeated several times over the following months.[450] But the autonomous status remained suspended. Tadeusz Rutowski was well respected and quite popular among Poles.

His appointment as government commissioner initially calmed the mood. But in the spring of 1918 Rutowski suffered a severe stroke that left him incapable of continuing work. Several options were now available: (1) reinstatement of the disbanded city council: this option was what the majority party, a confederation of civil parties dominated by the National Democrats, would have preferred; (2) immediate elections: this was the option preferred by parties with very few or no representatives on the city council, in other words, the Social Democrats, the Ukrainian parties and the Zionists, because they expected to considerably increase the number of elected representatives from their parties; and (3) the appointment of an advisory council that would consist of the most important representative of all parties according to the level of their support in the population. The governor's office favored the third solution, in which a government commissioner would be appointed who would hold office with the support of an advisory council whose authority would be considerably expanded. In December 1917 the governor's office set the first steps in motion to establish the latter option. The parties put forward their candidates for the advisory council and the governor selected the members. Of the one hundred members of the council, sixty-one had been members of the old city council and thirty-nine seats were given to parties not previously represented on the city council. By and large, the governor tried to take account of the parties' preferred candidates. For the first time, Ukrainians were members of the city council. After some initial hesitation, most parties approved the compromise, and Władysław Stesłowicz from the Polish Democratic Party was appointed government commissioner.[451] But the new arrangement did not meet with unanimous acceptance. The Zionist member of the Imperial Council, Benno Straucher, protested that his party had been passed over. He demanded that the governor should appoint at least two or three Zionists.[452] The Zionists had expected that a snap election would have brought them a substantial increase in votes. The Yiddish newspaper *Tagblatt* suspected that the governor's office wanted to appoint the delegates Löwenstein, Diamand, and Reizes to the new advisory council. But the *Tagblatt* insisted that they did not represent the Jewish population: "It is clear that not a single Jew who truly feels Jewish in L'viv—and that applies to the great majority of the Jewish population of L'viv—will accept Dr. Löwenstein or Diamant [Diamand] as the Jewish representatives." The *Tagblatt* demanded that the governor appoint nationally minded Jews.[453]

Poles continued to take every opportunity to demonstrate their preeminence in the city and their national unity. As the governor had forbidden all political demonstrations, anniversaries and celebrations were taken as occasions for national manifestations. On October 13 and 14, 1917, a number of celebrations were held to commemorate the hundredth anniversary of the death of Tadeusz Kościuszko. Celebrations began on October 13 with a prayer service in the Latin Cathedral. In his sermon, Father Dziędzielewicz encouraged his listeners to emulate Kościuszko, to love the fatherland, and to be united. After Mass had finished, patriotic songs were sung, and the assembled congregation dispersed peacefully. On the same day, a Kościuszko exhibition was opened in the Ossolineum, and the municipal council decided to rename the municipal park Kościuszko Park. The main celebrations were held the next day with a High Mass in the Latin Cathedral celebrated by Archbishop Bilczewski. Special services were held at the same time in the Armenian Catholic cathedral, in the Protestant church, and in the temple of the Jewish progressive community. At the end of the High Mass, a commemorative plaque was unveiled on the wall of the cathedral. An imposing procession of several thousand people was formed, which was welcomed by rapturous crowds, also numbering several thousand, awaiting them in front of the Diet and in Kościuszko Park. After speeches by government commissioner Rutowski, representatives of the executive board of the Galician Diet and a representative of the peasants, the crowd joined in the singing of patriotic songs. The ceremony ended with the laying of the first stone of a monument to Kościuszko. That evening a gala performance was held in the city theater. The police noted with satisfaction that there had been no disturbances of the public order during the two-day celebrations.[454]

Just three weeks after these celebrations, the Russian October revolution changed the international framework again. The emergence of the Bolsheviks and of Soviet Russia represented a new power that would go on to play a key role in the politics of Eastern Europe. The situation in the lands to the east of the German and Austrian spheres of control began to spiral out of control. In the civil war that erupted soon after, the Bolsheviks fought the counterrevolutionary "White Armies" and the troops of the Ukrainian People's Republic. In its First Universal dated June 23, 1917, the Ukrainian Central Rada (the government of the Ukrainian People's Republic) first demanded the right of Ukrainian self-determination within a reformed Russia and followed this by proclaiming an autonomous Ukrainian Republic in a Third Universal issued on November 22, 1917. Finally, in the Fourth Universal of January 22, 1918, the Rada proclaimed Ukraine's full independence from Russia. For Galician Ukrainians, these developments in the Ukraïna opened the prospect of uniting the Ukrainian lands of the Habsburg monarchy with the new Ukrainian state.

On November 22, 1917, a meeting of the General Ukrainian Council, attended by members of the Imperial Council and about thirty representatives from all over the province was held in L'viv, chaired by Kost' Levyts'kyj. The members protested once again against any union of East Galicia with the Kingdom of Poland, remonstrating against "the subjugation of our people in our own land." The Poles were the "hereditary enemies" of the Ukrainians, who had never accepted Polish rule: "We demand the realization of the right to self-determination, we demand a free independent Ukraine."[455]

The Ukrainian parties also launched a debate in the Austrian House of Deputies, which culminated in Jevhen Levyts'kyj shouting, "The path to incorporation with Poland will only be over our dead bodies."[456]

By now, the Ukrainian Parliamentary Representation had won the power struggle against the General Ukrainian Council, which discontinued its activities. On December 25 and 26, 1917, fifty leading officials of the Ukrainian National Democratic Party came together in L'viv. The president of the Ukrainian Parliamentary Representation, Jevhen Petrushevych, reported that after the conservative Ernst Seidler Baron von Feuchtenegg had become the new minister-president, the Ukrainians would be able to hamstring the plans of their opponents. According to Petrushevych, Seidler was much more positively inclined toward the Ukrainians than his predecessor had been. The real goal of Ukrainian politics was the unification of East Galicia with the Ukrainian Republic. If the Habsburg monarchy would relinquish East Galicia, then it should not join Poland but the Ukraïna. In an ad hoc resolution, the meeting protested once again against any incorporation of East Galicia into Poland. If this were to happen, the Ukrainians demanded a vote on their nationality (citizenship). If the borders were to remain unchanged, the congress demanded the unification of East Galicia with North Bukovina and its promotion to an independent Ukrainian Crown land. The lawyer Volodymyr Okhrymovych, recently returned from Russian captivity, reported that representatives of the Ukrainian People's Republic (the chairman of the Central Rada, Hrushevs'kyj, and others) would demand the affiliation of East Galicia and Bukovina to Ukraine at the peace conference in Brest-Litovsk. Okhrymovych called on the Ukrainians in East Galicia to do the same. But Petrushevych and Sheptyts'kyj demurred. They believed that while it was important to maintain ties to eastern Ukrainians, it was also important not to dissolve the ties to the Austrian government. But the connections to the Ruthenian member for the Bukovina in the Imperial Council, Mykola Ritter Vasyl'ko, should be severed because of his fixation on Austria.[457] But only a short time later, Vasyl'ko was once again welcomed back into the fold, and he went on to play in important role as an intermediary during the peace negotiations between the Central Powers, Soviet Russia, and the Ukrainian People's Republic in Brest-Litovsk.

Brest-Litovsk and Recruitment to the National Cause

After the two revolutions in Russia in March and November 1917,[458] the Polish and Ukrainian question became more pressing. In L'viv and Galicia, 1918 began with a campaign of events launched by Poles. On January 11, Polish intellectuals held a meeting in the hall of the Polytechnic Association. Civil servants, professors, bankers, and other professionals discussed the future of Galicia. The speakers exhorted their listeners to remain vigilant and united to secure L'viv for the Kingdom of Poland. At the end of the evening the assembly cabled a message of support to the Polish Regency Council in Warsaw.[459] Six days later, seven hundred intellectuals, a number of workers, and representatives from various women's organizations held a meeting. The assembled group criticized the German (Prussian) policy toward Poland and the all too compliant Regency Council. One workers' representative declared "that Polish workers must stand together in solidarity with Polish intellectuals to prevent the spread of the Bolshevik movement to Poland."[460]

The majority of Poles were now keen to distance themselves from the Austrian government. Nevertheless, there were still politicians, particularly among the older generation of Cracow conservatives and the Podolian nobility, who remained steadfastly loyal to Austria. Among them were such prominent politicians as Rutowski, Land Marshal Niezabitowski, Prince Lubomirski, and Count Piniński. Supported by the government they formed the Klub Pracy Narodowej (Club of National Work), holding a meeting in L'viv on February 2. The aim of the club was a united Poland ruled by Emperor Charles. The National Democratic youth led by party heavyweights Głąbinski and Count Skarbek protested against this pro-Austrian initiative. The demonstrators kicked up a lot of noise in the streets, smashing several windows before moving on to various German institutions (the army postal service, the German Red Cross, and military administrative offices). A Polish high school student was shot, another high school student was seriously wounded, and eleven people were slightly injured. Up to that point, the demonstration had been primarily directed against Austria and its Polish supporters. After the shots, the hatred turned against citizens of the German Reich. Rioting youths demanded that the German Red Cross take down the German flag flying from its building. When this was rejected, high school students tore down the flag and burned it. German soldiers and officers were called names and stones were thrown at them. A rumor spread that German soldiers had fired the shots. On February 3 and 4, protesters assembled in front of the Mickiewicz monument to sing patriotic songs and listen to inflammatory speeches. Huge numbers of Poles attended the funeral of the high school student. The funeral procession was led by a cohort of Roman Catholic clergy. Soldiers and police stood by to prevent any rioting. The funeral was a demonstration directed against Germany. Mourning notices included the handwritten comment: "murdered by the Prussians." Countless funeral wreaths with inscriptions dedicating them "to the young hero, murdered by the enemy" were placed on the grave.[461]

The National Democratic deputies Skarbek and Głąbinski launched an urgent motion in the House of Deputies. The version they spread was that Prussian and Austrian military police had continually provoked the peaceful crowd. People of all social strata had been impelled to take part in the demonstration for purely patriotic reasons. The two National Democrats admitted that a few street urchins and certain "unknown individuals" had suddenly pushed to the front of the march and caused a disturbance. The deputies condemned the "unprincipled and barbaric actions" of the police and some of the Prussian officers.[462]

The government and the governor's office ordered high school directors to issue an appeal to their pupils, the parents of their pupils, and the teachers, admonishing them to prevent young persons from taking part in such street protests. The education authorities (Landesschulrat) ordered school directors to exert a moderating influence on their pupils.[463] The education authorities instituted their own investigation and learned the following. On February 2, an anonymous flyer had called on high school students to take part in a demonstration to be held that evening at seven o'clock in front of the Mickiewicz monument without stating the purpose of the demonstration. The crowd had attempted to move on to Hotel Krakowski, where Praca Narodowa (the Club of National Work) was holding a banquet. The pupils had not appeared to understand the purpose of their actions. They had only been told that it was a demonstration against "friends of the Prussians." Security guards had pushed the crowd into the poorly lit side street with the German army post office, which was where the shots had fallen. A rumor began to spread that the Prussians had killed two students, which had led to the anti-Prussian street demonstrations the next day. The education authorities suspended all classes on February 4, as none of the students came to school that day. The solemn funeral service of the killed student meant that all classes were also canceled on Wednesday, February 6. Polish high school teachers sided with their pupils and roundly condemned the actions of the police, demanding that all German soldiers' rest homes in L'viv and Galicia be closed down. But teachers also warned their pupils against participating in street demonstrations and political campaigns.[464] Classes recommenced the next day, however wild rumors continued to whip up emotions, fomenting unrest among students all across the country, and demonstrations began to be held in other cities as well. Marches were held in Cracow to protest the conditions of the peace treaty of Brest-Litovsk, which had just become more generally known. The demonstration ended with demonstrators laying waste to the German consulate general.[465] After a detailed investigation and careful questioning, the Department of Public Prosecutions found that the two high school students had been injured and killed by a Polish sergeant major of the Austrian police, who had misread the situation and overreacted. The officer had believed that he was being attacked and fired shots into the crowd. German officers had only fired a few warning shots, which had not harmed anyone.[466]

But these events were only a foretaste of the popular indignation among Poles against the terms of the peace treaty of Brest-Litovsk. In Brest-Litovsk, representatives of the Central Powers negotiated with delegates of the Soviet Russian government about the terms for a separate peace. Against the wishes of the Soviet Russian delegation the Central Powers also consulted with representatives of the Central Rada, the government of the Ukrainian People's Republic (Ukraïns'ka Narodna Respublika, UNR), which had only been recognized by a few states. The Central Powers concluded a peace treaty with the Central Rada even before they signed the peace agreement with Soviet Russia. Neither Polish representatives nor representatives of Galician Ukrainians had attended the negotiations. At the urging of the Ukrainian delegation, the head of the German delegation, state secretary Richard von Kühlmann, and the head of the Austrian delegation, foreign secretary Otto Count Czernin, agreed to allow the Ukrainian Reichsrat deputy for Bukovina Mykola Ritter Vasyl'ko to come to Brest-Litovsk as an advisor. Vasyl'ko was an important landowner and had recently fallen out with the Ukrainian Parliamentary Representation because of his unwavering loyalty to Austria. This was now irrelevant, and he informed the delegation from the UNR of the wishes of the Austrian Ukrainians.[467] The Ukrainian delegates successfully persuaded Czernin to agree to the creation of a separate Ukrainian Crown land composed of East Galicia and Bukovina in a secret supplementary agreement. But this general promise was not linked to a specific timetable and was kept secret to avoid antagonizing the Polish population and setting them against the government. But even the territorial agreements with the Central Rada were sufficient to provoke a storm of indignation among the Polish population. Podlasie, the Chełm region, and Volhynia had been handed over to the Ukrainian People's Republic. All of these areas had formerly been part of Poland–Lithuania and had large minority Polish populations. Governor Karl von Huyn anticipated that an uproar would follow and appealed in vain to Czernin to delay publication of the terms of the peace treaty until the governor's office could make arrangements to deal with the expected furor.[468]

The Regency Council in Warsaw immediately protested against the planned incorporation of the Chełm region in Ukraine. The Polish newspapers in L'viv sported thick black mourning borders. Their editorials sharply criticized the territorial decisions. There were riots and demonstrations in the Generalgouvernement. Pictures of the German and the Austrian emperors were burned during a demonstration in Lublin, and military governor Stanisław Count Szeptycki, a Polish patriot and brother of the Greek Catholic archbishop, requested his discharge.[469] On the night of February 15–16, 1,600 officers, noncommissioned officers, and soldiers of Brigade II of the Polish Legions stationed at Rarańcza defected to the enemy. The remaining troops numbering some 5,500 men were interned or thrown out of the Austrian army.[470]

Indiscretions meant that even the secret additional clause concerning the creation of a Ukrainian Crown land under Habsburg rule along with the planned partition of Galicia quickly became generally known, infuriating the Galician Poles. The terms of the treaty provoked "an immoderate storm of resentment and indignation in the Polish population of Galicia and more particularly in the provincial capital of L'viv" that swept through all classes of society. The mood was inflamed further by the Polish daily press, which preventive censorship did little to restrain. All Polish parties opposed the agreement but their political preferences differed. The National Democrats aspired to a greater Polish state without regard to the Central Powers, while the Conservatives and the Democrats continued to keep the Austro-Polish option open.[471] Imperial-royal symbols were now regularly attacked and defaced all over Galicia.[472] Police director Reinlender reported that "among the Polish population in L'viv there was a tremendous depression and the greatest ferment." On February 12, 1918, various dignitaries and representatives of different parties met in the city hall. During the meeting, one speaker described the peace with the Ukraine as an act of "treason committed against the Poles." Government commissioner Rutowski called on the assembled persons to "protest most keenly against the severance of the Polish territories." The meeting decided to appeal to the leaders of all Polish parties to proclaim February 18, 1918, as a day of national mourning as a sign of protest and to combine it with a general strike. At the end of the meeting, the 1,500 persons who had attended dispersed quietly.[473]

More protest meetings were held the next day. Around noon, the students of the university deliberated in the hall of the Polish Pedagogical Association. They denounced the peace treaty as a "violation of the people's right of self-determination," an act of violence, and a betrayal of the Polish nation. At the same time, Rutowski had called together representatives from all Polish parties to launch a concerted protest against the terms of the treaty. The same evening there was a gathering chaired by Count Czartoryski with a meeting held in parallel in the assembly room of the Polish Sokół Association. Speaking there, Głąbiński referred to the treaty as the "greatest misfortune" and as an indication of the German urge for territorial expansion. He called on his fellow patriots to oppose the government without compromise.[474] The campaign of protests continued in the days that followed: demonstrations were held by the actors of the municipal theater (February 18), by civil servants of the Executive of the Galician Diet (February16), by officials of the judicial courts (February 15 and 21), by members of Polish cultural societies (February 16), the Pedagogical Society, the board of trade, the Polytechnic Society, the Polish scientific societies (February 21), the Liga Kobiet (Women's League) and the Komitet prac obywatelskiej kobiet (Women's Committee for Civic Work; February 18). High school teachers solemnly swore to educate Polish youth in the spirit of the nation and show their pupils the crimes that had been perpetrated against the Polish nation: "We swear before the entire world to persist in the defense of our fatherland by unanimously expressing our abhorrence of the duplicitous policies of the Central Powers."[475]

The protests took hold across all of Galicia. In Cracow, the authorities even had to declare a state of emergency on February 13 and 14. The police lost control of the streets. All across the region, pictures of the emperor were destroyed and the imperial eagle taken down. An image of "Christ on the Cross" flanked on either side by a picture of the Austrian and of the German emperor was set up on the Ringplatz in Cracow. The inscription read "Jesus Christ, never have you hung on the cross in the company of two such villains." In schools, the pictures of the emperor were removed and replaced by pictures of Piłsudski. Ominously, the government could no longer depend on the loyalty of its Polish officials because many civil servants were also participating in the demonstrations.[476] From the standpoint of the Polish elite, it was not that they had rescinded their loyalty to the empire; rather, the government had violated Polish rights. Those who had supported the empire felt particularly betrayed. Their rejection of Austria was initially expressed by a rejection of Austrian symbols. The administration of the Crown land received more than seven hundred Austrian medals returned by their holders. Over the following days and weeks, symbols of the state and pictures of the emperor and his family were repeatedly attacked and defaced. In some schools, the pictures were removed and only subsequently rehung after interventions by the police.[477]

Foreign Minister Czernin criticized the fact that Polish newspapers were permitted to express such sharp criticisms of the government and the peace treaty. After consulting with the minister-president, Czernin requested Governor Huyn to enforce much stricter censorship.[478] But the wave of protests had already been unleashed and could no longer be stemmed by censorship. In the House of Deputies of the Imperial Council, the Polish deputies now attempted a policy of obstruction. They protested against the terms of the peace treaty, whereupon the Ukrainian deputies accused them of disloyalty to Austria.[479]

On February 18, protest rallies and strikes were held in West Galicia and in most East Galician towns with Polish majorities in response to the call for protests issued by an all-party commission. In L'viv, the protests kicked off with Masses held in all Roman Catholic churches and services held in the synagogues of the progressive Jewish community. A crowd gathered, stretching from Market Square to the Ringplatz. Platforms had been erected in front of the mayoralty, on Halicka Street, and in front of the Mickiewicz monument, from which speakers uttered fiery denunciations of the treaty. Representatives of all the Polish parties gathered at the Ringplatz. As usual, the Boy Scouts and schoolchildren, the Sokół, and the veterans of the January uprising of 1863 had come in full uniform. The Polish press reported euphorically that the rural population had also participated in great numbers, describing this as a sure sign that the entire nation had been mobilized and celebrating the fact that on this issue of national importance, class conflicts and differing political views appeared to play no role. Representatives from the Jewish community also participated in the protests. The assembled crowds then moved to the building of the Diet, where they listened to speeches by members of various parties, civil servants, teachers, and professors and sang patriotic songs. About twenty thousand people of all classes took part in the demonstration. Banners demanded the release of Piłsudski and of detained members of the Polish Legions and carried anti-Prussian slogans such as "Down with Prussian Militarism." Leaflets written in German and Polish demanded a separation from Austria. All Polish schools, private institutions, banks, businesses, restaurants, and coffeehouses were closed. Only military personnel and Ukrainians showed up for work in the railway workshops. Rail services were limited, and only a few trains were cleared and dispatched. A few Ukrainian businesses and institutions remained open but suffered no harassment. The police had put extensive security measures in place, and there were no large-scale disturbances.[480] According to other reports, pictures of the emperor and Austrian flags were burned, and anti-Semitic leaflets were distributed. A few incidents occurred, with stones thrown at houses in which Jews were living.[481] As a precautionary measure, a troop of 150 heavily armed Hungarian soldiers were sent to guard the German consulate.[482] All work between the hours of five in the morning and eight at night was halted in the war telegraph and telephone exchange in L'viv. This affected some 270 public officials; of these, only nine telegraph operators and five telephone switchboard operators came to work that morning. The Polish employees leaned heavily on their non-Polish colleagues, backing up their pressure with concrete threats.[483] In the beginning, Ukrainian and Jewish public officials had rejected the idea of a strike, but Jews in particular gave in to pressure, fearing a pogrom if they continued to refuse. Only German and Ukrainian civil servants arrived punctually at work. The authorities tried unavailingly to ensure that enough electricity from the power station and enough gas from the gas works was available to maintain emergency operations.[484] Many officials of the judicial courts also took part in the demonstrations as did civil servants from other administrative bodies and from the governor's office, some of them even striking as a body. As other public officials were not reprimanded, judicial employees were also not subjected to disciplinary action.[485]

In Przemyśl, all classes of the Polish population participated in the protest demonstrations held on February 17 and 18. The district commissioner, the Roman Catholic bishop, the government commissioner, and large numbers of civil servants also participated. One leaflet depicted the Polish eagle flanked by pictures of the two emperors hanging from a gallows. Numerous uncensored newspaper articles criticizing the government were published. The speakers at the demonstrations described the peace treaty as a betrayal that had defrauded the Polish people. The clergy took a particularly aggressive stance. One bishop called on his listeners to fight against this injustice "to the last drop of [their] blood." A privy councilor (Geheimrat) declared "that the Polish people could feel confident that it would be supported by the Polish clergy in this battle in every respect."

After the bishop had finished, representatives of all parties gave speeches. At the request of one of the speakers, the crowd uncovered "their heads, lifted their hands to take the oath, and pledged to fight for national unity, union and independence to the last drop of blood." Schoolchildren were particularly impressed by the clergy administering the oath. Many men and women sobbed and wept. The procession then continued to the bishop's residence. All public offices of the civil administration were closed, as were all businesses from nine o'clock in the morning. Jews and Ukrainians kept their heads down and caused no disturbances. The public authorities had declared their solidarity. All in all, the imperial-royal military command in Przemyśl considered the situation to be extremely alarming, reporting that the Polish population had become alienated from Austria and was now anti-German.[486]

In Rawa-Ruska, about two thousand people participated in the demonstration. In Nowy Sącz, the Austrian eagle was torn down from official buildings. In Nowy Targ, rioting occurred because of difficulties with supplies, while Jasło remained largely quiet. No symbols of the state were attacked in Jasło, but the windows of Jewish homes were smashed. In Rzeszów, the windows of Jewish dwellings were smashed, but the windows of other residences were similarly broken at random. Almost all Austrian eagles were removed from official buildings. A mood of "general exasperation" was reported for Skole. The mood among the lower classes was also volatile because of the lack of supplies. An impressive demonstration attended by two thousand people was held in Dobromil. Pamphlets attacking the Jews were distributed in Radymno.[487]

In March 1918 the Poles prepared for a second large demonstration. This time, attempts were made to persuade the Jewish population to participate. The regional conference for Galician Zionists had been planned for March 8 through 10, during which a Zionist-Polish union would allegedly be effected. The Polish press declared that the anti-Semitic leaflets and pamphlets hailed from Berlin and had been distributed by German agitators to incite Jewish hatred against the Poles. The Polish National Democrats also attempted to woo Jewish refugees in Vienna, where they numbered some sixty to seventy thousand persons, and to induce them to hold a pro-Polish rally. The attempted rapprochement between National Democrats and Jews was a purely tactical move and came to nothing. At the same time, Polish nationalists were disseminating a leaflet showing a Polish eagle wearing a yarmulke and holding a money bag in its right hand and a menorah in its left hand. The leaflet was directed against Jewish Polish politicians who supported an independent Poland under Habsburg rule. At the beginning of March pictures of the emperor and Austrian flags were burned in front of the Mickiewicz monument in L'viv and at other sites.[488] Governor Huyn considered the excesses directed against state symbols to be symptomatic of the anti-Habsburg mood in the Polish population: "The demonstration on February

18 made it apparent that the entire Polish civil service, the professors, teachers and the clergy consider themselves only as Poles, the Austrian idea was nowhere to be found."[489]

But Huyn showed himself conciliatory toward his civil servants. He made allowances for them, believing that "under the enormous impression of the moment [they] were at the moment under the spell of national exaltation." The civil servants of Polish nationality had kept aloof from the excesses staged by radical elements, and Huyn hoped that they would be more reticent in future.[490] Huyn believed that it would be inopportune to discipline public officials sharply. The important thing was to restore the peace and public order and to allow such outlets to prevent an irreparable breach between Polish society and the Austrian state. Huyn defended his approach against criticisms by the minister of the interior, declaring that drastic measures would have discredited the Austro-Polish solution. But the popular mood remained unchanged, and the calm was merely superficial.[491]

In March 1918 Governor Huyn reported pervasive agitation by Polish nationalists, particularly in the towns. The minister of the interior had previously informed Huyn that military agencies were providing the minister with better information on the events in Galicia than Huyn's own reports. Huyn defended himself by declaring that the entire body of public servants in Galicia was strongly Polish nationalist and that at least 80 percent of them supported the All-Polish (National Democratic) party. An objective coverage of events could not be expected from them under these circumstances. "It [the civil service] will always endeavor to mitigate or even entirely conceal acts which would be detrimental to the assessment of their own nation."[492]

A police report dated March 2, 1918, commented that "the tension in L'viv is immense." Both the Poles and the Ukrainians were reportedly planning to hold demonstrations the following Sunday. The Jews feared a pogrom and hid their possessions. Schoolchildren wore either white-and-red (Polish) or yellow-and-blue (Ukrainian) ribbons and armbands.[493]

In contrast to the Poles, the Ukrainian elites were satisfied with the terms of the peace treaty and organized demonstrations of thanks.[494] While the majority of Polish demonstrations were held in West Galicia, in East Galicia it was the Ukrainians who took to the streets. Overlaps occurred in L'viv and also in Przemyśl. On the day the peace treaty was announced, Ukrainians in L'viv gathered in front of the Prosvita building on Market Square and the chairman of the Ukrainian National Committee Kost' Levyts'kyj gave a short speech. An orchestra composed of Ukrainian railroad men played to the assembled crowd, and the enthusiastic crowd marched down Kopernikus Street to the building of the Lysenko Musical Society. Another celebration was held on February 12, during which the speakers criticized the Polish reactions to the peace treaty, commenting that the Poles were laying spurious claims to Ukrainian territories.[495]

The demonstrations showed to what an extent national mobilization had now also taken hold in the villages. On February 23, nine thousand peasants came together in Gródek Jagielloński, most of them young men and elderly women from the surrounding villages. About fifty and sixty intellectuals also attended the meeting. The tenor of the speeches was loyal to the Habsburg dynasty but aggressively anti-Polish. Between four and five thousand peasants, most of them women from the surrounding countryside, converged on Żółkiew, where they cheered the Ukrainian People's Republic and shouted their support of an "independent Ukrainian state in Austria." At the meeting, Poles, particularly the landowners, were again sharply criticized. Approximately three thousand Ukrainians, most of them adolescents of both sexes and older women, assembled in Przemyśl. As in other locations, the intellectuals spoke out against the Poles and declared their loyalty to Austria. The governor's office and Poles who observed the scenes had to admit that peasants were participating in the meetings in significant numbers. But the old patterns of perception persisted. Ruthenian peasants continued to be considered politically passive, as a mass that could only be persuaded to take part in political demonstrations by the enticement of material gain. The governor's office was happy to believe the rumors that every peasant in Gródek Jagielloński had received six krone, and every peasant in Przemyśl had received four krone to take part in the demonstration.[496] But which Ukrainian organization could have raised such a sum of money?

One of the largest demonstrations with twelve thousand participants was held in L'viv. Half of all persons participating came from the surrounding villages. The celebrations started with Masses held in all Greek Catholic churches. Longin Tsehel's'kyj, standing in front of St. George's Cathedral, expressed his joy at the creation of a Ukrainian state. Finally, the crowds moved to the Ringplatz in the town center, where Kost' Levyts'kyj welcomed the peace treaty and demanded the partition of Galicia. The rally was peaceful and concluded with the crowd cheering the name of Emperor Charles.[497]

In Jarosław, the first rally was held on March 3; it was attended by 1,200 people, mainly peasants from the surrounding villages. After a morning service of thanksgiving, Greek Catholic priests gave patriotic speeches. They accused the Poles of having stolen Ukrainian lands and of having made Ukrainians their bondsmen and -women. They then celebrated that on that day, Ukrainians had become so strong that they wished to rule themselves, either in a state of their own within the Habsburg Empire or in a united, independent Ukraine. "The Poles should just grab their Jews and leave Ukrainian territories." At the end of the day, the intellectuals went on to hold their own private celebration, staging a musical evening in honor of the Ukrainian national poet Taras Shevchenko.[498]

In Drohobycz, twenty thousand people held a rally that began, as usual, with a Mass, followed by a procession with Sich and Sokil formations carrying blue-and-gold banners and singing patriotic songs. In an address to the Emperor Charles, speakers demanded the unification of Ukrainian territories under his rule. The celebrations ended the same evening with a concert.[499] In Śniatyn on March 3, ten Greek Catholic priests celebrated a thanksgiving Mass, with twenty thousand people taking part in the solemn procession. Ukrainian and Austrian flags were waved, and the emperor's hymn and patriotic songs were sung.[500]

The vehemence of the Polish protests against the incorporation of the Chełm region in Ukraine had taken the government by surprise. The government subsequently showed itself to be willing to accommodate Polish demands and took the failure of the Ukrainian People's Republic to provide promised grain supplies as a welcome excuse not to hand over the Chełm region. The entry of the Red Army into Kiev also played a part, and the German supreme command in the east (Ober Ost) abandoned the Central Rada, installing the aristocratic landowner Pavlo Skoropads'kyj as Hetman of Ukraine. In a supplementary protocol to Brest-Litovsk dated March 4, 1918, the Chełm region was removed from the territory of Ukraine in return for a promise of military assistance for Ukraine.

After the terms of the treaty were changed and the Chełm region was withdrawn, the Ukrainian mood darkened. The Przemyśl military command noted that the Ukrainians were deeply upset, but that most politicians, despite their considerable misgivings, continued to militate in favor of Austria. "People in Ukrainian towns, particularly the clergy, have been agitating quite strongly from house to house and also in the churches against the Poles and in support of the separation of Middle and East Galicia and their transfer to Ukraine ... In general, it must be stated that despite various attempts by both sides to bring about a rapprochement between Poles and Ukrainians, the differences are becoming ever more acute and are becoming apparent also in many aspects of daily life."[501]

On March 8, 1918, the Austrian police cavalry captain L. Hintz reported on the resentful and acrimonious mood among Ukrainian intellectuals in L'viv. His remarks provide a good insight into the Ukrainian political scene. All political parties, Hintz believed, shared the same radical national and anti-Polish attitude. This also applied to the clerical and Austrophile Ukrainian Christian Social Party, whose main supporters tended to be civil servants rather than Greek Catholic clergy. Because of its uncritical loyalty to the Habsburg monarchy the Christian Social Party enjoyed little grassroots support. The Ukrainian Radical Party, "a party of the peasantry with anti-clerical and socialist affectations" enjoyed more support among small farmers. The Radical Party adopted an aggressive style in public but was incapable of publishing a party newspaper. The Ukrainian Social Democratic Party was insignificant in Galicia, because even the urban Ruthenian proletariat was largely Polonized. The National Democratic Party was the largest Ukrainian party, and it published two daily newspapers and a weekly paper in L'viv. It was headed by a national committee chaired by Kost' Levyts'kyj, a member of the Imperial Council. Hintz commented that "nationally inclined Ukrainians" were dissatisfied with the results of their conciliatory policy. Radical elements had now assumed control of the party. The overwhelming majority of Ukrainian intellectuals in L'viv supported the Ukrainian Parliamentary Representation: "Their eyes are fixed on the increasing successes of the Russian Ukrainians, from whom they expect all salvation for the Ukrainian people . . . The disenchantment of Ukrainians because of the behavior of the government is universal. It is only that not all intelligent Ukrainians have yet drawn the obvious conclusions."[502]

On March 25, Jevhen Petrushevych, working on behalf of the Ukrainian Parliamentary Representation, called the deputies, politicians, and other representatives of Ukrainian society together to a meeting in L'viv for consultations. Approximately five hundred delegates from East Galicia and Bukovina assembled in the Ukrainian Musical Institute and repeated their demand for a new Crown land, which would consist of East Galicia, northern Bukovina, the Chełm region, and Podlasie. The discussions on setting up Ukrainian troops were inconclusive. But in the expectation that Galicia would be divided and its eastern half would become Ukrainian, local Ukrainian cooperatives, party groups, and institutions were galvanized into action and established contacts to the district administrations. Even more important was the growing network of Ukrainian representatives at the district and the municipal level who took instructions from central Ukrainian institutions in L'viv.[503]

Instability and Loss of Authority

Supply Problems

Any focus that looks exclusively at the ethno-political situation in the city, at the Polish–Ukrainian conflict, and the growing anti-Semitism only captures one aspect—albeit a central one—of the experience of war. But in everyday life during the war ethnic boundaries became blurred, with all sides experiencing hardship and misery. In many cases, social class determined experience. To some extent, social conflicts fused with national and ethnic conflicts, but there were also areas where these different conflicts overlaid one another. All ethnic groups faced the same problems of insufficient supplies and a lack of food, but how these hardships were interpreted and experienced differed between groups. After the war, the discourse of memory focused only on ethnic and political conflicts, not on the material deprivation experienced during the war. But this deprivation was an important aspect of war experiences.

The city administration tried to ensure sufficient supplies of food to the city; the longer the war continued, the more the city administration came into conflict with local military authorities and the government in Vienna. The Austrian authorities could no longer compensate for the shortfall in supplies and now had to deal with hunger rallies, economically motivated strikes, and demonstrations all over Austria-Hungary. Although many municipal workers and employees had been conscripted, the city administration in L'viv was still able to make up for its manifest lack of staff and keep the municipal water, electricity, and gas supplies going and the streetcars running. But the city was continually faced with new duties and functions. On one hand, it had to satisfy the army's needs; on the other hand, it had to ensure the survival of the impoverished population and of tens of thousands of destitute refugees. The city had already subsidized or organized soup kitchens for the poor during the Russian occupation and set up shops where foodstuffs were sold at fixed prices. The city continued to operate public soup kitchens, and private charitable contributions were strongly encouraged. The Austrian government gave the city a loan of 6.5 million krone and contributed 2.5 million krone for the building of roads, orphanages, and other social services.[504]

But by 1915/1916, the supply situation was worse than under Russian occupation, and the military authorities in L'viv urged the introduction of ration cards for flour and bread.[505] Refugees who were only able to subsist with the help of public welfare, many of them impoverished Jews, were sent back to their home towns and villages to relieve the supply situation in the city.[506] But 18,846 refugees remained in L'viv, initially housed in temporary accommodation. L'viv was swarming with beggars, and accommodation could only be found for about 250 of them.[507] According to a report by the municipal department of supplies, in August 1917, only 157,000 civilians were living in L'viv.[508] But the department expected that approximately twenty thousand refugees would return, placing a serious strain on housing and food supplies. In a report sent to the Ministry for Foreign Affairs, the population was described as close to despair.[509] Despite the city's good railroad and transport connections, the authorities were unable to bring sufficient supplies to the city, and living conditions steadily deteriorated. There were no longer regular supplies of grain to East Galicia, and the population could only be fed because the authorities tacitly accepted smuggling. L'viv required five railcars of flour every day, but even after much pleading, the military administration only provided three cars. And despite the bitter cold, many inhabitants of L'viv were forced to "subsist without coal or wood."[510]

As L'viv was not far from the front and providing supplies to the troops was the top priority, the municipal administration could not act without the permission of the army command. Flour and bread rationing started in the summer of 1915. Shortly afterward sugar and fat were also rationed, followed by coffee and petrol; finally, in the fall of 1916, rationing also included potatoes. When the grain trade collapsed, the city administration itself became a wholesale dealer, increasing the number of its shops from twenty-two to forty-three. The Supplies Department provided thirty thousand loaves of bread every day, which were produced in twenty-three bakeries. In 1916 half of the entire sugar allocation was sold in municipal shops. Sourcing sufficient supplies of potatoes was now the most important issue as they had become the main staple food. In the first four months after the region was recaptured by Austria, the Supplies Department was able to obtain five hundred railcars with potatoes. However, the supply of milk was extremely inadequate and was nowhere near to meeting the population's needs. The public soup kitchens were a vital element in feeding the population. The Supplies Department continued to expand and took on more and more responsibilities. In 1914 the value of distributed goods amounted to 7 million krone, but by 1915, that figure had increased to 22,625,000, and in the first half of 1916 alone the sum was 46 million krone.

Notwithstanding these problems, in 1915 the city was able to secure regular supplies of coal again, after coal supplies had collapsed during the Russian occupation. In August 1915 the connection to Hungary was reestablished, and livestock transports began to reach L'viv again. Despite its strained financial circumstances, the city spent three million krone on culture, education, and grants to theaters and museums in 1915/1916.[511]

In 1916 the city continued to receive fairly regular supplies, but by winter the situation once more began to become critical. Problems started with the supply of petrol.[512] Repeated riots broke out because the amount of food available for distribution was insufficient. On January 27, 1917, eight hundred demonstrators, most of them women, converged on the military command in the city in protest because they had missed out during the free distribution of potatoes that morning.[513] The censor's office in the Ministry of the Interior noted a general mood of war-weariness among both Poles and Ukrainians. Rising prices and food shortages had led to a general deterioration in the economic situation. The Ukrainian peasants complained about the seizure of grain supplies. Fewer complaints about problems with supplies and inflation were reported among the Jews.[514]

In March 1917 deputy government commissioner Schleicher, now released from Russian captivity, sounded the alarm. The federal authorities continued to govern from Biała; banks and insurances had shifted their headquarters to their branch offices in Cracow. This only increased the general mood of depression. The formerly prosperous appearance of L'viv had given way to an appearance of visible poverty. Its people were desperate and disheartened: "The places of those who have left the city are taken by new throngs of poor and desperate people from all of East Galicia, who have only been able to save their naked skins, leaving behind all their worldly belongings and increasing the numbers here in the capital of those who are dependent on public charity."[515]

The situation did not change in the following months. When Józef Białynia-Chołodecki, keeper of the archives, returned to L'viv after his release from prison in Kiev, the city was a dismal sight. The remnants of building destroyed during the war were still visible everywhere. The streets were dirty and empty; most of the shops were closed. He noted a general air of depression and want.[516]

The statutory ration of 1,260 grams of bread per person and per week was reduced to 1,000 grams because there was not enough flour. As promised deliveries failed to materialize, in March 1917 rations were again decreased by a further 20 grams per day. The public soup kitchens only remained open because they were able to obtain a quantity of sorghum and buckwheat from the Kingdom of Poland. Flour and pulses were so scarce that potatoes and meat became even more important. But these, too, were in short supply. The potato ration cards introduced in the fall of 1916 only provided half a kilo per person and day. But by the spring of 1917, the city was no longer able to provide even this allowance of food. The supply of meat halved between January and March 1917, and the cards for fat rations could no longer be redeemed. The supply of milk dropped from 60,000 liters per day before the war to a mere 6,500 liters. Butter and cheese were almost unobtainable. The inadequate diet increased the numbers of persons suffering from disease, and the first cases of epidemic typhoid were diagnosed. The conditions were insupportable, and famine appeared imminent. New public soup kitchens were essential.[517] In the spring of 1917, approximately fifty thousand people or one-quarter of the population required some form of support.[518]

In March 1917 the inadequate supply situation triggered protests and riots. On March 14, 1,600 people were already waiting in front of the Ferdinand Barracks at six in the morning for the distribution of potatoes. Within two hours, the queue had grown to more than three thousand people. Five kilos of potatoes were distributed per person. But all that was available was one wagon load of 11.9 tons of potatoes. About 1,200 people had to be turned away. The crowd was persuaded to leave peacefully, but some of the people waiting shouted that they had not eaten for three days.[519] Three months later, Schleicher complained that the promised help had again failed to arrive. Now about thirty thousand families comprising more than one hundred thousand people no longer earned enough to pay for their basic rations of food. At the same time, food that was brought every day into the city with great difficulty was being transported outside the city again, both by the military and by civilians. In L'viv, potatoes—which had become the staple food for most people—were rationed to two kilos per week and per person. About twenty thousand people were fed in municipal soup kitchens in return for minimal payments or even for free.[520]

A meeting held in the council chamber of the town hall on August 23, 1917, demanded that three hundred kilograms of potatoes be distributed per person per year. It was proposed that consumers be allowed to buy food directly from the producers.[521] Another meeting on December 11 protested against the inadequate supply situation. Citizens urged that L'viv's autonomy be reinstated and demanded that drastic measures be taken against profiteering.[522] Instead, in October 1917, the police seized food that women had procured from surrounding villages. In response, several hundred women gathered in front of the town hall, protesting loudly. The police director feared further unrest.[523]

By the middle of January 1918, the supply situation had deteriorated even further, and Schleicher asked Minister-President Ernst von Seidler for help. No flour had been distributed during the two previous weeks, and no other foodstuffs were available as substitutes. While the population was inured to deprivation, the complete lack of bread could not be compensated. By that time, more than 160,000 people out of a total population of 220,000 were dependent on assistance. Schleicher urged the government not to wait "until the population, driven to desperation, takes steps and commits excesses which would be regrettable in the interest of the state." Schleicher demanded that illegal imports of legumes be released for general sale as this could contribute to decreasing prices. Meat supplies had also dropped. This was particularly critical because meat had been primarily used in the public soup kitchens for want of other food supplies. The closure of all soups kitchens was imminent as the limited stocks of vegetables and potatoes were running out. Prices for meat, fat, and bacon had risen to astronomical heights.[524] The state of affairs with regard to coal supplies was equally desolate. Barely one-quarter of the necessary quantities reached the city. Schleicher's previously polite and pleading requests began to sound a more demanding and critical note. According to Schleicher, the government rationing system had failed. He demanded immediate deliveries of foodstuffs and proposed that the city administration be given a free hand.[525]

In the spring of 1918, the closure of the public soup kitchens again appeared imminent. By March 1918, the population had not received any flour for ten weeks.[526] In June 1918 the Jewish relief committee counted 59,655 Jews living in L'viv. In total, 7,500 families numbering 30,000 people required help, half of which was given for free.[527] But the government had little scope to assist L'viv by sending additional deliveries of food. All of Austria-Hungary was suffering from supply problems. Providing sufficient supplies to the army and to the city of Vienna took priority above all else. The fruits of the "bread peace" of Brest-Litovsk could not be harvested yet. Neither the Central Rada nor the subsequent Hetman regime provided the promised supplies of foodstuffs. Riots, which started in the morning and lasted till the afternoon, broke out on the streets of L'viv on June 9, 1918. The rioting kicked off after about five hundred women and youths gathered at the Ringplatz and smashed some of the windows of the city hall. The police scattered the crowd and hustled them away, pushing them into the side streets, where shop windows were smashed and the goods on display plundered. Patrols arrested twenty-two rioters, most of them women. Riots were anticipated on the following days, and precautionary measures were taken.[528]

The railroad workers had gone on strike several times since October 1917 to enforce their demands for higher wages and higher food allowances. Their demands were fulfilled because of the importance of the railroads for the continuation of the war effort.[529] But the calm was only temporary. On January 17, 1918, the railroad employees began another strike which was to last rather longer.[530] Even more ominous for the government was the combination of economic and political demands. On January 23, the workers of the electricity plant joined the strike. They demanded the release of Piłsudski and protested against the German delegation in Brest-Litovsk. The striking workers of the electricity plant returned to work after a meeting had been arranged with the government commissioner, but the railroad workers continued their strike and were joined by 150 workers from the railroad maintenance unit and 150 boiler house operators. A five-man delegation traveled to Vienna to present their demands to the Polish club in the House of Deputies.[531] The strike only ended after the delegation had returned.[532]

After the railroad workers did not receive their full rations of bread and flour either in March or in April 1918 and only 700 loaves of bread were available for distribution on April 22 instead of the promised 3,200, the workshop staff again downed their tools. According to the Ministry for Railroads, there could be no question of insufficient food supplies at the time, because several wagonloads of potatoes, sauerkraut, legumes, buckwheat and meat were available from the shops at the food depot. But the workers demanded their full bread rations and to be allowed to travel freely to the countryside to obtain food supplies. The executive board of the national railroads managed to reroute some supplies of food and have them delivered to L'viv at short notice. But the politicization of demands, which had already been noted, continued in parallel to developments in other parts of Austria and in the German Empire. On April 24, 350 conscripted workers joined the strike and elected a soldiers' council. The next day, a number of civil servants also attended a strike meeting. The strikers now demanded not only better food supplies but also the immediate cessation of the war. By April 26, 4,400 loaves of bread had arrived, but the workers still did not return to work. At this point, the shunters, switchmen, and train drivers also went on strike. By the afternoon of April 27, thirty-seven freight trains were unable to pull into L'viv. On April 26 and 27, the strike movement spread to Rawa-Ruska and Przemyśl. Fifty-four percent of train cars were now halted for repairs; only fifteen locomotives were still operational. To prevent the strike from spreading further the Ministry for Railroads called a halt to further procedures and demanded that the L'viv railroad workers be conscripted as military workers, a request the army command complied with on the same day. Thereupon the railroad workers declared their willingness to return to work if they could be guaranteed sufficient supplies of food. On April 28, the Ministry for National Defense ordered the forced conscription of all workers employed by the administration of state railroads (Staatsbahndirektion) L'viv. Many of them returned to work on the same day, but they only resumed work after the public announcement of the conscription of railroad workers.[533]

The Ministry of the Interior considered the complaints of railroad workers about the lack of food supplies to be justified and criticized the Staatsbahndirektion in L'viv for not having devoted enough attention to the problem. "Because of this workmen are losing the last vestiges of confidence in government organizations." Like the military command of Przemyśl, the Ministry of the Interior suspected that this was precisely what the *Staatsbahndirektion* and other civil authorities in Galicia intended.[534]

Fear of the Bolsheviks and Anti-Semitism

After the October revolution, the Austrian-Hungarian government feared the rise of revolutionary movements in their own territories. The terms *Bolshevik*/Bolshevist and *bolshevism* became labels that were also used in various ethnic and national conflicts with the aim of discrediting opponents in the eyes of the government in Vienna and of the world. The authorities were afraid of both social unrest and of nationally motivated upheavals. The October revolution fueled the fear of a socialist revolution, alarming citizens and aristocrats alike. Major General Eduard Fischer[535] from the gendarmerie command for Galicia and Bukovina reported in March 1918 that rumors of a revolt had been circulating but that the situation had calmed down again. Middle-class politicians mistrusted the Social Democrats and feared the Bolshevik example. The landowners were afraid of the Ukrainian peasantry. Fischer anticipated further strikes by Polish railroad workers and by the staff of the post and telegraph offices. But he considered Ukrainian civil servants as "not much imbued with socialism" and believed the peasants to be conservative and loyal to the emperor. Fischer discerned strong currents of socialism among the workers in the petroleum industry in Borysław, where he foresaw a threat of hunger riots—and anticipated that rioting would carry strong undercurrents of anti-Semitism.[536]

In the spring of 1918, agricultural riots broke out in the region of Rawa-Ruska. The landowners feared the twenty thousand prisoners of war who had returned from Russia, suspecting them of bringing Bolshevik ideas.[537] The Austrian high command similarly viewed the former prisoners of war as a seditious element. Bolshevism, in the opinion of the high command, was also affecting the rural population, whose hunger for land was fueled by the news about the land distribution in Russia. The high command similarly ascribed food riots and pogroms to the adoption of Bolshevik sentiments.[538]

Reinlender, the police director of L'viv, rejected the rumors of an imminent putsch. Abandoning the national and political neutrality incumbent upon him, he expressed some sympathy with the popular outrage directed against the terms of the peace treaty of Brest-Litovsk. His depictions of Ukrainians were correspondingly negative. As he described it, the Ukrainian masses were strongly influenced by the impression made by the revolutionary changes in Russia and Ukraine. Although Reinlender was not prepared to acknowledge that irredentism might be a problem, he was nevertheless worried by the potential for social unrest in the city and the countryside following the "Russian or Ukrainian example." But at that point Reinlender considered inadequate food supplies to be the most pressing problem. The lack of supplies was exhausting the population's patience, and there were people willing to exploit this to incite unrest. The issue of security was equally important. Gangs of deserters and fugitive Russian prisoners of war were terrorizing whole districts. Because of their limited numbers, police agents and trained police officers were unable to get the problem under control, and military assistance had failed to materialize.[539] The military authorities suspected the Polish intelligentsia of inciting soldiers to desert. Deserters apprehended by the gendarmerie were often poorly guarded, making it easy for them to escape again.[540]

The police authorities in L'viv were also attempting to hunt down the people disseminating anti-Jewish leaflets and pamphlets that demanded the "dejudaization of Poland." An unknown man had asked the owners of several shops to take the pamphlets on commission and display leaflets. Based on his appearance witnesses believed him to be a priest.[541] Despite these rather vague clues, the police found the man. He was a priest named Zdzisław Łuczycki from Lublin Province. He had become an Austrian citizen in 1896 and had moved to live permanently in L'viv in 1911. A search of his apartment produced unequivocal proof. Łuczycki had not only disseminated pamphlets; he had also drafted anti-Semitic articles and proclamations himself.[542] When the priest returned from a trip to Lublin, he was brought to the police directorate for questioning. He defended himself by claiming that his aims had been entirely idealistic, arguing that because of their intrinsic nature, the Jews were harming the Polish nation both morally and materially. He insisted that he had no wish to incite racial hatred but only wanted to encourage Polish society to defend itself.[543] The police regarded the calls for a boycott as ideas imported from the Kingdom of Poland. Anti-Semitic activities had increased in Galicia in 1916 and 1917. The police believed that the brochures and proclamations had been especially adapted to the situation in Galicia. The priest must have had helpers who had smuggled in the pamphlets and distributed them.[544]

But matters did not rest with the distribution of anti-Semitic pamphlets. In 1918 reports of physical attacks on Jews in West Galicia became more frequent. The police and the gendarmerie struggled to maintain law and order in the region. Jews were held to blame for the rising prices and food shortages, while Polish nationalists interpreted the loyalty of the Jewish population to Habsburg as a betrayal of the Polish national cause. In the spring, the governor's office and the Ministry of the Interior received repeated reports about the anti-Semitic mood of the population, about attacks on Jews, and anti-Jewish comments made on train journeys. The dissemination of anti-Jewish pamphlets in L'viv continued, and the windows of Jewish shops in Rzeszów were smashed.[545]

In January, February, and April 1918, three large demonstrations marched through the streets of Cracow. The first demonstration was held to protest against the food shortages; the second was triggered after the terms of the treaty of Brest-Litovsk had become known to the public. The third demonstration was also caused by food shortages but had a distinctly anti-Jewish character. On April 16, 1918, a rumor spread that food on Market Square was being sold to Jews at lower prices than to Christians. The result was an immediate uproar that spread rapidly across the city. The police were taken by surprise because until that point, anti-Jewish brochures and leaflets had not appeared in the city.[546] In the days that followed, Jewish shops were plundered and destroyed, and Jews traveling on public transport were beaten up. The Viennese newspaper *Neue Freie Presse* commented that these excesses were not food riots but an actual pogrom following the pattern set in Russia.[547] A new spate of attacks occurred at Market Square on April 20. Four women attacked and beat a Jew who took refuge in a hospital. A further two hundred people shouting slogans such as "beat the Jews" converged on Market Square and attacked anyone whose appearance marked them out as Jewish. A rumor had spread that Jews had killed a priest and wanted to tear down churches.[548] In addition to the charge of murder, the mob accused Jews of having provoked Poles with calls such as "You may have the legions but we have the millions." The police identified a young woman as the source of the rumor and took her into custody. The crowd subsequently dispersed.[549] The interior minister ordered Huyn to prevent anti-Jewish riots in future.[550]

This was easier said than done. The state's loss of authority permitted the latent anti-Semitic mood to deteriorate into open violence in other places as well.[551] Repeated attacks occurred on trains traveling between Przemyśl and L'viv in the spring of 1918. Jews attempted to board trains carrying large items of luggage filled with food, some of which they wanted to sell in L'viv. Their Christian fellow passengers often prevented them from boarding the train and threw their luggage off the train, citing problems caused by the luggage obstructing the aisles. One railroad official distributed anti-Jewish caricatures and had to be moved to another job after Jewish officials complained about him to the director of the national railroads.[552]

Police agents and local authorities submitted conflicting reports on the political mood among the Jewish population. Some of their reports were also anti-Semitic and appeared oblivious to the internal inconsistencies of their accusations. Anti-Semitism was widespread in the local authorities, the army, and the state administration. In July 1917 the general of the gendarmerie, Fischer, reported that the Zionists' sympathies lay almost without exception with the Entente. Anti-Semitic stereotypes are obvious in statements such as the following: "With regard to politics, the majority of the Jewish population is, as is always the case, on the side of the stronger party, on the side of the Poles." Other assertions included the stereotypical accusation that Jews were continuing to rake in profits and were less involved in politics. The majority of Jewish students were considered Zionists. Jews were believed to adapt cleverly to the situation, of favoring Poles in the cities and more likely to support Ukrainians in the countryside. In addition, Jews were accused of eagerly engaging in all manner of illicit trading.[553]

That such comments were not isolated cases is borne out by a report by Rittmeister Hintz, who opined in March 1918 that all Galician Jews supported the Entente. He went on to assert that, just as they had done under Russian occupation, Jews had informed on harmless Ukrainian peasants to the authorities. Almost in the same breath, Hintz first referred to Jews as protégés of the Poles and then went on to accuse them of harboring a deep affection for revolutionary Russia.[554] The Przemyśl military command, however, reported that Jews, particularly urban schoolchildren, were increasingly supporting Zionism.[555]

Jewish deputies to the Imperial Council repeatedly raised the issue in parliamentary inquiries to the government. But Reinlender, writing from L'viv, found no evidence for an increase in anti-Jewish sentiment in L'viv.[556] Reinlender's comments were too hasty. In May 1918 anti-Jewish leaflets were once again being circulated.[557]

During a meeting held in the House of Deputies on July 22, 1918, Jewish members accused the Galician authorities of failing in their duties and of not taking action against anti-Jewish excesses. They drew attention to the anti-Semitic tendencies of the Polish parties that were inciting the population against Jews. The Jewish deputies described a looting and robbery spree in Wilówka that had occurred on February 18, 1918. Peasants from surrounding villages who had been peaceable up until that time had been stirred up by "so-called members of the intelligentsia." Armed with flails, pitchforks, millstones, and branches the peasants had attacked Jews, beaten them up and stolen their property. The Jews had been accused of any number of things: they were held to have betrayed Poles, were considered responsible for the cession of Chełm, and blamed for the war and the food shortages. It was alleged that Jews dodged military service and received more and better food. The Polish press often denied that any pogroms or anti-Jewish attacks had occurred. A meeting of Jewish citizens and of representatives of the Jewish community was subsequently held in L'viv to discuss how to prevent anti-Semitic pogroms from spreading to the city. All of the speakers were very aware of the danger and set up a committee that would be responsible for the safety of the Jewish population in L'viv.[558]

The Polish and Ukrainian populations believed that food was not being fairly distributed and blamed this on corruption in the distribution centers. Jews stood accused of having received special privileges under Austrian rule. Re-sentiment directed against the authorities was widespread. The general opinion was that excessive numbers of Jews had managed to dodge military service and had found employment in the supply services. The resentment also extended to landowners who were accused of hoarding supplies: "These circumstances have led to the looting of food stores and in this context to pogroms against Jews, which were also caused by the one-sided preference given to Jews during the distribution of food."

As the authorities did not show much interest in intervening, Jews began arming themselves and fighting back.[559] At the end of August 1918, Major General Fischer wrote about a general feeling of political disaffection among Poles, which they vented by attacking Jews. Fischer, himself an anti-Semite, accused Jewish traders of forcing up prices, which he ascribed to the "unbridled acquisitiveness of Jewish merchants."[560]

The anti-Semitic mood was not restricted to Galicia. The antagonism between Jews and Poles also increased in the Kingdom of Poland. The Jewish press ascribed this to the intensified economic and social competition, commenting that it was common for Poles to seek to eliminate Jews from business and social life. Jews were increasingly referred to as alien and foreign to prevent them from sharing in civil liberties.[561]

The Zionist deputy to the House of Deputies of the Imperial Council, Straucher, wrote on August 9, 1918, to the Austrian minister-president that the excesses and attacks on Jews in Galicia were continuing. All interpellations had been to no avail. The treatment of Jews by the authorities was reprehensible, and he requested that this be redressed immediately.[562] Two months later, Straucher protested against a statement by the Jewish Polish deputy Löwenstein. In an audience with the emperor, Löwenstein had declared that the Galician Jews supported the Polish national demands. Straucher criticized that as a member of the Polish club in the House of Deputies, in other words, "a foreign nationalist organization," Löwenstein was not entitled to speak in the name of the Jews. The overwhelming majority of the Jewish population was Jewish nationalist in feeling; only a tiny Jewsh upper class was not. Orthodox Jews were also "Jewish national" (*jüdischvölkisch*) but had hesitated to express their sentiments as long as the local authorities had been dominated by Poles. "Collectively the Jewish community of Galicia and Poland is frequently subjected to brutal, hateful and humiliating treatment, repression, contempt and persecution, politically, administratively, and socially." Straucher also protested against the biased information given to the emperor on the Jewish question. "The Jews cannot be reduced to a simple religious community; they are a people, a nation, and therefore, just like the other Austrian nations, they claim the right of self-determination."[563]

Turning their Backs on Austria

In July and August 1918, the problem of feeding the population temporarily abated. But the harvest was poor, and the lack of fodder meant that livestock owners were forced to reduce stock numbers. At the end of August 1918, one member of the governor's office described the miserable conditions, the lack of food and the political impact of this to the Ministry of the Interior. Prices for food and clothing had shot up and were now at astronomical heights. Cereal crops were particularly prone to price gouging as the authorities had been obliged to turn a blind eye to trading for months because supplies from the government remained inadequate. In addition, thousands of refugees had returned to formerly embattled regions. It was unclear how they could be supplied with food and how they could be helped to rebuild their farm buildings and houses. The issue of the partition of Galicia continued to keep Ukrainians and Poles in suspense. The problem of insufficient food supplies might trigger rioting, but a "widespread grassroots movement across the country is only conceivable if prompted by political and immaterial considerations." He described the workers and railroad employees as socialists but added that the latter group was currently satisfied. He could offer no information on any organized revolutionary movements.[564]

All Austrian sources tell of high levels of national mobilization among the Poles in the spring and summer of 1918. The Austro-Polish solution for the Polish question no longer enjoyed much support among wide sections of the population.[565] Most Poles were betting on an Entente victory and the reestablishment of Poland in its old borders. Only a few of the more conservative noblemen and some of the higher civil servants still felt some attachment to Austria.[566] Combined with the problem of inadequate food supplies this gave a special impetus to the progressive nationalization of political and social relations.

The Przemyśl military command accused Galician officials, teachers, and clergy of instilling subversive ideas in the population. The army suspected officials of stirring up hatred against state institutions. Teachers in particular were believed to be systematically inculcating their pupils with anti-Habsburg and anti-Austrian sentiments. It was felt that although the Poles were keeping quiet, they continued to disseminate Polish nationalist ideas within their organizations and societies. With the exception of the peasants, the population was strongly politicized. The military command believed that the Poles were counting on the Entente powers: "There is great resentment and direct hostility in All-Polish circles against Ukrainians and their ambitions. These antagonisms are even spilling over into social and private life."[567]

In July 1918 Statthalter Huyn commented that the military intelligence agency in Przemyśl was living in pathological fear of revolutionary uprisings, seeing conspiracies everywhere. The situation was not as bad as the military command painted it.[568] Military agencies reported increasing numbers of incidents of "incitement of Polish schoolchildren." The private Polish secondary school in Leżajsk had engaged in nationalist propaganda for some time. Pupils repeatedly released imprisoned deserters and attacked Jews. In Łancut, secondary school pupils refused to attend Mass on the empress's name day and birthday, and only peasants, mainly women, continued to sing the Austrian anthem in church, while pupils and their teachers remained silent. On the days of national celebrations on February 18 and May 3, "Boże coź Polskę" was sung enthusiastically. In Rzeszów, on the occasion of the empress's name day, pupils had sung the Austrian anthem with dwindling enthusiasm until the singing had finally died away before the end of the first verse.[569] In L'viv, an appeal signed by "the Polish Youth" was distributed to schoolchildren, calling on them to boycott religious services: "We will hold aloft the banner of national honor and subdue those who dare to thrust it down from the heights into the mire. During the days of imperial celebration the churches should be empty. Polish schoolchildren will not be coming to church and will not be singing the hymn honoring the conqueror."[570]

On May 30, collections were held on the streets and squares of the city in aid of members of the legions who were facing court martial. Even officers participated, and the authorities did not intervene to stop these collections for the "mutineers." The collections were held, of all times, during Emperor Charles week, which aroused little enthusiasm in L'viv. A Polish flyer called on the population to boycott all events and meetings.[571] In contrast, the collections taken up in support of the members of the legion were a huge success. The majority of the population kept away from the Austrian celebrations in Kiliński Park. Instead, the masses flocked to the Polish national celebrations that were held at the same time in the same park.[572]

Rittmeister Hintz of the gendarmerie command for Galicia and the Bukovina in Czernowitz had the impression that the Galician authorities wanted to create a fertile soil for a revolutionary uprising, and surmised that this was the reason they did nothing to improve the difficult situation created by the inadequate supplies of food to the cities. The indigent population in Czernowitz had not received any bread for days, even though bread could be bought—at exorbitant prices—on the free market. He suspected the autonomous authorities of the state and the city of deliberately stoking the animosity of civil servants and employees by paying them cost-of-living allowances that were insufficient to their needs. This was also the main reason for the complaints voiced during a meeting of elementary school teachers held on May 27 and 28 in L'viv and at a similar meeting of middle school teachers on May 25. Although the focus of the respective meetings was on the current privations, the sessions ended with the attendees fiercely abusing the Austrian state.[573]

Major General Fischer reported on the increasing politicization of young people and of civil servants, teachers, university professors, secondary school teachers, and Roman Catholic and Greek Catholic clergy. All of them were now seeking to promote "national policies":[574] "The clergy—from the bishops to the country priests—are promoting national policies irrespective of creed and are misusing the pulpit to incite national passions."[575]

The governor's office also noted that the Polish national movement had grown and expanded to include civil servants at all levels, along with many Roman Catholic priests. The Liga Kobiet (Women's League) and Polish youth were fervently nationalist.[576] Fischer confirmed the reports: many Poles no longer considered themselves part of the imperial-royal state. Large numbers of Polish middle school and elementary school teachers were tirelessly exhorting their pupils, in contrast to Ukrainian teachers, the majority of whom continued to behave loyally. The Roman Catholic clergy was reported to be secretly spreading political propaganda. Bandurski, the retired auxiliary bishop of L'viv, was reputed to be particularly active. The announcement that he would be returning to L'viv had elicited an enthusiastic response from nationalist clergymen.[577]

Outwardly, the army command declared, the Poles seemed quiet and appeared to be biding their time. However, the All-Polish parties had become much stronger and the clergy was starting to widen its propaganda activities to include more rural areas. The Social Democratic Polish Socialist Party (PPS) was believed to be marching in step with the All-Poles. Latterly, the army command had even observed attempts by Polish National Democrats to achieve a rapprochement with Ukrainians, although Ukrainians reacted with hostility to the overtures.[578] The Ministry for National Defense was also of the opinion that Galician Poles, without exception, sided with the All-Poles.[579]

In July 1918 the Austrian government demanded that Hetman Skoropads'kyj, head of the government of Ukraine since April, should ax the additional agreements to the peace treaty of Brest-Litovsk, in which the Austrian government had declared its willingness to create a Ukrainian Crown land, thus agreeing to a partition of Galicia. After vainly protesting these changes, Skoropads'kyj agreed. This led to a further estrangement of Galician Ukrainians from the government in Vienna but did not succeed in wooing back the Polish elites who had turned away from Austria.[580]

After the changes to the peace treaty, the mood in the Ukrainian population was very gloomy. Their trust in Austria-Hungary had been shaken with the resurgence of the Austro-Polish option. Fischer believed that he could detect a certain reticence on the part of the Hetmanate: it too expected little or nothing from the Entente powers, and the tenor of the political mood was "<u>a complete despondency and disorientation.</u>"[581]

Only vestigial remnants of the Russophile movement remained in the summer of 1918. The Ukrainian Radical Party had declined considerably while the Social Democratic Party attempted to organize the Ukrainian railroad and oil workers. The National Democratic Party was by far the most influential, despite the fact that it was split into two factions. The moderate wing was led by Kost' Levyts'kyj, and the radical left wing was headed by Jevhen Petrushevych. Both factions based their aims on the treaty of Brest-Litovsk. As far as Fischer could find out, Ukrainian peasants were preoccupied more with social than with national issues and pressed for estates to be divided up and parceled out. The better-off peasants preferred using lawful means, while the more indigent peasants were not averse to Bolshevik ideas. However, in the wake of the October revolution, Fischer noted a "progressive increase in national consciousness" among the Ruthenian peasantry. But he believed that, by and large, the Ukrainians were friendly to Austria.[582] According to the information collected by the governor's office, although bolshevism had gained a foothold, support for it was not widespread. In Galicia, national conflicts of interest trumped other political aims. The mood among Ukrainians was depressed, their opposition to the Poles was becoming ever more pronounced. However, the governor's office did observe an increase in national self-awareness.[583]

In August, the leadership of the Ukrainian National Democratic Party began secret preparations in anticipation of future conflicts with the Poles on the future of East Galicia. A secret Ukrainian military general commissariat was formed in L'viv. Members of the Ukrainian Sich riflemen and young, previously little-known politicians joined the new organization. They hoped—vainly—that the current commander of the Ukrainian Sich rifleman, Wilhelm von Habsburg, would also lead the new general commissariat. Until he was prepared to join, it was planned that Captain (Sotnyk) Dmytro Vitovs'kyj would deputize for him. The members of the committee approached Ukrainian soldiers serving in the imperial-royal army and attempted to make contact with the units of Sich riflemen stationed in East Ukraine.[584] In the countryside, Ukrainian legionaries began spreading nationalist propaganda,[585] and the Ukrainian intelligentsia became increasingly active: "Their opposition to the Poles who attempt with all the means at their disposal to hamper their cultural ascent has become almost insurmountable."[586]

Finally, in October 1918, the peasantry began demonstrating in support of an independent Ukraine. A Polish observer in Tłumacz was astonished by the "excellent manner in which the Ukrainian village was organized" when a "huge crowd of peasants on horseback and on foot marched on our Tłumacz, in military order, singing battle songs, and shouting their cheers in support of an independent Ukraine."[587]

Notes

1. A popular L'viv song from the winter of 1914/15. Stanisław Rossowski, *Lwów podczas inwazyi* (Lwów: H. Altenberg et al., 1916), 10.
2. Kramarz, *Samorząd Lwowa w czasie pierwszej wojny światowej*, 32.
3. Maria von Gember, "Die Russen in Lemberg," in *An den Grenzen Rußlands: Elf Abhandlungen aus der Sammlung "Der Weltkrieg"* (Mönchengladbach: Volksvereins-Verlag, 1916), 153–68, especially 153. For a Ukrainian perspective, see the memoirs of the Greek Catholic priest and politician Jaroslav Levyts'kyj, "Z dnïv rosyjs'koï invazyï," serialized in *Dilo*, November 11–December 15, 1915, here: November 28, 1915.
4. The General Ukrainian National Council (Allgemeiner Ukrainischer Nationalrat) consisted of the Ukrainian members of the Imperial Council and the Galician Diet and the chairmen of Ukrainian cooperatives and associations in Galicia and the Bukovina. Helga Grebing, "Österreich-Ungarn und die 'Ukrainische Aktion,' 1914–1918," *Jahrbücher für Geschichte Osteuropas* 7 (1959): 270–96, especially 283–84.
5. The Ukrainian associations of riflemen developed out of the gymnastics and fire fighter associations Sich. The Sich associations were started in spring 1900 by one of the leaders of the Ukrainian Radical Party, Kyrylo Trylovs'kyj. In December 1912 Sich was transformed into the Ukrainian Sich Union, which revived Cossack traditions and aimed to strengthen the national solidarity of its members. In January 1913 the journal of the Sich Union called on all member associations to prepare themselves to fight in the ranks of the Austrian-Hungarian army against tsarist Russia. Michał Klimecki, *Lwów 1918–1919* (Warsaw: Bellona 1998), 16.
6. TsDIAL, f. 581, op. 1, spr. 90, ark. 1-3: Report in the Governor's office, n.d. (probably end of August 1914). See also Teophil Hornykiewicz, ed., *Ereignisse in der Ukraine 1914–1922, deren Bedeutung und historische Hintergründe*, 3 vols, here: vol. 1 (Philadelphia: W. K. Lypynsky East European Research Institute, 1966), 129–43.
7. Klimecki, *Lwów 1918–1919*, 17–18.
8. Holovna Ukraïns'ka Rada, in 1915 renamed Zahal'na Ukraïns'ka Rada (General Ukrainian Council).
9. From a resolution of the Ukrainian Main Council quoted in Orest Mazur and Ivan Pater, "L'viv u roky peršoj svitovoï vijny," in *L'viv: Istorychni narysy*, 304-24, here 304–305.
10. John-Paul Himka, "Hope in the Tsar: Displaced Naive Monarchism among the Ukrainians of the Habsburg Empire," *Russian History/Histoire Russe* 7 (1980): 125–38. Wendland, *Die Russophilen in Galizien*, 497–98.
11. Pastoral letter by Archbishop Sheptyts'kyj, August 21, 1914, in *Ereignisse in der Ukraine 1914–1922*, vol. 2, 424–26.
12. Jakób Schall, *Żydostwo Galicyjskie w czasie inwazji rosyjskiej (w latach 1914–1916)* (L'viv: I. Madfes, 1936), 4.
13. Excerpt of the speech (in Ukrainian translation) in the Ukrainian newspaper *Dilo*, August 21, 1914, 6. The Jewish community (Kahal) also gave fifty thousand krone to the Polish legions. Kramarz, *Samorząd Lwowa w czasie pierwszej wojny światowej*, 30.
14. *Dilo*, August 22, 1914: "'Polski Lwów—polskim legionom.'" TsDIAL, f. 309, op. 1, spr. 2028, ark. 6–8: Ukrainian report on Polish-Ukrainian relations, n.d. (probably December 1915).
15. TsDIAL, f. 146, op. 4, spr. 7687, ark. 138: presidium of the governor's office to all starostas (heads of local rural administration), August 4, 1914. On the Russophiles in the first few months of the war, see Wendland, *Die Russophilen in Galizien*, 540–64.

16. TsDIAL, f. 146, op. 6, spr. 1370, ark. 591–93: k. u. k. military command L'viv to the governor's office, August 14, 1914.
17. See the diary entries and documents on the repressions against Ruthenians in Thalerhof Almanac (*Talergofskij Al'manakh*). The Thalerhof Almanac was published by a committee of former prisoners in L'viv (1924–1932). See also TsDIAL, f. 408, op. 1, spr. 112: Report of Greek Catholic priest Kyryl Levyts'kyj (1914). TsDIAL, f. 146, op. 6, spr. 1376, ark. 505–506: presidium of the Ukrainian parliamentary representation to the k. u. k. High Command (copy), August 11, 1915. Veryha, *Vyzvol'ni zmahannja v Ukraïni 1914–1923 rr.*, vol. 1, 24–33. Wendland, *Die Russophilen in Galizien*, 540–47.
18. K. u. k. Kriegsüberwachungsamt (Military Office for Surveillance) to the governor's office in Graz, November 9, 1914, in *Talergofskij Al'manakh: Propamjatnaja Kniga*, vol. 4, part 2 (L'viv: Talergofs'kij Komitet, 1932), 134–37.
19. TsDIAL, f. 462, op. 1, spr. 90, ark. 1–4: memorandum of the Ukrainian Citizens' Committee (Bürgerkomitee), December 4, 1920.
20. Hornykiewicz, *Ereignisse in der Ukraine 1914–1922*, vol. 1, 20–22: Note from Baron Giesl (representative of the Austrian-Hungarian Foreign Office with the Army High Command, AOK) on conversations with Polish and Ukrainian politicians in L'viv (copy), August 31, 1914. Ibid., 20: Berchtold (k. u. k. Foreign Ministry) to Baron Giesl, August 26, 1914. The High Command informed Emperor Franz Josef about the assumed Russophile sentiments in the Ruthenian population. It blamed the Polish elites and their support for the Russophile movement before the war. Ibid., 22–24: k. u. k. Army High Command (Archduke Friedrich) to Franz Josef I: Presentation on the reasons of Russophilism in East Galicia and request to transfer the administration of this Crown land to a senior general, October 14, 1914. Veryha, *Vyzvol'ni zmahannja v Ukraïni*, vol. 1, 24–33.
21. Leopold Ferdinand Freiherr von Andrian zu Werburg was an Austrian writer and diplomat. In 1915 he was the Austrian-Hungarian representative at the German Central Administration of the occupied Polish territories. Ursula Prutsch and Klaus Heyringer, eds., *Leopold von Andrian (1875–1951): Korrespondenzen, Notizen, Essays, Berichte* (Vienna: Böhlau, 2003).
22. AVA, MdI, Präsidiale, Allgemeine Angelegenheiten, 22/2116: Report by Legationsrat Baron Andrian on his trip to East Galicia, Cracow, July 26, 1915.
23. Grebing, "Österreich-Ungarn und die 'Ukrainische Aktion' 1914–1918," 273–76.
24. Gember, "Die Russen in Lemberg," 154.
25. TsDIAL, f. 309, op. 1, spr. 2029, ark. 1–29: Ukrainian memorandum on the Polish administration in Galicia, summer 1915.
26. TsDIAL, f. 581, op. 1, spr. 90, ark. 1–3: Report in the governor's office, n.d. (probably end of August 1914).
27. TsDIAL, f. 146, op. 6, spr. 1370, ark. 663: k. u. k. minister of the interior to the governor of Galicia, October 27, 1914. The letter mentions the order of the Army High Command from April 28, 1915.
28. In Przemyśl, an Austrian officer destroyed two signs with inscriptions in Ukrainian, thinking the inscriptions were in Russian. TsDIAL, f. 146, op. 6, spr. 1376, ark. 505–506: presidium of the Ukrainian parliamentary represention to the k. u. k. High Command (copy), August 11, 1915.
29. TsDIAL, f. 309, op. 1, spr. 2028, ark. 1–2: Order of the k. u. k. High Command (Archduke Friedrich), January 13, 1915.
30. Consisting of about seventy Greek Catholic priests who had fled Galicia.
31. HHStA, P.A.I., 931, Bl. 55–64: Letter of protest of the Viennese "Representation of the Ukrainian Catholic Clergy," n.d. (probably end of 1914). The letter was sent to the em-

peror, the representative of the pope in Vienna, important politicians, and all Catholic bishops of Austria-Hungary.

32. TsDIAL, f. 146, op. 6, spr. 1376, ark. 505–506: Executive committee (Präsidium) of the Ukrainian parliamentary representation to the Army High Command (copy), August 11, 1915.
33. A Ukrainian memorandum from summer 1915 also mentions attacks by an unspecified "Jewish mob" on Ukrainians. TsDIAL, f. 309, op. 1, spr. 2029, ark. 1–29.
34. Levyts'kyj, "Z dnïv rosyjs'koï invazyï," *Dilo*, December 1, 1915.
35. Ibid. See also TsDIAL, f. 146, op. 6, spr. 1376, ark. 505–506: executive committee of the Ukrainian parliamentary representation to the Army High Command (copy), August 11, 1915.
36. Levyts'kyj, "Z dnïv rosyjs'koï invazyï," *Dilo*, December 1, 1915.
37. Grebing, "Österreich-Ungarn und die 'Ukrainische Aktion' 1914–1918," 270–96.
38. On the league, see ibid., 276–80. Ivan Pater, "Sojuz Vyzvolennja Ukraïny: zasnuvannja, polityčhna platforma ta orijentatsija," *Visnyk L'vivs'koho Universytetu: Serija istoryčhna* 34 (1999): 331–39.
39. Rossowski, *Lwów podczas inwazyi*, 3–6. Adolf Beck, *Uniwersytet Jana Kazimierza we Lwowie podczas inwazji rosyjskiej w roku 1914–15* (L'viv: Uniwersytet Jana Kazimierza we Lwowie, 1935).
40. Józef Białynia-Chołodecki, *Wspomnienia z lat niedoli i niewoli 1914–1918* (L'viv: Author, 1919), 5–6. TsDIAL, f. 694, op. 1, spr. 10, ark. 1–65: Russocki, diary entry, September 2, 1914.
41. Gember, "Die Russen in Lemberg," 154.
42. Schall, *Żydostwo Galicyjskie w czasie inwazji rosyjskiej*, 10.
43. Levyts'kyj, "Z dnïv rosyjs'koï invazyï," *Dilo*, November 30, 1915. TsDIAL, f. 694, op. 1, spr. 10, ark. 1–65: Russocki, diary entry. Kramarz, *Samorząd Lwowa w czasie pierwszej wojny światowej*, 34–36.
44. Gember, "Die Russen in Lemberg," 155. Levyts'kyj, "Z dnïv rosyjs'koï invazyï," *Dilo*, November 29, 1915. Bohdan Janusz, *293 dni rządów rosyjskich we Lwowie (3.IX.1914–22.VI.1915)* (L'viv: Księgarnia Polska, 1915), 3–4. Kramarz, *Samorząd Lwowa w czasie pierwszej wojny światowej*, 36f.
45. Gember, "Die Russen in Lemberg," 155. Levyts'kyj, "Z dnïv rosyjs'koï invazyï," *Dilo*, November 30, 1915. Zygmunt Zieliński, *Lwów po inwazyi rosyjskiej: Wrzesień-Grudzień 1914* (Vienna: Z. Machnowski, 1914), 2. Janusz, *293 dni rządów rosyjskich we Lwowie*, 1–2.
46. Janusz, *293 dni rządów rosyjskich we Lwowie*, 4–5. Marzell Chlamtacz, *Lembergs politische Physiognomie während der russischen Invasion, 3.9.1914–22.6.1915: Erinnerungen und Betrachtungen* (Vienna: R. Lechner und Sohn, 1916), 22–25. TsDIAL, f. 694, op. 1, spr. 10, ark. 1–65: Russocki, diary entries, September 2 and 3, 1914.
47. Schall, *Żydostwo Galicyjskie w czasie inwazji rosyjskiej*, 5.
48. Chlamtacz, *Lembergs politische Physiognomie*, 22–26.
49. DALO, f. 350, op. 1, spr. 3609, ark. 1–2: police directorate in L'viv to the governor's office (draft, handwritten), September 1915. Kramarz mentions the figure forty thousand. Kramarz, *Samorząd Lwowa w czasie pierwszej wojny światowej*, 36.
50. Chlamtacz, *Lembergs politische Physiognomie*, 22–26.
51. Janusz, *293 dni rządów rosyjskich we Lwowie*, 4–5, 13. Levyts'kyj, "Z dnïv rosyjs'koï invazyï," *Dilo*, November 29, 1915; November 30, 1915. TsDIAL, f. 694, op. 1, spr. 10, ark. 1–65: Russocki, diary entry. Rossowski, *Lwów podczas inwazyi*, 3–6. TsDIAL, f. 408, op. 1, spr. 112: report of Greek Catholic priest Kyryl Levyts'kyj (1914). Kramarz, *Samorząd Lwowa w czasie pierwszej wojny światowej*, 41.

52. Schall, *Żydostwo Galicyjskie w czasie inwazji rosyjskiej*, 5–6. Teofil' Melen', "Z pobutu pid rosijs'koju invazyju u L'vovi," *Dilo*, July 24, 1915. Prusin, *Nationalizing a Borderland*, 24–28.
53. Gember, "Die Russen in Lemberg," 156.
54. Rossowski, *Lwów podczas inwazyi*, 11–15.
55. Białynia-Chołodecki, *Wspomnienia z lat niedoli i niewoli 1914–1918*, 8. Gember, "Die Russen in Lemberg," 156. Zieliński, *Lwów po inwazyi rosyjskiej*, 9. Schall, *Żydostwo Galicyjskie w czasie inwazji rosyjskiej*, 5. Piotrowski (first name unknown), *Wpływ wojny na moralność ludności* (unpublished memoirs, written after 1920, found in Stefanyka Library (L'viv), O/N, Nr. 38, ark. 1–17. "Najbliższe zadania kahału lwowskiego," *Chwila*, January 29, 1919.
56. Chlamtacz, *Lembergs politische Physiognomie*, 21. *Słowo Polskie*, September 10, 1914.
57. Białynia-Chołodecki, *Wspomnienia z lat niedoli i niewoli 1914–1918*, 8.
58. Piotrowski, *Wpływ wojny*.
59. AVA, MdI, Präsidiale, Allgemeine Angelegenheiten, 22/2116: report by Legationsrat Baron Andrian on his trip to East Galicia, Cracow, July 26, 1915. Piotrowski, *Wpływ wojny*.
60. On the entry of Russian troops in Krasno: "The Moskals robbed [everything] and destroyed what they could not carry." TsDIAL, f. 408, op. 1, spr. 112: report of Greek Catholic priest Kyryl Levyts'kyj (1914).
61. Piotrowski, *Wpływ wojny*.
62. HHStA, P.A.I., 931, Bl. 83–91: k. u. k. ambassador to the apostolic see (Vatican) to k. u. k. Foreign Minister Count Berchtold, November 18, 1914.
63. TsDIAL, f. 146, op. 8, spr. 1893, ark. 16–22: protocol of the interrogation of two Jewish merchants from Stanislau concerning the Russian occupation of the city from September 3, 1914, to February 21, 1915, recorded on March 19, 1915.
64. All dates in Russian documents follow the Julian calendar. In the twentieth century, it differed from the Gregorian calendar by thirteen days. The document is dated August 20, 1914 (Julian calendar), and September 2, 1914, according to the Gregorian calendar. TsDIAK, f. 361, op. 1, spr. 132, ark. 2: general military governor Bobrinskij to the commander-in-chief of the armies of the Southwestern Front (copy of a telegram), August 20, 1914.
65. The committee "Jüdisches Kriegsarchiv" (Jewish War Archive) was founded in Vienna in 1915. It collected information on the situation of Jews in the war zone and under Russian occupation. It published many reports on anti-Jewish violence in its bulletin "Jüdisches Kriegsarchiv."
66. Schall, *Żydostwo Galicyjskie w czasie inwazji rosyjskiej*, 18. Piotrowski, *Wpływ wojny*. Prus, *Nationalizing a Borderland*, 26-27. See also the report of the Russian Jewish writer and journalist S. Ansky. He traveled to the region to organize help for Galician Jews. S. Ansky, *The Enemy at his Pleasure: A Journey through the Jewish Pale of Settlement during World War I* (New York: Metropolitan Books, 2003) (first published in Yiddish in Warsaw in 1925), 63-82.
67. Schall, *Żydostwo Galicyjskie w czasie inwazji rosyjskiej*, 9.
68. Ibid., 8–9, 17.
69. For Stanislau: protocol of the interrogation of two Jewish merchants from Stanislau concerning the Russian occupation of the city from September 3, 1914, to February 21, 1915, recorded on March 19, 1915.
70. Gember, "Die Russen in Lemberg," 156. Zieliński, *Lwów po inwazyi rosyjskiej*, 5. Rossowski, *Lwów podczas inwazyi*, 7. Kramarz, *Samorząd Lwowa w czasie pierwszej wojny światowej*, 39.

Chapter 2 ♦ 115

71. Schall, Żydostwo Galicyjskie w czasie inwazji rosyjskiej, 6.
72. Zieliński, *Lwów po inwazyi rosyjskiej*, 2. TsDIAL, f. 146, op. 6, spr. 118, ark. 413–23: the town major of L'viv, Major General Riml, on his impressions after the reconquest of the city, July 26, 1915 (excerpts printed in *Ereignisse in der Ukraine 1914–1922*, vol. 1, 72–80).
73. TsDIAL, f. 694, op. 1, spr. 10, ark. 1–65: Russocki, diary entry, September 3, 1914. Teofil' Melen', "Z pobutu pid rosijs'koju invazyju u L'vovi," *Dilo*, July 24, 1915.
74. Janusz, *293 dni rządów rosyjskich we Lwowie*, 20.
75. TsDIAL, f. 694, op. 1, spr. 10, ark. 1–65: Russocki, diary entry, September 3, 1914.
76. Levyts'kyj, "Z dniv rosyjs'koï invazyï," *Dilo*, December 1, 1915. Similar: Melen', "Z pobutu pid rosijs'koju invazyju u L'vovi," *Dilo*, July 24, 1915.
77. Białynia-Chołodecki, *Wspomnienia z lat niedoli i niewoli 1914–1918*, 8. Gember, "Die Russen in Lemberg," 157. Zieliński, *Lwów po inwazyi rosyjskiej*, 6. Janusz, *293 dni rządów rosyjskich we Lwowie*, 29–32.
78. Gember, "Die Russen in Lemberg," 158. Chlamtacz, *Lembergs politische Physiognomie*, 34–35. Kramarz, *Samorząd Lwowa w czasie pierwszej wojny światowej*, 40.
79. TsDIAK, f. 361, op. 1, spr. 132, ark. 2: Bobrinskij to the commander-in-chief of the armies of the Southwestern Front (copy of a telegram), August 20, 1914.
80. Zieliński, *Lwów po inwazyi rosyjskiej*, 11–12.
81. Veryha, *Vyzvol'ni zmahannja v Ukraïni 1914–1923 rr.*, vol. 1, 33–34.
82. TsDIAL, f. 694, op. 1, spr. 10, ark. 1–65: Russocki, diary entry, September 5, 1914. Kramarz, *Samorząd Lwowa w czasie pierwszej wojny światowej*, 42.
83. TsDIAL, f. 79, op. 1, spr. 5, ark. 15: proclamation of the general governor for Galicia, November 24, 1914.
84. Melen', "Z pobutu pid rosijs'koju invazyju u L'vovi," *Dilo*, July 24, 1915.
85. Janusz, *293 dni rządów rosyjskich we Lwowie*, 117. Kramarz, *Samorząd Lwowa w czasie pierwszej wojny światowej*, 43.
86. Lwów w ogniu walki, *Słowo Polskie*, September 10, 1914.
87. Straszliwe odblaski, *Gazeta Wieczorna*, September 9, 1914.
88. Georgij A. Bobrinskij was a cousin of the president of the Galician-Russian Benevolent Society Vladimir A. Bobrinskij. Vladimir was also chairman of the nationalist faction in the State Duma.
89. Janusz, *293 dni rządów rosyjskich we Lwowie*, 156ff.
90. RGVIA, f. 2005, op. 1, d. 8, l. 6–8: report of Chamberlain Bazili, September 16, 1914. See also the proclamation of the Russian supreme commander Grand Prince Nikolaj Nikolaevich "To the Russian people in Austria." Stepan Makarczuk, "Lwów w warunkach rosyjskiej okupacji 1914–1915," in *Lwów: Miasto—społeczeństwo—kultura*, vol. 1, 131–137, here: 135–136.
91. The government, army, and Church shared this opinion, as did the liberal opposition in the Duma. RGVIA, f. 2005, op. 1, d. 8, l. 22–23: The members of the State Duma and the State Council M. A. Stakhovich, Count V. M. Pushkin, V. A. Miljukov, N. N. L'vov, and N. A. Khomjakov to Count G. A. Bobrinskij, October 25, 1914. Bakhturina, *Politika Rossijskoj Imperii*, 10–19, 57–69.
92. The speech is quoted in Janusz, *293 dni rządów rosyjskich we Lwowie*, 156–58.
93. RGVIA, f. 2005, op. 1, d. 8, l. 3–5: Janushkevich to Goremykin, September 19, 1914.
94. RGVIA, f. 2005, op. 1, d. 12, l. 48–49: Bobrinskij to A. F. Zabelin, October 19, 1914.
95. Zieliński, *Lwów po inwazyi rosyjskiej*, 6–7. Kramarz, *Samorząd Lwowa w czasie pierwszej wojny światowej*, 36–40. Janusz, *293 dni rządów rosyjskich we Lwowie*, 17.
96. Chlamtacz, *Lembergs politische Physiognomie*, 21. Russocki uses the word "shame" when referring to Mayor Neumann, who had left the city before Russian troops arrived. TsDIAL, f. 694, op. 1, spr. 10, ark. 1–65: Russocki, diary entry, September 3, 1914.

97. RGVIA, f. 2005, op. 1, d. 12, l. 6–10: Bobrinskij to Janushkevich, October 20, 1914.
98. RGVIA, f. 2005, op. 1, d. 8, l. 6–8: report of Chamberlain Bazili, September 16, 1914. Janushkevich forwarded the report to the Council of Ministers.
99. Dimitrij Vergun, "Galizien und Polen: Die Organisation Galiziens," in HHStA, P.A.I., 931, Bl. 58–67). This is the German translation of an article published by Dimitrij Vergun in the St. Petersburg Journal Novoe Vremja, December 11, 1914.
100. Zieliński, *Lwów po inwazyi rosyjskiej*, 6.
101. RGVIA, f. 2005, op. 1, d. 13, l. 1–2: note on administrative questions of the general governorate in Galicia, November 5, 1914.
102. RGVIA, f. 2005, op. 1, d. 8, l. 6–8: report of Chamberlain Bazili, September 16, 1914. Janushkevich forwarded the report to the Council of Ministers.
103. RGVIA, f. 2005, op. 1, d. 8, l. 3–5: the chairman of the Council of Ministers I. L. Goremykin to Janushkevich, October 3, 1914.
104. Zieliński, *Lwów po inwazyi rosyjskiej*, 6
105. Gember, "Die Russen in Lemberg," 166.
106. Beck, *Uniwersytet Jana Kazimierza we Lwowie*, 65–66.
107. RGVIA, f. 2005, op. 1, d. 12, l. 15: resolution (postanovlenie) of the Russian general governor of Galicia, August 31, 1914.
108. Rutowski referred to the costs this would cause and the lack of appropriate manufacturing workshops in L'viv. Finally, he also gave aesthetic reasons why these changes should not be implemented. DALO, f. 3, op. 1, spr. 5905, ark. 47–48: Rutowski to Bobrinskij, January 15, 1915. Ibid., ark. 57: Rutowski to Bobrinskij, February 11, 1915.
109. TsDIAK, f. 361, op. 1, spr. 99, ark. 30: Bobrinskij to Rutowski, February 2, 1915.
110. Levyts'kyj, "Z dniv rosyjs'koï invazyï," *Dilo*, December 4, 1915. Malyts'ka, "Na khvyljach svitovoï vijny," *Dilo*, March 27, 1937. HHStA, P.A.I, 931, Bl. 32–35: Police Commissioner Pajączkowski (in the town of Skole) to the presidium of the k. u. k. police directorate in Biała, November 7, 1914.
111. Zieliński, *Lwów po inwazyi rosyjskiej*, 32–33.
112. TsDIAK, f. 361, op. 1, spr. 677, ark. 4–5: the chief of the provisional administration of the gendarmerie (constabulary) of the military general governate in Galicia to the military general governor, April 27, 1915.
113. Gember, "Die Russen in Lemberg," 165. HHStA, P.A.I, 931, Bl. 32–35: Police Commissioner Pajączkowski (in the town of Skole) to the presidium of the k. u. k. police directorate in Biała, November 7, 1914. TsDIAL, f. 694, op. 1, spr. 10, ark. 1–65: Russocki, diary entry.
114. TsDIAL, f. 146, op. 6, spr. 118, ark. 413–23: the town major of L'viv, Major General Riml, on his impressions after the reconquest of the city, July 26, 1915 (excerpts printed in *Ereignisse in der Ukraine 1914–1922*, vol. 1, 72–80).
115. For example, TsDIAL, f. 408, op. 1, spr. 112: report of Greek Catholic priest Kyryl Levyts'kyj (1914).
116. Janusz, *293 dni rządów rosyjskich we Lwowie*, 248–49. TsDIAL, f. 694, op. 1, spr. 10, ark. 1–65: Russocki, diary entry.
117. Gember, "Die Russen in Lemberg," 166.
118. Vergun, "Galizien und Polen: Die Organisation Galiziens."
119. RGVIA, f. 2005, op. 1, d. 8, l. 22–23: Stakhovich and others to Bobrinskij, October 25, 1914. Russian nationalists criticized the cautious policy of the military general governor. Wendland, *Die Russophilen in Galizien*, 555–64.
120. RGVIA, f. 2005, op. 1, d. 12, l. 89–92: Russian Ministry of the Interior to Janushkevich, October 1914.
121. RGVIA, f. 2005, op. 1, d. 8, l. 6–8: report of Chamberlain Bazili, September 16, 1914.

122. Zieliński, *Lwów po inwazyi rosyjskiej*, 18–19. Janusz, *293 dni rządów rosyjskich we Lwowie*, 159.
123. Quoted in a confiscated article in the journal *Prykarpatskaja Rus'* (Polish translation), January 3, 1915, found in TsDIAL, f. 79, op. 1. spr. 12, ark. 115.
124. Janusz, *293 dni rządów rosyjskich we Lwowie*, 77. Beck, *Uniwersytet Jana Kazimierza we Lwowie*, 10–16.
125. TsDIAK, f. 361, op. 1, spr. 99, ark 30: Bobrinskij to Rutowski, February 2, 1915. RGVIA, f. 2005, op. 12, l. 77–78: Bobrinskij to Janushkevich, February 3, 1915.
126. Chlamtacz, *Lembergs politische Physiognomie*, 48–50.
127. TsDIAL, f. 146, op. 6, spr. 118, ark. 413–23: Major General Riml on his impressions after the reconquest of the city, July 26, 1915.
128. RGVIA, f. 2005, op. 1, d. 8, l. 19–21: Polish members of the Russian State Council and the State Duma to Bobrinskij, October 9, 1914.
129. TsDIAK, f. 361, op. 1, spr. 132, ark. 39–40: Bobrinskij to Janushkevich, December 25, 1914.
130. TsDIAK, f. 361, op. 1, spr. 132, ark. 51: Janushkevich to Bobrinskij, January 4, 1915.
131. TsDIAK, f. 361, op. 1, spr. 132, ark. 52–53: Bobrinskij to Janushkevich, January 30, 1915. Ibid., ark 57: Bobrinskij to Prince Sergej Dmitrievich, February 24, 1915.
132. RGVIA, f. 2005, op. 1, d. 12, l. 11–12: the Russian military general governor to the provincial governors, October 27, 1914. Levyts'kyj, "Z dnïv rosyjs'koï invazyï," *Dilo*, December 4, 1915. Zieliński, *Lwów po inwazyi rosyjskiej*, 11–12.
133. RGVIA, f. 2005, op. 1, d. 13, l. 1–2: note on administrative questions of the general governerate in Galicia, November 5, 1914.
134. RGVIA, f. 2005, op. 1, d. 12, l. 111–15: Bobrinskij to Janushkevich, April 17, 1915.
135. See, for example, the activities of the state attorney of the Warsaw Law Court Gesse. Backed by the Russian Ministry of Justice, he tried to russify the Galician law courts and came therefore into conflict with Bobrinskij's more moderate policy. RGVIA, f. 2005, op. 1, d. 13, l. 430–31: Bobrinskij to Janushkevich, March 8, 1915. Ibid., l. 436–437: Gesse to Janushkevich, April 4, 1915. Ibid., d. 8, l. 439–440: Janushkevich to Bobrinskij, April 16, 1915.
136. RGVIA, f. 2005, op. 1, d. 12: Janushkevich to Bobrinskij, January 5, 1915. Ibid., l. 77–78: Bobrinskij to Janushkevich, February 3, 1915.
137. RGVIA, f. 2005, op. 1, d. 12: Janushkevich to Bobrinskij, January 5, 1915.
138. RGVIA, f. 2005, op. 12, l. 77–78: Bobrinskij to Janushkevich, February 3, 1915.
139. Beck, *Uniwersytet Jana Kazimierza we Lwowie*, 8–16, 51–65.
140. TsDIAK, f. 361, op. 1, spr. 162, ark. 22–23: Bobrinskij to Evlogij, September 29, 1914. RGVIA, f. 2005, op. 1, d. 12, l. 11–12: circular of the military general governor to the governors, October 27, 1914. RGVIA, f. 2005, op. 1, d. 8: Bobrinskij to *Kamer-junker* (valet de chamber) S. A. Bazarov, October, 12, 1914.
141. Vergun, "Galizien und Polen: Die Organisation Galiziens." Chlamtacz, *Lembergs politische Physiognomie*, 80–81.
142. AVA, MdI, Präsidiale, Allgemeine Angelegenheiten, 22/2116: report by Legationsrat Baron Andrian on his trip to East Galicia, Cracow, July 26, 1915.
143. Janusz, *293 dni rządów rosyjskich we Lwowie*, 181–83. TsDIAL, f. 694, op. 1, spr. 10, ark. 1–65: Russocki, diary entry.
144. RGVIA, f. 2005, op. 1, d. 8, l. 19–21: Polish members of the State Council and the State Duma to Bobrinskij, October 9, 1914. Ibid., l. 22–23: Stachovich et al. to Bobrinskij, October 25, 1914.
145. DALO, f. 3, op. 1, spr. 5905, l. 30: Rutowski to Bobrinskij, December 30, 1914.
146. RGVIA, f. 2005, op. 1, d. 8, l. 341–42: Bobrinskij to Janushkevich, December 25, 1914.

147. TsDIAK, f. 361, op. 1, spr. 99, ark. 30: Bobrinskij to Rutowski, February 2, 1915.
148. RGVIA, f. 2005, op. 1, d. 8, l. 328: the commander-in-chief of the armies on the Southwestern Front to the supreme commander Grand Duke Nikolaj Nikolaevich, November 5, 1914.
149. DALO, f. 3, op. 1, spr. 5904, ark. 12–13: Rutowski et al. to Bobrinskij, February 11, 1915.
150. Ibid., ark. 15a–15v: Rutowski to Bobrinskij, February 18, 1915.
151. Malyts'ka, "Na khvyljach svitovoï vijny," *Dilo*, March 27, 1937. Janushkevich also noted Rutowski's complacency about the interests of the Ukrainian (from Russian perspective: Russian) schoolchildren. RGVIA, f. 2005, op. 1, d. 12, l. 75–76: Janushkevich to Bobrinskij, January 5, 1915.
152. Zieliński, *Lwów po inwazyi rosyjskiej*, 10. "Kronika z miasta," *Gazeta Wieczorna*, September 9, 1914.
153. Makarczuk, "Lwów w warunkach rosyjskiej okupacji 1914–1915," 134.
154. Janusz, *293 dni rządów rosyjskich we Lwowie*, 184. DALO, f. 350, op. 1, spr. 3609, ark. 1–2: police directorate in L'viv to governor's office (handwritten draft), September 11, 1915.
155. Gember, "Die Russen in Lemberg," 162-63. "Kronika z miasta," *Gazeta Wieczorna*, September 9, 1914.
156. Gember, "Die Russen in Lemberg," 162–63. Zieliński, *Lwów po inwazyi rosyjskiej*, 28.
157. Levyts'kyj, "Z dniv rosyjs'koï invazyï," *Dilo*, December 6, 1915. Zieliński, *Lwów po inwazyi rosyjskiej*, 22–23.
158. Janusz, *293 dni rządów rosyjskich we Lwowie*, 60–63.
159. Gember, "Die Russen in Lemberg," 164.
160. Levyts'kyj, "Z dniv rosyjs'koï invazyï," *Dilo*, December 1, 1915. Malyts'ka, "Na khvyljach svitovoï vijny," *Dilo*, March 27, 1937.
161. Gember, "Die Russen in Lemberg," 163.
162. Janusz, *293 dni rządów rosyjskich we Lwowie*, 94.
163. Levyts'kyj, "Z dniv rosyjs'koï invazyï," *Dilo*, December 1, 1915. Malyts'ka, "Na khvyljach svitovoï vijny," *Dilo*, March 27, 1937.
164. Levyts'kyj, "Z dniv rosyjs'koï invazyï," *Dilo*, December 4, 1915.
165. Zieliński, *Lwów po inwazyi rosyjskiej*, 24–25; DALO, f. 350, op. 1, spr. 3617: k. u. k. city captain to police directorate in L'viv, October 28, 1915.
166. Zieliński, *Lwów po inwazyi rosyjskiej*, 21.
167. Janusz, *293 dni rządów rosyjskich we Lwowie*, 14–17.
168. Zieliński, *Lwów po inwazyi rosyjskiej*, 35. TsDIAL, f. 694, op. 1, spr. 10, ark. 1–65: Russocki, diary entry.
169. TsDIAL, f. 694, op. 1, spr. 10, ark. 1–65: Russocki, diary entry.
170. Chlamtacz, *Lembergs politische Physiognomie*, 66–68.
171. TsDIAK, f. 361, op. 1, spr. 677, ark. 4–5 (also in RGVIA, f. 2005, op. 1, d. 12, l. 42): the head of the provisional administration of the gendarmerie of the military general governorate in Galicia to the military general governor, April 27, 1915.
172. Janusz, *293 dni rządów rosyjskich we Lwowie*, 224. Chlamtacz, *Lembergs politische Physiognomy*, 97–98. TsDIAL, f. 146, op. 6, spr. 118, ark. 413–23: Major General Riml on his impressions after the reconquest of the city, July 26, 1915.
173. TsDIAK, f. 361, op. 1, spr. 677, ark. 4–5: the head of the provisional administration of the gendarmerie of the military general governorate in Galicia to the military general governor, April 27, 1915.
174. Gember, "Die Russen in Lemberg," 162.
175. Zieliński, *Lwów po inwazyi rosyjskiej*, 20–21.

176. Schall, Żydostwo Galicyjskie w czasie inwazji rosyjskiej, 11.
177. Gember, "Die Russen in Lemberg," 165. Chlamtacz, Lembergs politische Physiognomie, 96–97.
178. Chlamtacz, Lembergs politische Physiognomie, 97–98. For Russian corruption in provincial towns, see Kyryl Levyts'kyj. TsDIAL, f. 408, op. 1, spr. 112: report of Greek Catholic priest Kyryl Levyts'kyj (1914).
179. Levyts'kyj, "Z dniv rosyjs'koï invazyï," Dilo, December 6, 1915. Janusz, 293 dni rządów rosyjskich we Lwowie, 13.
180. DALO, f. 3, op. 1, spr. 5905, ark. 4–13: Rutowski to Bobrinskij, November 10, 1914.
181. Rutowski to Bobrinskij, December 1, 1914; ibid., ark. 18–19.
182. Bobrinskij to Rutowski, January 14, 1915 (copy); DALO, f. 3, op. 1, spr. 5906, l. 10.
183. RGVIA, f. 2005, op. 1, d. 13, l. 1–2: note on administrative questions of the general governerate in Galicia, November 5, 1914. Ibid., l. 387–88: Bobrinskij to Janushkevich, December 15, 1914. Zieliński, Lwów po inwazyi rosyjskiej, 8–9.
184. Janusz, 293 dni rządów rosyjskich we Lwowie, 219–23.
185. Ibid., 79–82.
186. Rossowski, Lwów podczas inwazyi, 27–28, 62. Janusz, 293 dni rządów rosyjskich we Lwowie, 84–85.
187. Beck, Uniwersytet Jana Kazimierza we Lwowie, 22–24.
188. Rossowski, Lwów podczas inwazyi, 102–104.
189. Białynia-Chołodecki, Wspomnienia z lat niedoli i niewoli 1914–1918, 24. Gember, "Die Russen in Lemberg," 158.
190. Gember, "Die Russen in Lemberg," 159. Levyts'kyj, "Z dniv rosyjs'koï invazyï," Dilo, December 6, 1915.
191. DALO, f. 3, op. 1, spr. 5905, ark. 18–19: Rutowski to Bobrinskij, November 11, 1914.
192. Schall, Żydostwo Galicyjskie w czasie inwazji rosyjskiej, 15–16. Kramarz, Samorząd Lwowa w czasie pierwszej wojny światowej, 49–50.
193. Schall, Żydostwo Galicyjskie w czasie inwazji rosyjskiej, 15–16. Ansky, The Enemy at his Pleasure, 125–27.
194. There was a club of historians at the Pasaż Mikolascha; other eating places served artists, teachers, members of the Jewish intelligentsia, Ukrainians, or civil servants. Kramarz, Samorząd Lwowa w czasie pierwszej wojny światowej, 49–51.
195. Rossowski, Lwów podczas inwazyi, 54.
196. DALO, f. 3, op. 1, spr. 6013, ark. 31–36: Deputy Mayor Schleicher to Bobrinskij (copy), February 19, 1915.
197. Levyts'kyj, "Z dniv rosyjs'koï invazyï," Dilo, December 6, 1915.
198. Kramarz, Samorząd Lwowa w czasie pierwszej wojny światowej, 50–51.
199. Janusz, 293 dni rządów rosyjskich we Lwowie, 200–202.
200. DALO, f. 3, op. 1, spr. 6518a, ark. 2–9: report by the statistical office of L'viv city administration on causes of death for the years 1914–1916.
201. Kramarz, Samorząd Lwowa w czasie pierwszej wojny światowej, 44.
202. RGVIA, f. 2005, op. 1, d. 12, l. 6–10: Bobrinskij to Janushkevich, October 20, 1914.
203. Ibid., l. 75–76: Janushkevich to Bobrinskij, January 5, 1915.
204. Ibid., l. 77–78: Bobrinskij to Janushkevich, February 3, 1915.
205. Janusz, 293 dni rządów rosyjskich we Lwowie, 42ff.
206. Zieliński, Lwów po inwazyi rosyjskiej, 5. On atrocities during the first days of Russian rule, see Schall, Żydostwo Galicyjskie w czasie inwazji rosyjskiej, 6.
207. Zieliński, Lwów po inwazyi rosyjskiej, 12–13. Józef Białynia-Chołodecki, Lwów w czasie okupacyji rosyjskiej (L'viv: Wschód, 1930), 105–106.
208. Melen', "Z pobutu pid rosijs'koju invazyju u L'vovi," Dilo, July 24, 1915.

209. Janusz, *293 dni rządów rosyjskich we Lwowie*, 166.
210. The municipal authorities gave the wrong date for the pogrom (September 29, 1914). DALO, f. 3, op. 1, spr. 6518, ark. 3: the municipal authorities to the k. u. k. army command (handwritten), June 26, 1917.
211. Gember, "Die Russen in Lemberg," 161. Levyts'kyj, "Z dnïv rosyjs'koï invazyï," *Dilo*, December 3, 1915, December 4, 1915.
212. Janusz, *293 dni rządów rosyjskich we Lwowie*, 171. Melen', "Z pobutu pid rosijs'koju invazyju u L'vovi," *Dilo*, July 24, 1915.
213. Schall, Żydostwo Galicyjskie w czasie inwazji rosyjskiej, 1–2, 16. "Die Juden Lembergs," *Jüdisches Archiv* 8–9 (1917): 8–10. Prusin, *Nationalizing a Borderland*, 30–31.
214. Zieliński, *Lwów po inwazyi rosyjskiej*, 12–13. Schall, Żydostwo Galicyjskie w czasie inwazji rosyjskiej, 14.
215. Melen', "Z pobutu pid rosijs'koju invazyju u L'vovi," *Dilo*, July 24, 1915.
216. Schall, Żydostwo Galicyjskie w czasie inwazji rosyjskiej, 10.
217. Ibid., 20–21. DALO, f. 30, op. 1, spr. 3933, ark. 45–47: Helene Rosner to k. u. k. war ministry, October 28, 1915.
218. Eric Lohr, "The Russian Army and the Jews: Mass Deportations, Hostages and Violence," *Russian Review* 60 (2001): 404–419. Mark von Hagen, *War in a European Borderland: Occupations and Occupation Plans in Galicia and Ukraine, 1914–1918* (Seattle: University of Washington Press, 2007), 28–31.
219. RGVIA, f. 2005, op. 1, d. 8, l. 3–5: Janushkevich to the chairman of the Council of Ministers, I. L. Goremykin, September 19, 1914. Ansky, *The Enemy at his Pleasure*, 5–6.
220. RGVIA, f. 2005, op. 1, d. 12, l. 111–15: Bobrinskij to Janushkevich, April 17, 1915.
221. Prusin, *Nationalising a Borderland*, 40–41.
222. RGVIA, f. 2005, op. 1, d. 8, l. 3–5: Goremykin to Janushkevich, October 3, 1914.
223. R. Ganelin, "Evrejskij vopros vo vnutrennej politike Rossii v 1915 godu," *Vestnik evrejskogo universiteta v Moskve* 1, no. 14 (1997): 41–65.
224. RGVIA, f. 2005, op. 1, d. 8, l. 6–8: report of Chamberlain Bazili, September 16, 1914.
225. Levyts'kyj, "Z dnïv rosyjs'koï invazyï," *Dilo*, December 3, 1915.
226. Janusz, *293 dni rządów rosyjskich we Lwowie*, 11.
227. HHStA, P.A.I, 931, Bl. 32–35: Police Commissioner Pajączkowski (in the town of Skole) to the presidium of the k. u. k. police directorate in Biała, November 7, 1914.
228. TsDIAL, f. 309, op. 1, spr. 1399: diary of Je. Kalytovs'kyj aus Stryj (in Ukrainian), diary entry, September 11, 1914.
229. TsDIAK, f. 361, op. 1, spr. 677, ark. 1: Janushkevich to the staff of the supreme commander, February 3, 1915.
230. RGVIA, f. 2005, op. 1, d. 8, l. 439–40: Janushkevich to Bobrinskij, April 16, 1915.
231. Ibid., l. 441: Bobrinskij to Janushkevich, May 4, 1915.
232. Ibid., l. 442: Janushkevich to Aleksander Gesse, May 8, 1915.
233. RGVIA, f. 2005, op. 1, d. 12, l. 118: note on the deportees, April 16, 1915.
234. Ibid., l. 111–15: Bobrinskij to Janushkevich, April 17, 1915.
235. TsDIAK, f. 361, op. 1, spr. 161, ark. 1–6: the military governor of Czernowitz to Bobrinskij, November 26, 1914.
236. TsDIAL, f. 694, op. 1, spr. 10, ark. 1–65: Russocki, diary entry.
237. Schall, "Żydostwo Galicyjskie w czasie inwazji rosyjskiej," 19.
238. The text was first published in *Ukrainische Nachrichten*. Cited after Schall, Żydostwo Galicyjskie w czasie inwazji rosyjskiej, 27.
239. Prusin, *Nationalizing a Borderland*, 51–54. Wendland, *Die Russophilen in Galizien*, 550.
240. Cited after Schall, "Żydostwo Galicyjskie w czasie inwazji rosyjskiej," 23.

241. TsDIAL, f. 408, op. 1, spr. 112: report of Greek Catholic priest Kyryl Levyts'kyj (1914).
242. RGVIA, f. 2005, op. 1, d. 8, l. 3–5: Janushkevich to Goremykin, September 19, 1914. CDIAK, f. 361, op. 1, spr. 162, l. 65–67: the chief of staff of the commander-in-chief of the Southwestern Front to Bobrinskij, September 23, 1914. RGVIA, f. 2005, op. 1, d. 13, l. 323–25: oral report to Janushkevich, November 1914. RGVIA, f. 2005, op. 1, d. 8, l. 3–5: the chairman of the Council of Ministers, I. L. Goremykin to Janushkevich, October 3, 1914.
243. Malyts'ka, "Na khvyljach svitovoï vijny," *Dilo*, March 27, 1937.
244. HHStA, P.A.I., 931, Bl. 9–16: report by the governor's office for the Austrian Ministry of the Interior on "The Atrocities of the Russians against the Ukrainian Nation in Galicia," October 5, 1915.
245. Melen', "Z pobutu pid rosijs'koju invazyeju u L'vovi," *Dilo*, July 24, 1915.
246. RGVIA, f. 2005, op. 1, d. 8, l. 6–8: report by Chamberlain Bazili, September 16, 1914.
247. Janusz, *293 dni rządów rosyjskich we Lwowie*, 56–57.
248. Levyts'kyj, "Z dniv rosyjs'koï invazyï," *Dilo*, December 7, 1915. Malyts'ka, "Na khvyljach svitovoï vijny," *Dilo*, March 27, 1937.
249. Among those arrested were Jaroslav Levyts'kyj, Bohdan Barvins'kyj, Volodymyr Okhrymovych, Stepan Fedak, and Kost' Pan'kivs'kyj. Levyts'kyj, "Z dniv rosyjs'koï invazyï," *Dilo*, December 11 and 12, 1915. Konstantyna Malyts'ka was also arrested. Malyts'ka, "Na khvyljach svitovoï vijny," *Dilo*, March 27, 1937.
250. Levyts'kyj, "Z dniv rosyjs'koï invazyï," *Dilo*, December 14, 1915.
251. RGVIA, f. 2005, op. 1, d. 12, l. 6–10: Bobrinskij to Janushkevich, October 20, 1914. Janusz, *293 dni rządów rosyjskich we Lwowie*, 149.
252. TsDIAK, f. 361, op. 1, spr. 237, ark. 1–4: the minister of the interior N. A. Maklakov to Bobrinskij, September 30, 1914.
253. TsDIAK, f. 361, op. 1, spr. 94, ark. 9–10: memorandum of Dudykevich, September 1, 1914.
254. RGVIA, f. 2005, op. 1, d. 8, l. 494–96: the minister of the interior N. A. Maklakov to Janushkevich, November 7, 1914. On the Russian policy toward the Greek Catholic Church, see Bakhturina, *Politika Rossijskoj Imperii*, 142–83.
255. Bakhturina, *Politika Rossijskoj Imperii*, 147. Wendland, *Die Russophilen in Galizien*, 557–64.
256. RGIA, f. 821, op. 12, d. 150, l. 70: Archbishop Evlogij to the minister of the interior Maklakov, January 1915 (cited after Bakhturina, *Politika Rossijskoj Imperii*, 143). See also Evlogij, arkhiepiskop Volynskij, *Obrashchenie k galitsko-russkomu narodu i dukhovenstvu*, 1.
257. Bakhturina, *Politika Rossijskoj Imperii*, 159–61. See also Evlogij's memoirs *Put' mojej zhizni: Vospominanija Mitropolita Evlogija (Georgievskogo), islozhennye po ego rasskazam T. Manukhinoj* (Moscow: Moskovskij Rabochij, 1994, first published in Paris: 1947).
258. For example, in 1914 (before the war), Archbishop Antonij (Khhrapovitskij) on a session of the Galician-Russian Benevolent Society (cited after Bakhturina, *Politika Rossijskoj Imperii*, 157).
259. Bakhturina, *Politika Rossijskoj Imperii*, 156–59.
260. Ibid., 162–63.
261. Vergun, "Galizien und Polen: Die Organisierung Galiziens."
262. Bakhturina, *Politika Rossijskoj Imperii*, 158–59.
263. RGIA, f. 821, op. 150, d. 35, l. 23: The supreme commander Nikolaj Nikolaevich to Janushkevich (telegram), September 13, 1914 (cited after Bakhturina, *Politika Rossijskoj Imperii*, 160).

264. Bakhturina, *Politika Rossijskoj Imperii*, 160. RGVIA, f. 2005, op. 1, spr. 8: Nikolaj II to the military general governor of Galicia (telegram, copy), September 15, 1914.
265. TsDIAK, f. 361, op. 1, spr. 162, ark. 1: Janushkevich to Bobrinskij, September 14, 1914. RGVIA, f. 2005, d. 8: Bobrinskij to Janushkevich, September 17, 1914.
266. RGVIA, f. 2005, d. 8: Bobrinskij to Janushkevich, September 17, 1914. On Bobrinskij's policy in religious affairs, see the interview in *Birzhovye Vedomosti*. Published in Polish translation in *Słowo Polskie*, October 21, 1914 and November 3, 1914.
267. The villagers received two white slips of paper. They were asked to make one cross if they wanted to have an Orthodox priest and two crosses if they wanted to stay with the Greek Catholic Church. TsDIAL, f. 694, op. 1, spr. 1, ark. 7: circular of the military general governor for Galicia and the Bukovina, October 1914. Vergun, "Galizien und Polen: Die Organisierung Galiziens."
268. TsDIAL, f. 694, op. 1, spr. 1, ark. 7: circular of the military general governor for Galicia and the Bukovina, October 1914.
269. RGVIA, f. 2005, op. 1, d. 8: Bobrinskij to Evlogij, October 6, 1914. Vergun, "Galizien und Polen: Die Organisierung Galiziens." Bakhturina, *Politika Rossijskoj Imperii*, 144.
270. RGVIA, f. 2005, op. 1, d. 8: Bobrinskij to Evlogij, October 6, 1914.
271. TsDIAL, f. 694, op. 1, spr. 1, ark. 7: circular of the military general governor to the military governors, November 20, 1914.
272. RGVIA, f. 2005, op. 1, d. 8: Bobrinskij to Bazarov, October 12, 1914.
273. RGVIA, f. 2005, op. 1, d. 12, l. 11–12: circular of the military general governor to the military governors, October 27, 1914.
274. Levyts'kyj, "Z dnïv rosyjs'koï invazyï," *Dilo*, December 8, 1915.
275. HHStA, P.A.I, 931, Bl. 32–35: Police Commissioner Pajączkowski (in the town of Skole) to the presidium of the police directorate in Biała, November 7, 1914.
276. Bakhturina, *Politika Rossijskoj Imperii*, 164.
277. RGVIA, f. 2005, op. 1, d. 13, l. 472–73: on the question of the unification of the Russian Galicians with the Orthodox Church, September 19, 1914.
278. Evlogij, *Put' mojej zhizni*, 243 (cited after Bakhturina, *Politika Rossijskoj Imperii*, 166).
279. Bakhturina, *Politika Rossijskoj Imperii*, 168–69.
280. Levyts'kyj, "Z dnïv rosyjs'koï invazyï," *Dilo*, December 7 and 8, 1915. HHStA, P.A.I., 931, Bl. 32–35: Pajączkowski to the governor's office, November 7, 1914.
281. HHStA, P.A.I., 931, Bl. 89: k. u. k. ambassador to the Holy See to Foreign Minister Count Berchtold (third supplement: "Nachrichten aus Lemberg"), November 18, 1914.
282. On the discussions about the best way to handle Sheptyts'kyj, see Bakhturina, *Politika Rossijskoj Imperii*, 145–53. Evlogij, *Put' moej zhizni*, 233–35.
283. Levyts'kyj, "Z dnïv rosyjs'koï invazyï," *Dilo*, December 1, 1915.
284. TsDIAK, f. 361, op. 1, spr. 162, ark. 22–23: Bobrinskij to Evlogij, September 29, 1914.
285. RGVIA, f. 2005, d. 8: Bobrinskij to Janushkevich, September 17, 1914. TsDIAK, f. 361, op. 1, spr. 162, ark. 22–23: Bobrinskij to Evlogij, September 29, 1914.
286. Bakhturina, *Politika Rossijskoj Imperii*, 160–61.
287. TsDIAK, f. 361, op. 1, spr. 162, ark. 22–23: Bobrinskij to Evlogij, September 29, 1914.
288. Levyts'kyj, "Z dnïv rosyjs'koï invazyï," *Dilo*, December 8, 1915.
289. *Prikarpatskaja Rus'*, December 8, 1914. Levyts'kyj, "Z dnïv rosyjs'koï invazyï," *Dilo*, December 8, 1915. Bakhturina, *Politika Rossijskoj Imperii*, 170.
290. *Prikarpatskaja Rus'*, December 8, 1914. Bakhturina, *Politika Rossijskoj Imperii*, 171.
291. Bakhturina, *Politika Rossijskoj Imperii*, 171–72.
292. RGVIA, f. 2005, op. 1, d. 8: Vicar General Bilets'kyj to Bobrinskij (in Russian), December 23, 1914. Ibid., l. 513: collegiate assessor Olfer'ev to the head of the chancellory of the Russian Foreign Office, Baron M. F. Shilling (copy), December 27, 1914.

RGVIA, f. 2005, op. 1, d. 13, l. 509–10: Bobrinskij to Janushkevich, December 30, 1914. Ibid., l. 319: Bobrinskij to Janushkevich (telegram), January 26, 1915.
293. TsDIAL, f. 408, op. 1, spr. 112: report of Greek Catholic priest Kyryl Levyts'kyj (1914).
294. HHStA, P.A.I., 931, Bl. 9–16: report by the k. u. k. governor's office for the Austrian Ministry of the Interior on "The Atrocities of the Russians against the Ukrainian Nation in Galicia," October 5, 1915. Ibid., Bl. 16: The k. u. k. governor's office in Biała to Minister-President Count Berchtold in Vienna, November 6, 1914.
295. RGVIA, f. 2005, op. 1, d. 8: Bobrinskij to Evlogij, October 6, 1914.
296. TsDIAL, f. 408, op. 1, spr. 112: report of Greek Catholic priest Kyryl Levyts'kyj (1914).
297. HHStA, P.A.I., 931, Bl. 20: Governor Korytowski (Biała) to the Austrian Ministry of the Interior (copy), October 18, 1914. Ibid., Bl. 26–27: k. u. k. minister for education to k.u.k. minister-president, October 20, 1914.
298. RGVIA, f. 2005, op. 1, d. 8, l. 539–40: The ober-procurator of the Holy Synod to Janushkevich, January 2, 1915.
299. RGIA, f. 797, op. 84, otd. 2, st. 3, Nr. 510, l. 37–38: Evlogij to the Holy Synod, fall 1914 (cited after Bakhturina, *Politika Rossijskoj Imperii*, 144). RGIA, f. 821, op. 12, d. 150, l. 135: a member of the Russian Ministry of the Interior in L'viv to the Department for Ecclesiastic Affairs of the Ministry of the Interior, fall 1914 (cited after Bakhturina, *Politika Rossijskoj Imperii*, 144).
300. Bakhturina, *Politika Rossijskoj Imperii*, 161, 169–70.
301. HHStA, P.A.I., 931, Bl. 3–4: protest of the Ukrainian Parliamentary Representation of Galicia (Vienna) against the Russian violation of the freedom of religion of the Ukrainian people in Galicia, October 6, 1914.
302. Bakhturina, *Politika Rossijskoj Imperii*, 172.
303. Dean Warren Lambert, "The Deterioration of the Imperial Russian Army in the First World War, August 1914–March 1917," PhD dissertation, University of Kentucky, 1975.
304. AVPRI, f. 135, op. 474, d. 142, l. 45 ob. (cited after Bakhturina, *Politika Rossijskoj Imperii*, 172–73.
305. Bakhturina, *Politika Rossijskoj Imperii*, 173. New rules were introduced in February 1915. Believers were now told to appeal directly to Evlogij, which would then be followed by a vote held in the parish.
306. Bakhturina, *Politika Rossijskoj Imperii*, 174.
307. Levyts'kyj, "Z dniv rosyjs'koï invazyï," *Dilo*, December 13, 1915. The k. u. k. authorities agreed, see the reports from Chyrów, near Przemyśl. HHStA, P.A.I., 931, Bl. 83–91: k. u. k. ambassador to the Holy See to Foreign Minister Count Berchtold, November 18, 1914. AVA, MdI, Präsidiale, Allgemeine Angelegenheiten, 22/2116: report by Legationsrat Baron Andrian on his trip to East Galicia, Cracow, July 26, 1915. The new Austrian governor of Galicia, General Hermann von Colard, also believed that the Ruthenian population had not understood the difference between the Greek Catholic Church and the Russian Orthodox Church. AVA, MdI, Präsidiale, Allgemeine Abteilung, 22/2117: Governor Colard to the Austrian minister of the interior, Heinold von Udyński, December 2, 1915.
308. Levyts'kyj, "Z dniv rosyjs'koï invazyï," *Dilo*, December 13, 1915. The Polish general of the Jesuit order Ledóchowski noticed that the Russian occupiers had exploited the similarity of the Greek Catholic and Russian Orthodox rites. PA, R-8975: report by Victor Naumann on a conversation with Ledóchowski, August 26, 1915.
309. Malyts'ka, "Na khvyljach svitovoï vijny," *Dilo*, March 27, 1937.
310. Bakhturina, *Politika Rossijskoj Imperii*, 166–67.

311. AVA, MdI, Präsidiale, Allgemeine Angelegenheiten, 22/2116: report by Legationsrat Baron Andrian on his trip to East Galicia, Cracow, July 26, 1915.
312. Levyts'kyj, "Z dniv rosyjs'koï invazyï," *Dilo*, December 9, 1915.
313. Gember, "Die Russen in Lemberg," 160. Levyts'kyj, "Z dniv rosyjs'koï invazyï," *Dilo*, December 4, 1915.
314. Janusz, *293 dni rządów rosyjskich we Lwowie*, 91, 112.
315. Levyts'kyj, "Z dniv rosyjs'koï invazyï," *Dilo*, December 4, 1915. Janusz, *293 dni rządów rosyjskich we Lwowie*, 233–34. Schall, Żydostwo Galicyjskie w czasie inwazji rosyjskiej, 18–19.
316. Levyts'kyj, "Z dniv rosyjs'koï invazyï," *Dilo*, December 3, 1915. TsDIAL, f. 694, op. 1, spr. 10, ark. 1–65: Russocki, diary entry.
317. RGVIA, f. 2005, op. 1, d. 12, l. 323–25: protocol of a meeting of a commission chaired by Major General Baron Knorring, November 7, 1915.
318. With twelve Polish, ten Ukrainian, and sixteen Jewish hostages. Białynia-Chołodecki, *Wspomnienia z lat niedoli i niewoli 1914–1918*, 28–80. The local authorities in L'viv only knew of thirty-two hostages. DALO, f. 3, op. 1, spr. 6518, ark. 3: city administration L'viv to k. u. k. high command (handwritten), June 26, 1917.
319. Białynia-Chołodecki, *Wspomnienia z lat niedoli i niewoli 1914–1918*, 28–80. "Der verschleppte Vize-Bürgermeister: Erinnerungen des Dr. Ph. Schleicher," *Neue Lemberger Zeitung*, June 22, 1917.
320. "V spravi vyvezenykh Rosijanami," *Dilo*, February 16, 1916. See also the list of names in HHStA, P.A.I., 931, Bl. 9–16: report by the k. u. k. governor's office for the Austrian Ministry of the Interior on "The Atrocities of the Russians against the Ukrainian Nation in Galicia," October 5, 1915.
321. Levyts'kyj, "Z dniv rosyjs'koï invazyï," *Dilo*, December 15, 1915. Malyts'ka, "Na khvyljach svitovoï vijny," *Dilo*, from March 28, 1937 to April 6, 1937.
322. DALO, f. 3, op. 1, spr. 6518, ark. 3: city administration L'viv to k. u. k. high command (handwritten), June 26, 1917.
323. RGVIA, f. 2005, op. 1, d. 12, l. 323–25: protocol of a meeting of a commission chaired by Major General Baron Knorring, November 7, 1915.
324. Białynia-Chołodecki, *Wspomnienia z lat niedoli i niewoli 1914–1918*, 27. Gember, "Die Russen in Lemberg," 167. Chlamtacz, *Lembergs politische Physiognomie*, 98–99.
325. Gember, "Die Russen in Lemberg," 166–67. Levyts'kyj, "Z dniv rosyjs'koï invazyï," *Dilo*, December 15, 1915. Wendland, *Die Russophilen in Galizien*, 562–66.
326. HHStA, P.A.I., 931: staff officer of the gendarmerie in L'viv to "K.-Stelle of the k. u. k. Etappenkommando" of the Second Army, October 19, 1915.
327. AVA, MdI, Präsidiale, Allgemeine Angelegenheiten, 22/2116: report by Legationsrat Baron Andrian on his trip to East Galicia, Cracow, July 26, 1915. TsDIAL, f. 694, op. 1, spr. 10, ark. 1–65: Russocki, diary entry.
328. TsDIAL, f. 408, op. 1, spr. 112: report of Greek Catholic priest Kyryl Levyts'kyj (1914).
329. DALO, f. 3, op. 1, spr. 6518, ark. 3: city administration L'viv to k. u. k. high command (handwritten), June 26, 1917.
330. PA, R-8977: the German consul in L'viv, Heinze to the German Chancellor Michaelis, August 31, 1917.
331. Gember, "Die Russen in Lemberg," 161. Kramarz, *Samorząd Lwowa w czasie pierwszej wojny światowej*, 53.
332. RGVIA, f. 2005, op. 1, d. 8, l. 3–5: Janushkevich to Goremykin, September 19, 1914.
333. RGVIA, f. 2005, op. 1, d. 8, l. 6–8: report of Chamberlain Bazili, September 16, 1914.
334. See letters of Rutowskis to Bobrinskij from November 1914 to January 1915; DALO, f. 3, op. 1, spr. 5905.

335. TsDIAL, f. 408, op. 1, spr. 112: report of Greek Catholic priest Kyryl Levyts'kyj (1914).
336. Ibid.
337. AVA, MdI, Präsidiale, Allgemeine Angelegenheiten, 22/2116: report by Legationsrat Baron Andrian on his trip to East Galicia, Cracow, July 26, 1915. HHStA, P.A.I, 931, Bl. 32–35: Police Commissioner Pajączkowski (in the town of Skole) to the presidium of the police directorate in Biała, November 7, 1914.
338. AVA, MdI, Präsidiale, Allgemeine Angelegenheiten, 22/2116: report by the k. u. k. inspector of the gendarmerie on the mood of the population in Galicia, December 21, 1915.
339. AVA, MdI, Präsidiale, Allgemeine Angelegenheiten, 22/2116: report by Legationsrat Baron Andrian on his trip to East Galicia, Cracow, July 26, 1915.
340. Ibid.
341. Ibid.
342. TsDIAL, f. 146, op. 6, spr. 1388, ark. 317–21: k. u. k. military command Przemyśl: political report on the mood of the population, November 19, 1916.
343. Janusz, *293 dni rządów rosyjskich we Lwowie*, 105.
344. Malyts'ka, "Na khvyljach svitovoï vijny," *Dilo*, March 27, 1937. RGVIA, f. 2005, op. 1, d. 12, l. 89–92: the Russian Ministry of the Interior to Janushkevich, October 1914.
345. TsDIAL, f. 309, op. 1, spr. 1399: Je. Kalytovs'kyj from Stryj, diary entry from September 11, 1914.
346. TsDIAL, f. 408, op. 1, spr. 112: report of Greek Catholic priest Kyryl Levyts'kyj (1914).
347. DALO, f. 350, op. 1, spr. 3933, ark. 45–47: Helene Rosner to k. u. k. War Ministry, October 28, 1915. On the corruptibility of the Russian town captain of L'viv E. N. Skalon, see Ansky, *The Enemy at his Pleasure*, 122–23.
348. Wendland, *Die Russophilen in Galizien*, 552.
349. RGVIA, f. 2005, op. 1, d. 12, l. 131: A. Terovskij (Petrograd) to Valerian Nikolaevich, October 19, 1915.
350. TsDIAK, f. 361, op. 1, spr. 677, ark. 4–5 (also in RGVIA, f. 2005, op. 1, d. 12, l. 42): the head of the provisional administration of the gendarmerie of the military general governorate in Galicia to the military general governor, April 27, 1915.
351. Schall, Żydostwo Galicyjskie w czasie inwazji rosyjskiej, 23–25. On the fear of being deported to Russia, see TsDIAL, f. 694, op. 1, spr. 10, ark. 1-65: Russocki, diary entry.
352. Janusz, *293 dni rządów rosyjskich we Lwowie*, 259–60. TsDIAL, f. 694, op. 1, spr. 10, ark. 1–65: Russocki, diary entry. Ansky, *The Enemy at his Pleasure*, 120–24.
353. TsDIAL, f. 694, op. 1, spr. 10, ark. 1–65: Russocki, diary entry. TsDIAL, f. 146, op. 8, spr. 1913: report on the activities of the local authorities in L'viv between July 1, 1915 and December 31, 1916.
354. Gember, "Die Russen in Lemberg," 168.
355. Schall, "Żydostwo Galicyjskie w czasie inwazji rosyjskiej," 26.
356. Levyts'kyj, "Z dniv rosyjs'koï invazyï," *Dilo*, December 15, 1915.
357. "Po zdobutju L'vova," *Dilo*, June 26, 1915.
358. TsDIAL, f. 146, op. 6, spr. 118, ark. 413–23: Major General Riml on his impressions after the reconquest of the city, July 26, 1915.
359. AVA, MdI, Präsidiale, Allgemeine Angelegenheiten, 22/2116: report by the k. u. k. inspector of the gendarmerie on the mood of the population in Galicia, December 21, 1915.
360. TsDIAL, f. 146, op. 6, spr. 1388, ark. 317–21: k. u. k. military command Przemyśl: political report on the mood of the population, November 19, 1916.
361. AVA, MdI, Präsidiale, Allgemeine Angelegenheiten, 22/2116: report by Legationsrat Baron Andrian on his trip to East Galicia, Cracow, July 26, 1915. AVA, MdI, Präsidiale,

Allgemeine Abteilung, 22/2117: gendarmerie major Schmidt (L'viv) to the inspector of the gendarmerie (Vienna), July 27, 1915.
362. Ibid.
363. TsDIAL, f. 146, op. 6, spr. 118, ark. 413–23: Major General Riml on his impressions after the reconquest of the city, July 26, 1915.
364. AVA, MdI, Präsidiale, Allgemeine Abteilung, 22/2117: gendarmerie major Schmidt (L'viv) to the inspector of the gendarmerie (Vienna), July 27, 1915.
365. TsDIAL, f. 146, op. 6, spr. 118, ark. 413–23: Major General Riml on his impressions after the reconquest of the city, July 26, 1915.
366. AVA, MdI, Präsidiale, Allgemeine Angelegenheiten, 22/2116: report by Legationsrat Baron Andrian on his trip to East Galicia, Cracow, July 26, 1915. TsDIAL, f. 146, op. 6, spr. 118, ark. 413–23: Major General Riml on his impressions after the reconquest of the city, July 26, 1915.
367. TsDIAL, f. 146, op. 6, spr. 118, ark. 413–23: Major General Riml on his impressions after the reconquest of the city, July 26, 1915.
368. AVA, MdI, Präsidiale, Allgemeine Angelegenheiten, 22/2116: report by Legationsrat Baron Andrian on his trip to East Galicia, Cracow, July 26, 1915. Similar in TsDIAL, f. 146, op. 6, spr. 118, ark. 413–23: Major General Riml on his impressions after the reconquest of the city, July 26, 1915.
369. AVA, MdI, Präsidiale, Allgemeine Angelegenheiten, 22/2116: report by Legationsrat Baron Andrian on his trip to East Galicia, Cracow, July 26, 1915.
370. Chlamtacz, *Lembergs politische Physiognomie*, 15–17.
371. Ibid., 30.
372. AVA, MdI, Präsidiale, Allgemeine Angelegenheiten, 22/2116: report by Legationsrat Baron Andrian on his trip to East Galicia, Cracow, July 26, 1915.
373. Ibid.
374. AVA, MdI, Präsidiale, Allgemeine Abteilung, 22/2117: Governor Colard to the Austrian minister of the interior, Heinold von Udyński, December 2, 1915.
375. TsDIAL, f. 146, op. 4, spr. 7687, ark. 174–76: Governor Diller to the Army High Command, November 30, 1916.
376. Ibid.
377. Ibid., ark 162–163: Army High Command to the presidium of the Council of Ministers (copy), March 27, 1918.
378. Ibid.
379. PA R-8975: report by the German consul general in L'viv, Heinze, February 1917.
380. AVA, MdI, Präsidiale, Allgemeine Abteilung, Unruhen, und Exzesse, 22/2119: notes of a police agent "Aus meinen Kriegserlebnissen in Galizien," from July 1 to December 15, 1916 (copied in the Army High Command, January 30, 1917).
381. HHStA, P.A.I., 931: staff officer of the gendarmerie in L'viv to "K.-Stelle of the k. u. k. Etappenkommando" of the Second Army, October 19, 1915.
382. PA, R-8975: Consul Heinze to the German ambassador in Vienna, Leonhard von Tschirschky und Bögendorff, February 21, 1916.
383. DALO, f. 350, op. 1, spr. 3628, ark. 18: report on collaborators at L'viv University (copy), April 28, 1916.
384. Białynia-Chołodecki, *Wspomnienia z lat niedoli i niewoli 1914–1918*, 27–28.
385. PA, 8975: *Kurier Lwowski*, August 30, 1918 (translation by the German consulate in L'viv).
386. AVA, MdI, Präsidiale, Allgemeine Abteilung, 22/2116: memorandum of the Ukrainian National Council (excerpts), October 11, 1915.

387. AVA, MdI, Präsidiale, Allgemeine Abteilung, 22/2116: presidium of the governor's office (Biała) to the Ministry of the Interior, November 24, 1915.
388. TsDIAL, f. 146, op. 8, spr. 1913: report on the activities of the local authorities in L'viv between July 1, 1915, and December 31, 1916. TsDIAL, f. 146, op. 4, spr. 5177, ark. 41–45: Józef Neumann and fifty-four L'viv councilors to the governor, July 1, 1915.
389. DALO, f. 3, op. 1, spr. 6011, ark. 21 ob: military command in L'viv to the government commissioner in L'viv, December 10, 1915. AVA, MdI, Präsidiale, Allgemeine Abteilung, 22/2117: report on the situation in L'viv from a source that the Foreign Ministry held to be reliable. The Foreign Ministry sent the report to Minister-President Karl Stürgkh, December 30, 1915.
390. Memorandum on the situation in L'viv (copy), sent by the Ministry of the Interior to Minister-President Karl Stürgkh, December 28, 1915.
391. TsDIAL, f. 146, op. 6, spr. 121, ark. 1266: Governor Count Huyn to the minister of the interior, August 16, 1918.
392. Białynia-Chołodecki, *Wspomnienia z lat niedoli i niewoli 1914–1918*, 16, 82–84.
393. Levyts'kyj, "Z dniv rosyjs'koï invazyï," *Dilo*, November 30, 1915.
394. Schall, Żydostwo Galicyjskie w czasie inwazji rosyjskiej, 26.
395. TsDIAL, f. 146, op. 6, spr. 118, ark. 413–23: Major General Riml on his impressions after the reconquest of the city, July 26, 1915.
396. AVA, MdI, Präsidiale, Allgemeine Angelegenheiten, 22/2116, Bl. 306–307: anonymous letter to the Ministry of the Interior, Vienna, n.d. (summer 1915).
397. Letters of the Zionist Executive Committee to the government, May 5, 1915, and July 25, 1915, *Jüdische Volksstimme*, August 20, 1915, 5 (cited after Gaisbauer, *Davidstern und Doppeladler*, 524–25).
398. Emphasis original. AVA, MdI, Präsidiale, Allgemeine Angelegenheiten 22/2116, 293–96: k. u. k. Statthaltereirat Galzewski in *Dziennik rozporządzeń c.k. Starostwa i Rady szkoln. ork. w Dolinie* 8, no. 3 (June 15, 1915) (translation from Polish to German). Appended to a letter of the Jewish National Association to the Ministry of the Interior, September 3, 1915.
399. AVA, MdI, Präsidiale Allg. Abt. 22/2117: presidium of the governor's office in Biała to the minister of the interior, December 1, 1915. AVA, MdI, Präsidiale, Allgemeine Abteilung 22/2116: protocol in the Ministry of the Interior, August 12, 1915. TsDIAL, f. 146, op. 1, spr. 1884, ark. 26–31: anonymous letter that reached the governor's office on August 12, 1915, the governor of Galicia to the Ministry of the Interior (draft with handwritten corrections), December 1, 1915.
400. AVA, MdI, Präsidiale Allg. Abt. 22/2117: police department of the district administration (Bezirkshauptmannschaft) in Przemyśl to the presidium of the governor's office, August 15, 1915.
401. Ibid.: District administration Tarnów to the presidium of governor's office, September 6, 1915.
402. Ibid.: District administration Sanok to the governor's office, August 26, 1915.
403. Ibid.: District administration Rzeszów to the governor's office, March 20, 1916.
404. Ibid.: District administration Sambor to the governor's office, September 24, 1915.
405. Ibid.: Director of Police Reinlender to the governor's office, September 22, 1915.
406. Ibid.
407. AVA, MdI, Präsidiale, Allgemeine Abteilung, 22/2116: anonymous report sent by the police directorate in Vienna to the Ministry of the Interior, July 9, 1915. Ibid.: note to the Ministry of the Interior, August 3, 1915.
408. Ibid.: Report by Legationsrat Baron Andrian on his trip to East Galicia, Cracow, July 26, 1915.

409. RGVA, f. 483, op. 1, d. 85, l. 11–17: Żydzi przeciw napaściom antypolskim, O.K.N.K.N., July 9, 1915.
410. TsDIAL, f. 701, op. 3, spr. 431, ark. 11: appeal by Dr. Emil Parnas and Herman Feldstein, March 1, 1917.
411. TsDIAL, f. 146, op. 6, spr. 1388, ark. 317–21: k. u. k. military command Przemyśl: political report on the mood of the population, November 19, 1916. See also ibid., ark. 324–25: k. u. k. city captain (Stadthauptmann) in Przemyśl to the governor's office, February 8, 1917.
412. AVA, MdI, Präsidiale, Allgemeine Abteilung, Unruhen, und Exzesse, 22/2119: report of the police agent Theodor Ahne: Aus meinen Kriegserlebnissen in Galizien, from July 1 to December 15, 1916 (copy); January 30, 1917.
413. "V uvil'nenim L'vovi," *Dilo*, July 24, 1915.
414. AVA, MdI, Präsidiale, Allgemeine Angelegenheiten, 22/2116, Bl. 316–17: report of the Ministry of the Interior, August 13, 1915. Ibid., Bl. 329: Minister of the Interior Heinold to the minister of trade and the minister of agriculture, August 13, 1915.
415. TsDIAL, f. 146, op. 4, spr. 7687, ark. 154–60: memorandum of the General Ukrainian National Council on the National House (Narodnym Dim), October 1915. Ibid., ark. 174–76: Governor Diller to the Army High Command, November 30, 1916.
416. Kost' Levyts'kyj, "Ukraïns'kyj narid u svitovij vijni," *Dilo*, January 7, 1916, 1–2.
417. For politics, economy, culture, education, public health, and for the occupied territories.
418. DALO, f. 350, op. 1, spr. 4042: police directorate in L'viv to the governor's office, April 19, 1916.
419. DALO, f. 350, op. 1, spr. 4232, ark. 2–22: k. u. k. Kriegsüberwachungsamt (Military Office for Surveillance) to governor's office (Biała), January 20, 1916. Ibid., ark. 23: protocol of a conversation with Polish journalists, April 30, 1916.
420. Memoranda of the General Ukrainian National Council (Vienna), August 1915 and October 29, 1915, in *Ereignisse in der Ukraine 1914–1922*, 84–92, 97–107, 107–109.
421. *Ereignisse in der Ukraine 1914–1922*, vol. 1, 335–87.
422. DALO, f. 350, op. 1, spr. 4232, ark. 2–22: k. u. k. Kriegsüberwachungsamt (Military Office for Surveillance) to the governor's office (Biała), January 20, 1916. Ibid., ark. 23: protocol of a conversation with Polish journalists, April 30, 1916.
423. TsDIAL, f. 146, op. 8, spr. 1924, ark. 1–3: General Ukrainian National Council to the governor of Galicia, General Hermann von Colard, October 1, 1915.
424. DALO, f. 1, op. 52, spr. 185: minister of the interior to the governor of Galicia, December 16, 1917.
425. *Dilo*, January 17, 1916.
426. Dr. Stefan Baran, Dr. Sydir Holubovych, the priest Oleksander Stefanovych, and Dr. Volodymyr Bachyns'kyj.
427. *Dilo*, April 23, 1916.
428. TsDIAL, f. 146, op. 4, spr. 5195, ark. 20–21: Police director Reinlender to the governor's office, December 17, 1916. TsDIAL, f. 146, op. 4, spr. 9, ark. 55–60: Reinlender to the governor's office, March 3, 1917.
429. *Kurier Lwowski* (morning edition), November 8, 1916.
430. DALO, f. 350, op. 1, spr. 4052: police directorate to governor's office, November 6, 1916.
431. *Kurier Lwowski*, November 12, 1916.
432. DALO, f. 350, op. 1, spr. 4052, ark. 4–6: Reinlender to the governor's office, December 18, 1916.
433. *Kurier Lwowski* (morning edition), November 8, 1916.

434. PA, R-8976: the German ambassador in Vienna to Chancellor Bethman-Hollweg, November 11, 1916. Ibid.: the German consul in L'viv, Heinze, to Bethmann-Hollweg, November 16, 1916. Ibid.: memorandum of Mykhajlo Lozhyns'kyj on the special status of Galicia, November 1916 (appendix of Heinze's letter to Bethmann-Hollweg).
435. DALO, f. 350, op. 1, spr. 4042, ark. 31–34: Reinlender to the governor's office, November 16, 1916. *Dilo*, November 9–11, 1916. TsDIAL, f. 146, op. 6, spr. 1387, ark. 109–110: report from the office for censorship of the Ministry of the Interior on the mood in Galicia, based on censored correspondence (copy), January 10, 1917.
436. DALO, f. 350, op. 1, spr. 4042, ark. 31–34: Reinlender to the governor's office, November 16, 1916. *Dilo*, November 9–11, 1916.
437. DALO, f. 350, op. 1, spr. 4042, ark. 43: the Ministry of the Interior mentioned Romanchuk, Bachyns'kyj, Tsehel's'kyj, and Petrushevych. Ministry of the Interior to police directorate, Vienna, November 9, 1916.
438. Klimecki, *Lwów 1918–1919*, 20–21.
439. The meeting demanded the unification of the Chełm region with the other occupied Ukrainian territories, the legalization of the Ukrainian language in these regions, the establishment of a state-funded Ukrainian school system, the fulfillment of religious and cultural demands, and financial support for the local population.
440. AVA, MdI, Präsidiale, Allgemeine Abteilung 22, Unruhen und Exzesse 2117, Bl. 304–11: police directorate in L'viv to the governor's office, February 6, 1917.
441. TsDIAL, f. 146, op. 4, spr. 5195, ark. 20–21: Reinlender to the governor's office, December 17, 1916. TsDIAL, f. 146, op. 4, spr. 9, ark. 55–60: Reinlender to the governor's office, March 3, 1917.
442. *Wiek Nowy*, February 6, 1917. PA, R-8975: Consul Heinze to Chancellor Bethmann-Hollweg, November 7, 1916.
443. *Dilo*, February 4, 1917.
444. "Ukraïnski syroty i uprava L'vova," *Dilo*, March 11, 1917. *Dilo*, March 15, 1917.
445. PA, R-8977: Heinze to Chancellor Michaelis, September 12, 1917. *Dilo*, September 9 and 10, 1917 (translated into German in PA, R-8977). *Gazeta Lwowska*, September 11, 1917 (translated into German in PA, R-8977).
446. DALO, f. 350, op. 1, spr. 4339, ark. 3–4: police directorate to the governor's office (Biała), May 15, 1917.
447. TsDIAL, f. 146, op. 6, spr. 1401, ark. 1026–31: report by the military command in Przemyśl, sent by the Ministry of the Interior to the governor's office, May 1918.
448. DALO, f. 350, op. 1, spr. 3607, ark. 54–58: police directorate to the Ministry of the Interior, May 1, 1917 (draft).
449. TsDIAL, f. 146, op. 4, spr. 5174, ark. 69–76: Advisory Council of the city of L'viv to the governor's office, August 31, 1917.
450. Ibid.: ark. 101–104: presidium of the Civic Committee to the governor's office, October 20, 1917. Ibid., ark. 112-118: report on the activities of the municipal council during the war, October 20, 1917. TsDIAL, f. 146, op. 4, spr. 5177, ark. 105: resolution of a meeting of citizens, October 20, 1917. Ibid., ark. 65–66: Chlamtacz et al. to the governor's office, November 21, 1917.
451. TsDIAL, f. 146, op. 4, spr. 7174, ark. 141–46: Governor Huyn to the minister of the interior, March 16, 1918.
452. TsDIAL, f. 146, op. 4, spr. 5177, ark. 174–75: member of the House of Deputies Dr. Straucher to k. u. k. minister-president (copy), January 20, 1918.
453. TsDIAL, f. 146, op. 4, spr. 5174, ark. 148–51: *Jüdisches Tagblatt* 296, December 31, 1917 (translation by the governor's office from Yiddish into German).

454. DALO, f. 350, op. 1, spr. 4341, ark. 4–7: police directorate in L'viv to the Ministry of the Interior (draft), October 15, 1917.
455. TsDIAL, f. 146, op. 4, spr. 197, ark. 1–2: Reinlender to the Ministry of the Interior, January 11, 1918. "Gegen eine Vereinigung mit Polen," *Ukrainische Korrespondenz* 4, no. 42/43 (November 28, 1917), 1–3.
456. "Die Debatte im Abgeordnetenhaus," *Ukrainische Korrespondenz* 4, no. 42/43 (November 28, 1917), 4–10.
457. A police spy overheard private conversations that showed that the participants were worried Vasyl'ko might organize meetings in the Bukovina to protest against the decisions of the congress and the unification of the Bukovina with East Galicia. They intended to urge deputies Spanul and Lukashevych (both from the Bukovina) to try to neutralize, if necessary, Vasyl'ko's activities. TsDIAL, f. 146, op. 6, spr. 1395, ark. 12–17: Police Director Reinlender to the Ministry of the Interior, December 28, 1917.
458. According to the Julian calendar that was still used in the Russian Empire at the time, the two revolutions occurred in February and October, respectively.
459. TsDIAL, f. 146, op. 4, spr. 5197, ark. 4–6: Reinlender to the Ministry of the Interior, January 13, 1918.
460. Ibid., ark. 14–16: police directorate in L'viv to the Ministry of the Interior, January 18, 1918.
461. PA, R-8978: Consul Heinze to German Chancellor Count Hertling, February 6, 1918. Ibid.: German Embassy in Vienna to Hertling, February 7, 1918. Ibid.: Berckheim from the "The Great Headquarters" in Spa to the Foreign Office, February 7, 1918. AVA, MdI, Präsidiale, Allgemeine Abteilung, 22/2119, Bl. 770–71: First Lieutenant Boelling to the plenipontary of the Royal Prussian Ministry of War at the k. u. k. Ministry of War, February 7, 1918.
462. AVA, MdI, Präsidiale, Allgemeine Abteilung 22/2118: parliamentary inquiry of the members of the Austrian Imperial Council (House of Deputies) Dr. Głąbinski and Count Skarbek, February 1918.
463. Ibid.: the minister for culture and education to the Ministry of the Interior, February 27, 1918.
464. TsDIAL, f. 717, op. 1, spr. 59, ark. 1: association of secondary school teachers to the Polish club in the Austrian parliament, February 12, 1918.
465. AVA, MdI, Präsidiale, Allgemeine Abteilung 22/2118: presidium of the education authorities in Galicia (Landesschulrat) to the Ministry of the Interior, February 19, 1918.
466. AVA, MdI, Präsidiale, Allgemeine Abteilung 22/2119, Bl. 98–117: report by the district attorney's office in L'viv, May 20, 1918.
467. Józef Skrzypek, "Ukraińcy w Austrii podczas wielkiej wojny i geneza zamachu na Lwów," *Niepodległość* 20, no. 53 (1939): 349–87, here 352–55.
468. AVA, MdI, Präsidiale, Allgemeine Abteilung 22/2118: Governor Huyn to the Ministry of the Interior, March 4, 1918.
469. TsDIAL, f. 146, op. 4, spr. 7687, ark. 162–63: k. u. k. Army High Command to k. u. k. presidium of the Council of Ministers (copy), March 27, 1918. PA, R-8978: Consul General Heinze to Chancellor Hertling, February 14, 1918.
470. Klimecki, *Lwów 1918–1919*, 22.
471. AVA, MdI, Präsidiale, Allgemeine Abteilung 22/2118: the president of the Galician Law Court, Adolf Czerwiński, to the governor of Galicia (copy sent to the Ministry of the Interior), February 25, 1918.
472. TsDIAL, f. 146, op. 4, spr. 7159, ark. 134–36: report from Wadowice for the governor's office, February 26, 1918.

473. DALO, f. 350, op. 1, spr. 4052, ark. 46–49: Reinlender to the Ministry of the Interior (draft), February 13, 1918.
474. Ibid., ark. 50: police directorate in L'viv to the Ministry of the Interior, February 14, 1918 (draft).
475. AVA, MdI, Präsidiale, Allgemeine Abteilung 22/2118: the president of the Galician Law Court, Adolf Czerwiński, to the governor of Galicia (copy sent to the Ministry of the Interior), February 25, 1918. *Gazeta Wieczorna*, February 23, 1918.
476. TsDIAL, f. 146, op. 4, spr. 7162, ark. 63–67 or AVA, MdI, Präsidiale, Allgemeine Abteilung 22/2118: reports about the actual situation in Galicia (excerpt), March 1918.
477. TsDIAL, f. 146, op. 6, spr. 1395, ark. 229–30: Huyn to the cabinet chancellery of the emperor (copy), February 17, 1918. *Neue Lemberger Zeitung*, February 19, 1918.
478. TsDIAL, f. 146, op. 6, spr. 1395, ark. 206–207: Czernin to Huyn, February 15, 1918.
479. Skrzypek, "Ukraińcy w Austrii podczas wielkiej wojny i geneza zamachu na Lwów," 358–60.
480. "Manifestacja Lwowa przeciw zaborowi Ziemi Chełmskiej i Podlasia," *Kurier Lwowski*, February 20, 1918. DALO, f. 350, op. 1, spr. 4052, ark. 55–56: Police directorate in L'viv to the Ministry of the Interior (draft), February 18, 1918.
481. TsDIAL, f. 146, op. 4, spr. 7162, ark. 63–67. Auch AVA, MdI, Präsidiale, Allgemeine Abteilung 22/2118: reports about current events in Galicia, March 1918.
482. PA, R-8978: Heinze to Chancellor Hertling, February 20, 1918.
483. Three Germans, ten Ukrainians, and one Jew had come to work. DALO, f. 257, op. 2, spr. 234, ark. 3–4: k. u. k. *Kriegstelegrafen- und Telefonzentrale* in L'viv to the representative of the *Chef des Feldtelegrafenwesens* in L'viv (copy), February 20, 1918.
484. Ibid., ark. 5–6: the representative of the *Chef des Feldtelegrafenwesens* in L'viv to *Chef des Feldtelegrafenwesens* (copy), February 21, 1918.
485. AVA, MdI, Präsidiale, Allgemeine Abteilung 22/2118: the president of the Galician Law Court, Adolf Czerwiński to the governor of Galicia (copy sent to the Ministry of the Interior), February 25, 1918.
486. TsDIAL, f. 146, op. 6, spr. 1396, ark. 315–24: military command in Przemyśl to the governor's office, February 19, 1918. AVA, MdI, Präsidiale, Allgemeine Abteilung 22/2118: the president of the Galician Law Court, Adolf Czerwiński, to the governor of Galicia (copy sent to the Ministry of the Interior), February 25, 1918.
487. Ibid.: reports from different Galician court districts, March 1918.
488. Ibid: report on riots in Galicia, March 1918.
489. Ibid.: Governor Huyn to the Ministry of the Interior, March 4, 1918.
490. Ibid.: Huyn to the Ministry of the Interior, June 1, 1918.
491. Ibid.: Huyn to the Ministry of the Interior, March 4, 1918.
492. Ibid.
493. AVA, MdI, Präsidiale, Allgemeine Abteilung 22/2118: report on riots in L'viv, March 2, 1918.
494. TsDIAL, f. 146, op. 6, spr. 1396, ark. 315–24: military command in Przemyśl to the governor's office, February 19, 1918.
495. "Ukraińcy lwowscy prowokują," *Gazeta Wieczorna*, February 14, 1918. PA, R-8978: Heinze to Chancellor Hertling, December 14, 1918. Skrzypek, "Ukraińcy w Austrii podczas wielkiej wojny i geneza zamachu na Lwów," 357.
496. TsDIAL, f. 146, op. 4, spr. 7159, ark. 121: report in the governor's office of Ukrainian manifestations (reported by the district captains—*Bezirkshauptleute*, by phone), February 23, 1918.
497. Ibid.: ark. 122: Police director Reinlender (L'viv) to the Ministry of the Interior, February 23, 1918. AVA, MdI, Präsidiale, Allgemeine Angelegenheiten 22/2118: report by

the head of the division for East Galicia in the Ministry of Justice, Hofrat von Dworski, March 3, 1918.
498. TsDIAL, f. 146, op. 4, spr. 7159, ark. 161–62: report by a member of the governor's office from Jaroslaw for the presidium of the governor's office, March 4, 1918.
499. Ibid., ark. 163–64: report by a member of the governor's office from Drohobycz, March 4, 1918.
500. Ibid., ark. 180–82: head of the district authorities in Śniatyn to the governor's office, March 4, 1918.
501. TsDIAL, f. 146, op. 6, spr. 1401, ark. 1026–31: report by the military command in Przemyśl, May 1918.
502. DALO, f. 257, op. 1, spr. 22, ark. 16–18: report by the Austrian Rittmeister of the gendarmerie, L. Hinz, March 8, 1918 (copy, excerpt).
503. DALO, f. 350, op. 1, spr. 4042, ark. 49–65: police directorate in L'viv to the Ministry of the Interior (draft), March 26, 1918. Skrzypek, "Ukraińcy w Austrii podczas wielkiej wojny i geneza zamachu na Lwów," 370.
504. TsDIAL, f. 146, op. 8, spr. 1913: record of the activities of the administration of the royal capital L'viv between July 1, 1915, and December 31, 1916.
505. DALO, f. 3, op. 1, spr. 6013, ark. 48: k. u. k. city command L'viv to k. u. k. government commissioner in L'viv, August 7, 1915.
506. DALO, f. 350, op. 1, spr. 3879: k. u. k. city command L'viv to the presidium of the police directorate (Präsidium der Polizeidirektion), L'viv, August 25, 1915.
507. The municipality also had to provide accommodations for officers. Between July 1915 and December 1916, there were 72,000 cases of billeting or quartering of troops. TsDIAL, f. 146, op. 8, spr. 1913: record of the activities of the administration of the royal capital L'viv between July 1, 1915, and December 31, 1916.
508. *Dilo*, February 15, 1916.
509. AVA, MdI, Präsidiale, Allgemeine Abteilung, 22/2117: report on the situation in L'viv, December 30 or 28, 1915.
510. Ibid.
511. TsDIAL, f. 146, op. 8, spr. 1913: record of the activities of the administration of the royal capital L'viv between July 1, 1915, and December 31, 1916.
512. DALO, f. 3, op. 1, spr. 6173, ark. 66–71: Schleicher to the Petroleum Center (Petroleum-Zentrale) in Vienna, January 3, 1917.
513. DALO, f. 350, op. 1, spr. 4329, ark. 11: Policeman Franz Schromm to the office of the military police in L'viv, January 27, 1917.
514. TsDIAL, f. 146, op. 6, spr. 1387, ark. 109–10: report by the office for censorship of the Ministry of the Interior on the mood in Galicia, based on censored correspondence (copy), January 10, 1917.
515. DALO, f. 3, op. 1, spr. 6213, ark. 6–9: City Administration L'viv to k. u. k. High Command, March 8, 1917.
516. Białynia-Chołodecki, *Wspomnienia z lat niedoli i niewoli 1914–1918*, 80–81.
517. DALO, f. 3, op. 1, spr. 6213, ark. 6–9: City Administration L'viv to k. u. k. High Command, March 8, 1917.
518. Ibid., ark. 10–13: protocol of a meeting of the municipal provision commission with members of the provisional city council at the governor's office in Biała on April 17.
519. DALO, f. 350, op. 1, spr. 4329, ark. 18: military police in L'viv to the police directorate in L'viv, March 14, 1917.
520. DALO, f. 3, op. 1, spr. 6213, ark. 17–24: Schleicher to the Presidium of the Council of Ministers, June 10, 1917.
521. Ibid., ark. 27–28: resolution of a meeting of citizens, August 23, 1917.

522. Ibid., ark. 50: resolution of a meeting of citizens, December 11, 1917.
523. AVA, MdI, Präsidiale, Allgemeine Abteilung 22/2117: police directorate in L'viv to the Ministry of the Interior, October 17, 1917.
524. Fifty krone for one kilogram of butter and forty krone for one kilogram of bacon.
525. DALO, f. 3, op. 1, spr. 6173, ark. 68–75: Schleicher to the Austrian government, January 15, 1918.
526. Ibid., ark 77–81: City Administration L'viv to the minister for Galicia, Juliusz Twardowski, March 21, 1918
527. TsDIAL, f. 505, op. 1, spr. 54: report of the Committee for the Assistance of the Victims of the Pogrom in L'viv.
528. AVA, MdI, Präsidiale, Allgemeine Angelegenheiten 22/2118: police directorate in L'viv to the Ministry of the Interior (telegram), June 9, 1918.
529. DALO, f. 350, op. 1, spr. 4328, ark. 2 and 6: police directorate in L'viv to the Ministry of the Interior (two telegrams), October 9, 1917.
530. Ibid., ark. 14: police directorate in L'viv to the Ministry of the Interior (telegram), January 17, 1918.
531. Ibid., ark. 16–18: police directorate to the Ministry of the Interior (telegram, draft), January 23, 1918.
532. Ibid., ark. 20–21: police directorate to the Ministry of the Interior (telegram), January 28, 1918.
533. AVA, MdI, Präsidiale, Allgemeine Abteilung 22/2119: Ministry for Railroads to the Ministry for National Defense (Landesverteidigung) (copy), June 26, 1918.
534. TsDIAL, f. 146, op. 6, spr. 1401, ark. 1026–31: k. u. k. minister of the interior to Governor Huyn based on a report by the military command in Przemyśl, May 12, 1918.
535. Before the war, Major General Fischer was a staff officer in the national gendarmerie (13th gendarmerie command). At the beginning of the war, he organized the defense of the Bukovina. After the retreat of the Russian troops, he created a network of agents in Galicia that operated independently from the respective military agencies. He had spies in L'viv, Cracow, and various provincial towns. His reports were sent to the Army High Command and the military chancellery of the emperor. More information on Fischer in DALO, f. 257, op. 2, spr. 234.
536. AVA, MdI, Präsidiale, Allgemeine Abteilung 22/2119, Bl. 453–57: report by Major General Fischer (gendarmerie command for Galicia and the Bukovina) to the Ministry for National Defense (Landesverteidigung), March 20, 1918.
537. AVA, MdI, Präsidiale, Allgemeine Abteilung 22/2118: Governor Huyn to the Ministry of the Interior, April 14, 1918.
538. AVA, MdI, Präsidiale, Allgemeine Abteilung 22/2118: report by the Intelligence Department (Nachrichtenabteilung) of the Army High Command to the Ministry of the Interior, June 2, 1918. TsDIAL, f. 146, op. 6, spr. 1402, ark. 1236–31: Summary of the intelligence report for the district captains (Bezirkshauptleute), September 15, 1918.
539. TsDIAL, f. 146, op. 6, spr. 1405, ark. 1950–56: Reinlender to the governor's office, May 25, 1918. Skrzypek, "Ukraińcy w Austrii podczas wielkiej wojny i geneza zamachu na Lwów," 357.
540. AVA, MdI, Präsidiale, Allgemeine Abteilung 22/2119: Ministry for National Defense (Landesverteidigung) to the Ministry of the Interior, May 30, 1918.
541. TsDIAL, f. 146, op. 8, spr. 2688a, ark. 13–15: Reinlender to the district attorney in L'viv, February 26, 1918.
542. TsDIAL, f. 146, op. 8, spr. 2684, ark. 67-69: Reinlender to the district attorney in L'viv, June 19, 1918.

543. Ibid., ark. 92–96: presidium of the police directorate in L'viv, protocol of the questioning of the priest Zdisław Łuczycki (German translation from Polish), July 4, 1918.
544. Ibid., ark. 88–91: police directorate to the district attorney in L'viv, July 4, 1918.
545. AVA, MdI, Präsidiale, Allgemeine Abteilung 22/2118: report on riots in Galicia, March 1918. The district captain (Bezirkshauptmann or starost) of Rzeszów reported that not only had the glass windows of Jewish shops been smashed but also those of Catholic shops. He argued that therefore the violence was not inspired by anti-Semitism but was the result of supply problems. TsDIAL, f. 146, op. 8, spr. 2684, ark. 92: Starost of Rzeszów to the governor's office. On anti-Semitic violence, see Frank Golczewski, *Polnisch-jüdische Beziehungen 1881–1922: Eine Studie zur Geschichte des Antisemitismus in Osteuropa* (Wiesbaden: Steiner, 1981).
546. TsDIAL, f. 146, op. 8, spr. 2683, ark. 53–55: presidium of the police directorate in Cracow to the governor's office (copy), June 16, 1918.
547. AVA; MdI, Präsidiale, Allgemeine Abteilung 22/2119, Bl. 632–37: parliamentary question in the House of Deputies (Vienna) by Straucher et al., June 21, 1918.
548. TsDIAL, f. 146, op. 8, spr. 2684, ark. 58–60: the Jewish lawyer Leon Adler to the governor's office, April 20, 1918.
549. Ibid., ark. 55–57: report of the police clerk Tomasz Fedorowicz on anti-Jewish riots in Cracow, May 31, 1918.
550. TsDIAL, f. 146, op. 8, spr. 2683, ark. 51: minister of the interior to Count Huyn (telegram), April 23, 1918.
551. TsDIAL, f. 146, op. 4, spr. 7162, ark. 83: Starost of Strzyzów to the heads of the village and town administrations, March 11, 1918.
552. TsDIAL, f. 146, op. 8, spr. 2684, ark. 112–15: report by the office of the inspector general of the Austrian Railroads for the Ministry for Railroads (copy), June 19, 1918.
553. DALO, f. 257, op. 2, spr. 234, ark. 13–14: report by Fischer no. 190, July 22, 1918.
554. DALO, f. 257, op. 1, spr. 22, ark. 20: report by Rittmeister L. Hintz, March 8, 1918 (copy).
555. TsDIAL, f. 146, op. 6, spr. 1401, ark. 1026–31: report by the military command in Przemyśl, sent by the Ministry of the Interior to the governor's office, May 1918.
556. TsDIAL, f. 146, op. 8, spr. 1684, ark. 81: Reinlender to the governor's office, June 3, 1918.
557. DALO, f. 350, op. 1, spr. 4052, ark. 83: minister of the interior to the governor's office (excerpt), May 16, 1918.
558. AVA, MdI, Präsidiale, Allgemeine Abteilung 22/2119, Bl. 632–37: parliamentary question in the House of Deputies by Straucher et al., July 22, 1918.
559. AVA, MdI, Präsidiale, Allgemeine Abteilung 22/2118: report by the intelligence department (Nachrichtenabteilung) of the Army High Command to the Ministry of the Interior, June 2, 1918.
560. DALO, f. 27, op. 2, spr. 234, ark. 13–17: report by Major General Fischer, August 22, 1918.
561. HHStA, P.A.I. 931, Bl. 407–19: intelligence department of the military governorate (Militärgouvernment) in Poland: report on Jewish newspapers, August 4, 1918.
562. AVA, MdI, Präsidiale, Allgemeine Abteilung 22/2119: the member of the Imperial Council (House of Deputies) Dr. Straucher to the minister-president, August 9, 1918.
563. Ibid.: Straucher to the minister-president, October 14, 1918 (copy).
564. TsDIAL, f. 146, op. 4, spr. 5197, ark. 138–44: presentation of an official of the governor's office (Statthaltereirat Wenz) at a meeting in the Ministry of the Interior in Vienna, August 28, 1918.

565. TsDIAL, f. 146, op. 6, spr. 1402, ark. 1262–64: k. u. k. Ministry of War, intelligence department of the Army High Command to the Ministry of the Interior, June 16, 1918.
566. AVA, MdI, Präsidiale, Allgemeine Abteilung 22/2118: report by the command of the gendarmie on events in Galicia for the Intelligence Department of the Army High Command, June 2, 1918.
567. TsDIAL, f. 146, op. 6, spr. 1401, ark. 1026–31: report by the military command in Przemyśl, sent by the Ministry of the Interior to the governor's office, May 1918.
568. TsDIAL, f. 146, op. 6, spr. 121, ark. 1266: Governor Count Huyn to the minister of the interior, August 16, 1918.
569. AVA, MdI, Präsidiale, Allgemeine Abteilung 22/2119: Ministry for National Defense (Landesverteidigung) to the Ministry of the Interior, May 30, 1918. TsDIAL, f. 146, op. 8, spr. 2690, ark. 3–6: Gendarmerie command no. 5 (L'viv) to the Ministry for National Defense, June 1, 1918.
570. TsDIAL, f. 146, op. 8, spr. 2696, ark. 10–16: Proclamation "An die polnische Schuljugend" (translated from Polish to German by Rittmeister Schicke, copy), May 12, 1918.
571. TsDIAL, f. 146, op. 8, spr. 2690, ark. 3–6: command of the gendarmerie (*Landesgendarmeriekommando*) no. 5 to the Ministry for National Defence (*Landesverteidigung*) (copy for the Ministry of the Interior), June 1, 1918. TsDIAL, f. 146, op. 6, spr. 1402, ark. 1262–63: intelligence department of the Army High Command to the War Ministry, June 16, 1918.
572. DALO, f. 257, op. 2, spr. 234, ark. 13–14: report by Major General Fischer no. 190, July 22, 1918.
573. AVA, MdI, Präsidiale, Allgemeine Abteilung 22/2118: report by the intelligence department (Nachrichtenabteilung) of the Army High Command to the Ministry of the Interior, June 2, 1918.
574. DALO, f. 257, op. 2, spr. 234, ark. 13–14: Report by Major General Fischer no. 190 (copy, excerpt), July 22, 1918.
575. Ibid.
576. AVA, MdI, Präsidiale, Allgemeine Abteilung 22/2118: report by the intelligence department (Nachrichtenabteilung) of the Army High Command to the Ministry of the Interior, June 2, 1918.
577. DALO, f. 27, op. 2, spr. 234, ark. 13–17: report by Major General Fischer no. 330 (copy, excerpt), August 22, 1918.
578. HHStA, P.A.I. 931, Bl. 325–27: Army High Command to the representative of the Foreign Ministry, July 27, 1918.
579. TsDIAL, f. 146, op. 6, spr. 1403, ark. 1428–32: Ministry of National Defense (Landesverteidigung) to the Ministry of the Interior (copy), September 4, 1918.
580. Klimecki, *Polsko-ukraińska wojna o Lwów i Galicję Wschodnią 1918–1919*, 42–43.
581. AVA, MdI, Präsidiale, Allgemeine Abteilung 22/2118: report by the intelligence department (Nachrichtenabteilung) of the Army High Command to the Ministry of the Interior, June 2, 1918. TsDIAL, f. 146, op. 6, spr. 1402, ark. 1262–64: k. u. k. Ministry of War, intelligence department (Nachrichtenabteilung) of the Army High Command to the Ministry of the Interior, Vienna, June 16, 1918.
582. DALO, f. 257, op. 2, spr. 234, ark. 13–14: report by General Major Fischer no. 190, July 22, 1918.
583. HHStA, P.A.I. 931, Bl. 325–27: Army High Command to the representative of the Foreign Ministry, July 27, 1918.
584. Klimecki, *Lwów 1918–1919*, 29–30.
585. TsDIAL, f. 146, op. 6, spr. 1402, ark. 1236–39: governor's office to all district captains (starosty, in Polish), September 15, 1918.

586. DALO, f. 27, op. 2, spr. 234, ark. 13–17: report by Major General Fischer no. 330 (copy, excerpt), August 22, 1918.
587. TsDIAL, f. 837, op. 1, spr. 71, ark. 15–20: report by a Polish man from Tłumacz, after 1919.

CHAPTER 3

The Fight for the City

Маніфестантам польськости Львова[1]
Чого ви кричите? Ми віримо, панове,
Що перлою для вас був до согодня Львів.
З часу, як вас сюди ваш Казимір привів,
Було в нім серед нас житте для вас шодкове?

To the manifestants of Polishness in L'viv
Why are you shouting?
We believe, gentlemen,
that up to the present day L'viv is a jewel for you.
Since the time when your Kazimierz led you here,
Was life harmful for you there in our midst?

Third Regime Change: The Ukrainian Coup d'État

The Last Days of Austrian Rule

By October 1918 the defeat of the Central Powers was sealed and the dissolution of the Habsburg Empire imminent. Even civil servants had begun deserting the monarchy en masse. The cost-of-living allowance in September had fallen far short of expectations and "resentment [was] enormous." State employees went on strike to demand substantial wage increases. Around five thousand Polish and four hundred Ukrainian government employees held separate meetings on October 6 to discuss the matter after previously coordinating their demands. Economic and class interests still trumped national differences.[2] Polish government employees—which included important railroad officials and municipal and regional civil servants—demanded a doubling of their inflation compensation. Only with difficulty was the chairman of the meeting able to deter the assembled protesters from marching on the governor's office. A representative of the Ukrainian government employees declared that they supported the demands of their Polish colleagues. At the Ukrainian meeting held at the same time, a Polish speaker declared his solidarity with his Ukrainian colleagues.[3]

But this amity between Polish and Ukrainian civil servants remained an isolated episode. In the days that followed, events began to unfold at breakneck speed. At the heart of everything lay the decision about which nation would exercise control over East Galicia in the future. The Regency Council in Warsaw issued a statement on October 7 to prepare the way for complete independence. The Polish population of L'viv responded enthusiastically: "The Proclamation of the Warsaw Regency Council has elicited much enthusiasm among the Polish population in the Crown land, which manifests itself in greater or fewer numbers of flags displayed on houses, in solemn Masses, and in the sessions of autonomous corporations."[4]

Polish political parties used every opportunity to call for mass demonstrations. It was a matter of occupying the public space both symbolically and physically. One such opportunity presented itself with the return of the Polish legionaries released from captivity and their arrival at L'viv's main station on the evening of October 9. They were welcomed by several thousand people who escorted them to the Mickiewicz monument, where speakers invoked the Polish tradition of martyrdom as the moral legitimation for a rebirth of the Polish state.[5]

At two well-attended meetings held on the same day, representatives of the National Democratic Party and some of the city's dignitaries discussed the proposals for peace tendered to the Entente by Germany and Austria on October 4. The meeting's participants agreed that the creation of a new Polish state was imminent. In anticipation of this event, both meetings issued identical resolutions, declaring that Galician Poles henceforth considered themselves citizens of an independent Poland. All ties at variance with their loyalty to Poland—in other words, all obligations towards Austria—were considered to be dissolved. The celebratory mood of the Poles was reflected on the streets of the city. Many private residences were decorated with red and white flags, and the police authorities noted the population's buoyant mood.[6] Less than one week later the National Democrat Stanisław Głąbiński and the Social Democrat Ignacy Daszyński declared in the House of Deputies of the Imperial Council that Polish deputies would henceforth also consider themselves to be citizens of Poland. The qualification "also" had been included at the urging of conservative members from Cracow who did not wish to break all ties with Austria. But the overwhelming majority of Polish deputies no longer attached any importance to this reservation.[7]

Everything appeared to point to East Galicia being included in the new Polish state. But the Polish elites had reckoned without Ukrainian nationalism. Ukrainian party leaders were only prepared to begin negotiations based on the partition of Galicia. The governor of Galicia, Count Karl von Huyn, feared that if no concessions were made to the Ukrainians "riots of the Bolshevik kind" would break out, which would be directed against the big landowners and the urban intelligentsia.[8] In Galicia, armed gangs of deserters and former prisoners of war continued to roam the countryside and menace the rural population. The military authorities also feared a Bolshevik revolution.[9]

The Ukrainian National Council was opposed to the way events were unfolding and began making its own preparations in parallel to its Polish opponents for the momentous day when the future of Galicia would be decided. Both sides invoked the people's right of self-determination postulated by the American president Woodrow Wilson as the organizing principle for the postwar era in his fourteen-point program published on January 8, 1918. Although all relevant groups on the Polish side had now settled on an independent Polish state, which would include the entire Crown land, opinions among Ukrainians were divided.

On October 16, Emperor Charles launched a last-ditch attempt to save the monarchy. An Imperial Manifesto proposed transforming the Cisleithanian part of the empire into a confederation. The following day, during a session of the Ukrainian National Council, a bitter altercation erupted between a minority of delegates who demanded the immediate incorporation of East Galicia into the Ukrainian People's Republic and the majority who continued to back an Austro-Ukrainian solution, even though the emperor had still not committed to partitioning the Crown lands. Emperor Charles had only offered to create a Ukrainian curia, a block of reserved seats for Ukrainian delegates, in the Diet.[10] The members of the Ukrainian constituent assembly met up for preliminary discussions on October 18. The fifty-seven-man delegation consisted of Ukrainian members of the Austrian House of Lords, deputies from the Ukrainian Parliamentary Representation, Ukrainian delegates to the Diet and three representatives from each of the Ukrainian political parties (National Democratic Party, Radicals, Social Democratic Party, and Christian Social Party). The secret consultations even included a few Hungarian Ukrainian representatives. But the secrecy of these proceedings left much to be desired: one member of the group was an informer who kept the gendarmerie fully informed of the progress of the talks. Archbishop Sheptyts'kyj was present but largely abstained from the discussions. However, his presence together with that of two more Greek Catholic bishops showed that the Greek Catholic Church broadly supported Ukrainian attempts to set up a state. The Ukrainian Parliamentary Representation and numerous delegates from Bukovina, all of whom favored an Austro-Ukrainian solution, were in the majority. After a fierce and controversial discussion, the assembly approved union with Austria against the stated wishes of party representatives from the rest of the Crown land. Advocates of the Austro-Ukrainian solution justified their decision by pointing out that in the event of the region being incorporated in Ukraïna, they anticipated that only part of East Galicia, extending to the Bug River, would be ceded to them. But if the Ukrainian question was to be solved as proposed in the Imperial Manifesto, the Ukrainian delegates had understood the Austrian government officials as having promised that East Galicia would not be divided. The borders of the new state, which would be affiliated with Austria, would be the San, Zbrucz, and Serit Rivers, borders that included areas in Hungary inhabited by Ukrainians. The small Social Democratic Party opposed the plan. It had loosened its ties to Austria earlier than any of the other parties had and was backing a national policy and the revolutionary agrarian demands. At a well-attended meeting Semen Vityk, a delegate to the Imperial Council, demanded the immediate unification of Ukrainian territories and the abolition of large estates in the new states. To achieve these aims, the party urged people to break with the principle of national solidarity, resolving "to begin the class war against the bourgeois Ukrainian parties using all available means." The party proposed appealing to East Ukrainians for support and mobilizing Ukrainian workers, students, and peasants' sons in a collective struggle to abolish large landed estates. But the majority parties were unfazed.[11] On October 19, the constituent assembly held its opening session. It laid claim to all areas east of the San River, including the Lemko region, northwest Bukovina, and Transcarpathian Rus, which was part of Hungary. The chairman of the constituent assembly, Jevhen Petrushevych, proclaimed the creation of a Ukrainian state within the borders of these territories. In contrast to the Habsburg Empire, the constituent assembly accepted Jews as a nation in their own right. The Ukrainian constitution was based on democratic principles and incorporated prevailing ideas about the protection offered to minorities. The cornerstones of the constitution were universal, free, and equal suffrage and voting by secret ballot; minorities were to be given cultural autonomy and would be entitled to send representatives to the Ukrainian National Council. The Austrian foreign ministry was henceforth denied the right to speak on behalf of Ukrainian territories.[12] Notwithstanding this rejection of Austrian rule, it was proposed that the new state would initially be associated in some unspecified way with the Austro-Hungarian monarchy. This Austro-Ukrainian plan was only pushed through in the teeth of strong resistance by a minority of the delegates, who, in their turn, demanded immediate unification with the Ukrainian People's Republic. After unavailingly demanding a power of veto, the Social Democrats declared their intention of seceding and walked out on the assembly.[13] The next day, Petrushevych traveled to Vienna to speak for Ukrainian interests, while Kost' Levyts'kyj remained in L'viv to head up a six-man committee that would push on with creating a Ukrainian administration.

The Ukrainian elites were still uncertain under which form of government they would ultimately exist as a nation. But they were certain of one thing: "that under no circumstances" would the territories they claimed be associated in any shape or form with a Polish state. "Polish rule in these territories will now end forever. That is how matters stand and it cannot be otherwise; the guarantee for this is given by those millions of sons and daughters of the Ukrainian nation [*narid*] in this country who know today that the worst terms of opprobrium will be directed against our generation by future generations if we are not all prepared to come together and raise our heads and shed our blood for the freedom of our country, for the descendants of the Fatherland, for our grandsons and great-grandsons."[14]

The Poles, according to the Ukrainian newspaper *Dilo*, faced a choice between war and peace. The Ukrainians were prepared to offer them minority rights—the same rights offered to Jews and Germans—and an "equitable life" in a Ukrainian state.[15] Jevhen Petrushevych and Kost' Levtys'kyj had already threatened in the House of Deputies on October 4 and 9 to unite East Galicia with Ukraïna if the Austrian government made any attempt to hand over the whole of the Crown land to the Poles.[16]

The Polish public failed to recognize how serious the Ukrainian attempts were to create their own state, considering such Ukrainian pronouncements as only the words of a minority group which did not speak for the mass of the "Ruthenian" population. The general mood of euphoria among the Poles contributed to this dangerous self-deception. The momentous, historical day of the "rebirth of Poland" was imminent. On October 20, 1918, the members of the L'viv city council met in solemn assembly in the town hall at noon. Without mentioning, even in passing, the recent proclamation of a Ukrainian state, the deputy government commissioner for L'viv, Marceli Chlamtacz, read out a resolution "in which the city council on behalf of the population of Lwów expresses its sincere delight with the manifesto of the Regency Council, as it views therein the realization of the fervent ambitions of the Poles concerning the unification of all Polish territories." The resolution was adopted by "tumultuous acclamation." Only the Ukrainian member of the advisory council, the Greek Catholic clergyman Teodosij Lezhohubs'k'yj, protested on behalf of Ukrainians "against every unlawful attempt on East Galicia by Poland." But he hoped that "both closely related peoples can live in harmony and work for the good of their own citizens." He declared that both Poles and Ukrainians should have their own state.[17] But on the publicly posted bills the municipal council confirmed the city's loyalty to the state of Poland: "Polish Lwów remains, as it always was, loyal to Poland." The city council justified the Polish claims by pointing to the sacrifices made for the city by generations of Poles and to the blood that had flowed in its defense. The "great felicity of the people is the fruit of the suffering and the immeasurable sacrifices of our ancestors." The mistakes of the past and the disputes and bickering between parties were condemned, and the nation's unity was evoked. The main goal now had to be "to live and die for the Polish state whose citizens we consider ourselves to be." The municipal council of L'viv demanded that the

Polish nation be accorded equal status with other nations "just as we recognize and wish to recognize other nations, particularly the citizens of the fraternal clan living together with us on this soil as an equal nation." But this was to be the only reference to the Ukrainians. The municipal council avoided direct confrontations with the remaining imperial-royal authorities and troops. It was keen to ensure a peaceful and orderly transfer of power. Until the day when the relationship to the Austrian state would be finally settled, the municipal council intended to tolerate the continuing authority of the Austrian state in Galicia. This was made much easier by the fact that authority rested predominantly in the hands of "ardently Polish citizens." Finally, the municipal council, speaking on behalf of the population of the ancient "bulwark of the republic," declared its solidarity with the Regency Council and announced its intention of sending a delegation to Warsaw to pay its respects to the Regency Council. The session ended with the delegates cheering an independent Polish state. Between fifteen and twenty thousand people gathered in front of the town hall; after the resolution was read, the crowd cheered the Regency Council and began singing patriotic songs. Between one and two thousand students then progressed to the Mickiewicz monument, where yet more speeches were made and more songs sung. Finally the crowd dispersed peacefully.[18]

At the same time three thousand Ukrainians had assembled in front of St. George's Cathedral to celebrate the proclamation of a Ukrainian state which had occurred the previous day. Kost' Levyts'kyj gave a brief speech and affirmed that the current Austro-Ukrainian solution did not preclude subsequent unification with Ukraïna. However, Vityk, the Social Democratic delegate to the Imperial Council, argued for the immediate unification with Ukraïna and made a scathing attack on the Poles, particularly the Polish nobility. After singing a number of patriotic songs the crowd also dispersed peacefully.[19]

In the days that followed, the frenzy of activities in the Crown land's capital continued. On October 24, the Polish Citizens Club called for a mass demonstration in front of the building of the Sokół sports club. About ten thousand people, most of them shopkeepers, tradesmen, workmen, members of the intelligentsia, and students, assembled to applaud a resolution in which L'viv was referred to as a Polish city. Most Polish shops were closed for the duration of the rally to emphasize the importance of the demonstration.[20] *Dilo* accused the Poles of using such rallies and similar demonstrations to mask the fact that in East Galicia, the Poles were in the minority. The newspaper argued that this amounted to co-opting the Ukrainian inhabitants of L'viv against their will. The Poles were not interested in coming to an understanding; instead, as a national minority living on Ukrainian soil they wanted to rule over the Ukrainians. They were usurpers.[21]

Governor Huyn continued his attempts to ensure peace and order in the region. On October 28 he sent an urgent appeal to all district commissioners, sympathizing with their conflict of loyalty. He asked them to continue to do their duty until a Polish state was set up. He did not fail to point out that the Ukrainians also wished to exercise their right to an independent existence. Huyn warned obliquely of the possibility of a Ukrainian or Polish coup. To prevent anarchy it would be necessary for the outgoing state authorities to continue to wield power until power could be transferred to a new state organization in an orderly manner. After five years of war, much suffering, and many privations it was very understandable that people found it difficult to accept such balanced reasoning. But it was the duty, in particular of political civil servants, to ensure peace and order until the imminent day of peace would arrive.[22]

Huyn's pleas for moderation were unsuccessful. The proclamation of a Czechoslovak Republic in Prague on October 28, 1918, impressed the Polish elites. On the same day, after many difficult negotiations, representatives from the biggest Polish political parties came to an agreement in Cracow, whereby a Polish Liquidation Committee (Polska Komisja Likwidacyjna, PKL) would be set up and would assume government of the Austrian part of partitioned Poland. The committee would be based in L'viv. The head of the People's Party (Stronnictwo Ludowe–Piast), Wincenty Witos, was chosen to head the new committee. An endless succession of Polish and Ukrainian delegations streamed in and out of the governor's office during the next few days, all of them urging the governor to transfer power to them by legal means. However, Governor Huyn did not want to preempt orders from Vienna.[23]

On the afternoon of October 31, Polish authorities received the information that the Ukrainians were planning to seize power in the city. The Society for Mutual Assistance of the Legions was quickly informed, and the most important members of the secret military organizations discussed the options open to them with a group of officers but without coming to any definite conclusion. They were not even able to agree on who would serve as supreme commander. However, some officers began planning for the expected coup by mobilizing former legionaries and volunteers so that they would be able to resist, if necessary.[24]

November 1918

Members of the Polish Liquidation Committee had given notice that they would be arriving on November 1 to start preparations for the incorporation of East Galicia into the state of Poland. The plan was that the highest-ranking Polish officer in every town would take charge, and all Austro-Hungarian emblems and insignia would be replaced by Polish emblems and symbols. The Ukrainian National Council, realizing that a Polish coup might be imminent,[25] decided to seize power in L'viv and East Galicia itself. For once, no information about the Ukrainian plans reached the police authorities or the governor's office, although rumors about a planned Ukrainian "attack" (Polish: *zamach*) floated through the city. Even the usually well-informed German consul Heinze knew nothing.

The disbanding of the Polish Legions meant that there were no longer any genuinely Polish units in the armies of the Habsburg Empire. Secret military organizations such as the Polska Organizacja Wojskowa (Polish Military Organization, POW) with its close ties to Piłsudski or the National Democratic Polskie Kadry Wojskowe (Polish Military Cadre, PKW) could not compensate for this. Matters stood rather differently with the Ukrainians. The Ukrainian Sich riflemen were a battle-seasoned unit of highly motivated Ukrainian soldiers and officers. However, the Sich riflemen were not stationed in L'viv but in the Bukovina. Later, they became some of the strongest units of the Ukrainian Galician Army. But it just so happened that in October 1918 the units based in the city consisted largely of Ukrainian soldiers and only a few Polish soldiers, together with a number of multinational troops, which included many Hungarians, Czechs, and German Austrians, giving the Ukrainian side military ascendancy. The secret Ukrainian military organization under Captains (Sotnyk) Dmytro Vitovs'k'yj and Dmytro Paliïv of the Ukrainian Sich riflemen had been planning to seize power for some time and had established an extended network of connections across the predominantly Ukrainian units. On the night of October 31–November 1, the Ukrainian commanders pounced.[26]

At four o'clock in the morning the Ukrainian soldiers left their barracks. They had fastened yellow-and-blue armbands to their Austrian uniforms. These were the only signs that they were now no longer acting as imperial-royal troops but as the armed forces of the newly proclaimed Ukrainian state. One group of soldiers moved to detain Governor Huyn and the commander of the garrison, Colonel Rudolf Pfeiffer. Huyn steadfastly refused to formally hand over power to the Ukrainian National Council. Police director Reinlender was detained and confined to his own apartment. He refused the offer to continue as head of the police force. Despite his refusal his house arrest was lifted the next day. Stepan Baran took over formally as head of police, but only Ukrainian police, who were few in number, remained on duty. Ukrainian units then raised the golden (yellow)-and-blue flag on the town-hall tower and moved to occupy all government buildings and key positions, such as the main train station, the train station in Podzamcze, and the main post office.[27]

For the Poles in L'viv the blow came "like a thunderbolt out of the blue."[28] Stunned passersby watched as Ukrainian soldiers patrolled the streets.[29] One Polish witness later recalled the morning of November 1: "For a time it appeared as though everyone in the apartment had lost the power of speech. That is impossible! . . . We had walked a little way into Łyczakowska Street when we saw a soldier with a yellow-blue cockade who was busy taking away the weapons of all passing military persons. . . . When we beheld the Ukrainian flag on the city hall, what inconceivable feelings shocked us to the core. How dare they . . . , that is impossible. Lwów is ours and must be ours!"³⁰

The Ukrainians living in L'viv, according to the memoirs of Oleksa Kuz'ma, had "tears of joy in their eyes."³¹ Things remained calm on November 1. Only a few shots were fired and no one was killed.³² It looked as though the coup would be bloodless. The Ukrainian National Council announced that "through the will of the Ukrainian nation a Ukrainian state would be created in the Ukrainian territories of the former Austro-Hungarian state" and that the National Council had assumed power in the capital city L'viv and across the entire territory of the state of Ukraine. The National Council appointed Kost' Levyts'kyj as chairman of the Provisional Secretariat of State (Tymchasovyj Derzhavnyj Sekretarijat) and thus of the government. The National Council called on the population to remain calm and comply with the council's decrees. The council went on to offer the Polish and Jewish populations one seat each in the government and promised them full citizenship and minority rights. For the Jewish population the offer represented a revolutionary reform. They had not previously been recognized as a separate nation within the Habsburg Empire. *Ukraïns'ke Slovo* optimistically printed the front-page headline: "Jews go along with Ukrainians." On the next page, the article continued: "The Jewish population sympathizes with the Ukrainian nation." These statements were wrong and were to have devastating consequences for the Polish perceptions of Jewish behavior.³³

By November 7, Ukrainian units had seized power across all of East Galicia.³⁴ *Ukraïns'ke Slovo* exhorted the population to continue to keep the peace and maintain order so that "nobody can accuse us of uncultured behavior and Bolshevik methods": "The world's nations must look on and acknowledge that the Ukrainian nation is doing nothing else than what other nations do: ensuring that it becomes mistress in her own country while assuring other nations that they will have full rights, that our brother Poles and Jews can live together with us. These nations must feel at home in a Ukrainian state."³⁵

Non-Polish and non-Ukrainian units, including many Hungarian troops, declared themselves neutral; they were then partially disarmed by Ukrainian troops and sent home. Their weapons were brought to the Ukrainian National House (Narodnyj Dim) and other collection points. According to the Ukrainian high command, they commanded only eight hundred combat-ready soldiers, with the same number, most of them elderly or ill, only capable of being deployed locally.³⁶ But in November 1918 rumors of much higher numbers were making the rounds. The Poles believed that up to six thousand Ukrainian soldiers were involved. Because of the limited numbers of Ukrainian officers in the Austro-Hungarian army, the Ukrainians had relatively few officers. The number of soldiers in the units fluctuated wildly. Although many soldiers participated in the initial takeover of the city, many of them then opted to return to their villages.³⁷ Even before the coup, Ukrainian commanders had attempted to obtain more reinforcements from the Ukrainian Sich riflemen. Wilhelm von Habsburg, whose regiment included around 1,500 Ukrainian riflemen deployed in Bukovina, responded to the request for assistance and allowed eight hundred Sich riflemen to depart; the riflemen arrived in L'viv on November 3.[38]

Ukrainian politicians and military officers had refrained from taking hostages from the ranks of Polish elites to ensure the peaceful transfer of power. As the first day had been calm, the Ukrainian National Council believed that the Polish population had accepted the coup "quietly and with resignation."[39] Officers of the imperial-royal army strolled through the streets and allowed themselves to be disarmed without resistance. They included Polish officers home on leave to celebrate the upcoming All Saints' Day.[40]

On All Saints' Day, Poles flocked to the cemeteries and the churches, passing Ukrainians "armed to the teeth" on their way there.[41] A rumor persisted in the city that Governor Huyn had voluntarily handed over power to the Ukrainians and was part of a Ukrainian–German–Austrian conspiracy. Huyn protested against these imputations.[42] Leading Ukrainian politicians, most of them lawyers used to the standard legal procedures of the Diet and Imperial Council, continued to struggle to find some legal means of transferring power. On November 2, they finally found a solution acceptable to Huyn. Huyn declared himself unable to continue performing his official duties and relinquished his official powers to his Ukrainian deputy Volodymyr Detsykevych, who, in turn, immediately relinquished them to the Ukrainian National Council. While this procedure at least paid lip service to the principle of legality and bolstered the legitimacy of the new rule, it had no impact on the Polish–Ukrainian struggle for power. After the Polish military organizations had recovered from their initial shock, they began shooting at Ukrainian patrols. The Ukrainian government was forced to recognize that it was not in control of all of the city. At the start of hostilities those on the Ukrainian side still believed that they were merely dealing with individual acts of resistance committed against the Ukrainian state by irregular troops. Moreover, particularly in the early stages, Polish fighters often wore civilian clothes without any signs identifying them as combatants.[43]

Celebratory masses were held on November 3 in all Greek Catholic churches in the L'viv archdiocese to mark the proclamation of a Ukrainian state. Archbishop Sheptyts'kyj celebrated mass in St. George's Cathedral accompanied by the entire cathedral chapter and voiced his support of the attempt to create a Ukrainian nation in a "highly patriotic sermon." At the end of Mass, the congregation sang the hymn "Bozhe Velykyj Jedynyj" ("Great and Only God").[44] At almost the same time, the Polish resistance was also receiving clerical backing. In the Church of St. Nicholas in Szukalski, a Polish priest called on the Polish population to fight the Ukrainians by any means necessary to save the fatherland "from the Ukrainian invasion."⁴⁵

As the Polish military organizations began coordinating their resistance, this signified the beginning of the "fratricidal war"⁴⁶—a descriptor frequently used in the Polish and Ukrainian press. A handful of Poles occupied buildings that became rallying points for additional volunteers. Because most able-bodied men were away serving in the Austrian army, most volunteers were students, schoolchildren, or members of various military committees. To start with, the volunteers had few weapons. They made up their deficiencies—as did the Ukrainians—by taking weapons from barracks and gendarmerie stations; occasionally they managed to disarm Ukrainian patrols.⁴⁷ The Polish resistance also had an avowedly international significance, making it impossible for the Ukrainians to assert that they had seized power in L'viv without any resistance on the part of the city's Polish inhabitants.

On November 1, all Jewish organizations, from the Zionists to the Social Democratic parties and various Jewish Poles, took the decision together with the Kahal to set up a security committee to search for ways to maintain order and preserve the public peace in the Jewish districts. The members of the committee were of the opinion that the Jewish population must not side with any of the opposing parties to avoid putting a strain on future relations with their Christian neighbors. The security committee therefore called on all Jews to maintain "strict neutrality." To protect Jewish districts from looters, the Kahal set up a militia consisting of Jewish soldiers from the Habsburg army and quartered them in local buildings. Some Jews reported feeling emotional on seeing a blue-and-white flag flying from the building of the Kahal for the first time as a demonstration of Jewish autonomy. During the night of the November 1–2, the Jewish militia already took a few looters into custody.⁴⁸ Both Polish and Ukrainian commanders explicitly recognized the neutrality of the Jewish militia and acknowledged its right to provide security and maintain order in the Jewish districts. Militiamen wore a white armband on their left sleeves.⁴⁹ A few Poles of Jewish faith opposed the creation of the militia, proclaiming their solidarity with the Polish community and demanding the resignation of the head of the Jewish community, although this was only proposed on November 22.⁵⁰

Polish politicians, city councilors, officers, and the heads of military organizations had already met in the rooms of the state credit association on the morning of November 1. Representatives of the Podolians, the National Democratic Party, and the People's Party formed a Citizens' Committee (Komitet Obywatelski). After a tumultuous discussion, the politicians approved the military high command organized by Mączyński. In the afternoon, a representative from the Social Democrats also joined the committee.⁵¹

A Polish national committee consisting of members of the mayoralty, the Diet executive, politicians, and delegates was set up in the area of the city under Ukrainian control. The committee was dominated by the National Democrats. The Ukrainians tolerated the committee and permitted it to hold its meetings unmolested in the building of the Chamber of Industry and Commerce. A Committee for Security and Public Welfare was set up in the Polish part of the city on November 7, which in addition to National Democrats included various Social Democrats and members of the People's Party. The committee had contacts to the Polish National Committee and its representatives were included in the joint delegations holding talks with the Ukrainian National Council.[52]

By this time, the city had been divided into three zones. The town center was in Ukrainian hands, the Jewish militia controlled Cracow Suburb, and pockets of Polish resistance had developed in the southwestern part of the city. The Ukrainian National Committee argued its case based on the right of national self-determination and legitimized the seizure of power by referring to the proclamation of a Ukrainian state on October 19 and the Imperial Manifesto of October 16.[53] But its attempt to woo Polish and Jewish support was unavailing. Not a single member of the Polish and Jewish elites could be induced to join the provisional Ukrainian government. But the Jewish Kahal also evaded Polish blandishments. Editorials and articles in the *Neue Lemberger Zeitung* regularly emphasized the Jewish stance of neutrality to counter any accusations that the Jewish population was siding with the new Ukrainian rulers.[54] On November 14, the Jewish militia began setting up a second company.[55] The white armbands of the Jewish militiamen were stamped with Jewish, Polish, and Ukrainian letters.[56]

The Ukrainians had set up their headquarters in the Ukrainian National House. During the first few days, Polish journalists also entered and left the house without hindrance. They reported that the corridors were full of students and academics. Female members of Ukrainian rifle clubs were milling around, and carbines collected by soldiers and brought in on peasant carts were piled high in the courtyard.[57]

Bands of deserters and the urban criminal community took advantage of the confusing situation to loot railroad cars and shops. This only served to increase the uncertainty, finally prompting Polish and Ukrainian politicians to attempt to reach some form of amicable settlement.[58] On the afternoon of November 1, Lord Marshall (Landesmarschall) Stanisław Niezabitowski betook himself together with members of the Diet executive to the Ukrainian National Council in the Stauropygian Institute. Niezabitowski urged his counterparts, among them Kost' Levyts'kyj and Archbishop Sheptyts'kyj, to withdraw their troops from the streets and return to the status quo ante. In the interim period, in other words, until the final decision was taken concerning the city's fate, which would be determined at a peace conference, the "mutual relationship between both nationalities" should be based on "good will and constant cooperation on both sides." A lengthy discussion ensued, in which the Ukrainian participants appeared inclined to begin negotiations on this basis. But finally they demanded that the Poles recognize the sovereignty of the Ukrainian state and the takeover of power in L'viv and issued a calming statement to the Polish population. In return, the Ukrainian negotiators promised to preserve self-administration in L'viv and guaranteed the Poles generous minority rights within the Ukrainian state. But the Polish delegation had no mandate to act with authority. Its primary concern was to get life in the city back to normal and prevent any excesses. They did not believe that they had the authority to give the desired assurances. The Ukrainian National Council elected a committee, headed by Kost' Levyts'kyj, to continue negotiations with the Poles. In the same session, Lev Hankevych was admitted to the National Council as the representative of the Ukrainian Social Democratic Party. This restored Ukrainian unity, with all parties now represented on the National Council. On November 2, the Ukrainian National Council invited the deputy government commissioner for L'viv, Filip Schleicher, to a meeting. Filip Schleicher was responsible for maintaining food supplies to the city. The National Council asked him to continue to carry out his duties as before. But Schleicher was not prepared to continue without consulting the mayoralty. The Ukrainian National Council accepted his decision. During the preparations for the takeover the council had not considered the possibility that there might be problems with food supplies and it was shocked when Schleicher declared that the available supplies would only last one more day. Shortly thereafter, a request was sent to government commissioner Stesłowicz asking him to meet with the National Council. Stesłowicz came directly from consultations with the mayoralty, which had been holding a session in the building of the Chamber of Industry and Commerce. The Ukrainian National Council wanted the mayoralty to resume its duties. That afternoon, the entire mayoralty repaired in a body to one of the members of the National Council and presented him with the following demands as a precondition for continuing their work: all municipal civil servants must be allowed to visit the town hall unhampered, the town hall must be handed over entirely to the municipal authorities, the Ukrainian soldiers must withdraw, and the Ukrainian flag must be replaced by the city's flag. Just how confusing the situation was, was later demonstrated when a member of the municipal council attempted to enter the town hall armed with a letter of safe conduct issued by the Ukrainian National Council. The sentry on duty declared that he could not read and that the letter of safe conduct was therefore irrelevant to him. After lengthy negotiations, a literate corporal was found who permitted the council member to enter. That evening more than one hundred Polish dignitaries and politicians, among them Archbishop Józef Bilczewski, members of the Diet executive, Lord Marshall Niezabitowski, many deputies of the Diet, the entire mayoralty, numerous councilors, the rectors of the university and the polytechnic, the chairmen of various societies and a number of distinguished citizens met up again in the great hall of the Chamber of Commerce. The assembly approved the position of the mayoralty and the Diet executive and authorized both agencies to begin negotiations without delay based on the status quo ante.[59]

Negotiations had at least led to a truce being declared twice on November 2. Both Polish and Ukrainian elites were still strongly influenced by the non-belligerent tradition of resolving conflicts within the Habsburg Empire. There was a good prospect that the worst could be avoided. Only a few lives had been lost. Both sides agreed to set up a Ukrainian–Polish committee that would try to settle the dispute amicably and prevent further bloodshed. The Polish interests in this joint security council (Komitet bezpieczeństwa) were represented by Stesłowicz, Schleicher, and Stahl, while the Ukrainian side sent the National Democratic priest and deputy chairman of Prosvita Teodosij Lezhohubs'kyj, Longin Tsehel's'kyj, and Stepan Fedak.[60] The security council's first act was to draw up a declaration announcing its formation and its intention of jointly maintaining peace and order in the city. In addition to the members of the security council, the declaration was also signed by Niezabitowski, Józef Neumann, and Kost' Levyts'kyj.[61] But in the days that followed, negotiations stalled. One cause of the impasse was the assertion by Polish fighting organizations that the Polish delegation had no authority to conduct negotiations. Only the provisional government in Cracow, by which they meant the Polish Liquidation Committee, was entitled to make binding agreements. The Polish fighters initially did not consider themselves as belligerents but as "townspeople who do not want to submit to Ukrainian rule."[62]

As the days passed, the conflict developed a momentum of its own. Both Polish and Ukrainian military commanders felt strong enough to try to resolve the dispute by force of arms. The Ukrainian city command blamed the bloodshed on the Poles. The Ukrainians had not taken hostages and had even been prepared to raise the siege on November 2. But now they had to defend themselves against attacks by Polish legionaries and civilians who were taking potshots at Ukrainian soldiers from behind gateways and windows.[63] The Ukrainian commander in chief threatened civilians who attacked Ukrainian soldiers with summary execution under martial law.[64] In an unsigned declaration, the Polish side rejected the idea that it was responsible for the bloodshed. Ukrainian soldiers had shot at the windows of innocent residents. All Poles aspired to a peaceful solution. The Ukrainian soldiers should vacate all public buildings and withdraw to barracks in their part of the town. Public safety should be maintained by a militia composed equally of Ukrainians and Poles. The declaration was particularly worried about ethnically mixed families in which "brother [is] hostile to sister, son [is set] against mother." The Poles were not claiming any Ukrainian territories but wanted to live together with Ukrainians in peace, but the whole world knew that

L'viv was a Polish city. The handbill called on the Polish population to hurry to assist the "heroic struggle" of the legionaries.[65]

The Ukrainian National Council informed the Polish population about the proclamation of a Ukrainian state. But it is unlikely that the historical arguments cited by the Ukrainian side made much impression. In the Ukrainian view, East Galicia had been Ukrainian (Ruthenian) until 1387, and "from an ethnographic standpoint it has remained so up until the present day." The descendants of this Ukrainian population had the right to determine their own affairs in their own country. Part of the Polish population had defied the Ukrainian state by taking up arms. But the Polish majority in the city could not be allowed to "determine the affiliation and political fate of the country and its large Ukrainian majority." The mutual bloodshed was benefitting no one and was only bringing "anarchy, hunger and misery" to the city. Such acts were also futile because the population of L'viv itself—the Poles and the Ukrainians—could not decide the ultimate fate of the city. This final decision must be subject to an agreement between both states or settled as part of a general peace conference. The National Council therefore called on its "Polish fellow citizens" to immediately end the unhappy Polish–Ukrainian struggle.[66]

While battles on the streets continued, the Ukrainian National Council managed to adopt a provisional constitution for the West Ukrainian People's Republic (Zakhidno-Ukraïns'ka Narodna Respublika, ZUNR) on November 13, in which it once again laid claim to all ethnic Ukrainian territories in the Habsburg Empire. Until the election of a constituent assembly, state authority would continue to be vested in the Ukrainian National Council and the state secretariat. The Ukrainian National Council also agreed to set up national secretariats for Jews and Poles and proposed that the heads of these secretariats would be members of the government.[67] The Ukrainian government promised the Poles of L'viv that it would protect their "national property." The city of L'viv was promised self-administration, as were Polish cultural and economic institutions.[68]

It was an odd war. The combatants accused each other of committing atrocities and of violating the laws of war, but at the same time members of the city council and of the Polish National Committee were able to meet unhindered in the building of the Chamber of Commerce and Industry, located in the part of the city under Ukrainian control. Although subject to occasional searches, Polish societies were also able to continue their work in areas controlled by Ukrainians and were able to provide logistical support for their co-nationals in other districts of the city. Binational committees controlled the water works and the power station and ensured that supplies to the city continued. Ceasefires were agreed, allowing the inhabitants of contested streets to go out and obtain food. In the first few days, some Ukrainian and Polish troop leaders even preferred to smoke cigarettes together rather than let their young soldiers shoot at each other.[69] The matinée performance in the city theater on November 1 passed off without disruption. It took until the evening of the same day before Ukrainian soldiers appeared in the theater after the first act and sent the audience home.[70] On November 1, it was still possible to walk through the streets wearing the uniform of the Polish legions without being immediately arrested by Ukrainian patrols. But by November 5, all this had changed. The situation was becoming increasingly dangerous and the streets were deserted. Only patrolling soldiers could be seen. Almost all the shops were closed; the few that had remained open sold only apples and cucumbers, and the population faced a real risk of hunger. Many people did not dare leave their houses for days on end because they feared becoming trapped between the front lines. The hospitals were overcrowded; they too lacked food supplies.[71] But even at that point, a number of curious episodes occurred. During a truce on November 15, Polish and Ukrainian fighters in Kraszewski Street allowed themselves to be photographed together before returning to shoot at each other again after the ceasefire had ended.[72]

A seemingly antiquated code of honor persisted, but violations of the law of war also occurred. Some Ukrainian officers released Polish prisoners if they gave their word not to take part in the fighting again. But not all of the freed prisoners kept their promise; they felt themselves bound by their oaths as Polish riflemen or considered it their patriotic duty to break their word of honor in this special case. One officer who had been released after giving his word of honor was captured again and killed.[73] Fighting around the main train station was temporarily suspended to avert bloodshed among the soldiers of the Austro-Hungarian army who were returning home and to prevent the demobilized soldiers from proceeding into the city to rob and plunder.[74] One Polish unit took advantage of the national reverence of its Ukrainian opponents by placing a bust of Taras Shevchenko on top of a chest of supplies. The Ukrainian soldiers were unable to bring themselves to shoot at the image of their national poet, and the chest reached the frontline unharmed.[75]

A propaganda war started with each of the warring sides accusing the other side of committing atrocities.[76] The Ukrainian newspaper *Dilo* vilified the Polish resistance, describing it as enjoying the support of the dregs of society and the backing of chauvinist legionaries. Rapacity and bloodlust were cited as the prime motivators of this "Polish scum." It was asserted that these "bandits" had even shot at Ukrainian medical patrols.[77] The Ukrainian high command accused the Polish side of using "dumdum bullets" all along its front lines.[78] The Poles in their turn accused Ukrainians of disregarding Red Cross insignia and shooting at medical staff.[79] Both Ukrainians and Poles accused each other of mistreating and shooting prisoners and of taking every opportunity to rob and plunder. Polish units controlled St. George's Cathedral and the seat of the metropolitan bishop, where, according to Ukrainian reports, they behaved atrociously.[80] These offenses were described using terms such as *lack of culture* and *barbarity*. Conversely, the Polish newspapers wrote of the "savagery and barbarism of the Ruthenians" and of the "Ukrainian beast."[81] The Ukrainians reacted defensively as they wanted to prove that they were a "civilized people," while the Poles showed more self-assurance. Ukrainian newspapers wrote ironically about the misconduct of Polish soldiers as a manifestation of Polish culture (*kul'turnist'*).[82] The Polish newspaper *Kurier Lwowski* published a report on the depredations carried out by Ukrainian soldiers in L'viv's town hall. After their withdrawal, their "vandalism" was documented on camera. The pictures were described as an "eternal document of the shame of Ukrainian culture." The damage to city property which occurred during the three weeks of fighting was calculated as amounting to almost five million krone.[83]

Positions on both sides hardened. After one week the negotiating Polish delegation demanded that a Polish garrison under the control of the Regency Council in Warsaw be stationed in L'viv. The Ukrainians rejected the proposal; while they were prepared to grant a degree of autonomy they refused to countenance the presence of a foreign authority on Ukrainian territory. As a compromise the Poles again proposed setting up a Polish–Ukrainian militia whose composition would mirror the respective groups' share of the population. This would have given the Polish side an overwhelming majority in the militia. The Ukrainians declared that they were prepared to agree to a joint militia but insisted on a mixed Polish–Ukrainian–Jewish militia. This meant that only around half of the militiamen would be Polish. This proposal in turn was rejected by the Polish negotiators.[84] On the afternoon of November 14, the adversaries again attempted to reach a truce. On the Polish side a military delegation now also participated in the discussions alongside the civilian negotiators, prompting the *Neue Lemberger Zeitung* to hope "that this time an agreement will be reached."[85] The Polish side was finally prepared to accept the Jewish militia and to countenance the idea of three hundred Polish militiamen under Ukrainian command. But it continued to insist on a garrison under the command of the Polish National Council. The Ukrainians were not prepared to agree to this demand. However, the *Neue Lemberger Zeitung* anticipated that the Poles would give way on this point. The newspaper had received the information that Ukrainian reinforcements were on their way to L'viv. But on November 15 the Polish delegation did not show up for negotiations.[86]

The fighting on the streets had continued all the while, unaffected by the negotiations. The Polish organizations not only managed to hold their ground, they even began to slowly improve their positions. Many civilians had been injured or killed. Stocks of food and other necessities were dwindling. The gasworks had ceased operations; the power station and the waterworks were still functioning, but the lack of coal threatened to shut them down as well.[87] The Ukrainian press attempted psychological warfare. *Dilo* lamented the terrible repercussions of war on the city's population. The inhabitants living in combat areas did not dare leave their homes; they were living in fear, going hungry and suffering great hardships. The Jewish population was particularly badly affected. Many had lost their lives in the shooting and now their bodies lay unburied in their houses. In contrast, all was calm in the part of the city under Ukrainian control. Life in the Ukrainian areas was continuing as normally as could be expected under the circumstances, and the supply situation was improving. However, in the other part of the city Polish bandits were not only ransacking businesses and shops, they were even targeting private homes.[88] With the permission of the Ukrainian government, a Jewish committee finally assumed responsibility for the delivery of supplies to the Jewish population. Sellers were given Ukrainian passes.[89] In the meantime, regular ceasefires were agreed to give the inhabitants of areas where fighting was taking place the opportunity to obtain food during the lull in the fighting.[90]

The Polish and Ukrainian Social Democrats were in a difficult position as members of the only party which had continued to attend each other's events in 1918 and which had retained a modicum of transnational class solidarity. Their dilemma was expressed in an appeal issued by the local council of worker delegates of the Polska Partia Socjalno-Demokratyczna Galicji i Śląska (Polish Social Democratic Party of Galicia and Silesia, PPSD) in the first days of the fighting. The Polish workers' representatives called on "the working population of the city of Lwów" to end the fighting immediately and pointed to the dangers of further bloodshed that threatened L'viv's future. They denounced the Ukrainian coup. Only a peaceful agreement arrived at through a constituent assembly composed of the Polish and Ukrainian nations could resolve the Ukrainian–Polish question. But they also reminded their readers that L'viv was "in its overwhelming majority a Polish city" and that the coup had taken place against the will of this majority. They therefore called on all workers to defend their civil liberties. The appeal ended with an accolade lauding a "free and independent people's Poland" alongside a salute to the "brotherhood of nations" and "international social democracy." Effectively, despite the proclamation's rhetoric of peace, it was an appeal to Polish workers to fight against the Ukrainians, should it become necessary.[91]

After a little hesitation the Ukrainian Social Democratic Party of Galicia and Bukovina supported the formation of a Ukrainian state and sent one delegate to the Ukrainian National Council. The Ukrainian Social Democratic Party was as uncomfortable with the bloodshed as the Polish Social Democrats, but the executive committee of the Ukrainian Social Democratic Party placed the blame squarely on the opposing side. "But irresponsible elements of the Polish population in the city of L'viv have begun a terrible, barbarous, fratricidal battle and call upon the working masses to this end." The workers should make use of their rights as citizens but should not allow themselves to become embroiled in a futile battle about the alleged "Polishness [*pol's'kost'*] of Lwów." "The relative Polish majority in the city of L'viv cannot impose its will and decide on the future of the overwhelming majority of the Ukrainian population in the entire country." The executive committee ended the declaration with expressions of its enthusiastic support of the "freedom and brotherliness of all nations," of a "free, united, independent Ukrainian republic" and of "international revolutionary social democracy."[92]

The situation for Greek Catholics who considered themselves as Poles and for the children and spouses in mixed Ukrainian–Polish marriages was difficult. Both sides treated them with suspicion, which explains the low proportion of Greek Catholics among the Polish "Defenders of Lwów," even though a considerable number of Greek Catholic Poles lived in the city.[93]

After the Polish inhabitants had recovered from their initial shock, they supplied their fighters with food. Young women fought as frontline combatants, cared for the wounded, smuggled messages and passed on information, and procured weapons and ammunition.[94] Oleksa Kuz'ma, who participated in the fighting on the Ukrainian side, later praised the solidarity of the Poles, which had transcended class barriers and political parties. Even the Polish Social Democrats had formed an alliance with the class enemy.[95] The Ukrainian troops did not enjoy the same level of support. The Greek Catholic minority in the city could not be persuaded to take up arms against their Roman Catholic neighbors, and attempts by Ukrainian commanders to mobilize more of the population met with only limited success. Kuz'ma blamed the failure on an insufficient national consciousness and the effects of Polonization.[96]

The German consul Heinze described the Ukrainian mode of warfare as "rather haphazard." The Ukrainian officers and commanders were inexperienced, the composition of the high command changed several times. On November 5 Hryhoryj Kossak, the colonel of the Ukrainian Sich riflemen, replaced Vytovs'kyj as commander in chief. But he was unpopular among the Sich riflemen and was replaced shortly thereafter by Hnat' Stefaniv, who continued to command the Ukrainian troops until their withdrawal.[97] On November 18 the Ukrainian commander in chief desperately requested additional troops from the district commander. The capital city L'viv must be held at all costs. The commanders promised to send more soldiers but very few arrived in L'viv.[98]

Most Ukrainian soldiers came from rural areas and, in contrast to the young Polish fighters, found it difficult to get their bearings in the city. And so, unsurprisingly, the scales began to tip in favor of the Poles. East Galicia was controlled almost entirely by Ukrainian units. But the Ukrainian fighters in L'viv received little support from the district administrations of the West Ukrainian People's Republic proclaimed on November 13. All appeals for help were unavailing.[99] The peasants wanted to rid themselves of the landowners and gendarmes, the fate of L'viv did not move them enough to want to risk their lives for it.

The Poles of L'viv were considerably more determined. The Joint Committee of Polish Women already demanded in the early days of November that there be no negotiations. "It is the duty of all men to place themselves at the disposal of the high command of the Polish troops in Lwów; it is the duty of every Polish woman to send her husband, brother, father, betrothed to the defense of the beloved city."[100] One Polish commander had his soldiers swear their loyalty to the Polish state and pledge to be worthy of their ancestors and not cede even a hand's breadth of Polish soil.[101]

But not all Poles were quite as self-sacrificing. Many of the soldiers and officers who had no personal connections to L'viv often had no great inclination to hazard their lives again, now that the world war had ended. During the first few weeks it was not uncommon for Polish and Ukrainian soldiers who were returning home not to take part in the fighting, either because they did not understand the purpose of the war or because they had no wish to shoot at their former comrades in arms with whom they had, until recently, been serving in the Austro-Hungarian army.[102] Several contemporary witnesses report that most of the demobilized Polish soldiers and officers only wanted to return home and simply walked past the combatants. More importantly, a number of high-ranking Polish officers of the Austro-Hungarian army were in L'viv and refrained from taking part in the fighting.[103] Despite their keen motivation the inflow of untrained youths and volunteers also led to disciplinary problems. Many were discontented with their deployment and disappeared again without informing their commanders.[104] After the first week the inrush of volunteers abated.[105] On November 11, a total of 239 officers and 3,044 noncommissioned officers and soldiers were fighting on the Polish side, aided by 132 officers, 1,679 soldiers, civil servants, and women. The total number of "Defenders of Lwów" rose from 5,094 on November 11 to 5,472 on November 21.[106]

According to data compiled in 1938, 6,022 people of the city were accepted as having been "Defenders of Lwów." Of these, 67.4 percent were younger than twenty-five (23.6 percent were not even eighteen years old) at the time, 25.5 percent were between twenty-five and forty-two, and 5.3 percent were older than forty-two years; 22.7 percent (1,374) were either still at school or were students. Insofar as it is possible to determine their occupations, 12 percent (774) were civil servants or teachers, of whom 136 were professors or teachers, 11 were priests and 10 were monks; 21.3 percent worked in industry, in trade, or as craftspeople; and 157 were members of the free professions. About half had no previous military training. More than 1,000 were proved to be soldiers, including 739 officers or noncommissioned officers. There were 5,595 men and 427 women. Of the men, 3,994 actively participated in the fighting, with 1,601 providing ancillary services. Only 17 of the women took up arms, with 410 providing ancillary services. Nine "Defenders of Lwów" were Armenian Catholics, twenty-five were Greek Catholics, and forty-nine were Jewish. A further fifty were of other Christian denominations, and one had no affiliation to any denomination. The overwhelming majority, totaling 3,931, were Roman Catholics; the denomination of a further 1,947 persons could not be determined.[107] To put these figures in perspective: in the fall of 1918 L'viv had a population of about 194,000; of these approximately one hundred thousand were Roman Catholics, thirty-four thousand were Greek Catholics, and fifty-seven thousand were Jewish.

Between 1918 and 1920, 439 people on the Polish side were killed in battles for L'viv, 172 of whom were born in L'viv with 41 born in the district of L'viv; 412 were Roman Catholics, 6 were Greek Catholics, 1 was Armenian, 2 were Protestants, and 6 were Jewish. The denomination of twelve could not be determined. Twelve women were killed. Between November 1 and 22, 194 fighters were killed. No one died on November 1, and only one person was killed each day on November 12, 15, and 19. The greatest numbers of persons killed on individual days died on November 5 (eighteen), November 9 (twenty-one), November 14 (twenty-four), and November 22 (twenty-six).[108]

On November 16 *Dilo* declared that all was calm in the territories of the West Ukrainian People's Republic with the exception of "the capital city of the republic, the ancient Ukrainian town of L'viv." This was the only place where skirmishing between the troops of the republic and Polish combat units still continued. The rebellion had proceeded from "Polish islands" in a "Ukrainian sea" and was the result of the "centuries old rule of Poland over our land and over our nation [*narid*]." The Poles had taken up arms "against the right of the Ukrainian nation to have a national life in an own state to defend the so-called 'historical rights of Poland' to rule over the Ukrainian nation for centuries": "The Polish reactionaries—the Polish szlachta, Polish capitalism, Polish bureaucracy—are fighting for dominance over the Ukrainian nation—over the Ukrainian peasants and workers. The old order of subjugation is fighting against the new order, which has manifested itself in the founding of the West Ukrainian People's Republic."[109]

Ukrainian propaganda linked the national struggle for independence to the struggle for a more equal society and attempted to appeal to Roman Catholic peasants. The fight was not directed against the Polish population per se as Poles enjoyed the same legal protections as the Ukrainian population. But the Poles appeared to be of the firm opinion that "the Ukrainian nation should be Poland's slave." The Polish units were not merely fighting against Ukrainian troops; they were attacking "the entire Ukrainian nation."[110] On November 19, the Ukrainian high command exhorted its soldiers to stand firm. The entire Ukrainian nation, millions of peasants and workers, were backing them. The Polish insurgents were acting in the interests of factory owners and landowners and were fighting against the People's Republic, which gave land to the peasants and protected workers from oppression and misery. The peasants were asked to impose order in their villages and districts and deal with insurgents.[111]

A final attempt, involving the French officer Henri Villaimé, was made to negotiate a settlement. Villaimé had travelled to L'viv as a private citizen without a mandate from his government, but the Ukrainian side was unaware of this. Villaimé sided with Poland, unnerving the Ukrainian leadership, which received the impression that the Entente had already committed itself to supporting the Polish claims.[112] When Polish relief troops advanced on the city from the west, the Ukrainian soldiers and their government left L'viv on November 22. The Poles were overjoyed to see the white-and-red flag flying from the town hall. They welcomed the young fighters with flowers, fruits, sweets, and home-baked food.[113]

Fourth Regime Change: Polish Lwów and the Pogrom

Throughout the period of fighting, Jewish shops in the areas under Polish control were subjected to attacks. The Jewish militia fought the attackers in an attempt to protect Jewish shopkeepers.[114] The Polish military commander accused the Jewish militia of having fired not only at bandits but also at regular Polish troops. Jewish militiamen were denounced as having fraternized with Ukrainian soldiers; they were accused of acting in a hostile manner toward Polish soldiers, of taking them prisoner and handing them over to the Ukrainians.[115] As it happened, there had been repeated skirmishes between Polish units and the Jewish militia. It was difficult for the Jewish militia to differentiate between military operations and attempts at looting.[116] Polish soldiers could readily conclude—not least because of the reports put out by their military newspaper *Pobudka*—that the Jewish militia and the Jewish population in general were hostile to them.

The violence in the city did not end with the departure of the Ukrainian troops. In the early hours of the morning, Polish units began occupying Jewish neighborhoods. The Jewish militia had allowed itself to be disarmed without resistance. But almost immediately the rumor spread that the Jews were offering resistance, ambushing and shooting at Polish soldiers or pouring boiling water over them. The Polish population believed the reports. The press later repeated the accusations over and over again, with such tales serving to place the blame for the subsequent pogrom squarely on the Jews themselves. The reports of attacks by Jewish civilians on Polish soldiers corresponded to the archetypal patterns of anti-Semitic rumors, which had led to riots in various rural areas in the prewar period and served as justification for plundering and killings. These patterns of thinking had hardened into interpretive schemes that governed Polish interpretations of Jewish behavior.

But the alleged pro-Ukrainian behavior of the Jewish population was only the trigger, not the underlying reason for the pogrom. As discussed in the previous chapter, anti-Jewish resentment had increased during the war and had taken on a racist hue. The same litany of accusations were constantly leveled against the Jews: that they had enriched themselves during the war; that they had profited from the misery of the Christian population by demanding exorbitant prices; and that they had collaborated with all of the occupying powers and informed on Poles. During the Polish–Ukrainian fighting, Jews were believed to have helped the Ukrainians and attacked Polish soldiers.[117] The Polish military newspaper *Pobudka* stoked such resentment even more and reported, even before the Ukrainian troops had left the city, that Polish soldiers had been doused with boiling water and shot at in Jewish neighborhoods.[118] The declaration by the Jewish community that it would remain neutral had aroused much indignation in Polish society. Many Poles viewed Jewish neutrality in itself as a hostile act, indeed as an act of betrayal directed against Poland.[119]

As soon as Polish patrols entered the Jewish neighborhoods, bandits newly released from the prisons, marauding militiamen, soldiers, officers, and civilians began looting and pillaging Jewish businesses and homes, abusing, raping, and killing Jews. The marauders told their victims that requisitioning had been permitted by their Polish commanders as a just punishment for the Jewish collaboration with the Ukrainians. The Jewish quarter had previously been sealed off by a military cordon. The subsequent pogrom lasted three days. According to conservative estimates, it resulted in seventy-three deaths and several hundred seriously injured persons. Many houses were set on fire and many Jewish shops were looted.[120]

Although some attacks had occurred previously, the pogrom surpassed all previous attacks in L'viv with regard to the extent of atrocities committed, and the rapacity and destructiveness of the perpetrators. For the Jewish population in L'viv the pogrom was a catastrophe that eclipsed all their previous sufferings experienced during the war. Members of the Jewish community documented the pogrom. They set up a "rescue committee," which systematically questioned all the victims of the pogrom. The interviews were done by Jewish lawyers, who compiled protocols of the statements.

Within a very short space of time, all Jewish shops had been looted. But the patrols also searched homes, mistreated Jews and extorted money and valuables. The victims reported that Polish citizens had joined in the attacks: "It is an interesting and sad business that in addition to members of the military, persons from the so-called 'superior middle classes' also joined in the attacks, the women wearing fur coats and gloves; among those doing the plundering you could see civil servants, high school teachers, persons who were attending university, etc."[121]

Mechl Zorn was visited several times by patrols on November 22 and 23; they robbed him of four thousand krone in cash and goods to the value of twenty thousand krone. One sergeant was particularly cruel, using his sword to slash at a woman holding a baby and causing serious injuries to several people. On November 23, Zorn received a warning from the Polish caretaker of his house that it would be the turn of all Cracow Suburb that day. Zorn could not believe it and remained at home. But the caretaker had been right. Only a short time later, four apartment buildings were ablaze in Ulica Bożnica, the street where Mechl Zorn was living. Before being set on fire, the buildings had been ransacked and their residents mistreated to extort money and valuables. Finally Zorn found himself, together with his family, on the street where he observed the mob watching the fire: "On the other side of the street a crowd of people were standing, civilians and soldiers, and among this mob [pospólstwa] there were also many citizens, whose appearance indicated that they could be members of the intelligentsia. I observed that all were watching the Jewish houses burning with pleasure and laughter. And so I passed along there below the burning house to observe this crowd which was so hostile to Jews, [this] horrified me more than the fire itself."[122]

But some soldiers condemned the behavior of their comrades. One soldier approached Zorn and requested him to warn the Jews in one of the neighboring streets as their house would also be set on fire. The soldier accompanied Zorn's family to prevent anyone from harming them and subsequently refused the reward offered him.[123] Another Jewish homeowner was less lucky. As her house started burning, she asked a sergeant for help. The sergeant replied that he had orders not to save Jewish houses.[124] It was the lack of any substantial support from Poles, which shocked the Jews most. Very few Poles attempted to curb the attacks and the killing.[125]

The preferred approach was to extort money. The butcher Adolf Meisel reported that he had been attacked in his apartment by a patrol. Their leader stated that he was a lieutenant and demanded five thousand krone. He gave Meisel ten minutes to comply, threatening that otherwise he would shoot the entire family.[126] Another patrol entered an apartment in which twenty-five Jews had gathered. The soldiers threatened to shoot everyone if they were not given money. When the women and children resisted the search, the soldiers announced that they would set fire to the house. When the soldiers learned that another patrol had already stolen all the money, they repeatedly struck one man in the face with a revolver and then set fire to the living room. The assembled Jews escaped to the Chasidim synagogue, where some seventy persons had already fled. After a few minutes, the same band of marauders came to the synagogue, searched all persons present, sent the women and children outside, and threatened to set fire to the building if they did not receive thirty thousand krone within five minutes. One man still had thirty krone and handed them over. He was stripped to his shirt, and the soldiers demanded more. Then they hung up a rope and simulated his execution. He was finally released, but the soldiers then demanded paper, which they used together with copies of the Talmud to set fire to the synagogue. They gave the assembled

Jews one minute to hand over twenty thousand krone. When the heavy smoke forced the soldiers to vacate the synagogue, they left, locking the gate. The soldiers did not know that there was a rear exit that allowed the Jews to escape.[127]

The teacher Stella Agid had to put up with visits from several different patrols in her apartment on Plac Krakowski. The first troop was already at her door at seven in the morning on November 22. The soldiers extorted money at gunpoint. This patrol and the following one stole numerous articles of value. The fourth patrol was particularly brutal, murdering Stella's husband Moses Agid. The son of the victim believed that he recognized the murderer as the son-in-law of a rich Polish butcher. Another witness confirmed that she had previously often seen the murderer in the butcher's shop. He was wearing a military uniform when he murdered Moses Agid but, a few days later, was seen walking around in civilian clothes again. When Agid fled into the corridor with four women, the perpetrator shot him four times. Prior to the murder, the perpetrator was said to have rampaged through the house, yelling that he needed to kill a Jew. When one of the soldiers reproached him for killing an innocent man, the murderer kicked the body and left the room.[128]

Polish L'viv appeared to be imbued with hatred of the Jews. Even outside Jewish neighborhoods it was impossible for Jews to walk freely on the streets without risking threats and insults from civilians.[129] Salomon Rawicz was living among Christian neighbors. On November 22, a Polish officer accompanied by a soldier knocked on Rawicz's door at six in the morning. The officer informed Rawicz that "the Israelites had been shooting from apartments." A contribution had therefore been imposed on the Jewish population, which he was now here to demand. Persons who refused to pay would be shot. The officer obtained eleven thousand krone. When Rawicz contended that the money was not his and had only been given him for safekeeping, the officer returned three thousand krone and announced that he would return later with a receipt for the money but failed to return. The next day, when Rawicz heard the news that robbery and murder had begun to spill over from the Jewish quarter into his own neighborhood, he betook himself together with two of his neighbors to see the commander of the local vigilante group (*Bürgerwehr*). The commander promised to be responsible for their safety in return for a fee. The commander insisted that shots had been fired from Jewish houses at Polish soldiers and that dozens of Polish soldiers had already died. The commander maintained that he had seen this with his own eyes. He informed Rawicz that the different units had divided the districts into areas where they would carry out a "punitive action." He demanded money to pay the commander of the designated unit. That evening he came to Rawicz's apartment and accepted one thousand krone.[130]

Such extreme acts of violence were directed exclusively against Jews. Although the Ukrainian population of L'viv was subjected to many acts of hostility, there were no murders. However, a number of Ukrainians were arrested. Because the Poles believed that the German government had supported the Ukrainians in their attempt to seize power, the employees of the German consulate were at risk of their lives. Consul Heinze fled, placing himself under the protection of Archbishop Bilczewski, where he remained until his departure from L'viv. The consulate and Heinze's private residence were vandalized and plundered. His two daughters were kidnapped until a Polish officer took them into protective custody and sheltered them in his own family. Although German civilians were not attacked, German members of the military were "treated dishonorably" by the crowds and then expelled back to Germany.[131]

The first meeting of the provisional city council after the withdrawal of the Ukrainian troops was already held on November 25, 1918, one day after the pogrom had ended. The Social Democrat Mykola Hankevych was the only Ukrainian representative to appear at the council. The other Ukrainian council members had sent messages refusing to participate in the work of the council. Public interest in the meeting was enormous; the viewing gallery was packed. Government commissioner Stesłowicz opened the session by giving a brief outline of the events of the past three weeks, rejecting the Ukrainian claim to L'viv as being without legal basis. L'viv was a purely Polish city, and after three weeks' suffering the city was now free again, because of the "heroism of our young people." The assembled councilors responded with a standing ovation. Stesłowicz then thanked the most important commanders, listing them by name, and the Polish institutions involved in the relief of the city. The mention of Piłsudski's name elicited enthusiastic clapping. Finally, the government commissioner expressed his regret about the "incidents of robbery and violence," by which he meant the pogrom. He ascribed the acts of violence to the fact that prior to withdrawing the troops the Ukrainians had released many bandits from prison. At the time, the Polish troops had had to pursue the enemy and had been very tired at the end of the three weeks' fighting. It was now the duty of the city council to restore order again and repair the damage. Speaking in the name of all of the Polish parliamentary groups, Professor Maksymilian Thullie proclaimed the union of L'viv with the Polish republic and acclaimed the "Defenders of Lwów," Polish youth and the "heroic women together with the heroic workers" who had helped in the city's defense. Finally Thullie read the following resolution: "The city council utterly condemns the acts of violence and the robberies perpetrated against the Jewish population, because in free Poland the law of justice and tolerance should reign. The city council solemnly declares that society has nothing in common with these acts of violence."

The representative of the PPSD placed a different slant on the affair. While he spoke of his pleasure that L'viv was once again "our city," he also expressly acknowledged that the Ukrainians were a distinct and self-contained nation. He recalled the attempts made by Social Democrats to end the fighting and still wanted to negotiate a settlement with the Ukrainians. The proletariat was fighting against nationalism and did not encourage hatred toward other nations, denominations, or races. He strongly objected to ascribing the blame for the pogrom to the behavior of "Jewish nationalists."[132]

Mykola Hankevych then took the floor, speaking "as a Ukrainian socialist, as a representative of the Ukrainian socialist proletariat." He lamented the fact that Polish and Ukrainian students had shed their blood fighting against one another in the war: "But it was one hundred times more serious, one hundred times more terrible when the unarmed, unhappy, hapless population of the Jewish ghetto fell victim to a barbaric, savage pogrom! For two days and two nights the violence raged, old people, women and children died, their goods and chattels disappeared in the fire, houses and buildings were transformed into fire-ravaged wreckage and ruins, Jewish beggars were ruined by robbery and murder! A truly Dantesque hell opened up before our very eyes in those two terrible days and nights!"

He protested against the imputation that Ukrainian soldiers had been involved in the violence. "It is a fact that under the Ukrainian regime over a period of three weeks there were no Jewish pogroms." Responding to loud interjections by the Polish majority on the council, Hankevych continued: "Gentlemen! The damage wreaked by nationalism is strong and powerful. You don't want to hear the voice of a socialist!"[133]

The Jewish members of the council proposed a proclamation whereby the city council would utterly condemn the pogrom and comprehensively distance itself from all persons who had participated in the pogrom or supported it morally. The council should express its deepest sympathy to the Jewish population, push for justice and compensation, and do everything to prevent such things from happening again. All victims must be registered, and the perpetrators should be called to account immediately. Until the power of the new state had been established, the mayoralty should be assisted by a council whose members would be drawn from the Jewish population. But no decisions concerning these proposals were taken; instead, the suggestions were passed on to a commission for further consultation. In the end, the resolution strongly condemning the pogrom, which had been read out at the start of the session was published, but without touching on the role of Polish soldiers as perpetrators.[134] Instead, the newly formed Polish provisional government commission published an improbable ethnic breakdown of the perpetrators, according to which 60 percent of arrested persons were Greek Catholics, 30 percent Roman Catholics, and 10 percent were Jewish.[135]

On November 25, Archbishop Józef Bilczewski publicly condemned the violence in the Jewish districts but avoided using the term *pogrom*. Assuredly—he opined—no true Christians had participated in the violence. He considered it possible that Jews shared some responsibility for the attacks but felt that he must leave the decision to what extent Jews had incurred some guilt themselves to the judgment of God and the courts of law.[136]

One week after the end of the pogrom the Polish Committee of Women Citizens (Komitet Obywatelski Kobiet) published the following declaration: "It is the truth that the Jewish population behaved in a provocative manner. It is the truth that a large part of this Jewish population does not recall the benevolent protection which they always enjoyed on Polish soil. It has adopted a very unfriendly stance towards Polish society and has assisted the Ukrainian rapists in their shameful work. Nevertheless, Polish society does not strive for such a settlement of accounts and, above all, it is not out to take revenge on the poorest and perhaps least guilty population."[137]

With its declaration the committee was only expressing opinions which were widely held in Polish society. The commanders played down the pogrom and claimed to have taken drastic measures against marauders. They repudiated the suggestion that they had known anything about the pogrom. They had done everything they could to combat the excesses and mitigate the consequences.[138] Apparently Polish patrols had arrested some 2,700 persons over the two days of rioting.[139]

But other exculpation strategies were also pursued. In a report drawn up for the international community, the commanders of the Polish units claimed that their soldiers had come under fire when they entered Jewish neighborhoods. This had then led to a fierce gun battle, which prevented the soldiers from deterring dubious characters from attacking Jewish shops and homes and had stopped the soldiers from purging the Jewish quarter of these elements. But the total number of Jews killed by shooting or other attacks was not more than thirty-five at the most. No pogrom had therefore occurred in L'viv "in the literal sense of the word." Some robberies had occurred, and there had been some incidents where people had taken personal revenge against hostile individuals. As they supported Austria and Germany, the representatives of the Jews had exaggerated events to stir up international hatred against Poland.[140]

The pogrom did indeed elicit considerable response abroad and was a severe blow to Poland's international reputation. The high level of publicity generated by the pogrom was used to reproach the Jewish population and was interpreted as a further sign of Jewish disloyalty. The *Kurier Lwowski* considered it particularly perfidious that Jews had appealed to the international community to criticize Poland. Just when in L'viv "the flower of Polish youth was dying in the struggle for national honor and existence" the Jews had "thrust a dagger into the back" of Polish youth.[141]

The press department of the Council of Ministers in Warsaw reacted on November 30. It admitted that it did not have precise information, but it assumed that "a part of the Jewish population had turned their weapons against Poles out of solidarity with the Ukrainians," a course of action which had provoked "understandable indignation among the majority Polish population of Lwów." But the press department sharply criticized the subsequent excesses, viewing them as committed by criminal groups keen to create a provocation, and added that "the rule of law, justice and tolerance shall prevail in free Poland." The government in Warsaw announced that a detailed investigation would be held and that the guilty parties would be severely punished. But at the same time it tempered the severity of its recriminations by adding the rider that civil rights also involved duties towards the Polish state and the Polish nation. The Jews must refrain from anything that could arouse the indignation (*rozgoryczenie*) of the Polish population.[142]

The *Kurier Lwowski* also regretted and condemned the incidents that had occurred in the Jewish quarter, but refrained from using the term *pogrom*. The newspaper blamed Ukrainian politicians and officers and the Jews themselves for the excesses that had been committed by the "dregs of society." The Ukrainian government was held to be partly to blame because it had thrown open the prisons. By launching its "attack" on November 1, it had behaved "with barbaric thoughtlessness" and upset the equilibrium that directed the complicated organism of a "big, modern city." The newspaper repudiated the accusations leveled against Polish society and the Polish authorities. When the excesses had kicked off, there had been no Polish authority in place. This, too, could be laid at the door of the Ukrainians. In addition, through their previous acts the Jews had incurred guilt. The *Kurier Lwowski* argued the case for exonerating the Poles on several different levels. The newspaper began by placing the violence in the context of the war, recalling the organized murder sprees of German troops and the atrocities committed against civilians in Belgium. It then pointed to the Bolshevik cruelties perpetrated in Russia. The newspaper blamed these on the Jews because "it was common knowledge" that the Bolsheviks were headed by Jews. The Polish daily newspaper was drawing on an influential and long-lasting stereotype. The Jews were associated with social revolution and upheaval. The Jews of L'viv were collectively held to be responsible for acts committed by revolutionaries of Jewish descent who—it was insinuated—controlled the Bolshevik party and the Soviet state. This interpretive model would later play an important role in the Second World War. The *Kurier Lwowski* cleverly cited some of the criticisms leveled against Zionist neutrality by Jews and "Polish philosemites." Then the newspaper went on to claim that Jews had indeed been shooting at Polish soldiers from behind and went on to invent a story whereby machine guns had been concealed in one of the synagogues. This was proof enough for the newspaper that the Jews had been providing assistance to the Ukrainians during the fighting. As further proof the *Kurier Lwowski* quoted the Ukrainian newspapers which had reported that "the Jews are with us."[143] Just how little truth there was in these accusations leveled at the Jewish population and its militia later became evident in the attempts at explanations put forward by Polish soldiers who had entered the Jewish quarter. One fighter considered it suspicious that the Jewish population had not poured out into the streets to welcome the Polish soldiers. They had, he said, "obviously something on their conscience." His story included nothing about any attacks committed by Jews when Polish troops had entered the city.[144]

The daily newspaper *Wiek Nowy* showed more sympathy. The entire population was shocked by the terrible events. There was not a single Polish person who did not condemn the cruel acts that had transpired in the Jewish quarter. Above and beyond all politics, there must surely be sympathy: "On both sides the seeds of hatred were sown. On the receptive soil of nervous excitation falls the poison of reckless cutting words, promises of revenge, the threat of further massacres, destruction—annihilation." *Wiek Nowy* urged calm, ascribing the febrile atmosphere to the war. Over the last five years, so many explosive issues had accumulated in society that every demand for revenge had serious consequences. At the same time *Wiek Nowy* continued to report new incidents and provocations.[145]

After he was arrested, just before Christmas 1918, Lev Hankevych overheard conversations between Polish soldiers in which he discerned no hatred against the Ukrainians but a "terrible thirst for blood" directed against the Jews.[146] Nor did his impressions deceive him. Violence, looting, and requisitioning continued for weeks after the end of the pogrom. Members of local vigilante groups and troops participated in the attacks. Nocturnal searches of houses and illegal confiscations were common. Jews, many of them elderly or academics, were usually the first to be conscripted when men were needed to dig trenches:[147] "Today in the fourth week of Polish government in L'viv Jews are as little safe with regard to their lives and property as in the first days of the pogrom. The arrests continue, robbery is the order of the day, and the taking of prisoners on the streets for different purposes and under different pretexts along with searches and all types of persecutions and harassments has not stopped for a single moment."[148]

The entire Jewish neighborhood was living in a state of "panic-stricken fear." The searches which continued nightly were combined with robberies and extortions without any weapons ever being found among the Jews.[149]

On January 2, 1919, Rafał Buber brought up the pogrom and its consequences during a session of the municipal council. The city council had unanimously condemned the pogrom but the attacks on Jews persisted. Buber cited numerous examples showing how Jews of all ages and social class were being hounded on the streets and marched away to do forced labor. Money and valuables were stolen during arbitrary searches. After it had become apparent that the reports of Jewish attacks on Polish soldiers could not be verified, the range of accusations had simply been expanded. Now it was being said that bolshevism was spreading through the Jewish quarter and that the Jews were plotting to revenge themselves for the pogrom and were planning an armed attack on Polish troops together with the Ukrainians. But no Jewish Bolshevik had been arrested yet, nor had there been any arrests of Jews who had shot at Polish units or who had poured boiling water on them. Buber opined that General Rozwadowski and Colonel Sikorski had lost the authority to command their own troops. It was not the Jews but the troops who were behaving like Bolsheviks.[150] This sharp criticism led to some units being disbanded at the beginning of January 1919, including the reconnaissance troop of the quartermaster's battalion and the security service (Straż bezpieczeństwa) of the local military commander.[151]

On January 5, every Jewish member of the city council, the Jewish Assistance Committee and the Kahal threatened to resign en masse if the discriminations, arbitrary house searches, confiscations and attacks on Jews did not stop immediately. The way they saw it, the pogrom was still continuing and had become a "permanent institution." "No Jew can stroll along the street unless he wants to run the risk of being captured like an animal; no Jew can go to bed calmly because he cannot know whether the night will bring an illegal investigation or a robbery." Twenty-nine robberies targeting Jews occurred between November 25, 1918, and January 3, 1919; in eleven cases, apartments were robbed; in eleven cases, entire houses were plundered. These figures did not include the robberies committed against fifty Jewish families in Sokolniki, the theft of food supplies from one hundred L'viv Jews in Gródek, thirty-eight cases of illegal confiscations, numerous wrongful arrests, and a number of rapes.[152]

It is difficult to say to what extent these incidents were "normal" crimes and to what extent they were motivated by anti-Semitism. After the November pogrom the Jewish population and its representatives were disposed to impute anti-Semitic motives to every attack, robbery, or arbitrary measure. The situation in the city and in the surrounding countryside remained dangerously unsettled, and Poles and Ukrainians were as likely to fall victim to attacks as Jews.[153] Although the potential anti-Semitic motivation behind these crimes and discriminations cannot be resolved in retrospect, anti-Semitism played a key role in the violations discussed in the following section.

Polish troops desecrated the graves of the Jewish cemetery. The cemetery's caretakers and visitors to the cemetery were humiliated, and men were subjected to a forcible shaving of their beards. The city council complained to General Iwaszkiewicz about the behavior of the Polish units, pointing out that they had also profaned the graves of Jewish Polish legionaries and heroes of the insurrection.[154] The troops of General Haller and the troops from Poznań were particularly prominent in attacks on Jews. In May 1919 Jewish shops were attacked and looted twenty-nine times, with thirteen assaults occurring on May 14 alone. In seven cases, soldiers from General Haller's units were involved in attacks on Jews, during which the beards of Jewish men were cut off and some men were additionally beaten.[155]

Chwila, a new Polish language daily newspaper with Zionist sympathies, declared that the forcible conscription of the "strictly neutral" Jewish population to dig trenches and reinforce defenses was contrary to international law. But by mid-January 1919, the newspaper saw some evidence of a slow improvement in Polish–Jewish relations. Impelled by a sense of justice, a few important Polish politicians had perceived the necessity of protecting the Jewish population from persecution and attacks. But the paper decried the strongly hostile attitude to Jews in the regular Polish press, which continued to poison the social climate.[156]

Jews continued to be blamed for rising prices and the lack of supplies. *Chwila* objected to generalized accusations that the Jews held a "usurious monopoly." Most Jewish traders charged fair prices; the price hikes were due to increases in retail costs.[157]

The actions of the Polish high command in East Galicia show just how certain the army was that the Jewish population was on the enemy's side. The quartermaster had received information about planned hostile actions by Jews and Ukrainians and ordered five hostages to be seized from both ethnic groups. Polish newspapers painted a picture of a Jewish–Ukrainian alliance that was planning a coordinated attack on L'viv from within and without. Representatives of Jewish organizations reminded them that thus far the Jews had not resisted; they complained to the government about the attacks and discriminations by the state and military authorities and demanded that those responsible be punished.[158] Four Jewish hostages were still under arrest in mid-January 1919. *Chwila* argued that taking hostages from a neutral nation was a breach of international law.[159]

On January 26, the Jewish Assistance Committee complained to Chief of State Józef Piłsudski and Prime Minister Ignacy Paderewski that the acts of violence and discriminations had not ceased. The pogrom had become a permanent institution. The committee demanded that there must be an end to discrimination and to the "anti-Jewish excesses" of the press if any future coexistence were to be successful. The committee complained that the press accused Jews of all manner of evil deeds, from the speculative misappropriation of sugar and providing millions to fund the Ukrainian resistance to concealing weapons and ammunition. No evidence for any of these accusations had been found; no Jew had been charged with attacking Polish soldiers. Across the board, Jews were the victims of extortion and blackmail and were being robbed of their last pennies. Forced conscription to dig trenches was another Jewish "privilege," with Jews only permitted to refuse if they paid bribes of between twenty and fifty krone. They were suffering a truly "Dantesque hell." Some twenty thousand Jews had suffered violence or robbery in the last six weeks. The Jews were entirely powerless against a "bestial marauding soldiery" and the "pathological mood of local Polish opinion." Many Jews had been deprived of their very means of existence. Although some of the worst units had been disbanded, "nevertheless a pogrom atmosphere exists, an atmosphere of hatred and vilification exists . . . , agitation against Jews together with the imputation of all manner of imagined crimes exists; a moral pogrom exists and continues."[160]

Reports of attacks on Jewish shops continued throughout the spring.[161] Greed and covetousness were the main motives, as was also shown during a pogrom that occurred in Grzybów on May 12, 1919. Around two thousand people had assembled, but only between three or four hundred of them took part in the looting, the majority of them former soldiers of the Austrian army, teenagers, and women. The gendarmes proved unable to control the disturbance. People eager for plunder even arrived from the surrounding villages.[162]

During those weeks and months, Jewish politicians and dignitaries were not merely fighting to end such attacks; they also wore themselves out in the battle against false and unjustified accusations. The pogrom had shaken the self-perception of Jewish Poles. They had not envisaged that such anti-Semitic violence could occur in a civilized city like L'viv with its long tradition of resolving conflicts peacefully. Jewish lawyers and representatives of the Jewish community set up a "Committee for the Assistance of the Victims of the Pogrom in L'viv" (hereafter, the Assistance Committee) already mentioned here several times previously. At the request of the authorities, who objected to the word *pogrom*, the committee was renamed Jewish Assistance Committee for the Victims of the Disturbances (*rozruchów*).[163] The committee's chairman was the provisional head of the Kahal Emil Parnas. Tobiasz Askenaze; two rabbis, Leib Braude and Samuel Guttmann; the banker Wiktor Chajes, the historian Mojżesz Schorr; and the lawyer Ozyasz Wasser served as deputy chairmen. The shock of the indifference of Polish society cut deep. Tobiasz Askenaze, a lawyer and burning Polish patriot, became a spokesman for the Jewish population. Already in 1918, he compiled a detailed memorandum based on statements made by victims of the pogrom. "My pen trembles in my hand when I begin to record all the atrocities and murders, the full orgy of the bestial mob which raged ceaselessly on the Jewish streets."[164]

Askenaze denounced the behavior of the Polish military and Polish society. "The attitude of the majority of the Polish population in L'viv was not what could have been expected. Quite the contrary; the Polish middle classes adopted an attitude which even the greatest pessimist could not have foreseen."[165] Nobody had raised their voice during the pogrom to protest the events. One might even be excused for harboring the impression that the majority silently approved of everything that happened. "This is perhaps the saddest moment of all in the calamity, that the population did not draw a demarcation line between their own deeds and feelings and those of the unleashed marauding soldiery." In partial mitigation, Askenaze was willing to believe that the Christian majority was not fully informed about the extent of the catastrophe. But he charged the Polish population with continuing to assume that the Jews had deserved their ill treatment.[166]

Askenaze pointed out that Jewish organizations had announced that Jews would remain strictly neutral and that they had adhered to this declaration. He additionally listed examples, starting from the very first day, of Jews "who felt themselves to be Polish" who had spilt "their blood in the service of Poland." The initial claim by Ukrainians that the Jews were fighting alongside them had been false. The Jewish militia had only protected Jewish property from attacks by Polish bandits.[167] If the Jews had wanted to fight on the side of the Ukrainians, the Zionist newspaper *Chwila* affirmed, they would have called on the many Jewish officers and demobilized soldiers to arms themselves and not limited themselves to a mere two hundred militiamen.[168] *Chwila* emphasized that the Jews were not interested in repudiating well-founded criticisms of individual Jews that had mutated into generalized accusations directed against Jews; rather, they rejected the accusations in their entirety. "We want justice—and nothing else."[169] Askenaze and the Assistance Committee demanded an official "entire and complete rehabilitation of the Jews" and a "complete rehabilitation of the Jewish militia."[170]

L'viv was being temporarily administered by a provisional government committee headed by Leonard Stahl. In December 1918 the committee set up a Commission for Jewish Affairs, and Tobiasz Askenaze attended the first session of the newly formed commission. Askenaze was anything but pleased with what he heard there, writing a letter of remonstrance to Stahl, the contents of which were subsequently approved by the Jewish Assistance Committee. Askenaze criticized that despite the best intentions of members of the commission the proposed projects were unable to resolve the "pathological paroxysm" which had gripped society. For six weeks Askenaze had been forced to intervene continually because of crimes committed against Jews. "The source of this illness is the defamation of the entire Jewish population, the artificial but false conviction insinuated to the entire Christian society that the Jews were greatly culpable in that great Polish-Ruthenian commotion [*awantura*], while in fact not the slightest blame attaches or was attached to the Jewish side."

Nor had the commission's claim that the Jews had been guilty but should be forgiven done anything to lessen the pogrom mood. Askenaze was passionately opposed to any such resolution of the Polish–Jewish dispute. The Jews, he said, could tolerate almost unlimited suffering and pain, but nobody could destroy their "feeling of inner dignity." And, therefore, the Jews would continue to fight to their last breath until they received the acknowledgment that they were completely blameless. Askenaze demanded the "entire and full rehabilitation of the Jews." All Jewish hostages must be released immediately because they were victims of this social psychosis.[171]

Askenaze delivered his extensive memorandum to the French General Barthélémy, who had come to L'viv at the head of a commission to mediate between Poles and Ukrainians.[172] He also handed the memorandum to the Polish high command in L'viv in mid-February 1919 and passed a copy of his memorandum in French to a French–British relief committee.[173] The National Democratic newspaper *Słowo Polskie* accused Askenaze of having harmed Poland by his memorandum. Askenaze sharply repudiated the accusation. His report had been compiled at the behest of the Jewish Assistance Committee, and with the assent of the Polish government. General Barthelémy had requested a copy and had received it with the Polish authorities fully advised of the fact. The report had not been intended for publication.[174]

On January 4, 1919, the Jewish Assistance Committee received a letter from Quartermaster Władysław Sikorski, expressing his regrets about the pogrom. But Sikorski again asserted that the Jews had taken sides against the Poles during the Polish–Ukrainian fight and that the Jewish militia had taken up arms and fought against Polish soldiers. Sikorski had heard that the Jews in Tarnopol had formed "revenge battalions." He insinuated that the Jews had passed information about troop movements in the city to Ukrainian units and ascribed the violence against the Jews to this behavior. The pogrom, he believed, had mainly been carried out by bandits wearing military uniforms. He viewed the observations of the Assistance Committee as an indication of the generally unfriendly mood toward the Polish army. Moreover, in contrast to what was implied by its name, the Jewish Assistance Committee was not caring only for victims of the pogrom. If this behavior did not change he would be obliged to take steps to ensure the safety of the combat troops by bringing the members of the Assistance Committee before a court martial.[175] Sikorski's threats did not have the desired effect of intimidating Askenaze. Writing back on behalf of the Assistance Committee, Askenaze described the accusations as "entirely unfounded" and was incensed at the threat to bring the Committee's members before a military court. The reports of "revenge battalions" in Tarnopol were yet another instance of the usual unfounded rumors. The Assistance Committee had not accused the Polish army in toto but had specifically named certain units that had attacked Jews. If the Assistance Committee would be obliged to limit its aid only to victims of the pogrom and not be permitted to support the victims of later atrocities, the Committee's work would become impossible.[176] Sikorski responded by backpedaling. In an addendum to his letter sent on January 4, he declared that the accusations that the enemy was constantly receiving information on troop movements in L'viv was not leveled against the Assistance Committee. Nor were the accusations directed against all Jewish people. Moreover, he supported the philanthropic activities of the Assistance Committee.[177] Askenaze replied, objecting to both the praise and the censure. The military was not called on to judge his civic and social commitment. He again emphasized his wish not to allow the information he had collected to pass outside L'viv.[178]

During a meeting with a delegation of Jews from L'viv, the Polish government represented by Chief of State Piłsudski and Prime Minister Paderewski condemned the pogrom. Paderewski announced that the perpetrators would be punished. He deplored the existing bad relations between Jews and Poles, which he viewed as unacceptable in the long term and detrimental to Jews and Poles alike. While he believed Jews should receive all civil rights and liberties, he had no sympathy with Jewish demands for national self-determination.[179] Nevertheless, the delegation was satisfied with the outcome of the discussions.[180] But different reports about the exact contents of the talks soon began to circulate. The Jewish daily press did not dwell much on the accusations served up by the two Polish politicians, reporting on them in mild words. In contrast, the Polish newspaper *Głos Narodu* published a much more acrimonious version. According to its report, Piłsudski had accused the Jews of acting in a hostile manner against the Poles. The Jews had mobilized the foreign press against Poland and exaggerated the extent of the pogroms while keeping silent about pogroms in other countries. "The Polish masses are actually incapable of carrying out pogroms, despite their strongly anti-Zionist mood." Most pogroms, the newspaper continued, could be laid at the door of the Ukrainians. As soon as the war started, the Jews should have sided with Poland. The chief of state had requested the delegation to appeal to the Jews of L'viv to stop their hostile activities abroad against Poland.[181] The Jewish National Council for East Galicia in Vienna did not formulate its comments based on the account of the discussions given in the Jewish press but on the accounts of the Polish press and accused Piłsudski of anti-Semitism: "The statements by Piłsudski sufficiently indicate the spirit of the Polish people whose aim it is to entirely expel all Jews from Poland through the hounding of Jews using the basest form of demagoguery."[182]

The Jewish press in Poland, however, avoided fueling the flames further and refrained from criticizing the government. *Chwila* was willing to credit the government with positive intentions but considered it to be poorly informed about Jews and their national demands.[183]

The international response to the L'viv pogrom forced Warsaw to act. In December 1918 the foreign ministry sent a fact-finding committee to L'viv. The committee largely agreed with Askenaze and came to a shocking conclusion: "It was true barbarism, entirely medieval. We must painfully state that there were a certain number of officers who participated in the murders and robberies."[184] The commission found that many professional criminals who had recently been released fought on the Polish side and took the opportunity to loot and plunder. The commission strongly criticized the military leadership. They had not done their duty during the days of the pogrom.[185] At the beginning of January a new fact-finding commission traveled to L'viv. It consisted of the president of the Polish Supreme Court, Dymowicz; regional federal prosecutor, Wesołowski; the examining magistrate Koss; Lieutenant Colonel Wacław Bielski; and Judge Stefan Liskowski, who represented the Polish War Ministry.[186]

The Assistance Committee was able to provide them with a more detailed list of victims and an inventory of the economic losses suffered. The list included the names of seventy-three people known to have been murdered during the pogrom. The committee did not include the names of those who died later of their injuries in their list. In total, 443 wounded persons were registered, among them 27 women and children. The highest number of dead (36) and wounded (104) were to be found among the merchants and tradesmen, but the list also included craftsmen, employees, unemployed persons, civil servants, lawyers, doctors, and peddlers. By the end of January 1919, losses amounting to 103 million krone had been reported. The greatest losses, totaling some 82 million krone, were the result of plundering and looting, with damages amounting to 15.7 million krone caused by fire, and willful damage accounting for a further 5.3 million krone. Merchants and tradesmen had been hit the hardest; the value of their plundered goods alone was almost fifty million krone. But much of the damage had not even been registered yet; the committee had only finished evaluating 3,620 of 5,000 completed questionnaires. But it was already clear that at least 13,375 persons, approximately 20 percent of the Jewish population, had suffered losses. The interim report documented 2,815 attacks. In 1,916 cases, the attacks had been perpetrated by common soldiers; in 494 cases, by patrols headed by an officer; and in 391 cases, by soldiers and civilians working together. Attacks carried out only by civilians were relatively rare. A key motivator was greed, borne out by the fact that businesses and well-off families were the primary targets of attacks.[187]

It is difficult to find information about the civilian perpetrators. Women participated in the attacks in only ninety-eight cases; fourteen of these women were Red Cross nurses. In fifteen cases, the attackers were known to be students; in five cases the attacks were committed by academics; in seventeen, by railroad workers; and in three cases, by employees who worked on the municipal streetcars. Other civilians listed among the attackers included a postman and two members of the local vigilante group. Fifty-four soldiers, eighteen officers, and thirty-one civilians were identified by name, including a doctor, two high school teachers, a student, a police inspector, and two well-known footballers. One hundred seventy-three people were recognized, but their names could not be determined with certainty, among them fifty-one municipal employees.[188] The L'viv Police Department compiled a list of persons arrested in connection with the November events that included the names of more than 180 civilians. As most of the victims on the list bore Jewish names, it can be assumed that the majority of arrests were linked to involvement in the pogrom. The number of men and women arrested were approximately even. The arrested persons consisted of 108 Roman Catholics, 47 Greek Catholics, 7 Jews, and 2 Protestants, while the religious affiliation of the rest is not known. A closer look at the age of the arrested persons shows that the majority of them were between eighteen and forty years old. But two dozen children and adolescents aged ten and older were also included in the list. Only about thirty of those arrested were older than forty. Almost all were from the lower classes: blue-collar workers, prostitutes, petty craftspeople, or unemployed. The most commonly cited occupation was janitor. With the exception of one student, none of the persons arrested was from the educated classes. About thirty had previous convictions.[189]

The Assistance Committee launched an appeal to the Jewish population for donations and emergency aid. In "the name of the ideals of Judaism and of humanity as a whole," the committee asked for donations of food, clothing and cash to help the victims of the "incidents." Omitting the word *pogrom* was a concession to the Polish daily newspapers who printed the appeal. The appeal was signed by leading Jewish supporters of assimilation to Polish culture, including Tobiasz Askenaze, Wiktor Chajes, and Rabbi Guttmann.[190]

The pogrom continued to be played down in Polish public life. The press made no attempt to keep the topic in the public eye. However, the newly formed Polish government did attempt to track down and punish the perpetrators. After Polish rule had been established in the city, the police department and the judicial authorities began moving against the perpetrators. In November 1919 the Department of Public Prosecutions provisionally took stock of the investigations against civilians: sixty-six verdicts resulted in sentences ranging from fourteen days' to seven years' imprisonment and the release of ten people. Verdicts on forty-nine further people were still pending.[191] This largely concluded the legal examinations and actions taken in connection with the pogrom. Late in the summer of 1920 the Department of Public Prosecutions reported that more than two hundred civilians had been arrested in connection with the anti-Semitic excesses of 1918 and 1919, and a total of eighty-four criminal proceedings had been instigated against alleged perpetrators, the majority of which had ended with the conviction of the accused. It was not possible to ascertain how many proceedings were initiated by military courts.[192] In mid-December forty soldiers accused of murder or robbery were in prison awaiting the verdict of their court martial.[193] Given the magnitude of the pogrom, in the end only a small percentage of the perpetrators faced judicial proceedings.

The Polish–Ukrainian War

Siege

The battle to rehabilitate the Jewish population and punish the offenders occurred in an atmosphere of ethnic hatred amid numerous new discriminations and attacks on Jews and Ukrainians. After the Ukrainian troops had withdrawn from the city, L'viv continued to be besieged for several more months. Recapturing L'viv was paramount for the government and the army of the West Ukrainian People's Republic. All military efforts were directed toward regaining the "old capital of the Ukrainian-Galician-Volhynian state" and the capital city of the new republic. It was hoped that the "Polish occupation of L'viv" represented only a transient "episode in the process of the creation of the Ukrainian state."[194]

Ukrainian units now no longer cared whether supplies could reach the city and went on to disrupt the city's main water supply. Artillery fire damaged many building and killed many civilians, among them women and children.[195] The artillery fire on February 26, 1919, was particularly fierce. The city's inhabitants cowered in the entrances of houses and sought shelter in cellars. Shell after shell crashed down, killing, and injuring the town's residents.[196] With the main water supply disrupted, long queues formed at fountains and standpipes. One eyewitness described how much the city had changed. The streets were deserted, and artillery and rifle fire could be heard in the distance.[197]

The Polish press adopted a vehemently anti-Ukrainian stance. The conflict was described as a battle against "bands of haidamaks" and "Ukrainian murderers." The newspapers insisted that the Ukrainians viewed themselves as the descendants of the Sich Cossacks who would rampage through "Polish Lwów" just as their forebears had done before them.[198] *Haidamak* and *Khmel'nyts'kyj* were terms that had long served to scare Polish children; even in private documents the unexpectedly firm attempts to set up a Ukrainian state were equated with social rebellion (haidamaks) or treason committed against Poland (Khmel'nyts'kyj).[199]

The daily newspaper *Dziennik Ludowy* accused the Ukrainians of firing poison gas shells at the city. The newspaper deduced this from reports that six horses and ten rabbits had been found dead with no external signs of injury.[200] Almost all Ukrainian newspapers, even those written in Polish, were forbidden, making it impossible to respond to such unfounded accusations.[201] Only the Social Democratic newspaper *Vpered* was still allowed to appear. But newspaper vendors were frequently attacked.[202] All Ukrainian cultural institutions and societies had been closed down. Their buildings were subjected to regular searches, their contents destroyed or plundered. By May 1919, there had been twenty-nine raids on the Stauropygian Institute alone. Even Greek Catholic monasteries were forced to tolerate multiple searches for weapons. In December, the Ukrainian Social Democratic daily newspaper *Vpered* reported that not a single Ukrainian house had escaped inspection.[203] Polish passersby attacked Ukrainians talking in their mother tongue in the street. People speaking Ukrainian risked being arrested as potential spies.[204] Ukrainians were forced to work on Greek Catholic holidays, and over Easter many Ukrainians were interned. The Ukrainians, according to one memorandum, no longer enjoyed the protection of the law. Ukrainian authors described these events as a pogrom directed against the Ukrainians of L'viv and urged a peaceful solution to the conflict, as Poles and Ukrainians would be obliged to continue living alongside one another in the future. They demanded that civil rights be extended to Ukrainians and that Ukrainians be shielded from the attacks of the Polish press.[205] The Ukrainian population, Archbishop Sheptyts'kyj wrote to Ritter Vasyl'ko, was living "in constant fear of arrest, raids or similar" incursions. Some prominent Ukrainian politicians were interned for a time.[206]

The Polish high command in East Galicia passed regulations discriminating against Ukrainians. Banks were ordered not to pay out more than one thousand krone per day to Ukrainian individuals or institutions. No more than four thousand krone could be paid out per person per month. Any higher amounts required the permission of the army quartermaster.[207] The administration was almost completely Polonized, with all government employees required to swear an oath of allegiance to Poland. As most Ukrainian civil servants refused, they were summarily dismissed without pension rights.[208] The Ukrainian members in the city council resigned their seats in May 1919 to protest against the fact that the fifty newly appointed council members did not include a single Ukrainian and that they had not been invited to participate in electing the mayor. After their resignation, the city's Ukrainian inhabitants were not represented on the city council until 1927.[209]

During the siege, the civil and military authorities already began working to improve security in the city. A civilian security force was set up to relieve the military; it consisted of three groups: a civilian militia operating in rural areas, a government militia, and a civilian militia, which operated in L'viv.[210] The men were armed and wore tall hats and long overcoats, reminding one visitor of nothing so much as the literary character Rinaldo Rinaldini, an Italian bandit chieftain.[211]

The Poznań Assistance Committee for L'viv sent a transport of sixty-one freight cars with food and other relief supplies to L'viv at the end of January 1919. A few Catholic clergy escorted the transport and the delegation was welcomed by Archbishop Bilczewski. The priests accompanying the relief supplies explained that the relief supplies were provided by Greater Poland to help fellow Poles as part of a determined effort to preserve the city's Western culture. The supplies were therefore exclusively earmarked for the hungry Polish Christian population, in other words, not for Jews or Ukrainians. Some of the food was distributed free of charge to orphanages, charitable institutions, and other organizations, and some was sold at reduced prices.[212] Destitute Ukrainians did not benefit from such donations. Ukrainian orphanages and welfare institutions suffered great deprivations during the siege because they no longer received any aid from the city authorities.[213]

The mayoralty called on the population to hold out and not lose heart.[214] Polish organizations and parties called on the male population to volunteer as fighters. Historical arguments played an important role in the recruitment propaganda. National Democratic politicians called on the populace to ensure that the "sacrifices made on behalf of Poland" would not be in vain. Their current efforts gave meaning to the past and would make it possible to have a national future. These authors were placing themselves in a long tradition that called on them to act. Attempts to achieve a peaceful compromise were criticized as the result of false notions of "universal human ideals": "Let us go then, young and old, let us stand in rank and file, let us take up our weapons, which are enough for thousands, let us not reach a point where we could be accused of lacking sympathy for the national interest or of having a false notion of so-called universal human ideals, which surely cannot exist without a national ideal, or—even worse—where we could today be accused of cowardice, and by a single word be condemned by future generations."[215]

The city council also solemnly swore that it would not slacken in its "defense of the holiest national ideals." It upheld the "holy and glorious tradition of the ancestors" and "the Polish identity of our city which has existed since time immemorial and which has been fortified anew by the blood of our most treasured children."[216] On March 18, 1919, Polish reserve troops were able to lift the siege of L'viv. The road from Cracow to L'viv was now clear and supplies could reach the city again. But even in April the city was still within range of Ukrainian artillery.

Ukrainian Rule

In November/December 1918 Ukrainian troops controlled all of East Galicia with the exception of L'viv. They were now in control of a large part of the area previously defined as comprising the territory of the West Ukrainian People's Republic (ZUNR).[217] With the exception of L'viv, there were very few areas where Poles took up arms to resist the Ukrainian seizure of power. The Ukrainians already lost Przemyśl in the first week of November. There was also fierce fighting in the oil-producing region around the city of Borysław. But there the defiant Polish workers faced a far more numerous Ukrainian militia.

The population of the ZUNR numbered about four million people, three million of whom were Ukrainians. The Bukovina was occupied by Romanian units, while Transcarpathia initially remained under Hungarian control. The Polish population boycotted the elections to the Ukrainian National Council, which were held from November 22 to November 26. Jewish and Galician German inhabitants also refused to participate in the elections so as not to become embroiled in the Polish–Ukrainian dispute. The 150-strong council therefore consisted almost exclusively of Ukrainians. The Ukrainian historian Oleh Pavlyshyn has analyzed the social composition of the council and of local representative bodies. He was able to find information on 187 of the councilors. The largest contingent consisted of lawyers who accounted for fifty-five council members, followed by teachers (forty-one), farmers (twenty-seven), priests (twenty-four), civil servants (nine), journalists (seven), railroad employees (six), engineers and students (four), and doctors (two). Of the deputies, 78 percent had completed secondary school, and 42 percent had studied at university. Fifty-two deputies had a PhD, most of them in law. At the top levels of the district administration—the district commissioners—the picture was not much different. Twenty-two of the forty-eight commissioners had a PhD, with lawyers again predominating. The existing information on the social backgrounds of all 124 councilors confirmed the same story. Forty-five of the deputies came from clerical families, thirty-seven from peasant families, and seventeen from families in which one parent had been a teacher. The overwhelming majority (95 of 165) were members of the Ukrainian National Democratic Party. Thirty-five were members of the Ukrainian Radical Party, twenty-four were members of the Ukrainian Social Democratic Party, seven were members of the Christian Social Party, and seven belonged to the Ukrainian People's Party (Ukraïns'ka Narodna Partija). The only two women delegates (both of them teachers) were from the Bukovina. One in three deputies had formerly been a member of the Imperial Council or the Diet.[218]

The Ukrainian National Council elected lawyer and former delegate to the Imperial Council Jevhen Petrushevych as its head, thus making him the president of the republic. Stanislau (Stanyslaviv) was chosen as the republic's provisional capital.[219] The governments of East and West Ukraine concluded an agreement on the unification of the two states on December 1, 1918. However, unification was only officially and formally proclaimed on January 22, 1919, in the square in front of St. Sophia's Cathedral in Kiev. The West Ukrainian People's Republic was accorded the status of an autonomous region within the Ukrainian People's Republic (Ukraïns'ka Narodna Respublika, UNR), which had superseded the Hetman regime. Its new name was now Western Region of the Ukrainian People's Republic (ZOUNR). Its subordination to Kyïv (Kiev) had little practical significance; the government of the ZOUNR continued to act largely autonomously. The UNR under Volodymyr Vynnychenko and later under the directorate of Symon Petljura was precarious and had to defend itself against the superior Red Army and initially also against various Polish troops. In its battle against Poland, the ZOUNR was more or less on its own.[220]

After the initial chaos the Ukrainian elites began to set up a system of public administration. They took the old Austrian administrative structures as their template but filled all top positions in the administration with Ukrainians. The positions of municipal and district commissioner were uniformly held by Ukrainians. Polish specialist staff were kept on, but many Poles refused to serve in the new state administration. The greater the successes clocked up by Polish troops, the less willing the Polish population was to cooperate. Civil servants and railroad employees used obstructionist tactics. There was even a Polish underground resistance movement that carried out acts of sabotage. The Ukrainian authorities responded by setting up detention centers where Poles were interned. As the old administrative staff was unreliable or often no longer even turned up to work, local Ukrainian elites were forced to improvise. In some places, specialist administrative departments were set up, in others the respective national councils created administrative departments, and in a few other places workers' councils were set up.[221] Despite all the deficiencies, forming administrative bodies of their own was a significant step in Ukrainian nation building and served to exacerbate the conflicts with Poles living in East Galicia. It was the first time Greek Catholic peasants had ever seen a Ukrainian administrative authority. The imagined national community became tangible with the creation of the administrative bodies of the West Ukrainian People's Republic and the Ukrainian Galician Army (Ukraïns'ka Halyts'ka Armija, UHA), which took on the role of a "forge of the nation."

The units of Sich riflemen functioned as the predecessors of the UHA; they had laid the groundwork for the nationalization of Ukrainian soldiers. Officers, the majority of them members of the Ukrainian intelligentsia, not only held courses in which they taught illiterate Ukrainians to read and write; they also gave lessons on the history and geography of Ukraine. In the first half of 1918, Ukrainian units were stationed in Volhynia, where they set up educational and cultural institutions. They were in contact with local politicians and intellectuals from Central and East Ukraine. Such national educational work was supported by their commander, Wilhelm von Habsburg, also referred to as Wilhelm (Vasyl) Vyshyvanyj because of his Ukrainian sympathies.[222] The Sich riflemen formed the strong and combat-ready nucleus of the UHA. After the fall of L'viv, the Ukrainian National Council ordered the general mobilization of all male Ukrainians between the ages of eighteen and thirty-five years. Although this goal was not achieved, the number of soldiers in the UHA reached an all-time high of one hundred thousand men. However, only forty thousand of them could be deployed in battle. Their weapons and equipment came from the Austro-Hungarian army or had been taken from demobilized soldiers who had crossed the area of the ZOUNR in their tens of thousands. The lack of battle-tried officers in the UHA was a serious deficiency. Only two out of every one thousand Ukrainian soldiers had held a commission in the Austrian army, and most commissions had only been for the lowest rank of officer. In contrast, twenty-seven out of every one thousand Polish soldiers were officers. The severe lack of officers in the UHA could only partly be compensated for by the recruitment of German Austrian and other non-Ukrainian officers from the imperial-royal army. In the aftermath of the L'viv pogrom, a number of Jews, predominantly Zionists, enlisted in the UHA. They were joined by high-ranking Ukrainian officers from the Russian army, such as General Mykhajlo Omeljanovych-Pavlenko, who at one point commanded the UHA.[223]

The constitutional principles and legislation of the ZUNR were liberal and democratic. The National Council reserved 30 percent of the seats in the future parliament for national minorities, who were granted extensive rights. But the election boycott by the Polish, Jewish, and Galician German population meant that no minorities were represented in the first elected National Council.[224]

The authorities did not treat the region's Polish inhabitants gently. Mirroring Polish reactions to the use of Ukrainian in L'viv, speaking Polish in Ukrainian-held territories was unwelcome and considered suspicious. Poles were not permitted any form of assembly.[225] But the Ukrainian authorities behaved no worse toward the Polish population than the Polish government did toward Ukrainians. The majority of Poles rejected any form of allegiance to the Ukrainian state and were discriminated against for their refusal, but there were no systematic acts of violence or massacres.

The military conflicts were accompanied by a propaganda war between Poles and Ukrainians. The combatants accused one another of human rights abuses and violations of the laws of war. The Polish press equated Ukrainians with the Bolsheviks. The distribution of the estates of former landowners among the peasantry, sometimes with the approval of the Ukrainian authorities, in some areas the result of spontaneous land grabs, contributed to this perception. The *Kurier Lwowski* reported that the entire Polish intelligentsia living in areas close to the front and that priests in particular had been interned by the Ukrainians, who carried out frequent house searches, usually accompanied by looting. The newspaper asserted that bands of soldiers had vandalized valuable libraries and art collections, torched estates, and destroyed buildings. They had killed prisoners of war and taken their revenge on anyone who had offered shelter to Polish legionaries.[226] The *Gazeta Poranna* also reported the destruction of all traces of Polish culture, the devastation and looting of museums and libraries and demanded that all Ukrainian museums and art collections in L'viv be confiscated in retribution.[227]

The *Kurier Lwowski* reported in February 1919 from Brody that local Polish schools had been closed, private lessons prohibited, and Ukrainian inscriptions placed everywhere. The Ukrainians had seized all national assets and property in Brody. The peasants were cutting down forests and requisitioning the livestock of Polish landowners. Sixty-seven members of the Polish intelligentsia had been arrested and interned in a house. Arrests of Poles were also being reported from Chołojów and Radziechów. The newspaper believed that "the Ukrainian Bolshevik movement" was increasingly running amok in the region. Ruthenian peasants were attacking and robbing wayfarers. Nowhere was safe. If gendarmes captured a deserter, a contribution of ten thousand krone was levied against the local community, and the owner of the house where the deserter was seized was brought before a court martial.[228]

General Rozwadowski, commander in chief of the Polish troops in East Galicia, accused the enemy of murdering prisoners of war, systematically firing on medical units, behaving brutishly to civilians, killing innocent women and children, and inciting the rural population to murder Polish soldiers. Rozwadowski threatened to treat Ukrainian prisoners of war as criminals and to shoot two Ukrainians for every Polish prisoner of war who was shot.[229]

What of the relations between Jews and Ukrainians in the Ukrainian-held regions? Following the example of L'viv, Jewish communities in many towns formed Jewish militias to protect Jewish property from looting. Many areas set up Jewish national councils, who declared their intention of remaining neutral in the Polish–Ukrainian conflict.[230]

The Polish press was incensed by these declarations of neutrality. The *Kurier Lwowski* reported that all Jews living in areas under Ukrainian control favored the Ukrainians. The newspaper insisted that young Zionists were often to be found as members of Ukrainian units. But the paper also noted that not all Ukrainians behaved kindly towards their Jewish supporters. Small groups of Cossacks from the Ukraïna traveled to Galicia where they carried out robberies and pogroms. Without the militia's support, Jewish tradesmen would be unable to keep their shops open. In various small towns, Ukrainian soldiers had dragged Jews off the street to do forced labor. Some Jews had only managed to secure their own release by paying one hundred krone. In one place, a Jew had been given sixty lashes of the whip. A judge who protested against it was sentenced to twenty-five lashes but had been able to buy his way out by paying five hundred krone. Several dozen Jews, among them members of the intelligentsia, had been brought into the building of the Ukrainian gendarmerie to clean the toilets. One Jew who had refused to do the work had been whipped. The newspaper assured its readers that all of these stories chronicled true events. The *Kurier Lwowski* then recounted the rumor that Ukrainians in Berdyczów had carried out a six-day pogrom of Jews and Poles. According to the paper's implausible report, about one thousand Jews had fallen victim to the pogrom.[231] The Jewish community in Sambor complained of acts of repression under Ukrainian occupation in a detailed memorandum.[232] But the Polish starost (the head of the county administration) later commented that the Jews had been privileged compared with the situation of the Polish population. With the exception of two persons, everybody gave his or her nationality as Ukrainian in the Ukrainian census.[233]

By February 1919, the press in Warsaw was already reporting that Jews everywhere were hostile to the Ukrainian government. The wooing of Zionists by Ukrainians had been replaced by mutual hatred. Greek Catholic priests whipped up the antipathy against the Jews and called on Ukrainians to boycott Jewish shops. The anti-Semitic propaganda had triggered various robberies, and none of the peasants were still selling to Jews.[234]

As the military and economic situation became increasingly critical, attacks and discriminations increased, something the Polish press seized on and described in exaggerated detail. Anti-Semitic attacks were more common in West

Galicia than in East Galicia. Collective attacks on Jews occurred in thirty-seven different places west of the San River in December 1918.[235]

The state secretariat for internal affairs of the ZOUNR admitted that Jewish shops in Stanislau had been looted, naming recruits of a supply unit and Cossacks as the perpetrators. The state secretariat ordered the authorities to take strong action against such attacks and to prevent all forms of anti-Jewish agitation that foreign countries could use against the Ukrainian state.[236] In March 1919 the newspaper of the Ukrainian Radical Party reported on robberies committed against Jews in Tarnopol, Złoczów, Kolomea, and Stanislau.[237] But contrary to the horror stories spread by the Polish press, no large-scale pogroms occurred in the ZOUNR that matched those that took place in West Galicia or those committed later on by certain Polish and Ukrainian units during the Polish–Soviet war. Attacks on Jews did occur, some of them committed by peasants, some by soldiers, many of them East Ukrainian auxiliaries, but the Ukrainian Galician Army and Ukrainian administrative bodies were able to restrain the tide of ethnically motivated and anti-Semitic violence in their territory.

The Polish population could not reconcile itself to being part of a Ukrainian republic. During the first phase of the war, which lasted until February/March 1919, the battle was still between the Ukrainian Galician Army and the Polish inhabitants of East Galicia. At this stage, the fall of L'viv still appeared to be only a matter of time. After the collapse of the Central Powers, West Ukrainian politicians placed their hopes on the Entente and its willingness to promote the right of nations to self-determination. As mentioned earlier, a French delegation headed by Joseph Barthélemy traveled to L'viv to mediate between Poles and Ukrainians. The French government had a strong interest in settling the conflict, as a settlement would free up forces and unite them to fight against the Bolsheviks. Barthélemy's sympathies clearly lay with the Poles. The negotiated ceasefire exclusively benefitted the Poles, offering them a brief respite and the opportunity to muster their forces anew. The negotiations in Paris in April and May 1919 also yielded no results. A commission of the Entente powers proposed partitioning East Galicia, which would have left L'viv in Poland. The Ukrainians accepted the proposal, but Dmowski and Paderewski rejected it on the grounds that the administration of the West Ukrainian People's Republic had proved to be incompetent and was committing atrocities against the Polish population. The civil war in East Galicia was developing into a war between Poland and the western territories of the Ukrainian People's Republic. Haller's Army, an army of former Polish prisoners of war set up in France which also included French officers, began to intervene in the fighting. The Entente had originally only given permission for Haller's Army to be deployed against "the Bolsheviks." But the Polish government ignored these restrictions, attempting to maintain a pretense of compliance by equating West Ukrainians with Bolsheviks. The reinforcements gave the Polish side the decisive advantage.[238]

The rejection by Poles of any form of cooperation meant that there was an enormous lack of doctors in western Ukraine. Typhus and the Spanish flu began to spread. Military discipline among the soldiers slackened and mass desertions followed as the government's authority crumbled. On April 14 and 15, 1919, the Ukrainian National Council approved a land reform that would have entailed the distribution of large estates among the peasants. The planned reform was fiercely opposed by conservative National Democrats and the Greek Catholic Church, itself the owner of extensive landholdings. The National Council caved in and postponed the decision on land reforms until the future constitution of a state legislative assembly. Such halfhearted reforms did not satisfy the peasants. The first Congress of the Ukrainian Workers' and Peasants' Union, which had Bolshevik sympathies, met in Stanyslaviv (Stanislau) on May 30 and 31, 1919. The Congress demanded closer ties to the Soviet Ukrainian government and proposed continuing the war against Poland. The National Council was able to suppress a rebellion launched by Ukrainian soldiers against their officers in Drohobych with the help of loyal units of the UHA and prevent the development of a second, internal front. About 1,200 insurgents were arrested. The Social Democrat Semen Vityk, a sworn opponent of Petrushevych, was held responsible for the uprising. Vityk fled to Kam'janets'-Podil's'k (Kamieniec-Podolski) where he placed himself under the protection of the resident directorate of the UNR.[239]

Polish units broke through the ring of troops besieging L'viv in the spring of 1919. The UHA was forced to retreat in the direction of the River Zbrucz and regroup. The new commander in chief of the UHA, General Oleksander Grekov, launched another offensive to recapture L'viv in June 1919. The push for L'viv started successfully but had to be abandoned because of a lack of ammunition and a new influx of Polish reinforcements. The Ukrainian population gave its troops an enthusiastic welcome and set up guerilla units in some areas. But nothing availed. By mid-July 1919 a large part of East Galicia was in Polish hands. Some of the UHA troops had scattered, but about twenty-one thousand men moved to the territory of the Ukrainian People's Republic, where they joined Petljura. Petrushevych had recently proclaimed himself dictator and also repaired to Kam'janets'-Podil's'k together with part of his administration. Around one hundred thousand Ukrainians moved to eastern Ukraine. The war for East Galicia had cost about fifteen thousand Ukrainian and ten thousand Polish lives.[240]

The main enemy of the UNR was Soviet Russia, but the main enemy of the West Ukrainian state was Poland. It was impossible to withstand both of them at the same time. After the defeat of the UHA Petljura stopped his support of Ukrainians in Galicia as he sought to reach some form of accommodation with Poland at the expense of western Ukraine. On June 16, 1919, a Polish–Ukrainian armistice was concluded; on June 25, the Council of Allied Foreign Ministers approved the occupation of all of East Galicia by Polish troops; and on December 2, a delegation of the UNR in Warsaw agreed to the River Zbrucz as the border between Poland and Ukraine. The Galician members responded by leaving the diplomatic mission in protest. On April 21, 1920, the UNR formally relinquished East Galicia.[241]

Reprisals and Resistance

The Polish government attempted to obtain a general idea of the conquered territories in July 1919, requesting information from the returning municipal and district commissioners. The government was particularly interested in the mood among the Ukrainian population. The answers give an inconsistent picture. The head of the gendarmerie in Dolina reported that the peasants had welcomed the establishment of Ukrainian authorities, but the peasants' initial enthusiasm had turned to rejection because of the incompetence and venality of the Ukrainian authorities. However, the distribution of landed estates had won over many peasants to the new Ukrainian government. Most of the commentators were agreed that there could be no question of Ukrainian peasants having a generalized hatred of Poland. For one thing, there were many intermarriages between the two groups. Ukrainian and Polish peasants were united in their hatred of the aristocratic estates, which barred their access to woods and meadows. But the heads of administration did not detect a categorical hatred of Polish authorities. Most Polish district commissioners (starosti) were of the opinion that setting up Polish administrative bodies had not been received unfavorably. The peasants were war-weary, exasperated by the "confusion" of the Ukrainian period and wished above all for peace and security. Only one person detected a foundation for bolshevism. The starost of Rava-Ruska thought that the Ukrainian peasants were not afraid of their Polish neighbors but feared that in any future land reform the estates would be divided up among the Polish colonists (who were also referred to as *masury*, Masurians). But almost all starosti noted an enormous hatred of Jews among both the Polish and the Ukrainian peasantry. The starost of Drohobycz opined that the Jews had turned their backs on the West Ukrainian authorities because of the numerous attacks Jews had been subjected to. Some starosti reported that the Ukrainian intelligentsia had lost its influence over the peasants; others were of the opinion that the Ukrainian intelligentsia still had considerable influence as members of the intelligentsia themselves were descended from the peasant class.[242] In the district of Sokal, the "mood among the local Ruthenians with regard to the government [was] constantly hostile." Not a day passed without colonists arriving and asking for land. Almost all landowners were selling only to Poles. When Polish troops marched into the city a procession was held in which the Polish population participated and "Masurians" paraded in their national dress, but no Jews took part.[243]

When Polish troops captured Sambor, they carried out numerous acts of violence and robberies against Jews. The attacks continued for a whole day until the commander of the troops intervened. The government commissioner proved himself to be hostile to the Jews, who made up 35 percent of the population. No Jews were employed by local authorities or were allowed to be part of any local institutions of self-government; Jews were even dismissed from the civil service if they had continued to work under Ukrainian rule. Some Jews were interned, and most were not permitted to travel.[244] The starost admitted that he had dismissed Jewish teachers but argued that he had only done this because they had worked for the Ukrainian authorities and had signed Ukrainian declarations. The starost refused to hear a word about the Jewish population having been loyal to Poland. He believed that with very few exceptions all Jews had sided with the Ukrainians.[245]

The Polish inhabitants of East Galicia took issue with the decision passed by the Entente on July 21, 1919, whereby East Galicia was only placed under Polish administrative rule for a period of twenty-five years. They did not want a mandate; they had expected that the territories would finally be integrated into the state of Poland. The treaty was considered a provisional constitution until the new constitution became law. It included extensive minority rights, which were subsequently also incorporated in the March Constitution.[246] A mass demonstration was promptly held in L'viv—as usual, in front of the Mickiewicz monument. The speakers ensured their listeners that, if necessary, the "inhabitants of heroic Lwów" were prepared to take up arms again to defend the incorporation of East Galicia into Poland. The demonstrators then marched to the army headquarters where the assembled protestors cheered the Polish army, praised the defense of L'viv, and shouted their approbation of the heroes, "child defenders," and the eastern borderlands.[247]

The Ukrainian organizations also protested the decision of the Parisian peace conference. They were incensed that the Poles had been authorized to occupy East Galicia. However, they were not able to publicly express their protest and indignation in L'viv but had to resort to memoranda, which they sent in great numbers to the Entente powers and various international organizations. Ukrainian representatives hoped that these reports might persuade the Entente to revisit its decision. They submitted historical and legal arguments and launched a scathing critique of their experience of Polish rule. Ukrainian society, it was pointed out, had been subjected to a wave of arrests and lawsuits. Many members of the Ukrainian intelligentsia and many peasants and workers were in prison or in detention camps. One memorandum accused the Polish state of permitting its military units to destroy villages and Greek Catholic churches and carry out brutal acts of violence. The "Polish occupation" constituted an attack on the "classe cultivée" and the "vie intellectuelle" of Ukrainians. In July, the Brigydka prison in L'viv alone held more than two thousand Ukrainians, among them more than two hundred priests. Ukrainian newspapers were forbidden, and Ukrainian politicians had been attacked. In summary, the memorandum stated that Ukrainians had no rights under Polish rule.[248]

Another memorandum came to similar conclusions: "The Ukrainian civilian population is outside the protection of the law. During the time of the Polish-Ukrainian war on the territory of East Galicia from November 1918 to October 1919 each and every Polish soldier could with impunity kill any Ukrainian civilian without distinction of age, sex or social class." The report went on to list more than forty cases where Polish soldiers had allegedly murdered Ukrainian civilians.[249]

Even Polish eyewitnesses noted that the soldiers requisitioned what they wanted at will, beat the peasants, and clearly sided with the landowners. On December 15, 1919, the Council of Ministers attempted a gesture of reconciliation and ordered that all interned persons be released. A revision commission subsequently released 2,224 prisoners, among them most of the interned priests. Only seven Greek Catholic clergymen remained in custody.[250]

The government was less conciliatory on the question of Ukrainian civil servants. In the spring of 1919, Ukrainian state employees refused to take the required oath of allegiance to the Polish nation and the Polish state to prevent the government from making the case that West Ukrainians were prepared to accept the final incorporation of their territory into Poland. Following this widespread refusal to take the oath, thousands of civil servants and state employees (including 5,000 railroad employees, 1,500 of them in L'viv) were dismissed on April 1. The authorities justified the dismissals with the need to consider the mood of the Polish population, which would not understand if, for example, gendarmes who had served in the ZUNR, were accepted into the civil service.[251] But after the Entente had granted the mandate to Poland to occupy East Galicia, giving a conditional legitimacy to Polish rule, Ukrainians wanted to return to the civil service. Ukrainians were even prepared to take a modified oath swearing allegiance to the Polish state. But by October 1920, many Ukrainians had still not been reinstated (including 2,500 railroad employees, 700 of them in L'viv).[252]

The State Police Command for Lesser Poland opined in January 1920 that the Ukrainian and Jewish populations were beginning to reconcile themselves to Polish rule. The security situation had improved, even if in some regions banditry and looting had increased. Disaffection because of the inadequacy of available supplies was rife among the lower and middle classes, creating a fertile soil for revolutionary propaganda. The state police had not observed open agitation in support of bolshevism or communism, despite the proximity to areas under Bolshevik control. It was only among railroad employees in L'viv, in the district of Sokal, among Jews and landless peasants that the state police found Bolshevik propaganda.[253]

Banditry continued to be a significant problem in L'viv. Contributing factors included the continued outage of the street lighting due to the destruction of the electric power station. The police force was notoriously understaffed and was not even capable of enforcing closing hours. To compensate for the lack of police, a municipal citizens' protection force (MSO) stepped in to control the bars and keep an eye on "shady lowlifes." The MSO was soon in competition with the state police and involved in disputes with the police directorate. It lost this power struggle, was subordinated to the police and finally dissolved..[254]

The War with Soviet Russia

For a long time, it was unclear where the precise borders of the Second Polish Republic would be. In the wake of the Poznań uprising in January 1919, the Poles controlled almost the entire province of Poznań, creating a fait accompli in the west, which the Entente had to accept. In areas with mixed German and Polish populations, the question of national affiliation was decided by plebiscite. Prior to a plebiscite in Silesia, Poles attempted to influence the decision in their favor by staging three uprisings. Finally, although the results of the vote favored Germany, the province of Silesia was partitioned, and the economically more important part was given to Poland. The overwhelming majority of the population in the Eastern Prussian districts of Allenstein and Marienwerder voted to remain with Germany. In the dispute with Czechoslovakia for the region of the former Duchy of Teschen (Cieszyn), Poland lost out, with the Allies deciding to award Poland only the eastern part of the territory it had laid claim to.

In Warsaw, Józef Piłsudski began setting matters straight. He was by far the most popular Polish politician. The Regency Council had transferred power to him shortly after his arrival in Warsaw. The competing seats of power, that is, the Liquidation Committee in Cracow and the Provisional People's Government of the Republic of Poland under the Social Democrat Ignacy Dąszyński, deferred to his authority as chief of state (Naczelnik Państwa). Piłsudski had come to a temporary arrangement with his long-standing opponent, the National Democrat Roman Dmowski. Dmowski was an extremely able advocate of Polish interests at the peace conference in Paris. After Piłsudski had established himself as the undisputed head of the new state, Polish troops occupied Vilnius and Belarusian territories as far as Minsk in April 1919. On December 8, 1919, the Supreme Allied Council presented a plan whereby the eastern border of Poland would follow the course of the Bug and San Rivers. This plan (later named after the British foreign secretary Lord Curzon) was based on ethnographic considerations and would have left those territories where the majority of the population was Polish with Poland. But Piłsudski had far more ambitious goals. He hoped to bring the eastern border as close as possible to the former borders of 1772 and proposed a federation of states under Polish leadership, which would include Belarus, Lithuania, and Ukraine. After Piłsudski came to an initial agreement on the proposed border with the Soviet government, he concluded a defensive military alliance on April 21, 1920—in opposition to the wishes of the National Democratic Party—with the Ataman of the Ukrainian People's Republic, Symon Petljura, against Soviet Russia. Piłsudski promised Petljura to support the establishment of a Ukrainian state outside the borders of 1772. At this point, Petljura had already lost the war against the Red Army and only had a few thousand soldiers left, most of them on Polish territory. In February 1920 these forces were combined and by the beginning of March there were two Ukrainian divisions consisting of eight thousand men. The offensive by Polish and Ukrainian troops was launched on April 25, 1920. It was initially successful, capturing Kiev in the first week of May.[255] However, at the end of June 1920, the Red Army started a counteroffensive whose momentum took the Polish leadership by surprise. Two separate forces, one in the north and one in the south, pushed westward, driving the Polish army in front of them. One of the goals of the Bolsheviks was, in the words of the commander in chief of the troops on Soviet Russia's western front, Mikhail Tukhachevskij, to kindle a "world conflagration" in the west over "the corpse of White Poland." The Red Army was not strong enough to attempt a march on Berlin, but Lenin hoped that smashing Poland would topple the Versailles system and trigger revolutionary uprisings across Western Europe. In the southwest, the Red Army invaded East Galicia and threatened L'viv.[256]

The Red Army was assisted behind the lines by the Communist Party of Poland, which had been formed on December 16, 1918 out of the revolutionary Social Democratic Party of the Kingdom of Poland and Lithuania (SDKPiL) and the left wing of the PPS. The Communist Party attempted to induce the workers to go on strike. Even before the Red Army marched into East Galicia, the Bolsheviks had created a Galician Revolutionary Committee, based in Tarnopol, to act as a provisional government. The Revolutionary Committee was headed by the Ukrainian Bolshevik Volodymyr Zatons'kyj. Zatons'kyj informed Lenin at the end of July 1920 that the Ukrainian population, including the Ukrainian intelligentsia, would welcome the Red Army as "liberators from the rule of the *Pane* [masters]." This was a little premature. Although Ukrainian peasants perceived Polish rule as an occupation, their welcome of the Bolsheviks was far from unanimous. The antireligious policies of the Bolsheviks, the arrests and murders of clergymen, were unlikely to elicit much sympathy among the general population. The West Ukrainian population remained largely passive. Only landless peasants and impoverished villagers, irrespective of their nationality, expected to benefit from a Bolshevik government. The Galician Revolutionary Committee gave the peasants land; set up its own administrative organization, a security service, and a militia; and began a recruitment drive to encourage people to join the Galician Red Army. The Galician Revolutionary Committee implemented these policies in the sixteen districts occupied by the Red Army in the summer of 1920.[257]

At a secret meeting of the Ukrainian National Council in L'viv on May 19, 1920, the discussion revolved around the feelings of West Ukrainians towards the Polish–Ukrainian union and the war against the Soviet Russia. Archbishop Sheptyts'kyj was the first to speak and opined that they would first have to agree on who they considered the greatest enemy of Ukraine: Russia or Poland. Only then would it be possible to deliberate further. In the discussion that followed, all agreed that Russia was the greater enemy. Everyone present agreed to give his or her utmost support to Petljura.[258] However, police director Reinlender reported that some West Ukrainian politicians did not share this general opinion and were in contact with Rakovs'kyj's Soviet Ukrainian government as they supported a union between East Galicia and Soviet Ukraine.[259]

In July 1920 a Central Relief Committee for the Defenders of Eastern Lesser Poland was formed in L'viv, renaming itself the Citizen's Executive Committee for the Defense of the State in L'viv on July 27. The committee's chairman was the delegate general of the government of Eastern Lesser Poland, Kazimierz Gałecki. Faced with the looming threat of the Red Army, the political parties temporarily abandoned their wrangling. Czesław Mączyński, recently promoted to colonel, launched an appeal for the population to join the Lesser Poland Units of the Voluntary Army. All men between the ages of sixteen and sixty were called on to enlist. In the end, more than forty thousand men from East Galicia took part in the fighting. Substantial numbers joined, with 13,440 men, among them 1,503 Greek Catholics, joining the Voluntary Army and a further 15,321 men joining various civilian militias. But it proved almost impossible to mobilize the poorest villagers, most of whom deserted as soon as the opportunity arose.[260]

If the police reports were to be believed, the population was exhausted and apathetic. But preparations for the battle with the Red Army began everywhere. The police command of Lesser Poland noted a readiness to serve their country among well-educated people and the working class. But the members of the peasantry appeared to lack any understanding of their own and their country's interests. They did not join the army and generally attempted to avoid making any financial contributions. The effect of Bolshevik propaganda on the Polish population worried the police command.[261] In the opinion of the police command, the exhaustion of parts of the population and the hopes placed in the Red Army were helping "Ukrainian–Jewish–Communist propaganda." But irrespective of whether they lived in occupied or free territories the Polish population and all persons who felt themselves to be Polish behaved impeccably. "Even consciously Polish workers understood their obligations to the fatherland and did not allow themselves to be seduced by Bolshevik agitators."[262]

The worsening security situation compounded the military threat. In the district of Rudki, there were reports in August of Jewish chandlers allegedly trading on people's fears to buy livestock and grain cheaply. Security was poorest in the villages. Livestock was stolen and the bigger estates were looted. Ukrainians targeted colonies of Polish Masurians and carried out acts of sabotage.[263] Robberies, murders, and illegal requisitioning were the order of the day.[264] After the families of some of the civil servants fled to the west in fear of the Red Army, village women carrying cloths and baskets turned up at the deserted houses and apartments to loot them. Many armed deserters were hiding out in the forests from where they carried out random attacks. The military police and the gendarmerie found it very difficult to get the problem under control.[265] Yet another security problem was created by scattered groups of Polish and Ukrainian soldiers from the UNR who robbed and raped with impunity. The Petljura troops were often from East Galicia, and they were loud in their declarations that they would soon be settling scores with the Poles.[266] The Polish inhabitants of the borderlands lived in terrible fear of soldiers of the UNR. Their headquarters were in the district of Buczacz, where numerous attacks on Polish institutions by Ukrainian soldiers were reported. The starost of Czortków believed that West Ukrainians were cherishing hopes hostile to Poland and requested that troops be dispatched to preserve the peace and restore order. It was the only way to keep the Poles from panicking. In the eastern part of the district, the population was being forced to accept Ukrainian banknotes, and signs bearing Polish inscriptions were being pulled down.[267]

The successful attack by the Red Army raised the hopes of some Ukrainian intellectuals that there would be a repeat of the Ukrainian seizure of power in East Galicia. But Ukrainian peasants suffered under the raids and plunderings, not least from the attacks carried out by Petljura's troops, and were not given to hostile acts against Poles. Most people had had enough of politics and wished for peace at all costs.[268] But the "Ukrainian–Galician agitation" continued to increase in intensity and its influence over the Ukrainian population had grown. The police command was of the opinion that the Ukrainian intelligentsia was entirely hostile to Poland and prepared to cooperate with any enemy of Poland. Landless peasants and peasants who did not have enough land looked to bolshevism for both personal and national reasons.[269]

In June 1920 the starost of Jaworów believed that he had also detected silent supporters of bolshevism among the Jewish and Ukrainian intelligentsia and noted a rapprochement between Ukrainians and Jews which was directed against Poland.[270] Two months later he observed "delight among the Ukrainian population and parts of the Jewish population because of the approaching Bolsheviks."[271]

The state police believed that the invasion had proved that the Ukrainian intelligentsia would never accept the incorporation of Eastern Lesser Poland into the state of Poland and would use all and any means at its disposal to launch another armed rebellion. The Social Democratic newspapers *Vpered* and *Ukraïns'ki Holos* had even been prepared to countenance East Galicia joining Soviet Ukraine.

The hatred of Poland persisted even after victory. In contrast, villagers and rural populations were viewed as "inherently passive" but not as particularly hostile. The state police described the Ukrainian populace as not very intelligent and willing to follow where the Jews and Ukrainian leaders led.[272]

Jewish inhabitants of small Galician towns were unhappy with Polish rule. They were frequent victims of requisitioning by troops of the UNR or the Polish army. Many Jewish communists had ties to the Bund. They were happy to exploit the dissatisfaction rife among Jews and called on them to boycott the Polish army and the Voluntary Army, tearing down propaganda bills and agitating against the Polish state in the villages. The authorities responded in mid-July 1920 by arresting members of the Bund and other organizations sympathizing with the Bolsheviks in L'viv and other Galician cities.[273] The police was unsure how to rate the Jews. In some areas, they went along with the Bolsheviks; in other areas they remained passive, while in other areas they worked alongside the Polish population. But despite these contradictory reports, the police command remained convinced that the Jews were resentful and hostile to the Polish state. The police command accordingly considered Jews to be the most important organizers behind the revolutionary committees.[274]

The police command for Lesser Poland believed that a heavy hand would be needed as this was the only means of protecting and maintaining Polish rights in East Galicia. All hopes of coming to some form of accommodation with the Jews and Ukrainians were illusory. The Jews in particular, it was said, set their hopes on a dictatorship of the proletariat under which they expected to claim an important share in government. They evaded being drafted, purchased no government bonds, spread panic, and bought real estate and other property at knockdown prices from worried Poles. "The Jews are a demoralizing ferment .." Jews were believed to have secreted Bolshevik proclamations and to be carrying out "criminal, anti-government activities" in the villages and among the working class.[275]

The attitude of Jews toward the Polish army in the areas nearer the frontline was ambivalent. There were numerous anti-Jewish excesses, in which units from Poznań and from Haller's Army played particularly prominent roles. A number of pogroms occurred during the retreat, which may have cost the lives of several thousand Jews. Army commanders attempted to stop such excesses. The command of the Sixth Polish Army ordered that Jews must not be collectively called to account for assisting the Red Army. On July 30, 1920, General Kazimierz Sosnkowski, the minister for military affairs, threatened to punish anyone severely who participated in anti-Jewish excesses. A few people were even sentenced to death.[276] The end of September and the beginning of October 1920 saw a fresh wave of attacks and assaults committed against Jews in many of the southern districts of East Galicia by some of Petljura's troops. The Ukrainian military command imposed harsh punishments on the perpetrators.[277]

The Jewish population—according to the account of the police command for Lesser Poland—still continued to act "always to the detriment of the Polish state" but was beginning to lean toward the Polish side the under the impression of the atrocities committed by both the Red Army and the Petljura troops. But there was still no concrete proof that the Jews had conclusively changed their inclinations. "The overwhelming majority of the Jewish intelligentsia, who are drawn from the professions, and the majority of Jewish workers continue to be hostile to us and are prepared at any moment to pursue aims unfavorable to us."[278]

The Polish press and the Polish police collectively accused Jews of providing aid to the Red Army. But this perception was wrong. The main council of the Association of Poles of Jewish Faith in all Polish Territories issued an appeal to the Jewish population on July 11, 1920, to assist in the defense of Poland. The coalition of Zionist organizations also called on Jews to carry out their civic duties. Orthodox Jews were afraid that a victory by the Red Army would result in the destruction of Jewish religion and culture.[279]

The delegate general of the government of East Galicia commented that the Bolshevik invasion, chaos, and anarchy had changed the attitude of Jews toward the Polish state. Now all Jews, whether they were Polish, nationalist, or unaffiliated, were prepared to accept the permanent incorporation of East Galicia into the Polish Republic.[280] The police command for Lesser Poland confirmed that Jewish political affiliations were inclining more towards Poland. A closer acquaintance with bolshevism had resulted in bolshevism losing many of its supporters. "All of society without distinction of nationality or party allegiance noted any peace activity with a feeling of relief and visible satisfaction and awaits a permanent peace."[281]

The behavior of Jews was as inconsistent as that of Poles and Ukrainians. In Tarnopol, the temporary headquarters of the Bolshevik Revolutionary Committee for East Galicia, the Jewish population often came to the assistance of Poles.[282] The soldiers' newspaper *Gazetka Żołnierska* reported that in Tarnopol Poles, Ruthenians and Jews had collectively celebrated the ousting of the Red Army. More than ten thousand inhabitants enthusiastically welcomed the Polish army and listened to Polish, Ukrainian, and Jewish speakers accusing the Red Army of numerous crimes, robberies, acts of terror, and murders.[283]

Finally, in October 1920, Jewish inhabitants came together in thirty cities to vote for the union of East Galicia with Poland. A resolution from Tarnopol proclaimed, "After the experiences of recent years and sick of Bolshevik 'governments' we hold the deep conviction that . . . only within the Polish state will we find a refuge where we may live and have a chance to exist."[284]

What were the reactions to the Polish–Soviet war in L'viv? As the Red Army approached in September 1920, the mayoralty of L'viv called on the city's inhabitants in this time of great danger to do their duty for "the beloved fatherland."

The battle against their "ferocious enemy" meant defending Poland against the "flood of eastern barbarism." It reminded its readers of the recent heroic deeds performed in the battle for the Polish character of L'viv: "We call upon you, citizens of Lwów, without distinction of class, age, sex or denomination, to stand by us as we hold watch for the honor of the city, to come and join the ranks of the defenders of the fatherland, the defenders of western civilization."[285]

Poland was once again standing tall in the "defense of Christian civilization and culture against the fierce attacking hordes."[286] The Red Army was unable to take L'viv. In the early days of the battle for L'viv, one battalion captained by Bolesław Zajączkowski held its ground near Zadwórze on August 17 until the last bullet was spent. Three hundred eighteen officers and young soldiers, most of them from L'viv, were cut down and battered to death by Cossack troops wielding sabers and rifle butts. This event went down in the heroic story of L'viv as the "Polish Battle of Thermopylae."[287] The renewed defense of L'viv represented a significant turning point in the war. The Soviet Russian Southwestern Army was determined to conquer the city instead of coming to the assistance of the Soviet armies of the Northwestern Front as Tukhachevskij demanded. This created the conditions for the Polish victory in the battle for Warsaw, subsequently often referred to as the "Miracle at the Vistula." After its defeat, the Red Army was forced to pull back from East Galicia.

The Polish authorities were unsure how they should proceed with collaborators in East Galicia. Initially it was proposed to bring all persons who had cooperated with the Soviets, worked for the local authorities, or registered for the citizens' militia before a court-martial. But this proved unfeasible; even the district commissioners advised against carrying out the idea, as many people had only cooperated with the Soviets under duress. Moreover, this would also have implied calling the Polish workers to account who had sabotaged the war effort with strikes. In the end, only 407 people in all of East Galicia were sentenced because of their behavior during the war.[288]

Negotiations for a cessation of hostilities began on September 16, 1920. While the Soviet Russian leadership was keen to conclude peace quickly as this would free up their armies to fight against the remaining counterrevolutionary armies, opinions in Poland were divided. Suggestions ranged from continuing the war to securing what had been achieved by that point through a peace settlement. But plans were still being mooted to create a federation that would include Lithuania, Belarus, and Ukraine. In the end, the desire for peace prevailed. Piłsudski relinquished his Ukrainian policies and reluctantly jettisoned Petljura. In the Treaty of Riga signed on March 18, 1921, Poland received territories with Belarusian and Ukrainian majority populations extending up to 150 kilometers beyond the Curzon line. The war in East Galicia only ended with the conclusion of this treaty.

Notes

1. "Manifestam pol's'kosty L'vova," *Dilo*, October 25, 1918.
2. TsDIAL, f. 146, op. 8, spr. 5329, ark. 1: presidium of the police directorate (Präsidium der Polizeidirektion) L'viv to the Ministry of the Interior, September 26, 1918.
3. DALO, f. 350, op. 1, spr. 4434, ark. 33–38: police directorate L'viv to the Ministry of the Interior, October 7, 1918.
4. Governor Huyn to the Ministry of the Interior, October 16, 1918, in *Ereignisse in der Ukraine 1914–1922*, vol. 4, 41–42.
5. TsDIAL, f. 146, op. 6, spr. 1404, ark. 161–66: Reinlender to the Ministry of the Interior, October 10, 1918.
6. Ibid.
7. Skrzypek, "Ukraińcy w Austrii podczas wielkiej wojny i geneza zamachu na Lwów," 367. Michał Klimecki, "Das Ende der österreichische Souveränität in Galizien im Oktober–November 1918," in *Między Wiedniem a Lwowem: Zwischen Wien und Lemberg. Die Vorträge der polnisch-österreichischen Tagung zum 80. Jahrestag des Ausbruchs des Ersten Weltkriegs, Warschau, den 17. November 1994*, ed. Andrzej Rzepniewski (Warsaw: Austriacki Instytut Kultury we Warszawie, Wojskowy Instytut Historyczny, 1996), 163–70.
8. K. u. k. Governor Count Karl von Huyn to the Ministry of the Interior (Vienna), October 16, 1918, in *Ereignisse in der Ukraine 1914–1922*, vol. 4, 41–42.
9. PA, R-8980: the liaison officer of the German Army in L'viv, Rittmeister Gebsattel, to Major von Berghes (office of the quartermaster general in Berlin), October 1, 1918.
10. DALO, f. 257, op. 234, ark. 41–43: commander of the k. u. k. gendarmerie in Galicia and the Bukovina to k. u. k. Army High Command (Nachrichtenabteilung), October 21, 1918. On the Imperial Manifesto and the regulations concerning East Galicia, see Klimecki, *Polsko-ukraińska wojna*, 45–47. Mroczka, *Spór o Galicję Wschodnią 1914–1923*, 63–65.
11. DALO, f. 257, op. 234, ark. 41–43: commander of the k. u. k. gendarmerie in Galicia and the Bukovina to k. u. k. Army High Command (Nachrichtenabteilung), October 21, 1918. PA, R-8980: Rittmeister von Gebsattel to Chancellor Max von Baden, October 21, 1918.
12. Vasyl'ko to Archduke Wilhelm, October 19, 1918, in *Ereignisse in der Ukraine 1914–1922*, vol. 4, 44–45. Veryha, *Vyzvol'ni zmahannja v Ukraïni 1914–1923 rr.*, vol. 1, 406–409.
13. DALO, f. 257, op. 234, ark. 41–43: commander of the k. u. k. gendarmerie in Galicia and the Bukovina to k. u. k. Army High Command (Nachrichtenabteilung), October 21, 1918. Vasyl'ko to Archduke Wilhelm, October 19, 1918, in *Ereignisse in der Ukraine 1914–1922*, vol. 4, 44–45.
14. "Zhydy i Nimtsi," *Dilo*, October 17, 1918.
15. "Vybyrajte: vijny chy myr?" *Dilo*, October 10, 1918.
16. Klimecki, "Das Ende der österreichische Souveränität in Galizien," 165.
17. Police director Reinlender to the Ministry of the Interior, October 20, 1918, in *Ereignisse in der Ukraine 1914–1922*, vol. 4, 45–46.
18. DALO, f. 350, op. 1, spr. 4506, ark. 13: declaration by Schleicher and resolution of the L'viv city council, October 20, 1918. Report of the police directorate L'viv (by phone) for the presidium of the Ministry of the Interior, Vienna, October 20, 1918, in *Ereignisse in der Ukraine 1914–1922*, vol. 4, 45–46. DALO, f. 2, op. 22, spr. 1911, ark. 685: protocols of the sessions of the provisional city council in 1918. Józef Klink, "W przededniu listopadowej obrony Lwowy," in *Obrona Lwowa*, vol. 2, 637. Henryka

Kramarz, "Ze sceny walk polsko-ukraińskich o Lwów," in *Galicja i jej dziedzictwo*, vol. 1, 102–103. On October 24, 1918, another Polish manifestation took place. Ten thousand listened to the deputy government commissioner for L'viv, Józef Neumann, who emphasized the "Polish character of the city of L'viv" and demanded the unification of East Galicia with the Polish state. TsDIAL, f. 146, op. 8t, spr. 2679, ark. 2: police directorate L'viv to the Ministry of the Interior, Vienna, October 24, 1918.
19. Reinlender to the Ministry of the Interior, October 20, 1918, in *Ereignisse in der Ukraine 1914–1922*, vol. 4, 45–46.
20. TsDIAL, f. 146, op. 8t, spr. 2679, ark. 2: Reinlender to the Ministry of the Interior, October 24, 1918.
21. "Borot'ba za Skhidnu Halychynu," *Dilo*, October 24, 1918.
22. DALO, f. 350, op.1, spr. 4434, ark. 41: appeal of the governor of Galicia to the department heads of the governor's office and to all district commissioners (*Kreishauptleute*), October 28, 1918.
23. Klimecki, "Das Ende der österreichische Souveränität in Galizien," 163–70. Mroczka, *Spór o Galicję Wschodnią 1914–1923*, 93–94. Torsten Wehrhahn, *Die Westukrainische Volksrepublik: Zu den polnisch-ukrainischen Beziehungen und dem Problem der ukrainischen Staatlichkeit in den Jahren 1918 bis 1923* (Berlin: Weißensee Verlag, 2004), 127–53.
24. Recollections of an anonymous participant of the fighting "Pierwsze dni walk o polski Lwów," *Gazeta Poranna*, December 6, 1918. Klimecki, *Polsko-ukraińska wojna*, 65.
25. "Pol's'kyj zamach," *Dilo*, November 1, 1918. "Jak Ukraïns'ka Natsional'na Rada perejjala vlast' u svoï ruky u L'vovi," *Dilo*, November 3, 1918.
26. Veryha, *Vyzvol'ni zmahannja v Ukraïni 1914–1923*, vol. 1, 410–11. Klimecki, *Polsko-ukraińska wojna*, 62–63. Kost' Levyts'kyj, *Velykyj zryv* (L'viv: Samoosvita, 1931). Dmytro Paliïv, *Lystopadova revoljutsija: Z moïkh spomynyv* (L'viv: Novyj Chas, 1929).
27. "1 Listopada r. 1918," *Gazeta Poranna*, November 1, 1919. "Z przed roku: 1 listopada (piątek)," *Słowo Polskie*, November 2, 1919. *Wiek Nowy*, November 3, 1918. Mroczka, *Spór o Galicję Wschodnią 1914–1923*, 96–97.
28. TsDIAL, f. 837, op. 1, spr. 71, ark. 44–45: recollections of a Polish fighter, after 1919.
29. DALO, f. 257, op. 2, spr. 1515, ark. 27–29: recollections of Józef Rafalski (1933).
30. DALO, f. 257, op. 2, d. 1657, ark. 30–47: memoirs of Janina Chomówna, n.d. (probably 1935).
31. Oleksa Kuz'ma, *Lystopadovi dni 1918 r.* (L'viv: Chervona Kalyna, 1931), 71.
32. See also the statistical information in *Obrona Lwowa*, vol. 3, 437.
33. "Ukraïns'ka Natsional'na Rada obnjala vlast' u L'vovi i kraju!" *Ukraïns'ke Slovo*, November 2, 1918. "Do naselenja mista L'vova! Energichno i v ladï!" *Ukraïns'ke Slovo*, November 2, 1918. "1 Listopada r. 1918," *Gazeta Poranna*, November 1, 1918.
34. Veryha, *Vyzvol'ni zmahannja v Ukraïni 1914–1923*, vol. 1, 410–14.
35. "Energichno i v ladï!" *Ukraïns'ke Slovo*, November 2, 1918.
36. "Zamach ukraiński na Lwów w świetle ukraińskich pamiętników z czasów oblężenia Lwowa," *Gazeta Poranna*, May 10, 1920.
37. Polish newspapers counted six thousand Ukrainian and four thousand Polish fighters. "Siły i straty po obu stronach," *Gazeta Wieczorna*, November 4, 1918. Mroczka, *Spór o Galicję Wschodnią 1914–1923*, 97.
38. Klimecki, *Polsko-ukraińska wojna*, 86.
39. "Shche w l'vivs'kych perezhyvan," *Dilo*, November 7, 1918.
40. TsDIAL, f. 841, op. 1, spr. 169-a: Dr. Marceli Prószyński, "Ze wspomnień listopadowych" (clipping from an unknown Polish newspaper).

41. Tadeusz M. Nilman, "Niezapomniana chwile," *Gazeta Lwowska*, November 1, 1919. "Kronika," *Gazeta Wieczorna*, November 4, 1918.
42. "Eine Erklärung des Statthalters," *Neue Lemberger Zeitung*, November 3, 1918.
43. "Zvidomlennja Nachal'noï Komandy Ukraïns'kykh Vijs'k," *Dilo*, November 9, 1918.
44. *Dilo*, November 4, 1918.
45. Cited after *Dilo*, November 4, 1918.
46. "Ciężkie dni Lwowa," *Wiek Nowy*, November 3, 1918.
47. Józef Klink, "Historyczna noc (Wrażenia i przeżycia z 31 października na 1 listopada," *Gazeta Lwowska*, November 1, 1919. Adam Schwetz, "Ze zdarzeń d. 2 listopada 1918," *Gazeta Lwowska*, November 4, 1919.
48. "Der jüdische Sicherheitsausschuss," *Neue Lemberger Zeitung*, November 3, 1918. "O neutralność," *Chwila*, January 12, 1919.
49. The Jewish militia protected the area bordered by the following streets: Kleparowska; Weteranów; Pod Dębem; Panienska, Zborowskich, Kąpielna; Zamkowa; Klasztorna; Podwale; Sobeskiego; Karola Ludwika; Jagiellońska; Kołątaja; Kazimierska; Kleparowska. DALO, f. 257, op. 2, spr. 1497, ark. 12: contract between the Jewish militia and the Polish troops (copy), November 10, 1918.
50. The deputy rector of the university Adolf Beck and Dr. Schlenker. Klimecki, *Polsko-Ukraińska wojna*, 80. "Zhydy-Poljaky suproty l'vivs'kych podij," *Dilo*, November 29, 1918.
51. Klimecki, *Polsko-Ukraińska wojna*, 74.
52. Mroczka, *Spór o Galicję Wschodnią 1914–1923*, 114.
53. "Urjadovyj akt ukraïns'kij natsional'nij radi, November 1," 1918, *Dilo*, November 7, 1918.
54. For example "Die jüdische Miliz," *Neue Lemberger Zeitung*, November 14, 1918.
55. "Vom Tage," *Neue Lemberger Zeitung*, November 15, 1918.
56. "Die jüdische Miliz," *Neue Lemberger Zeitung*, November 17, 1918.
57. "W 'Głównej kwaterze' Ukraińskiej," *Wiek Nowy*, November 3, 1918.
58. "Die polnisch-ukrainischen Verhandlungen," *Neue Lemberger Zeitung*, November 3, 1918.
59. "Rokowania," *Wiek Nowy*, November 3, 1918. *Dilo*, November 3, 1918. "Verhandlungen des ukrainischen Nationalrates (übernommen aus Dilo)," *Neue Lemberger Zeitung*, November 3, 1918. See also Marceli Chlamtacz, "Relacja o obronie Lwowa w listopadzie 1918 r.," in *Obrona Lwowa*, vol. 2, 113–20. Klimecki, *Polsko-ukraińska wojna*, 83–84. Mroczka, *Spór o Galicję Wschodnią 1914–1923*, 114–18. W. Kutschabsky [Vasyl' Kuchabs'kyj], *Die Westukraine im Kampfe mit Polen und dem Bolschewismus in den Jahren 1918–1923* (Berlin: Junker and Dünnhaupt, 1934), 56–60.
60. "Rokowania polsko-ukraińskie," *Gazeta Wieczorna*, November 4, 1918. On the military developments, see Klimecki, *Polsko-ukraińska wojna*. Kozłowski, *Zapomniana wojna*. Łukomski, Partacz, and Polak, *Wojna polsko-ukraińska 1918–1919*. Mykola Lytvyn, "Ukraïns'ko-pol's'ka borot'ba za L'viv: vijs'kovo-politychnyj aspekt (Lystopad 1918–sichen' 1919 rr.)," in *L'viv: Misto—suspil'stvo—kul'tura*, vol. 3, 462–68. Mykola Lytvyn, "Stolytsa Zakhidno-ukraïns'koï Narodnoï Respubliky," in *L'viv: Istorychni narysy*, 330–56. Antin Krezub, *Narys istoriji ukraïns'ko-pol'skoï vijny 1918–1919* (New York: Oko, 1966). Mychajlo Lozhyns'ky, *Halychyna w rokach 1918–1920* (Vienna: Institut Sociologique Ukrainien, 1922). *Obrona Lwowa, 1–22 listopada 1918*, all 3 vols.
61. "Do ludności miasta Lwowa!" *Gazeta Wieczorna*, November 4, 1918.
62. "Die Kämpfe in der Stadt," *Neue Lemberger Zeitung*, November 3, 1918.
63. Ibid.

64. "Eine Warnung des ukrainischen Stadtkommandos," *Neue Lemberger Zeitung*, November 3, 1918.
65. TsDIAL, f. 201, op. 1t, spr. 249, ark. 2–3: Polish proclamation from November 7, 1918.
66. "Do pol's'koho naselennja mista L'vova!" *Dilo*, November 9, 1918.
67. "Die westukrainische Republik," *Neue Lemberger Zeitung*, November 15, 1918. Veryha, *Vyzvol'ni zmahannja v Ukraïni 1914–1923*, vol. 1, 419–26. Kutschabsky, *Die Westukraine im Kampfe mit Polen und dem Bolschewismus*, 45–46.
68. "Pershyj tyzhden' ukraïns'koï derzhavnoï vlasty," *Dilo*, November 9, 1918.
69. DALO, f. 257, op. 2, d. 1512, ark. 3–6: recollections of the engineer Witold Zaborowski, n.d. (probably 1934).
70. "Das Stadttheater," *Neue Lemberger Zeitung*, November 3, 1918.
71. "Piąty dzień walk we Lwowie," *Gazeta Wieczorna*, November 6, 1918.
72. TsDIAL, f. 837, op. 1, spr. 71, ark. 46–53: report by Józef Duda, n.d. (after 1919).
73. Józef Klink, "Historyczna noc (Wrażenia i przeżycia z 31 października na 1 listopada)," *Gazeta Lwowska*, November 1, 1919.
74. T. M. Nittman, "Walka o Lwów," in *Obrona Lwowa*, vol. 2, 269. Klimecki, *Polsko-ukraińska wojna*, 88. Mroczka, *Spór o Galicję Wschodnią 1914–1923*, 103.
75. TsDIAL, f. 837, op. 1, spr. 71, ark. 59–65: report by Feliks R. Buna about November 1918 in L'viv, n.d. (December 1918 or January 1919).
76. The High Command of the Polish troops, for example, had received news that on November 8 Ukrainian soldiers had executed six Polish prisoners of war. Mączyński demanded that the Ukrainian High Command respect international law, otherwise Polish troops would react accordingly. DALO, f. 257, op. 2, spr. 1497, ark. 62: Mączyński to the command of the Ukrainian troops in L'viv (copy), November 8, 1918. The Ukrainian High Command wrote back that there had been no executions of prisoners and asked for evidence. Ibid., ark. 63: Ukrainian High Command to the Polish High Command (copy), November 8, 1918.
77. "Z kim vojujemo," *Dilo*, November 13, 1918. "Otzhe z kym vojujemo?" *Dilo*, November 15, 1918.
78. DALO, f. 257, op. 2, spr. 1497, ark. 64: Ukrainian High Command to the Polish High Command (copy), November 18, 1918.
79. Ibid., ark. 57–58: report by Professor Hornowski for the Polish High Command, November 12, 1918.
80. "Z kim vojujemo," *Dilo*, November 13, 1918. "Novynky," *Dilo*, November 13, 1918. See also the correspondence between the two archbishops Andrij Sheptyts'kyj and Józef Bilczewski. *Nieznana korespondencja arcybiskupów metropolitów Lwowskich Józefa Bilczewskiego z Andrzejem Szeptyckim w czasie wojny Polsko-Ukraińskiej 1918–1919* (L'viv: Wydawnictwo Bł. Jakuba Strzemię Archidiecezji Lwowskiej Ob. Łac, 1997). Franciszek Salezy Krysiak, *Z dni grozy we Lwowie (1–22 listopada 1918)* (Rzeszów: Dextra, 2003; first edition Cracow: G. Gebethner, 1919), 99–118.
81. Cited after "Otzhe z kym vojujemo?" *Dilo*, November 15, 1918. Klimecki, *Polsko-ukraińska wojna*, 94.
82. "Z kim vojujemo," *Dilo*, November 13, 1918. "Novynky," *Ukraïns'ke Slovo*, November 13, 1918. "Otshe z kym vojuemo?" *Dilo*, November 15, 1918.
83. "Ratusz w czasie inwazji ukraińskiej," *Kurier Lwowski*, March 4, 1919.
84. "Ukrainisch-polnische Verhandlungen," *Neue Lemberger Zeitung*, November 13, 1918.
85. "Polnisch-ukrainische Verhandlungen," *Neue Lemberger Zeitung*, November 15, 1918.
86. "Polnisch-ukrainische Verhandlungen," *Neue Lemberger Zeitung*, November 17, 1918.
87. "Der Kampf um Lemberg," *Neue Lemberger Zeitung*, November 15, 1918. PA, R-8980: record of the German Consul Heinze, December 12, 1918.

88. "Do choho vojny dovodjat," *Dilo*, November 15, 1918.
89. "Vom Tage," *Neue Lemberger Zeitung*, November 17, 1918.
90. DALO, f. 257, op. 2, spr. 1497, ark. 54: Polish High Command to the commander of the Ukrainian troops (copy), November 15, 1918.
91. DALO, f. 257, op. 2, spr. 1155, ark. 9: proclamation of the council of worker's delegates of the PPSD in L'viv (copy), n.d. (early November 1918).
92. Proclamation of the executive committee of the Ukrainian Social Democratic Party of Galicia and the Bukovina (Osyp Krupa, Antin Chernets'kyj, and Semen Vityk), "Do robitnykiv m. L'vova, November 5, 1918," *Dilo*, November 6, 1918.
93. Mroczka, *Spór o Galicję Wschodnią 1914–1923*, 106.
94. Recollections of Helena Ciechowska, April 12, 1932; DALO, f. 257, op. 2, spr. 1657, ark. 53–64. DALO, f. 257, op. 2, spr. 1573, ark. 62–66: recollections of Jadwiga Białkowska, 1934.
95. Kuz'ma, *Lystopadowi dni 1918 r.*, 226. DALO, f. 257, op. 1, spr. 332, ark. 1–14: recollections of Marja Wójcikiewiczowa, secretary of the Liga Kobiet, after 1919.
96. Kuz'ma, *Lystopadovi dni 1918 r.*, 307–308. L. Katrich, "Z lystopadowich boïv," *Dilo*, November 1, 1928.
97. Klimecki, *Polsko-ukraińska wojna*, 96–97. PA, R-8980: report by the German consul in L'viv, December 12, 1918.
98. TsDIAL, f. 581, op. 1, spr. 206, ark. 1: the state secretary for domestic affairs Roman Perfets'kyj and the state secretary for military affairs D. Vitovs'kyj to all district commissioners and military commanders of the West Ukrainian People's Republic, November 18, 1918.
99. TsDIAL, f. 581, op. 1, spr. 206: correspondence of the state secretary for domestic affairs of the West Ukrainian People's Republic with the district authorities. Kuz'ma, *Lystopadovi dni 1918 r.*, 250.
100. "Odezwa Kobiet Polskich," *Dziennik Ludowy*, November 23, 1919.
101. "Listopad 1918: Ósmy dzień walki," *Gazeta Lwowska*, November 9, 1919. Kuchabs'kyj believed the reason for the Polish victory lay in the higher level of national consciousness among Poles and their pugnacious traditions. Kutschabsky, *Die Westukraine im Kampfe mit Polen und dem Bolschewismus*, 50–52.
102. Mroczka, *Spór o Galicję Wschodnią 1914–1923*, 106.
103. TsDIAL, f. 837, op. 1, spr. 71, ark. 15–10: report by a volunteer from Tłumacz, after 1919. Antoni Jakubski, "Walki listopadowe we Lwowie w świetle krytyk," in *Obrona Lwowa*, vol. 1.
104. TsDIAL, f. 837, op. 1, spr. 71, ark. 15–20: report by a volunteer from Tłumacz, after 1919.
105. *Obrona Lwowa*, vol. 3, 434–35.
106. Ibid.
107. Ibid., 13–15, 431–33.
108. Ibid.
109. "Za shche ide borot'ba?" *Dilo*, November 16, 1918.
110. "Nenavyst' pol's'koï dushi," *Dilo*, November 19, 1918.
111. "Voroh Ukraïns'koho Narodu," *Dilo*, November 20, 1918.
112. Mroczka, *Spór o Galicję Wschodnią 1914–1923*, 119–21.
113. DALO, f. 257, op. 1, d. 332, ark. 1–14: recollections of Marja Wójcikiewiczowa (excerpt), January 11, 1932.
114. DALO, f. 257, op. 2, spr. 504, ark. 23–59: memorandum by Dr. Tobiasz Askenaze, November/December 1918.

115. DALO, f. 257, op. 2, spr. 162: "Brigada Lwowska: Wypadki w dzielnicy żydowskiej we Lwowie w listopadzie 1918," n.d. The Polish press repeated these accusations. For example, "Echa pogromów żydowskich we Lwowie," *Wiek Nowy*, January 3, 1919.
116. "Milicya żydowska w świetle prawdy," *Chwila*, January 10, 1919.
117. DALO, f. 257, op. 2, spr. 1624: "Brigada Lwowska: Wypadki w dzielnicy żydowskiej we Lwowie w listopadzie 1918," n.d. The Polish commander of the Obrona Lwowa Czesław Mączński passed this report in 1933 to the archive of the Society for the Study of the History of the Defense of Lwów and the southeastern voivodeships (*Towarzystwo Badania Historii Obrony Lwowa i wójewództw południowo-wschodnich*). See also Ludwik Mroczka, "Przyczynek do kwestii żydowskiej w Galicji u progu Drugiej Rzeczypospolitej," in Żydzi w Małopolsce, 297–308, here 303. On the economic reasons for the pogrom, see William W. Hagen, "The Moral Economy of Ethnic Violence: The Pogrom in Lwow, November 1918," *Geschichte und Gesellschaft* 31 (2005): 203–26.
118. DALO, f. 257, op. 2, spr. 504, ark. 23–25: memorandum by Askenaze, November/December 1918, 9.
119. "O neutralność," *Chwila*, January 12, 1919.
120. Josef Bendow, *Der Lemberger Judenpogrom* (Vienna: Hickl, 1919). Abram Insler, *Dokumenty fałszu* (L'viv: I. Jaeger, 1933). Golczewski, *Polnisch-jüdische Beziehungen 1881–1922*, 185–205. German newspapers reported thousands of victims, and Warsaw newspapers reported 150 victims. *Wiek Nowy* estimated that forty-one persons had directly or indirectly become victims of the pogrom. "Echa pogromów żydowskich we Lwowie," *Wiek Nowy*, January 3, 1919.
121. DALO, f. 257, op. 2, spr. 504, ark. 23–59: memorandum by Askenaze, November/December 1918.
122. TsDIAL, f. 505, op. 1, spr. 201, ark. 57: record no. 273 (Mechl Moses Zorn), December 12, 1918.
123. Ibid.
124. Ibid., ark. 46: record no. 25 (Sali Katz), December 3, 1918.
125. "Smutna rocznica," *Chwila*, December 6, 1920.
126. TsDIAL, f. 505, op. 1, spr. 201, ark. 30–31: record no. 64 (Adolf Meisel), December 1918.
127. Ibid., ark. 71: record no. 248 (Israel Deutscher, Mayer Deutscher, Abraham Hersch Kessler), December 9, 1918.
128. DALO, f. 271, op. 4, spr. 446, ark. 84–85: record (Stalla Agid with witnesses Antonina and Laura Piątek), n.d. (probably December 1918).
129. DALO, f. 257, op. 2, spr. 504, ark. 23–59: memorandum by Askenaze, November/December 1918.
130. TsDIAL, f. 505, op. 1, spr. 201, ark. 80–81: record (Dr. Salomon Rawicz), January 7, 1919.
131. PA, R-8980: report by the German consul general in L'viv, Heinze, December 12, 1918.
132. *Gazeta Wieczorna*, November 26, 1918. "Vibrannja tymchasovoï mis'koï Rady," *Dilo*, November 28, 1928.
133. "Ostanni podji u L'vovi," *Vpered!* November 29, 1918.
134. *Gazeta Wieczorna*, November 26, 1918.
135. *Dilo*, November 29, 1918.
136. Appeal by Archbishop Józef Bilczewski, November 25, 1918, *Kurier Lwowski*, December, 1918.
137. Appeal by the (Polish) Women's Citizens' Committee (*Komitet Obywatelski Kobiet*) from December 1, 1918; cited after TsDIAL, f. 505, op. 1, spr. 23, ark. 3–158: Lwów pod znakiem pogromów żydowskich: Dokumenty chwili zebrał i zaopatrzył w uwagi i

komentarze Z. Komrat, Cz. 1: Pogrom lwowski w dniach 22 i 23 listopada 1918, June 1, 1919.
138. Appeal by the Provisional Government Committee to the population of L'viv, *Gazeta Lwowska*, November 28, 1918. See also the justification strategy of Czesław Mączyński, *Boje lwowski*, 3 vols. (Warsaw: Spółka wyd. Rzeczpospolita, 1921). Bolesław Roja, *Legendy i fakty* (Warsaw: Nakł. Księg. F. Hoesicka, 1931).
139. DALO, f. 257, op. 2, spr. 504: report no. 2 on the events in November 1918. It is not clear who actually wrote this report. The information is therefore not reliable.
140. DALO, f. 257, op. 2, spr. 1624: "Brigada Lwowska: Wypadki w dzielnicy żydowskiej we Lwowie w listopadzie 1918," n.d.
141. "W imię prawdy," *Kurier Lwowski*, December 1 and 3, 1918.
142. Appeal of the Polish government to the Jewish population, November 30, 1918, *Kurier Lwowski*, December 2, 1918.
143. "W imię prawdy," *Kurier Lwowski*, December 1 and 3, 1918.
144. TsDIAL, f. 837, op. 1, spr. 71, ark. 59–65: report by Feliks R. Buna on the events of November 1918 in L'viv, December 1918 or January 1919.
145. "Nie budzić nienawiści," *Wiek Nowy*, December 5, 1918.
146. TsDIAL, f. 462, op. 1, spr. 41, ark. 18–21: record by Lev Hankevych on his prison stay, early 1919.
147. DALO, f. 257, op. 1, spr. 48, ark. 2–45: Żydowski Komitet dla niesienia pomocy ofiarom rozruchów i rabunków w listopadzie 1918 we Lwowie (Jewish Assistance Committee for the Victims of the Riots and Robberies in November 1918 in L'viv) to Kwatermistrzowstwo Naczelnej Komendy Wojsk Polskich we Lwowie (office of the quartermaster of the Polish Army High Command in L'viv), December 16, 1918, in Dokumenty Chwili: part 2: Okres popogromowy od 24. listopada do 31. grudnia 1918. TsDIAL, f. 505, op. 1, spr. 24, ark. 1–9: Jewish Assistance Committee to Quartermaster of the High Command W. Sikorski, December 20, 1918.
148. DALO, f. 257, op. 1, spr. 48, ark. 2–45: Dokumenty Chwili: part 2: Okres popogromowy od 24. listopada do 31. grudnia 1918, December 20, 1918.
149. DALO, f. 257, op. 1, spr. 48, ark. 2–45: Czy już jest istotnie po pogromie, December 20, 1918, in Dokumenty Chwili: part 2: Okres popogromowy od 24. listopada do 31. grudnia 1918. "Czy zwrot ku lepszemu?" *Chwila*, January 12, 1919.
150. DALO, f. 257, op. 1, spr. 48, ark. 46–91: interpellation of city councilor Dr. Rafał Buber, January 2, 1919; in Dokumenty Chwili, part 3: Rok 1919.
151. DALO, f. 257, op. 1, spr. 48, ark. 46–91: press communiqué of the Polish Army High Command, January 4, 1919, in Dokumenty Chwili, part 3: Rok 1919.
152. DALO, f. 257, op. 1, spr. 48, ark. 46–91: communiqué of the Jewish Assistance Committee to all newspapers in L'viv, January 1, 1919 in Dokumenty Chwili, part 3: Rok 1919.
153. DALO, f. 2, op. 26, spr. 13, ark. 9–11: the city council was worried about the catastrophic security situation. Decision of the city council, May 28, 1919.
154. TsDIAL, f. 701, op. 3, spr. 506, ark. 5–6: the Jewish Kahal to the delegate general of the Ministry of the Interior, Gąlecki, May 30, 1919. DALO, f. 2, op. 26, spr. 2, ark. 37: presidium of the city of L'viv to the commanding general W. Iwaszkiewicz, June 2, 1919.
155. DALO, f. 271, op. 1, spr. 445, ark. 13–15: Jewish Assistance Committee to the police directorate of L'viv, July 29, 1919.
156. "Czy zwrot ku lepszemu?" *Chwila*, January 12, 1919.
157. "Walka z paskarstem," *Chwila*, February 20, 1919.

158. DALO, f. 257, op. 1, spr. 48, ark. 2–45: Protest mężów zaufania i reprezentatów żydowskich organizacyj (Protest by men of trust and representatives of Jewish organizations), December 14, 1918, in Dokumenty Chwili, part 2. Ibid.: men of trust and representatives of Jewish organizations to the Polish government, December 24, 1918. "Alians żydowsko-ukraiński," *Głos Narodu*, December 15, 1918 (cited after DALO, f. 257, op. 1, spr. 48, ark. 2–4: Dokumenty Chwili, part 2).
159. "W obronie neutralności," *Chwila*, January 15, 1919.
160. DALO, f. 257, op. 1, spr. 48, ark. 46–91: Jewish Assistance Committee to the head of state and the prime minister, January 26, 1919, in Dokumenty Chwili, part 3: Rok 1919.
161. DALO, f. 271, op. 1, spr. 445, ark. 10 and 12: police commissariat in Zamarstynów to the presidium of the police directorate in L'viv, May 1 and 3, 1919.
162. TsDIAL, f. 146, op. 8, spr. 3852, ark. 9–10: district captain (*starost*) to the delegate general of the government, May 12, 1919.
163. DALO, f. 257, op. 1, spr. 48, ark. 2–45: Dokumenty Chwili, part 2.
164. Memorandum by Askenaze, November/December 1918; DALO, f. 257, op. 2, spr. 504, ark. 23–59. The Jewish Assistance Committee has distributed seventeen hundred questionnaires to victims of the pogrom. By the end of the year, twelve hundred reports had been examined. According to initial estimates, about five thousand had been affected by blackmail, arson, or robberies.
165. Ibid.
166. Ibid.
167. Ibid.
168. "Milicya żydowska," *Chwila*, January 31, 1919.
169. "Przed sąd," *Chwila*, January 22, 1919.
170. DALO, f. 257, op. 1, spr. 48, ark. 46–91: statement of Dr. Tobiasz Askenaze and letter from the Jewish Assistance Committee to the Provisional Government Committee in L'viv (Dr. Leonard Stahl), January 5, 1919, in Dokumenty Chwili, part 3, Rok 1919.
171. DALO, f. 2, op. 26, spr. 2, ark. 29–31: Jewish Assistance Committee to the Provisional Government Committee in L'viv. The quotes come from a letter sent by Askenaze on January 4, 1919, to the Government Committee. Jewish newspapers insisted that the Jewish militia had behaved correctly. "Milicya żydowska," *Chwila*, January 31, 1919.
172. DALO, f. 257, op. 2, spr. 504, ark. 23–59: memorandum by Askenaze, November/December 1918.
173. Ibid.
174. "Odpowiedź Dra Tobiasza Aszkenasego," *Chwila*, February 25, 1919. The Jewish Assistance Committee confirmed the veracity of Askenase's account. The following members of the committee signed the letter: Dr. Tobiasz Askenaze, Leon Appel, Dr. Rafał Buber, Dr. Karol Einäugler, Dr. Juliusz Fell, Adolf Freund, Dr. Józef Parnas, Ingenieur (engineer) Anzelm Reiss, Dr. Henryk Rozmarin, Dr. Mojżesz Schorr, Dr. Dawid Schreiber, Mojżesz Silber, Dr. Rubin Sokal, and Dr. Ozyasz Wasser. "Echa zajść listopadowych," *Chwila*, February 20, 1919. See also "Bluff," *Chwila*, February 26, 1919.
175. DALO, f. 2, op. 26, spr. 2, ark. 32–33: Quartermaster Władysław Sikorski to the Jewish Assistance Committee, January 4, 1919. Also printed in DALO, f. 257, op. 1, spr. 48, ark. 46–91: Dokumenty Chwili, part 3: Rok 1919.
176. DALO, f. 257, op. 1, spr. 48, ark. 46–91: Jewish Assistance Committee to Quartermaster Sikorski, January 7, 1919, in Dokumenty Chwili, part 3: Rok 1919.
177. DALO, f. 2, op. 26, spr. 2, ark. 34: Quartermaster Władysław Sikorski to the Jewish Assistance Committee, January 9, 1919.
178. DALO, f. 2, op. 26, spr. 2, ark. 28: Jewish Assistance Committee (Askenaze) to the mayor of L'viv, January 9, 1919.

179. *Nowy Dziennik*, February 11, 1919.
180. Interview with the member of the delegation Ozyasz Wasser, *Goniec Krakowski*, February 12, 1919.
181. "Naczelnik Państwa o Żydach," *Głos Narodu*, February 20, 1919. See the reports about the conversation between Marshall Piłsudski and Prime Minister Ignacy Paderewski and a Jewish delegation from L'viv: *Nowy Dziennik*, February 11, 1919. *Goniec Krakowski*, February 12, 1919. "Czy zwrot ku lepszemu?" *Chwila*, January 12, 1919. See also Golczewski, *Polnisch-jüdische Beziehungen 1881–1922*, 200–202.
182. Piłsudski held the Jews responsible for the fact that the Polish population perceived them as "alien" and tried to exclude or eliminate them. He argued that the only reason why there had not been more pogroms was due to the peaceful nature of the Polish peasantry. He accused the Jews of being hostile to the Polish state, otherwise they would not have trumpeted the pogroms to the whole world. When asked for proofs of this supposedly hostile attitude of the Jewish population, he answered that that was how the Polish people felt. DALO, f. 257, op. 2, spr. 24, ark. 37–38: report by the press office of the delegation of the Jewish National Council for East Galicia, November 23, 1920.
183. "Premier Paderewski o sprawie żydowskiej," *Chwila*, February 25, 1919.
184. Archiwum Akt Nowych, Warsaw (AAN), Komitet Narodowy Polski, no. 159, k. 103–108: "Raport Delegacji Ministerstwa Spraw Zagranicznych R.P. w sprawie wystąpień antyżydowskich we Lwowie, December 17, 1918," in Jerzy Tomaszewski, "Lwów, 22 listopada 1918," *Przegląd Historyczny* 75 (1984): 279–85. The credibility of this document is (unconvincingly) questioned by Leszek Tomaszewski, "Lwów—Listopad 1918: Niezwykłe losy pewnego dokumentu (Listy do Redakcji)," *Dzieje Najnowsze* 25, no. 4 (1993): 163–73.
185. The commission believed (wrongly) that at least 150 Jews had been murdered. It reported that 50 houses had been burned down, 500 shops plundered, and that 200 people had lost their homes. Several dozen women had reported that they had been raped. The commission suspected that there had been more cases of rape. Many women were too ashamed to go to the police. About 70 children had lost both parents and 7,000 families had been affected by the pogrom, in "Raport Delegacji Ministerstwa Spraw Zagranicznych R.P.," 279–85.
186. "Komisya urzędowa w sprawie wypadków listopadowych," *Chwila*, January 10, 1919.
187. DALO, f. 257, op. 2, spr. 24: report no. 9 of the press office of the delegation of the Jewish National Council for East Galicia, March 1, 1919; "Prawda o pogromach lwowskich," *Chwila*, January 29, 1919. "Odbudowa dzielnicy żydowskiej," *Chwila*, January 30, 1919.
188. DALO, f. 257, op. 2, spr. 24, ark. 24: report no. 9 of the press office of the delegation of the Jewish National Council for East Galicia, March 1, 1919. DALO, f. 257, op. 1, spr. 48, ark. 46–91: statistical analysis of 3,620 questionnaires about the pogrom in Dokumenty Chwili, part 3: Rok 1919.
189. TsDIAL, f. 146, op. 8, spr. 1917, ark. 18–23: list of names of people who were arrested in connection with robberies in November 1918, n.d. (early 1919).
190. "Do Żydów," *Kurier Lwowski*, December 5, 1918.
191. TsDIAL, f. 205, op. 1r, spr. 1122, ark. 28: state prosecutor at the district court in L'viv to the state prosecutor at the court of appeals in L'viv, November 30, 1919.
192. Ibid., ark. 56–57: state prosecutor at the district court in L'viv to the state prosecutor at the court of appeals in L'viv, August 31, 1920. Other contemporary documents report about one thousand or two thousand arrests. "Raport Delegacji Ministerstwa Spraw Zagranicznych R.P.," 279–85.
193. "Raport Delegacji Ministerstwa Spraw Zagranicznych R.P.," 279–85.

194. "Nashe teperishne politychne polozhennja," *Dilo*, November 28, 1919. Klimecki, *Polsko-ukraińska wojna*, 146–88. On the military side, see also Maciej L. Jagóra, "Walki o Lwów w listopadzie i grudniu 1918 roku," *Dzieje Najnowsze* 25, no. 3 (1993): 83–96.
195. "Posiedzenie Tymcz. Rady miejskiej," *Dziennik Ludowy*, March 12, 1919.
196. "Ostrzeliwanie miasta," *Dziennik Ludowy*, February 26, 1919.
197. Stefan Rayski, "Z wędrówek po Lwowie," *Dziennik Ludowy*, February 11, 1919.
198. "Lwów po inwazyi ukraińskiej!" *Gazeta Wieczorna*, December 15, 1918.
199. TsDIAL, f. 841, op. 1, spr. 128, ark. 36–39: see, for example, the diary entry of an unknown Polish woman, February 27, 1919.
200. "Ukraińcy strzelają na miasto trującemi bombami," *Dziennik Ludowy*, March 12, 1919.
201. TsDIAL, f. 368t, op. 1, spr. 103, ark. 1–2: Archbishop Sheptyts'kyj to Vasyl'ko, January 17, 1919.
202. TsDIAL, f. 462, op. 1, spr. 253: excerpts from *Vpered*, December 1918.
203. TsDIAL, f. 462, op. 1, spr. 22: record of searches in the monastery of Basilian nuns on Zyblikewicz Street, the Stauropygian Institute, and the Greek Catholic theological seminary. The newspaper of the Ukrainian Social Democratic Party *Vpered* reported that between November 22 and December 13, the Stauropygian Institute had been searched 147 times. TsDIAL, f. 462, op. 1, spr. 253: excerpts from *Vpered*, December 1918.
204. TsDIAL, f. 462, op. 1, spr. 253: excerpts from *Vpered*, December 1918.
205. Ibid., ark. 152–58: excerpts from Ukrainian newspapers on the oppression of Ukrainians in L'viv, 1918–1921. TsDIAL, f. 146, op. 6, spr. 1406: Lev Hankevych et al. to the general commissioner of the Polish Republic in Cracow, Kazimierz Gąlecki, May 21, 1919. TsDIAL, f. 462, op. 1, spr. 249, ark. 4–10: record of the Ukrainian Civic Committee in L'viv, June 1, 1919.
206. For example, Lev Hankevych, Julijan Romanchuk, and others. TsDIAL, f. 368T, op. 1, spr. 103, ark. 1–2: Archbishop Sheptyts'kyj to Vasyl'ko, January 17, 1919.
207. TsDIAL, f. 462, op. 1, spr. 236, ark. 2: order of the quartermaster of the High Command of Polish troops in Galicia, W. Sikorski, November 28, 1918.
208. TsDIAL, f. 462, op. 1, spr. 236, ark. 28–29: record of the Ukrainian Civic Committee in L'viv, probably March 1919.
209. Ibid., ark. 17: Ukrainian Civic Committee in L'viv to the mayoralty in L'viv, March 2, 1919. Kramarz, "Ze sceny walk polsko-ukraińskich o Lwów," 113.
210. "O odbudowe życia gospodarczego," *Gazeta Wieczorna*, November 30, 1918.
211. Stefan Rayski, "Z wędrówek po Lwowie," *Dziennik Ludowy*, February 11, 1919.
212. "Wielkopolska dla Lwowa," *Kurier Lwowski*, February 1, 1919. Figura, *Konflikt polsko-ukraiński w prasie Polski Zachodniej w latach 1918–1923*.
213. TsDIAL, f. 462, op. 1, spr. 236, ark. 28–29: record of the Ukrainian Civic Committee in L'viv, probably March 1919.
214. "Do ludności m. Lwowa," *Wiek Nowy*, January 3, 1919.
215. "Obywatele—Rodacy!" *Gazeta Wieczorna*, November 30, 1918.
216. "Z Tymcz. Rady miejskiej," *Kurier Lwowski*, March 4, 1919.
217. On the West Ukrainian People's Republic, see *Die Westukrainische Volksrepublik*, 161–218. B. Tyshchyk and O. Vivcharenko, *Zakhidnoukraïns'ka Narodna Respublika 1918–1923 rr.* (Kolomyja: Svit, 1993). Mykola Lytvyn and Klim Naumenko, *Istorija ZUNR* (L'viv: OLIR, 1995).
218. Oleh Josyf Pavlyshyn, *Formuvannja ta dijal'nist' predstavnyts'kykh orhaniv vlady ZUNR-ZOUNR (zhoten' 1918–cherven' 1919 rr.). Avtoreferat dissertatsiï na zdobuttja naukovoho stupenja kandydata istorychnykh nauk* (L'viv: L'viv University, 2001), 16–18.
219. Kutschabsky, *Die Westukraine im Kampfe mit Polen und dem Bolschewismus*, 66–68.

220. Ibid., 90–94. On Petljura and the Ukrainian People's Republic (UNR), see Rudolf A. Mark, *Symon Petljura und die UNR: Vom Sturz des Hetman Skoropads'kyj bis zum Exil in Polen* (Wiesbaden: Harrassowitz, 1988).
221. Pavlyshyn, *Formuvannja ta dijal'nist' predstavnyts'kykh orhaniv vlady ZUNR-ZOUNR*, 15.
222. Klimecki, *Lwów 1918–1919*, 18. On Wilhelm von Habsburg, see Timothy Snyder, *The Red Prince: The Fall of a Dynasty and the Rise of Modern Europe* (London: Bodley Head, 2008).
223. Kutschabsky, *Die Westukraine im Kampfe mit Polen und dem Bolschewismus*, 234–36. Klimecki, *Polsko-Ukraińska wojna*, 136, 151.
224. Pavlyshin, *Formuvannja ta dijal'nist' predstavnyts'kykh orhaniv vlady ZUNR-ZOUNR*, 18–19.
225. "Kałusz pod panowaniem ukraińskiem," *Kurier Lwowski*, February 16, 1919. "Na 'swobodzie' ukraińskiej," *Gazeta Poranna*, February 21, 1919.
226. "Tyranja ukraińska," *Kurier Lwowski*, February 13, 1919.
227. *Gazeta Poranna*, May 30, 1919.
228. "Bolszewizm ukraiński we wschodniej Galicji," *Kurier Lwowski*, February 1, 1919.
229. "Zarządzenia odwetowe: Komunikat Naczelnego Dowództwa Wojsk Polskich na Galicyę wschdonią," *Wiek Nowy*, January 3, 1919.
230. "Der westukrainische Staat," *Neue Lemberger Zeitung*, November 13, 1918. "Die jüdische Miliz," *Neue Lemberger Zeitung*, November 13, 1918. "Der westukrainische Staat," *Neue Lemberger Zeitung*, November 14, 1918. "Kałusz pod panowaniem ukraińskiem," *Kurier Lwowski*, February 16, 1919.
231. "Bolszewizm ukraiński we wschodniej Galicji," *Kurier Lwowski*, February 1, 1919.
232. TsDIAL, f. 146, op. 8, spr. 3025, ark. 1–16: memorandum of the Jewish Kahal in Sambor, July 31, 1919.
233. TsDIAL, f. 146, op. 8, spr. 3029, ark. 51–53: office of the district captain (*starost*) of Stary Sambor to the governor's office, August 7, 1919.
234. "Koniec idylli ukraińsko-żydowskiej," *Wiek Nowy*, February 27, 1919.
235. Mroczka, "Przyczynek do kwestii żydowskiej w Galicji u progu Drugiej Rzeczypospolitej," 301. Golczewski, *Polnisch-jüdische Beziehungen 1881–1922*, 200–208.
236. Instruction of the state secretariat of the interior to all district commissioners, March 10, 1919, *Kurier Lwowski*, July 14, 1919.
237. *Narid*, March 30, 1919 (cited after *Kurier Lwowski*, July 14, 1919).
238. Klimecki, *Polsko-Ukraińska wojna*, 169–81, 208–209. Veryha, *Vyzvol'ni zmahannja v Ukraïni 1914–1923*, vol. 1, 471–80.
239. Veryha, *Vyzvol'ni zmahannja v Ukraïni 1914–1923*, vol. 1, 466–67. Janusz Szczepański, *Społeczeństwo Polski w walce z najazdem bolszewickim 1920 roku* (Warsaw: Pułtusk, 2000), 80.
240. Klimecki, *Polsko-Ukraińska wojna*, 198–241.
241. Ibid., 235. Szczepański, *Społeczeństwo Polski w walce z najazdem bolszewickim 1920 roku*, 86–87.
242. TsDIAL, f. 146, op. 8, spr. 3029, ark. 15–17: district captain in Rawa Ruska to the governor's office in L'viv, July 18, 1919. Ark. 21–28: district captain in Drohobych to the governor's office, July 21, 1919. Ark. 29–35: district captain in Brody to the governor's office, July 25, 1919. Ark. 36–38: district captain in Stanislau to the governor's office, July 25, 1919. Ark. 41–44: district captain in Gródek to the governor's office, July 30, 1919. Ark. 45–49: district captain in Stryj to the governor's office, July 30, 1919. Ark. 51–53: district captain in Stary Sambor to the governor's office, August 7, 1919. Ark. 54–55: the head of the gendarmerie in the district of Dolina to the district captain in

Dolina, August 8, 1919. Ark. 55–61: district captain in Dolina to the governor's office, August 12, 1919. Ark. 67–69: office of the district captain in Podhajce to the governor's office, August 25, 1919. Ark 79–80: district captain in Skałat to the governor's office, October 20, 1919. See also ark 1–2: report of the press department of the headquarters of Polish troops in East Galicia, June 16, 1919. Szczepański, *Społeczeństwo Polski w walce z najazdem bolszewickim 1920 roku*, 78.
243. TsDIAL, f. 146, op. 8, spr. 3027, ark. 58–59: district captain in Sokal to the governor's office, May 17, 1920.
244. TsDIAL, f. 146, op. 8, spr. 3025, ark. 1–16: memorandum by the leaders of the Jewish community in Sambor, July 31, 1919.
245. Ibid., ark. 24–37: district captain in Sambor to the governor's office, October 28, 1919.
246. Papierzyńska-Turek, *Sprawa Ukraińska w Drugiej Rzeczypospolitej 1922–1926*, 37–44.
247. "Cały Lwów protestuje!" *Gazeta Poranna*, December 10, 1919.
248. Memorandum on the "Polish acts of destruction" in East Galicia, sent to the French prime minister Georges Clemenceau, July 15, 1919, in *Ereignisse in der Ukraine 1914–1922*, vol. 4, 66–84.
249. TsDIAL, f. 581, op. 1, spr. 139, ark. 1–14: unsigned report from 1920. Ark., 34–38: report on other murders in L'viv district, February 15, 1920.
250. Szczepański, *Społeczeństwo Polski w walce z najazdem bolszewickim 1920 roku*, 84.
251. TsDIAL, f. 146, op. 8, spr. 3395, ark. 32: head of the gendarmerie in L'viv to the delegate general of the Polish government Gąlecki, July 27, 1919. Ark. 33: delegate general to the Ministry of the Interior, September 14, 1919.
252. Memorandum on public functionaries of Ukrainian origin locked out by the Polish occupation authorities, October 12, 1920; TsDIAL, f. 462, op. 1, spr. 5, ark. 137–39. "Rusini galicyjscy powrócić chcą do służby państwowej," *Dziennik Ludowy*, December 3, 1919.
253. TsDIAL, f. 146, op. 8, spr. 3027, ark. 22–26: command of the state police for Little Poland: report on the political, economic, and security situation in Little Poland for December 1919, January 6, 1920. Ibid., ark. 10-17: Police Director Reinlender to the governor's office, February 26, 1920. Ibid., ark. 9. Report of the police command for Little Poland, February 28, 1920.
254. TsDIAL, f. 146, op. 8, spr. 4040, ark. 7–10: memorandum by the command of the local civil defense group, February 17, 1920.
255. Szczepański, *Społeczeństwo Polski w walce z najazdem bolszewickim 1920 roku*, 86–87.
256. Ibid., 169–72. Zbigniew Karpus, Waldemar Rezmer, Emilian Wiszka, eds., *Polska i Ukraina. Sojusz 1920 roku i jego następstwa* (Toruń: Wydawnictwo Uniwersytetu Mikołaja Kopernika, 1997). Michał Klimecki and Gerard Położyński, *Czas próby: Wojna polsko-sowiecka 1919–1920 r.* (Warsaw: Vipart, 2000).
257. Szczepański, *Społeczeństwo Polski w walce z najazdem bolszewickim 1920 roku*, 309–24.
258. TsDIAL, f. 146, op. 6, spr. 1407, ark. 36: Police Director Reinlender to the Polish Ministry of the Interior in Warsaw, May 21, 1920.
259. TsDIAL, f. 146, op. 6, spr. 1409, ark. 330–32: Reinlender to the Ministry of the Interior, July 14, 1920. On such deliberations by the West Ukrainian government-in-exile in Vienna, see Wehrhahn, *Die Westukrainische Volksrepublik*, 271–86.
260. Szczepański, *Społeczeństwo Polski w walce z najazdem bolszewickim 1920 roku*, 275–82.

261. TsDIAL, f. 146, op. 8, spr. 3822, ark. 2–10: report of the police command for Little Poland on the general situation in July 1920, sent to the delegate general of the Polish government, August 6, 1920.
262. Ibid., ark. 11–18: report of the police command for Little Poland on the general situation in August 1920, sent to the delegate general of the Polish government, September 9, 1920.
263. TsDIAL, f. 146, op. 8, spr. 3027, ark. 106–109: district captain in Rudkace to the governor's office, September 13, 1920.
264. TsDIAL, f. 146, op. 8, spr. 3822, ark. 11–18: report of the police command for Little Poland on the general situation in August 1920, sent to the delegate general of the Polish government, September 9, 1920.
265. TsDIAL, f. 146, op. 8, spr. 3027, ark. 86: office of the district captain in Jaworów to the governor's office, August 30, 1920. Szczepański, *Społeczeństwo Polski w walce z najazdem bolszewickim 1920 roku*, 82.
266. TsDIAL, f. 146, op. 8, spr. 3822, ark. 2–10: report of the police command for Little Poland on the general situation in July 1920, sent to the delegate general of the Polish government, August 6, 1920.
267. TsDIAL, f. 146, op. 8, spr. 3823, ark. 52–54: district captain in Czortków to the governor's office, July 12, 1920. Szczepański, *Społeczeństwo Polski w walce z najazdem bolszewickim 1920 roku*, 280–81.
268. TsDIAL, f. 146, op. 8, spr. 3822, ark. 11–18: report of the police command for Little Poland on the general situation in August 1920, sent to the delegate general of the Polish government, September 9, 1920.
269. TsDIAL, f. 146, op. 8, spr. 3822, ark. 2–10: report of the police command for Little Poland on the general situation in July 1920, sent to the delegate general of the Polish government, August 6, 1920.
270. TsDIAL, f. 146, op. 8, spr. 3027, ark. 5: district captain in Jaworów to the governor's office, June 29, 1920.
271. TsDIAL, f. 146, op. 8, spr. 3027, ark. 86: office of the district captain in Jaworów to the governor's office, August 30, 1920.
272. TsDIAL, f. 146, op. 8, spr. 3822, ark. 31–41: report of the police command for Little Poland on the general situation in September 1920, sent to the delegate general of the Polish government, October 10, 1920.
273. TsDIAL, f. 146, op. 8, spr. 3822, ark. 2–10: report of the police command for Little Poland on the general situation in July 1920, sent to the delegate general of the Polish government, August 6, 1920. Szczepański, *Społeczeństwo Polski w walce z najazdem bolszewickim 1920 roku*, 283.
274. TsDIAL, f. 146, op. 8, spr. 3822, ark. 31–41: report of the police command for Little Poland on the general situation in September 1920, sent to the delegate general of the Polish government, October 10, 1920.
275. TsDIAL, f. 146, op. 8, spr. 3822, ark. 2–10: report of the police command for Little Poland on the general situation in July 1920, sent to the delegate general of the Polish government, August 6, 1920.
276. Szczepański, *Społeczeństwo Polski w walce z najazdem bolszewickim 1920 roku*, 242–51, 468.
277. Ibid., 465–66.
278. TsDIAL, f. 146, op. 8, spr. 3822, ark. 11–18: report of the police command for Little Poland on the general situation in August 1920, sent to the delegate general of the Polish government, September 9, 1920.

279. Szczepański, *Społeczeństwo Polski w walce z najazdem bolszewickim 1920 roku*, 242–51.
280. DALO, f. 2, op. 26, spr. 2, ark. 40–41: the delegate general of the Polish government (governor's office) to all district captains, October 18, 1920.
281. TsDIAL, f. 146, op. 8, spr. 3822, ark. 44: report of the police command for Little Poland on the general situation in October 1920, sent to the delegate general of the Polish government, November 10, 1920.
282. TsDIAL, f. 146, op. 8, spr. 3822, ark. 31–41: report of the police command for Little Poland on the general situation in September 1920, sent to the delegate general of the Polish government, October 10, 1920.
283. "Święto oswobodzenia Tarnopola," *Gazetka Żółnierska*, October 8, 1920. Szczepański, *Społeczeństwo Polski w walce z najazdem bolszewickim 1920 roku*, 467–68.
284. Cited after Szczepański, *Społeczeństwo Polski w walce z najazdem bolszewickim 1920 roku*, 468.
285. "Apel Prezydyum miasta do mieszkańców," *Gazeta Poranna*, July 10, 1920.
286. M. Thullie, "Modły za Polskę?" *Gazetka Żółnierska*, September 24, 1920.
287. Józef Białynia-Chołodecki, "Obrona Lwowa przeciw najazdowi bolszewików w r. 1920," in *W dziesiątą rocznicę bitwy pod Zadwórzem* (L'viv: We Lwowie, 1920). Artur Leinwand, "Obrona Lwowa w 1920 roku," in *Rocznik Lwowski* (Warsaw: Instytut Lwowski, 1991), 30–31.
288. Szczepański, *Społeczeństwo Polski w walce z najazdem bolszewickim 1920 roku*, 466.

CHAPTER 4

Reconstruction and Remembrance, 1920–1939

> They [the Ukrainians] have strong sympathies for all things German and Germany . . . But terrible, blind, dull hatred, an entirely brutish hatred of Poles squirts out of many of them . . . L'viv is a lively western modern medium-sized town; its streets are peaceful and bustling with activity. But then there is something strange there which suddenly confronts me. This city lies in the arms of two enemies, and each wants to dominate it. Subterranean enmity and violence are fermenting in the background.[1]

The Impact of War

The Second Polish Republic was not a homogeneous nation state. National minorities made up 30 percent of the population (see table 4.1). The Ukrainians were the largest minority, followed by Jews and Germans. Most Ukrainians lived in Volhynia, Podlasie, and East Galicia, where they constituted the majority of the population.[2]

East Galica was now known as Małopolska Wschodnia (Eastern Little Poland) and was divided into three voivodeships: Lwów (L'viv), Stanisławów (Stanyslaviv), und Tarnopol (Ternopil). Losses during the war and emigration had considerably reduced the population (see table 4.2).

Ukrainian politicians calculated that between 1914 and 1921, about two hundred thousand Galician Ukrainians had lost their life as a consequence of the war (see table 4.3).

The number of Ukrainians in L'viv also decreased for these but also for additional reasons. Thousands of Ukrainians had left the city while Polish and West Ukrainian troops were still fighting each other for the control of Galicia. After the

Nationality (based on mother tongue)	Census of 1921*		Census of 1931		Modern estimate for 1931	
	Number	%	Number	%	Number	%
Poles	18,814,200	69.2	21,993,000	68.9	20,644,000	64.7
Ukrainians (Ruthenians)	3,898,400	14.3	4,441,600	13.9	5,114,000	16.0
Jews	2,110,400	7.8	2,732,600	8.6	3,114,000	9.8
Belarusians	1,060,200	3.9	989,900	3.1	1,954,000	6.1
Germans	1,059,200	3.9	741,000	2.3	780,000	2.4
Lithuanians	68,700	0.3	83,100	0.3	83,000	0.3
Russians	56,200	0.2	137,700	0.4	139,000	0.4
Tutejszi (i.e., "from here")	49,400	0.2	707,100	2.2	—	—
Czechs	30,600	0.1	38,100	0.1	38,000	0.1
Other	29,200	0.1	50,300	0.2	50,000	0.2
Total	27,176,700	100	31,915,800	100	31,916,000	100

* Ukrainian politicians had called on the Ukrainian population to boycott the 1921 census, and many Ukrainians followed this recommendation. The number of Ukrainians is therefore only an estimate.

Table 4.1. Nationalities in the Second Polish Republic.[3]

Voivodeship	1910	1921	Losses	%
Lwów	2,866,321	2,724,327	141,994	4.95
Stanisławów	1,513,390	1,334,630	178,760	11.81
Tarnopol	1,613,087	1,419,355	193,732	12.01

Table 4.2. Population of East Galicia/Eastern Little Poland.[4]

	Soldiers	Civilians
First World War	100,000	
Executed for "treason" or died in Austrian internment camps		25,000
War-related casualties (diseases, epidemics, etc.)		25,000
Victims of the Polish–Ukrainian war	20,000	
Died in Polish internment camps	30,000 (including civilians)	

Table 4.3. War-related deaths of Ukrainians in Galicia (1914–1920).[5]

war ended, Greek Catholics who identified with the Polish nation often converted to Roman Catholicism.

The Polish census of 1921 questioned respondents about their nationality. Out of 219,388 inhabitants of L'viv, 136,519 (62.4 percent) considered themselves Poles, 19,866 (9.2 percent) considered themselves Ruthenians,[6] 60,431 (27.6 percent) Jewish, and 1,626 (0.8 percent) German (see table 4.4). Considering themselves Poles were 24,659 non-Roman Catholic residents, meaning that more than one-quarter of Greek Catholics and one-third of Jews identified with the Polish nation.[7] The number of Greek Catholics had dropped, but their identification with the Ukrainian nation had become stronger. In 1910 only 48.2 percent of Greek Catholics gave Ruthenian as their main language. The national affiliation (if there was one) of more than 50 percent was questionable. In 1921 72.8 percent of Greek Catholics identified with the Ruthenian (Ukrainian) nation.[8]

The number of conversions increased dramatically. In cases where national affiliation and religious denomination appeared to contradict each other, people converted to the denomination that indicated their national affiliation. To better understand the impact of the war the number of conversions before the war and in the immediate postwar period need to be looked at.

In the two years before the war, fewer than three hundred Greek Catholics and twenty Jews converted annually to Roman Catholicism (see table 4.5). The number of conversions after the war was much higher. Table 4.6 shows the con-

	1910	%	1921	%	1931	%
Roman Catholic	105,469	51.17	111,860	50.99	157,490	50.44
Greek Catholic	39,314	19.07	27,269	12.43	49,747	15.93
Jewish	57,387	27.84	76,854	35.03	99,595	31.90
Other	3,943	1.91	3,405	1.55	5,268	1.69
Total	206,113		219,388		312,231	

Table 4.4. Population of L'viv in 1910, 1921, and 1931 (religion/denomination, percentage).[9]

Year	Total	RC→GC	GC→RC	RC→Jewish	Jewish→RC	GC→Jewish	Jewish→GC
1910	362	4	261	2	13	—	—
1911	391	6	292	—	20	1	3
1922	761	3	568	7	36	1	1
1923	803	3	559	6	43	—	—
1924	594	4	386	3	38	1	—
1925	623	5	461	4	35	2	1

Note. GC = Greek Catholic; RC = Roman Catholic.

Table 4.5. Religious conversions in L'viv, 1910–1911 and 1922–1925.[10]

Year	Total	Roman Catholic			Greek Catholic			Jewish		
		To	From	Balance	To	From	Balance	To	From	Balance
1912	396	331	24	+307	16	279	−263	5	52	−47
1913	424	377	24	+353	9	332	−323	8	45	−37
1914	385	336	24	+312	8	292	−284	5	42	−37
1915	286	284	8	+276	5	247	−242	0	31	−31
1916	265	239	10	+229	4	207	−203	3	32	−29
1917	231	194	25	+169	4	163	−159	4	21	−17
1918	370	317	34	+283	12	263	−251	3	39	−36
1919	2,329	2,239	48	+2,191	6	2095	−2,089	6	130	−124
1920	995	865	90	+775	18	731	−713	11	104	−93
1921	894	761	93	+668	6	665	−659	6	78	−72
1922	761	645	84	+561	5	578	−573	8	56	−48

Table 4.6. Conversions in L'viv 1912–1922.[11]

versions for 1912 through 1922. Before 1918, between 194 and 317 people in L'viv joined the Roman Catholic Church annually. The enormous rise in the number of conversions in 1919 is particularly striking, with 2,239 people converting to Roman Catholicism and 2,095 persons leaving the Greek Catholic Church. In all probability, these were Greek Catholic Poles who renounced their Ruthenian heritage after the Polish–Ukrainian war. Between 1919 and 1929, 234 people left the Jewish community. Most of them converted to Roman Catholicism while a few joined Protestant churches. It can safely be assumed that most of them were Jewish Poles who now became Roman Catholic Poles.

There was no significant difference between the sexes with regard to the percentage of conversions. More women converted during the war; in peacetime, the number of men who converted was higher. In total, 3,175 men and 2,674 women left the Greek Catholic Church between 1912 and 1922. The greatest impact was during 1919, with 1,335 men and 760 women leaving the Greek Catholic Church. In the same period (1912–1922), 239 men and 223 women left the Roman Catholic Church, and 346 men and 285 women ceased being Jews.[12]

Before the war, marriages between Roman Catholics and Greek Catholics were fairly common. In 1910 and 1911 there were more than three hundred mixed marriages every year, making up almost 17 percent of all marriages. The Polish–Ukrainian war and the increasing enmity between Poles and Ukrainians reduced the number of mixed couples. Between 1922 and 1925 only 5 to 7 percent of all marriages were between Greek Catholics and Roman Catholics. This percentage increased to 9 to 12 percent in the 1930s but still did not reach prewar levels. Marriages between Jews and Christians were extremely rare. The difference in religion made mixed marriages difficult, preventing the creation of familial ties between Jews on the one hand and Greek Catholics and Roman Catholics on the other. Crossing the boundary between Roman Catholicism and Greek Catholicism was much easier and there were many familial ties between Poles and Ukrainians.[13]

The war had also had a significant and tangible impact on the cityscape. About 7.7 percent of the city's buildings were destroyed, and 20.5 percent were damaged. In December 1918 the Ukrainian troops had disrupted the city's water supply by destroying the water pipes. Repairing the damaged pipes took until July 1921. In the meantime, the people were forced to haul their water from public and private wells. The power station had also been damaged, and even in 1923 it still produced less electricity than before the war, which had an additional negative impact on public transport. In 1921 there were fewer passengers in the city's streetcars than in 1912, and streetcars were only operational on 50 percent of the tracks. The city was still spending money to repair war-related damages in 1929.[14] Financially, the city was bankrupt. Its expenditure in 1918/1919 was three times higher than its revenues. The annual deficit from 1919 to 1923 ran between 22 and 40 percent. The Polish state had to step in to save the city from financial collapse.[15]

The war had also ended L'viv's role as the capital of a large territory (the crown land). During the Russian occupation banks, insurance companies and other organizations had already begun moving their headquarters to Cracow, and they did not return, even after L'viv was retaken. Cracow grew in importance and Warsaw became the undisputed political, cultural, economic, and administrative center of Poland. Many politicians, civil servants, scientists, and artists moved to Warsaw. L'viv was now merely the capital of one of the country's southeastern voivodeships.

The L'viv municipal council made the case for receiving additional resources from the center by arguing that only the patriotism and heroism of L'viv Poles had saved the eastern provinces for Poland. This outpost of Polish culture—so the argument went—needed to be preserved. On November 23, 1925, a monument was unveiled in the garden of the L'viv Polytechnic, which bore the inscription "Remember Warsaw, remember fatherland—that we fell at Lwów."[16] The Polish government was happy to pay tribute to the heroism of the Poles of Lwów. In 1922 the city was awarded the highest Polish military decoration: the Virtuti Militari. The government also granted the municipal council the right to include the title "Leopolis—semper fidelis" (always faithful) in its coat of arms.

L'viv was given material help, even if building the port of Gdynia and other projects in western and northern Poland took priority. The train lines to L'viv were improved and a small airport was built. But these investments were not sufficient to overcome the city's structural problems. The region was still predominantly agricultural, and industrialization failed to take off.[17]

The municipal council was in a difficult position. Its democratic legitimacy was questionable because the last elections to the council had been held under Austrian rule. A number of members on the city council had been chosen by the simple means of "Austrian" councilors co-opting new members or were government appointees. For a while, the municipal council was headed by a government commissary. This unsatisfactory situation only ended when new elections were held on May 27, 1934. Sixteen Jewish, five socialist, five National Democratic (Polish), and forty-six government candidates were elected.[18]

L'viv continued to be a focal point in the Polish–Ukrainian conflict. The Ukrainian population experienced Polish rule as oppressive. According to Ukrainian sources, some 3,000 Ukrainian political prisoners were still languishing in Polish prisons in December 1920, 1,200 of whom were interned in L'viv.[19] By 1921, fifty thousand soldiers of the Ukrainian Galician Army and twenty thousand civilians (including eight hundred Greek Catholic priests) had been temporarily interned.[20] The three Greek Catholic bishops sent protest notes to the League of Nations complaining about the arrest of Greek Catholic priests and the pressure put on the Greek Catholic population to convert to Roman Catholicism. They accused the authorities of giving trading licenses or jobs in the civil service exclusively to Roman Catholics.[21]

Former officers of the Ukrainian Galician Army set up a Ukrainian Military Organization (UVO), which began attacking government offices and other official buildings. The Ukrainian Student Union (founded in 1921) and the Union of Ukrainian Nationalist Youth (Sojuz Ukraïns'koï Natsionalistychnoï Molodi) provided the UVO with new recruits.[22] The most spectacular attack occurred on September 25, 1921. Chief of State Józef Piłsudski had traveled to L'viv to open a trade fair. He was accompanied by the voivode of the L'viv region, Kazimierz Grabowski. Stepan Fedak, a Ukrainian student, shot Grabowski, slightly injuring him. The attack was followed by a wave of arrests. Thirteen Ukrainians were accused of having conspired to kill the head of state and were put on trial. They were defended by thirteen Ukrainian lawyers, who argued that the attackers had not committed treason as legally East Galicia was not part of Poland.[23]

Minority policy and land reform lay in the hands of the national government and parliament. Poles were no longer the subject of imperial minority policies but were now responsible for formulating their own policies for the minorities living in the new Polish nation state. The government formally acknowledged the national rights of Ukrainians and promised the Entente and the League of Nations to grant autonomy to Eastern Little Poland.[24] Trusting that this promise would be carried out, on March 15, 1923, the Allied Council of Ambassadors recognized the sovereignty of Poland over East Galicia.

The Polish government was in a difficult situation. It had promised autonomy but placed no faith in the loyalty of the Ukrainian population. The government hoped to consolidate Polish rule in its eastern borderlands by promoting the settlement of demobilized Polish soldiers, privileging ethnic Poles in the land reform, and offering cheap credit to Polish settlers.[25] According to Ukrainian estimates, around two hundred thousand settlers arrived in Volhynian and East Galician villages in the period up until 1938, and a further one hundred thousand Poles moved to the towns and cities. Polish sources only give a figure of one hundred thousand colonists, which was still a sizable number but far from sufficient to change the ethnic balance of the borderlands.[26]

The Polish authorities curtailed the rights of Ukrainian cooperatives. Ukrainians had little or no chance to get a job in the public sector. Ukrainian schools were put under pressure to either adopt Polish as the sole language of teaching or increase Polish language teaching.[27] In 1920 there were forty-five Polish state primary schools in L'viv but only one Ukrainian state primary school. Ukrainians funded private primary schools for 1,580 children, but 1,126 Ukrainian children were obliged to attend Polish schools. The only Ukrainian secondary school was given a provisional home in the Ukrainian National House.[28]

In 1919 all Ukrainian-language chairs in L'viv University were abolished. The government broke its promise to create a Ukrainian university and tried to suppress the private Ukrainian university, where former Ukrainian professors and lecturers from the main university were teaching.[29] In the aftermath of the wave of repressions following the attack on Piłsudski and Grabowski, the Polish authorities closed down the private Ukrainian university, forcing it underground. According to Ukrainian sources, in 1922/1923 the university had 1,500 students and 54 professors and lecturers.[30] After the authorities closed down the secret university in 1925, Ukrainian students were forced to study at the universities of L'viv (in 1925/1926, 15.6 percent of all students were Ukrainian) or Cracow or go abroad.[31]

Once the Allied Council of Ambassadors had recognized Polish sovereignty over East Galicia, the Ukrainian national movement had to adapt to the new situation. The West Ukrainian government in exile in Vienna became less important. The Ukrainian political parties in Poland tried to defend and rebuild the cooperative system and uphold the interests of the Ukrainian population. This approach created a rift between legal Ukrainian parties and the UVO, which still pursued a policy of noncooperation with the Polish authorities.

The new Polish government of 1924 was dominated by the National Democrats. The government dissolved the Ukrainian Social Democratic Party. Ukrainian institutions, including some of the Prosvita reading clubs, were closed down.[32] Stanisław Grabski, a former L'viv professor of law, was appointed minister for education. He tried to expand the use of the Polish language in East Galicia. The so-called Lex Grabski created a legal framework to transform most Ukrainian schools into *utraquist* (bilingual) Polish Ukrainian schools. Ukrainian-language teaching was now completely banned in L'viv University and in higher education in general, notwithstanding the promises made to the Entente.[33] In 1912 there were 2,400 Ukrainian primary schools in East Galicia. In 1927 this figure dropped to 352 and decreased even further to 144 by 1939. While there was one secondary school for every 16,000 Poles, one Ukrainian secondary school served 230,000 Ukrainians.[34]

But these events only cover part of the story. The second half of the 1920s also saw the Ukrainian cooperative system flourish and Ukrainian parties develop and prosper, accompanied by a reinvigoration of the Greek Catholic Church. The dominant Ukrainian party was the National Democratic Party. After merging with a few of the smaller parties, it renamed itself in 1925 as the Ukrainian National-Democratic Union (Ukraïns'ke Natsjonal'no-Demokratychne Objed"nannja, UNDO). Most leading politicians from the older generation of Ukrainian politicians joined the UNDO. The party's ultimate goal was still the establishment of an independent Ukraine, but the UNDO was willing to cooperate with the Polish state to improve the political, cultural, and economic situation of the Ukrainian minority in Poland. The UNDO was under pressure from the Polish state and Ukrainian nationalist youth but won around six hundred thousand votes in every national election. The second-most important Ukrainian party was the Ukrainian Radical Party, which received around 280,000 votes. The Ukrainian Social Democratic Party still existed but enjoyed no mass support. [35]

The concordate between the Polish Republic and the Vatican on February 10, 1925, improved the situation of the Greek Catholic Church. The Greek Catholic Church had four million members in some three thousand parishes, a network of youth and women's organizations, and published a number of magazines. It even had its own party—the Ukrainian Catholic National Party (Ukraïns'ka Katolyts'ka Narodna Partija)—and a theological academy in L'viv.[36]

Piłsudski's coup d'état in May 1926 initially had positive repercussions on Polish–Ukrainian relations as he was more tolerant of national minorities than the Polish National Democratic Party. Piłsudski seized power to end the economic and political crisis that had engulfed Poland. Supported by the army he overthrew the government headed by Wincenty Witos, the leader of the peasant party. Piłsudski installed an authoritarian regime with the avowed aim "to heal" public life. In December 1927 his supporters formed the Nonpartisan Bloc for Cooperation with the Government (Bezpartyjny Blok Spółpracy z Rządem). Piłsudski hoped to achieve reconciliation between the national minorities and the Polish state. He appointed Henryk Józewski as voivode of Volhynia. Józewski made concessions to the Ukrainian peasants to win them over to the Polish state. His policy, however, was not implemented in East Galicia. Volhynian

Ukrainians were perceived as less nationally aware and more malleable than East Galician Ukrainians.[37]

There was a generational conflict within the Ukrainian national movement. While the Ukrainian parties, which continued to operate within the framework of the Polish state, were dominated by the "fathers," many "sons" adopted a militant nationalism based on the ideas of the East Ukrainian immigrant Dmytro Dontsov. Dontsov was an integral nationalist who believed all things should be subordinated to the central aim of establishing an independent Ukrainian state. All means were justified to achieve this end.[38] In the winter of 1929, representatives of various Ukrainian radical nationalist groups met in Vienna to found the Organization of Ukrainian Nationalists (OUN). The OUN was set up to resemble an underground army, with a military-style leadership and an emphasis on strict discipline and conspiratorial methods. Its command center remained outside Poland and it was headed by Jevhen Konovalets, a former officer of the Sich riflemen. Stepan Bandera, a veteran of the Ukrainian Galician Army, headed the OUN in Poland. The OUN did not have many members (not more than twenty thousand in 1939) but managed to launch a terrorist campaign against Polish rule in East Galicia.[39]

Between July and November 1930, supporters of the OUN carried out more than two thousand acts of sabotage and attacks on Polish estate owners, military settlers, and officials.[40] By mid-September the Polish government had had enough and began sending police units and military detachments to East Galicia to end the rebellion by force. Repression was based on the principle of collective retribution. Reprisals, referred to as "pacifications," hit whole villages. Village halls and reading rooms were destroyed, property was seized, and any resistance was met with violence.[41] More than two thousand Ukrainians, many of them minors, were arrested, and about one-third were sentenced to lengthy prison terms. The spiral of violence continued as militant nationalists attacked representatives of the Polish state. Between 1921 and 1939 the OUN carried out sixty-three assassination attempts, which cost the lives of twenty-five Poles, one Russian, one Jew, and thirty-six Ukrainians. The OUN murdered Polish politicians along with local Polish civil servants and Ukrainians who attempted to reach a compromise with Poland. In 1931 the OUN killed the chairman of the government bloc, Tadeusz Hołówko, one of the most important advocates of granting concessions to the Ukrainians. In 1933 a secretary of the Soviet consulate in L'viv was murdered in retribution for the famine in Soviet Ukraine. In 1934 the OUN succeeded in killing the minister of the interior, Bronisław Pieracki. Legal Ukrainian organizations and parties opposed such terrorist acts as they precipitated repressions and reprisals by the authorities.[42]

Notwithstanding this violence, attempts were also made to settle the conflict peacefully. The Polish minister-president Wacław Jędrzejewicz admitted that the government had made mistakes in its policy toward the Ukrainian minority, and the Ukrainian National Democratic Union temporarily stopped demanding autonomy for Ukrainian regions and acknowledged the validity of some of the Polish national interests. UNDO deputies voted for the budget and the government allowed more UNDO politicians to stand in parliamentary elections. The new Sejm had fourteen Ukrainian deputies, and Ukrainian organizations and cooperatives were given government loans at favorable conditions. But radical UNDO members and the OUN rejected such attempts at normalization. Attempts to improve relations were also foiled by the local and regional Polish authorities in East Galicia, who continued to discriminate against Ukrainians. The Polish military viewed Ukrainians as a security risk and was similarly opposed to granting them more concessions.[43]

The Ukrainian cooperative movement, however, flourished. All activities of daily life were covered by Ukrainian organizations, shops, and products. In 1939 the Ukrainian cooperatives had seven hundred thousand members and employed fifteen thousand people. About 90 percent of Ukrainian cooperatives were in East Galicia; in Volhynia, the Chełm region, and in Podlasie, Ukrainians had to join Polish cooperatives. The government supported Polish cooperatives, which were financially much stronger than their Ukrainian counterparts.[44] Education societies played an important role in Ukrainian self-organization. In 1938 Ridna Shkola maintained forty private secondary and vocational schools and had one hundred thousand members. The educational society Prosvita had more than 360,000 members and maintained a dense network of reading rooms. It promoted Ukrainian culture and engaged in national (i.e., Ukrainian) education and publishing.[45]

Ukrainians were the majority nationality in the three southeastern Polish voivodeships, but in L'viv the Jewish community was more important. L'viv was home to the third-largest Jewish community in Poland (after Warsaw and Łódź). The Jewish community was divided into assimilationists (who advocated assimilation to Polish culture), Zionists, supporters of Hasidism, Orthodox Jews, and various types of socialists.[46] In 1924 the non-Zionist organizations created a civil committee to check the growing influence of the Zionist movement within the Jewish community (Kahal). The strongest Jewish middle-class party was the Economic Bloc, which later—after Piłsudski's coup d'état—supported the new (Sanacja) regime. The bloc cooperated with the religious Orthodox group and its strongest organization Agudat Israel, which was supported by about 20 percent of the Jewish population (according to estimates by the Polish police). The different Zionist parties enjoyed strong support but never achieved a majority in the Kahal.[47] The Zionists themselves were politically divided. Leon Reich, whose power base was in Galicia, refused to form parliamentary alliances with other minorities against Polish parties and fought for Jews to be accorded full minority rights. Reich was even prepared to form alliances with the Polish National Democrats. On the other side, Izaak Grünbaum, the leader of the Zionists in the former

Kingdom of Poland, wanted to transform Poland from a nation-state into a state of nationalities and formed alliances with the Bloc of Minorities in parliament.[48]

The L'viv Kahal controlled several education and welfare societies, religious schools and synagogues. In 1929 bank director Wiktor Chajes, a Jewish Pole, became head of the Kahal administration. The headquarters of many Jewish organizations, sports clubs, cooperatives, newspapers, and many Polish, Yiddish, or Hebrew journals were located in L'viv.[49]

Jewish parties and organizations were politically divided but they were united in their fight against anti-Semitism. Anti-Semitism permeated the Polish National Democratic Party and its youth and student organizations. From the end of the 1920s on, it became almost traditional at the beginning of every university year in L'viv for National Democratic students to beat up Jews and attack Jewish shops and institutions. The Jewish youth defended themselves, and fights between Jewish and National Democratic Polish students were a regular occurrence. Sometimes knives were used, but the clashes rarely ended with casualties. The violence had not yet become deadly, but anti-Semitism was growing. Anti-Semitic Polish nationalists tried to exclude Jews from society, restrict the number of Jews studying at university, and, by the second half of the 1930s, force Jewish students to sit separately from other students. In 1925 the law faculty of L'viv University introduced a *numerus clausus* for national minorities, whereby 60 percent of law students had to be Roman Catholics. The faculty refused to increase the proportion of Ukrainian and Jewish students when it proved to be impossible to fill the places with Poles.[50] Between 1921/1922 and 1938/1939 the number of Jewish students at Polish universities decreased from 24.6 percent (8,400) of all students to 8.2 percent (4,100).[51]

While anti-Semitism weakened the assimilationist movement, cultural Polonization was also taking place. For many Jews, Polish became their most important daily language, and the importance of Yiddish decreased. Jews increasingly began to detach themselves from their former religious environment but without being able to find a secure place within Polish society.[52] Unsurprisingly, Zionism was growing. In the 1921 census, 78.7 percent of the Jewish population in L'viv declared themselves as being of Jewish nationality (60,417 of 76,783 people of Jewish faith). In rural areas around L'viv, only 47 percent (5,440 of 11,568) considered themselves as being of Jewish nationality. In the 1929 parliamentary elections, the Jewish National Union (Zionists) won 29.3 percent of the vote. The union was the strongest party in L'viv. Its share of votes was 4 percent higher than the share of the next strongest party, the Government Bloc.[53]

The Ukrainian population was not free from anti-Semitic tendencies but there were no violent clashes between Ukrainians and Jews in the interwar period. Some Ukrainian organizations participated in boycotts of Jewish shops, but Jewish and Ukrainian minority politicians also occasionally cooperated in parliament.

Contested Memories

The military victory of the Polish troops put an end to the Polish–Ukrainian war. But once the war was over, the battle over symbols and the meaning of the war began.[54] This debate was waged in historical books and in the press, through symbols and material representations, the building of chapels and churches, festivities, the design and creation of cemeteries, and the political cult of the dead. The struggle over the interpretation had both an internal and an external aspect. Internally, the remembrance of heroism, of magnificent victories and tragic defeats could bolster or even engender a sense of national identity. Externally, the issue could take the form of a claim to a nation-state (Ukrainians), the defense of the territory acquired (the Poles) or the favorable positioning of an ethnic group within a new state (the Jews). The external aspect impinged on both the public sphere in the Second Polish Republic and the international arena of politics, where the belated decision, not taken until 1923, about which state East Galicia should be part of still hung in the balance.

November 1918 was the central historical reference point for the city's main ethnic groups. The Polish–Ukrainian war, the proclamation of the West Ukrainian People's Republic, the Polish Obrona Lwowa (Defense of Lwów), the pogrom, and the establishment of the Second Polish Republic were key events that all had lived through. They altered the previous experiences of the Great War while shaping the ongoing experiences of the present. World War I was reinterpreted and downgraded into a kind of prelude leading up to November 1918. Public discourse on memory absorbed only what could be combined teleologically with the successful or abortive (re)birth of a Polish or Ukrainian state. Every subsequent November, feelings and emotions ran high. Polish festivities began on November 1 and lasted for about three weeks. The Polish political cult of the dead concentrated—with the exception of the members of the Polish legions—on the national heroes who had fallen in the wars fought over national borders in the period between 1918 and 1920. These dead were firmly placed in the tradition of the heroes of previous Polish uprisings and victorious battles. The victory in the battle for Lwów was the first military victory of the Second Polish Republic. It bridged the stateless period, smoothly linking the present to the glorious past of the First Republic. The battle for Lwów was inscribed as within the tradition of the battles of Chocim (1621 and 1673), Częstochowa (Jasna Góra, 1665), and Zbaraż (1649). Although there was no Nobel laureate like Henryk Sienkiewicz on hand to immortalize the new heroes in a national epic, this did not interfere with the nationalist appropriation of the glorious Obrona.

The Ukrainians in their turn created a political cult of the dead, which centered on medieval Ruthenian princes, heroes of the Cossack wars, and the Haidamak uprising, as their way of infusing the *Listopadovyi chyn*[55] (November deed) with tradition. Only the Jews tried in vain to find some meaningful reading of the pogrom.

For Poles and Ukrainians, November 1918 fulfilled the basic functions of a political myth. It legitimated claims, provided a justification for authority, and offered orientation. It functioned as a "filter of perception," facilitating the formation of a consensus by reducing political complexity and thereby increasing the ability to take action. The Polish and Ukrainian myth tellers were themselves part of their respective societies, integrated by the myths and believing in the supreme national significance of their tale and the correctness of their interpretation.

Ukrainian and Polish elites wove myths around the events of that fateful November. Their accounts found an interested public that willingly participated in the process. In Polish society, memorialization was rapidly institutionalized. Already by November 21, 1920, an Association of the Defenders of L'viv (Związek Obrońców Lwowa) had been set up, supported by the municipality, the banks, the universities, and the high schools.[56] Under the umbrella of the league a multitude of small veteran organizations kept the memory of the Obrona alive. Beginning in November 1928, the Society for the Study of the History of the Defense of Lwów and the Southeastern Voivodeships (Towarzystwo Badania Historii Obrony Lwowa i wójewództw południowo-wschodnich) began collecting original documents from archives and private persons and encouraged those who had taken part in the fighting to record their memories for posterity.[57] Their search led to a series of publications, culminating in three volumes on the Obrona Lwowa, published between 1933 and 1938.[58] The well-known artist Wojciech Kossak painted scenes from the Obrona Lwowa and a canvas titled *The Eagles in Battle*.[59]

The Związek set up a Commission of Verification, which laid down the criteria that would allow a person to be formally classified as a "Defender of Lwów." The title betokened social recognition. Unsurprisingly, many tried to acquire this "social capital." In total, 10,599 applications were submitted to the commission, of which 6,355 were recognized, 6,022 from the city of Lwów and 333 from the ranks of the relief troops. More than four thousand persons were denied official recognition as a "Defender of Lwów."[60]

The Polish press called the Ukrainian seizure of power a German–Austrian–Ukrainian machination,[61] a "Ruthenian–Prussian–Austrian assault"[62] and an "act of alien, German inspiration."[63] Such descriptions aimed to convince the Entente that a Ukrainian state building in East Galicia was not an ambition held by the Ruthenian/Ukrainian population but the result of German and Austrian intrigues.[64] Polish authors differentiated between Ukrainian agitators and politicians and the ordinary Ruthenian peasants who—they believed—had been loyal to Poland.[65] Their enemies were "the Ukrainians," not the Ruthenians. The newspapers referred to "Ukrainian" atrocities, "Ukrainian" terror, and "Ukrainian" usurpers.[66]

The national democratic newspaper *Słowo Polskie* blatantly denied the existence of a Ukrainian nation in East Galicia. "People" had exploited the divide et impera policy of the Austrian government and Polish carelessness to cobble together a nation and advance historical claims. "On this fiction they based their plan, an impudent scheme rare in history, to create an own independent state for a historically non-existent nation." The Ukrainian seizure of power was referred to as an "assault" (*zamach*), often with the add-on "treacherous."[67] Brother had taken up arms against brother.[68] According to this discourse, the Polish victory was a blessing for the Ukrainians because it had not only saved Poland but also the "Ruthenian brother nation" from falling into the hands of the Bolsheviks.[69]

Separate from this discourse, which emphasized the childlike naivety of the Ruthenians, were the numerous reports about Ukrainian atrocities which had already began circulating in the first two days after the takeover. These stories aimed to exclude Ukrainians from the family of cultured European nations, to justify Polish retributions and support the Polish claim to ethnically Ukrainian territories.[70] The authors tried to counter the Ukrainian claim that the takeover on November 1 had been smooth and passed off without bloodshed. Ukrainian writers argued that only the armed resistance of Poles had escalated the conflict. Their claim was justified, as a Polish statistic from 1938 showed that there had been no casualties on November 1, 1918.[71] But for the Poles the Obrona Lwowa was not only a fight for the future of Lwów and East Galicia but was also a spontaneous act of self-defense against a Ukrainian attack. The newspaper *Słowo Polskie* wrote of noisy gunfire and—falsely—of "innocent victims" and "innocent blood" that had been spilled in the first few hours.[72] "The Ukrainian"—the newspaper added—had no feelings of common humanity. Whosoever wore a Polish cockade risked being shot by the "Ruthenian soldiery."[73]

For Polish society it was important that it had been children who had voluntarily saved "beloved Lwów" from the treacherous "Ukrainian usurpation." With their deeds the children had demonstrated to the world that Lwów was Polish and that they were the worthy successors of the Polish heroes of the past.[74] Heroism accumulated over generations had ultimately led to victory, culminating in the rebirth of the Polish state. This interpretation was given expression in a play, written for secondary school children by the teacher Jan Niemiec in 1919. The hero of the play is a fourteen-year-old boy, Antoś Nieborski. The story was based on the life of the famous youngest "Defender of Lwów" Jurek Bitschan.[75] In 1928 the author Zofja Lewartowska published the play *Lwów—Pride of the Nation*.[76] The play tells the story of the children of a widowed Polish mother who, with the exception of the youngest son, died in the battle for Lwów. The mother had also raised a Ruthenian orphan who joins the Ukrainian side after his love is rejected by the eldest daughter. In the end, he perfidiously kills the daughter before he is killed himself. In the second act, the remaining youngest son Jozio has an apparition. An old man appears in Jozio's dream and shows the twelve-year-old boy the past as a continuous line in which the Obrona Lwowa has its place. Polish rulers who had taken or regained Lwów march past Jozio. The following six scenes evoke historical events, showing how Lwów has defended herself in the past against attackers—mostly from the east—and acquired its title as "always faithful" (i.e., to the Polish crown): *Leopolis—semper fidelis*. The longest scene depicts the siege of Lwów by Cossack troops under Hetman Bohdan Khmel'nyt'kyj, establishing a line of continuity from the fearsome seventeenth-century Cossacks to the Ukrainian Galician Army in the twentieth century. Lwów is presented as an eternally Polish city and its inhabitants as staunch defenders of the Polish nation and Roman Catholic faith. Lewartowska did not fail to include the famous Polish poem "Rota" (The Oath) in her play, in a new version adapted to current needs:

> We will not forsake Lwów—this is our city—
> We will not allow our language to be buried,
> We are children of Lwów—the Polish nation
> from the royal line of Piast!
> We will not let the enemy oppress us.
> So help us God!
> So help us God!

The Obrona Lwowa and the reconstitution of the Polish state represented the consummation and fulfillment of the sacrifices of all the previous uprisings, or, to use a religious terminology, it was the redemption and the previous unsuccessful uprisings were the tests. The defeats suffered in previous rebellions were thus negated; indeed, they retroactively became the necessary preconditions for victory. Heroism accumulated over generations ultimately led to victory. And November 1918 became "the greatest date in our history."[77]

In the process of mythicizing the Obrona Lwowa, the discourse became separated from its historical subject. The concrete enemy and the historical context no longer played any role for the substance of the myth. Instead, the Obrona was infused with a more profound national significance. Newspaper articles, speeches, and sermons continually repeated the same themes, which centered on the concepts of unity, education, struggle, and sacrifice. These four key foci correlated with the function fulfilled by the memory of the Obrona Lwowa. Unity referred to the strengthening of solidarity within the group and was particularly aimed at the generation that had consciously experienced the Obrona. Education involved the transfer of experience from one generation to the next. Sacrifice and struggle were exemplary modes of behavior held up as motivations to Polish youth to encourage them to emulate such examples.

The topos unity had two aspects: unity during the struggle and unity in sacrifice. The bonds between Polish participants had developed spontaneously from below and had not emanated from the leadership: "We arose as one man to engage in a struggle for life and death."[78] The blood that was spilled united people across political and social boundaries.[79] The symbol of the Obrona Lwowa was meant to reconcile a Polish population, politically divided and ridden with social divisions, under the unifying canopy of the nation, an alchemy which would allow conflicting interests to disappear. This is why a recurrent central theme in the memorial practice was that *all* social strata had defended the city, understood as an indication that only unity in the present would guarantee future success.[80] The Obrona Lwowa was a "symbol of the unification of the nation" (*Symbol zjednoczenia narodu*).[81]

This projected unity of 1918 was the yardstick with which to measure the present. In 1933 the leading national democratic daily newspaper *Słowo Polskie* wrote that it was necessary to examine one's conscience to determine "whether within us today the spirit of the Defenders of Lwów" still beats strongly."[82]

At a meeting of the Association of the Defenders of Lwów on November 21, 1923, one member caused an uproar by casting doubt on the consensus that all of Polish society had defended the city. He provoked additional displeasure by expressing the—well-founded—opinion that the Ukrainian–Polish war had been a game of cat and mouse compared with the Great War. The indignation of the audience was tremendous, so great, in fact, that the meeting had to be suspended for half an hour until tempers cooled. Then the head of the association took to the rostrum to declare that all Poles had participated in the defense of Lwów.[83] The previous speaker had violated the unwritten rule not to make different views on the Obrona a subject in commemorative practice and not to raise doubts about their function. The Obrona Lwowa was far too important an element in the Polish myth of November and of the place of the Lwów Poles within the Polish state.

There was also a particularly active collective cult that focused on the youth of Lwów. This was the area in which the second leitmotif—education—played a central role. The Obrona was enshrined within the tradition of Polish heroism. Children at school were presented with the story of the Obrona Lwowa as a living textbook of "the most idealistic patriotism and most unselfish heroism." Memorialization was designed to deepen the "love for the fatherland."[84]

One of the myth's most celebrated heroes was Jurek Bitschan, a fourteen-year-old boy killed in battle. Another important hero was Roman Feldstein-Felsztyn, who—of Jewish origin—had fought on the Polish site. He fell, nineteen years old, in the spring of 1919, leaving behind a number of poems. His "Song on the Future Life" ("Pieśń o przyszłym życiu"), written four years earlier, became very popular and exemplifies the attitude of his generation and class toward death and sacrifice.

And death shall be beautiful and wonderful /
Equally beautiful will be my life. /
And all strings of the soul will be played. /
And in each the noble tone will secretly be lost.

A śmierć ma będzie piękna i wspaniała /
Jakoteż pięknem będzie moje życie. /
I na dusz wszystkich będzie strunach grała. /
I w każdej traci ton szlachetny skrycie.[85]

While, on one hand, the cult of the Obrona was a cult about the youth of Lwów, on the other hand, it was instrumentalized to educate contemporary youth: "Our young generation shall read about the history of the Defense of Lwów, taking the heroism of the Lwów eagles as a model for emulation."[86]

This transfer of experience was explicitly discussed. The "history of this bloody, sacrificial and heroic deed" would be passed on from generation to generation, by "the children to the children, the grandchildren to the grandchildren." The "blood of those Lwów eagles" was a "revitalizing, healing fountain for the soul of the entire nation."[87]

Pathos was the appropriate emotion when contemplating and commemorating the Obrona. Discourse became a celebratory rhetoric of the uprising: young people in 1918 perceived the chance to redeem the constantly repeated promises, and from being only admirers of the heroes of yore, they became honored heroes themselves. That also explains the sense of joy and exhilaration the young fighters recalled. Descriptions of comrades dying and of sadness and loss are accompanied by accounts of joyful and jubilant episodes, of singing, laughing, and high spirits during the three weeks when the battles raged for the defense of neighborhoods and houses. Some had died "with a smile on their lips."[88]

Grief and triumph also went hand in hand in the practice of remembrance. *Słowo Polskie* wrote that "these were terrible days but they were beautiful days, radiant, just as every noble uplifting of the spirit, ready for sacrifice, and every common effort, has its own beauty."[89] *Wiek Nowy* wrote that despite all the pain and sorrow, the pilgrimage to the graves of sons and brothers on November 22 was more than anything else "a day of joy and cheerfulness" stemming from a deep sense of having done one's duty for a just cause.[90]

An important function of commemoration was to give meaning to the losses suffered by families by interpreting them as an act of service for the sake of the nation: "Happy the family nests, the aeries from which these eagles flew forth, despite the sacred pain! Happy the city that can boast such children, theirs the hearts of heroes! Happy the nation, those who marched in the front ranks to struggle for freedom, paving the way to liberty by the blood they spilled in its attainment."[91]

The third and fourth motifs—sacrifice and struggle—served to remind subsequent generations of their duty because whether the past sacrifice would continue to have meaning in the present would depend on them. *Słowo Polskie* was dissatisfied with the first four years of independence. It argued that if nothing changed, then the sacrifices had been in vain.[92] The motifs of sacrifice and struggle were not only meant to mobilize people, but they also functioned as a model for action. Future generations, the newspaper declaimed, might also be called on to sacrifice their lives for the fatherland. In the practice of remembrance, young people could see just how the nation honored this sacrifice. They could experience the tributes paid to past heroes as an anticipation of their own future sacrifices. In 1926 the former commander of the Obrona Lwowa, Czesław Mączyński, formulated this as follows: "The first and most important duty of the nation which strives to live in keeping with that ideal is to honor its dead. This is a cardinal duty. The future of the nation depends on its fulfillment."[93]

Słowo Polskie identified certain distinctive Polish features: a "burning love for the fatherland, and boundless dedication to the point of self-sacrifice." For the paper, this "community prepared for sacrifice" was the hallmark of the "Polish national soul."[94]

Yet even in Polish society the memory of November 1918 was not without its conflicts and controversies. Dozens of protagonists struggled to obtain some recognition of the part they had played in the victory and for an appropriate representation of their roles in the public image of history. But such disputes did not disturb the core of the myth. What was at issue in these disputes was which group would gain the most "symbolic capital" from the Obrona Lwowa. Which group had contributed more to the victory: the Endecja or the Piłsudski camp?[95]

Feelings ran high after the publication of the first volume on the Obrona Lwowa in 1933. Members in the Piłsudski camp cast doubts on the undivided heroism of Polish Lwów. They presented themselves as the heroes and accused the Polish National Committee (which had been dominated by National Democrats) of having been defeatist.[96]

Słowo Polskie had always emphasized the role of national democratic organizations and criticized liberal politicians and Piłsudski supporters: "On 22 November 1918, we also prevailed over the neutrality of 40% of the population of Lwów, over our own weakness, indecision, demoralization, opportunism."[97]

National Democrats and Piłsudski supporters alike attacked the moderate politicians who had attempted to find a peaceful settlement for the Polish–Ukrainian conflict. After the victory this counted as defeatism, and the existence of such attempts was ignored during the annual celebrations evoking national unity. A willingness to negotiate and find peaceful solutions to conflicts is not popular in times when heroes are made.[98] *Słowo Polskie* wrote in November 1919 that "antiquated Austrophiles" had advised not to resist and, instead, to await the decision of the international peace conference, but an "overwhelming majority at once understood, or rather felt with unerring national instinct, that the fight was imposed on us, despite the desperate conditions."[99] The armed fight and the success of the Obrona had become an untouchable myth, which could no longer be called into question by supporters of a peaceful solution and opponents of the bloodshed.[100]

Despite the different attempts at political instrumentalization, the Obrona became a symbol of national unity—although only the unity of Roman Catholic Poles. The lost national unity was restored in rituals of remembrance and refashioned into something that could be re-experienced through participation in the festivities. The Ukrainian elites made similar attempts, albeit under far less favorable conditions.

After the end of the Polish–Ukrainian war, the Ukrainians produced competing interpretations of the conflict and were able to negotiate a consensual reading of the war within the internal discourse of their own group. The media employed in this discourse were the organs of the press, although they were partly hindered by censorship. Closed meetings and get-togethers in venues such as Greek Catholic church buildings served the same purpose.

Initially, the Ukrainians rejected the political insinuation that they had been controlled by the Austrians. They contended that the aim of the coup was to prevent, through Ukrainian resistance, East Galicia from falling into Polish hands.[101] The Ukrainian seizure of power was meant to demonstrate the upsurge of a Ukrainian national movement to the Entente. It was to drive home the realization that the permanent inclusion of East Galicia in Poland was not in keeping with the wishes of the local population. The West Ukrainians seized on the Polish epithet "haidamaks,"[102] using it deliberately to refer to themselves. They chose to stand proudly in the tradition of the hetman Bohdan Khmel'nyts'kyj, the Cossack uprisings against the Polish crown in the seventeenth century, and the haidamak uprising in the eighteenth century. During clashes with the Polish police in the interwar period, Ukrainians often sang militant songs such as "My Haidamaki."[103]

In their variant of the November myth, the Ukrainian elites emphasized the same values as their Polish competitors. Their November deed (*Lystopadovyj chyn*) was the seizure of power in L'viv and the establishment of a West Ukrainian People's Republic. The discourse among Ukrainians also revolved around unity, education, sacrifice, and struggle. However, in the Second Polish Republic, they were unable to formulate their position publicly in a form that differed sharply from the Polish interpretation. Nonetheless, hundreds of articles, memoirs, and literary works on the November events and the Polish–Ukrainian war were published in Ukrainian newspapers, almanacs, calendars, and brochures.[104]

For the Ukrainian newspaper *Dilo* (*The Deed*), unity was one of the central experiences of November 1918.[105] As on the Polish side, heated confrontations and debates took place in the Ukrainian political arena during the interwar period.

Ukrainian society at the time was far from united. It was thus all the more important to create a space of experience every November in which, against a backdrop of continuous political infighting, the longed-for unity could be experienced in festive acts and the practice of commemoration. The Ukrainian soldiers had experienced this unity in the shared battles and the comradeship of the Ukrainian Galician Army. Such encounters were repeatedly emphasized as special experiences.[106]

In its consideration of the meaning of November 1918, *Dilo* found no political beliefs, only the "conscious members of the nation and of the nation alone." For the Ukrainian elites, November 1, 1918, was a "symbol of the unification of the entire nation." Participation in memorial religious services and meetings was an expression of allegiance to the Ukrainian nation and community with fellow Ukrainian citizens. November would live on for all times in the heart and soul of the nation "which is immortal!"[107]

November 1918 was solidly anchored in Ukrainian collective memory. The memory of the *Lystopadovyj chyn* and the Polish–Ukrainian war was made a living presence in the anniversary celebrations, and the experience gained at the time was passed on to younger generations. There was a clear educational aspect here, a commemorative pedagogy. Children knew about the events from the tales of their fathers, brothers, and relatives. The contrast between the heroic period of struggle and the reality of the Second Polish Republic was painful.[108] Yet even in the darkest times, the paper claimed, the memory of the *Lystopadovyj chyn* provided hope and inspiration for future generations.[109]

The motifs of sacrifice and struggle were even more important for the defeated Ukrainians than for the victorious Poles. Armed struggle was meritorious in itself, and the Polish–Ukrainian war was considered the forge of the nation. Until that time, *Dilo* argued, Ukrainians had generally been disinclined to take mortal risks. But in 1918/1919 they had put their lives on the line; they had salvaged the "dignity of the Ukrainian nation." The battle had led them on the path for independence.[110] The paper gave a precise definition of what nation building entailed: "Consciousness decides whether a people remains an ethnographic mass or is transformed into a nation according to the modern understanding of the concept."[111]

In Ukrainian discourse, the Polish–Ukrainian war functioned as a national foundation myth. As a rule, such a mythical narrative references an event outside historical time, but the Ukrainian national movement lacked an archaic, genuine, and undisputed "Ukrainian" foundation myth.[112] That gap was filled over the short term by the November deed. As *Dilo* saw it, the "legend of the glorious days" had arisen "from the graves of the heroes on the battle fields." The newspaper stressed that the groundwork for the battle had been laid by many years of hard work in which several generations of Galician intellectuals had participated. The work had transformed the rural masses into a nationally conscious force fighting for its freedom.[113]

Other characteristic motifs of the Polish discourse are also found in the Ukrainian discourse. Although the "blood of the finest sons of the nation" had been shed for the ideal of a pan-Ukrainian state,[114] the military defeat retrospectively became a moral victory and a guarantor of future success. That was why commemoration of November 1918 should not be an occasion for mourning and sadness: "There are no vain sacrifices nor, as citizens and sons of the nation, is there any tragedy or mournful anniversaries for us."[115]

It was not the prospect of victory that was decisive, but the readiness to fight, the willingness to lay down one's own life for the nation. The extent to which people were willing to make this "ultimate sacrifice" indicated the nation's level of maturity. The *Lystopadovyj chyn* was important because "identification with the national community was manifesting itself not only in speech or platonic sympathy but in armed action, in the spilling of one's own blood":[116] "The hecatombs of sacrifices, laid on the altar of liberation, did not die in vain; they proved our national dignity, our maturity, placed us within the circle of those nations of the world which know and appreciate their right to live, and finally they gave us great spiritual nourishment for whole generations and laid the foundation for a new national tradition and national education."[117]

But why had the defeat occurred? Reflections on this occupy a substantial portion of the Ukrainian discourse on the wars of independence. Participants in this debate saw the greatest deficit as existing precisely in those spheres celebrated in the context of the remembrance festivities as the greatest achievements of the wars of independence: the Ukrainian nation's willingness to struggle and endure sacrifices. The newspaper *Dilo* suggested the importance of learning as much as possible for the future from the defeat. West Ukrainians developed a "culture of defeat,"[118] viewing the failure as an opportunity to obtain greater benefits over the longer term than the victors would derive from their victory.[119] What had gone wrong?

Criticism of their own behavior solidified over time into the convictions formulated in anniversary articles which went on to become part of a lasting Ukrainian interpretation of the events. The argument ran roughly as follows: in November 1918 the Ukrainians had had an army, real power, and genuine initiative. But their leaders had been caught unawares by the "great moment"; they had reacted without a plan; they had been at a total loss and had not exploited the favorable constellation.[120]

An article in *Dilo* published on the fifteenth anniversary of November 1918 summarized the reasons for the defeat: the commanding officers had made mistakes, the politicians had been undecided, and the masses had not been sufficiently prepared for a revolution. The other reasons for the defeat were outside Ukrainian control: the unfavorable international context, the superiority of the Polish troops and leadership, and the low level of organization. The newspaper employed social Darwinist concepts of the struggle for survival between nations. In the view propounded by the newspaper, not only had two national ideologies been pitted one against the other but two different types of social psyche as well, with differing national characters rooted in different traditions and cultures. Preparing for a potential military battle was part of the fabric of Polish tradition, so the Polish readiness to fight was greater. "Every Pole, from the children to the street urchins and up to the highest of gentlemen" had engaged in the battle. In contrast, there had been no true mass participation among the Ukrainians. That was why a last heroic resurgence against the imminent defeat had failed to materialize. The anniversary of the lost war should be used to educate the youth in the tradition of fighting and sacrifice.[121]

Activists and ideologues of militant Ukrainian nationalism such as Dmytro Paliïv and Dmytro Dontsov also voiced incisive criticisms of the behavior of the Ukrainian political and military leadership in 1918/1919. In Dontsov's view, the adherence of the older generation of politicians to humanist ideas and a patriotic idealization of culture had been responsible for the failure to establish a viable Ukrainian state. Dontsov espoused the idea of a national egoism in which all means would be justified as long as they served to realize national ends. The Ukrainian defeat had, in his view, been brought about by a lack of the requisite passion. The old humanist values should now be replaced by an unconditional will to victory and power.[122]

In one respect, Dontsov was right. The leading Ukrainian politicians, like their moderate Polish counterparts, had a strong preference for legalistic procedures. Many were lawyers, and all of them had been socialized in Austria-Hungary. The politicians on both sides knew each other well from sessions of the Diet and the parliament in Vienna. They had hoped that it would be possible to achieve a peaceful settlement of the Polish–Ukrainian conflict. The West Ukrainian state builders of November 1918 did not want to establish absolute Ukrainian domination but championed a tolerant and democratic Ukrainian state that recognized Polish and Jewish cultural and political rights. "Ethnic cleansing" and systematic terror against ethnic minorities were not means they were prepared to use.

The Jewish Discourse

For the Jewish population, November 1918 was inextricably bound with the memory of the pogrom. It had come as a complete surprise to the Jewish Poles and dealt an almost lethal blow to the Jewish movement for assimilation. Ukrainian troops were still besieging L'viv when Jewish politicians began criticizing the Polish interpretation of the pogrom in memoranda and letters and in personal conversations. The most important Jewish daily in L'viv founded in 1919 by moderate Zionists, the Polish-language *Chwila*, tried to explain the difficult situation the Jewish community faced in November 1918 to its Polish readers: "The Jews finally came under attack from both sides, and were therefore in a very dangerous situation; they could only shake this off by proclaiming their neutrality."[123]

The stance of Jewish neutrality was contested. In 1919 Tobiasz Askenaze, a Jewish Pole, accused the Zionists of having been too passive. They had surrendered all agency by simply waiting to see which side would prevail in the conflict. Neutrality should only be a temporary option. The terrible pogrom made it more difficult to follow the "right path." If the Jews had joined the Polish side, the Polish–Ukrainian fight would soon have been over.[124] The journalists of *Chwila* were not convinced. They accused Askenaze of having spoken from the position of a Jewish Pole (Żyd-Polak). Supporting Poland endangered the Jewish population living in the territories controlled by Ukrainians. *Chwila* reminded Askenaze that the Ukrainians had been the first to recognize the Jews as a nation and had not harmed the Jewish population while they controlled L'viv.[125]

The pogrom traumatized the Jewish population. The Jewish press only used the first few anniversaries as occasions to speak about the pogrom.[126] One year after the pogrom, the Zionists tried to glean some basis for Jewish unity out of the experience of the pogrom.[127] At the invitation of the Zionist executive, representatives of all Jewish strata and groupings gathered to show "the unity of all of Jewry in times of threat and grief." *Chwila* wrote, "But the tears were not in vain. They washed away what was bad, weighing down the Jewish soul, they tightened the bonds between the individual and the nation. Jewish society became conscious of its unity. Without concern for partisanship, all rose to lend a hand, to dry the tears of the Jewish people."[128]

The composition of the Jewish Relief Committee for the Victims of the Pogrom, which spanned all political parties and religious camps, was in the eyes of *Chwila* a prime example of Jewish unity.[129] In 1919 memorial services of mourning were held in the three largest synagogues. The memory was still fresh. Thousands attended these religious services, creating such a throng that many of the faithful had to stand outside the synagogue and the lines of worshippers extended all the way down the street.[130]

But the attempt of Zionists to inscribe the pogrom with a unifying function failed. The traumatic experience was sealed off, impervious to any meaningful interpretation. The practice of memorialization manifested itself in grief and declarations of "never again": "At a time when for all the world the hour of resurrection had come, a merciless hell opened wide its gates for the Jews of L'viv. The Jewish city was paralyzed with pain, speechless with horror. . . . There was a sea of deprivation and distress, blood and desperation in the Jewish quarter, a hell in which mothers, children and old men died, on the lips of the innocent the petrified question of why?"[131]

At a meeting of the L'viv city council on February 2, 1919, the Zionist Dawid Schreiber brought up the subject of the pogrom. His argument was similar to that later advanced by *Chwila*: a lack of knowledge had made the pogrom possible in the first place. Polish society, he argued, was unfamiliar with the wishes of the Jewish nation and thought the Jews all wanted to be assimilated into Polish society. They did not. Polish disappointment had been great when this bubble burst. There was no "wall of granite" between the Polish and Jewish nations. The pogrom in L'viv had been a disaster for Jewish society, but even more painful for Jewish society was the attitude of Polish society toward these events and their behavior afterward, because no one had been ready to condemn the pogrom unconditionally. In Schreiber's view, in the end the Jews themselves were blamed for the suffering they had endured. A productive existence where Jewish and Polish society could work together was only possible if these blanket criticisms of the Jews were retracted and the behavior of the Jews in November 1918 fully and completely rehabilitated.[132]

The Jewish discourse developed out of the confrontation with Polish criticism. Jewish authors found it especially regrettable that the Polish government, the L'viv notables, or the press had not dealt self-critically with the pogrom. Instead, they had accused the Jewish community of harming Polish interests by publicizing the pogrom abroad. But the Jewish community had not done this. In October 1919 the Kahal sent a letter of complaint to the mayor of L'viv, Józef Neumann. Neumann and other Polish politicians had claimed in an open letter to the Entente powers that in November 1918, L'viv Jews had shot at Polish units. The Kahal protested against the insinuation in private but did not go public with its protests. It demanded that its letter be kept in the city's archives.[133]

Polish organizations tried desperately to find proof of Jewish attacks on Polish units but in vain.[134] Some eyewitness accounts stated that there had been attacks but these could not be confirmed. In October 1919 a Polish court rehabilitated eight Jewish militiamen who had been accused of having collaborated with the Ukrainians. It was proved that the eight men had only crossed the demarcation line to the Ukrainian side because they were investigating certain criminal attacks. They had not fired a single shot on Ukrainian-controlled territory. The trial collapsed when the lawyers of the accused found out that the main witness for the prosecution was a wanted criminal who was accused of having shot a Polish officer.[135]

In the Polish public sphere, the pogrom was played down; privately this served as a way to avoid having to deal with the stigma tainting the Obrona Lwowa. In his unpublished memoirs, a Catholic priest stated that the role of the Jews had been outrageous and perfidious. Many of the supposed pogrom victims had, he alleged, died of an epidemic of typhoid fever.[136]

The L'viv Jews argued about what conclusions could be drawn from this denial and from the behavior of Polish society. Several Jewish Poles who had been directly involved in the Obrona Lwowa espoused an extreme position. In a peculiar twisting of the facts, Tadeusz Feldstein accused his fellow Jews of using the incidents after the withdrawal of the Ukrainians to vent their anger against the Poles: "Today in Poland everyone—even a person who up until now was the greatest philosemite—understands that the Jews are the most dangerous, threatening and immediate enemy of Poland." The idea of assimilation as espoused by the previous generation was bankrupt. Now there remained only two opposing camps: Poles and Jews. There was no third camp. Jewish Poles had to decide whether they wanted to be Poles or Jews, and if they opted for one camp, they would have to stop being in the other. Feldstein placed himself squarely on the side of Poland.[137]

Only a small proportion of Jewish Poles shared his view. In February 1919 the L'viv city council held an inquiry into the "Jewish question." Representatives of different political directions in the Jewish community presented their views. Some recommended assimilation to the Polish nation; others demanded national cultural autonomy. The Jewish Social Democrat Samuel Herschtal accused the Zionists of being partly responsible for the growing anti-Semitism in Polish society. He believed that Zionism and anti-Semitism bore a shared responsibility for the fact that assimilation appeared to have reached an impasse. Wiktor Chajes supported this view. Without anti-Semitism, he argued, Jews would tend to assimilation. But he did not believe that assimilation would ever become a mass phenomenon and therefore recommended recognizing the Jewish nationality and granting them equal rights and minority rights. There should be Jewish primary schools, but teaching at secondary school should be in Polish, and the schools should be supervised by the Kahal. Dawid Schreiber spoke for the Zionists and demanded full recognition of the Jewish nation with minority rights and full civil rights in Poland.[138]

The subsequent speech by the Polish national democrat Jan Pieracki demonstrated the resistance the Jews faced on the issue of assimilation but also with respect to national cultural autonomy. Pieracki declared that Poles should be the masters in their state. The Jews, he continued, were an alien element. It would be in Poland's interest to promote Jewish emigration and prevent Jewish immigration. Jews who did not identify with the Polish nation should be considered foreigners. He wanted to make it easier for Jewish Poles to adopt a Jewish nationality than for Jews to become Poles.[139]

For the Jewish population, the experience of the pogrom overshadowed the Obrona Lwowa. While the Ukrainian elites created their own November myth, the Jews soon fell silent. Although Jews and Poles were unable to agree on an interpretation of the pogrom, there was a tacit agreement between the elites not to broach the pogrom again in public. In private, however, the nightmare was remembered. Its lasting function for the Jewish experience of the war is manifested in diaries and memoirs. The Jewish Pole and longstanding deputy mayor of L'viv, Wiktor Chajes, wrote in his diary on November 1, 1938, that he, like almost all other Jews, had not spoken about the pogrom in public. He hoped that by these means the wounds would heal quicker.[140]

Jewish Poles were in a particular quandary. On one hand, they were regarded by the Zionists as traitors to the Jewish nation, but on the other hand, some sections of Polish society refused to accept them as Poles. Because of that, Jewish Poles attempted to document the activity of Jews in the Polish war of independence and the uprising in articles, brochures and books. They were supported in this endeavor by Zionists who were also interested in emphasizing the role of Jews in the Polish struggle for freedom.[141] Jews were only able to celebrate the Obrona Lwowa if the pogrom remained shrouded from sight. The motif of "sacrifice" was emphasized primarily when the sacrifices involved were those Jews had made for Poland. The same held true when it came to the motif of "struggle" as a pattern of action. The attorney Isaak Bürger accused Polish critics of the Jews that they had forgotten the blood shed by "Jewish youth, shoulder to shoulder with the Polish eagles in the trenches, to preserve the Polish character of our Lwów." He claimed that no one now remembered the long roster of Jewish participants in the uprisings, Jewish independence fighters, Jewish volunteers, Jewish fighters for Poland, Jewish defenders of Lwów.[142] The progressive Jewish Community in L'viv celebrated the anniversary of Poland's independence every year with a festive service in the temple, and Jewish Poles took part in the Polish commemorations of the Obrona.[143]

Because the subject of the pogrom was not touched on in the official Polish festivities, Polish descriptions of the Obrona Lwowa in particular provoked public reactions. The Jewish elites reacted immediately when journalists or politicians engaged in pogrom denial[144] or sought to blame Jews for the excesses.[145]

In 1931 Isaak Bürger wrote bitterly, "Anti-Semitic propaganda is gradually even taking over historiography. It continues its unceasing work of slander, insinuation and unjustified generalization of facts, all based on unproven accusations. Were such facts to actually exist, they would cast an indelible pall over attempts by Poles and Jews to live together."[146]

But attempts to reach any agreement on the issue of the pogrom and Jewish attitudes had long since become hopeless. The majority of Poles were convinced that the Jews had collaborated with the Ukrainians and that the Jewish militia had shot at Polish soldiers and had thus failed the Jewish population in Poland. For the overwhelming majority of Jews it was clear that the Jewish militia had maintained strict neutrality and not harmed Poles. The only differences in opinion were those between Jewish Poles and Zionists as to whether at some point it would have been necessary to espouse the Polish cause.

The Political Cult of the Dead

In the interwar period, the public space in L'viv was permeated with Polish symbols and monuments along with mementos of the Polish victory in the Obrona Lwowa. The Ukrainian war experience was not present in the public space, and its expression was confined to Greek Catholic churches and the graves of fallen Ukrainian soldiers. Cemeteries and graves became central spaces and sites of remembrance where memory condensed or, as the Polish newspaper *Gazeta Lwowska* put it, "These many rows of crosses erected in the Cemetery of the Defenders of Lwów will stand for all eternity as emblems of grief for the sacrifices laid upon the altar of the fatherland. And their names will be inscribed with golden letters in the annals of Lwów and Poland."[147]

The graves of the heroes played such an important role in the staging of celebrations and the practice of commemoration that their design was carefully planned. A Society for the Protection of the Graves of Polish Heroes (Straż Mogił Polskich Bohaterów) was set up in L'viv in July 1919. One of the society's first projects was to design a cemetery for the "Lwów Eagles." Immediately after the end of the fighting there was already a general consensus that all Poles killed in battle should be buried in a special cemetery near Łyczaków Cemetery. This field of graves soon came to be known as the "Cemetery for the Defenders of Lwów" (Cmentarz Obrońcow Lwowa, COL).[148] Over the subsequent months and years, the last remains of Polish fighters killed in the fighting were transferred to that final resting place. As a rule, such transfers were accompanied by commemorative religious services and festive processions.[149]

The provisional and makeshift character of the small cemetery was not in keeping with the significance that Polish society ascribed to the Obrona Lwowa.[150] With the assistance of the Architects Club, the municipality organized a design competition that caught the interest of Rudolf Indruch, who had himself participated in the Obrona. In subsequent years, the cemetery was altered in accordance with his plans. He designed a military cemetery located on a slope with a round white chapel, catacombs with arcades, a triumphal arch, and high pillars arranged in a semicircle. The entrance to the cemetery was via a stairway interspersed at various levels by terraces.[151]

The Cemetery of the Defenders was such a popular burial place that the municipal council already had to close it in February 1922. Final resting places for the dead who had been awarded the Cross for the Defense of Lwów or who had taken part in the November battles were arranged next to the Cemetery of the Defenders.[152] In addition, all "false" heroes were removed from the cemetery. Thus, in December 1937, the remains of five persons who had not taken part in the Defense of Lwów were transferred elsewhere.[153]

On All Saints' Day and All Souls' Day the impression on the onlookers must have been overwhelming. Candles were lit on all of the graves. Polish girls and boys were brought up on stories of the Obrona and spent innumerable hours during their school years in the presence of those who had died for the fatherland. Kazimierz Żygulski (born in 1919) recalled that every year on All Souls' Day his entire class would make a pilgrimage to the grave of the youngest hero of the Obrona, Jurek Bitschan. "The Łyczaków Cemetery thus formed for me a strange supplement to various history books and the debates on Polish history."[154]

Alma Heczko wrote in her diary that on November 1, 1938, an endless crowd of persons flowed through Piekarska Street toward the cemetery: "The atmosphere in the Cemetery of the Eagles is exceptional, not commonplace. The mood is exalted, people remain in silence and contemplation at the graves of those who sacrificed their lives for us. The graves swim in a sea of a thousand flickering lights. This festival is beautiful but sad."[155]

In 1925 the commemoration of the fallen "Defenders of Lwów" received an additional boost and shot to national prominence. The Polish government had decided to build a central war memorial that would take the form of a Tomb of the Unknown Soldier. The body of a Polish soldier whose identity could not be verified would be brought to the nation's capital and buried there under the arcades of the Saxon Palace, the seat of the war ministry at the time. This entwined the Obrona Lwowa with the newly emerging cult of the Unknown Soldier.[156]

On May 4, 1925, a ceremony was held in the Great Hall of the Polish War Council in Warsaw. The youngest bearer of the Virtuti Militari, the highest military order of the Second Polish Republic, removed one slip from an urn containing fifteen slips bearing the names of fifteen battlefields. All the battles were fought between 1918 and 1920 during the Polish state-building wars; none of the slips bore the name of any of the battles of World War I. The Polish authorities wanted to make sure that their Unknown Soldier had fought and died for Poland and not for any imperial power. No unidentified soldier of the Great War could guarantee this. The minister of military affairs Władysław Sikorski unfolded the paper and read aloud: "Bojowisko Lwowskie"—The Battle of Lwów. This meant that the Polish Unknown Soldier would come from the Cemetery of the Defenders of Lwów and that he had fallen in the Polish–Ukrainian war in 1918/19.

Poland was emulating a European trend that had started in 1920. Following the examples of France and Britain, many countries built a central tomb to house the remains of an unidentified soldier. These tombs became national shrines, with the Unknown Soldier standing at the heart of a political cult of the dead and representing all those who had died for the nation, not only in the Great War but also in other, previous wars and those who would die in future wars. The Unknown Soldier was a powerful symbol that, in Britain or France, appeared to unite the majority of the nation behind it.[157] In all countries, religious metaphors played a very prominent role in the cult. The Unknown Soldier was implicitly compared to Christ. By giving his life the Unknown Soldier had redeemed his nation. Poland was no exception. The sacrifice of the Unknown Soldier was celebrated as "life-giving." One author let the Unknown Soldier say, "My silent death was the birth of a new life for my nation."[158] Another newspaper viewed the cult of the Unknown Soldier as an expression of gratitude for the soldier's sacrifice and as proof of the nation's "spiritual rebirth."[159] The reburial of the remains gave Polish Lwów the opportunity to express its gratitude to the Defenders of Lwów. Tens of thousands of people lined the streets as the body of the Unknown Soldier was brought to the train station. Church services were held, and the event was marked with patriotic speeches and public addresses. The city was full of Polish symbols and Polish colors.[160]

The Ukrainian population was excluded from the celebrations and boycotted the ceremonies. The Polish Unknown Soldier had fallen in the war against Ukrainians, and his sacrifice served to reinforce the fact that East Galicia was now part of Poland. The symbol united the Poles but did not appeal to Ukrainians. The Jewish population had problems with the fact that the Polish Unknown Soldier came from L'viv. It was not unthinkable that prior to his death he had participated in the November 1918 pogrom. In the end, only progressive Jews participated in the cult, detaching it from a narrowly Polish interpretation and giving the symbol of the Unknown Soldier a more general humanist meaning.[161]

The Polish cult of the heroic dead that dominated the public sphere almost completely submerged Jewish mourning and grief for the victims of the pogrom. But within the Jewish cemetery a small space was made over for the victims. A plaque bearing their names was put up. In December 1919 and 1920, thousands of people and representatives from almost all Jewish organizations attended memorial events held at the Jewish cemetery. Jewish sources are silent about the extent the memory reverberated down the years that followed and what meaning the mourning for the victims of the pogrom held for Jewish society in L'viv.[162] The Ukrainian elites focused on their own slain soldiers, not out of piety alone but for political reasons as well. The aim was to use memorialization to plant the idea of the nation in people's hearts: "The earth, bathed in the breath of memories that conjure up the laurel wreaths of the dying heroes, brings forth the life-nourishing grain, just as the burial of life gave birth to the driving force of the nation."[163]

However, the opportunities for action open to Ukrainians were limited. Not until they had their own state, *Dilo* argued, would it be possible to freely honor the memory of those who had fallen for this national cause.[164] Until that time, the Ukrainian elites had created and cultivated what Foucault has termed a counter-memory. Ukrainian public memorialization contradicted the dominant Polish constructions of continuity.[165] In this respect, Ukrainian remembrance much resembled the Polish commemoration of its heroes. The graves of fallen soldiers were sites of pilgrimage visited by the masses on special anniversaries. The Ukrainian processions were political demonstrations that the state sought to prevent.

Similar to the Poles, for Ukrainians the political cult of the fallen soldiers was closely associated with specific spaces. The permeation of space with constructed markers of memory increased the impact of the political cult of the dead. It is not the simple material character of a space that awakens memory. It is its symbolic infusion that calls up memory, especially when the space has become the site of a ritual.[166]

Shortly after the end of the war, Ukrainians set up a Regional Committee for the Preservation of War Graves (Krajevyj komitet okhorony voennykh mohyl u L'vovi), although it was not registered by the Polish authorities. In 1921 the committee published a small book titled *In Eternal Memory of the Heroes* (*Na vichny pamjat' herojam*). It contained numerous poems and prose pieces that were typical manifestations of the Ukrainian political cult of the dead. The poet, literary scholar, and president of the private Ukrainian University in L'viv Vasyl' Shchurat published a short article on the graves of the "fallen heroes." In his article, he stated that Ukrainians had fallen in thousands of places, and these sites had, by virtue of that sacrifice, become "an eternal possession for which they paid with their own blood." For posterity, these places would be "sacred unto all eternity." No foreigner could doubt any longer to whom the country belonged.[167]

In 1927, after much effort, the Ukrainians succeeded in finally registering their Society for the Preservation of War Graves (Tovarystvo okhorony vojennykh mohyl) in L'viv. At their founding meeting, the chair and editor in chief of *Dilo*, Ivan Nimchuk, presented a paper on the "cult of the fallen heroes" in which he emphasized the necessity of covering the country with Ukrainian emblems of remembrance. He focused on the need to strengthen national identity and achieve international acknowledgement of Ukrainians as a "civilized people," along with recognition of the legitimacy of their national claims.[168] Nimchuk regretted the fact that many thousand Ukrainian graves had vanished over the past decade. The most treasured possession, the "greatest moral capital" to emerge from World War I and the wars of liberation, the "graves of our heroes" were in danger. Even in those areas where they still existed, most were extremely neglected: "On our national territory, among us, there are incredibly few Ukrainian monuments, in fact almost none which might lift and fire our spirits, and which might have some educational influence on our nation [*narid*], especially on the younger generation. That would be proof of our maturity, our culture, our gratitude to those who have given service for the good of the nation."

Instead, the monuments of their neighbors (i.e., the Poles) stood on the land as proof of their "cultural dominance, their piety vis-à-vis their forebears and heroes." Only churches and cemeteries remained as testimonies to the Ukrainian past.[169]

Nimchuk suggested copying the Poles, whose cult of insurgents, legionaries, and, indeed, all of their dead he considered exemplary. Monuments, Nimchuk continued, were important to strengthen the national consciousness and served to link the interrupted historical tradition to the war of liberation. "One has just to think what influence it could have on the young Ukrainian generation, mostly taught in alien schools . . . if in every church, in every village and town, a sign made of durable material with appropriate inscriptions and a complete list of the fallen would be installed."

Nimchuk recommended intensifying the "cult of our tradition"; paying tribute to the fallen soldiers was an important part of "the cult of the meritorious forefathers, the cult of heroes." As he was at pains to stress, only "nations at the lowest cultural level" did not concern themselves with monuments to the past. For that reason, plaques "in honor of the fighters for the freedom of Ukraine" should be mounted everywhere, and crosses should be erected.[170]

Nimchuk's appeal did not go unheeded. The Society for Preservation of War Graves took an active interest in caring for the most important gravesite of Ukrainian soldiers. The Society for Fallen Ukrainians erected 440 concrete crosses in the second most important cemetery in L'viv, the Janowski Cemetery (*Janivs'kyj tsvintar*), adding another 20 in 1930.[171]

Celebrations and Rituals of Remembrance

Polish Lwów celebrated its victory every year. Memorial services were held on All Souls' Day and All Saints' Day and on November 22 during which the fallen were celebrated and remembered. Dignitaries, representatives of the different political parties, and veterans' organizations participated in the annual rituals, and Roman Catholic priests preached sermons on the "value of the great sacrifice which the children of Lwów had made" and the obligations which this sacrifice imposed on the living.[172] These memorial services were often followed by processions to the Cemetery of the Defenders of Lwów.[173]

Public Ukrainian celebrations of their November deed were forbidden,[174] but the authorities did not dare to forbid the church services or religious processions with which the Ukrainian celebrated their seizure of L'viv and the proclamation of the West Ukrainian People's Republic and commemorated their fallen compatriots. After a service on All Souls' Day held in St. George's Cathedral, a procession formed which moved on to the Ukrainian Heroes' Cemetery in Janowski (Janivs'kyj) Cemetery. All other manifestations outside the church were prohibited.[175]

In 1928 both Ukrainians and Poles began gearing up for the tenth anniversary of the November events. The Polish elites wanted to demonstrate their dominance of the public space and show the whole world that the city was Lwów, not

L'viv or Lemberg. Ukrainian nationalists tried to undermine both of these intentions, directing their actions against monuments that were visible symbols of the Polish victory. On the evening before November 1, two members of the Ukrainian Military Organization tried to blow up the Obrona monument on Persenków hill. The attack did not cause much damage, except for injuring one guard and wounding him in the leg. Another Polish monument was defaced with ink. Ukrainian activists not only attacked monuments but placed temporary Ukrainian symbols in prominent sites to demonstrate the Ukrainian claim to L'viv. By this simulation of the *Lystopadovyj chyn* Ukrainians symbolically controlled L'viv. For a brief time yellow-and-blue Ukrainian flags fluttering in the wind were visible on top of the hill of the Union of Lublin and on the main building of the university. But by five o'clock on the same morning, the police, who had been alerted betimes, had already replaced them with Polish flags. In the afternoon, small groups of Ukrainians wearing yellow-and-blue armbands strolled through the city.[176]

The Ukrainian demonstrations continued with a service held in the Greek Catholic Cathedral of St. George. Ten thousand Ukrainians, many of them from neighboring towns and villages, had traveled to L'viv. The cathedral could not hold the throng of people, and many gathered on the cathedral forecourt to listen to the mass, which was celebrated by thirty Greek Catholic priests. What happened next is contested. Polish newspapers reported that Ukrainian youths started an illegal demonstration and began marching in the direction of the city center.[177] According to Ukrainian reports, it was not a youthful demonstration but a religious procession to the Ukrainian graves in Janivs'kyj Cemetery. Whatever the truth of the matter, mounted police troops appeared and attempted to disperse the three hundred participants. Some Ukrainians suffered kicks by the horses and had to be treated in hospital; the rest were forced back on to the cathedral's forecourt. The police later argued that unknown persons within the press of people had fired pistol shots, injuring several Polish students and police. The Ukrainian organizations hotly denied the accusation. While the police were still dealing with the demonstration or procession, depending on the point of view, Polish students began gathering at the Mickiewicz monument to revenge the Ukrainian attacks on Polish monuments.[178] It was as if the days of November 1918 had returned. The students tried to present themselves as "Defenders of Lwów." They had been raised on the stories of the heroic deeds of their older siblings and fathers and grasped the opportunity to reconquer the city and symbolically retake it—albeit with much less risk—from the Ukrainians.

The newspaper *Słowo Polskie* reported that 4,600 students participated in the riots that followed, although the Jewish daily *Chwila* only counted 1,000 participants. The Polish demonstrators marched to the Ukrainian students' hall, where Ukrainian students had already barricaded the doors and windows. Rumors circulated that shots had been fired, injuring two Polish students. The remaining

Polish students entered the building, wrecking the ground floor.[179] Only then did the police finally arrive; they stopped Ukrainian students from leaving but did not try to arrest the rioting Polish students. The Polish students then marched on Ukrainian shops and the buildings of Ukrainian organizations, leaving a trail of devastation. They tore down the signs of Ukrainian lawyers and smashed Ukrainian printers' shops, the buildings of the Scientific Shevchenko organization, the Prosvita, and the Ukrainian insurance company Dnister. The police blocked all the roads leading to Ukrainian institutions and pushed the demonstrators back to Market Square, where the demonstration then dispersed. It was past midnight before the situation was finally brought under control. About fifty people had been injured. In the days that followed, Polish students continued to smash the windows of Ukrainian institutions.[180]

Reactions in Polish society were divided. The National Democrats defended the students,[181] while liberal newspapers and those close to the government criticized them. It was suggested that the actions of the students had harmed Poland's international reputation. The situation had fundamentally changed since the days of November 1918. The Poles now had their own state, and it was the police's job to punish attacks and actions that threatened the security of the state. The Poles had to rid themselves of old habits dating from the times of Poland's partition. It was nonsense—the paper *Dziennik Lwowski* argued—to take the law into one's own hand in one's own state.[182] The police, however, turned a blind eye to certain activities. While Polish students escaped unpunished, the police arrested about eighty Ukrainian students.[183]

The riots were also discussed in the Polish parliament. The Polish minister of the interior defended the actions of the police against the accusations leveled by Ukrainian deputies. The number of victims—he argued—spoke for themselves: only nine Ukrainians had suffered slight injuries, while eight Poles (including four police) had suffered gunshot wounds. Thirty Poles (among them twenty-six police) had been badly injured.[184] In the end, a handful of Ukrainians were sentenced.[185] The riots were not repeated in the years that followed, not the least because the police increased its presence and placed guards at Polish monuments.

Tensions between Ukrainians and Poles were not the only reason for riots. Growing anti-Semitism in Polish society also sometimes led to violence. In 1929, on the day of Corpus Christi, a Roman Catholic procession was passing a Jewish secondary school for girls. The girls watched the procession from the school windows. They were loud, there was laughter, and some pieces of paper and a few pieces of bread rained down on the procession. The Polish participants interpreted this as a deliberate act and an attempt to profane the Roman Catholic Church. Members of the procession were incensed and complained to the director of the school, but nothing more happened. The following Monday, however, the National Democratic daily *Lwowski Kurier Poranny* came out with the headline that the Jewish girls had tried to profane the Catholic religion. The National Democratic students had been waiting for just such an opportunity, and the same evening they stormed the school, wrecking the ground floor before moving on to the halls of residence of Jewish students, which they similarly vandalized. They were stopped by police, and thirty-two of them were arrested. During the days that followed, student groups and National Democratic newspapers demanded the release of the prisoners.[186] The students elected a committee, which then called a strike. The committee declared that "Polish academic youth believes that all of Jewish society is responsible for the purposeless provocation by Zionist Jewish girls . . . , as Jewish society, which has long since been thoroughly steeped in hostility against our state, is educating its brood in a reptilian hatred of all things Polish and Catholic, and its criminal behavior in the time of the Defense of Lwów in the year 1918 vividly remains in the memory of Polish society."

The committee went on to demand that all Polish universities should close their doors against the unlimited influx of "this Jewish youth" and that the offending secondary school for girls be "shut down as a nest of felonious instincts which has offended the religious feelings of the Polish population." The students also castigated the critical coverage by *Chwila* as "Jewish press hooliganism," alleging that the newspaper in its "Semitic impertinence" had criticized the "healthy uproar" of Polish academic youth.[187]

During the following days, repeated clashes occurred between Polish and Jewish students. The government set up a special committee on June 5 and ordered the police to patrol the city on foot and on horseback. Jewish establishments were guarded by police with fixed bayonets. The pro-government press and the National Democratic press fought a propaganda war against each other. On June 7, the minister of the interior flew to L'viv to get a firsthand impression of the situation himself. The fierce crackdown by the government made an impression and the mood became calmer. In the end, the public prosecutor's office put thirty-two rioters on trial for unlawful entry and criminal damage to property. Fourteen well-known National Democratic lawyers offered their services free of charge to the accused rioters to defend them in court.[188]

The most violent clashes between Polish National Democratic and Jewish students took place in 1932 when Polish students called for a boycott of Jewish shops and tried to enforce it. On November 12, Polish students smashed the windows of fifty-nine Jewish shops after the unveiling of a plaque commemorating the Obrona Lwowa. Two weeks later, a Polish veterinary medicine student was fatally injured after being stabbed with a knife during a nighttime clash between Polish and Jewish students. In the days that followed, no public place and no street in the city were safe. National democratic students divided into groups, each group several dozen strong, and attacked Jewish passersby and Jewish establishments and shops in several areas of the city. The police declared a state of emergency and only managed to get the situation under control after several days' unrest and after having strongly increased the police presence on the streets. The police arrested 256 persons—150 Roman Catholics, 56 Greek Catholics, and 47 Jews—in connection with the attacks. Prosecuting the offenders, however, proved to be difficult. The majority of student perpetrators were members of the All-Polish Youth Organization and covered for each other. In the end, very few were brought to trial.[189]

In 1938 Polish society was badly in need of national integration and self-reassurance: outside Poland, Nazi Germany was looking increasingly threatening, while in Poland itself, the death of Marshal Piłsudski had left the Sanacja government "orphaned." The desire to experience tangible demonstrations of the "Polishness" (polskość) of the city increased among the Poles of L'viv. New monuments and a new museum celebrating the Defense of Lwów were planned; streets were renamed after the heroes and events of the Obrona. That November the local radio station also began broadcasting the commemorative events.[190] This massive demonstration of Polishness forced Ukrainians into clandestine, conspiratorial activities, pushing them out of the public sphere and into cooperatives, clubs, and meetings held at home.[191]

Wiktor Chajes wrote in his diary on November 1, 1938, that he had not wavered in his Polishness, even in November 1918, although he had seen the atrocities of the "Abraham people, Mączynskis, etc." with his own eyes. But the growing anti-Semitism had overtaken Chajes. The pro-government Obóz Zjednoczenia Narodowego (OZN) had prevented him from being elected to the committee for the preparation of the twentieth anniversary of the Obrona Lwowa. Even an ardent Polish patriot such as Chajes was now excluded from the Polish community of memory because of his Jewish religion. He wrote bitterly in his diary that now the committee was "judenrein" (German term in the original).[192]

This focus on ethnic conflicts might convey the impression that the history of L'viv in the years before World War II was nothing but a succession of ethnically motivated acts of violence. That was not the case. For most of the time everyday life in the multiethnic city was peaceful. There were numerous places where the different social classes and ethnic groups met and mixed, did business with each other, and talked and drank coffee. Poles, Jews, and Ukrainians all frequented the cafés Roma, Szkocka, and Sztuka or bought confectionery from Zaleski. Well-to-do guests put up at Hotel George. Ukrainians, Jews, and Poles all enjoyed the popular radio broadcasts of L'viv comedians Szczepko and Tońko. The chronic economic crisis and persistently high levels of unemployment in the 1930s exacerbated existing social conflicts, but these did not erupt along the fault lines of ethnic and national conflicts. In the spring of 1936, a number of clashes occurred between striking workers, unemployed persons demonstrating for work and the police, which resulted in the deaths of thirty-one workers, both men and women; a further eighteen later succumbed to their injuries. More than three thousand workers were arrested.[193] In their battles with the authorities, the working classes of all three ethnic groups moved closer together. Working-class leaders attended each other's meetings and declared their solidarity with victims. In March 1936 about three thousand Polish and Ukrainian workers jointly protested against the attacks on Jews and the national oppression of Ukrainians. Repeated strikes broke out in the spring of 1936 with demonstrations of up to twenty thousand people, increasing to sixty thousand demonstrators on May 1.[194]

The student body was polarized. Polish National Democratic students declared certain days to be "days free of Jews" and intercepted Jewish students at the entrance gate to the university.[195] Most students preferred to remain neutral. Only a few Polish students defended their Jewish classmates, and those Polish students who aligned themselves with their Jewish fellow students were beaten up by national democratic students. A *numerus clausus* for Jews was introduced in medicine and in all subjects taught at L'viv Polytechnic. The general principle was to have Jewish students constitute no more than 10 percent of any department. This was not a statutory rule; it was the result of the university's own self-regulation. In accordance with this self-imposed code, only three Jewish students were accepted to study medicine in the 1938/1939 academic year. Another important goal of the anti-Semites was the creation of so-called ghetto benches. The rector of Jan Kazimierz University, Professor Stanisław Kulczyński, resisted their introduction, and anti-Semitic students had pelted him with eggs for this. He resigned and his successor, Professor Edmund Bulanda, professor of archeology, assented to the setting up of "ghetto benches." Jewish students were now only permitted to sit in one of the two last rows on the left-hand side of the lecture hall. Many Jewish students only attended lectures in groups for their own safety, preferring to stand rather than to sit on the "ghetto benches." Jewish students were given special dates on which to sit their examinations to ensure students who appeared on their own would not be subjected to attacks.[196] The Ukrainians, as former student Bronisława Witz-Margulies remembered, did not want to become involved in the quarrel and usually sat on both sides of the lecture halls. Some professors refused to tolerate ghetto benches and expelled disruptive troublemakers from the room.[197] Jan Feuerman, a student at the time, summed up the situation as follows: "Studying under those conditions was a nightmare."[198]

But there were also occasional episodes when democratic or socialist-inclined Polish and Jewish students stood shoulder to shoulder. On the evening of February 9, 1939, a public meeting of the Democratic Youth and the Independent Socialist Youth was held in Skarbek Theater, attended by about seven hundred men and women; half the participants were Polish, and half were Jewish. The speaker for the Democratic Youth criticized the rector of the university for having, in effective, handed over control of the university to the All-Polish Youth Organization. The meeting passed a resolution protesting against the All-Polish terror.[199] On the evening of February 16, fifteen young men roamed the city's streets chanting slogans against the National Party.[200] But the nationalist groups set the tone at the university. As long as their aggression was directed against Jews, socialists or Ukrainians, the state treated violent young Poles leniently; only organized labor could have opposed them with any prospect of success.[201] Brawls repeatedly broke out between National Democrats and workers. But ultimately the workers' parties concentrated on championing social interests and on battling the authoritarian government.

Some of the attacks on Jewish students ended fatally. In 1938 the pharmacy student Karol Zellermayer was stabbed on the grounds of the university. The Polish physiology lecturer Bieliński risked his life to pull the victim away from his attackers. Only a few weeks later, Samuel Proweller, a student at the polytechnic, was murdered. For some time thereafter no more fatalities occurred. But in the spring of 1939 another student from the polytechnic, Markus Landesberg, was beaten to death on the university grounds.[202] Landesberg was buried in the Jewish cemetery on May 28, 1939. His funeral turned into a huge memorial demonstration in which twelve thousand people participated, among them many Poles who wanted to demonstrate their solidarity.[203]

The Road to War

On Poland's borders Hitler, with his aggressive revisionary policies, was threatening Poland's safety. The German–Polish nonaggression treaty of 1934 slightly improved German–Polish relations, but the reoccupation of the demilitarized Rhineland by German soldiers in 1936, the Anschluss of Austria in March 1938, and the annexation of the Czechoslovak Sudetenland seriously worsened Poland's political situation. The Polish government could not resist the temptation to exploit Czechoslovakia's weakness and incorporated the Zaolzie area of Cieszyn Silesia (formerly part of the Duchy of Teschen) into Poland. Slovakia and Carpatho-Ukraine declared their autonomy within Czechoslovakia. These foreign policy changes also affected the Polish–Ukrainian relationship. The autonomy status of Carpatho-Ukraine raised the hopes of West Ukrainians. A special service attended by four thousand people was held in St. George's Cathedral on October 11, 1938, in honor of the occasion. One of the priests referred to Carpatho-Ukraine as the cradle of an independent Ukraine and voiced the hope that "our land here will become free" as well. After the service had ended, several hundred young Ukrainians proceeded to move into the city center chanting their support of Ukraine. The police soon dissipated the demonstration but smaller groups immediately formed again. One group smashed the windows of the editorial office of the Polish national democratic newspaper *Słowo Narodowe*. The All-Polish Youth Organization could not let this incident pass. About three hundred students gathered at the Mickiewicz monument to protest against these demonstrations of Ukrainian nationalism. One of the speakers opined that the Lwów Eagles had not died that Ukrainians could now roam through the city and cheer for Ukraine. On their way to St. George's Cathedral, the Polish students smashed forty-nine windows of Jewish and Ukrainian institutions and buildings.[204] The following evening three hundred Polish students demonstrated again in the city center, chanting, "Away with the haidamaks." At the Ukrainian hostel, they were met with a hail of stones. The police moved in and occupied the building. The demonstrators moved on, again smashing the windows of Jewish and Ukrainian establishments. The police arrested six Ukrainians and three Poles.[205] The next day, the All-Polish Youth Organization held a meeting to protest the behavior of the police for having protected a Ukrainian demonstration "in the heart of Lwów." It was surely a disgrace that "Ukraine rules in the City of the Eagles." And, therefore, it was incumbent for Polish youth to rise up and fight to defend the Polish nature of the city and the *kresy*.[206] In the weeks that followed, National Democratic students repeatedly provoked new incidents and incited new unrest.[207]

The Ukrainian organizations responded with a butter strike, demonstrating the power of their cooperatives.[208] L'viv and other cities remained without butter for three days. The authorities reacted with mass arrests, which were followed by further violent riots. In rural areas, Poles could not venture on the streets or speak Polish. Several Polish farms were burned down. The government now ordered punitive expeditions, so-called pacifications, to crush the resistance. In the villages, men and women, young and old were arrested indiscriminately, chained to one another and herded through the village streets. Farms were razed to the ground. Ukrainian politicians estimated that at the end of 1938 about thirty thousand Ukrainians were being held in Polish prisons. The intensification of ethnic violence and the government's brutal policies of repression boosted the support for nationalist Ukrainian organizations. The proscribed OUN attracted a lot of new members and followers. According to rough estimates, in 1939 the OUN had approximately twenty thousand members, but the number of its sympathizers was far higher.[209] The authorities continued to hound Ukrainian nationalists with further waves of arrests. At the beginning of the war, many leading OUN activists were still in jail.[210] Many Greek Catholic priests were also arrested. In the spring of 1939, six hundred Greek Catholic priests were allegedly still in prison.[211]

In May 1938 the leader of the OUN Jevhen Konovalets was assassinated in Rotterdam by a Soviet agent. As the months passed, serious cracks appeared in the unity of the OUN. The fault line lay between the older generation of OUN politicians, now in exile, who made up the organization's leadership and the younger generation who were working clandestinely in Poland. The OUN leadership in exile chose Andrij Mel'nyk, a close associate of Konovalets, as their new leader. The OUN in Poland preferred a younger man, Stepan Bandera, who had only recently been released from a Polish jail. Yet, there was no outright rift between the factions.[212]

The German embassy in Warsaw reported that every Ukrainian considered it a disgrace to shop in Polish stores or marry a Polish man or woman. The UNDO controlled the legal organizations, but the OUN was more dynamic and its influence was spreading. The Front of National Unity, founded in 1935 by Dmytro Paliïv, stood in even greater contrast to the UNDO. The German Embassy categorized Paliïv's party as fascist. Paliïv accused the UNDO of having breached national solidarity by its readiness to compromise. According to the information available to the embassy, the overwhelming majority of the younger generation of Ukrainians supported the OUN. Many distrusted Paliïv's personality. The Greek Catholic Church and Archbishop Sheptyts'kyj, considered by some as the "uncrowned king of Polish Ukrainians," still played a central role.[213]

The last elections to L'viv municipal council were held on May 21, 1939, and clearly indicated the extent of the government crisis and the confrontational mood in L'viv. The election campaign highlighted the lines of conflict crisscrossing the city. The dominant topic in the election was the accusation, directed against the city authorities and the government, that national minorities were given preferential treatment. The National Democrats accused the government camp of dividing Polish society, which was under threat from Jews and Ukrainians.[214] On April 23, some two hundred supporters of the National Catholic Bloc held an election rally. One of their speakers, a young student, called upon the bloc to support the All-Polish Youth and its attempt at a "de-Jewification of Lwów" (odżydzenie Lwowa).[215] Nationalist groups repeatedly took to the streets chanting "Away with the Jews and the council." On May 29, about three hundred nationalist Poles assembled in front of the Mickiewicz monument to chant slogans directed against Ukrainians and Germans.[216]

In L'viv, the Polish National Democrats considerably increased their share of the vote, obtaining twenty-one seats. But despite the loss of twenty council seats, the pro-government coalition of Mayor Ostrowski remained the strongest group, with twenty-five councilors. The Polish Socialists and Democrats won ten seats together (they had previously held five). The Jewish ticket obtained sixteen seats. Not a single Ukrainian was elected to the council. The constitutive session of the newly elected council was scheduled for the fall of 1939, but because of the war, the council never met.[217]

In March 1939 Hitler decided to invade and occupy the rest of Czechoslovakia, and German soldiers entered Prague. The majority of Czech territories became the Protectorate of Bohemia and Moravia while Slovakia was permitted to form a separate client state dependent on Germany. Carpatho-Ukraine declared its independence on March 14 but was immediately occupied by Hungarian troops, an occupation fiercely resisted by Ukrainian fighters. Many young Ukrainians from East Galicia traveled to Carpatho-Ukraine to fight the occupiers.[218]

Ukrainian political parties still had only limited opportunities to appear in public.[219] But they made good use of every legal chance to raise their public profile. A church consecration festival was held in St. George's Cathedral on May 6, 1939; it was attended by approximately three thousand people, the majority of them peasants from the surrounding areas. One priest called on the Ukrainians to stand firm in those difficult hours. He believed that after the long darkness, day would soon be dawning again for Ukrainians, prophesying a united Ukraine.[220]

There had been contacts between various German authorities and Ukrainian emigrant organizations throughout the interwar period. The Hetman group around Skoropads'kyj was headquartered in Berlin. The UNDO and the OUN also kept in touch with the German ministry of foreign affairs. After Hitler's seizure of power, the German military intelligence agency under Admiral Wilhelm Canaris established contacts to Ukrainian nationalists.[221] The German Reich took over many of the assets of the former state of Czechoslovakia, appropriating the Czechoslovak consulate in L'viv. From then on, the German consul Gebhard Seelos sent regular reports and firsthand information on the ethnopolitical situation in East Galicia to Berlin.[222]

The consul believed that after they recovered from their disappointment about Carpatho-Ukraine the mood among most Ukrainians would be pro-German again. The Ukrainians were placing their hopes of achieving an independent Ukrainian state on Germany's help. But the Ukrainian leaders were not planning to revolt because they wanted to keep the Ukrainian national strength unbroken. His conclusion was that "[t]he glue which binds Ukrainians together in despite of all internal dissension is their hatred of the Poles."[223]

Notes

1. Alfred Döblin, *Reise in Polen 1924*, second ed. (Munich: dtv, 1993), 191–92.
2. Ukrainian politicians had called on the Ukrainian population to boycott the 1921 census, and many Ukrainians followed this recommendation. The number of Ukrainians is therefore only an estimate.
3. The table was compiled by Łucja Kapralska based on the published censuses of 1921 and 1931. Łucja Kapralska, *Pluralizm kulturowy i etniczny a odrębność regionalna Kresów południowo-wschodnich w latach 1918–1939* (Cracow: Nomos, 2000), 98. *Rocznik statystyki RP* (Warsaw: Nakładem Głównego Urzędu Statystycznego, 1926), 26, table 5. "Drugi powszechny spis ludności z dnia 9 XII 1931 r.: Mieszkania i gospodarstwa domowe, ludność, stosunki zawodowe," in *Statystyka Polski*, seria C, zeszyt 62 (Warsaw: Główny Urząd Statystyczny, 1937), 27. The modern estimate comes from Zbigniew Landau and Jerzy Tomaszewski, *Robotnicy przemysłowi w Polsce 1918–1939* (Warsaw: Książka i Wiedza, 1971), 35. Jerzy Tomaszewski, *Rzeczpospolita wielu narodów* (Warsaw: Czytelnik, 1985), 35.

4. AAN, Ambasada RP w Londynie, 430: Polish Ministry of Foreign Affairs to the Polish Embassy in London, November 28, 1921.
5. TsDIAL, f. 462, op. 1, spr. 23, ark. 33–36: human losses of the Ukrainian population in Galicia, early 1921.
6. The census used the ethnonym Ruthenian, not Ukrainian.
7. *Wiadomości statystyczne o mieście Lwowie*, vol. 16: 1923–1925 (L'viv: Gmina Lwowa, 1928), 261.
8. Ibid.
9. Andrzej Bonusiak, *Lwów w latach 1918–1939* (Rzeszów: Wydawnictwo Wyższej Szkoły Pedagogicznej w Rzeszowie, 2000), 191. In 1931 the suburbs were incorporated into "Great Lwów," which substantially increased the city's population. The census of 1931 shows that the share of Greek Catholics had increased and now almost reached the level of 1914. Grzegorz Hryciuk, "Zmiany demograficzne ludności polskiej we Lwowie w latach 1931–1944," in *Wschodnie losy Polaków*, vol. 1, ed. Stanisław Ciesielski (Wrocław: Instytut Historyczny Uniwersytetu Wrocławskiego, 1991), 14, 76.
10. *Wiadomości statystyczne o mieście Lwowie*, vol. 14: 1910–1911 (L'viv: Nakladem gminy krol. stol. M. Lwowa, 1914). *Wiadomości statystyczne o mieście Lwowie*, vol. 15: 1912–1922 (L'viv: Gmina Lwowa, 1926). *Wiadomości statystyczne o mieście Lwowie*, vol. 16.
11. Ibid.
12. *Wiadomości statystyczne o mieście Lwowie*, vol. 15, 84.
13. *Wiadomości statystyczne o mieście Lwowie*, vols. 14 and 16.
14. Bonusiak, *Lwów w latach 1918–1939*, 19–25, 137–50.
15. DALO, f. 2, op. 26, spr. 1851, ark. 1–86: report on the activities of the mayoralty in L'viv between 1919 and 1923. On the interwar period, see Andrzej Bonusiak, "'Niedemokratyczna demokracja': Rzecz o Lwowie w latach 1918–1934," in *Lwów: Miasto—społeczeństwo—kultura*, vol. 2, 215–34.
16. "Siódma rocznica," *Słowo Polskie*, November 24, 1925.
17. Bonusiak, *Lwów w latach 1918–1939*, 277–78.
18. Ibid., 83–92.
19. TsDIAL, f. 462, op. 1, spr. 90, ark. 1–4: memorandum by the Ukrainian Civic Committee, December 4, 1920.
20. TsDIAL, f. 462, op. 1, spr. 23, ark. 33–36: human losses of the Ukrainian population in Galicia, early 1921.
21. TsDIAL, f. 462, op. 1, spr. 222, ark. 126–28: the three Greek Catholic archbishops to the Council for the League of Nations in Geneva, n.d. (probably 1921).
22. John A. Armstrong, *Ukrainian Nationalism*, second ed. (Littleton, CO: Ukrainian Academic Press, 1980), 21. Mykhajlo Shvahuljak, "L'viv: vid stolytsi zakhidnoukraïns'koï derzhavy do politychnoho tsentru Ukraïntsiv Halychyny (1918–1939 rr.)," in *L'viv: Misto—suspil'stvo—kul'tura*, vol. 3, 469–92, here 481.
23. TsDIAL, f. 205, op. 1, spr. 889: record of the attorney at the Court of Appeals in L'viv for the Polish minister of the interior (including many documents), October 3, 1921. TSDIAL, f. 462, op. 1, spr. 91, ark. 1–2: the collegium of the lawyers defending Fedak to the "Nations of Culture of the World," April 13, 1922. TSDIAL, f. 205, op. 1, spr. 889, ark. 58–63: the attorney of the Court of Appeals to the District Court in L'viv, June 25, 1922.
24. Papierzyńska-Turek, *Sprawa Ukraińska*, 118. For a good overview of the Polish political parties in L'viv, see Grzegorz Mazur, *Życie polityczne polskiego Lwowa 1918–1939* (Cracow: Księgarnia Akademicka, 2007).
25. Papierzyńska-Turek, *Sprawa Ukraińska*, 167.

26. Orest Subtelny, *Ukraine: A History* (Toronto: University of Toronto Press, 3rd edition, 2000), 428–29. Jaroslav Hrycak, *Historia Ukrainy 1772–1999* (Lublin: Instytut Europy Środkowo Wschodniej, 2000), 188.
27. *Dilo*, November 2, 1923.
28. TsDIAL, f. 146, op. 8, spr. 3806, ark. 56–58: police report of a meeting of the city committee of the Ukrainian Social Democrats in L'viv, March 15, 1920. *Dilo*, March 16, 1920.
29. *Gazeta Wieczorna*, October 27, 1921. On the secret Ukrainian university, see Vasyl' Mudryj, *Zmahannja za ukraïns'ki universytety v Halychyni*, esp. 134–40.
30. DALO, f. 110, op. 4, spr. 849, ark. 45–47: Agency 5-F of the police command of L'viv to director of police Reinlender: report of discussions of Ukrainian politicians concerning the secret Ukrainian university, February 15, 1923.
31. AAN, Ambasada RP w Londynie, 1435, 97–98: Polish Foreign Ministry to the embassy in London, January 27, 1926.
32. Papierzyńska-Turek, *Sprawa Ukraińska*, 217–18.
33. Hrycak, *Historia Ukrainy*, 190. Subtelny, *Ukraine*, 192. Papierzyńska-Turek, *Sprawa Ukraińska w Drugiej Rzeczypospolitej 1922–1926*, 220–37, 257–69.
34. Subtelny, *Ukraine*, 438–39. Hrycak, *Historia Ukrainy*, 190. TsDIAL, f. 355, op. 1, spr. 28, ark. 1–20: L'Association de L'Ukraine Occidentale pour la Société des Nations: La situation de la population ukrainienne en Pologne, June 27, 1924.
35. On the Ukrainian parties in the interwar period, see Shvahuljak, "L'viv: vid stolytsi zakhidnoukraïns'koï derzhavy do politychnoho tsentru Ukraïntsiv Halychyny (1918-1939 rr.)," 469–92. Subtelny, *Ukraine*, 434–46. Papierzyńska-Turek, *Sprawa Ukraińska w Drugiej Rzeczypospolitej 1922–1926*, 53–80.
36. Subtelny, *Ukraine*, 440–41. Shvahuljak, "L'viv: vid stolytsi zakhidnoukraïns'koï derzhavy do politychnoho tsentru Ukraïntsiv Halychyny (1918–1939 rr.)," 488–89.
37. Hrycak, *Historia Ukrainy*, 189–203. On Józewski, see Timothy Snyder, *Sketches from a Secret War: A Polish Artist's Mission to Liberate Ukraine* (New Haven, CT: Yale University Press, 2007). On Polish policy in the northeastern borderlands, see Werner Benecke, *Die Ostgebiete der Zweiten Polnischen Republik: Staatsmacht und öffentliche Ordnung in einer Minderheitenregion 1918–1939* (Cologne: Böhlau, 1999).
38. Alexander J. Motyl, *The Turn to the Right: The Ideological Origins and Development of Ukrainian Nationalism 1919–1929* (New York: Columbia University Press, 1980), 50–53. Armstrong, *Ukrainian Nationalism*, 19–21. Amir Weiner, *Making Sense of War: The Second World War and the Fate of the Bolshevik Revolution* (Princeton, NJ: Princeton University Press, 2001), 241–42.
39. Armstrong, *Ukrainian Nationalism*, 19–21. Subtelny, *Ukraine*, 443–46. Hrycak, *Historia Ukrainy*, 198–203. Shvahuljak, "L'viv: vid stolytsi zakhidnoukraïns'koï derzhavy do politychnoho tsentru Ukraïntsiv Halychyny (1918–1939 rr.)," 481–82, 489–90.
40. Władysław A. Serczyk, "Die sowjetische und die 'polnische' Ukraine zwischen den Weltkriegen," in *Geschichte der Ukraine*, ed. Frank Golczewski (Göttingen: Vandenhoeck and Ruprecht, 1993), 202–23.
41. Pavlo Olijnyk, *Zoshyty* (Kyïv: Instytut Ukraïns'koï arkheografiï na dzhereloznavstva im. M.S. Hrushevs'koho NAN Ukraïny, 1995), 48.
42. Subtelny, *Ukraine*, 428–46. Hrycak, *Historia Ukrainy*, 191–200.
43. Subtelny, *Ukraine*, 430–46. Hrycak, *Historia Ukrainy*, 200–201. Stępień: Ukraińska Reprezentacja Parlamentarna, 230.
44. Subtelny, *Ukraine*, 437–46. Papierzyńska-Turek, *Sprawa Ukraińska w Drugiej Rzeczypospolitej 1922–1926*, 80–84. Mirosław Sycz, *Spółdzielczość ukraińska w Galicji w okresie II wojny światowej* (Warsaw: Pracownia Wydawnicza, 1997), 17–56.

45. Subtelny, *Ukraine*, 439–46. Hrycak, *Historia Ukrainy*, 195. Papierzyńska-Turek, *Sprawa Ukraińska w Drugiej Rzeczypospolitej 1922–1926*, 84–94. Myroslava Djadjuk, *Polityzacija Ukraïnskoho zhinochoho ruchu w Halychyni: 1921-1939 rr. Avtoreferat dysertatsiï na zdobuttja naukovoho stupenja kandydata istorychnykh nauk* (L'viv: unpublished manuscript, 2002).
46. Melamed, *Evrei vo L'vove*, 167–77.
47. DALO, f. 110, op. 4, spr. 124, ark. 3–13: police report on Jewish organizations in L'viv, 1930. Melamed, *Evrei vo L'vove*, 137–42, 166–77.
48. On the (short-lived) agreement between the Grabski government and the Jewish Club, see Paweł Korzec, "Das Abkommen zwischen der Regierung Grabski und der jüdischen Parlamentsvertretung," *Jahrbücher für Geschichte Osteuropas* 20 (1972): 331–66. Dietrich Beyrau, "Antisemitismus und Judentum in Polen, 1918–1939," *Geschichte und Gesellschaft* 8 (1982): 205–32, here 219. On Jewish life in Poland in the interwar period, see Ewa Kurek, *Polish-Jewish Relations 1939–1945: Beyond the Limits of Solidarity* (Bloomington, IN: iUniverse, 2012), 15–170. Antony Polonsky, *The Jews in Poland and Russia*, vol. 3: 1914–2008 (New York: Littmann Library, 2012). Celia S. Heller, *On the Edge of Destruction: Jews of Poland between the Two World Wars* (New York: Columbia University Press, 1977). Harry M. Rabinowicz, *The Legacy of Polish Jewry: A History of Polish Jews in the Inter-War Years, 1919–1939* (New York: T. Yoseloff, 1965). Ezra Mendelsohn, "Jewish Politics in Interwar Poland: An Overview," in *The Jews of Poland between the Two World Wars*, ed. Yisrael Gutmann, Ezra Mendelsohn, Jehuda Reinharz, and Chone Shemruk (Waltham: Brandeis University Press, 1989), 9–19. Antony Polonsky, "A Failed Pogrom: The Demonstrations in Lwów, June 1929," in *The Jews of Poland between the Two World Wars*, 113–14. Józef Lichten, "O Asymilacji Żydów w Polsce od wybuchu pierwszej wojny światowej do końca drugiej wojny (1914–1945)," *Zeszyty Historyczne* 42 (1977): 96–134.
49. Melamed, *Evrei vo L'vove*, 137–39. Szyja Bronsztejn, "Polish-Jewish Relations as Reflected in Memoirs of the Interwar Period," *Polin* 8 (1994): 66–88.
50. Pavel Korzec, "Das Abkommen zwischen der Regierung Grabski und der jüdischen Parlamentsvertretung," *Jahrbücher für Geschichte Osteuropas* 20 (1972): 355–56.
51. Beyrau, "Antisemitismus und Judentum in Polen, 1918–1939," 227.
52. Katrin Steffen, "Jüdische Identität in Polen zwischen den Weltkriegen: Studien zur polnischsprachigen jüdischen Presse," in *Nationalismus und nationale Identität in Ostmitteleuropa im 19. und 20. Jahrhundert*, ed. Bernard Linek and Kai Struve (Marburg: Herder Institut, 2000), 113–34. Beyrau, "Antisemitismus und Judentum in Polen, 1919–1939," 214–15.
53. Albert Lichtblau and Michael John, *Jewries in Galicia and Bukovina, in Lemberg and Czernowitz* (http://czernowitz.org/Lichtblau/lichtblau.html). Polonsky, "A Failed Pogrom," 115. Paweł Korzec, "The Steiger Affair," *Soviet Jewish Affairs* 3, no. 2 (1973): 38–57.
54. An earlier and shorter English version of this subchapter can be found here: Christoph Mick, "War and Conflicting Memories – Poles, Ukrainians and Jews in Lvov 1914–1939 " *Simon Dubnow Institute Yearbook*, 4 (2005), 257-78.
55. In Ukrainian historiography, the seizure of power in L'viv and East Galicia and the declaration of the West Ukrainian People's Republic are called *Lystopadovyj chyn*.
56. *Gazetka Żołnierska*, November 20, 1920, 3. DALO, f. 257, op. 2, spr. 5, ark. 6–8: protocol of a session of the TBHOL, June 23, 1934.
57. *Dziennik Lwowski*, November 20, 1928.
58. *Obrona Lwowa*, 3 vols. (L'viv: 1933–1938; reprint Warsaw: Volumen, 1991). *Materiały do bibliografii Historii Obrony Lwowa i województw południowo-wschodnich* (L'viv:

Towarzystwo Badań Historii Obrony Lwowa i Województw Południowo-Wschodnich, 1935). *Rocznik Towarzystwa Badania Historii Obrony Lwowa* (L'viv: Towarzystwo Badania Historii Obrony Lwowa i Województw Południowo-Wschodnich, 1936, 1937). Eugeniusz Wawrzkowicz and Józef Klink, *Walczący Lwów w listopadzie 1918* (L'viv: Książnica-Atlas, 1939).

59. Some poems are quoted in Stanisław Sławomir Nicieja, *Łyczaków: Dzielnica za Styksem* (Wrocław: Zakład Narodowy im. Ossolińskich, 1998), 368–71. Stanisław Łempicki, "O panoramę Orląt," *Gazeta Poranna*, August 27, 1934.
60. *Obrona Lwowa*, vol. 3, 6–7, 431–32.
61. "Niech żyje, niepodległa i zjednoczona!" *Gazeta Poranna*, November 2, 1919. "Przed listopadową rocznicą (Z kół obywatelskich)," *Gazeta Lwowska*, October 30, 1919.
62. "W rocznicę listopadową?" *Słowo Polskie*, November 2, 1919.
63. *Dziennik Lwowski*, November 23, 1928.
64. AAN, Ambasada RP w Londynie, 433, 10–12: the Polish Ministry of Foreign Affairs to the Polish Embassy in London, October 15, 1921. On the Ukrainian question at the peace conference in Paris, see Przemysław Piotr Żurawski vel Grajewski, *Sprawa Ukraińska na konferencji pokojowej w Paryżu w roku 1919* (Warsaw: Semper, 1995).
65. "W rocznicę wiekopomnego zwycięstwa?" *Wiek Nowy*, November 23, 1919. *Dziennik Lwowski*, November 23, 1928.
66. "Skąd wyszła inicjatywa do obrony Lwowa?" *Gazeta Poranna*, November 2, 1919. "Listopad 1918: Jedenasty dzień walki," *Gazeta Lwowska*, November 12, 1919. "Dwa lata," *Gazeta Lwowska*, October 31, 1920.
67. TsDIAL, f. 837, op. 1, spr. 71, ark. 44–45: recollections of a Polish participant in the *Obrona Lwowa*.
68. "1 Listopada R. 1918," *Gazeta Poranna*, November 1, 1919. "W rocznicę wiekopomnego zwycięstwa?" *Wiek Nowy*, November 23, 1919.
69. *Słowo Polskie*, November 23, 1923.
70. "Przed listopadową rocznicą (Z kół obywatelskich)," *Gazeta Lwowska*, October 30, 1919. "W rocznicę listopadową," *Słowo Polskie*, November 2, 1919. "W trzecią rocznicę," *Słowo Polskie*, November 2, 1921. Józef Białynia-Chołodecki, "Boje o Lwów," in *W obronie Lwowa i kresów wschodnich* (L'viv: Nakładem Straży Mogił Polskich Bohaterów, 1926), 29. *Gazeta Poranna*, November 2, 1919. "Dwa lata," *Gazeta Lwowska*, October 31, 1920.
71. *Obrona Lwowa*, vol. 3, 437.
72. "W przededniu drugiej rocznicy," *Gazeta Lwowska*, October 31, 1920.
73. "W trzecią rocznicę," *Słowo Polskie*, November 2, 1921.
74. "Dziecko Lwowskie," *Gazeta Lwowska*, November 1, 1919.
75. Nicieja, *Łyczaków*, 371.
76. Zofja Lewartowska, *Lwów chlubą narodu: Dramat w 4 aktach na tle obrony Lwowa w roku 1918* (L'viv: Małopolska Straż Obywatelska, 1928).
77. "Polski listopad," *Gazeta Lwowska*, November 4, 1928.
78. Z. Zygmuntowicz, "W noc listopadową," *Kurier Lwowski*, November 1, 1920.
79. "Niech żyje, niepodległa i zjednoczona!" *Gazeta Poranna*, November 2, 1919.
80. "Święcenie rocznicy walki o polskość Lwowa," *Gazetka Żołnierska*, November 3, 1920. "W trzecią rocznicę," *Słowo Polskie*, November 2, 1921.
81. *Dziennik Lwowski*, November 23, 1928.
82. "Na cmentarzu Obrońców Lwowa," *Słowo Polskie*, November 3, 1933.
83. *Kurier Lwowski*, November 25, 1923.
84. Stefan M., "Obrona Lwowa," *Słowo Polskie*, November 2, 1919.
85. "Tom poezyi Romana Feldsztein-Felsztyna," *Gazeta Wieczorna*, November 23, 1919.

86. DALO, f. 257, op. 1, d. 3, ark. 112: Związek Oficerów Rezerwy Rzeczypospolitej Polskiej—Zarząd Okręgu Śląskiego Katowice to Główny Komitet Obchodu 10-cio lecia Obrony Lwowa, November 20, 1928.
87. Speech by General Malczewski on November 23, 1925, *Słowo Polskie*, November 24, 1925.
88. TsDIAL, f. 837, op. 1, spr. 71, ark. 59–65: report by Feliks R. Bursa on November 1918 in L'viv, December 1918 or January 1919. Ibid., ark. 46–53: report by Józef Duda, after 1919.
89. "W rocznicę listopadową," *Słowo Polskie*, November 2, 1919.
90. "W rocznicę wiekopomnego zwycięstwa?" *Wiek Nowy*, November 23, 1919.
91. Speech by General Malczewskis on November 23, 1925, *Słowo Polskie*, November 24, 1925.
92. "Cztery lata temu i dzień dzisiejszy," *Słowo Polskie*, November 2, 1922.
93. Czesław Mączyński, "Słowo wstępne," in *W obronie Lwowa i kresów wschodnich*, 7.
94. Stefan M., "Obrona Lwowa, *Słowo Polskie*, November 2, 1919.
95. See, for example, the memoirs of the National Democrat Czesław Mączyński. According to his memoirs, he won the fight more or less single-handedly: Czesław Mączyński, *Boje lwowskie*, 2 vols., part 1: *Oswobodzenie Lwowa* (Warsaw: Nakł. Spółki Wyd. Rzeczpospolita, 1921). Czesław Mączyński, "Odpowiedź na kwestionariusz o listopadowej obronie Lwowa," in *Obrona Lwowa*, vol. 1, 310–39.
96. Władysław Brzozowski, "Obrona Lwowa w świetle relacji uczestników," *Gazeta Polska*, October 9, 1933. Article of Władysław Brzozowski, *Gazeta Polska*, November 10, 1933. Article of Al. Kawałkowski, *Gazeta Polska*, December 18, 1932. "Lwowski Listopad," *Słowo Polskie*, November 1, 1920. Antoni Jakubski, "Walki listopadowe we Lwowie w świetle krytyk," in *Obrona Lwowa*, vol. 1, 99–240. See also the reactions to Jakubski in *Obrona Lwowa*, vol. 2. In November 1918 Antoni Jakubski was Mączyński's second deputy chief of staff.
97. *Słowo Polskie*, November 23, 1928.
98. Jakubski, "Walki listopadowe we Lwowie w świetle krytyk," 172–73. Jakubski, "W obronie prawdy," in *Obrona Lwowa*, vol. 2, 798–815. Mączyński, "Odpowiedź na kwestionariusz o listopadowej obronie Lwowa," 334–37.
99. "W rocznicę listopadową?" *Słowo Polskie*, November 2, 1919.
100. Marceli Chlamtacz, "Wyjaśnienie i sprostowanie w związku na marginesie relacji Prof. Dr. Antoniego Jakubskiego pt. 'Walki listopadowe we Lwowie w świetle krytyki,'" in *Obrona Lwowa*, vol. 2, 763–79.
101. *Dilo*, November 4, 1928.
102. The term *haidamak* is of Turkish origin and was coined in the eighteenth century. It was the name for the Orthodox rebels resisting Polish rule. It can mean "partisan" or "brigand," depending on the perspective. Andreas Kappeler, *Kleine Geschichte der Ukraine* (Munich: Beck, 1994), 103.
103. DALO, f. 110, op. 4, spr. 100, ark. 2–3: For example, on May 28, 1928, when the police broke up a meeting of deputies of the UNDO. The commander of the police in the voivodeship L'viv to the administration of the voivodeship L'viv, May 29, 1928.
104. See the bibliography of Ukrainian publications "Zherel do istoriï ukraïns'koï vyzvol'noï vijny 1914–19" on the "war of liberation," published since 1929 in *Litopys Chervono Kaliny*.
105. First page of *Dilo*, November 1, 1923 (partly censored).
106. For example, in *Al'manakh Chervona Kalyna* (L'viv: Chervona Kalyna, 1934).
107. "Najbil'sha data nashykh dniv," *Dilo*, November 1, 1934.
108. "U Velyki rokovyny," *Dilo*, November 2, 1932.

109. *Dilo*, November 1, 1924.
110. "U Velyki rokovyny," *Dilo*, November 2, 1932.
111. "Najbil'sha data nashykh dniv," *Dilo*, November 1, 1934.
112. Wolfhart Pannenberg, "Christentum und Mythos," in Wolfhart Pannenberg, *Grundfragen systematischer Theologie: Gesammelte Aufsätze*, vol. 2 (Göttingen: Vandenhoeck & Ruprecht, 1980), 13–65, here 15–16.
113. "Rokovyny," *Novyj Chas*, November 1, 1934.
114. First page of *Dilo*, November 1, 1923 (partly censored).
115. *Dilo*, November 1, 1924.
116. Petro Sahajdachnyj, "Jednist' dumky i chynu," in *Istorychnyj kalendar-al'manakh 'Chervonoï Kalyny 1938 rik* (L'viv: Chervona Kalyna, 1937), 3–9, here 3.
117. "Velyki rokovyny," *Dilo*, November 1, 1929.
118. Wolfgang Schivelbusch, *Die Kultur der Niederlage: Der amerikanische Süden 1865—Frankreich 1871—Deutschland 1918*, second ed. (Berlin: A. Fest Verlag, 2001), 12–14.
119. Koselleck, "Erfahrungswandel und Methodenwechsel," 51–53.
120. First page of *Dilo*, November 1, 1923 (partly censored). "U Velyki rokovyny," *Dilo*, November 2, 1932.
121. "U 15-littja lystopadovoho chynu," *Dilo*, November 1, 1933. Evhen Javorivs'kyj, "Sto dniv u bojakh pid L'vovom (zapysnyk frontovnyka)," part 5, *Novyj Chas*, November 6, 1937. "Najbil'sha data nashykh dniv," *Dilo*, November 1, 1934.
122. Dmytro Dontsov, *Natsionalizm*. (London,: Ukraïns'ka vydavnycha spilka, 1966 [first published in Zhovkva in 1926]). Excerpts translated into English by Ralph Lindheim and George Luckyj, in *Towards an Intellectual History of Ukraine: An Anthology of Ukrainian Thought from 1710 to 1995*, ed. Ralph Lindheim and George S. N. Luckyj (Toronto: University of Toronto Press, 1995), 260–68.
123. "O neutralność," *Chwila*, January 12, 1919. "O pokój wewnętrzny," *Chwila*, August 1, 1919.
124. Tobiasz Askenaze, "Gdybym był syonistą," *Chwila*, January 23, 1919.
125. "Odpowiedź Redakcyi," *Chwila*, January 23, 1919.
126. "Smutna rocznica," *Chwila*, December 6, 1920. "Uczczenie pamięci ofiar rozruchów listopadowych," *Chwila*, December 7, 1920.
127. "Ofiary," *Chwila*, December 16, 1919.
128. "W smutną rocznicę," *Chwila*, December 17, 1919.
129. Ibid.
130. "W bożnicach," *Chwila*, December 16, 1919.
131. "Smutna rocznica," *Chwila*, December 6, 1920.
132. Stefanyk Library, L'viv, f. 102, Savch. 1, ark. 89–153: protocol of a meeting of the provisional government committee for L'viv on the Jewish question in Poland, February 2, 1919.
133. TsDIAL, f. 701, op. 3, spr. 505, ark. 1–2: members of the religious council to Mayor Józef Neumann, October 15, 1919.
134. DALO, f. 257, op. 1, spr. 48, ark. 46–91: Dokumenty Chwili, part 3: Rok 1919, Order no. 52 of the command of the local defense force, January 14, 1919. DALO f. 257, op. 2, spr. 1513, ark. 7–8: record of Stanislaw Voelpel, n.d. Voelpel reported that his unit was shot at when entering the Jewish quarter. See also DALO, f. 257, op. 2, spr. 1516, ark. 67–76: recollections of the engineer Michał Zerebrecki, 1933. TsDIAL, f. 837, op. 1, spr. 71, ark. 44–45: recollections of a Polish fighter. DALO, f. 257, op. 2, spr. 1515, ark. 27–29: recollections of Józef Rafalski, 1933.
135. "Rehabilitacya milicyi żyd. przez sąd polski," *Chwila*, October 21, 1919. "Prawda zwyciężą," *Chwila*, October 22, 1919.

136. DALO, f. 257, op. 2, d. 1657, l. 1–20: recollections of the priest Romuald Chłopecki, n.d. (1932).
137. Open letter of Tadeusz Feldstein to Marya Feiles, *Wiek Nowy*, December 19, 1918 (copy in DALO, f. 257, op. 1, spr. 4, Dokumeny Chwili: part 2, 8).
138. "Ankieta w sprawie polsko-żydowskiej (Czwarty dzień)," *Chwila*, February 11, 1919. "Ankieta w sprawie polsko-żydowskiej," *Chwila*, February 20, 1919.
139. Ibid.
140. Diary entries from November 1, 1933, and November 1, 1938, in Chajes, *Semper Fidelis*, 152 and 226.
141. Udział Żydów w walkach o niepodległość Polski; *Chwila*, November 12, 1933. Katrin Steffen, "Jüdische Identität in Polen zwischen den Weltkriegen," 113–33.
142. DALO, f. 257, op. 2, spr. 1573, ark. 95–99: Izaak Bürger to TBHOL, n.d. (possibly fall 1933).
143. "Uroczyste nabożeństwo w temple," *Chwila*, November 14, 1933.
144. For example, Mączyński, *Boje lwowskie*, part 1.
145. For example, Antoni Jakubski, "Walki Listopadowe we Lwowie w świetle krytyk," 179–81, and Czesław Mączyński, "O stanowisku Żydów w czasie walk listopadowych," 816–29.
146. DALO, f. 257, op. 2, spr. 1573, ark. 95–99: Izaak Bürger to TBHOL, n.d. (possibly fall 1933).
147. "Dwa lata," *Gazeta Lwowska*, October 31, 1920.
148. On the history of the cemetery, see Nicieja, *Łyczaków*, 375–98.
149. "Gdy orlęta chwyciły za broń. . . ," *Gazeta Wieczorna*, November 4, 1919. "Cześć poległym bohaterom!" *Gazeta Lwowska*, November 4, 1919.
150. Władysław Kubik, "O cmentarzyku obrońców Lwowa?" *Gazeta Poranna*, November 1, 1919.
151. Ibid.
152. DALO, f. 257, op. 2, spr. 183, ark. 1: L'viv city administration to the president of the Straż mogił Polskich Bohaterów, Neumann, February 27.
153. Ibid. ark. 21: TBHOL to the war graves department of the administration of the voivodeship, November 4, 1937. Ibid., ark. 23: administration of the voivodeship to TBHOL, December 2, 1937.
154. Żygulski, *Jestem z lwowskiego etapu* (Warsaw: PAX, 1994), 21. See also AW, II/1773, Alma Heczko, Dziennik-pamiętnik: diary entry, November 1, 1937.
155. AW, II/1773, Alma Heczko, Dziennik-pamiętnik: diary entry, November 1, 1938.
156. Christoph Mick, "Der Kult um den 'Unbekannten Soldaten' im Polen der Zwischenkriegszeit," in *Nationalisierung der Nation und Sakralisierung der Religion im östlichen Europa*, ed. Martin Schulze-Wessel (Stuttgart: Steiner Verlag, 2006), 181–200. Jay Winter, *Sites of Memory, Sites of Mourning: The Great War in European Cultural History* (Cambridge: Cambridge University Press, 1995), 102–104. Volker Ackermann, "'Ceux qui sont pieusement morts pour la France. . .' Die Identität des Unbekannten Soldaten," in *Der politische Totenkult: Kriegerdenkmäler in der Moderne*, ed. Reinhart Koselleck and Michael Jeismann (Munich: Fink, 1993), 281–314. George L. Mosse, *Fallen Soldiers: Reshaping the Memory of the World Wars* (New York: Oxford University Press, 1990), 94–98.
157. Ken S. Inglis, "Entombing Unknown Soldiers: From London and Paris to Baghdad," *History and Memory* 5 (1993): 7–31; Mosse, *Fallen Soldiers*, 94–97.
158. *Słowo Polskie*, October 1, 1925.
159. *Kurier Lwowski*, November 1, 1925.
160. Mick, "Der Kult um den 'Unbekannten Soldaten.'"

161. *Chwila*, November 1, 1925.
162. "Ofiary," *Chwila*, December 16, 1919. "Uczczenie pamięci ofiar rozruchów listopadowych," *Chwila*, December 7, 1920.
163. First page of *Dilo*, November 1, 1924.
164. "1-go listopada," *Dilo*, November 1, 1922.
165. Michel Foucault, *Language, Counter-Memory, Practice* (Ithaca, NY: Cornell University Press, 1977), 139–64.
166. Pierre Nora, "Between Memory and History: Les Lieux de Mémoire," *Representations* 26 (1989): 7–24.
167. Vasyl' Shchurat, "Dlja tykh, shcho vstanut...,'" in *Na vichny pamjat' herojam* (L'viv: unknown publisher, 1921), 9.
168. Ivan Nimchuk, "Kul't poljahlykh heroïv," *Dilo*, May 13–17, 1927.
169. *Dilo*, May 13, 1927.
170. *Dilo*, May 14, 1927.
171. "Zhyvi svidky nedavn'ominuloï slavy," *Novyj Chas*, November 1, 1934.
172. "Gdy orlęta chwyciły za broń...," *Gazeta Wieczorna*, November 4, 1919.
173. "Dzisiejsze uroczystości," *Słowo Polskie*, November 2, 1919.
174. "Przed listopadową rocznicą (Z kół obywatelskich)," *Gazeta Lwowska*, October 30, 1919. "Svjato 1-ho listopada na emigratsiji," *Novyj Chas*, November 30, 1927.
175. TsDIAL, f. 485, op. 1, spr. 485, ark. 1: the administration of the L'viv voivodeship to Archbishop Sheptyts'kyj, October 31, 1925. On the celebrations, see also Mazur, Życie polityczne polskiego Lwowa, 121–24.
176. "Nieudałe prowokacje," *Gazeta Lwowska*, November 2, 1928. "Demonstracje ukraińskie," *Chwila*, November 3, 1928. See also Mazur, Życie polityczne polskiego Lwowa, 123–24.
177. *Słowo Polskie*, November 3, 1928. *Dziennik Lwowski*, November 3, 1928.
178. *Dziennik Lwowski*, November 3, 1928.
179. *Dziennik Lwowski*, November 3 and 4, 1928.
180. "Strzały na pl. Jura i ul. Supińskiego," *Chwila*, November 3, 1928. TSDIAL, f. 355, op. 1, spr. 85, ark. 1–9: the president of the Ukrainian National Council Petrushevych to the president of the League of Nations (in French).
181. *Słowo Polskie*, November 4, 1928. DALO, f. 110, op. 4, spr. 108, ark. 192: appeal of a meeting of citizens, November 15, 1928. Ibid., ark. 189: police report on the meeting, November 16, 1928. Ibid., ark. 190–91: report by an assistant to the city captain (*starost*), November 16, 1928.
182. *Dziennik Lwowski*, November 3, 1928.
183. *Dilo*, November 4–24, 1928.
184. *Dziennik Lwowski*, November 8, 1928.
185. *Dziennik Lwowski*, November 23, 1928.
186. DALO, f. 126sc, op. 3, spr. 453, ark. 1–3: three letters by the commander of the police in L'viv to the office of the district attorney, June 4, 1929. Ibid., ark. 4: proclamation of Polish students to the Polish youth, June 5, 1929. On the context of these events, see Antony Polonsky, "A Failed Pogrom," 109–25.
187. DALO, f. 121, op. 3, spr. 453, ark. 5: proclamation of Polish students to the Polish youth, June 5, 1929.
188. TsDIAL, f. 205, op. 1, spr. 1123, ark. 14–27: bill of indictment of the district attorney of L'viv, July 15, 1929.
189. DALO, f. 110, op. 4, spr. 372, ark. 2–15: police command L'viv to the L'viv city captain (*starost*), December 20, 1932. *Chwila*, December 8, 1932. DALO, f. 110, op. 4, spr. 370, ark. 3: police protocol of a statement by Dr. Filip Rubin, December 13, 1932.

DALO, f. 110, op. 4, spr. 372, ark. 16–27: reaction of the police to the accusations, December 20, 1932. DALO, f. 110, op. 4, spr. 437, ark. 2–5: the commander of the police in L'viv to the district attorney in L'viv, April 1, 1933.
190. *Gazeta Lwowska*, November 22, 1938. DALO, f. 2, op. 26, spr. 1631, ark. 2–4: proclamation no. 32 of the mayor of L'viv, Stanisław Orlowski, November 25, 1938.
191. Chajes, *Semper Fidelis*, 227: diary entry, November 20, 1938.
192. Chajes, *Semper Fidelis*, 226.
193. Articles from Polish workers' newspapers in Russian translation in *Istorija L'vova v dokumentach i materialach*, ed. Uljana Jedlins'ka (Kiev: Naukowa Dumka, 1986), 199–205. For the Soviet version of events, see *Istorija L'vova: Korotkyj narys* (L'viv: Vydawnytstvo L'vivskoho Universytetu, 1956), 205–13.
194. Eyewitness account of a Polish worker, after April 4, 1936, in *Istorija L'vova v dokumentach i materialakh*, 196–99.
195. For example, in October 1938: TsDIAL, f. 205, op. 1, spr. 494, ark. 59–63: daily police report from October 17, 1938.
196. Elesar J. Feuerman, "Moi Lwowscy profesorowie," *Zesztyty Historyczne* 117 (1996): 55–72.
197. Bronisława Witz-Margulies, "Jan Kazimierz University 1936–1939: A Memoir," *Polin* 14 (2001): 223–36. AW, II/1773, Dzennik-pamiętnik of Alma Heczko, third part: diary entries from November 14 and 27, 1937, and December 9, 1937.
198. Feuerman, "Moi lwowscy profesorowie."
199. TsDIAL, f. 205, op. 1, spr. 498, ark. 152–54: daily police report, February 10, 1939.
200. Ibid., ark. 176–77: daily police report, February 17, 1939.
201. TsDIAL, f. 205, op. 1, spr. 500, ark. 72–75: daily police report, May 14, 1939.
202. Feuerman, "Moi lwowscy profesorowie."
203. TsDIAL, f. 205, op. 1, spr. 500, ark. 148–50: daily police report, May 31, 1939.
204. Ibid., ark. 31–33: daily police report on the political situation, October 11, 1938.
205. Ibid., ark. 39–44: daily police report on the political situation, October 13, 1938.
206. Ibid., ark. 55–58: daily police report on the political situation, October 16, 1938.
207. Ibid., ark. 125–28: daily police report on the political situation, January 28, 1939. Ibid., ark. 100–102: daily police report, February 1, 1939.
208. Zdzisław Pawluczuk, "Ukraińska Spółdzielczość w Polsce do 1939 roku," *Przegląd Wschodni* 2 (1992/93): 863–72.
209. PA, R-104149: German embassy in Warsaw to the Foreign Office in Berlin, November 15, 1938. Torzecki, *Polacy i Ukraińcy*, 22–25. Subtelny, *Ukraine*, 444.
210. Torzecki, *Polacy i Ukraińcy*, 22.
211. PA, Konsulat Lemberg, 54, March 1939–July 1939, R-104149: report of the German consulate in L'viv for the German Foreign Office, n.d.
212. Torzecki, *Polacy i Ukraińcy*, 23.
213. PA, R-104149: German embassy in Warsaw to the Foreign Office in Berlin, November 15, 1938.
214. TsDIAL, f. 205, op. 1, spr. 498, ark. 167–69: daily police report, February 15, 1939.
215. TsDIAL, f. 205, op. 1, spr. 499, ark. 254: daily police report, April 24, 1939. TsDIAL, f. 205, op. 1, spr. 500, ark. 92–95: daily police report, May 18, 1939.
216. TsDIAL, f. 205, op. 1, spr. 500, ark. 140–43: daily police report, May 30, 1939.
217. Bonusiak, *Lwów w latach 1918–1939*, 92.
218. Olijnyk, *Zoshyty*, 64.
219. TsDIAL, f. 493, op. 1, spr. 18, ark. 90: overview of the Wydział Narodowościowy of the Ukrainian press, March 10, 1939.
220. TsDIAL, f. 205, op. 1, spr. 500: daily police report, May 7, 1939.

221. Wolodymyr Kosyk, *The Third Reich and Ukraine* (New York: Peter Lang, 1993), 54–57. Frank Golczewski, *Deutsche und Ukrainer 1914–1939* (Paderborn: Schöningh, 2010).
222. PA, Konsulat Lemberg, 54: report of the German consulate in L'viv for the Foreign Office in Berlin, n.d.
223. Ibid.: consulate in L'viv to the Foreign Office, June 3, 1939.

CHAPTER 5

World War II

On August 21, 1939, the German Consulate in L'viv reported that mass arrests, persecution, and mistreatment had so inflamed the Ukrainians that a revolutionary crisis was possible.[1] Two days later, the German–Soviet nonaggression treaty was signed on August 23, 1939, and a wave of patriotism swept through Poland. Tens of thousands of young men immediately joined the army. The leaders of Jewish organizations urged the Jewish population to support Poland. The legal Ukrainian parties appealed to the Ukrainian population to maintain their silence and not to confront the authorities. The appeal was successful. Almost all Ukrainian soldiers—between 100,000 and 120,000 men—fought alongside their Polish comrades.[2]

The quick advance of the German army took the population by surprise. A few hours after the German invasion had begun, the first air strike hit L'viv, heavily damaging the train station. Over the next few days, an endless series of air alerts wore down the nerves of the population. The bombing of the airport alone killed eighty-three people.[3] On September 12, the German artillery began firing shells at the city. Two days later, the city's water and gas supply collapsed, and after six days power was cut. About eight hundred people died each day. The German troops were already in the city's western suburbs when the Red Army's invasion of eastern Poland on September 17 altered the political and military situation. The collapse of the Polish state led to chaos and anarchy. In towns or villages with Polish majority populations, militias were formed to fill the power vacuum. In other places, Ukrainian peasants took revenge on estate owners and Polish settlers for past humiliations, economic exploitation and state-sanctioned violence. The Red Army exploited the social and ethnic conflicts and encouraged Ukrainian peasants and the lower stratum of the urban population to form revolutionary committees, with the aim of destroying the old social and political structures "from below." There was no clear-cut front line, and Polish and Soviet troops moved through the country. Polish soldiers killed Ukrainian peasants in villages where triumphal arches had been constructed to greet the Red Army or where Poles had been attacked. Some sections of the population welcomed the creation of Soviet power structures because they hoped this would restore law and order.[4]

The Soviet troops met with little resistance and were soon standing at the outskirts of L'viv. On the evening of September 21, the Polish commander General Władysław Langner decided to hand over the city not to the Germans but to the Red Army. As a quid pro quo the Soviet high command granted Polish generals and officers the right to leave the city.[5]

Fifth Regime Change: The First Soviet Occupation

The Entry of the Red Army

At 1 p.m. on September 22, the Red Army marched into L'viv. All in all, the occupation went smoothly, save for a few instances of hostile fire from Polish stragglers. Soviet reports referred to them as "bourgeois elements" who were resisting "the entry of our troops."[6] There were other, more serious incidents. A Soviet unit attacked and killed a number of unarmed Polish police on their way to a registration office on Zielona Street.[7] One eyewitness remembered Soviet soldiers using their rifles to bludgeon wounded police. Some police were detained by Ukrainians, robbed, then handed over to Soviet soldiers.[8] Similar stories were reported about the Jews. According to a 1942 report by the Polish resistance, Soviet troops had barely reached the outskirts of the city when Jews began attacking Polish soldiers, disarming them and tying them up.[9] Another eyewitness, a Zionist, confirmed that some Jews openly showed their dislike of Poles: "For us Jews it was politically very unwise that part of Jewish society behaved very badly towards Polish society and towards Polish soldiers."[10]

The first Soviet units to enter L'viv treated the civilian population reasonably well.[11] Even the Polish underground later commented on "the initially quite favorable impression of the discipline of the entering Soviet troops and their tolerant attitude toward the population."[12] The first onlookers appeared on the streets at 5 p.m., many of them wearing red cockades.[13] When questioned about the living conditions in the Soviet Union, the soldiers always answered: "Everything is there" (*vse est*), just as they had been ordered to do by their political instructors. Their appearance, however, contradicted such statements. Their uniforms were of poor quality, often torn, and the soldiers looked malnourished.[14] This was "a terrible sight for all us Poles, they looked like the lowliest beggars, with horses without saddles, soldiers carrying heavy loads, old rifles slung over shoulders using ropes, in a word, a scene of poverty and desperation."[15]

Many Poles may have preferred a Soviet to a German occupation, but with the exception of a few communists and some of the working class, the sight of Red Army soldiers was no reason for celebration. It was clear to all that Poland had lost the war. One anonymous diary writer reported "complete chaos" and a sensation of "unfathomable tragedy."[16] On Market Square, Polish soldiers gathered to throw their rifles on a pile and left. Many were crying.[17]

The Polish underground was dissatisfied with the way the Soviet troops were welcomed by Ukrainians and Jews. Jews had welcomed them with visible joy,[18] sometimes even enthusiastically. The local group of the Home Army (Armia Krajowa, AK) only excluded the small group of Jewish Poles from their censure.[19] Other eyewitnesses reported that the Jewish and Ukrainian populations were divided. Railroad worker Władysław Zawiłło noticed that while Jewish communists talked to the Russian soldiers, the intelligentsia, "knowing what bolshevism is, avoided them and possibly repined as much as the Poles did, because they knew all about those Bolshevik benefits and the [Bolshevik] paradise."[20] The only joy that policeman Józef Mroczkowski noted was among the "lower classes and the urban rabble."[21] Police corporal Michał Klof linked social and ethnic categories by differentiating between Poles and the "social scum" which had welcomed the Red Army to the city: "The Soviet troops marched into L'viv on September 22, 1939 through Łyczaków Street with red flags, banners and flowers, welcomed by the city's social scum which consisted of Ukrainians and Jews."[22]

Other Polish eyewitnesses agreed with him, confident that no Poles among the crowds had welcomed the Soviet troops: "I saw Jewish and Ukrainian civilians on horses which had been taken from our cavalrymen, wearing red armbands, cheering the Red Army and at the same time strewing flowers at their feet and under the iron tanks."[23]

But there were also dissenting voices. Wanda Jóźwiak reported that children wearing Cracovian costumes presented flowers to Soviet soldiers holding rifles ready to fire.[24] Her account was confirmed by Lala Fishman, the daughter of an assimilated Jewish family: "Small wonder, then, that when the Red Army entered the city, it was a gala event and the cause of much rejoicing by the populace. Thousands of L'viv citizens turned out to greet the Soviet troops ... The Soviets marched in columns down one of the city's main thoroughfares, and the people who thronged the sidewalks clapped and shouted Polish hosannas while pretty girls skipped and capered alongside the soldiers, tossing flowers to them and strewing blossoms at their feet."[25]

It was not national identification but political and class beliefs that shaped the way Soviet troops were greeted. Bronisława Stachowicz, a teacher for Przysposobienie Wojskowe Kobiet (Military Training for Women) reported that not only Ukrainians and Jews but also Polish communists, and some workers had welcomed the Red Army. "Jews, Ukrainians, Polish communists who had been released from prison and a very small number of workers went to welcome [them]."[26]

The Polish underground organization Związek Walki Zbrojnej (Union for Armed Struggle, ZWZ) reported that initially there was not much difference between the Poles and the Ukrainians in the manner in which they welcomed the new masters of the city. The working class was enthusiastic, but its enthusiasm melted after Soviet officials took over the management of the factories.[27] Jewish eyewitnesses confirmed the Polish and Ukrainian reports that in addition to workers and communists, irrespective of nationality or religion, a considerable section of the Jewish youth also welcomed Soviet rule.[28] They explained this by pointing out that the alternative was German rule and by reminding readers of the Jewish experience of anti-Semitism in the years of the Second Polish Republic.[29]

Sovietization and Ukrainization

The Red Army had crossed the eastern Polish border as the "liberator of Slavic brothers from the Polish yoke," but in Soviet ideology this "yoke" was, in the first instance, social and, only in the second, national. The proletariat and peasantry had to be liberated from their domination by the Polish ruling elite, from the factory and estate owners, and from the capitalists. Soviet propaganda took aim at the "Poland of the masters" (*Pańska Polska*), not the "Poland of the people" (*Polska Ludowa*). The Second Polish Republic was subsequently reviled during meetings, in newspapers, posters, and radio broadcasts.[30] Every Polish officer was considered a potential spy. The workers were promised an end to all oppression.[31]

All political parties except the communist party were declared illegal. Independent social activities were no longer tolerated. Soviet trade unions, youth organizations (Young Pioneers and Komsomol), and unions for artists, writers, architects, and teachers pervaded all levels of society and helped control the population. Membership in such organizations spelled access to certain privileges and was a precondition for continuing to work in one's profession.

The integration of the eastern Polish territories into the Ukrainian Socialist Soviet Republic (UkrSSR) followed the blueprint provided by the Soviet nationality policies of the 1920s. The Ukrainians were the titular nationality, which meant that they took precedence over Poles and Jews in the administration, culture, and education. During so-called national operations against "diaspora nations" in the latter half of the 1930s, Poles in Soviet Ukraine had been classified as members of the newly introduced category known as "enemy peoples." Soviet Poles had lost their limited political rights of self-government; at least eighty-five thousand ethnic Poles were executed, and several hundred thousand were deported from areas where they had been long established.³² In contrast, Poles in the newly annexed territories were recognized as a national minority (as they had been in the 1920s) whose claims to cultural and educational representation had to be accorded some consideration.

Soviet politicians made it clear that the occupied territories would become part of the Ukrainian and Belarusian Socialist Soviet Republics. Formally, the decision was left to the population and the outcome of a special election. A Soviet-style election campaign was launched. Propagandists visited restaurants, coffeehouses and public kitchens, where they delivered lengthy speeches in Ukrainian, Polish, and Yiddish praising the wonderful quality of life in the Soviet Union. The population was amused and the campaign was soon halted. Public loudspeakers were installed, which broadcast propaganda all day. Public announcements, posters, red flags, and portraits of Lenin and Stalin were everywhere. Countless meetings were held, and those assembled had no choice other than to vote for the designated candidate. Attendance was compulsory. Those who did not comply were forced to do manual labor. The elections simulated participation by the population in the political decision making and were a first exercise in obedience.³³

On the afternoon of Election Day, October 22, 1939, representatives of the election commissions went to those persons who had not yet voted to convince them to "voluntarily" cast their ballots. Sick persons were brought to the polling stations. Voting was also linked to material incentives, with people permitted to buy scarce goods in improvised shops. Voter turnout in L'viv was 95.65 percent; 93.48 percent voted for the (only) list. The population believed that the results were faked, and there were rumors that ballot cards with crossed-out names had been replaced by new cards.³⁴

The overwhelming majority of deputies were local Ukrainians, followed by Poles. Jews were underrepresented. Just twenty Jews (1.3 percent of 1,495 deputies) were elected to the People's Assembly. The assembly voted for union with the UkrSSR, a request that was promptly accepted. Western Ukraine became part of Soviet Ukraine, and its inhabitants were given Soviet citizenship. The assembly decided to nationalize large estates and approved the distribution of land by peasants' committees. It retrospectively legalized the nationalization of banks and large factories and proclaimed that all land now belonged to the state.³⁵

After West Ukraine joined the UkrSSR, further elections were held in quick succession. These elections followed the principles of democratic centralism, whereby party organizations chose the candidates, mass meetings confirmed them, and the voters voted for the only list standing for election. The authorities used the elections to update the registers of residents. In March 1940 the western Ukrainian population elected deputies to the Supreme Soviets in Kiev (Kyiv) and Moscow and participated in elections for trade unions, professional organizations, and the People's Courts. Local and regional elections were held on December 15, 1940. They were to be the last elections before the German attack on the Soviet Union. In L'viv, 311,786 people had the right to vote. Voter turnout was 97.64 percent. The list of the "Bloc of Communists and Independents" received 98.51 percent of the vote. Three hundred and fifty-two ballot cards were pronounced invalid, and 4,005 voters had crossed out all names on the ballot paper. Elected to the L'viv municipal council were 274 Ukrainians (52.79 percent), 144 Poles (27.74 percent), 73 Russians (14.07 percent), 21 Jews (4.05 percent), and 7 others. The titular nation (Ukrainians) had the majority on the municipal council, despite making up less than 20 percent of the city population. Russians were also overrepresented. The Jewish population and the Polish population were disadvantaged.[36]

In the first few weeks after the Soviet invasion, the commander in chief of the occupying forces governed eastern Poland. In 1914/1915 the Russian occupiers had collaborated with the municipal authorities, and the municipal council hoped that the Soviet government would take a similar approach. On September 23, 1939, the municipal council met for the last time. The councilors discussed the supply situation, and the city administration informed them about the state of the city's public welfare institutions.[37] Not long after, Mayor Stanisław Ostrowski and some of the councilors were arrested. The Soviet authorities installed a provisional city administration headed by Soviet officials. On September 27, Fjodor I. Eremenko became chairman of the provisional municipal council. For a time, he was advised by vice-mayors Wiktor Chajes, Jan Weryński, and Franciszek Irzyk, but they too were soon arrested. Mykola H. Ma'tsko became chairman of the provisional administration of the voivodeship, and L. S. Hryshchuk was appointed first party secretary of the city and region of L'viv.[38]

Poles in key administrative and managerial positions were fired and replaced by newcomers from eastern Ukraine and other parts of the Soviet Union. Locals (twelve Ukrainians, eight Jews, and three Poles) occupied only twenty-three of the more important positions (mostly in the *rayons*). The Soviet leadership ordered the Red Army and the state and party in the eastern oblasts (regions) of the Ukrainian republic to identify cadres (3,500 in all) who could be sent to the occupied territories. To avoid the impression that Soviet rule was synonymous with Russian rule, a premium was put on officials with native Ukrainian language skills. Oblast leaders, however, tried to avoid sending their best people. In consequence, many Soviet administrators in western Ukraine were appointed to positions well above their training or experience, all of which contributed to the bad impression the new Soviet order was making on the local population and giving rise to many complaints about the low qualifications of Soviet staff.[39] Despite the sweeping dismissal of a large number of Poles from top positions, many experienced Polish administrators proved indispensable and were retained, particularly at the middle levels of bureaucracy.[40]

The Soviet administrative and judicial system was transferred to western Ukraine. The voivodeship L'viv became L'viv region (oblast'). The fourteen districts of the voivodeship were partitioned into thirty-six rayons. L'viv itself was divided into four rayons. The city's ten police districts were now headed by Soviet police commanders.[41] Cadres from the Soviet Union dominated the administration and police, but local Ukrainians were appointed as secretaries and chairmen of the village and district Soviets. The 828 village Soviets in L'viv region were chaired by 1,553 Ukrainians, 65 Poles, 18 Jews, and 3 Russians. Fifty-nine Ukrainians, twelve Jews, and three Poles headed the district Soviets. All sixteen chairmen of collective farms were Ukrainian.[42] In December 1939 the militia was renamed the "Workers' and Peasants' Militia." From February 1940, the leader of the militia was also the deputy head of the regional Narodnyj Komissariat Vnutrennikh Del (People's Commissariat for Internal Affairs, NKVD). The officers came from the Soviet Union, but most militiamen were locals. The exact ethnic composition of the militia is not known, but eyewitnesses reported that the majority of militiamen were Jews, followed by Ukrainians, while only a handful of Poles joined the militia.[43] In the fall of that year, the notorious Ivan Serov, a leading member of the Soviet security apparatus, became People's Commissar of the Ukrainian NKVD. He shared the responsibility for police operations in western Ukraine with the Deputy People's Commissar of the NKVD of the USSR, Vsevolod Merkulov. The head of the NKVD in L'viv region was also Deputy People's Commissar of the NKVD of the UkrSSR (after March 1940 this position was held by Major V. T. Serhijenko, followed by V. Sh. Lashenko and M. D. Djatlov).[44] Nikita S. Khrushchev (Ukr.: Mykola S. Khrushchov) was first secretary of the Ukrainian Communist Party. Khrushchev personally directed the integration of the occupied territories into the UkrSSR. He often traveled to L'viv to talk to regional party and NKVD functionaries and to deliver programmatic speeches at mass rallies.[45]

The cinemas showed documentaries and feature films from the Soviet Union.[46] In restaurants, cafés, and public soup kitchens propagandists told the bystanders about the good life enjoyed by citizens in the Soviet Union; public loudspeakers played propaganda broadcasts. Proclamations and posters, red flags, and portraits of Lenin and Stalin were everywhere.[47] One Polish woman wrote in her diary: "Since four days we are part of the partitioned region of the Muscovites. That is terrible but true. The red flag is flying from the town hall, the buildings have been decorated with red paint, the communists are walking around with red armbands, the pillars sport decrees written in Russian, Ukrainian and below in Polish. The streets are full of Soviet troops, tanks, weapons. There is a strange atmosphere in the city. You can see that strangers are in the city, that already we are no longer in charge."[48]

Private workshops, businesses, and trading companies were taxed out of existence. Factories, banks, and companies were seized, and their directors and managers fired. Their places were taken by cadres from the Soviet Union or by locals with the right proletarian class background.[49] The local population was skeptical about the qualifications of the new elite, and there were rumors that a doorman had been appointed director of the liquor monopoly and a road sweeper appointed head of the city's main bakery.[50]

The peasants had freely distributed the land taken from landowners. The subsequent legalization of these expropriations generated some support for the Soviet Union. But the peasants were soon disillusioned by the high quotas they were expected to deliver and the start of collectivization. However, only 13 percent of farms had been collectivized when Germany attacked.[51]

The new preeminence of Ukrainians was also apparent in the new cultural policy. On September 29, 1939, the new authorities called a meeting of the professors, lecturers, assistants, students and employees of the university. The gathering was held in the university's Collegium Maximum. The speech by the Ukrainian writer and cultural officer Oleksander Kornijchuk made a great impression on the Polish countess and university lecturer Karolina Lanckorońska. Kornijchuk emphasized the importance of science and art, talked of the great contributions of Polish culture to world culture, and honored Mickiewicz with "fine words." He professed his wish to reconciliate Polish culture with Ukrainian culture. The Polish listeners left the meeting buoyed by the hope that Jan Kazimierz University would be preserved. Sometime later, Lanckorońska heard that Kornijchuk had promised his listeners at a Ukrainian meeting on the very same day "to exclude all Polish elements from Lwów University."[52]

The university was promptly renamed Ivan Franko University, after the leading western Ukrainian politician and writer. A new rector was appointed and several Soviet Ukrainian professors arrived. Local Ukrainian scholars were appointed or promoted to more senior positions, but the administration was kept strictly under Soviet control.[53] All official announcements were made in Ukrainian, and pressure was put on lecturers and professors to hold their lectures in Ukrainian, although Polish professors were permitted to speak Polish if they could not speak Russian or Ukrainian.[54] By 1941 the composition of the academic staff had changed considerably. Staff were 40 percent Ukrainian and 40 percent Polish. The professors were mostly Polish; fifty-two Polish, twenty-two Ukrainian, and eight Jewish professors taught at L'viv University. At the Technical University, the proportion of Polish professors was even higher. Only three of sixty-nine professors were Ukrainian. However, in other institutions Ukrainization progressed more quickly. The Institute for Foreign Trade, for example, employed thirty-two Ukrainians, eight Poles, four Jews, and two Russians.[55]

Before the war, many obstacles had been put in the way of Ukrainians and Jews to limit their enrolment at Polish universities. This changed under Soviet rule. In December 1939 the composition of the student body still reflected the discrimination against Jews of the prewar years. At L'viv University Poles accounted for 77.9 percent of students, with Ukrainians and Jews making up 12.9 percent and 6.7 percent of the student body, respectively. By April 1941, Ukrainization and the end of anti-Jewish discrimination had dramatically altered the composition of the student body. Of 1,617 students, 540 were Ukrainians (33.40 percent), 362 were Poles (22.39 percent), and 715 were Jews (44.21 percent). The Technical University had a higher share of Poles, but only the Institute for Veterinary Medicine still had a majority of Polish students (303, or 58.72 percent). Under Soviet rule, class mattered as much as ethnicity. Out of 340 first-year students at the Medical Institute 39 percent had a working-class background, 20 percent came from the peasantry, and 40 percent were categorized as coming from "working-class intelligentsia" families, while only one student had a "bourgeois" background. Forty-eight percent of students were Ukrainians, 32 percent were Jews, and 16 percent were Poles.[56]

Coordination did not only affect universities. The Soviet authorities also reorganized the museums and privatized private collections. Historical and ethnographical museums underwent profound changes. Sovietization trumped Ukrainization. The Ukrainian museums Molodaja Hromada (Young Community) and Ukraïns'ka Vijs'ka (Ukrainian Troops) were closed because the Soviet authorities considered them too nationalist. The Museum of the City of L'viv displeased visitors from the Central Committee of the Ukrainian Communist Party. The museum was "too Polish" for their taste, and the areas describing the wars between 1918 and 1920 were downright "chauvinistic" and anti-Soviet. The museum was promptly closed. When it was reopened the museum showed L'viv as a Ukrainian city. Part of the exhibition was dedicated to the "liberation of the working people" (in September 1939) by the Soviet Union.[57]

Although the scientific Shevchenko Society was disbanded, institutes of the Ukrainian Academy of Sciences were set up in which members of the Society were given employment. Institutes for the history of Ukraine; Ukrainian literature, linguistics and Ukrainian folklore studies; archeology; and economy followed. Most of the facilities of former Polish scientific societies were handed over to these new institutes.[58] The well-known West Ukrainian historian and Hrushevs'kyj-pupil Ivan Kryp"jakevych was appointed director of the Institute for Ukrainian History.[59] The Ossolineum was placed under the control of the academy and partially Ukrainized.[60]

Important cultural buildings such as the Opera House were nationalized and handed over to the Ukrainian SSR. Ukrainian ensembles were given the best buildings and were elevated to the rank of "Ukrainian State Theaters." The Polish theaters and the Jewish theater in L'viv continued to operate, but Polish and Jewish theaters in other towns were closed.[61] The center of literary life was the Union of Soviet Writers, which, like other artists' unions, set up a branch in L'viv. Soviet Ukrainian writers were ordered to move to L'viv to see the "liberation of the working people in West Ukraine" with their own eyes as preparation for a later incorporation of the topic in literature. Local authors noted carefully who of these visitors spoke Ukrainian easily and without accent and who had a Russian accent.[62] Some local communist writers were accused of "Trotskyist deviation" and were put on trial. Some bourgeois writers were rejected because of their anti-Soviet attitude. This was equivalent to being banned from their profession, with rejected writers forced to find other jobs.[63]

A Polish eyewitness believed that the Soviet authorities wanted to bring up children in a Bolshevik spirit with a "hatred of all things Polish."[64] Polish schools were given specially developed teaching materials and Soviet schoolbooks. Between 1939 and 1940, the numbers of Polish primary schools in the southeastern voivodeships dropped from 4,907 to 984 while the numbers of Ukrainian schools increased correspondingly, rising from 371 to 5,336. The number of Yiddish elementary schools also increased, from just 23 in 1939 to 103 in 1940. East Galician Jews had formerly sent their children mostly to Polish-language primary schools. After the Ukrainization of education this was no longer an option. Other than Yiddish schools, Jewish parents only had a choice between Ukrainian and a few Russian schools. Many parents preferred to send their children to Yiddish schools, even though this made access to higher education more difficult for Jewish children when they had to move to Ukrainian secondary schools. In the spring of 1940, the Ukrainian ministry for education therefore opted to limit Yiddish-language educational establishments. Jewish children now had no other choice than to learn Ukrainian. Ukrainian was gradually introduced as the language of instruction in Yiddish primary schools but the teaching of Yiddish continued.[65]

The Bolsheviks replaced old symbols with new Soviet symbols. They started by removing all Polish symbols from the cityscape. Singing "Boże coś Polskę" in church was forbidden. This patriotic Polish song from 1816 had been the most important Polish hymn apart from "Jeszcze Polska nie zginęła" during the time of the Polish partitions and had a subversive aspect. In independent Poland, parishioners sang the line of the refrain as "God bless the free fatherland" (*Ojczyznę wolną pobłogosław Panie*). During the time of partition and during World War II, the line was replaced by the words "May God restore the free fatherland to us" (*Ojczyznę wolną racz nam wrócić Panie*). However, the Soviet authorities did treat some Polish monuments, for example, those of Kościuszko and Mickiewicz, with respect. Soviet propaganda was not directed against Polish culture per se.[66]

The most common language on the streets of L'viv remained Polish, although the number of Ukrainian speakers was on the rise.[67] Jews tended to speak Yiddish or Polish, depending on whom they were talking to, while Ukrainians—according to a Jewish eyewitness—always and everywhere spoke only Ukrainian.[68] The Soviet authorities took care to ensure that the cadres who were summoned to work in the occupied territories spoke Ukrainian as a reminder that Ukrainian territories had been "reunified." The literary scholar Myroslav Semchyshyn remembered how pleasant it was during the first days of Soviet rule to hear Ukrainian words and songs on the streets and to read signs written in Ukrainian. Academy member M. Voznjak felt similar feelings of elation when he heard Ukrainian spoken in administrative offices and in the halls of the university.[69]

But in many respects this vaunted Ukrainization was only external. Ukrainian streets signs were installed in May 1940, but streets were not always renamed. And so Mączyński Street remained, even though the street name was now written in Cyrillic. Mączyński, the commander of the Obrona Lwowa in November 1918, was hated by both Ukrainians and Jews. The Wały Hetmańskie in the city center was renamed Radians'kyj Bulvar (Boulevard of the Soviets). Other streets were given names referencing a Ukrainian heritage. There was now an Ivan Franko Street, a Lesja Ukraïnka Street, and an Ivan Bohun Street. Other street names cited Russian and Soviet traditions. The new rulers sought to leave their mark on L'viv's public spaces. Enormous posters were put up, and new monuments were erected all over the city. The monuments, however, were usually made of wood or plaster. Exposed to the elements, they quickly began to look dingy and shabby, giving rise to many jokes about the permanence of Soviet rule.[70] A monument of Lenin was commissioned for the plaza in front of the Opera House, but when Germany attacked in June 1941 only the pedestal had been completed. The Nazis later used it to set up a bust of Hitler.

In March 1940 the city's inhabitants were given Soviet passports. But instead of the planned issue of 40,000 passports, only about 1,500 passports were ready. Many people were afraid that they could lose their right to Polish citizenship by accepting a Soviet passport. But refusal was a risky business. Persons picked up without a valid passport ran the risk of being deported eastward, deep within the Soviet Union. Most refugees were given identity cards that bore the infamous Paragraph 11, forbidding them to settle in the border areas or bigger cities. They were obliged to leave L'viv and seek refuge in the more easterly areas of the UkrSSR.[71]

By the time of the German attack on Soviet Russia, the infiltration of the Ukrainian population by the party and other mass organizations had not progressed very far. In spring 1941, there were 5,804 party members and 2,993 candidates in the L'viv region, most of whom hailed from within the Soviet Union. The figures for three out of four quarters of 1940 show that 107 Russians, 251 Ukrainians, 56 Jews, 7 Belarusians, and 1 Pole were admitted to the Communist Party in this period. The Komsomol had a less restrictive acceptance policy, and by June 1941 it numbered around 30,000 members in L'viv region, of whom 6,300 were resident in L'viv.[72]

Repression

Sovietization did not end with the shaping of society and public life according to the Soviet model. It went further. Terror was an integral part of Stalinism, and the destruction of the "class enemy" and the neutralization of all real or potential opponents was a central part of Soviet occupation policy. The systematic terror began on September 25 after the NKVD had reinforced its numbers in the city. Until that point the relationship of the Soviet authorities to the population had been "fairly liberal."[73] After that it was "hell."[74] The first wave of arrests, which took place in the last quarter of 1939, hit Polish officers, civil servants, and estate owners hardest, followed by members of the social and political elite irrespective of nationality or creed. Former Polish prime ministers Leon Kozłowski and Aleksander Prystor and former National Democratic ministers Stanisław Grabski and Stanisław Głąbiński were arrested. Members of the mayoralty, the judiciary, the police, priests, and officers were also arrested, followed by civil servants, students, teachers, noncommissioned officers, factory owners, and politicians. The arrested officers, police officers, and administrative and court officials were mostly Polish, while Jews were overrepresented among real estate owners, manufacturers, merchants, and bank directors.[75] In the first days of the occupation, 145 leaders of Ukrainian organizations and parties were also arrested, among them the eighty-year-old doyen of Ukrainian politics Kost' Levyts'kyj.[76] In January 1940 the NKVD carried out a purge of intellectuals and left-wing groups in L'viv. Dozens of authors, journalists, and former members of the Communist Party of Western Ukraine were arrested. Together with scores of Polish authors they were accused of Polish chauvinism and anti-Soviet sympathies.[77]

The Polish population viewed these measures as an attack on the Polish nation. This perception was not wrong; the Soviet leadership was trying to destroy the prewar elite who had been the most ardent proponents of Polish independence. More than twenty-two thousand Polish officers, police, and members of the prewar elite were murdered by the NKVD in Katyn, Ostashkov, and elsewhere. Tadeusz Riedl, who was six years old at the start of the war, retrospectively described the "annihilation of the Polish intelligentsia" as one of the chief activities carried out by the new rulers.[78]

The NKVD also took a hard line against all local cells of the Organization of Ukrainian Nationalists (OUN). In December 1939 the OUN had between eight and nine thousand members in western Ukraine, according to present-day pro-OUN estimates. About 5,500 of them were controlled by the OUN leadership in L'viv.[79] Hundreds of OUN activists were arrested in the spring of 1940, with a further series of arrests taking place in September. On December 22 and 23, 1940, 520 people were arrested in L'viv oblast alone for suspected links to the OUN. A number of trials were held, many of which culminated in the accused being sentenced to death. The most important trial was of fifty-nine mostly younger supporters of the OUN in January 1941. When the verdict was handed down, forty-one defendants were sentenced to death, and seventeen were given ten years in prison. Sixteen of those who sentenced to death were executed shortly thereafter. A further twenty-one were executed in April.[80] The last wave of arrests in May 1941 also targeted Ukrainian nationalists. When Germany invaded the Soviet Union, many of these Ukrainians were still being held in local prisons. Some escaped using the confusion after the German attack; others were murdered by the NKVD.[81]

Underground Zionist organizations and Jewish politicians did not fare much better. The leaders of the Jewish Workers' Party Bund were considered "traitors to the Revolution." Zionist parties and organizations were overwhelmed with arrests.[82] At a trial held in L'viv in March 1941, seven members of the Socialist-Zionist youth organization Hashomer Hatzair received prison sentences ranging from seven to ten years. The Zionist youth organization Bnei Akiva was also persecuted and went underground.[83]

Using Soviet sources, Grzegorz Hryciuk and Jaroslav Stots'kyj have calculated that approximately 45,000 people—15,000 (39.5 percent) Poles, 15,300 (39.5 percent) Ukrainians and 8,000 (21 percent) Jews—were arrested in East Galicia, many of them when they tried to cross the German–Soviet demarcation line. In East Galicia and Volhynia 66,563 people were arrested (see table 5.1). Torture was commonplace in all prisons. Prisoners were beaten, crammed into overcrowded cells, and deprived of food.[84]

The Soviet occupiers used not only arrests and executions to terrorize the population but also the ever-present threat of mass deportations to Kazakhstan, northern Russia, or Siberia. Soviet authorities began deporting prewar Polish settlers from East Galicia in January 1940. The Polish state had promoted their settlement to strengthen the "Polish element" in East Galicia. Around thirty-five men had formerly served in the Polish army. The Soviet authorities viewed them

	Total	Poles	Ukrainians	Jews
Sept. to Dec. 1939	10,566	5,406	2,779	1,439
Jan. to Dec. 1940	47,403	15,518	15,024	10,924
Jan. to May 1941	8,594	1,121	5,418	801
Total	66,563	22,045	23,221	13,164

Table 5.1. Arrests in East Galicia and Volhynia, September 1939 to May 1941[85]

as counterrevolutionary elements who needed to be eliminated.[86] According to the inflated estimates of the AK, 120,000 colonists were deported between February 10 and February 12, 1940. Using Soviet transport lists, Hryciuk has calculated that least 68,624 persons were deported. About sixty-four thousand of them hailed from East Galicia.[87] These deportations took place in winter. Some of the cattle cars carrying colonists passed through L'viv, and townsfolk attempted to hand food and clothing to the prisoners, sometimes successfully but oftentimes prevented by the guards.[88] The deportation of the colonists was popular with the Ukrainian population, but only a short time later the more affluent Ukrainian peasants were also being deported.[89]

The second wave of deportations targeted the family members of persons who were already under arrest or had been deported. In April 1940, 32,000 people were deported from West Ukraine, among them more than 23,700 persons from East Galicia. On the so-called St. Bartholomew's Night of April 12–13, 1940, between 7,000 and 8,500 Poles were deported from L'viv alone, most of them family members of officers or police.[90] Alma Heczko wrote in her diary, "Poles are now living through hard times. The Muscovites are deporting us in huge numbers day and night. They are picking up the families of soldiers, policemen, doctors."[91] The following night, Jewish politicians and prominent Zionists were arrested and deported.[92]

The third wave of deportations was directed against refugees from the German-occupied territories of Poland. In May 1940 a German committee traveled to L'viv to register persons who had formerly lived in the territory of the Generalgouvernement for resettlement. In the first few weeks, 75 percent of the refugees applied for resettlement to the Generalgouvernement, among them a number of Jews. The Jews feared the Germans but were also afraid that later on they would never be permitted to return to their homes. Only ten thousand refugees accepted Soviet passports and settled in the province.[93] The German commissions were overwhelmed by the demand. They registered 66,000 people in West Ukraine who wished to return to the Generalgouvernement, although only 1,600 Jews were among them.[94] After registration had been completed the Soviet police spent ten days hunting down refugees who had no Soviet passports and bundling them into freight cars going east. According to Hryciuk's calculations, no fewer than 43,000 refugees were deported, of which at least 37,800 hailed from L'viv region (22,000 from the city itself). Many Jews and Poles had hidden refugees and provided food and clothing to the refugees penned into freight cars awaiting deportation to the Soviet Union.[95] Between 20 and 25 percent of refugees proved impossible to trace. They were later able to legalize their residence, although most of them were only given passports with the Paragraph 11 stamp and had to leave L'viv.[96] Only a few hundred Ukrainians and Jews were deported in the second half of 1940.

The fourth wave of deportations took place on May 22, 1941, and was directed primarily against the families of Ukrainians who had been arrested for nationalist activities. According to Soviet documents, 11,329 people were deported from western Ukraine, 2,216 of whom were from the L'viv region.[97]

Excluding the approximately twenty-two thousand refugees and using only the lowest figures cited, at least ten thousand inhabitants of the city of L'viv were arrested between 1939 and 1941, and more than eight thousand were deported. The Polish government in exile estimated that 1.2 million people, 700,000–750,000 of them Poles, were deported from Poland's eastern territories. Their figures are too high, as are the figures given by Archbishop Sheptyts'kyj, who believed that around four hundred thousand Ukrainians had been deported from East Galicia.[98] Based on Soviet documents Hryciuk arrived at much lower numbers, but numbers which nevertheless reveal the extent of the terror. According to his calculations, at least 140,000 people were deported from East Galicia.[99] Approximately ninety-five thousand were residents of East Galicia, and forty-thousand were refugees from central and western Poland. The majority of deported refugees were Jewish. Approximately eighty percent of deported local residents were Poles, ten to fifteen percent were Ukrainians, and five to ten percent were Jews.[100] Between 1939 and 1941, 220,000 people were deported from all of Poland's eastern territories, including Volhynia, Podlasia, and the Chełm regions, 25,000 of whom were Ukrainian.[101] The percentage of Ukrainians was much higher among the numbers of arrested and murdered persons but cannot be verified in detail. In East Galicia, fifty thousand Ukrainians, Poles, and Jews were sentenced to terms in prison, executed, or murdered without trial. The Ukrainian population also experienced the forced enlistment into the Soviet army as repression. Between thirty to fifty thousand young men, the majority of them Ukrainians, were forcibly conscripted into the Red Army.[102]

Viewed on its own, the number of persons affected says little about the impact this had on life in L'viv and on the families and friends of those executed, arrested, or deported. Night after night, the NKVD visited homes to arrest people. Every knock on the door could spell arrest or deportation. And night after night, Weliczker Wells and his father hid in their basement, "for we did not know whether we belonged to the "capitalist" group or not . . . During this period all of us would sit up all night, dressed and packed, so that if they came to take us away, at least we'd have all the essentials with us for the 'trip.' This went on for a few weeks. Then the arrests quieted down."[103]

For days and weeks after an arrest, family members went to the prisons or NKVD offices to find out the fate of their loved ones. Often they returned no news. Ilana Maschler's uncle Samek, the former owner of a candy factory, was among those arrested: "Aunt Bela spends many hours every day in front of the prison gate and tries without success to find out something about Uncle Samek's fate and to drop off a packet of food for him. She shares these experiences with a group of women, Poles and Jews, whose husbands or sons were arrested because they too had held higher positions or were officers in the Polish army."[104]

During her visits, Bela met the wives of several leading Zionists who had been arrested earlier. A few months later, Aunt Bela shared the fate of these women and was deported from L'viv.[105]

The New Soviet Life

The collapse of the Polish state, the arrests and deportations demoralized the population, and the rapid French defeat in June 1940 depressed Poles and Jews in particular; suicides were a daily occurrence. Living conditions deteriorated and unemployment was high. At the end of 1939, forty thousand people in L'viv were unemployed.[106] Over the next three months, nineteen thousand found jobs. The authorities attempted to convince many of the remaining unemployed to volunteer to work in industries inside the Soviet Union. By the end of 1939 more than 15,500 had moved east, with 13,400 of them relocating to the Donbass region. In the first quarter of 1940, a further 8,780 people found work in eastern Ukraine. But interest soon dropped off as news about the bad working and living conditions filtered back to L'viv. The work was hard and dangerous, and factories were generally unprepared for the influx of new workers, who often had to live in temporary shelters and huts. Of the first contingent, 85 percent (13,700 people) returned to L'viv before their one-year contract had expired.[107] They found a changed city.

The new Soviet life was a cultural shock for the population. Soon after the invasion large numbers of Soviet officials and cadres poured into the city.[108] Noting the influx, Countess Lanckorońska was careful to differentiate between eastern Ukrainians and Russians. In her opinion, it was Kiev, and not Moscow, that wanted to destroy Polish culture:

> Constantly and at every step of the way we sensed that, in our daily life, we were being ruled not from Moscow but from Kiev; that we were dealing not with Russia, but rather with the problems of our tragic seventeenth century, the legacy of the rebellion in the Ukraine led by the Cossack Hetman Bogdan Chmielnicki. From the east our lands were inundated (as they were after King Władysław IV) by a wave of socially inchoate barbarism, fighting against us under the banner of social slogans derived in a large part from a feeling of inferiority and a hatred of the indigenous culture which the invaders did not possess. Because that culture happened to be Polish, everything Polish had to be destroyed.
>
> So far as the business of everyday life was concerned, we had to contend far more often with simple and coarsely simplistic Ukrainian nationalism than with communism or Russian imperialism, which did not "get involved in trifling affairs."[109]

Many L'viv residents mocked the Russian's lack of "culture." Soldiers and party cadres were portrayed as uncouth and uncivilized. Very few of them had ever heard of using a handkerchief to blow their nose. The occupiers' physiognomies were pronounced "rustic" and "unintelligent." In streetcars, the new Soviet man did not offer his seat to women or the elderly.[110]

Sovietization changed everyday life in other ways as well. In November 1939 L'viv residents were already being forced to participate in *subbotniki*— work without pay carried out on workers' days off for the benefit of the state. Moscow time and a six-day workweek of forty-eight hours were introduced in December 1939, with the latter innovation lasting until June 1940. People had to start work two hours earlier; Sundays became workdays. Both changes upset traditional patterns of life. People had to get up in the middle of the night to arrive at their workplaces in time.[111] "This completely unexpected change shattered the general rhythm of life, preventing the continuation of customs that had existed for generations or of ordinary, familiar, friendly, sociable contacts."[112]

Religious and national holidays were replaced by Soviet days of commemoration and celebration. All Saints' Day (November 1) and Polish Independence Day (November 11) were ousted and supplanted by May Day (May 1), the anniversary of the October revolution (November 7), Stalin's birthday, and Lenin's birthday and death day. Workers were expected to attend political rallies and to help with preparations. Big celebrations were held on Stalin's sixtieth birthday (December 21, 1939), Lenin's death day (January 22) and the first anniversary of the "liberation of western Ukraine" (September 17, 1940). The city's inhabitants viewed these unfamiliar compulsory celebrations as an imposition. The Bolsheviks could not convince the population to replace the Christ Child, the Virgin Mary, and St. Nicholas with the Russian "little Father Frost."[113] Infringements of discipline at work were severely punished. If workers arrived more than fifteen minutes late to work on three occasions, they could be sentenced to prison. Offenders faced high fines for other infractions as well. Members of the working class were disillusioned. They had expected something else from the "fatherland of the proletariat."[114]

The Red Army soldiers had been well supplied with rubles. This reduced looting but increased the problem of supplying the city with enough foodstuffs and other necessaries. The parity exchange rate favored the ruble, which had a lower purchasing power in the Soviet Union than the złoty did in Poland. On December 11, 1939, the ruble became the only official currency, leaving the złoty worthless and accelerating the impoverishment of the local population. Flush with rubles, officers and soldiers emptied the shops, giving the lie to the assertions about the abundance of goods in the Soviet Union. Wristwatches were particularly popular, but officers and soldiers were also eager to obtain clothing and all forms of consumer goods.[115] Initially, the newcomers were easily recognizable by their shoddy and worn clothing. But within a short time the incomers had refurbished their wardrobes in the local shops and now drew attention to themselves by their "capitalist elegance."[116]

Stocks were soon depleted, and provisions were in short supply. People were forced to queue for hours for even the most basic goods. The normal waiting time for a loaf of bread was two to three hours, stretching to four to five hours for two pounds of sugar. Because the price of sugar on the black market was twenty-five times the official price, "professional" queuers, experts at pushing their way to the front of a queue, soon began to offer their services. The situation was even worse for textiles, clothing, and shoes. People often began queuing in the evening in preparation for the next day.[117] Persons branded as "class enemies" under the new regime and unable to find work attempted to convert their belongings into cash on one of the black markets.[118] Countess Karolina Lanckorońska recalled the emergence of Soviet black marketeers, describing them as a "fragment of Asia descended on Lwów." She regarded them as a tragic sign that the east "was devouring us."[119]

The new Soviet organizations could not compensate for the dissolution of Jewish, Polish and Ukrainian cooperatives. The supply situation continued to be bad.[120] In the cold winter of 1939/1940, fuel (coal and firewood) was in short supply.[121] The Soviet textiles arriving in the city were of poor quality and failed to convince the population of the superiority of Soviet civilization.[122]

Weliczker Wells reflected more generally on life under Soviet rule, noting, "All of us began to have new 'values' in life. Being 'happy' could now mean that you had had a successful day in the sugar queue, or that you had not been interrupted by the police during the night. Above all, we were satisfied as long as the family was together."[123]

Although living conditions in general had deteriorated, the plight of the many refugees who had come to L'viv was even worse. Even in "normal times" the number of refugees would have had a dramatic impact on life in the city. They presented a serious problem for the Soviet authorities. Housing was unavailable and most refugees were unemployed.

With the influx of refugees the number of inhabitants in the city increased to half a million. At the end of March 1940, the authorities had registered just under 39,000 refugees, including 26,000 Jews and 12,300 Poles. Two months later, 55,000 refugees were registered. More than 45,000 wanted to return to the German-occupied territories with just 9,000 preferring to remain in the Soviet Union.[124] The high percentage of Jewish refugees changed the face of the city. The streets were packed and there were more traditionally garbed Jews on the streets than ever before.[125] There were now as many Jews living in the city as Poles. This, too, contributed to residents experiencing the Soviet regime as "Jewish rule." That fact that refugees unable to find space with friends or relatives were living in collective accommodation centers did not change this perception. Barely any families still lived alone. Some apartments housed more than a dozen people. In mid-October 1939 the provisional city administration set up a committee to help refugees and the unemployed. The assistance committee was initially able to fund twenty-nine public kitchens, but by the beginning of December the difficulty of obtaining supplies had also begun to affect public welfare programs, and only twelve of the public kitchens remained open.[126]

The deportation of refugees eased the housing situation, but the refugees were not solely responsible for the shortage of housing. There was a great need to find accommodation for the newcomers from the Soviet Union. The plan was to nationalize 6,000 of the city's 15,578 buildings. The Red Army, the NKVD, and other administrative bodies in the city vied with one another to obtain housing. By November 27, 1939, the municipal administration had already taken over 2,649 apartments. What usually happened was that a committee went to the owner and declared that the house or apartment was now confiscated. About 1,000 apartments went to the NKVD and the Red Army.[127]

The authorities discriminated against the old economic and political elites. Members of the former "ruling class" had to pay more for gas, water, and electricity. The rents they paid per square meter were many times higher than the rents demanded from workers or craftspeople. The payment of pensions to higher civil servants, officers of the Polish army, judges, and the clergy was stopped, affecting 4,300 people in L'viv. State pensions, if they were paid out at all, did not even reach subsistence levels.[128]

The sanitary situation in the city in the winter of 1939/1940 was far from good. Garbage had not been collected for weeks, and the damage inflicted by the fighting and the rubble had not been cleared away. To combat this, the regional government (executive committee) launched a campaign in the spring of 1940 to clean up the streets and public places. The executive committee gave the chairman of L'viv city council, Eremenko, and the chairman of the municipal economic administration, Makarejko, deadlines of between ten and fifteen days to punish the parties responsible for the failures and to ensure that all streets, squares, and courtyards were cleaned up. Residents were obliged to enter into agreements to carry out socialist competitions and to ensure complete cleanliness in their area. The public parks too had to be entirely cleaned up within twenty days, and all inscriptions and slogans on houses, old posters, and advertisements by private companies removed.[129] The result was impressive. Jan Rogowski remembered that by the summer of 1940 the city was cleaner than it had ever been. House wardens were continually on the lookout to ensure that any garbage was removed instantly.[130]

The Soviet leadership did not wait long before it began implementing its antireligious policy. Religious communities were subjected to administrative repressions such as high taxes. Many parishes were unable to raise the necessary sums. Churches were closed down, and bell-ringing was strictly forbidden. Many rabbis and priests were arrested. Bishops were placed under house arrest. No preparations to forcibly reunite the Greek Orthodox Church with the Russian Orthodox Church were discernable.[131] Monasteries were dissolved, and the university's theological faculty was closed. But despite this, the churches continued to be filled to capacity on Sundays as people looked for comfort and at the same time demonstrated against the atheist system.[132] As so often in troubled times, hundreds of people visited miracle rabbis, thousands believed rumors of apparitions of saints or the Virgin Mary and made pilgrimages to holy sites. Sovietization did not reach the hearts of the people. Going to church or attending synagogue and believing in miracles and apparitions contradicted the regime's atheist ideology and could thus be considered a form of passive resistance.[133]

Cooperation and Resistance

The boundaries between unavoidable accommodation to new circumstances and collaboration are blurred. The Ukrainian population was pleased that Polish supremacy had ended, but their pleasure—according to Osyp Nazaruk, editor in chief of the Greek Catholic weekly newspaper *Nova Zorja*—was dimmed by the uncertain future.[134] Ukrainian activists tried to make some public demonstration of Ukrainian presence on the streets of L'viv so as not to leave the field to "Jews and communists." But on the advice of the Stadtkommandant (city captain) they decided against holding a demonstration.[135] Prominent Ukrainian academics and artists signed a letter to the first secretary of the Ukrainian Communist Party, Khrushchev, in the name of the "working-class intelligentsia," declaring their readiness to do all they could to contribute to the new Soviet life.[136] A delegation headed by Kost' Levyts'kyj offered to cooperate loyally with the Soviet Union. The Soviet city captain assured them that they had nothing to fear.[137] Ukrainian politicians set up a Council of Elders and an assistance committee and called on Ukrainian youth to join the militia. Nazaruk argued that otherwise the militia would have consisted exclusively of Jews.[138] But after only a few weeks all illusions had dissipated. Soviet alliance policies might potentially extend to include the national Ukrainian intelligentsia but certainly did not cover Ukrainian activists of any party. The leaders of Ukrainian nationalist parties were arrested with the exception of those who had managed to escape to the Generalgouvernement.[139] Ukrainians and Jews were permitted to hold public offices that had been closed to them under the Second Polish Republic. Jewish students still had unpleasant memories of the outbreaks of anti-Semitic attacks in L'viv in the last years before the war, but this did not mean that the Jewish youth was satisfied with the new regime or were immune from repression. Members of the Zionist youth organization Akiwa were persecuted and went underground.¹⁴⁰ Jewish teachers, however, had every reason to view the Soviet authorities positively.¹⁴¹ Formerly without any prospects of being employed as teachers in state schools, younger teachers were now able to join the teaching profession.¹⁴² Some local Jews and refugees from the German-occupied territories grasped the opportunities now available to them. For the first time, Ukrainians and Poles were confronted with a sizable number of civil servants and police who were Jewish.¹⁴³ For the Jewish population this signified an improvement compared to the prewar years. The postulated nondiscrimination of Jews and the fight against anti-Semitism were the most important reasons for the pro-Soviet sympathies of some Jews.¹⁴⁴ But when talking to Communist Party members, contemporary witnesses received the impression that party members, too, were not free of anti-Semitic sentiments.¹⁴⁵ Countess Lanckorońska met "very civilized officers of the Red Army, particularly native Russians" who did not trouble to conceal their antipathy toward the NKVD and its methods. She found them to be extremely anti-Semitic with regard to Jews in the NKVD who, in the opinion of the countess, were "numerically in the majority in this institution."¹⁴⁶

The Soviet authorities met with some successes in their attempts to garner the support of at least some sections of various national intelligentsias. Although most Jewish and Polish authors, among them Leon Pasternak, Ostap Ortwin, and Tadeusz Hollender, rarely if ever visited the club of the Soviet Writers' Union; socialist authors such as Wanda Wasilewska, Jerzy Borejsza, Jerzy Putrament, Stanisław Jerzy Lec, and Tadeusz Boy-Żeleński participated in union life and publicly sympathized with the Soviet Union. On September 17, 1940, the first anniversary of the Soviet invasion, fifty-eight L'viv authors joined the Writers' Union.¹⁴⁷ Pro-Soviet declarations from these authors only discredited them in the eyes of most Poles. Even decades later, eyewitnesses continued to express their contempt for the "false artistic and scientific elite," referring to them as "false moral authorities."¹⁴⁸

In the territories under Soviet rule, the willingness to cooperate with the occupiers went further than in the Generalgouvernement. The prospect of a socialist Poland was still better than subsisting as slaves under German rule. Moreover, until the discovery by the Wehrmacht of the mass graves in Katyn in April 1943 Polish society did not know about the murder of Polish prisoner-of-war officers.¹⁴⁹ The Jewish population had even more reason to hope for a continuation of Soviet rule. The refugee Stanisław Różycki, a Jewish Pole, initially wrote in his diary how much he felt his life inside the Soviet sphere of influence as a separation from civilized European culture.¹⁵⁰ But Różycki was even able to put a positive spin on the deportation of Jewish refugees to the east. In L'viv, the NKVD was terrorizing the population and people were going hungry. In the German-occupied territories, there was "war, hunger, disease, summary executions by shooting, the ghetto, the star of David, the camps." In Russia's heartland, there was nevertheless peace; there was employment, enough food, and equal citizenship rights. There were no differences between Jews and non-Jews.[151]

Once it became apparent that the strategy to win the sympathies of Ukrainians was faltering, Soviet policy changed tack. Galician Ukrainians tended to be anti-communists, and many of them sympathized with the Organization of Ukrainian Nationalists. In the summer of 1940, the Soviet authorities began granting Poles concessions with regard to cultural policies.[152] Writer Wanda Wasilewska believed that she was personally responsible for convincing Stalin during a private conversation that the regional authorities were making a mistake in their treatment of the Polish population. This kind of abrupt change of direction was typical of the Stalin era. On July 3, 1940, Stalin wrote to the L'viv oblast party committee that reports had come to his ears of "unlawful" and rough behavior by the authorities towards Poles, with suppression of the Polish language and Poles being forced to declare themselves as Ukrainians. Stalin called for a policy of "Polish-Ukrainian brotherhood." The oblast party leadership in L'viv promptly sent out the appropriate instructions to the lower levels in the party and state.[153] The propaganda against the "Poland of the masters" was toned down. Poles now had better chances of getting jobs in the administration, teachers were rehired, and Polish artists in particular were courted. In the fall, some of the families deported to Kazakhstan were even allowed to return. In higher education, Polish professors no longer faced reprisals for using Polish as their language of instruction. Some professors were invited to Moscow to learn about the Soviet university system. Much speculation was generated by the fact that former prime minister Kazimierz Bartel, a mathematician, also took part in the trip. Rumors circulated that he had been offered the opportunity to form a Soviet–Polish government. A further indication of the improved status of Poles was the expansion in the number of Polish publications. While *Czerwony Sztandar* remained the only daily Polish-language newspaper, the important literary journal *Nowe Widnokręgi* (*New Horizons*), appeared in print for the first time in 1941, together with the quarterly *Almanach Literacki* (*Literary Almanac*); the Communist Union of Youth newspaper *Młodzież Stalinowska* (*Stalinist Youth*), which appeared three times a week; and *Pionerzy* (*Pioneers*), a monthly magazine for children.[154]

The most significant event marking this change of policy was the celebration commemorating the eighty-fifth anniversary of the death of Adam Mickiewicz, Poland's national poet. At the end of August 1940, an organizational committee chaired by Tadeusz Boy-Żeleński was set up, and a series of commemorative events were held on November 25 and 26, 1940. An exhibition was opened in the former Ossolineum institute, a three-day conference was held at the university, and a special gala event, attended by top Soviet oblast officials, was staged in the Opera House, where well-known actors read passages from

Mickiewicz's works in Polish, Ukrainian, Yiddish, and Russian. The celebrations were broadcast live on L'viv radio. Polish schools and cultural centers also staged events in celebration of Mickiewicz. This reversal of policy showed that the Soviet Union was prepared to accept the Poles as a nationality and to grant them a degree of cultural freedom. These new policies in the summer of 1940 also indicated that at this point the Soviet government was still acting on the assumption that the Polish minority would remain in the occupied territories for a long time to come.[155]

The Sovietization of eastern Poland did not go smoothly and faced considerable opposition. A Polish resistance movement had formed prior to the occupation of L'viv. A local group of the Polish Organization for the Struggle for Freedom (Polska Organizacja Walki o Wolność) founded by General Marian Januszajtis-Żegota operated in L'viv between September and December 1939. The Paris-based government sent a delegate to L'viv in mid-December to create a local branch of the Union for Armed Struggle (Związek Walki Zbrojnej, ZWZ). A few days later, a representative of General Michał Tokarzewski-Karaszewicz arrived from Warsaw and appointed Lieutenant Colonel Jan Sokołowski head of the Service for Poland's Victory (Służba Zwycięstwu Polski). Sokołowski, however, refused to submit to the ZWZ leadership in Paris, and subsequently, there were two rival ZWZ organizations operating in L'viv, until Sokołowski founded his own group in the spring of 1940.[156]

It proved impossible to consolidate the Polish resistance movement. Its members had little experience of conspiratorial activities while the Soviet side was very experienced in discovering and destroying conspiracies of counter-revolutionary organizations, whether real or imagined. The NKVD relied on the willingness of opportunists and ideological fellow travelers to divulge information, together with torture and threats against the family members of prisoners, to create a vast network of informants. After a failed attempt to assassinate Wanda Wasilewska on April 26, 1940, and the wave of arrests that followed, the Polish underground was rendered largely inoperative until the Germans invaded.[157]

The expropriations, dismissals, arrests, and deportations demoralized the population, and the rapidity of the French defeat particularly depressed the Poles and the Jews. A wave of suicides followed. One contemporary witness described the despairing mood among young people who were "without any perspectives for the future."[158] The regional command of the Polish underground had a different impression and noted a sustained feeling of Polish patriotism among the working class and a "firm determination to perform an act of liberation" among Polish youth.[159]

Passive resistance to Soviet rule was widespread. Jokes about the disparities between propaganda and reality, the idiocies of the Soviet bureaucracy, and the low intelligence of Soviet bureaucrats were shared and enjoyed by many. The low caliber of the Soviet cadres may have been the reason for the widespread feeling of cultural superiority over the new masters. Many people in L'viv continued to sneer at the Russian lack of "culture." One popular, oft-repeated story described the wives of Russian officers attending the opera in their newly acquired nightgowns.[160] Many people listened to foreign radio broadcasts and read underground newspapers, and some hid refugees. The Polish underground attacked those it considered political collaborators.[161] Sometimes, during public gatherings, Polish patriotism was voiced despite the potential consequences. At one youth meeting, amid the usual speeches attacking the Second Polish Republic, a young man seized the microphone and began reciting the names of great events in Polish history, from the Battle of Grunwald when the Kingdom of Poland defeated the Teutonic Order in 1410, to the "Miracle at the Vistula," when the Poles had driven back the Red Army in 1920. The communists in the audience began singing "The International," but the sound of their singing was drowned out by Polish youths singing "Rota" (The Oath) and "My chcemy Boga" (We Want God).[162]

In the almost hopeless situation created by Soviet rule, Poles drew inspiration and confidence from their history, in particular from the memory of the 1918 "Defense of Lwów" (Obrona Lwowa). Lessons in Polish history at home counteracted the Soviet curriculum taught in schools. And the lessons from Polish history were, in their turn, linked to sites of memory. In 1940 Wanda Jóźwiak began attending the Sienkiewicz School: "My father told us the story of the battle for Lwów in 1918 when this school had been a military outpost. We were very proud to be educated here."[163]

On November 1 and November 22—All-Saints' Day and the day on which the Ukrainian troops had left L'viv, respectively—Roman Catholic churches were filled to overflowing, and a number of impromptu rallies were held.[164] The Cemetery of the Defenders of Lwów was an important site of patriotic demonstrations. In November 1939 Poles laid wreaths at the local Tomb of the Unknown Soldier in memory of those who had fought for Polish independence. The crowd spontaneously cheered an independent Poland, France, and England and acclaimed Władysław Raczkiewicz (the president in exile), General Władysław Sikorski (the premier in exile), and General Józef Haller (whose trooops had defeated the Galician Ukrainians in 1919). The participants in the demonstration sang "Dąbrowski's Mazurka" (the Polish national anthem) twice, "Rota," and "Boże coś Polskę" (God save Poland). The NKVD arrested some of the participants. Similar incidents occurred on November 1, 1940. Throughout the period of Soviet occupation, some unknown person or persons regularly laid wreaths on the graves of Polish soldiers who had died fighting the Soviets or Germans in 1939.[165]

Interethnic Patterns of Perception

The Soviet invasion had created a new space of experience, but traditional interpretive patterns, experiences from World War I and the interwar period, and expectations about the future influenced the way the local population perceived the Soviet occupation. The regional command of the Polish Home Army took the behavior of some Jewish youths as a basis for more generalized accusations.[166] The local command of the Home Army accused Jews of collaborating with the Soviets, of denouncing Poles, of profiting from their misery, and of taking over their positions.[167] Jewish communists in particular were accused of having used meetings to incite the "hatred of the Jewish masses" against the Polish population under the pretext of fighting the Polish bourgeoisie.[168] The phrase "Jewish masses" was shorthand for the general threat posed by Jews. One report by the Home Army from February 1940 depicted only impoverished Christian villagers and the Jewish underclasses as being pro-Soviet. According to the report, the "Jewish crowd" was not only showing its sympathies towards the occupiers, it was also seeking to get jobs in the administration and the militia. The general hatred of the Bolsheviks was leading to an increased hatred of Jews on the part of the peasants and lower middle classes.[169] Instances like the ones described in the following were laid at the door of the entire Jewish population. At an election rally of students from the polytechnic, Jewish students accused four of their Polish fellow students of being anti-Semites and members of nationalist organizations. The four students were beaten and subsequently arrested.[170]

The militia set up after the invasion of the Red Army was a particular object of the population's hatred as—at least until the NKVD units arrived—it exercised an arbitrary and despotic authority.[171] Militiamen wore red armbands, carried out searches and roadside checks, and helped the NKVD with its arrests.[172] According to Polish eyewitnesses the militia was primarily made up of "the scum of the suburbs of Ukrainian and Jewish communist nationality."[173] Contemporary Polish witnesses equated the militia with the Jewish population. The Jews—according to a report of the Home Army—had aroused the hatred and loathing of Polish society through their deeds. Polish society was convinced that the Jews bore the responsibility for Poland's misfortune.[174]

Concierges played an important role in controlling the population and as informers of the NKVD. Here again, Poles predominantly noted the presence of Jews and to a limited extent of Ukrainians in these roles or as informers in general.[175] "The great part of the Polish population hid to avoid arrests and was gripped by a denunciation psychosis. It truly viewed every unknown person as an informer of the NKVD. The NKVD left some Poles in office, exploited them, arrested them in the end and deported them deep into the heartland of Russia."[176] One eyewitness accused Ukrainians, "the grey Jewish multitude," and Polish criminals of having supported the NKVD in its persecution of Polish elites.[177] Others believed that the NKVD was recruited from the criminal classes and national minorities.[178]

Polish observers knew that many rich Jews and members of the Bund and of Zionist organizations had been arrested and deported, but this knowledge did not change their reports as they argued speciously that the Zionists had had "no influence on the masses."[179] The reports leave no doubt that Poles believed Jews were pursuing a policy hostile to Poland. In a memorandum from the summer of 1942, the Jewish population was still considered a "natural sphere of influence for Soviet Russia" and as the principal supporters of Bolshevik rule in eastern Poland.[180] Some counterexamples were noted, but these had no impact on the general opinion: "Among the Jews there are cases of active aid given to persecuted Poles, liberating them from the hands of furious and shouting Jewish mobs, but this behavior by certain Jewish groups can never take away their culpability for the behavior of Jews during the Bolshevik invasion."[181]

While Polish eyewitnesses promoted a differentiated view of the Polish population, Ukrainians and Jews were often collectively accused of collaboration.[182] The records of the policeman Mieczysław Jasiński show that it was possible to have a more discriminating view of the behavior of the Jewish population. He recognized that the relationship of the Jewish population to the Soviet authorities was cooling: "As far as the Jewish population is concerned, the poorer part showed itself satisfied with the invasion of the region of Lesser Poland by the Soviet Army, but within a short time, in other words, after restrictions were placed on the trades which earned them their livelihoods, they were disappointed and adopted a wait-and-see approach. In contrast, the rich Jewish class, when you consider their panic-fuelled fear of the Germans, was forced to pretend itself satisfied; but many were not prepared to do so, the majority were negatively disposed towards them [the Soviets]."[183]

The relationship between the Jewish and Polish populations increasingly deteriorated. A number of Poles broke off contacts to Jews and in the words of one Jewish author "a certain alienation" developed between them.[184]

Some Jewish Poles sharply criticized the behavior of their co-religionists. Stanisław Różycki even blamed Jews for the growing anti-Semitism in the Ukrainian and Polish populations. The relationship of the other nationalities to the Jews had always been "tense" to some degree, and he believed this was "exclusively caused by the Jews pressing for positions of leadership."[185] Another author was of the opinion that well-off Jews had occupied the majority of the top jobs as these offered the best protection against repressive measures.[186] Other sources reported that Jewish youth zealously attended Soviet events and that Jewish craftspeople, intellectuals, and workmen worked in state institutions.[187] Members of the Jewish population were also believed to have played an important role in banks and trusts. One eyewitness reported that 90 percent of persons working in banks and trusts were Jews.[188] Many Jewish teachers had gone into the countryside to help propagate the idea of collectivization. The peasants could therefore be excused for having the impression that everything was the fault of the Jews.[189] Despite all the problems, trade—according to another eyewitness—continued to flourish and persons working in trade, mainly Jews, profited.[190]

Jewish eyewitnesses also wrote in detail about the behavior of the other ethnic groups. The Jewish witnesses described the Ukrainization of the authorities and institutions of education but also noted that many Poles had retained their jobs.[191] Różycki observed that the Poles deeply hated the Bolsheviks and were suspicious of all overtures made to them by the Soviet side, while the Ukrainians were awaiting the Germans: "Only the Jews do not waver, regardless of their feelings or their rational and moderate attitude toward the union; although they suffered, their possessions were seized, and their families were deported, nevertheless they counted only on Russia, because everything is better than the Germans."[192]

One refugee described hearing about acts of vengeance against Poles carried out by Jews but had not personally seen or experienced such acts. Once while talking to an acquaintance in Polish he had been accosted by a Jewish passerby who asked him if he was perhaps dissatisfied with Soviet rule. Another time the refugee was approached by a well-known anti-Semite who asked him to forget the old tales of bygone events.[193] Another eyewitness commented that during the period of Soviet occupation, friendships with Jews were a good recommendation for Poles.[194]

The Polish underground organization did not only accuse Jews but also accused Ukrainians of disloyalty to the Polish state, of collaborating with the Soviets and of driving out Poles from the administration and from industry, trade, the universities, and the education system.[195] However, this behavior, if carried out by Ukrainians, was not interpreted as an expression of communist or pro-Soviet feelings, and Polish perceptions of it differed fundamentally from the Polish interpretation of Jewish behavior. One report explicitly stated that the Ukrainian elite remained entirely nationalist and kept its distance from the regime despite being granted privileges.[196]

Jewish authors also accused the Ukrainians of opportunism, but it was also understood that this opportunism took advantage of the additional freedoms obtained to pursue the Ukrainians' own nationalist interests. Ukrainian nationalism—one author commented—survived under a cloak of collaboration.[197] One Jewish eyewitness believed that the Soviets had alienated the Ukrainians and strengthened Ukrainian nationalism: all Ukrainians sympathized with Germany.[198]

The antagonism between Poles and Ukrainians decreased slightly during the final phase of Soviet occupation, when the Soviet occupying power became a common object of hatred.[199] At least at the universities, all Galicians—according to one Jewish author—were united by their distrust of their new colleagues from the Soviet Union.[200] This view is confirmed by the Ukrainian scholar Semchyshyn: "In short—it was US and the newcomers were THEM."[201]

The Polish and the Ukrainian population were—according to reports by the Polish underground—united not just by their common hostility to the regime but also by their shared hatred of Jews, who were perceived as having profited from Soviet rule. A Polish eyewitness called it a "sad paradox" that this hatred of Jews represented practically "the only bridge of communication between Poles and Ukrainians." This hatred, he continued, went beyond even the hatred directed against the Bolsheviks, and the mounting pressures were only awaiting the right moment to be released.[202]

The vague hope of a more general feeling of solidarity among the population of L'viv forged in the crucible of their common suffering ended abruptly with the German attack on the Soviet Union. The Ukrainian press published in the Generalgouvernement took up the old propaganda slogans of "Judeo-communism" and accused the Jews of profiting from the Soviet occupation and of denouncing Ukrainian resistance fighters to the Soviet security forces. This not only was consistent with the anti-Semitic attitude of the OUN[203] but also reflected the widespread mood of the Ukrainian population. Jews were seen as a "second-rate enemy" with links to bolshevism and were collectively held responsible for Soviet actions.[204] The Second General Congress of the OUN-B in April 1941 stated in its resolution: "The Jews in the U.S.S.R. constitute the most faithful supporters of the ruling Bolshevik regime and the vanguard of Muscovite imperialism in the Ukraine. The Muscovite-Bolshevik government exploits the anti-Jewish sentiments of the Ukrainian masses to divert their attention away from the true cause of their misfortune and to channel them in times of frustration into pogroms on Jews. The OUN fights the Jews as the props of the Muscovite-Bolshevik regime and it simultaneously makes them conscious of the fact that the principal foe is Moscow."[205]

However, other voices also persisted. Milena Rudnyts'ka, chairwoman of the women's organization Soiuz Ukraïnok, did not agree with the comprehensive accusation of collaboration leveled against the Jews. Rudnyts'ka was of the opinion that the "Jews as a whole are as dissatisfied as we are." Their middle class was being destroyed, as was their trade. However, Rudnyts'ka was able to derive something positive from the latter situation: "This is more important for us from a national standpoint than the dissolution of large landed properties. In the administrative bodies they [the Bolsheviks] have employed Jews, but with the exception of them [the Jews] they often have nobody else on whom they can depend."[206]

This revives a theme in Polish and Ukrainian nationalist discourse which goes back to the end of the nineteenth century. According to this train of thought, the strong position of Jews in the free professions and in the middle class was perceived as hindering the rise of a Polish or Ukrainian middle class, thereby preventing the modernization of both Poles and Ukrainians.[207]

In Ukrainian and Polish sources, it is notable that when they rate Jewish behavior, neither Ukrainians nor Poles take account of the specific situation of the Jewish population in September 1939. Poles interpreted Jewish cooperation in Soviet institutions as a betrayal of the Polish state, and for both Poles and Ukrainians it served as the final piece of evidence whereby Jewishness was identified with bolshevism. While Poles and Ukrainians were prepared—despite all their enmity—to concede that both had a right to promote the interests of their own respective group, they refused to acknowledge that Jews might have the same right. Christian citizens collectively held all Jewish fellow citizens liable—not just for the activities of L'viv Jews working in Soviet institutions but also for the activities and acts committed by Soviet cadres of Jewish origin newly come to the city.

The Soviet occupation policy was driven primarily by socio-political and power political considerations and only in the second instance by ethnopolitical categories. But the perceptions of the local population were governed by ethnic patterns of perception. And Soviet actions were construed and reinterpreted accordingly. All ethnic groups were affected when the Soviet authorities pursued class-war policies against the prewar elites, but Poles were affected most by such measures because of their dominant position before the war. Survival strategies, which were observed with understanding if followed by members of the person's own group, were used to reproach "the others" and were categorized based on the traditional patterns used to interpret the behavior of other ethnicities. Only actions that confirmed these stereotypes were "experienced" and cemented. Contradictory information was noted but did not flow into the process of interpretation. And so it was primarily the Jews who were classified by the other two major groups as protégés or even accomplices of the Soviet regime. Reports about the confiscation of Jewish property, the arrests of Jewish political leaders and many rabbis, and the deportation of tens of thousands of Jewish refugees were duly noted, but no conclusions were drawn from these events. But the actions of some Jewish youths and of Soviet officials of Jewish origin and the willingness of refugees to accept jobs in the Soviet administration and militia were collectively laid at the door of Jews and used to reproach the Jews of L'viv.

Sixth Regime Change: Racial Policies, Exploitation, and Genocide

Invasion

The Jews could not yet know the terrible fate awaiting them, but they were horrified by the German attack. Refugees prepared to flee again and the few local Jewish communists left.²⁰⁸ But the roads were blocked by the departing Red Army, making escape almost impossible.²⁰⁹ On the day of the German invasion, the NKVD and the NKGB carried out all pending death sentences; 108 persons were shot in L'viv alone. At the same time, the NKVD prepared to remove some five thousand detainees. When rapid advance of the Wehrmacht prevented their deportation, the regional NKVD head ordered his officials to quit the city and leave the prisoners behind in locked cells. In Łącki Prison, run by the NKGB, the shooting of the prisoners commenced immediately. A few of the prisoners managed to survive under the bodies of their murdered fellow prisoners. On June 24, the approximately 3,700 prisoners held in the now unguarded Brygidki Prison attempted to flee. When an NKVD patrol noticed this, the patrol blocked the exit, and a company of soldiers drove the prisoners back into their cells. Only about 220 to 362 people were able to flee. The NKVD now also began shooting the political prisoners, dangerous criminals, and all persons who had committed "crimes against socialist property." The rest of the prisoners were released. The majority of victims were Ukrainians, about one-quarter were Poles. A considerable number of Jewish prisoners were also murdered. Using Soviet sources, the Polish historian Grzegorz Hryciuk has come to the conclusion that between 3,100 and 3,500 prisoners were murdered. Eyewitnesses spoke of four to seven thousand victims.²¹⁰ The Polish historian Krzystof Popiński has estimated that in the summer of 1941, between twenty and thirty thousand of the one hundred thousand prisoners in the occupied regions of eastern Poland were murdered or did not survive the hardships of deportation.²¹¹

Prior to the entry of the Wehrmacht, Ukrainian nationalists attempted an uprising, taking advantage of the general confusion to attack Soviet officials but also to carry out their first attacks on Jews.²¹² The NKVD and the Red Army quickly brought the situation under control again, and until the Wehrmacht arrived no further attempts were made to launch an uprising.²¹³ After the withdrawal of the Soviet Army, L'viv was in chaos. Shops and empty flats were looted. Numerous robberies, fights, and murders occurred. Some used the period of anarchy when all authority was absent to revenge themselves on collaborators and Soviet agents.²¹⁴ Jewish eyewitnesses observed that the mood of the Polish population appeared contradictory. On one hand, there was a certain feeling of schadenfreude toward the Jews, Bolsheviks, and Russians; on the other hand, the Poles secretly feared the Ukrainians and Germans.²¹⁵

Poles had good reason to be afraid. According to Różycki, Ukrainians controlled every house and handed Jews and Poles over to a newly created Ukrainian militia.²¹⁶ Long queues began forming in front of grocery shops. Jews standing in the queues were insulted and pushed out of the queue.²¹⁷ Some Ukrainians and Poles stopped greeting Jews. However, not everybody behaved like that. Różycki noticed that many workers and intellectuals had not changed their behavior. He came to the conclusion that the Ukrainians actually only hated the Poles, but from base motives, they were also prepared to carry out anti-Jewish pogroms.[218] Another witness, writing in Yiddish, feared not only the Ukrainians but also the Poles, viewing both groups as "capable of sinking their teeth into the Jews."[219]

The first German troops reached the outskirts of L'viv on June 30, 1941. The Jewish population huddled fearfully in their homes.[220] Eyewitnesses agreed that the Ukrainian population greeted the German units enthusiastically; in the words of one author, "the Ukrainians welcomed the Germans with flowers, laughter, joy, full of hope and illusions, as rescuers and liberators."[221] Opinions differed regarding the behavior of the Polish population. Some reported that the Poles—with certain exceptions—remained indifferent.[222] One Jewish author reported that the Poles greeted the German soldiers joyfully and that the whole Polish population hurried to them bearing flowers in their hands.[223] No other eyewitness reports such a reception, but the L'viv Command of the Home Army confirmed that the Germans were received in a friendly manner, sometimes even with sympathy.[224] Eyewitnesses were impressed by the German soldiers. In contrast to the Soviet soldiers, the German soldiers were well nourished, their uniforms were clean, and their equipment was good.[225] The gold-and-blue Ukrainian flag flew next to the swastika. Posters by the Bandera faction of the OUN calling for a "Ukraine for the Ukrainians" were everywhere.[226]

"Samostijna Ukraïna"[227] and the Pogrom

The Ukrainian flags and posters had been put up by Ukrainian nationalists who had arrived in L'viv together with the German army. The OUN, which had been based in German-occupied central Poland, had split in early 1940, but both OUN factions—the OUN-B (consisting largely of the movement's younger members around Stepan Bandera) and the OUN-M (consisting mostly of the movement's older members and loyal to Andrij Mel'nyk)—continued to push for a united, independent Ukrainian state by joining forces with the German Reich.[228] There had been several previous attempts by Ukrainian politicians to unite the Ukrainian national movement. Volodymyr Kubijovych, chairman of the Ukrainian Central Committee (Ukraïns'kyj Tsentral'nyj Komitet, UTsK) in Craców,[229] wanted to unite all forces (with the notable exception of the Bandera faction) according to the "Führer principle." Bandera, on the other hand, planned to create a Ukrainian National Committee (but without the Mel'nyk faction) that would negotiate with the German government. The German authorities did not care for these initiatives. The Reich Security Main Office (Reichssicherheitshauptamt, RSHA) ordered that "every departure of important Ukrainians in this context for the newly occupied territories" had to be prevented to postpone the constitution of an All-Ukrainian council.[230]

But the security forces and the Wehrmacht had no objections to the creation of two Ukrainian battalions (known, respectively, as Nachtigall and Roland) by the German military counterintelligence service, Abwehr, with seven hundred men. At the same time the OUN-B organized several hundred small so-called expeditionary groups (*pokhidni hrupy*), each between seven and twelve men strong, which entered the newly conquered territories in the wake of the Wehrmacht. These Ukrainian expeditionary groups worked for the German army as translators and intermediaries to the local population but they also had a hidden agenda. Stepan Bandera, the head of the OUN-B, had ordered them to set up a Ukrainian administration and lay the foundations for a Ukrainian state. The aim was to confront the German authorities with a fait accompli.[231]

Bandera's emissary Jaroslav Stets'ko ignored German orders to go to Chełm, traveling instead to L'viv. He met with various local Ukrainian leaders in the Prosvita building to proclaim a Ukrainian state.[232] A short time later, two German Abwehr officers (Hans Koch and Wilhelm Ernst zu Eickern), who had learned of Stets'ko's intentions when they arrived at the residence of the Greek Catholic archbishop, succeeded in entering the building through a side entrance. The main entrance was blocked by a large crowd. The assembly greeted them with "boundless enthusiasm." Hans Koch addressed the meeting but was careful to avoid any recognition of the proclamation: "Koch ended with a *Sieg Heil* for the *Führer*, in which he was enthusiastically joined by the chairman and the meeting." When Stets'ko followed this up by calling for cheers for Stepan Bandera, Ernst zur Eickern and Koch left the meeting. Stets'ko did not let this dampen his enthusiasm. He betook himself directly to L'viv radio station, where he persuaded the German duty officer to broadcast the news of the creation of a Ukrainian government. Over the next few days Stet'sko tried hard to obtain German approval of the proclamation but failed. There was no room in the German plans of a "*Lebensraum* in the East" for an independent or even semi-independent Ukrainian state.[233]

While Stets'ko was proclaiming a Ukrainian state, members of the Ukrainian expeditionary groups and local people went to the prisons to look for friends and relatives, where they discovered the mass graves of executed prisoners. The culprits—Soviet prison guards—had already left the city, but many Ukrainians and Poles believed that the NKVD was controlled by Jews and held the Jews collectively responsible for the prison murders and other Soviet crimes. The *pokhidny hrupy* had helped to set up a local militia, which now turned its ire against the Jewish population.[234] Ukrainian patrols rounded up Jews in the street, beating men and women, young and old. From the window of his house, on July 1, 1941, retired law professor Maurycy Allerhand saw militiamen, using sticks and whips, beating Jews. He recognized them as Ukrainians, not just by their blue and gold armbands but also by the Ukrainian insults they shouted at the Jews. Women and men, children and old people were chased down, beaten, and taken to the prisons.²³⁵ Anastasja Klymkova remembered: "Men, young Ukrainian men wearing stickers in the colors blue and gold on their marine blue epaulettes entered the houses and took Jewish lawyers, doctors, merchants and others to Łącki Street from whence they never returned." False rumors about prisoners who had been terribly tortured and crucified circulated in the city.²³⁶

An enormous crowd assembled in front of the prisons; Jews were made to run the gauntlet of the crowd.²³⁷ Allerhand's adult son Jonatan was captured by Ukrainians and taken to Brygidka Prison by a German soldier. His wife and son were able to escape with the help of a German officer, but in Brygidka Jonatan Allerhand and about one thousand other Jews were forced to remove and clean the bodies. German soldiers wearing gas masks watched the scene. Ukrainian militiamen beat Jews and constantly threatened to shoot them. Jonatan Allerhand was one of very few to survive. Twelve wounds were counted on his body after he returned home.²³⁸ It is not known how many Jews were murdered during this pogrom. Estimates range from four to eight thousand victims.²³⁹ Holocaust survivor Jakub Dentel described the events: "I saw thousands of mutilated Jews beaten in the most brutal fashion, women stripped until they were completely naked and children covered in blood, I saw old men bleeding to death on the streets and German heroes who delighted in this terrible spectacle and photographed it."²⁴⁰

The anti-Semitic violence was tolerated by the German military authorities and played into the hands of the SS. A secret order by Reinhard Heydrich, chief of the security service and security police and head of the Reich Security Main Office (Reichssicherheitshauptamt, RSHA), had recommended inciting the local population to commit acts of anti-Jewish violence, but there is no evidence that German agitators were responsible for the L'viv pogrom. The first Nazi killing squad, the Sonderkommando 4b, arrived in L'viv after the pogrom had already started.²⁴¹

Some observers reported that the Ukrainian Nachtigall battalion had marched through the streets chanting, "Death to the Muscovite-Jewish commune."²⁴² For Różycki, the Ukrainians were collectively responsible for the pogrom.²⁴³ Other authors did not blame the entire Ukrainian population. They accused "janitors, Ukrainian youths, hysterical women and simple people from the criminal community," absolving the Polish population and the Ukrainian intelligentsia of any responsibility for such acts:²⁴⁴ "The pogrom and repressive activities were only carried out by the lower classes, the scum of the Ukrainians."²⁴⁵ According to a report by the Polish underground, the pogrom had been ordered by the Germans and "had been carried out by Ukrainian and Polish scum."²⁴⁶ This viewpoint, according to Maurycy Allerhand, was shared by the Ukrainian elite, even if they did not directly accuse Polish antisocial elements of being among the offenders.²⁴⁷ Allerhand himself believed that the German frontline soldiers had not behaved badly on the first day but that the military had given the Ukrainian population a free hand to carry out this "legal pogrom."[248]

Another eyewitness believed that "sinister Ukrainians, Petljura supporters and old pogromists" had begun the pogrom on their own initiative. But Allerhand and other eyewitnesses also reported the active participation of German soldiers, who, in some streets, helped Ukrainians to round up Jews. German soldiers and officers watched the atrocities; some took photographs and there was even a film crew present.[249] According to Jewish eyewitness reports, individual soldiers and members of the SS also participated directly in the murders.[250] The Germans later used the films and some of the photographs for propaganda purposes to show how deeply the Ukrainians hated the Jews.[251]

According to reports by the German Army, the pogrom had not been instigated but had erupted spontaneously. The duty log of the First Mountain Division, the first German unit to reach L'viv, noted on June 30 (1:15 p.m.), "There is frantic bitterness among the population about the infamous deeds of the Bolshevists, and these feelings are vented against the resident Jews of the town who have always worked together with the Bolshevists."[252] The following day, at seven in the evening, the commanding officers of the First Mountain Division held a meeting on L'viv's Castle Hill. The comment entered into the divisional duty log reads as follows: "At the urging of the Ukrainian population, there was a veritable pogrom against Jews and Russians in L'viv on 1.7. . . . During the officers' meeting one could hear shooting in the G.P.U. prison in L'viv, where Jews had to bury the Ukrainians (several thousands) murdered in the past few weeks by the Russians after Jewish denunciations."[253]

The report of the commander of Battalion 800 for July 1was very similar: "The butcheries by the Reds have aroused the utmost rage. On 30.6.41 and 1.7., there were increased acts of violence against Jews. The deployed police forces [the Ukrainian militia] showed themselves to be not up to the job. They stirred up the population with their brutal and offensive behavior against defenseless persons."[254]

With very few exceptions, the German soldiers, officers, and officials arriving in East Galicia had no knowledge of the language or country. They viewed the local ethnic relationships through the prism of anti-Semitism acquired during eight years of Nazi rule. The soldiers were therefore predisposed to believe that the pogroms were a spontaneous expression of popular will. Jonatan Allerhand talked with a German soldier who was firmly convinced that Jews had murdered the Ukrainian prisoners. The soldier was astonished when Allerhand explained the true circumstances.[255] Allerhand's father and other Jewish eyewitnesses also noted that both soldiers and officers firmly believed that Jews had been the mainstay of Soviet rule and were to blame for the murders in the prisons.[256]

Already in the first days of German occupation, the Germans began flooding western Ukraine with anti-Semitic pamphlets, posters, caricatures, and proclamations. These tropes were taken up and disseminated further in radio broadcasts and the legal Ukrainian press.[257] Apart from the propaganda articles in the press, it is difficult to find any contemporary Ukrainian documents that refer to the pogrom or discuss Jewish–Ukrainian relations during the war. I therefore must rely here primarily on contemporary memoirs. Semchyshyn held "urban scum" to be responsible for the bloody pogrom, believing that many of the people wearing badges in the Ukrainian colors yellow and blue were not Ukrainians.[258] Just how difficult it was for the urban Ukrainian elite to accept the fact that the pogrom had been carried out by Ukrainians is shown by the reports of conversations between Jewish eyewitnesses and their Ukrainian acquaintances.[259] The Greek Catholic archbishop Andrij Sheptyts'kyj evaded the question about the participation of Ukrainians in his letter to Pope Pius XII, written in August 1942. He merely noted that at the beginning of the war the German occupying forces had tried to prove that local citizens or police were the offenders, but the Germans had then began to kill their victims on the streets in full view of all bystanders without any sign of shame.[260]

L'viv was not an exceptional case. Pogroms, the majority carried out by Ukrainians, occurred in many East Galician cities. In L'viv, the NKVD prison murders were an important motive for the pogrom, but pogroms also occurred in villages and towns where no prison murders had taken place. Therefore, one has to look for additional reasons. The Ukrainian *pokhidny hrupy* played an important role in inciting the local population and creating a Ukrainian militia, but it is not clear whether they had been instructed to instigate a pogrom by leaders of the OUN. As in most pogroms, one of the most important motives was greed. Jews were not only beaten but also robbed and blackmailed.[261] Although in Buczacz members of the Ukrainian intelligentsia called on their fellow Ukrainians to take revenge on the Jews, no similar appeals are known to been issued by the Ukrainian intelligentsia in L'viv.[262]

The pogrom was only the beginning of Jewish suffering. The chief of the security service (Sicherheitsdienst, SD) and the security police (Sicherheitspolizei, SiPo) and head of the RSHA, Reinhard Heydrich had given the order to the Einsatzkommandos, the special ops killing squads, to kill all members of the Jewish intelligentsia and all Communist Party functionaries during the advance.[263] The chief of the SiPo and the SD in the Generalgouvernement reported at the end of July that the Jews in the newly conquered territories "continued to behave provocatively."[264] The mass murders of Jews are mentioned almost incidentally: "Despite ongoing liquidations impudent and brazen behavior." The Jews were said to be the originators of "anti-German rumors."[265] Jews were described as continuing to behave "rebelliously" and as sabotaging German orders.[266]

During the advance, reports "of sightings of Russian paratroopers, gangs and hidden Bolshevists" became increasingly frequent. The German security services did not believe all the reports but commented that "in many cases the total cleansing of localities of Bolshevists, Jews and antisocial elements following complaints was successful." The head of police blamed the exaggerations on "what could be termed the childish inability of the population" to express itself "clearly and unequivocally." By this he meant the scruples of people who did not want to be responsible for the deaths of their neighbors, with repeated instances of informers retracting their statements when they realized that the lives of the accused were at stake.[267]

The chief of the SiPo and the SD identified three main sources of danger for the German occupiers: "subversive Bolshevik activities," the "passive resistance by disappointed peasant masses," and "the Jews." Even the immediate "one hundred percent eradication of the Jews" would not eliminate the political source of danger. "Bolshevist work depends on Jews, Russians, Georgians, Armenians, Poles, Latvians, Ukrainians; the Bolshevist organization is in no way identical with the Jewish population." He believed that the goal of "political and police protection will fail if the principal task of destroying the communist organization were to be given only secondary or tertiary priority behind the operationally easier task of eliminating the Jews. Moreover the concentration on Bolshevist functionaries robs the Jews of their ablest bodies, with the solution to the problem of the Jews more and more becoming a purely organizational problem."[268]

But the chief of the SiPo and the SD considered the immediate murder of the Jews neither economically expedient nor useful for the occupation. The Jews were needed for the reconstruction of industrial production and the municipal administration. Heydrich therefore recommended "solving the Jewish problem through extensive use of the labor of Jews." This would "result in the gradual liquidation of the Jews."[269]

On Heydrich's order, the Einsatzkommandos of the Security Police murdered tens of thousands of people in July 1941. The Einsatzgruppen—military death squads—murdered 1726 inhabitants between July 21 and 31 in the L'viv region alone. The data are incomplete, but by September 9, a further 2,500 inhabitants had been murdered.[270] The victims, principally Jews, were shot "for communist activities as political commissars in the Red Army, for being murderers of nationalist Ukrainians, or being NKVD agents."[271] On July 12, all Jewish men living in St. Anna Street were hanged because shots had been fired at a police patrol from one of the houses.[272]

The German authorities approved a period of three days—July 25 to July 27—during which it was permissible to torture, kill and rob Jews without fear of reprisal. Auxiliary Ukrainian police were joined by Ukrainian peasants and by individual Poles greedy for robbery and murder. These so-called Petljura days—the name given to them by the occupiers—were not spontaneous outbursts; the auxiliary police specifically targeted members of the Jewish intelligentsia. Police went from house to house, driving men, women, and children like cattle to the Gestapo prisons. In the prisons, the Jews were tortured and subsequently often murdered. The massacre cost the lives of approximately two thousand people.[273] It was the last time the occupiers enlisted the participation of the population in the mass murder of Jews.

On July 29, 1941, the commander of the Rear Area of Army Group South, General Karl von Roques, ordered the use of "the most harsh measures to prevent" soldiers of the Wehrmacht from taking part in excesses "instigated by certain groups of the civilian population." Unauthorized acts of violence directed against the civilian population in pacified areas were "purely arbitrary acts." Excesses of the civilian population against other sectors of the population and mob law also had to be prevented.[274] The destruction of the Jews of L'viv was now organized bureaucratically and was left to the designated police units.

Under Nazi Occupation

Until the end of July, the general authority in L'viv was in the hands of the German military administration. On June 30, the Stadtkommandant (town major) appointed the Ukrainian professor for geography Jurij Poljans'kyj as mayor.[275] On July 9, the region was placed under the control of the commander of the Rear Area of Army Group South (until July 8: 103) General Karl von Roques, who set up area and regional commands (Feld- und Ortskommandanturen) assisted by Security Divisions (Sicherungsdivisionen) 444 and 454. Oberfeldkommandantur 365 was responsible for the military administration of East Galicia and its subordinate Feldkommandantur 603 was the military administration of the city of L'viv.[276]

Ernst-Anton von Krosigk, chief of general staff (Generalstabschef) for the Rear Army Area (rückwärtiges Heeresgebiet) 103, instructed the military administration that the "Ukrainian territory" should be considered the "*Lebensraum* [literally; living space] of a friendly [*befreundet*] people." Krosigk forbade unauthorized confiscations and ordered that the "religious beliefs of the population" should be respected. The "Ukrainians' urge to engage in political activities" should be directed into the "channels of social charitable activities. Public demonstrations by Ukrainians (e.g. declarations of independence and the like) are no longer appropriate after orderly conditions were restored by the mil. authorities and must therefore cease in future."[277]

The German authorities were dissatisfied with the Ukrainian units in the Abwehr as they had "in contravention of their Abwehr mission, already appointed mayors or other administrative bodies everywhere, which were to some degree harmless but basically had to be considered as obedient elements of the OUN."[278] These mayors and commanders of Ukrainian militia units shot objectionable persons, confiscated whatever they wanted, and issued identification papers on their own authority.[279] The behavior of the militia in some areas was such "that they are referred to by the Ukrainian peasants as 'Bolshevist mobs.'"[280] In certain areas, Ukrainian militia units had equated Poles with the Jews and demanded that they wear armbands. In L'viv, the OUN sold stamps for battle funds (*Kampffondmarken*) and issued leaflets demanding the return of Bandera and a "free and independent Ukraine."[281] In some areas, the security police disciplined the militia, but elsewhere the SiPo used them to fight against "gangs" (*Banden*).[282] In the end, the Ukrainian militia units were dissolved and some of their leaders arrested.

The occupying Germans created a Ukrainian auxiliary police, which was partly controlled by the Einsatzkommandos, partly by the respective Stadtkommandant (town major) or Ortskommandant.[283] On July 14, the Stadtkommandant of L'viv ordered the formation of a city militia that would report to the provisional mayor. City militiamen wore white armbands with a blue-and-yellow border and the coat of arms of the city of L'viv on a white background. A second militia "for special tasks" was set up under the command of the German Einsatzkommando z.b.V. Lemberg. This second militia was assigned yellow-and-blue armbands marked with an official stamp. It is doubtful, however, whether this purported separation between the two militia units was maintained in practice.[284] The Ukrainian auxiliary police was formally established on August 31, 1941. It initially numbered 425 members, rising to 874 members after L'viv was expanded by the inclusion of several villages in 1943/44. These figures were augmented by around 420 students from the Ukrainian police academy set up in L'viv. The official duties of the Ukrainian auxiliary police included pursuing the perpetrators of petty crimes and providing assistance during house searches and for manhunts.[285]

The Ukrainian auxiliary police were hated by Jews and Poles alike.[286] They ransacked homes, controlled, bullied, and murdered numerous Jews and Poles. One Jewish writer believed that the members of the auxiliary police had been recruited from the lowest dregs of society, describing the police as morally degraded, with no sense of responsibility and with a bestial propensity for robbery and violence.[287] But another Jewish commentator was of the opinion that the Ukrainian militiamen had partly been recruited from among the masses of students who only a short time before had invoked the brotherhood of nations alongside their Jewish fellow students, had received Soviet educational grants, and had held positions in the Komsomol. They were now showing their true, bloody, nationalist, and anti-Semitic face.[288] However, the OUN and other Ukrainians had a very different perception of the Ukrainian police. The OUN-B commented that the Poles greatly respected the police. In a report from March 1944, the Ukrainian police are referred to as "ours" (*nashi politsianty*). Previously, several hundred auxiliary police in Volhynia had defected to the nationalist Ukrainian partisans.[289] Evidence for the fact that Ukrainians did not view the auxiliary police as hostile can be deduced from a diary entry written by Arkadij Ljubchenko dated April 7, 1943. He notes that the majority of Ukrainian police in Galicia were people with middle and higher levels of education. Many engineers, teachers, and scientists had joined the police force, raising the general level of the auxiliary police. "In addition, one sees in it [the police] here the new seed of the Ukrainian army. They hate Poles, and the yellow and blue badge with its trident is a knife in the heart of every Pole."[290]

On July 19, 1941, a Führer Decree incorporated the larger part of East Galicia into the Generalgouvernement, while eastern Ukraine became a separate administrative area to be known as Reichskommissariat Ukraine. The security police reported that "a whispering campaign" was portraying the Führer Decree as a "German betrayal of Ukrainian culture." The decree had provoked "extreme despondency."[291] The Ukrainians feared that the incorporation of East Galicia into the Generalgouvernement might be the precursor to establishing a Polish state.[292] The Bandera faction was still undecided how it should behave toward the Reich. On one hand, it had recommenced its clandestine activities, but on the other hand, it was trying to maintain contacts to the authorities. The peasants—as long as they had not been seduced by Bandera propaganda—were "very pro-German." The Bandera group—the report continued—was the "agent of all hostile currents among Ukrainians."[293]

To sooth matters, the Wehrmacht had permitted the establishment of a Ukrainian Council of Seniors chaired by Archbishop Andrij Sheptyts'kyj.[294] On the night of July 22–23, 1941, the Council of Seniors held a meeting lasting several hours in the official residence of the Greek Catholic archbishop to protest against the planned incorporation of East Galicia in the Generalgouvernement. In a statement, the Council of Seniors declared that the incorporation would "undermine the cordial sympathy and the complete trust of the Ukrainians in the German Wehrmacht and government. The Ukrainians would sooner accept a German protectorate over all of reunited Ukraine and support it with the utmost devotion than the rebuilding of Poland to the detriment of Ukrainians." The Council of Seniors still hoped that the incorporation of East Galicia into the General Government could be prevented: "It is almost unbelievable that the Ukrainians, who are doubtless the most sincere and greatest friends of the German people are to be made a sacrificial lamb for the Poles or Russians."[295] Stets'ko, writing on behalf of his government, sent a letter of remonstration to Hitler: "The Ukrainian people and with it the Ukrainian government view this act of incorporation of Galicia, of this ancient Ukrainian territory where the Ukrainian princely state was able to hold out longest against the incoming tides of the Asian hordes, into the Generalgouvernement as a blow against its national feelings and it cannot give its assent."

Stets'ko hoped that in future "under the brilliant leadership" of Hitler, ethnic (*völkisch*) principles would be applied in the reshaping of Ukraine.[296] The chief of the SD and the SiPo, writing on July 31, 1941, reported "extreme reticence on the part of Ukrainian administrative bodies."[297]

The disappointment of the Ukrainians inversely mirrored the Polish hopes. Some Poles believed that the establishment of a Polish state or at least of a protectorate was imminent. But this did not mean that Poles had any sympathy for Germany. According to information of the Reich Security Main Office (Reichssicherheitshauptamt, RSHA) the Poles continued to place all their hopes in an Allied victory.[298]

On August 1, 1941, East Galicia formally left the area of military operations to become part of the Generalgouvernement under the name District of Galicia. The government of the Generalgouvernement took the opportunity to hold a grand state ceremony in L'viv "which will demonstrate to the world the incorporation of Galicia into German sovereign territory."[299] The commander of Rear Army Area South, Karl von Roques, handed over the civil administration to the government of the Generalgouvernement.[300] Karl Lasch, previously head of the District of Radom, was appointed governor of the new district (East Galicia), with SS and Police Leaders Ludwig Losacker and from October Friedrich Katzmann reporting to him. The official language was now German; however, use of Ukrainian and Polish was permitted in dealings with the authorities. Decrees were issued in all three languages.[301] SS-Obersturmführer Hans Kujath was appointed Stadthauptmann (city captain—head of administration) of L'viv.

The Bandera Group was much stronger in East Galicia than the OUN-M and continued to make difficulties for the Germans. After the murder of several of Mel'nyk's supporters, the OUN-M issued leaflets accusing Bandera of murder. The security police reported that the Mel'nyk Group and member of the "older intelligentsia" had proposed "arresting the entire leadership of the Bandera Group and liquidating the main culprits."[302] The SiPo believed that the general population was prepared to "work together under all circumstances" with the Germans.[303] In February 1942 police stations across eastern Ukraine were sending reports to the RSHA that Mel'nyk and Bandera supporters were mutually informing on each other to the German authorities. While the RSHA noted a "very extreme nationalist-chauvinist attitude" in both arms of the OUN, the OUN-B was particularly uncooperative. It was impossible to "engage the supporters of the Bandera movement in any form of positive cooperation." It was felt that the only option left was to utterly destroy the movement.[304]

Bandera was arrested in Cracow on July 5, brought to Berlin for questioning and then was placed under house arrest. On July 9, the SD also arrested Jaroslav Stets'ko and Roman Il'nyts'kyj. Bandera was subsequently interned in Sachsenhausen concentration camp where he remained until September 1944.[305] But the Mel'nyk faction had only two months to exploit their advantage. At the end of November 1941 the OUN-M organized a conference in Zhytomyr attended by leading representatives of the movement. The occupation authorities took the opportunity and arrested more than twenty persons attending the conference. All of them without exception were shot a short time later. At the same time the organizations of the Mel'nyk faction in Kiev, Poltava and Kamieniec Podolski (Kam"janets'-Podil's'kyj) were searched and shut down. Mel'nyk himself was arrested in January 1944 and, like Bandera, was taken to Sachsenhausen concentration camp.[306]

The German occupiers did not grant the Ukrainians additional or greater responsibilities in the administration, nor did they dissolve the hated collective farms or offer the Ukrainians any political perspectives. This left Ukrainian elites dissatisfied with the German occupation. On January 14, 1942, leading Ukrainian representatives appealed to Hitler.[307] Their letter highlighted the disappointment of Ukrainians who had hoped that after the defeat of Russia, Ukraine would have the opportunity to "join the political system of Europe." The authors complained about the "prohibition of Ukrainians from taking part in the armed struggle against their hereditary enemy." They additionally deplored the fact that in eastern Ukraine, Ukrainians has been robbed of "all opportunities for cultural-national development." Germany could not make the mistake of "preventing the Ukrainian people from fulfilling its historical task by supporting the enemies of Ukraine, Poland and Russia." Ukraine must be granted the right to an independent existence.[308]

But as long as the German troops continued to be victorious, such considerations were not on the agenda. East Galicia was part of that "*Lebensraum im Osten* [living space in the East]" designated in *Generalplan Ost* [Master Plan East] as a future German settlement area. Hitler viewed the region as German "cultural soil" (*Kulturboden*) whose affiliation with the German cultural sphere had been confirmed by 146 years of Austrian rule. Soon after the invasion by the Wehrmacht the new rulers began giving the streets German names or Germanizing existing names. By 1942, 156 streets and squares had already been "Germanized."[309] The occupiers claimed parts of the city for themselves, with officers and civil servants favoring the elegant residential district near Stryjski Park. Previous owners of houses—usually Poles—were forced from their homes. As in all occupied countries, the best hotels, restaurants, and cafés were "for Germans only." Theaters and cinemas now served the occupiers, although the occasional Polish performance and some Ukrainian theatrical productions were permitted. In cinemas, the population were usually shown productions from UFA studios, the most important German motion picture company, with the films flanked by newsreels.[310]

Although the decision had already been taken to annihilate the Jews, the policies pursued against Poles and Ukrainians were more differentiated and were determined by the military situation and the willingness to cooperate of the respective group. Although Ukrainians and Poles were considered "racially inferior," they had been accorded a subordinate place in the plans for a national socialist Europe.[311] Right from the start, the Germans continued the campaign against Polish intellectuals that had begun in the Generalgouvernement one-and-a-half years earlier. During the night of July 3–4, a special unit of the security service led by SS-Brigadeführer Karl Eberhard Schöngarth arrested twenty-three Polish professors from both universities in L'viv and murdered all of them, together with seventeen university employees, on the morning of July 4, sparing the life of only one of the group. A few days later two more professors were arrested and murdered. The former Polish prime minister and university professor Kazimierz Bartel was shot on July 26, 1941, on Hitler's personal order. Other university lecturers and one hundred students were also murdered.[312]

Shortly after the German invasion, Soviet time in L'viv was replaced by "German time" (actually, Central European Time). A curfew was maintained from 9 p.m. in the evening until 7 a.m. in the morning. But at the same time Polish habits and customs returned. From September the złoty was again used as currency. Private companies were also permitted again. The occupation authorities forbade the wearing of Polish medals or badges.[313] All Polish inscriptions in streetcars were replaced by German and Ukrainian inscriptions.

The occupiers issued identity cards to the inhabitants but certificates of employment were even more important than identification papers, as these provided Jews with a temporary means of survival and offered Ukrainians and Poles a certain amount of protection from compulsory conscription and deportation to work as Ostarbeiter in the Reich.[314] Work was compulsory for all persons between sixteen and sixty in the Generalgouvernement. On August 22, 1941, twenty-five thousand persons in L'viv were registered as unemployed. Even in February 1942 there were still 1,700 unemployed persons on the books, although only 600 of them were workers. Transports of Ostarbeiter to the Reich began in September 1941. In the beginning, recruitment advertising attracted some volunteers, but later the authorities resorted to hunting people down or dragging them off the streets. At a meeting of the heads of the labor exchanges in the Generalgouvernement it was announced that 350,000 people were required for work in the Reich, 65,000 of whom were expected to come from the District of Galicia (8,000 from L'viv).[315]

As the numbers of people volunteering for work in the Reich dried up, streets were closed and potential workers seized out of the midst of crowds. Ostarbeiter were sometimes forcibly recruited from groups of movie audiences.[316] The biggest hunt for forced laborers started on March 10, 1943, and continued for several more days. Passersby on the streets daily saw groups of men and women flanked by Ukrainian auxiliary police being brought to the labor exchange or the camp on Pieracki Street. According to information provided by the Polish Home Army, by the spring of 1943, 40,017 persons from the District of Galicia had been deported as forced laborers, of whom 7,588 came from the city of L'viv.[317] The hunt for foreign workers for the Reich continued even in the spring of 1944 and was among one of the most defining experiences of the war for the "Aryan" population.[318]

Ukrainians and Poles were given more cultural and economic leeway than their co-nationals in the rest of the Generalgouvernement or in the Reichskommissariat Ukraine.[319] Ukrainians and Poles competed against one another within the limited latitude allowed them by their occupiers, although in this battle the Ukrainians held the better cards. The Ukrainian authorities working under German supervision were anxious to "remove Poles from all cultural life and to utterly Ukrainize those institutes which had previously been controlled by Poles and where the majority of teaching staff was Polish."[320] The German occupiers promoted such attempts at Ukrainization as long as Germans experienced no disadvantages from these changes. In the first weeks of July, eight hundred employees working on the streetcars were fired and replaced by two hundred Ukrainians. The directorate for the municipal streetcars introduced the use of Ukrainian as its official language.[321] But if economic efficiency was threatened, the occupiers did not hesitate to employ Polish specialists. In the absence of Ukrainian specialists, the occupiers summarily appointed Poles as the administrators of collective farms, which, in turn, aroused discontent among the Ukrainian population.[322]

In January 1942 Governor Lasch was arrested on charges of corruption during his time as governor of Radom and replaced by Austrian lawyer Otto Wächter, who had previously been Personalkommissar (head of Human Resources) for the District of Cracow. Together with Wächter a number of other Austrians were given leading positions.[323] Stadthauptmann (city captain) Hans Kujath was replaced by the Austrian Egon Höller, who, until that date, had been Kreishauptmann (district captain) of Rural Cracow. The Stadthauptmann controlled the municipal administration, and the most important departments—those dealing with economic affairs and finances—were headed by Germans. The office of deputy mayor and the positions of departmental heads of twelve other departments were filled by Ukrainians. But Polish specialists continued to be employed. At the end of 1941, 759 people were working in the municipal administration, including 20 citizens of the German Reich or "ethnic Germans," 432 Ukrainians, and 307 Poles. Twenty-six Ukrainians but only eight Poles held senior positions in the administration. Municipal services were similarly Ukrainized, although the percentage of Poles was higher than in the city administration, with 74 Germans, 1,040 Ukrainians, and 2,909 Poles working in municipal services. At managerial levels there were 250 Poles as opposed to 84 Ukrainians. The percentage of German staff continued to increase until 1944. But this was also because many local Poles had German or Austrian ancestors who had become Polonized in the nineteenth century. More people registered in the Deutsche Volksliste (German People's List) in L'viv than in the regions of central Poland. Newly classified "*Volksdeutsche,*" that is, ethnic Germans, did not enjoy the full legal status of

German citizens from the Reich, but their status was significantly better than that of Poles or Ukrainians. On March 20, 1944, there were 171 Reichsdeutsche (Germans from the Reich) and 56 Volksdeutsche working in the city administration, with a further 96 Reichsdeutsche and 92 Volksdeutsche employed in municipal services. In 1943, 4,802 Ukrainians and 6,989 Poles were working in the city administration and municipal services.[324] In the railroad, post, and telegraph offices, the majority of employees were Polish. But senior and managerial positions were mainly held by either Germans or Ukrainians.[325] Eighty percent of postal workers in the postal district of L'viv were Polish, 10 percent were Ukrainian, and 10 percent German, mainly Volksdeutsche. The labor exchange employed 120 Poles, 80 Ukrainians, and 50 Germans.[326]

After the first wave of murders targeting members of the Polish intelligentsia had abated, over the next one-and-a-half years the occupiers refrained from carrying out extensive murder campaigns against Ukrainians and Poles.[327] Poles were permitted to set up a Rada Główna Opiekuńcza (Main Welfare Council), which began its work on September 1, 1941, initially in the form of a Polish aid committee. This Polish aid committee was mainly involved in charitable work but it also represented Polish interests vis-à-vis the occupiers.[328]

On the Ukrainian side several groups fought to control the national institutions.[329] After the occupation of the city, the Mel'nyk and Bandera groups set up separate "relief committees." The occupiers were dissatisfied by this turn of events and promoted the establishment of a Ukrainian aid committee, initially headed by a Mel'nyk supporter. The two existing committees joined the new aid committee, which performed only charitable duties.[330] Archbishop Sheptyts'kyj agreed with the German authorities when they finally decided to remove both OUN groups from the committee.[331]

The Ukrainian aid committee reported to the L'viv Office of the Ukrainian Central Committee (Ukraïns'kyj Tsentral'nyj Komitet, UTsK) headed by Kost' Pan'kivs'kyj. The Ukrainian Central Committee saw itself as the legal representation of the interests of the Ukrainian population, but was repeatedly criticized by the OUN-B for its close collaboration with the occupying forces.[332] Officially, the Central Committee had primarily humanitarian tasks; its main focus was on providing relief and assistance to the Ukrainian population and certain services to the occupiers such as the collection of winter clothing for the Wehrmacht or assisting in the collection of grain.[333]

One of the Central Committee's most important departments dealt with schools and education. Its activities testify to the relatively wide leeway granted to Ukrainians in the District of Galicia by the occupying authorities. In 1942 the department supervised 4,214 elementary schools (3,038 in the District of Galicia) with 8,408 teachers (3,088 in the District of Galicia). These schools were attended by 610,218 pupils (493,500 in the District of Galicia). In 1942/1943 there were 12 high schools with 26 parallel classes and 6,000 pupils, 9 teacher training colleges with 2,250 pupils, and 8 seminaries for kindergarten teachers. The 120 vocational colleges and professional schools had 11,556 students. In 198 agricultural colleges (167 in the District of Galicia), 399 full-time and 503 part-time teaching staff taught 67,059 pupils. In addition, at the end of 1943 there were 128 boarding schools with more than 5,000 pupils. The highest level of education permitted Ukrainians by the occupying authorities were specialized courses, taught in L'viv, which aimed to train up urgently required staff in the areas agriculture, engineering and medical care. These courses were attended by two thousand students. But such specialized courses also show the limits to the scope allowed Ukrainians. The establishment of specialist courses circumvented the need for university education. The occupying authorities also refused to permit the scientific Shevchenko Society to reopen its doors.[334]

From the start of the German occupation, the food situation in the cities and towns was terrible. At the beginning of July 1941, people had to queue for hours even for bread. Many families were hoarding food after extensive panic buying. Most peasants were only prepared to exchange foodstuffs in return for material goods.[335] At the end of July there was widespread "general dissatisfaction because of the need to queue in front of food stores and the limited rations." Supplies were insufficient; smuggling and illicit trading thrived.[336] The quotas on the ration cards could often not be fully utilized, even in the months that followed. Salaries and wages were low, and black market prices for foodstuffs constantly increased. Many L'viv residents tried their hand at trading or looked for illegal alternative sources of income.[337] The population sank into poverty. By the middle of 1942 between forty and seventy thousand Poles were dependent on food aid. At the beginning sixteen Polish soup kitchens were operating; their number later increased to twenty-one, and together they dispensed between three and five thousand meals every day, although the calorific value of the meals was low. The Polish aid committee additionally provided food to several thousand schoolchildren.[338] In 1944 the Ukrainian aid committee had eleven regular soup kitchens, which dispensed, on average, one thousand meals every day, four-fifths of which were handed out for free.[339]

The Murder of the Jews of L'viv

Not long after the invasion, the occupiers already had an overview of the ethnic composition of the population. Thus, in July 1941, 370,000 people were living in the city; of these 160,000 were Jewish, 140,000 were Polish and 70,000 were Ukrainian.[340] Between June and September 1941, numerous Jews were killed in pogroms and by German Einsatzgruppen (special task forces). All documents tell of endless hours of work, cruelty, murders, hunger, epidemics, and innumerable casualties among the Jewish population. From the start, Jews were given much less food than Poles and Ukrainians; by the middle of July 1941, Jews were ordered to wear special armbands and were only permitted to use the last car in streetcars; later they were not allowed to use any form of public transport. Some Poles and Ukrainians took advantage of the crisis, buying up valuable goods for little money and selling food for a lot of money to Jews. Denunciations and blackmail were common.[341] On July 28, 1941, the military administration imposed a tribute of twenty million rubles on the Jewish population. One thousand Jewish hostages were taken as "security."[342] The Jewish community finally managed to collect the required sum within the allotted time. Poles and even some German officers also contributed money. But the hostages were not freed; all were shot a short time later.[343]

Between October 1941 and June 1942, as measures were gearing up for the "*Endlösung*," murder campaigns focused on members of the Jewish intelligentsia and "unproductive" people. The L'viv ghetto was set up and mass murders intensified. Many Jews were deported to the Bełżec death camp. As was the case in all of the ghettos set up in the territories under German rule, the L'viv ghetto was much too small. Jews were forced to sell their former homes for a pittance or houses were confiscated outright. "Aryans" living in the designated ghetto area sold their apartments at excessive prices. Redistribution occurred on a huge scale. When Jews moved to the ghetto, they were robbed and beaten on their way there by Germans, Poles, and Ukrainians. Perpetrators entered Jewish homes, taking anything that took their fancy. In the fall of 1941, thousands of Jewish families moved to the ghetto carrying their belongings on their backs or stowed away on hand carts. At the border to the ghetto the Jews had to pass under a railroad bridge. Uniformed police (Schutzpolizei) standing there picked out several thousand old, ill and frail people and brought them to nearby sandpits where they were summarily shot. Ukrainian auxiliary police and Schutzpolizei searched homes on the hunt for old and ill people.[344] The deadline for Jews to move to the ghetto had to be extended twice because of organizational problems. Part of the Jewish population remained outside the ghetto until September 1942.[345] *Judenräte*, or Jewish councils, were set up, as were Jewish forced labor gangs. By setting up Jewish councils the occupiers shifted the immediate organization of the exploitation and decimation of the Jewish population to the Jewish community itself. As in other cities where Jewish councils had been set up, members of the L'viv Jewish Council and Jewish auxiliary police were trying to save their own lives. But they also believed that the unconditional fulfillment of demands, particularly if they could demonstrate the economic efficiency of Jewish labor, would make Jewish workers indispensable for the conduct of the war and could save at least part of the Jewish population from annihilation. According to differing sources, the Jewish Council had between fourteen and twenty-two departments and employed up to four thousand people.[346]

Most Jews were murdered in the Bełżec death camp, but mass executions were also common in the notorious Janowska camp and surrounding areas. The first to be killed were persons considered unfit for work or incapable of hard physical labor. This predominantly affected the old, the sick, women, and children. At the end of June 1942, approximately two thousand people were murdered, most of them elderly.[347]

Between July 1942 and June 1943, the ghetto was gradually scaled down and was finally liquidated. The largest massacres took place in August 1942. Some fifty thousand Jews were not issued new work cards or, as women and children, were no longer protected by the employment certificates of the husbands or fathers. The murderous campaign started on August 15, reaching its climax between August 17 and August 20. The ghetto was surrounded by uniformed German police and Ukrainian auxiliary police.

Jews hid in their apartments and in walled-up cellars. Most were found and dragged out of their hiding places. Many Jews were killed on the spot. In the evening, manhunts were held across the city with searches carried out of parks and cemeteries and even "Aryan" houses. According to initial information of the Polish Home Army fifteen thousand Jews were murdered; later reports cited figures of up to fifty thousand people killed during the campaign or deported to Bełżec death camp. Jews still capable of working who had not been given work cards by the Gestapo were sent to the Janowska forced labor camp. Old people, children, and sick people were transported to Bełżec. Executions of Jews by shooting also occurred sporadically in L'viv. On August 23, the Gestapo took away the entire medical and nursing staff of the Jewish hospital. The occupiers employed special SS forces, the Sonderdienst, the uniformed police, Ukrainian auxiliary police, and Lithuanian police to carry out these campaigns. The re-registration of Jewish workers by the SS was used to reduce the numbers of Jewish workers by 10 to 20 percent. The Ukrainian auxiliary police assisted the SS in bringing selected Jews to the Janowska camp.[348] From the spring of 1942, the Janowska camp functioned at once as a forced labor camp for Jews, and Ukrainians, a transit camp for Bełżec and a place of execution. The camp never held more than ten thousand prisoners at any one time. Slave laborers who were murdered or who died of hunger or disease were promptly replaced by new prisoners from the ghetto. The same appalling conditions typical for most German forced labor and extermination camps in eastern Europe prevailed in the Janowska camp.[349]

After Jewish resistance fighters killed a police agent in L'viv, the police hanged the chairman of the Jewish Council together with eleven members of the Jewish self-help organization. A further one hundred Jews, many of them members of the administration of the Jewish Council, were also murdered. Between January and December 1942 approximately 300,000 Jews, i.e. half of all Jews resident in the District of Galicia, lost their lives.[350] Maurycy Allerhand was murdered together with his wife in Janowska camp in August 1942. The emeritus professor for physiology and former rector of the university Adolf Beck died in the same month.[351] The "Aryan" population witnessed the murders of their Jewish fellow citizens.[352]

The August murders prompted Archbishop Sheptyts'kyj to denounce the national socialist genocide in a letter to Pope Pius XII. The archbishop listed the facts: robberies, thefts, confiscations, and corruption were the order of the day; about two hundred thousand Jews had already been murdered. Massacres took place in even the smallest villages across East Galicia, and not only Jews but also "non-Aryan Christians" and many other Christians had lost their lives. Mass executions by shooting, mass arrests and the deportations of workers to the German Reich must all be laid at the door of the Germans.[353]

In August 1942 the ghetto was reduced to one third of its former size and hermetically sealed off. Friedrich Katzmann, SS-Führer and Polizeiführer for the district, gave the order that all Jews had to have relocated to the ghetto by September 7. Any person attempting to hide Jews could expect to be killed.[354] Katzmann estimated that about eight thousand unregistered Jews were living in the ghetto. The death rate in the ghetto was high. The extreme overcrowding in the houses, the catastrophic sanitary conditions, and hunger led to recurrent outbreaks of disease and typhoid epidemics. People died in great numbers even without the assistance of the death squads. In the beginning, the Jewish hospital in the ghetto area still worked although it lacked medicines. But after the deportation of its doctors and nursing staff to Bełżec there was no longer any professional medical assistance in the ghetto.[355]

Another mass murder campaign was carried out in the L'viv ghetto on January 5 and 6, 1943; this time the primary targets were people who had no work cards. The Schutzpolizei, the Gestapo, and the Ukrainian auxiliary police set fire to houses, killing several hundred by burning them alive. All members of the Jewish Council were murdered. The ghetto was renamed and was now termed a "Judenlager" or Jewish camp. Survivors were housed in barracks and were assigned to specific companies. SS-Scharführer Josef Grzymek, who showed particular sadism in his dealings with the remaining Jews, was appointed commander of the Judenlager (Julag). Some of the members of the Jewish *Ordnungsdienst* (security staff) were murdered in February 1943. In March, forty Jews were shot in revenge for the murder of a Gestapo official; several dozen members of the Jewish *Ordnungsdienst* were hung from the balconies.[356]

In February 1943 the Home Army for L'viv reported on a new special operation carried out in the ghetto which cost a further 3,800 Jews their lives. Two hundred Jewish police and Jewish security guards, numbering some seven hundred people together with their families, were rounded up. On February 12, 1943, the Germans murdered a further seven hundred Jews. After these operations, only fifteen thousand people were still officially living in the ghetto.³⁵⁷ On March 17 and 18, 1943, many Jews were again murdered in the ghetto, among them twenty Jewish auxiliary police. Seven Jews were hanged in Łokietka Street.³⁵⁸

The liquidation of the Judenlager started on June 1, 1943. Several thousand young and healthy people had already been transferred to the Janowska camp a few weeks previously. Several companies had also arranged for their Jewish workers to be transferred to the camp to avoid losing them during the planned murder operations: "Jews were savagely hunted down on the streets and squares of L'viv. They were slain wherever they were found. All of this was done in line with well-known German methods. The Ukrainian militia zealously assisted—as, by the way, was usually the case—at these bloody murders."³⁵⁹

The liquidation of the ghetto lasted from June 1 to June 20, and the police units met with organized resistance. Every building, every house was searched. Instead of the registered twelve thousand Jews, about twenty thousand Jews were found to be living in the ghetto. Jews who were caught were either murdered on the spot or taken to the Janowska camp and murdered there. Numerous houses were set on fire. After the murder operation was finished, about three thousand bodies were found in various hiding places. Jewish resistance fighters managed to kill ten Germans and injure around a dozen.³⁶⁰ Katzmann reported to Berlin on June 23 that the District of Galicia, with the exception of the Jews in the camps overseen by the SS-Führer and Polizeiführer, was now *"judenfrei."*³⁶¹

Katzmann had warned the population against offering any assistance to Jews. But as the German defeat moved closer and the extermination of the Jews entered its final stages, the readiness of Poles and Ukrainians to help Jews also increased. Despite the threats, some Jews who had fled were hidden by their fellow citizens. Others hid in the city's sewer system, but a lack of food forced them to surface again and many were caught and shot. One group of ten managed to hold out in the city's sewer system until the German retreat. During all this time Polish sewer workers supplied them with food.³⁶²

After the ghetto had been liquidated, around twenty forced labor camps with twenty-one thousand inmates remained in the District of Galicia. By degrees, the Jewish inmates of these camps, with the exception of those who were able to flee, were also murdered or died of exhaustion, emaciation, and disease. The Oberfeldkommandantur, the divisional administration headquarters of the occupied territory, noted on September 17, 1943: "Now that no more Jews are employed by the Wehrmacht, civil businesses with the exception of [the] oil industry in the Drohobycz area have become judenrein. There are only 6000 Jews in the Judenlager Lemberg, of which 4000 are employed in the Deutsche Ausrüstungswerke [an SS-owned armaments company] and 2000 in the Ostbahn [Eastern Railroad]. The Jewish question in the District of Galicia should therefore be considered in the main as settled."³⁶³

On November 19, 1943, the Gestapo set about murdering the last Jews in Janowska camp. About three hundred men from the Gestapo, the Ukrainian auxiliary police, and a few dozen soldiers of the Waffen-SS took part in the extermination. The OUN-B estimated that at this point around 2,700 Jews were still living in the camp. The Gestapo ordered the Jews to undress completely. But Jews took that moment to attack the Gestapo men with knives. The Gestapo fired on the Jews with machine guns and threw hand grenades, killing almost all of them. A few Jews used the confusion to climb over the barbed wire fence and flee. Fifty Jews fled at the start of the carnage along with three hundred Russian SS-men, who were serving in the camp and had sold the Jews weapons and ammunition. The Gestapo was unable to get the situation under control by itself and called on the Ukrainian auxiliary police, which brought the surviving Jews to Lysnych. On the way there forty Jews overpowered the five-man guard and fled in the car.[364]

After the Wehrmacht retreated in July 1944, about eight hundred Jews emerged from their hiding places. Approximately eight hundred more came from the surrounding areas, so that on October 1, 1944 1,689 Jews were registered in L'viv. This meant that almost all the Jews living in the city in July 1941 had fallen victim to the genocide. A few thousand Jews had survived in the Soviet Union where they had been deported between 1939 and 1941. The death rate for deported Jews in Russia was also high, but the likelihood of surviving in the Soviet Union was incomparably higher than in the territories under German rule. According to estimates by the historian Aharon Weiss, out of 600,000 to 650,000 Jews living in the area later known as the District of Galicia at the time of the German invasion, only between 10,000 and 15,000 survived (see table 5.2)[365]

The Holocaust wiped out one of the three main ethnic groups that had helped shape the city over the previous six hundred years. Poles and Ukrainians benefited—even if for most of them the benefits were only temporary—from the persecution and murder of the Jews; a small percentage was complicit or actively assisted the Germans in their policy of extermination. Thousands of Ukrainians and Poles risked their lives to help their Jewish fellow citizens. Archbishop Sheptyts'kyj saved the lives of fifteen Jews by sheltering them in his official residence. The archbishop additionally directed Studite monasteries and nunneries to admit Jews who had fled; this saved the lives of 150 Jews, most of them children. According to a report by the German occupiers, one hundred Ukrainians were executed in Galicia between October 1943 and June 1944 for *Judenbegünstigung* (preferential treatment of Jews).[366]

A Shift in Occupation Policies

After the German defeat at Stalingrad, the Nazi occupiers changed their strategy and attempted to win over Poles, and more particularly Ukrainians, with the

Changes in population size		Chronological sequence	
Date	# of Jews in L'viv	Date	Number of victims
July 1, 1941	approx. 160,000	July 1–2, 1941	4,000–7,000 (pogrom)
July 31, 1941	approx. 150,000	July/August 1941	Several thousand killed in mass shootings carried out by Einsatzkommandos
		July 25–27, 1941	Around 2,000, mainly murdered by the Ukrainian auxiliary police ("Petljura days")
		August 1941	Murder of 1,000 Jewish hostages
October 1941	120,000	September 1941	Several thousand killed in mass executions
November 1941	109,000		
December 1941	106,000		
January 1942	103,000	March 1942	Approx. 15,000 killed in Bełżec
April 1942	86,000	May 5, 1942	Several thousand killed in mass executions
May 1942	82,000	June 27, 1942	Approx. 2,000 killed, mainly women
September 1942	36,000	August 10–22, 1942	Approx. 50,000 killed in Bełżec
October 1942	33,000	End of August/ beginning of September	Approx. 100 shot, several dozen hanged
November 1942	29,000	End of October	Several hundred murdered
December 1942	24,000	November 1942	Several thousand killed in Bełżec and in the Janowska camp
January 1943	approx. 20,000	January 5–6, 1943	Several thousand murdered or burned alive
February 1943	approx. 14,000 + approx. 1,500 illegal	March 1943	Shot or hanged
June 1943	12,000 + approx. 8,000 illegal	June 1–20, 1943	Several thousand murdered during the liquidation of the ghetto

Table 5.2. Number of Jews resident in L'viv 1941–1943 and their annihilation.[367]

hope of inducing them to contribute more actively to the war effort against the Soviet Union. The Oberfeldkommandantur reported in March 1943 that neither the Poles nor the Ukrainians wished for any return of the "Bolshevists." Many Ukrainians wanted to take part "in the armed fight against Bolshevism."[368] But at the same time, the report admitted that the Polish inhabitants and "to a certain extent and understandably the Ukrainian population are not favorably disposed" toward the Germans. "Otherwise little has changed. The Poles are seeking the return of their state and the majority of Ukrainians the establishment of a state of their own."[369]

For some time, the OUN-M and the collaborationist Ukrainian Central Committee had been urging that they be permitted to set up armed Ukrainian units to fight against bolshevism. Only now did Hitler finally agree. The two most important units were the Vlasov army composed of Soviet prisoners of war under former Soviet General Andrej Vlasov and the Ukrainian SS Schützen-Division Galicia. The decision to set up the SS Schützen-Division Galizien (*Halychyna*) announced on April 28, 1943, elicited a strong response among the Ukrainian population of East Galicia.[370] By the middle of May 1943, 42,000 Ukrainians had volunteered to enlist in the division, 36,823 of whom were accepted.[371] The departure of the volunteers to their places of deployment was staged as a public celebration, with fifty thousand people attending the formal ceremony in L'viv. After a Greek Catholic open-air mass tens of thousands of recruits marched in file to form ranks in front of the opera house, where the head of the military committee, Colonel Alfred Bisanz; the deputy head of the Ukrainian Central Committee, Konstantyn Pan'kivs'kyj; and Governor Otto Wächter had assembled to send off the officer cadets and noncommissioned officers.[372]

Citing historical antecedents, the head of the Ukrainian Central Committee Kubijovych appealed to the Ukrainian population to enlist in the SS-Division Galizien. He invoked the Polish–Ukrainian war and the fight of the Ukrainian People's Republic against the Red Army. Kubijovych placed the newly formed Schützen-Division in the tradition of the fight for independence. Twenty-five years before, Ukrainian fighters had been forced to lay down their arms. But the "blood spilled on the field of honor" by their comrades was calling on them to complete what had been started back then. Standing alongside the German army it was time for the "Jewish-Bolshevist pestilence" to be obliterated now and forever. He described bolshevism as "the worst enemy of the Ukraine and of all of mankind" against which the fathers and older brothers of the current Ukrainian soldiers had fought as "the first and only ones in Europe at the time." And finally Kubijovych also made direct reference to the Polish–Ukrainian war. After twenty-two years, the "Ukrainian youth of Galicia" must once again take up arms. Now the Ukrainians were fighting as part of the "new Europe" to defend Western civilization against communism.[373] But, rather than pro-German sympathies, the Home Army suspected that Ukrainian advocates of the SS-Division Galizien were prompted by nationalist motives.³⁷⁴ The Ukrainians were well aware of the speciousness of German promises, but they nevertheless considered the possession of arms an important trump card.³⁷⁵

The leaders of the OUN-B initially warned against enlisting in the SS division. With a German defeat not inconceivable and given the lack of any quid pro quo they considered the creation of the division a political mistake.³⁷⁶ In some cases, Bandera supporters were also said to have murdered Ukrainians who enlisted in the SS-Division Galizien. Nevertheless, enlistment proved highly popular. By mid-July 1943, eighty thousand volunteers had come forward, although about 10 percent had subsequently not shown up for the army physical. Only about 50 percent were considered physically fit enough for training.³⁷⁷ The OUN-B later changed its position. The SS would provide Ukrainians with weapons and military training. Both could become important assets in any future fight for an independent Ukrainian state.³⁷⁸

At the start of 1943 the German occupiers were once again courting the Ukrainian population. In sharp contrast to this and driven by a rise in the numbers of acts of resistance committed by the Home Army, from December 1942 the occupiers began increasing the pressure on the Polish population. The Janowska camp and the prisons of L'viv were soon filled with Poles. The Home Army received information, according to which three hundred Poles were shot in Łącki prison on December 11, 1942. At the same time Polish society faced the threat of further deportations of Poles to Germany as forced laborers.³⁷⁹ On February 6, 1943, three thousand people, the majority of them Poles, were brought from their homes and various camps to the Janowska camp.³⁸⁰ In the spring of 1943, numerous arrests were made in L'viv. The secret organization of the Polish National Democratic Party was almost completely crushed.³⁸¹

In the spring of 1943, some lower-ranking German representatives began talks with Polish representatives. The discussions did not yield any results but they were an indication of how nervous the occupiers were becoming after the defeat at Stalingrad.³⁸² The city captain of L'viv appointed an advisory council, consisting of five Polish and five Ukrainian members. The head of the Polish group was the seventy-eight-year-old professor of law Marceli Chlamtacz, while the Ukrainian group was headed by Stepan Bilak. But the council only met up infrequently and had no significant influence on the internal organization of the city.³⁸³

By mid-1943 it appeared as though there might be a shift in the policy toward Poles. Although, in the opinion of Abwehr officer Theodor Oberländer, after killing numerous members of the Polish elite and suppressing Polish life the Germans had forfeited any hope of Polish support, this could yet change under the banner of a battle to be waged against the Soviet Union.³⁸⁴ In another memorandum, the author demanded nothing less than a reversal of the German policies in the east, with the erstwhile foes united in a fight that would pit Europe against bolshevism. The immediate measures proposed by the author included land reform, an expansion of self-government, and positive cultural and social policies. The resettlement plans should not appear uncalculable because this would alienate the local population.[385] These and similar proposals circulated for a while in government circles of the Generalgouvernement but were not implemented.

The worsening situation on the front lines began to affect the everyday behavior of Germans. German children suddenly began greeting Poles with the words *dzień dobry* (hello, literally: good day). On being questioned, the children explained that their mothers had told them they should be polite to Poles. On the streets passersby excused themselves if they asked for information in German. The mood of the Polish population was correspondingly elevated, but hatred of Germans continually increased. The city and the country—in the opinion of the regional command of the Home Army—were impatiently awaiting the hour of revenge.[386] After the success of a counterattack, the Germans once again held their heads high and talked of an imminent victory. The Germans—the Home Army commented—were pursuing a stupid policy as they constantly allowed themselves to be guided by local conditions. In one place, they courted the Ukrainians, in another they flattered the Poles, and in each case they discriminated against the other group. And in this manner they managed to antagonize both groups.[387]

The head of the L'viv office of the Ukrainian Central Committee Kost' Pan'kivs'kyj also criticized the German policy at the end of 1943: "Up to the present day we still have no idea what will happen to us after the war. All social classes are suffering from a political hunger. The feeling of uncertainty has wider repercussions as it reduces the joy of working and work outputs."[388]

The occupiers additionally incensed the Ukrainian population by a number of small administrative provocations. In L'viv, for example, the Stadthauptmann forbade all Ukrainian celebrations on November 1, 1943 (the anniversary of the Lystopadovyj chyn), and any commemoration of the January 22, 1918 (the date of the declaration of independence of the Ukrainian People's Republic).[389] In several localities in the District of Cracow and in the city of Cracow itself, the authorities even forbade celebrations to commemorate Shevchenko. The Ukrainians were even more strongly affected by the prohibition of religious processions on Greek Catholic holidays.[390]

Polish underground organizations had an easier time under German occupation than under Soviet rule where state infiltration of the economy and society had left little latitude for free movement. Now Polish-owned private businesses and companies existed again and the Home Army was better able to disguise its activities. The Polish resistance created a well-organized "underground state" in L'viv and an effective underground army. Region no. 3 of the Home Army included the three southeastern voivodships and Volhynia from 1942 on. The regional command was based in L'viv. However, the Polish underground had to cope with several important handicaps. On one hand, it faced the continual threat of detection by the German police; on the other hand, it was at risk of espionage, denunciations, attacks, and murders by the Ukrainian auxiliary police and the OUN. Many Poles feared becoming involved in clandestine activities. Nevertheless, at the end of 1943, the regional Home Army had more than thirty thousand members.[391] In L'viv, the Home Army was strong and sometimes carried out spectacular acts. In one case, underground fighters raided a cinema where they held a collection in aid of the fight against the Germans.[392]

In the second half of 1943, the general security situation worsened. In addition to attacks by the Home Army and the Ukraïns'ka Povstans'ka Armija (Ukrainian Insurgent Army, UPA), raids carried out by bandits and criminals were also becoming more common.[393] In the fall of 1943, the occupiers therefore again resorted to carrying out harshly repressive acts directed against the local populations. The OUN-B noted that as a result of various fiascos and the lack of success on the frontlines, the Germans were becoming increasingly brutal. Assisted by the Ukrainian auxiliary police the occupiers fought the Polish and Ukrainian underground movements.[394] Everyone was waging war against everybody else. Poles, collaborators, Germans, and Ukrainians were murdered. On November 1, the Gestapo and the gendarmerie arrested Poles working in the oil refineries in Żółkiew Street. On October 25, Poles shot at Ukrainian auxiliary police. In the days that followed, the Gestapo and the Schutzpolizei shot many Poles and Ukrainians in broad daylight during controls. On the night of November 5, the Germans struck a serious blow against the Polish underground. Using a list of names and assisted by Ukrainian police they searched many homes. But across the District of Galicia Ukrainians were also shot and Ukrainian villages set alight.[395]

Public executions were held on November 4, 1943, the first—with the exception of the executions of Jews in the ghetto—to held in L'viv since the start of the war. Six Poles and two Ukrainians were executed. More public executions followed during the succeeding days. Seven Ukrainians and one Pole were shot for systematic evasion of labor and for absconding from their work on construction sites. A further thirteen people were executed on December 14, and on December 16 the police command announced publicly that fifty-five Poles and Ukrainians had been summarily tried for membership in underground organizations, possession of weapons, or hiding Jews. The majority of those condemned to death were Poles. In the end, thirty people were executed and fifteen pardoned. Over the following weeks further public executions were carried out. On January 19, 1944, ten Ukrainians were shot in revenge for the murder of a German noncommissioned officer. Two weeks later ten Polish hostages were executed for the same reason. On June 29, 1944, twenty-eight people were executed, although not publicly, in retaliation for the murder of SS-Rottenführer Karl Pommerenke. The executions and the wave of terror alarmed the Poles and Ukrainians in L'viv, who had suffered less from the Nazi terror policies over the previous one-and-a-half years than elsewhere in the Generalgouvernement. While in L'viv more Poles were murdered, in other areas of the District of Galicia Ukrainians were almost exclusively the victims of this new wave of terror.[396]

The wave of repressions and murders were a reaction to the continual decline in authority experienced by the occupiers in East Galicia, Volhynia and Podlasie. By the spring of 1943, the UPA controlled almost all of Volhynia with the exception of the larger cities. A comprehensive "pacification action" under General Erich von dem Bach-Zelewski cost the lives of around three thousand German soldiers between July and September 1943. The Ukrainian partisans lost six thousand fighters.[397]

In the eastern regions of the District of Galicia, the authorities had noted increasing tensions between Ukrainians and Poles in summer 1943. There had been some murders of Poles, although it was not clear whether the motives were nationalist or a result of the increased crime rates. The appearance of large Soviet partisan units under General Sidor Kovpak in the summer of 1943 led to a fundamental change in the mood of the population, resulting in a general loss of authority for the Germans. Many people eluded labor conscription. In one county, more than half of those conscripted to carry out construction work fled.[398] The "nationalist-Ukrainian attempts to become independent" increased over the following months. Further murders of Jews occurred in "strongly nationalist-Ukrainian regions." The Poles placed no reliance on the occupation authorities but began to take countermeasures.[399]

In the summer of 1943, the OUN-B realigned its policies. Nazi Germany was now viewed as an enemy of equal importance as the Bolsheviks. The third clandestine meeting held by the OUN in August 1943 adopted a program that had been adapted to the changed situation of the war and now included certain democratic elements to comply with the expectations of the Western powers. The new program's minority policy also promised tolerance. But the OUN-B had not completely abandoned the ideology of integral nationalism. Its new program was part of a political shift that aimed to create a rapprochement with the United States of America and Great Britain. At the same time, the OUN-B was attempting to escape a fatal association with Nazi Germany. One consequence of the meeting was the setting up of a Ukrainian Liberation Council (Ukraïns'ka Holovna Vyzvol'na Rada, UHVR).[400]

In November 1943 one of the county offices (Kreishauptmannschaft) in the eastern part of the district reported that while the majority of the population rejected bolshevism, it was nevertheless prepared—albeit reluctantly—to accept a new change of regime if this meant that the war would finally end. But the attention of "the masses" was "distracted by the civil war which smolders under the surface and claims numerous victims": "It was able to erupt when the march-through of the Soviet partisans revealed the weakness of the German executive authority, weakening German authority to an extent which could hardly be rectified. The two ethnicities, despite all attempts at combining them undertaken by one side or the other, fall apart again in enmity like certain chemical elements, with each side needing only a small push to begin murdering the other."[401]

The Ukrainian nationalists made good use of the loss of authority on the part of the German administration, using the power vacuum to settle old scores. The massacres in Volhynia in July 1943 had been the signal. From then on, reports of murders committed against Poles and Polish acts of retaliation became increasingly common (see table 5.3). The Ukrainian Central Committee (UTsK) attempted to find a means of counteracting the terror and fought against the Bandera movement. The partisans responded by killing representatives of the UTsK. One Greek Catholic priest was murdered after he read an appeal by the UTsK from the pulpit. But the latent civil war also mobilized criminal elements, heightening the general insecurity. The Kreishauptmann knew of some cases where Poles and Ukrainians had carried out attacks together.[402]

	Robberies	Gang attacks	Political murders	Acts of sabotage	Attacks on the Wehrmacht	Skirmishes
Sept. 16–Oct. 15, 1943	162	71	43*			
Oct. 16–Nov. 15, 1943	332	85	26*	10		
Nov. 16–Dec. 15, 1943	224	96	31*	10	10	
Jan. 16–Feb. 15, 1944	292	27	92	16	9	
Feb. 16–Mar. 15, 1944	395	114	194	16	9	
Mar. 16–Apr. 15, 1944	129	132	99	47	32	26

* Until the middle of December 1943 this category was classified under "murders of Poles."

Table 5.3. Development of the security situation in the area administered by Oberfeldkommandantur 365.[403]

German Occupation and Interethnic Relations

Between June 1941 and June 1943, interethnic relations were strongly affected by the ongoing extermination of the Jewish population. Jewish authors registered to what extent Ukrainians and Poles collaborated with the German occupiers and to what extent they participated in the murder of Jews. Jewish eyewitnesses noted that the relationship between Germans and Ukrainians had already begun to cool after the Germans annulled the proclamation of a Ukrainian state, took over the city, and began to give it a German appearance. The Ukrainian flag disappeared from the streets, leaving only the swastika.[404] However, Ukrainians were again given positions of authority in the city administration. One Jewish witness remarked that Poles were very busy trading, smuggling, and speculating: "And once again dreams come true: the Poles are in 'trade,' the Ukrainians are in the administration and the Jews do the physical work."[405]

One Jewish eyewitness noted that the Poles harbored feelings of revenge against the Jews and openly showed their feelings. The eyewitness had seen that many Poles participated in the murderous bullying. When the Jews were forced to relocate to the ghetto, on their way there they were robbed and beaten by Germans, Poles, and Ukrainians.[406] Maurycy Allerhand believed that Poles only participated in the plundering of Jewish homes in exceptional cases. He placed all the blame on the Ukrainians, who were trying to get rich by every means possible. As an example he cited the story that Ukrainians would go from house to house asking the caretakers whether any Jews lived there. They would then enter the houses and claim the flats for themselves, allowing themselves to be paid off with high sums of money. Poles—according to Allerhand—never participated in such activities.[407] But some Ukrainians also helped Jews: "In an atmosphere of brutal racist hatred, there were some cases, if not many, of humane behavior on the part of Poles and Ukrainians."[408]

Jewish eyewitnesses were also critical of Jewish ghetto police, the Jewish *Ordnungsdienst*, which helped the German authorities control the ghetto before the members of the *Ordnungdienst* themselves fell victim to the Holocaust. This Jewish police force was a great misfortune for the Jewish population, because it included many corrupt elements. Writing at the beginning of 1946 Philip Friedman commented bitterly that the Jewish police had behaved "worse than the Gestapo" toward the Jews.[409] Leon Weliczker Wells echoed this view in his memoirs: "Those who had any self-respect did not join this group, and it was basically made up of elements of the Jewish rabble."[410]

After the establishment of the L'viv ghetto, Jewish eyewitness accounts of the war break off or change in character. Now reports focus predominantly on hunger, misery, murders, and fear. Reflections on Jewish relations with other ethnic groups become rare. With the destruction of the L'viv ghetto, they stop altogether. On his flight by train to Warsaw, one author of a report who was traveling with fake papers met Aryan smugglers. Despite the whole-scale murder of Jews they still hated Jews: "The only area where we profit from the Germans is when they deal with the Jews."[411]

Despite the murder of tens of thousands of Jews from L'viv, a memorandum by the local command of the Home Army still thought in spring 1942 that the Jews posed a danger to the Poles. In this memorandum, stereotypes from the arsenal of prewar Polish anti-Semitic accusations are combined with anti-Semitic Nazi tropes. Jews are viewed as the most important internal enemy, whose final plan is to replace the Poles as the ruling class.[412] The memorandum argued that the Jews had not been defeated, only weakened, because only the weakest parts of Jewish society had been murdered. Indirectly, this had even somehow resulted in strengthening the Jews, because those who had survived were "not weighed down in the struggle of existence by these dead weights: One can say without reservation that the problem of the Jewish minority bears all the aspects of a difficult and chronic disease among us which upsets the normal functioning of the social organism." Traditional National Democratic anti-Semitic arguments are used here, even though the context had fundamentally changed. The existence of the Jewish minority—the report continued—prevented the development of an independent third estate and thus the modernization of society. The rise of talented Poles from the lower classes was being hampered by Jews. By these means Jews not only weakened Poland but were also barriers to the democratization of society.[413]

In the light of these perceptions of the Jews, the reactions of the Polish inhabitants of L'viv as reported to Warsaw and London by the regional command of the Home Army become more comprehensible.[414] The Poles did not support the murder of the Jewish population that took place in front their eyes. The L'viv command of the Home Army gave a detailed description of the so-called August action of 1942, during which the German police and Ukrainian auxiliary police murdered many Jews and deported at least forty thousand Jews to the Bełżec extermination camp. The scenes witnessed moved even people who were hostile to Jews: "The Aryan population witnessed this action with pain, even if a strong aversion had developed in the relationships to Jews after the Bolshevik invasion; nevertheless, when their own eyes saw what was done to Jews, it made a pitiful impression on them."[415]

The Home Army in L'viv described the German plan to eliminate the Jews as "ultra-bestial" (*ultrabestialski*).[416] The reaction of the masses to the murder of Jews was relatively uniform: "All condemn the bestiality and the premeditation with which the Jews are being murdered, but generally it is said that the Jews are getting their historical punishment." Polish society did not protest against what was happening: "There is no hot sympathy, only a rational cold condemnation of murder committed against the weak." Deep sympathy was often felt for individual Jews, who were sometimes helped even though helpers risked their own lives. But "with regard to the Jews in general, there is a subconscious satisfaction that there will be no more Jews in the Polish organism."[417]

There are very few contemporary sources which show how the Ukrainian population and the OUN perceived and interpreted the Holocaust. In February 1942 Archbishop Sheptyts'kyj protested in a letter to Himmler against the involvement of the Ukrainian auxiliary police in the murder of Jews. In November 1942 in a pastoral letter the archbishop emphasized the importance of the commandment "Thou shalt not kill." The timing and the line of argumentation taken in the missive made it clear to everyone that Sheptyts'kyj was referring to the murder of the Jews. He was directly appealing to the consciences of Greek Catholic believers.[418]

The numerous actions taken against Jews who had fled to the forests show that, despite the murders of hundreds of thousands of Jews, Ukrainian partisan groups were still strongly anti-Semitic and identified them with bolshevism.[419] However, already at the beginning of February 1942 the German police stations in eastern Ukraine were reporting that the OUN was trying to avoid being involved in "activities against Jews." Anti-Semitic sentences had even been deleted from some of the pamphlets of the Bandera faction.[420]

After the murder of the Galician Jews the Polish–Ukrainian conflict began to take center stage. The German Sicherheitspolizei noticed in August 1941 that the antagonism between Ukrainians and Poles had increased under German occupation.[421] In November 1942 there were 116,000 Poles and 54,000 Ukrainians living in L'viv; compared with 1938, the percentage of Ukrainians had increased by 30 percent. If the incorporated suburbs were included, 130,000 Poles and 87,000 Ukrainians were resident in Greater L'viv.[422] Their mutual hatred—described in the reports of the L'viv Command of the Home Army—permeated all social classes.[423]

Polish "general opinion" held the Ukrainians not only responsible for the deportation of Polish settlers and thousands of members of the Polish intelligentsia during the Soviet occupation, but also accused the Ukrainian auxiliary police—falsely—of complicity in the murder of twenty-five professors, which occurred in the first days of the German occupation.[424] One report listed numerous cases in which the Ukrainian auxiliary police had shot Poles. The regional command also believed Ukrainians to be behind numerous robberies and murders.[425] Ukrainians were additionally believed to be the Gestapo's primary informers and the "eyes and ears" of the occupying forces.[426]

The Polish underground recognized the fact that Ukrainian society was not monolithic. However, in their reports only the OUN appears as an actor, terrorizing the Ukrainian population, enforcing unconditional support and using the Germans to liquidate the Poles. Ukrainian youths were primed to fight the Poles "even if this battle should be lost."[427] Nevertheless, the Home Army was aware that the Bandera faction also fought against the Germans and noted the waves of arrests of Ukrainians in the winter of 1942/1943.[428]

At the beginning of 1943 hope germinated on the Polish side that a rapprochement might be possible.[429] Talks were held between the OUN-B and the Home Army as the fear of a return of the Bolsheviks softened the behavior of Ukrainians.[430] However, this convergence of interests was only of short duration. The talks clearly showed that positions were incompatible. Neither side was ready to renounce their claim to L'viv and East Galicia. Polish and Ukrainians underground organizations alike expected a new Polish–Ukrainian war.[431]

In the fall of 1942, nationalist Ukrainian partisan units in northwestern Ukraine merged to form the Ukraïns'ka Povstans'ka Armija (Ukrainian Insurgent Army, UPA), to be gradually joined by the armed units of both OUN factions and other partisan groups.[432] In the spring of 1943, Ukrainian nationalist partisans in Volhynia began attacking Polish villages and massacring the inhabitants. Their aim was to expel all Poles from these territories, as they claimed them for an independent Ukrainian state. The first refugees soon began arriving and the Volhynian murders became the talk of all Polish homes.[433] In July 1943 the wave of murderous attacks reached East Galicia.[434] The local command of the Home Army commented that "our Ukrainians" had assumed that this was their biggest opportunity yet to drive out all Poles.[435]

While the Home Army in L'viv considered the Germans as their main enemy, followed by "the Bolsheviks," the "next and the most terrible" enemy were "the Ukrainians." Polish society was "mortally tired." Its reserves of physical and psychological strength were dwindling and nerves were stretched to breaking point.[436] The majority of the Polish population was inclined to support a radical solution for the Ukrainian question. The average Pole—as the Polish underground had already noted at the end of 1941—was in favor of deporting all Ukrainians over the river Zbrucz to Soviet Ukraine. Any thoughts about a possible reconciliation were, at best, voiced by only a few members of the elites of both groups, but as soon as the question touched on the issue of a possible border between a Ukrainian and a Polish state, all talks ceased.[437] In their memoranda on the "solution of the Ukrainian question," the staff of the Home Army of L'viv mirrored the Polish population's mood. In July 1942 it recommended deporting between one and one-and-a-half million Ukrainians to the Soviet Union and settling the remainder in other parts of Poland. Any suggestions about a limited autonomy for Ukrainians, as were being discussed in Warsaw and London, would find no support among the local population.[438] The attacks by Ukrainian partisans on Polish villages in Volhynia and East Galicia increased the Polish determination to remove the Ukrainian population living in the eastern Polish areas by resettling them. One author commented that the conditions after the war would be ideal because the Ukrainians could expect to be punished for their criminal behavior. One report recommended expropriating the Ukrainian peasants and resettling them. Such a resettlement would guarantee a Polish majority in the *kresy* (borderlands). The battle against the Ukrainians and the Soviets was seen as rooted in the tradition of the "centuries-old battle to ensure that these areas belonged to Europe."[439] The authors still firmly believed in the civilizing mission of Poles in the east—"our historic mission is to bring religion and culture to the East"—with the Ukrainians considered as belonging firmly in the East.[440] The education of the Ukrainian intelligentsia at Polish, German, or Czech universities had not changed this perception nor had their Catholic affiliation, since Ukrainians were held to possess an "eastern, Byzantine mentality."[441]

Poles overheard Ukrainian police greeting each other in the summer of 1943 with the slogan "death to the *lachy* [Poles]—death." Similar slogans began appearing on many trains and on many walls. In June 1943 one slogan scribbled on the walls of L'viv ghetto read "The ghetto for Poles."[442] In August 1943 murders of Poles in the L'viv region began to increase. The primary targets of attacks were priests, doctors and other members of the intelligentsia. But the terror was also directed against ordinary Poles and included women and children.[443] There was now open warfare between the Home Army and the UPA.[444] But not all Ukrainians and Poles were willing to resort to violence. The Home Army noted that in rural areas attacks were predominantly driven by the younger generation. The older Ukrainian peasants were often opposed to the attacks on their Polish neighbors.[445]

From the fall of 1943 the OUN-B lived in the expectation of an armed Polish rebellion "[that] will be directed in the first instance against us as autochthons of western Ukraine. The work of the Polish underground is principally directed against us . . . The passive section of the Poles also takes its cue from England, but in panic-stricken fear of the Bolsheviks it weakly fears Ukrainian repressions in times of chaos. It constitutes only a minority among the Poles."[446] In November 1943 the OUN reported that Poles everywhere were increasing their activities and stepping up the armed struggle against Ukrainians.[447]

By November 1943, the population of East Galicia was already living in the expectation of the impending arrival of the Red Army. The mood in the city became increasingly nervous. The Ukrainian intelligentsia—the OUN underground reported—was already preparing to flee while the workers had generally decided to stay put. After the last Soviet military offensive the general mood had changed to panic. "In general the Germans continue to rely on the Poles and trust them more, although the latter do not much 'deserve' it."[448]

The L'viv Home Army held a different opinion. In their view, the situation of Poles at the beginning 1944 was worse than ever before.[449] On the night of February 28–29, 1944, forty Poles were murdered in L'viv. The rumor rapidly spread that in March there would be a large-scale slaughter of Polish people.[450] In the spring of 1944, there was indeed a new wave of killings.[451] The murders of members of the Polish population by the Ukrainian auxiliary police, UPA units, and other Ukrainian partisans became a formative experience for L'viv Poles.[452] In the end, the Poles had more reservations about the Ukrainian police than about the German police.[453]

In contrast, the OUN-B reported in March 1944 that the Poles were terrorizing the Ukrainian population and villages and were propagating the idea that the "west Ukrainian territories" belonged to Poland.[454] In the evenings, Poles patrolled the streets, checking people's identity cards and shooting members of the Ukrainian auxiliary police.[455] Polish inhabitants attempted to move to larger settlements where more Poles were living, as these offered them better opportunities to defend themselves. Some Poles proposed sending women and children to the west.[456] But the Home Army called on Poles to sit tight in the eastern territories; their duty to the nation demanded that they stay.[457] The Roman Catholic clergy remained in L'viv. One SS-Sturmbannführer quoted Archbishop Bolesław Twardowski as saying, "The priests will stay here and with them the Polish people."[458]

The approach of the Soviet Army unnerved the Ukrainian population. The intelligentsia was panic-stricken, and by February many were already trying to flee westward with their families. "Our intelligentsia in the majority, they are slaves who wear stiff collars."[459]

While the German occupiers slowly began to prepare for their evacuation and flight, the OUN/UPA and the Home Army were preparing for a repeat of the Polish–Ukrainian war of 1918/1919. The potency of the interpretive models created after November 1918 was so strong that both sides envisaged highly unlikely constellations. Only the simultaneous defeat of both Nazi Germany and the Soviet Union would have resulted in a power vacuum where a Polish–Ukrainian war for L'viv and East Galicia would make any sense.

In the summer of 1943, the Home Army began initial preparations to forestall a Ukrainian seizure of power.[460] In the opinion of the Home Army, the control of L'viv alone would determine the outcome of the fight with the Ukrainians. Military plans were developed and a training program set up to prepare for the fight.[461] The Home Army wanted to protect museums and libraries against Ukrainian attacks. The regional command calculated that the Ukrainians would want to destroy them because the Ukrainians were hostile to Polish cultural heritage.[462]

In June 1944 the Home Army noted a convergence of Ukrainian partisans around L'viv and expected an attack on the city after the Germans had withdrawn.[463] The Home Army estimated the strength of the OUN in L'viv as around four hundred men, with approximately seventy thousand fighters across the entire region. The duty of the Poles was to hold on to L'viv with all available means and to mobilize the Polish population to that end.[464] The Home Army even wanted to set up an alarm that would make it possible, when necessary, to evacuate Poles living in houses where the majority of the inhabitants were Ukrainian.[465]

The German occupiers provided the framework in which the Polish–Ukrainian conflict was staged. But rather than racism it was the ideology of integral nationalism, which dictated the anti-Polish actions of the OUN and UPA and kept the L'viv Home Army focused on the "Ukrainian question" until the summer of 1944. From the failure to build a Ukrainian state between 1918 and 1920, the OUN drew the conclusion that it had to remove the demographic basis for an incorporation of L'viv and East Galicia into Poland. The prerequisite for this to have any prospect of success was the murder of the Galician Jews by Nazi Germany. The Ukrainian terror directed against Polish peasants was intended to force them to leave Volhynia and East Galicia. While these policies were inspired by the cynical and murderous German population policies, they were not identical to them. The Polish underground reacted analogously. Particularly along the "Polish–Ukrainian front line" in L'viv the Polish population and significant elements of the regional Home Army could not imagine that it would be possible to live together with Ukrainians after the war. They therefore favored an "ethnic cleansing" of the city and the region, with the expulsion or resettlement of the Ukrainian population in the east.

Endgame

On March 18, 1944, the government of the Generalgouvernement ordered the evacuation of families and persons who were citizens of the Reich (*Reichsdeutsche*) and of ethnic Germans (*Volksdeutsche*) not working in strategic areas important for the war.[466] On April 9, 1944, Soviet planes flew attacks against airports, railroad tracks, and barracks. One hundred civilians died in the bombing, 120 were injured.[467] German civilians were panic-stricken, believing the fall of L'viv to be imminent.[468] Airstrikes occurred again at the beginning of May 1944, but the damage inflicted was minimal.[469]

The security situation continued to be precarious. There were numerous political murders but also many robberies and murders with no political motives. The OUN-B noted that the Polish underground was holding back as it had suffered serious losses the previous month. The OUN had also had two confrontations with the Germans, which resulted in heavy losses. Nevertheless, German military commanders never ceased attempting to persuade the Ukrainian underground to collaborate.[470] Toward the end of the war there were occasional instances of collaboration between the UPA and the Wehrmacht. Among other things, Ukrainian partisans provided intelligence and reconnaissance information.[471] Shortly before the Wehrmacht left Ukraine, it also handed over weapons to the UPA to be used in the fight against the Soviet Army.

Unfazed by the gradual approach of the front line, the occupiers celebrated Hitler's fifty-fifth birthday: "L'viv had donned a festive robe in honor of the Führer's birthday. In the forenoon, the Wehrmacht mustered on Adolf-Hitler-Square for an impressive ceremony. The guards of honor of the Wehrmacht and Organisation Todt lined up in open square formation facing the opera house."[472]

In the summer of 1944, the occupiers set up the Junak-SS, consisting of Ukrainian youths wearing yellow-and-blue armbands and blue uniforms. At the beginning of July 1944 the new formations marched through the town. In the theater, the young recruits stood onstage and sang Ukrainian folk songs, thunderously applauded by their listeners. The young Ukrainians subsequently marched to the officers' mess of the Stadthauptmannschaft, where they were given soup. "The parents had gathered, men with rough bear-like fists, women in city clothes from L'viv, and young girls in airy summer dresses. One could see at first glance that the entire local population had turned out in force. The young men come from all classes of the Ukrainian population."[473]

On July 9, 1944, just three weeks before they left, the occupiers celebrated the third anniversary of their invasion of L'viv or, in their own words, the "liberation" of the city. The celebrations were used to mobilize the local population one last time against "bolshevism." The rally was held in front of the opera with "workers' communities [*Gefolgschaften*]" marching there in closed formations. A Wehrmacht unit marched to the square "with drums beating" and took up its place on the *carrée* opposite the uniformed men of the East Railroad (*Ostbahn*) and the "German Postal Service East." More than ten thousand spectators clustered behind them. "The guests of honor from Party, state and Wehrmacht stood in front of the opera decorated with swastika flags and the colors of the city of L'viv. The flames of the sacrificial basin on the stone memorial which bears the Führer's name burned brightly up to the blue skies above."

Accompanied by his head of administration Josef Brandl, Governor Wächter slowly walked down the massed ranks. The Wehrmacht military band played "Die Himmel rühmen des Ewigen Ehre" ("The Heavens Praise the Glory of the Everlasting God"). The first speech was by city captain Höller, who described the event as commemorating a "memorable day which had brought the population together today on Adolf-Hitler-Ring." Three years ago the German troops had entered the city "welcomed by the inhabitants, with flowers showered upon them and feted as liberators from the Bolshevist yoke." All L'viv had breathed freely again in the knowledge "that the incubus of the Bolshevist terror had been lifted off it. When we drove the Bolshevists out of L'viv at the time, the joy of these people was like a single passionate cry by a liberated people . . . Never forget that it is the German soldier who protects you and your children from the renewed flood of bolshevism!" After Höller finished, the head of the municipal advisory council Bilak spoke next as the representative for the Ukrainians. Until the last moment the UTsK continued to be fixated on Germany. The OUN had long since outstripped the UTsK as the most influential political force among the west Ukrainian population, but the UTsK represented a number of well-known politicians who had worked together with the German occupiers. Bilak thanked Hitler for the liberation and Governor Wächter for the formation of the SS-Schützendivision Galicia. These had created the prerequisites that would allow the "defiant youth of this land, standing shoulder to shoulder with German soldiers, to secure the future of the homeland in the European family of nations." And finally, Marceli Chlamtacz gave his speech, speaking as the representative of the Polish population. His address differed fundamentally from Bilak's pronouncements, revealing the limits to any political collaboration by the Polish side. Chlamtacz emphasized the loyal attitudes of the Poles toward the German administration and invoked "Western values," but without clearly lining up in support of the Germans. He avoided referring to the occasion for the celebrations. He strung together empty phrases and emotional clichés: "As a member of the occidental cultural community, most closely linked culturally with western Europe and supported by its institutions, the Polish population also wants these priceless moral goods to survive. During the worldwide struggle of all the peoples of this globe, during the struggle for a new law of life, a new symbol of general global justice arises in compensation for all the sacrifices and all the hardships of this difficult time."[474]

His Polish audience listened to his performance with increasing amusement, interpreting the empty phrases as a successful satire. Nevertheless, the Home Army rebuked Chlamtacz for having even taken part in the celebrations.[475]

The insincere pathos of the celebrations was incapable of appealing to the Poles and Ukrainians of L'viv. The Polish population passionately maintained its own national traditions. The memory of the Obrona Lwowa offered moral support. The Cmentarz Obrońców Lwowa (Cemetery of the Defenders of Lwów) was the symbol of Polish L'viv. Thus, on the occasion of the death of General Władysław Sikorski, on the evening of July 14, 1943, Poles laid a wreath at the plaque in the Cmentarz Obrońców Lwowa commemorating the Unknown Soldier.[476] The Polish population also continued to adhere to its tradition of assembling at the cemetery every November. On November 1, 1943, Poles decorated the graves in the military cemetery for the 1918/1919 "Defenders of Lwów" with Polish flags and lit candles. On the twenty-fifth anniversary of the battle for L'viv, pamphlets appeared bearing titles such as "Leopolis—semper fidelis," calling for a "free Poland with a Polish Lwów." At the same time placards in Polish appeared on many walls of the city bearing the inscription "The Fighting Poland." On November 22, 1943, inscriptions and pamphlets appeared everywhere that included phrases such as "Poland lives and fights," "Lwòw—always faithful," "November 1918—1943," and "Lwòw fights."[477]

On July 20, 1944, the OUN-B L'viv reported on the last days of German occupation. The streets were clogged with tanks, cars and weapons. Vehicles were filled to the very last place and heavily laden. On July 17, "our SS-men" were also evacuated from the hospitals. According to the description, the Ukrainian intelligentsia became "completely panic-stricken." Their terror made them forget to go "into the forest," attempting instead to get seat reservations and escape from the oncoming Red Army by car or train. The evacuation frenzy reached its highpoint on July 18 and 19, 1944: "Dantesque scenes occurred at train stations, at cars, on account of seat reservations. Every form of transport from cars to carts cost colossal sums. The streets were jammed with refugees, many of them Ukrainian police who were being evacuated on trucks together with their families in the direction of Sambor. The Ukrainian police had been partly disbanded on Friday. One saw people with expressions of insensate terror whose only impulse was to save their own precious skin." The OUN-B praised the equanimity of the Ukrainian working classes, placing its hopes in those who awaited "the new evil" with dignity and calm.[478]

On Tuesday, July 25, the first shrapnel began bursting over the city. At the same time Soviet planes carried out air raids. On Wednesday afternoon the last evacuation train left the city and the general attack on L'viv began.[479] As they had done elsewhere in eastern Ukraine, German units had mined all important buildings such as the railroad station, the electricity plant and the water utility. But the explosives were never triggered. The Gestapo disappeared from the city on the evening of July 25. They had previously released some criminals but had taken the political prisoners with them to an unknown location.[480]

Consequences of German Rule

The Soviet power returned to a region convulsed by the Polish–Ukrainian conflict, ravaged, and partially depopulated by the German occupation. In Brody, where 25,000 people had lived before the war (70 percent of them Jews), the Red Army found only 150 inhabitants on their return.[481] Matters were somewhat different in L'viv (see table 5.4). The German occupiers had murdered more than one hundred thousand Jews from the city, but in the last months of German occupation tens of thousands of Poles had fled their villages and had come to the city to escape the terror of the UPA. The Soviet prosecutor took a figure of 136,000 Jews as his starting point, who had either been already living in L'viv in June 1941 or been brought there during the German occupation.[482]

According to Soviet calculations, approximately 150,000 people had been murdered or fallen victim to epidemics, disease, or hunger out of a population of more than 300,000 people living in the city. In the L'viv region, 75,425 civilians and 159,212 Soviet prisoners of war had been killed. In October 1947 the statistics listed 132,205 Soviet citizens who had been deported during the German occupation from the L'viv region "into German slavery" (usually to Germany for so-called *Ostarbeit*, or "eastern work"). Only 27,929 had returned by October 1, 1947, of whom 595 returned from France.[483]

Date	Total	Poles	Ukrainians	Jews	Germans
Sept. 1931	312,231	157,490	49,747	99,595	2,448
Aug. 1939	333,500	169,900	53,200	104,700	2,600
Jan. 1940	500,000	no data	no data	no data	no data
Mar. 1940	399,000	no data	no data	no data	no data
May 1940	433,838	no data	no data	no data	no data
Aug. 1941	327,400	no data	no data	no data	no data
Nov. 1941	325,458	150,058	64,315	104,126	5,923
Sept. 1942*	319,606	172,735	83,570	50,000	11,901
Mar. 1943*	283,690	153,066	81,583	20,722	19,013
Aug. 1944	149,000	92,500	52,100	-	1,300

* These data refer to the city of L'viv in its new borders.

Table 5.4. Changes in the population and ethnic composition of the city of L'viv during World War II.[484]

Seventh Regime Change: Re-Sovietization and Resistance

Invasion

On Friday, July 28, the first Soviet troops appeared in the Ulica Zielona. On Sunday, for the first time Soviet Army soldiers reached Market Square. Although the German soldiers did not display much enthusiasm to fight, there was still heavy fighting in Galicia Square and St. Mary's Square. The Wehrmacht continued to defend some of the streets in the western part of the city to cover the retreat. In contrast to September 1939, the Red Army soldiers made a "very good impression." They were armed with American guns and looked healthy and well fed. They were friendly to the local population.[485]

The regional command of the Home Army had ensured that the city was decorated with Polish flags. On the city's most important buildings, the Polish flag flew alongside the flags of the United States, Great Britain, and the USSR. By these means the Home Army was demonstrating the Polish claim to L'viv.[486] As part of Operation Burza (Tempest) the Home Army had taken control of the city after the departure of the Germans. In East Galicia, the Home Army commanded more than twenty-seven thousand fighters in July 1944, only a few less than the OUN and the UPA. The Home Army units were primarily concentrated in the cities, most notably in L'viv.[487] The first Polish pamphlets already started appearing within hours, welcoming the Soviet Army as an ally and liberator. At the same time "young, predominantly rather inexperienced Poles with red-and-white armbands" patrolled the streets armed with pistols, hand grenades, and other weapons. These self-appointed militia occupied several buildings and decorated them with white and red flags. This was done—in the opinion of the OUN—in order to prevail on the Bolsheviks to set up a Polish state in Galicia.[488] For their bases they used the commissariats of the former Ukrainian police. There were about eighty to one hundred people at every station, most of them aged between seventeen and thirty-five years. In the eyes of the OUN, this militia was made up of "scum," workers, a few students, and women. The activities of the militia had immediately been directed against Ukrainians. Searches, controls, and arrests took place. The Polish youths had murdered a few families and various individuals, most of them Ukrainians who had maintained contacts with the Germans. On the streets, the militia controlled Ukrainians and arrested them or put them against the wall and shot them. The OUN estimated that between fifty and one hundred people were murdered by Polish militiamen.[489]

The arriving Soviet cadres noticed the good mood among the Polish population in the early days after the Soviet arrival.[490] But the first disappointment arose when the Poles found no Polish officers in the Soviet Army and they asked about the whereabouts of Polish officers.[491] The OUN also noted the initial joy and the subsequent deep disappointment of the Poles in L'viv. The "Bolshevik-Polish idyll"—in the words of the OUN—had quickly ended. The Poles were obliged to remove their flag and the flags of the Western allies from the town hall. On Friday there were already fewer flags flying, and fewer armed Poles walking the streets. All national badges and insignia of the "Lwòw eagles" disappeared. In the OUN's view, the sympathies of the Poles were as follows: 70 percent of Poles trusted the government in exile in London. The older generation was more tolerant of the idea of a free Ukraine, but the younger generation reacted with hatred. All Poles unanimously rejected the concept of a Soviet Poland. Inscriptions such as "Poland fights" began appearing on the walls again—just as they had under German occupation. But the Soviets had recognized, the OUN continued, that this whole "obsequious community are all, essentially, zoologically Polish nationalists." The security organizations arrested three hundred Poles and shot several dozen of them, accusing them of having murdered Ukrainians.[492]

Once again, as the conditions changed Ukrainians and Poles were jockeying against each other for executive and leadership positions in hospitals, factories, companies and the administration. Some Poles used the anti-Soviet mood of the Ukrainian population to offer their services to the Soviet authorities as the more reliable partners. The OUN summarized the situation as follows: "The village fears the Bolsheviks—the city and the villages around L'viv [fear] the Poles."[493]

All the while, the OUN watched the unfolding of the "Bolshevik reality." While the first Red Army units were orderly (*kul'turnyj*), behaved well toward the local population, and refrained from stealing private property, they were followed by an apparently endless stream of new people who passed through the city and whose appearance, according to the commentators of the OUN, seemed to worsen progressively. Their weapons were poor and their uniforms shoddy, they drove old machines and tanks and were seated in primitive cars. They were much worse armed than the Wehrmacht, although numerically they far outnumbered the Germans. The author praised the Ukrainian soldiers in the Soviet army; they were friendly, did not rob the locals, and helped the population. The OUN believed they might be receptive to Ukrainian nationalist propaganda.[494]

The first Jews came out of hiding shortly after the Germans had finally left during the night of July 27–28, 1944. On August 1, 1944, 811 Jews who had survived in L'viv or the surrounding areas were registered. They were looking for jobs to work as managers or employees in trading or food companies. But many were ill and incapable of working. The OUN commented that Polish and Ukrainian inhabitants viewed the Jews "with unfriendly anxiety"; Poles and Ukrainians feared that the Jews would be privileged and would denounce their Christian fellow citizens because of their behavior under German rule. The OUN was reassured when Soviet soldiers revealed their open anti-Semitism in private conversations: "Among the fighters one could note—possible as a result of our propaganda—a hostile attitude towards the Jews." In some cases, soldiers had turned away Jews and not given them anything to eat. Some officers and soldiers said that Hitler had done the right thing with the Jews. They opined that the Bolsheviks had seen through the Jews and would relocate them to Palestine. The OUN even reported two cases in which Soviet soldiers had beaten Jews to death. In the one case, the Jew had previously beaten a German prisoner of war; in the other case, a Jew had demanded his money back from someone who had been keeping the money for him. "The sympathy for the Jews among the soldiers and commanders of the Red Army is not particularly great." The OUN carefully noted that not a single Jewish speaker had been present at the big public meeting held on July 30, 1944. Although about one thousand Jews had already been registered, no aid programs were set up for them, their sufferings were not remembered, and no materials were collected in order to document the anti-Jewish activities of the Nazis. In the opinion of the OUN, this showed that the attitude of the Bolsheviks toward the Jews had fundamentally changed. There were rumors of the mass liquidation of Jews in the USSR.[495]

The first NKVD units appeared in the city two days after the entry of the Soviet Army. Their initial activities were directed primarily against the Poles. But a few members of the Ukrainian Central Committee (the collaborationist Ukrainischer Hauptausschuß) were also arrested.[496] The NKVD attempted to prevail on

Poles to act as informers. One OUN report listed examples of Poles denouncing Ukrainians for collaborating with the Gestapo.[497]

In August, one OUN report again remarked on the huge difference between the frontline troops and the army units which followed. The second wave had consisted of an entirely different sort of people: dirty, carrying primitive weapons, poorly equipped, "racially mixed" soldiers. The NKVD officials and party members had been well fed and self-assured and had been accompanied by a host of Soviet women "covered with make-up and sporting unwashed perms." All in all, all this "civilization imported to us" consisted of "a few hundred primitive, antiquated cars, greasy shirts" together with numerous portraits of Stalin and other "holy idols" who looked down "on us all who were living 'under the sun of the Stalinist constitution' with 'happy smiles' on the squares and streets." The OUN described an entire "world of the darkest and lowest Russian and Mongolian tribes." Some of the newcomers were civilized (*kul'turnye*) people, the majority of them Ukrainians together with an occasional elderly Georgian, but such persons had no influence on the Soviet reality. As far as "our [Ukrainian] culture" was concerned, the neophytes hated "us" most while at the same time they envied "us." They perceived the superiority of "our life." The Poles were viewed by the incomers as temporary allies and not to be trusted.[498] Many Red Army soldiers happily acknowledged their Ukrainian nationality.[499] But Ukrainian society, the OUN opined, was under no illusions about its future under Soviet rule; it hoped that there would be changes after the war and put its trust in the UPA, which was becoming much more important. But the Ukrainian element in L'viv would only become active if victory was near, and it was currently listening intently to the news that could be obtained from the villages.[500]

The Soviet Perception

Sovietization picked up where it had left off in 1941. The inhabitants of East Galicia were considered Soviet citizens who had temporarily lived under enemy occupation. The base of Soviet power and the main targets for its propaganda and educational work were the poor and middle peasants, the workers, and members of the progressive intelligentsia.[501]

The party leadership identified "class enemies," *kulaks*, the bourgeoisie and priests as the backbone of the nationalist Ukrainian partisans. The challenge that the concept of *Samostijna Ukraïna* (i.e., independent Ukraine) presented to a Soviet Ukraine was explained using the language of class strife. The politburo of the Ukrainian Communist Party told the regional party committees to pay special attention "to the uncovering of sabotage by *kulaks*, dealers and other capitalist elements," because they were "the supporters and organizers of the gangs of Ukrainian-German nationalists."[502] The poor and middle peasants were to be gathered around the communist party and the Soviets, who would lead them in the "fight against *kulak* elements and their armed gangs—the Ukrainian-German nationalists." These classifications appeared mainly at the level of the regional party committees and in their reports to the Central Committee of the Ukrainian Communist Party. Social categories played a minor role in the actual fight against Ukrainian resistance. However, in addition to the enemies identified above and their families, another social category, the *kulaks*, also became a target. During a meeting in L'viv on May 15, 1945, Nikita Krushchev instructed the regional party secretaries and the heads of the regional administrations of the NKVD and the NKGB (People's Commissariat for State Security) that "the bandits are relying on kulaks, dealers, priests and other elements." It was made clear to the members of the administration that in the case of any 'bandit' activities in their village they would be arrested and banished, together with their families.[503] One important target for propaganda was young Ukrainians, because most fighters of the Ukrainian Insurgent Army were recruited from this group. The party leadership repeatedly complained about the poor links between party and society, in particular the lack of a good relationship to young Ukrainians, and reproached the Komsomol for its passivity. The inactivity of cadres was due, not least, to a fear of being active in rural areas where the representatives of Soviet rule risked being killed by partisans.[504]

Expulsion and Resettlement of the Poles

The party organizations in Moscow, Kiev, and L'viv considered the Poles, in contrast to the Ukrainians, as a homogeneous group. With the exception of the NKVD and NKGB, the party and state organizations did not try to infiltrate the Polish population. The authorities categorized the Poles as nationalists, whatever their class, and believed them to be loyal to the London government in exile.[505] Their reports showed that the Poles considered themselves as Polish citizens and the areas where they lived as part of Poland. One reason for the decision of the Soviet leadership to deport this section of the population was its strong loyalty to Poland. "Ethnic cleansing" prevented the emergence of a Polish irredenta in the Soviet Union.

During a public meeting in August 1944 the Soviets—to the great delight of the Ukrainians—emphasized that they considered L'viv to be a Ukrainian and Soviet city, not a Polish city. The Poles were accused of having Polonized the city for three centuries. The L'viv party secretary proposed restoring the "old Ukrainian character" of the city. To do this, Ukrainians, especially urban populations, should be resettled from Poland to L'viv and Poles should leave the city. Workers and members of the intelligentsia should be called in from eastern Ukraine. In western Ukraine, Krushchev denied the Poles the Polish schools that existed elsewhere in the Soviet Union. Soviet schoolbooks were forcibly introduced and lessons in all institutions of higher education were required to be held in Ukrainian or Russian.⁵⁰⁶

In September 1944 the Soviet government and the communist Polish Lublin Committee agreed on an exchange of Ukrainian and Polish populations. Poles were deported to the new Poland, Belarusians and Ukrainians from Poland were transferred to the respective Soviet republics. There can be no doubt that the resettlement of hundreds of thousands of Poles to the west and of Ukrainians and Belarusians to the east amounted to "ethnic cleansing." The Poles in the west of the Soviet Union were regarded as a "diaspora nation," which always would tend to Poland. In this understanding of the different ethnic groups, Ukrainians and Belarusians from Poland could, after careful reeducation, be included in the Soviet Belarusian and Soviet Ukrainian nations. The aim of resettlement was to reduce ethnic complexity for political reasons and prevent any form of irredentism.⁵⁰⁷

The regional party committee initially emphasized the voluntary nature of the departures. When Poles stubbornly refused to leave the country, the party committee reacted with threats and force. But to begin with, the duties implicit on Soviet citizens were also extended to the Polish population. Poles were called on to serve in the Red Army and were recruited for labor in eastern Ukraine. The regional organizations of the Home Army were rounded up, and many of the officers, as well as ordinary members, were arrested, deported, or recruited into the Soviet Army. After two months in solitary confinement and intensive interrogations, the delegate of the Polish government in exile, Adam Ostrowski, gave in and agreed to cooperate. He handed the NKVD a list with the names of Home Army members. All were arrested. Ostrowski was released and went on to forge a career in the People's Republic of Poland.⁵⁰⁸

The devotion of L'viv Poles to their city was so great that—according to Soviet reports—many were ready to stay, even if the city would now be part of the Soviet Union. It was the wave of new arrests that finally made the Poles give up. Almost all Poles registered that they wished to depart.⁵⁰⁹ The Poles of L'viv were allowed to take some of their monuments with them. The remnant, with the exception of two monuments, were demolished in 1947 as symbols of Polish power and as an "insult to Ukrainian national culture."⁵¹⁰

Ukrainian Resistance

After the German retreat deserters, bands of criminals, scattered groups of Ukrainian partisans and units of the Polish Home Army moved through western Ukraine. Initially the Soviet Union did not have enough people to pacify the conquered territories.⁵¹¹ The lack of sufficient numbers of Soviet forces made security organizations and authorities vulnerable. The population rejected Soviet rule. However, the officials bizarrely misjudged the mood of their new subjects.

Thus, the L'viv regional party secretary Hrushets'kyj reported to the Ukrainian party leader N. S. Khrushchev that the people had remained loyal to the Soviet state and were full "of confidence in their future life in the family of peoples of the great Soviet Union."[512]

Soviet propaganda repeated again and again that Ukrainian nationalists were Hitlerite tools and traitors, who tried to incite the Russian and Ukrainian brother nations to fight one another.[513] Members of the male population fit for military service were drafted into the Red Army. It was not just a question of filling up the army ranks; recruitment also aimed to cut off the reinforcements of young men to the UPA. Recruits were therefore carefully vetted in filtration camps. However, these measures were only partly successful because the OUN called on the Ukrainian population to evade recruitment.[514] Later, the UPA changed its tactics and recommended would-be recruits to infiltrate the Red Army and agitate non-Russian soldiers.[515]

The UPA urged Ukrainian society to protect "the souls of the young generation from moral aberrations." Pupils—lamented the UPA—were being exposed to Soviet propaganda and were subject to "the influence of a hostile culture." They ordered Ukrainian teachers not to teach "love for father Stalin" and to allow their pupils to sing Ukrainian folk songs instead of Soviet hymns. Teachers were threatened and those who did not oppose the Bolshevik slogans were regarded as traitors to the Ukrainian nation and risked punishment by the partisans.[516] In the second half of the 1940s, the Communist Party ordered almost forty-four thousand teachers from eastern Ukraine to move to the western territories. The party leadership wanted to reduce the risk of local teachers fomenting an anti-Soviet attitude among the youth of western Ukraine.[517]

The Ukrainian Insurgent Army was fighting to control the minds of the populace and opposed Sovietization by any means available. Representatives of the Soviet state were killed on a daily basis. The partisans showed no mercy for local Ukrainians who cooperated with the security organs or held functions in the Soviet administration.[518] The resistance movement did not cease when the war ended. The UPA calculated that a war between the Soviet Union and the United States and Great Britain was only a question of time. In the meantime, the UPA fought a partisan war because it was not able to meet the Soviet security forces and the Red Army in open battle.[519] The violence of the UPA and the Soviet forces escalated. Between February 1944 and December 1946 alone, partisans killed almost 12,000 officials and Soviet agents; 3,914 were wounded, and 2,401 reported missing, presumably kidnapped by partisans. The lower levels of the administration were hit particularly hard, undermining the willingness of the local population to cooperate with the Soviet occupiers. The ethnic or regional origin of victims was irrelevant for the UPA terror. More than 50 percent of the victims were local Ukrainians. Anyone working for the Soviet Union risked his or her life.⁵²⁰ According to recent estimates, by the end of 1945 the partisans had killed thirty thousand communists, soldiers, and local collaborators.⁵²¹

The security organizations reacted with merciless violence. No prisoners were taken. Between February 1944 and October 1945, they killed approximately one hundred thousand partisans. Very few were captured alive. By comparison, in the Baltic republics and in Belarus many more partisans were taken prisoner, and far fewer were killed. In Lithuania, approximately four thousand partisans were killed but more than fourteen thousand were captured alive.⁵²² In western Ukraine, the number of captured partisans seems to have gradually increased. The party leadership complained that partisans were often killed unnecessarily. This criticism was not the result of humane scruples; it was felt that large-scale killings negatively affected Soviet intelligence work as the lack of prisoners made tracking down other partisans more difficult.⁵²³ The warfare was accompanied by symbolic actions. Soviet units systematically devastated the graves of partisans to prevent them from becoming places of pilgrimage and sites that could spawn a cult of martyrs.⁵²⁴

Already in March 1944 Khrushchev ordered the deportation of families of partisans to Siberia. This led to some partisans leaving the woods and giving up.⁵²⁵ The local security organizations and party authorities made extensive use of this form of repression.⁵²⁶ The reasoning behind such actions was twofold: the first aim was to destroy the partisans' bases; the second was to deter the population from supporting the UPA. The Soviet *agentura* (secret service) knew that the young men filling up the ranks of the partisans were often replacing their brothers who had been killed or arrested. Over the course of 1946, collective liability was extended from families to entire villages. When a Soviet official was killed, the families of known partisans were first deported, followed by *kulak* families and finally randomly selected peasant families. In April 1947 a regional party secretary recommended deporting whole villages where necessary. One of the reasons for such reactions by the local authorities was because they had difficulty in assigning the UPA to a specific social class. Partisans did not only have the support of wealthy peasants, their social base was much broader. In one oblast, only 28 out of 416 people sentenced for partisan activities belonged to *kulak* families, 156 were middle peasants, and approximately 30 were poor peasants. If the Soviet security forces identified anybody as a helper of the partisans, it did not matter whether he was a poor peasant or a *kulak*. Most partisans were between eighteen and twenty-five years old. According to the official statistics of 1946 only 40 percent of all sentenced nationalists were men. The high proportion of women was due to the fact that the men often could not be caught and their wives were taken in their stead. Khrushchev finally concluded, "The enemy is in the midst of the population." However, by April 1947 Khrushchev wanted to restrict the deportation of families to the active helpers of the partisans.⁵²⁷

The security services were not given carte blanche. The NKVD and party cadres were held judicially liable if—during drunken excesses—they used excessive force, stole, or murdered. But the commandos behaved as though they were in enemy territory, carrying out acts of collective retribution against the local population notwithstanding their official status as Soviet citizens. The line between permissible and forbidden terror was unclear and not easily recognized by NKVD commanders. One unit was held to have overshot the mark when it revenged the killing of three comrades by shooting ten villagers between the ages of sixty and eighty and setting forty-five houses on fire, leading to an investigation by the regional party committee of Ternopil. The regional party leadership was especially annoyed because twenty of the destroyed houses belonged to the families of Red Army soldiers.[528] A defected partisan leader reported that the NKVD had no idea of the local conditions and usually arrested people who had nothing to do with the partisans. He complained that the NKVD waged war not only against "bandits" but also against completely innocent people and in this way discredited the Soviet authorities.[529]

Collective acts of retribution by local security forces show that the politics formulated in Moscow and Kiev could, at a local level, take on an ethnic dimension. The hostile attitude of the majority of West Ukrainians could not be understood if the interpretation was based only on class categories. The Soviet cadres had expected to meet with a favourably disposed population which was being repressed by a small minority and by the agents of foreign powers. The strength of the resistance showed that these expectations were false. Soviet officials had to learn how local populations differentiated between friends and enemies to be capable of fighting the partisans effectively. The official labeling of the UPA as "Ukrainian German gangs" did not help, because the Germans had already left the area, and once the Germans had surrendered the partisans could not be depicted as controlled by the enemy. The local Soviet cadres had to learn that ethnic categories were more important for the behavior of the native population than social stratifications and that they had to adapt their activities to local conditions. Although the local cadres explained their politics to Kiev and Moscow in the language of class struggle, in practice class categories were of minor importance.

The peasants reacted ambivalently to terror and counterterror. On one hand, the partisans were only able to hold out against the Soviet authorities for such a long time because they enjoyed the support of part of the local population. On the other hand, the UPA forced the population to provide support.[530] The security forces in their turn organized public executions with thousands of spectators to deter potential partisans, and party organizations reported that the population had welcomed the executions.[531] The security apparatus forced captured partisans to confess their deeds at public meetings. Soviet officials encouraged local populations to form militias in an attempt to protect their settlements against criminal gangs and nationalist partisans. Now and then, the peasants lynched partisans who had murdered village officials or had been the cause of acts of collective retribution carried out by Soviet forces against the village.[532] Sometimes peasants fought both Ukrainian partisans and criminal gangs.[533]

The local population was caught between a rock and a hard place. Any form of collaboration was dangerous, whether it was with the Soviet authorities or with the UPA. But the longer the fight lasted and the lower the hope of success, the more the population ceased to support the UPA. The population had had enough of war and terror and had to reckon with the retributive killing of local people and the deportation of whole families. How divided the population was can be shown by the example of a village nearby Drohobych. According to reports of the NKVD, sixty-one of its inhabitants fought in the ranks of the partisans in January 1946 while fifty-four had joined the Red Army.[534] Even the chairman of the village Soviet had joined the UPA. In some areas, the Soviet administration was paralyzed because of attacks on Soviet functionaries.[535]

In the spring of 1946, the OUN and the UPA noticed that the support of the population was beginning to waver under the impact of propaganda and terror.[536] Although the UPA was convinced that the majority of the population sympathized with its aims, it also noted that some of the local population had begun to enter the service of "the enemy."[537] But the resistance of the Ukrainian partisans was not easily broken. Collectivization measures strengthened the UPA. In the spring of 1946, many eastern Ukrainians, together with Russians and Belarusians, arrived in western Ukraine looking for food, after the areas they had been living in were hit by bad harvests. Western Ukraine had enjoyed a good harvest that year. The authorities were concerned that this would led to a setback for the acceptance of Soviet rule in western Ukraine; the UPA feared that this influx of new people would make it easier for soviet *agentura* to infiltrate the resistance movement. But the UPA used the famine to agitate against the *kolkhoz* system and against Soviet rule and tried to make the idea of an independent Ukrainian state palatable to eastern Ukrainians: "We will not create a Ukrainian state without the east." Instructions went out to agitate workers, intellectuals, "party members, *moskaly*, Georgians and all others and even NKVD cadres" under the slogan "Look to the east."[538] The terms *moskaly* and *Russians*, to which the attributes Bolshevik or Soviet were frequently affixed, began appearing in leaflets that stated that Muscovite imperialism and its puppets wanted to rob Ukrainian children of their last slice of bread.[539] As time passed the term *Bolshevik* began to be used more and more and the term *Russian* less and less. The partisan leadership even instructed its members to disseminate anti-Soviet propaganda among Russians as among all other nationalities. While ethnic categories were becoming more important for local Soviet authorities, ethnic categories no longer played such a prominent role in the propaganda of the UPA. *Moskaly* were no longer identified with Soviet rule. In the fight against the Soviet system, Russians could also become potential allies.

Immediately after the war, the security apparatus exploited the Ukrainian-Polish animosity by enlisting the help of Polish informers to help them in their fight against Ukrainian partisans. In the first months after the return of the Red Army, Home Army units sometimes cooperated with security forces. The Home Army tried to protect its compatriots from the terror of the UPA, which aimed to drive out the Poles. The UPA consequently accused Poles of collaborating with the NKVD. It registered that Poles cheered when Ukrainians were arrested.[540] However, one NKVD commander went too far by organizing a purely Polish battalion that, working as a Soviet unit, went on to attack Ukrainian villages. In the word of a Soviet district attorney, such methods stirred up the "national enmity between the Ukrainian and the Polish population," and the district prosecutor ordered the commander to reorganize the unit.[541] The few surviving Jews—reported the UPA—feared the Ukrainians and supported the NKVD. The majority of Jews wanted to leave the Ukraine because they were not sure if the authorities would be able to protect them from persecution.[542] The front lines in this undeclared war were vague and constantly shifting. In 1945/1946 selective alliances against the Red Army were also concluded between the UPA and the Polish Home Army.[543]

The fight between Soviet and UPA *agentura* was hard. Both managed to infiltrate their respective enemy organizations with double agents. But the NKVD and NKGB had considerably more experience of such operations. Soviet *agentura* contributed significantly to the eradication of the Ukrainian underground. The NKVD maintained a network of agents throughout the whole country and created a climate of general distrust in the UPA. In the end, everybody suspected everyone else. On July 1, 1945, the NKVD had 11,214 local officials and informers on its books.[544]

The work of the secret service organizations was suddenly made more difficult by the forced resettlement of the Poles. An important group of informers were no longer in the country. But in the long run this "ethnic cleansing" helped the cause of Sovietization. Land, houses and other forms of accommodation were now available and could be occupied by West Ukrainians; moreover, one of the aims of integral Ukrainian nationalism had been achieved, that of an ethnically "pure" western Ukraine. The NKVD used the ethnic conflicts to fight the Ukrainian partisans. But such policies were not one-dimensional. The Soviets did not systematically stir up ethnic conflicts. It was not a "central tactic of Soviet power."[545]

Sovietization

The security forces destroyed environments that were hostile to the Soviet Union. But the party did its best to win over the population through propaganda and education. By unifying all Ukrainian lands in a single state, the old dream of the

Ukrainian national movement was fulfilled. After the Holocaust and the flight and deportation of the Poles there were no competing ethnic groups left. There were no longer any obstacles facing the Ukrainization of towns, culture, education, science, the administration, and the economy.

During and immediately after the war the Soviet leadership exploited Ukrainian patriotism to mobilize the Ukrainian population against the German enemy. As in Russia, the propaganda made use of historical images whereby invaders from the west were beaten back by a heroic Ukrainian people. The fight against non-Russian aggressors and brotherhood with the Russian people were the acid test that decided whether a Ukrainian hero would find a place in the Soviet Ukrainian pantheon. All the Soviet nations practised this model. But the Ukrainians held a special place within the Soviet Union. Soviet Ukrainian elites were permitted to speak of the "great Ukrainian people" at a time when the public discourse was dominated by references to the greatness of the Russian people. In the hierarchy of Soviet nations, the Ukrainians occupied a place directly behind the Russians.[546]

Sovietization followed the standard pattern of Soviet nationality policy, that is, "national in form, socialist in content." However, the "socialist content" had a distinctly Russian flavor. One example of this is the policy toward the Greek Catholic Church and religion in general.

The Soviet leadership strove to unite the Greek Catholic Church with the Russian Orthodox Church. After an initial period of caution towards the Greek Catholic Church, in April 1945 the NKVD arrested the new Greek Catholic archbishop, Josyf Slipyj, together with all Greek Catholic bishops and many priests who opposed the union of the Russian Orthodox Church with the Greek Catholic Church. The arrests were accompanied by a campaign directed against the recently deceased Greek Catholic Archbishop Andrii Sheptyts'kyj, who was accused of having been an agent of the pope and the Germans at one and the same time.[547] However, a number of Greek Catholic priests supported the union. The Ukrainian government advised the Orthodox Church to send priests and bishops to western Ukraine who could speak Ukrainian and could read Church Slavonic texts with a Ukrainian accent. Church and government both hoped that this might make the Ukrainian intelligentsia in L'viv more conciliatory.[548]

By October 1945 an "Initiative Group" composed of priests who favoured unification had won over about six to eight hundred Greek Catholic clergymen.[549] Between March 8 and 10, 1946, a synod of unification was held in the cathedral of Saint George in L'viv, attended by 216 participants from the clergy and the laity.[550] The supporters of the union had other motives than those of the Soviet leadership. One Soviet informer reported that at a secret meeting Havryiïl Kostel'nyk, the founder of the Initiative Group, had recommended joining the Orthodox Church as a means of protecting believers. He argued that the Bolsheviks were striving to destroy the local intelligentsia and they could only escape danger by sheltering under the protective mantle of the Orthodox Church. During his visits to Kiev and Moscow he had seen how the Orthodox hierarchy wanted to learn from western Ukraine. The Church of western Ukraine would have to be the teacher of eastern Ukraine.[551]

The reaction of the Ukrainian intelligentsia to the coerced union was not uniform; some saw it as an opportunity to overcome the gulf that separated eastern and western Ukrainians and to consolidate the Ukrainian position within the Soviet Union.[552] Others sought protection for themselves and their faith under the mantle of the Russian Orthodox Church. However, most interpreted the unification as a form of Russification. Some believers announced they would prefer to become Roman Catholic because of their fear of Russification as a result of the union.[553] The historian Kryp"jakevych feared that the end of the Greek Catholic Church and the detention of the archbishop would mean the incarceration of the "national spirit," or even the incarceration of Galicia.[554] The peasants themselves were more concerned with the rites than with the canonical background of their priests. Many "unified" priests continued to hold masses in the traditional manner.[555] The UPA, however, threatened supporters of the union and wanted to expel the "priests from the east" from the villages. But the UPA's antiunion campaign does not appear to have led to any systematic terror against "unified" clergymen.[556] However, Kostel'nyk was considered a traitor by the nationalist Ukrainian underground and was assassinated in 1948.

The security organizations subsequently began coming down much harder on the opponents of the union. After the unification of the two churches in March 1946, Greek Catholic priests and monks opposing the union were arrested, and numerous priests were shot. All in all, more than half the of Greek Catholic clergy experienced some form of repression in the first two years after the war.

A peculiar population mix arose in former Polish or Jewish towns. Ukrainian peasants joined the established Ukrainian intelligentsia and lower classes; their numbers were augmented by Ukrainian refugees from Poland, as well as workers and functionaries from eastern Ukraine and other Soviet Republics. During industrialization the population of L'viv increased by leaps and bounds. But the previous heavy population losses, deportations, and forced migrations meant that in the mid-1950s only about 20 percent of postwar residents had been living in the city before the war. After the expulsion of the Poles the most important positions in politics, the administration, and the economy were occupied by newly arrived people from the east. The party leadership made sure that it was usually Ukrainians who were sent to western Ukraine. In March 1945, 12,000 workers arrived in the L'viv oblast alone; 4,250 were Communist Party members who were given the task of establishing local and regional party organizations. For many of the new arrivals, the transfer to the western region was an important step in their career. They were given leading positions for which they often were not qualified. At the time only eight hundred locals held any of the top positions.[557] One year later barely 12 percent of the fifteen thousand *nomenklatura* positions were held by local people. In August 1947 a mere 5,000 of the 17,275 members of the intelligentsia were local people.[558]

The party leaders of the eastern Ukrainian oblasti had to deal with a shortage of competent cadres. They had to exclude party members who had not fled to the Soviet hinterland in 1941 or joined the partisans. Reliable communists who could play a major role in the reconstruction of the economy and society were few and far between. The party leadership in Kiev and Moscow ordered some of the eastern Ukrainian cadres to be sent to the newly conquered areas in the west. But regional party leaderships decided to retain their best staff members and preferred to send people with less training who were also less reliable. Repeated criticisms by the Kiev party leadership had no effect.[559] Nevertheless, over the next few years hundreds of thousands of Soviet citizens moved to the newly acquired territories.

The party was in a quandary. It was essential that western Ukrainians should not feel colonized. But although it was important to promote local people, there was no existing western Ukrainian "proletarian" intelligentsia. Qualified local people tended to have a "petty bourgeois" background; a large percentage of the students came from families with close ties to the priesthood.[560] The party therefore began a campaign to encourage local people with the proper class background to study. For others from different backgrounds, access to higher education was restricted.[561]

Ukrainization measures were partly retracted in 1946, with priority given to Sovietization. This change reflected the new ideological climate at the center. From the summer of 1946 the category of "class" and the fight against class enemies determined the policies of party and state. While the new ideological ice age (called *zhdanovshchina,* after party secretary Andrej Zhdanov) was directed against "cosmopolitism" and "bourgeois" culture and society in Moscow and Leningrad, in the Ukraine this ideological campaign had an ethnic component. In the opinion of the Moscow party leadership, the Ukrainian elites in Soviet Ukraine had overemphasized Ukrainian patriotism, had slipped into "bourgeois nationalism," and thus had unwittingly helped the UPA and the OUN. The Ukrainian national intelligentsia had been courted, but after the summer of 1946 it came under strong pressure.[562] Regional party organizations noted that these measures led to widespread discontent. They recognized that the majority of the Ukrainian intelligentsia perceived the "fight for the improvement of the intellectual political level in literature and the fight against national narrow-mindedness" as an attack by Russian nationalism. Although the intellectuals had been impressed by the distribution of land to the peasants, the removal of the Polish settlers and the

Ukrainization of culture and education, they made a distinction between local people and newcomers from the east. They criticized the Russian inscriptions, the portraits of Russian artists in the artists' clubs and the use of Russian in public life as attempts to limit their national rights. The imputation was that Soviets intended to Russify L'viv, also through industrialization. Many intellectuals—the regional party leadership noted—did not understand why it was necessary to oppose the "anti-people theory" of the "bourgeois-national" historian Hrushevs'kyj. Collectivization and the potential underlying objectives of the collectivization were also discussed controversially.[563]

In October 1946 the Central Committee of the Ukrainian Communist Party discussed the problems of "ideological work" in western Ukraine. The main target was the "bourgeois-nationalist concepts of the so-called historical school of Hrushevs'kyj." The Central Committee ordered the Faculty of History of L'viv University to hold a general meeting. The meeting followed the ritual form of "criticism and self-criticism." The "main attack" was directed against Ivan Kryp"jakevych, professor for Ukrainian History at the university and director of the Historical Institute of the Department of the Ukrainian Academy of Science in L'viv and against Myron Korduba. Both men had been students of Hrushevs'kyj. Both refused to practice self-criticism and dared to openly defend their deceased teacher.[564] Three months earlier the dean of the History Faculty had already pledged to the regional party committee and the Department for Agitation and Propaganda of the Ukrainian Central Committee that he would dismiss Kryp"jakevych and Korduba. But in July 1946 the party protected both from sharp criticism. The regional party committee prevented the publication of a critical article by Dean Gorbatjuk.[565] Regional party leader Hrushets'kyj was therefore sharply criticized during the August plenum of the Central Committee of the Communist Party (Bolsheviks) of Ukraine, because he had not prevented the formation of a "bourgeois school" among L'viv historians and had not trained them in the spirit of Marxist-Leninist theory.[566]

Korduba died in 1947 and Kryp"jakevych was banished to Kiev. The stubborn refusal of both professors to dissociate themselves from Hrushevs'kyj was one reason why on October 28, 1946, the Ukrainian Academy of Sciences with the approval of the government of the UkrSSR dissolved the arts departments of the Ukrainian Academy in L'viv and transferred its most prominent members to Kiev. The local intelligentsia was horrified. They talked of the destruction of L'viv as a Ukrainian cultural center, of the "Russification of the city" and the "destruction of its Ukrainian physiognomy."[567] Some interpreted this as an attack by Jews and *moskaly* on Ukrainians. These remarks show how lastingly the decades of fighting along ethnic lines had shaped the perceptions of Ukrainian intellectuals. The Soviet leadership did not plan to Russify the city or region but intended to implement a Soviet model of society and to suppress any dreams of an independent Ukrainian state. As compensation they offered a form of Ukrainian particularism which was compatible with affiliation to the Soviet Union.

The campaign against "Ukrainian nationalist positions" in culture and science continued in 1947 and determined the repertoire played in opera houses and theaters and the history of literature taught in education and at the Historical Institute of the Ukrainian Academy of Sciences. The known Stalinist D. Z. Manuil'skij played a key role in this campaign. He was a politburo member of the Ukrainian Communist Party (from 1944 to 1952) and deputy chairman of the Ukrainian Council of Ministers (from 1944 to 1953). He reproached Kryp"jakevych, insisting that his "bourgeois nationalist distortions of the history of Ukraine" played into the hands of "Ukrainian bourgeois nationalism."[568] Similar reproaches were also directed against western Ukrainian writers and musicians.[569] At a meeting of the L'viv intelligentsia Manuil'skij and others attacked the composer Barvins'kyj, the historian Kryp"jakevych, and the writer Olena Stepaniv because they had published in the magazine *Chervona Kalyna*, which had been published under German occupation. Manuil'skij demanded absolute support for the Soviet Union and that the intelligentsia help in the fight against nationalist Ukrainian partisans. He claimed that the intelligentsia had confused the minds of the Ukrainian youth and accused intellectuals of having defended "that Polish magnate" Sheptyts'kyj who had been controlled by the Vatican and nationalist circles. He urged those being criticized to tell the young Ukranians that they had erred and ask their pardon for their faults and mistakes.[570] The audience applauded enthusiastically, but in private conversations not everyone shared these opinions. Some agreed with Manuil'skij's thesis, others perceived the accusations as a continuation of the "persecution of the Ukrainian intelligentsia." Kryp"jakevych remarked that he did not know what he could still do to silence such attacks. After all, he already had moved to Kiev and worked on the history of Ukraine as he had been told.[571]

Similar campaigns against "bourgeois Ukrainian nationalism" were carried out in all the larger towns in the incorporated areas.[572] In October 1947 Hrushets'kyj reported on his success to Kiev; the L'viv intelligentsia was on the way to becoming a Soviet intelligentsia and was waging a determined fight against the "bourgeois nationalist 'school' of Hrushevs'kyj and his successors and pupils in the persons of the graduate Voznjak, the professors Kryp"jakevych, Rudnyts'kyj, Barvyns'kyj, the assistant professor Terlets'kyj and others." The party leader praised those intellectuals who had opposed the "bourgeois-nationalist" standpoint during meetings. However, the majority of the intelligentsia, in Hrushets'kyj's opinion, did not have any firm views but moved closer every day to the Communist Party. As one example of this convergence the regional party leader named the writer Iryna Vil'de. But Hrushets'kyj still found many professors, assistant professors, and artists who persisted in retaining their "bourgeois nationalist views."[573]

The Soviet campaign against cosmopolitism also found an echo in L'viv. An assistant professor for electrical engineering was accused of often referencing American, English and German technology in his lessons and of not having mentioned the "brilliant GOELRO plan of Lenin." Professors in the Medical Institute stood accused of having talked too much about the scientific progress in the United States. In private conversations, the acting director of the Museum for Ukrainian art, M. D. Drahan, reproached Russian communists with behaving in the Ukraine like "hard-boiled imperialists, only under the cover of the flag of brotherhood related by blood."[574]

Until Stalin's death the scientific and artistic communities of the Ukraine continued to be hit by repeated waves of arrests and "cleansing." Nevertheless, the Ukrainization of higher education did not stop even during the high point of such campaigns. Professors were required to justify why they taught in Russian instead of in Ukrainian. However, it was not difficult to get a dispensation. In 1947, 97 of the 254 lecturers at L'viv University taught in Russian, and 85 did not understand Ukrainian at all.[575]

In the early years, eastern Ukrainians still had strong ties to Russian culture, but by the second generation a process of acculturation to their western Ukrainian surroundings had taken place. The Russians, on the other hand, formed a self-confident community of their own. They were not willing to adapt their language and behavior to their Ukrainian surroundings. The arrogance of Russians was proverbial. The western Ukrainian writer Iryna Vil'de wrote to Stalin that Russian children provoked their Ukrainian classmates: "Our technology is the best in the world, our music is the best in the world, our science is the best, and what do you have? You have no artists, no explorers, no famous musicians; in a word you have nothing." The Ukrainian children usually did not know how to respond in any other way than to defend their national honor with their fists.[576]

But the party categorized any criticism of the presence of Russians in western Ukraine and of the public use of the Russian language as an expression of wrong—in other words, bourgeois nationalist—consciousness. The party promoted historical publications and press articles which emphasized the deep attachment between Russians and Ukrainians. Hetman Khmel'nyts'kyj was stylized as common Russian Ukrainian hero whose treaty with the tsar historians were expected to praise; however, Hetman Mazepa, an ally of Charles XII of Sweden, was presented as a traitor and a symbol of misguided Ukrainian nationalism.[577] Russian culture was propagated in theaters and opera houses, newspapers and books. In countless performances, the brotherhood between Russians and Ukrainians was invoked. Nevertheless, it was always clear who remained the older brother in this relationship.

Russian cadres were inclined to regard any form of Ukrainian self-assertion as an expression of nationalist views. In 1949 Iryna Vil'de described

Russian arrogance in a letter to Stalin as "fertile soil which promoted the development of cosmopolitanism in Ukraine" and served to deepen the "antagonism between the two largest fraternal peoples who had the closest ties to one another."[578] After five years all western Ukrainians had learned "to speak Bolshevik," but just how different the historical experiences of western Ukrainians, eastern Ukrainians, and Russians remained is demonstrated by their conflicting views of history in which Sovietization and nationalist Ukrainian resistance played a key role.[579]

Notes

1. PA AA, 54, R-104149: German Consulate in L'viv to Foreign Office in Berlin, August 21, 1939.
2. Ryszard Torzecki, *Polacy i Ukraińcy: Sprawa ukraińska w czasie II wojny światowej na terenie II Rzeczypospolitej* (Warsaw: Wydawnictwo Naukowe PWN, 1993), 23–29. Oleksandr Luts'kyi and Kim Naumenko, "U roky Druhoï svitovoï vijny," in *L'viv: Istorychni narysy*, ed. Jaroslav Isajevych, Feodosij Steblij, and Mykola Lytvyn (L'viv: Ivan Krypjakevych Institute of Ukrainian Studies, 1996), 436.
3. Ośrodek "Karta," Archiwum Wschodni (AW), II/1773, Alma Heczko, Dziennikpamiętnik, part 3, September 1, 1939–September 10, 1939.
4. On the collapse of public order, see Gross, *Revolution from Abroad*, 35–40. Sudoł, *Początki sowietyzacji kresów wschodnich*, 34–38, 54–55. Torzecki, *Polacy i Ukraińcy*, 28–29, 38.
5. Hryciuk, *Polacy we Lwowie 1939–1944*, 15–16. Luts'kyj and Naumenko, "U roky Druhoï Svitovoï vijny," 435–38. Czesław K. Grzelak, *Kresy w czerwieni: Agresja Związku Sowieckiego na polskę w 1939 roku* (Warszawa: Neriton, 1998), 399–401.
6. Hryciuk, *Polacy we Lwowie*, 16. On Soviet occupation see also Christoph Mick, "Lviv under Soviet Rule, 1939-1941," in *Stalin and Europe: Imitation and Domination, 1928-1953*, ed. Timothy Snyder and Ray Brandon (Oxford: Oxford University Press, 2014), 138-162. On Soviet and German occupation see Christoph Mick, "Incompatible experiences: Poles, Ukrainians and Jews under Soviet and German Occupation," *Journal of Contemporary History* 46, no. 2 (2011), 336-363.
7. It is not clear how many policemen were actually killed: a few dozen at least, but not more than three hundred. AW, sygn. MINF 135, k. 163: report by Stefan Kuszpa (police officer). Ibid., k. 166–67: report by Antoni Pater (police officer). Ibid., k. 180–83: report by Eugeniusz Lipka. Ibid., k. 184–86: report by Franciszek Buciow. Ibid., k. 187–90: report by Andrzej Naja-Ostromirski. Ibid., k. 424: report by Dr. Adam Papée.
8. AW, sygn. MINF 135, k. 180–83: report by Eugeniusz Lipka (policeman).
9. AAN, AK-KOL, 203 (MF 2400/7), 20: report of AK-KOL on the political situation, July 1942. Memorandum on "the Ukrainian problem," December 1943, printed in Mikołaj Siwicki, *Dzieje konfliktów polsko-ukraińskich*, vol. 2 (Warszawa: Tyrsa, 1992), 74. AAN, AK-KOL, 203, 3–4: report in AK-KOL "On Jews," June/July 1942. In his report for General Sosnkowski dated January 9, 1940, General Tokarzewski mentioned attacks by "Ukrainian gangs and Jews," in *Armia Krajowa w dokumentach*, vol. 1, 64 (document 13). AW, sygn. MINF 135, k. 194–96: report by Bolesław Tobler. Ibid., k. 472: report by Stefan Robotycki. Ibid., k. 484–85: report by Jan Bałtro (train guard). See also Hryciuk, *Polacy we Lwowie,* 18.

10. *Archiwum Ringelbluma* (henceforth abbreviated AR). Account 40 (report by a Zionist refugee from Warsaw, translated from Yiddish to Polish), 771–87, quote from 772, written in Warsaw in March 1942.
11. AW, sygn. MINF 135, k. 439–40: report by Jan Palewicz (army major). Ibid., k. 464–65: report by Józef Weissenfeld. Ibid., k. 468: report by Tadeusz Borkowsky.
12. This impression was soon replaced by "great contempt." Colonel Rowecki to General Sosnkowski, February 8, 1940 (appendix: report on Soviet occupation), in *Armia Krajowa w dokumentach 1939–1945*, vol. 1: *September 1939–April 1941*, ed. Halina Czarnocka, Józef Garliński, Józef Żmigrodzki (London: Księgarnia SPK, 1960), 106.
13. AW, sygn. MINF 135, k. 194–96: report by Bolesław Tober; k. 424, report by Dr. Adam Papée.
14. AW, sygn. MINF 135, k. 158–60: report by Mieczysław Jasiński (member of the police of L'viv voivodeship). AW, sygn. II/171: reminiscences of Janina Kandeler. Karolina Lanckorońska, *Those Who Trespass against Us: One Woman's War against the Nazis*, trans. Noel Clark (London: Pimlico, 2005), 17. Adam Dotzauer, *Lwowskie wczesne dojrzewanie* (Wrocław: Sudety, 2000), 25. Ostap Tarnavs'kyj, *Literaturnyj L'viv, 1939–1944: Spomyny* (L'viv: Prosvita, 1995), 19. Gross, *Revolution from Abroad*, 45–53. Hryciuk, *Polacy we Lwowie*, 149.
15. AW, sygn. II/2696: reminiscences of Juliusz Jaszczuk (1992). See also Jadwiga Dabulewicz-Rutkowska, *Poezja, proza i dramat: Pamiętnik nastolatki: Lwów, 1939–1941* (Wrocław: W Kolorach Tęczy, 1998), 31.
16. AAN, 203/XV-34, 9a: eyewitness account (written in a diary), quoted in Hryciuk, *Polacy we Lwowie*, 17. See also AW, sygn. MINF 135, k. 171–72: report by Józef Mroczkowski (policeman). AW II/1773, diaries/memoirs of Alma Heczko: entry from September 22, 1939.
17. AW, sygn. II/1314: reminiscences of Wanda Jóźwiak (1993).
18. AAN, AK-KOL, 203 (MF 2400/7), 20: report in AK-KOL on the political situation, July 1942.
19. AAN, AK-KOL, 203 (MF 2400/5), 3–4: report in AK-KOL "On Jews," June/July 1942. AAN, AK-KOL, 203 (MF 2400/7), 20: report of AK-KOL on the political situation, July 1942.
20. AW, sygn. MINF 135, k. 492–93: report by Władysław Zawiłło (railway man).
21. AW, sygn. MINF 135, k. 171–72: report by Józef Mroczkowski (policeman).
22. AW, sygn. MINF 135, k. 474–75: report by Michał Klof (police corporal).
23. AW II/1773, diaries/memoirs of Alma Heczko: entry from September 22, 1939. AW, sygn. MINF 135, k. 440–41: report by Wiktor Adel. Ibid., k. 487–88: report by Władysław Chrobak (railway man). Ibid., k. 174–75: report by Jan Dobrochłop (head of a police station). Ibid., k. 424: report by Adam Papée. Ibid., k. 161: report by Krzysztof Izdebski (policeman). Ibid., k. 477–80: report by Stanisław Matiasz (noncommissioned officer of the Polish army).
24. AW, sygn. II/1314: reminiscences of Wanda Jóźwiak (1993).
25. Lala Fishman and Steven Weingartner, *Lala's Story: A Memoir of the Holocaust* (Evanston, IL: Northwestern University Press, 1997), 98.
26. AW, sygn. MINF 135, k. 480–82: report by Bronisława Stachowicz.
27. AAN, AK-KOL, 203 (MF 2400/7), 59–60: report in AK-KOL (excerpt), probably from the end of 1941.
28. The evidence comes from contemporary interviews with eyewitnesses and recollections of Jewish refugees from Eastern Poland, which were preserved in the archive of the Warsaw Ghetto by Emanuel Ringelblum. AR, vol. 3, no. 30, 516–37, here 517–18:

anonymous report of a young student from L'viv, Warsaw 1941/42. Ibid., no. 42, 792–885, here 808, 816: report on Jewish schools in L'viv during Soviet occupation (probably authored by Stanisław Różycki), Warsaw 1941/42. Similar stories are reported by Eliyahu Jones and based on Jewish memorial books kept in the archive of Yad Vashem. See Jones, *Żydzi Lwowa w okresie okupacji 1939–1945*, 24, 38.
29. AR, vol. 3, no. 30, 517. Maschler, *Moskauer Zeit*, 50. Jones, *Żydzi Lwowa w okresie okupacji 1939–1945*, 24.
30. AW, sygn. MINF 135, k. 437–38: report by Zygmunt Giercuszkiewicz (major in the Polish army).
31. AW, sygn. MINF 135: report by Bronisława Stachowicz. Lanckorońska, *Those Who Trespass against Us*, 2. Hryciuk, *Polacy we Lwowie*, 42–43.
32. Timothy Snyder, *Bloodlands: Europe between Hitler and Stalin* (New York: Basic Books, 2010), 103–104. Terry Martin, *The Affirmative Action Empire: Nations and Nationalism in the Soviet Union, 1923–1939* (Ithaca, NY: Cornell University Press, 2001), 311–13.
33. AW, sygn. MINF 135, k. 486–87: report by Marian Dąbrowski. Ibid., k. 484–85: report by Jan Bałtro. Ibid., k. 158–60: report by Mieczysław Jasiński (police official). On the elections, see also ibid., k. 161: Krzysztof Izdebski (policeman). Ibid., k. 161–62: report by Władysław Duszka (policeman). Ibid., k. 172–74: report by Bronisław Pawlus (head of a local police station).
34. AW, sygn. MINF 135, k. 161: report by Krzysztof Izdebski (policeman). Ibid., k. 161–62: report by Władysław Duszka (policeman). Ibid., k. 430: report by Stanisław Mrozek. Ibid., k. 480–82: report by Bronisława Stachowicz. Ibid., k. 474–75: report by Michał Klof (police corporal). Włodzimierz Bonusiak, "Powstanie i działalność władz okupacyjnych we Lwowie w okresie IX 1939–VI 1941," in *Lwów: Miasto—społeczeństwo—kultura*, vol. 2, 307–18, here 310. Sudoł, *Początki sowietyzacji kresów wschodnich*, 96–106.
35. Sudoł, *Początki sowietyzacji kresów wschodnich*, 91–92, 123–228. Jones, *Żydzi Lwowa w okresie okupacji 1939–1945*, 27.
36. Hryciuk, *Polacy we Lwowie*, 25. Bonusiak, "Powstanie i działalność władz okupacyjnych we Lwowie w okresie IX 1939–VI 1941," 310–12. Jones reports that the occupying power steered clear of giving Jews public roles to avoid fueling local anti-Semitism. Jones, *Żydzi Lwowa w okresie okupacji 1939–1945*, 32.
37. DALO, f. 2, op. 26, spr. 2350, ark. 1: protocol of a session of the municipal council, September 23, 1939.
38. Before his appointment, Hryshchuk worked with the Kiev party organizations. Later, the second secretary of the city party committee, Borys Kolesnychenko, became first secretary. After Kolesnychenko's death in January 1941, Ivan Sydorenko took over. Hryciuk, *Polacy we Lwowie*, 18–19, 27.
39. Bonusiak, "Powstanie i działalność władz okupacyjnych we Lwowie w okresie IX 1939–VI 1941," 307–308. The resolution of the politbureau is printed in Sudoł, *Początki sowietyzacji kresów wschodnich*, 404–11. The original is kept in the archives of the president of the Russian Federation (Resolution of the Politbureau of the VKP[b], October 1, 1939, no. 52, 57–61). Luts'kyj and Naumenko, "U roky Druhoï Svitovoï vijny," 451.
40. AR, vol. 3, no. 36, 688. AR, vol. 3, no. 30, 525–26. AW, sygn. MINF 135, k. 484: report by Jan Masztelarz (driver of the PKP). Hryciuk, *Polacy we Lwowie*, 21–25.
41. Osyp Nazaruk, *Zi L'vova do Varshava 2-13 zhovtnja 1939 roku* (L'viv: Naukove tovarystvo imeni Shevchenka, 1995), 14–16.

42. Bonusiak, "Powstanie i działalność władz okupacyjnych we Lwowie w okresie IX 1939–VI 1941," 312.
43. Contemporary Jewish, Polish, and Ukrainian sources agree on this. Jones, *Żydzi Lwowa w okresie okupacji 1939–1945*, 27.
44. Hryciuk, *Polacy we Lwowie*, 30–31.
45. "Memuary Nikity Sergeevicha Khrushcheva," *Voprosy Istorii*, no. 7 (1990): 99.
46. AW, sygn. MINF 135, k. 193–94: report by Marian Pryk. On cinema, see Hryciuk, *Polacy we Lwowie*, 116–18.
47. AW, sygn. MINF 135, k. 180–83: report by Eugeniusz Lipka (policeman).
48. AW II/1773, Dziennik-pamiętnik of Alma Heczko: entry from September 22, 1939.
49. AW, sygn. MINF 135, k. 486–87: report by Marian Dąbrowski. Luts'kyj and Naumenko, "U roky Druhoï Svitovoï vijny," 452.
50. AW, sygn. MINF 135, k. 491–92: report by Tadeusz Lipko (railway official). Oleksandr Luts'kyj, "Intelihentsija L'vova (veresen' 1939–cherven' 1941 rr.)," in *L'viv: Misto—suspil'stvo—kul'tura*, vol. 3, 574–91, here 580–81.
51. Torzecki, *Polacy i Ukraińcy*, 76. The anti-Soviet attitude of the peasantry is described by a Greek Catholic priest in Olijnyk, *Zoshyty*, 71–77.
52. Lanckorońska, *Those Who Trespass against Us*, 6. See also the recollections of Kazimierz Żygulski in *Jestem z lwowskiego etapu*, 114–15.
53. The following Ukrainian scholars received professorships or lectureships at L'viv University: historian Ivan Kryp"jakevych, ethnologist Filaret Kolessa, literary scholars Mychajlo Vozniak and Mychajlo Rudnyts'kyj, geographer Jurij Poljan'skyj, and physicists and mathematicians Volodymyr Levyts'kyj, Ja. Pasternak, V. Simovych, K. Studyns'kyj, V. Shchurat, Z. Khraplyvyj, and M. Zaryts'kyj. Luts'kyj, "Intelihentsija L'vova," 583. Luts'kyj and Naumenko, "U roky Druhoï Svitovoï vijny," 454–56. On the work at the university from a Polish perspective, see Lanckorońska, *Those Who Trespass against Us*, 5–10. Żygulski, *Jestem z lwowskiego etapu*, 130–37.
54. Milena Rudnyts'ka, *Zakhidnja Ukraïna pid Bol'shevikami* (New York: Naukove tovarystvo imeni Shevchenka v Amerytsi, 1958), 107, 187. O. S. Rubl'jov and Ju. A. Cherchenko, *Stalinshchyna j dolja zakhidnoukraïns'koï intelihenciï 20-50-ti roky XXst* (Kiev: Naukova Dumka, 1994), 194–95.
55. Hryciuk, *Polacy we Lwowie*, 130–35.
56. Ibid.
57. TsDIAL, f. 859, op. 1, spr. 10, ark. 10–13 (printed in *Kul'turne zhyttja v Ukraïni: Zakhidni zemli*, vol. 1: *1939–1953* (Kiev: Naukowa Dumka, 1995), 60–62: report by the representative of the TsK KP(b)U to the secretary of the TsK KP(b)U M.O. Burmistenkov on the reorganization of the museums of the western regions of Ukraine, n.d. (before October 25, 1939). Sudoł, *Początki sowietyzacji Kresów wschodnich*, 58–61.
58. Tsentral'nyj Arkhiv Akademiï nauk Ukraïny (TsAAN), f. 251, op. 1, spr. 75, ark. 171–75, 190 (printed in *Kul'turne zhyttja*, vol. 1, 65–68): protocol of the meeting of the presidium of the Academy of Science of the UkrSSR on the integration of the Scientific Shevchenko Society in the Academy of Science of the UkrSSR (excerpts), December 9, 1939.
59. TsAAN, L'vovskye uchrezhdenija AN USSR. Prykazy za 1940 h., ark. 10 (printed in *Kul'turne zhyttja*, 65–68). Instruction of the director of the Institute for the History of Ukraine of the Academy of Science of the UkrSSR on the creation of a L'viv branch of the Institute for History, February 1, 1940.
60. Hryciuk, *Polacy we Lwowie*, 120–22.

61. Decree of the Council of Ministers of the UkrSSR, December 19, 1939, printed in *Kul'turne zhyttja*, 68–72. AR, vol. 3, no. 40, 776. On the repertoire of the Polish theater, see Hryciuk, *Polacy we Lwowie*, 108–13. On the Jewish theater, see Jones, *Żydzi Lwowa w okresie okupacji 1939–1945*, 36–38.
62. For recollections of the poet Roman Kupchyns'kyj (1941), see *Kul'turne zhyttja*, 126–32. Sudoł, *Początki sowietyzacji kresów wschodnich*, 56–57.
63. Jones, *Żydzi Lwowa w okresie okupacji 1939–1945*, 34–35.
64. AR, vol. 3, no 40, 776. Record of a conversation with the refugee St.Au. (full name unknown) on the situation of Jews under Soviet occupation and the beginning of German occupation (Polish translation from Yiddish), Warsaw, early 1942, in AR, vol. 3, no. 43, 886–905, here 893–94.
65. Jones took the numbers from the Soviet Yiddish-language newspaper "Der Sztern." Jones, *Żydzi Lwowa w okresie okupacji 1939–1945*, 30–38. Hryciuk, *Polacy we Lwowie*, 122–35.
66. AW, sygn. MINF 135, k. 457–61: report by Augustyn Dębicz.
67. AR, vol. 3, no. 43, 893–94.
68. Recollections of Stanisław Różycki on his experiences in L'viv, June 1–September 29, 1941, 1941/42, in AR, vol. 3, no. 31, 538–89, here 549–50.
69. Myroslav Semchyshyn, *Z knyhy Leva: Ukraïns'kyj L'viv dvadtsjatych-sorokovych rokiv* (L'viv: Naukowa Tovarystvo im. Shevchenka, 1998), 65–69, 81–85. Ostap Tarnavs'kyj, *Literaturnyj L'viv 1939–1944*, 19. Luts'kyj, "Intelihentsija L'vova," 583.
70. Hryciuk, *Polacy we Lwowie*, 32–35. See also the list of essential and possible street names in the notes of the chairman of the organization committee of the Soviet Union of Writers in L'viv, Petr Panch, 1939, in *Kul'turne zhyttja*, 73–79.
71. Hryciuk, *Polacy we Lwowie*, 58–59.
72. Bonusiak, "Powstanie i działalność władz okupacyjnych we Lwowie w okresie IX 1939–VI 1941," 312.
73. AW, sygn. MINF 135, k. 158–60: report by Mieczysław Jasiński (police official). On the elections, see ibid., k. 161: report by Krzysztof Izdebski (policeman). Ibid., k. 161–62: report by Władysław Duszka (policeman). Ibid., k. 491–92: report by Tadeusz Lipko (railway official).
74. AW, sygn. MINF, k. 424: report by Ernest Bizanz (lieutenant colonel and engineer).
75. Report (probably by Stanisław Różycki) on the period of Soviet occupation in L'viv, in AR, vol. 3, no. 33, 614–66, here 617.
76. Luts'kyj, "Intelihentsija L'vova," 578.
77. Hryciuk, *Polacy we Lwowie*, 36.
78. Tadeusz Riedl, *We Lwowie: Relacje* (Wrocław: Sudety, 1996), 9
79. *Orhanizatsija Ukraïns'kykh Natsionalistiv i Ukraïns'ka Povstans'ka Armija*, ed. S. V. Kul'chyts'kyj (Kiev: Nauk. Dumka, 2005), 15.
80. Ljuba Komar, *Proces 59-ty* (L'viv: Naukove Tovarystvo im. Shevchenka, 1997).
81. Hryciuk, *Polacy we Lwowie*, 40–41.
82. Jones, *Żydzi Lwowa w okresie okupacji 1939–1945*, 39–42.
83. Hryciuk, *Polacy we Lwowie*, 153–54, 171.
84. AW, sygn. MINF 135, k. 171–72: report by Józef Mroczkowski (policeman). Ibid., k. 161: report by Krzysztof Izdebski (policeman). Ibid., k. 172–74: report by Bronisław Pawlus (head of a local police station). Ibid., k. 175–76: report by Bolesław Kusiak (head of a local police station). Ibid., k. 507–508: report by Antoni Trardochleb. Ibid., k. 158: report by Władysław Barski. Ibid., k. 177–78: report by Wojciech Olecki (head of a local police station). Ibid., k. 502–504: report by Władysław Zubrzyki (public trans-

port worker). Ibid., k. 158–60: report by Mieczysław Jasiński (police official). Prison experiences are summarized by Gross, *Revolution from Abroad*, 144–186. Hryciuk, *Polacy we Lwowie*, 36.

85. Based on data provided by Grzegorz Hryciuk and Jarosław Stoćkyj, *Studia nad demografią historyczną i sytuacją religijną Ukrainy* (Lublin: Instytut Europy Środkowo Wschodniej, 2000), 23.
86. Report by a refugee from Warsaw on the situation in L'viv between September 1939 and the of summer 1941, after December 7, 1941, in AR, vol. 3, no. 36, 614–66, 685–720, here 691.
87. Hryciuk and Stoćkyj, *Studia nad demografią historyczną i sytuacją religijną Ukrainy*, 27–30.
88. Lanckorońska, *Those Who Trespass against Us*, 28–34.
89. AAN; AK-KOL, 203 (MF 2400/8), 150–51: changes in the composition of the population in the Red Ruthenian territories, summer 1943.
90. Hryciuk and Stoćkyj, *Studia nad demografią historyczną i sytuacją religijną Ukrainy*, 30. The Polish underground believed that during Soviet occupation, 150,000 "capitalist elements and estate owners," including family members, had been deported. AAN; AK-KOL, 203 (MF 2400/8), 150–51: changes in the composition of the population in the Red Ruthenian territories, summer 1943. In Soviet sources, the number of 7,200 deportees from L'viv is mentioned. According to eyewitness accounts, 16,000 to 30,000 people were deported from L'viv. Hryciuk, *Polacy we Lwowie*, 40.
91. AW II/1773, Dziennik-pamiętnik of Alma Heczko: entry from September 22, 1939. Hryciuk, *Polacy we Lwowie*, 37–38.
92. Jones, *Żydzi Lwowa w okresie okupacji 1939–1945*, 28.
93. AR, vol. 3, no. 33, 631–34.
94. Hryciuk and Stoćkyj, *Studia nad demografią historyczną i sytuacją religijną Ukrainy*, 20–21.
95. AR, vol. 3, no. 33, 631–34. Contemporary sources report that between 60,000 and 70,000 refugees had been deported, 40,0000 from L'viv alone. According to Soviet sources, 22,000 refugees had been deported from L'viv. Hryciuk and Stoćkyj, *Studia nad demografią historyczną i sytuacją religijną Ukrainy*, 30. Hryciuk, *Polacy we Lwowie*, 40. Luts'kyj and Naumenko, "U roky Druhoï Svitovoï vijny," 457–58. According to their calculations, 20,770 refugees had been deported from L'viv.
96. AR, vol. 3, no. 36, 691–92. AR, vol. 3, no. 33, 628–29.
97. Hryciuk and Stoćkyj, *Studia nad demografią historyczną i sytuacją religijną Ukrainy*, 23.
98. Subtelny, *Ukraine*, 456. Torzecki, *Polacy i Ukraińcy*, 73.
99. 40 percent of all people were deported from the Polish eastern provinces. Hryciuk and Stoćkyj, *Studia nad demografią historyczną i sytuacją religijną Ukrainy*, 32.
100. Hryciuk and Stoćkyj, *Studia nad demografią historyczną i sytuacją religijną Ukrainy*, 32.
101. *Deportatsiï: Zakhidni zemli Ukraïny kintsja 30-ch—pochatku 50-kh rokiv: Dokumenty, spohady*, vol. 1 (L'viv: Instytut Ukraïnoznvastva im. Kryp"jakevycha NAN Ukrainy, 1996). Dieter Pohl, "Die Ukraine im Zweiten Weltkrieg," *Österreichische Osthefte* 42, no 3/4 (2000): 339–62.
102. Hryciuk and Stoćkyj, *Studia nad demografią historyczną i sytuacją religijną Ukrainy*, 32.
103. Leon Weliczker Wells, *The Janowska Road* (London: Jonathan Cape, 1966), 29.
104. Ilana Maschler, *Moskauer Zeit* (Göttingen: Steidl, 1995), 93.

105. Ibid., 130.
106. AW, sygn. MINF 135, k. 491–92: report by Tadeusz Lipko (railway official). Luts'kyj, "Intelihentsija L'vova," 580–81.
107. Hryciuk, *Polacy we Lwowie*, 60–67. Hryciuk and Stoćkyj, *Studia nad demografią historyczną i sytuacją religijną Ukrainy*, 21. Machler, *Moskauer Zeit*, 84–86.
108. Żygulski, *Jestem z lwowskiego etapu*, 125–26.
109. Lanckorońska, *Those Who Trespass against Us*, 22.
110. Hryciuk, *Polacy we Lwowie*, 151–52.
111. AK, sygn. MINF 135, k. 513–14: report by Jan Mazur (assistant machinist). Hryciuk, *Polacy we Lwowie*, 65–66, 144.
112. Żygulski, *Jestem z lwowskiego etapu*, 117.
113. Hryciuk, *Polacy we Lwowie*, 34–35, 60.
114. AK, sygn. MINF 135, k. 513–14: report by Jan Mazur (assistant machinist). Hryciuk, *Polacy we Lwowie*, 65–66, 144.
115. AW, sygn. MINF 135, k. 492–93: report by Władysław Zawiłło (Polish railways). AW, sygn. II/171: recollections of Janina Kandeler. AW, sygn. II/1314: recollections of Juliusz Jaszczuk (1992). Włodzimierz Bonusiak, "Sowietyzacja gospodarki Lwowa (IX 1939–VI 1941)," in *L'viv: Misto—suspil'stvo—kul'tura*, vol. 3, 562–73, here 568–69. Hryciuk, *Polacy we Lwowie*, 149.
116. Maschler, *Moskauer Zeit*, 101.
117. Weliczker Wells, *Janowska Road*, 27.
118. AW, sygn. MINF 135, k. 470–71: report by Leon Bylicki. Ibid., k. 489–91: report by Robert Pawelczyk (railway worker). AW, sygn. II/1314: recollections of Wanda Jóźwiak (1993). Ibid.: recollections of Juliusz Jaszczuk (1992). AW, sygn. II/1167: recollections of Halina Konopińska. Hryciuk, *Polacy we Lwowie*, 70–79.
119. Lanckorońska, *Those Who Trespass against Us*, 16–17.
120. Bonusiak, "Sowietyzacja gospodarki Lwowa (IX 1939–VI 1941)," 568.
121. AW, sygn. II/1314: recollections of Wanda Jóźwiak (1993).
122. Żygulski, *Jestem z lwowskiego etapu*, 117–18.
123. Weliczker Wells, *Janowska Road*, 30.
124. Hryciuk, *Polacy we Lwowie*, 88–89.
125. Lanckorońska, *Those Who Trespass against Us*, 18–19. Maschler, *Moskauer Zeit*, 67–68.
126. Hryciuk, *Polacy we Lwowie*, 88–89. Żygulski, *Jestem z lwowskiego etapu*, 118.
127. Hryciuk, *Polacy we Lwowie*, 80–81. Bonusiak, "Sowietyzacja gospodarki Lwowa (IX 1939–VI 1941)," 565.
128. Luts'kyj, "Intelihentsija L'vova," 581. Hryciuk, *Polacy we Lwowie*, 66, 82.
129. DALO, f. R-121, op. 1, spr. 68, ark. 13–14: Decree of the Executive Committee of Oblast L'viv, April 5, 1940.
130. Dział Rękopisów Biblioteki Zakładu Narodowego im. Ossolińskich: Jan Rogowski, W czerwonym Lwowie: Wspomnienia z czasów wojny, k. 2 (cited after Hryciuk, *Polacy we Lwowie*, 84–85).
131. AW, sygn. MINF 135, k. 443–45: report by Stefan Ludwig. Hryciuk, *Polacy we Lwowie*, 167–74. On the consequences of antireligous measures for the Jewish communities, see Jones, Żydzi Lwowa w okresie okupacji 1939–1945, 32.
132. AR, vol. 3, no. 43, 893–94. Hryciuk, *Polacy we Lwowie*, 170–71.
133. Hryciuk, *Polacy we Lwowie*, 126. Maschler, *Moskauer Zeit*, 68–70.
134. Nazaruk, *Zi L'vova do Varshava*, 14–16. Luts'kyj, "Intelihentsija L'vova," 582–83.
135. Nazaruk, *Zi L'vova do Varshava*, 14–16.

136. The letter was signed by the historian Ivan Kryp"jakevych, the composer Vasyl' Barvins'kyj, the author Jaroslav Halan, and others. Luts'kyj, "Intelihentsija L'vova," 582.
137. Luts'kyj, "Intelihentsija L'vova," 445–46, 577. Luts'kyj and Naumenko, "U roky Druhoï Svitovoï vijny," 435–85. Nazaruk, *Zi L'vova do Varshava*, 14–16.
138. Nazaruk, *Zi L'vova do Varshava*, 14–16. Polish eyewitnesses remembered that there were more Jews than Ukrainians in the militia. They reported that only a few Poles had joined the militia. Most commanders came from the Soviet Union. Hryciuk, *Polacy we Lwowie*, 30.
139. Nazaruk, *Zi L'vova do Varshava*, 14–16. Semchyshyn, *Z knyhy Leva*, 64.
140. AR, vol. 3, no. 42, 816, 821–22. AR, vol. 3, no. 30, 517–18. Jones, *Żydzi Lwowa w okresie okupacji 1939–1945*, 40.
141. AR, vol. 3, no. 42, 808.
142. Ibid., 792–95.
143. Dotzauer, *Lwowskie wczesne dojrzewanie*, 23–24.
144. AR, vol. 3, no. 36, 694. AR, vol. 3, no. 30, 517–18. AR, vol. 3, no. 42, 816. AR, vol. 3, no. 31, 538, 543–544.
145. AR, vol. 3, no. 36, 695. Jones, *Żydzi Lwowa w okresie okupacji 1939–1945*, 32.
146. Lanckorońska, *Those Who Trespass against Us*, 23, 30.
147. Hryciuk, *Polacy we Lwowie*, 100–101.
148. Żygulski, *Jestem z lwowskiego etapu*, 139. Mieczysław Inglot, "Obraz ojczyzny w liryce polskiej okupowanego Lwowa lat 1939–1945," in *Europa nie prowincjonalna: Przemiany na ziemiach wschodnich dawnej Rzeczypospolitej (Białoruś, Litwa, Łotwa, Ukraina, wschodnie pogranicze III Rzeczypospolitej Polskiej) w latach 1772–1999*, ed. Krzysztow Jasiewicz (Warsaw: Rytm, 1999), 168–180.
149. Hryciuk, *Polacy we Lwowie*, 145–49.
150. AR, vol. 3, no. 31, 538.
151. Ibid., 543–44.
152. Ibid. On the change of Soviet policy, see Hryciuk, "'Nowy kurs?'" 47–66.
153. Cited after Hryciuk, *Polacy we Lwowie*, 44–45.
154. Hryciuk, *Polacy we Lwowie*, 44–49. Agnieszka Cieślikowa, *Prasa okupanowego Lwowa* (Warsaw: Neriton, 1997), 91–98.
155. Hryciuk, *Polacy we Lwowie*, 47–48. Torzecki, *Polacy i Ukraińcy*, 88.
156. Grzegorz Mazur and Jerzy Węgierski, *Konspiracja Lwowska 1939–1944: Słownik Biograficzny* (Katowice: Wydawnictwo Unia, 1997), 10.
157. Sudoł, *Początki sowietyzacji kresów wschodnich*, 46–47, 117–18. Rafał Wnuk, "Polska konspiracja antysowiecka na Kresach Wschodnich II RP w latach 1939–1941 i 1944–1952," in *Tygiel narodów: Stosunki społeczne i etniczne na dawnych ziemiach wschodnich Rzeczypospolitej 1939–1953*, ed. Krzysztof Jasiewicz (Warsaw: Rytm, 2002), 157–249.
158. AW, sygn. II/2696: recollections of Juliusz Jaszczuk (1992).
159. Report from January 1940, in *Armia Krajowa w dokumentach*, vol. 1, 64-67.
160. AW, sygn II/171: memoirs of Janina Kandeler. Fishman and Weingartner, *Lala's Story*, 103. Weliczker Wells, *Janowska Road*, 27.
161. Hryciuk, *Polacy we Lwowie*, 158–67, 172–74.
162. Diary entry from October 15, 1939, by Jadwiga Dabulewicz-Rutkowska, *Poezja, proza i dramat*, 37–38.
163. AW, sygn. II/1314: recollections of Wanda Jóźwiak (1993).
164. Hryciuk, *Polacy we Lwowie*, 171.

165. Ibid., 153–54.
166. AAN, AK-KOL, 203 (MF 2400/9, XV-47), 34: report on Polish vested rights in L'viv, May 1943. On the Jewish reactions to the Soviet invasion, see Andrzej Żbikowski, "Jewish Reaction to the Soviet Arrival in the Kresy in September 1939," *Polin* 13 (2000): focusing on the Holocaust and its aftermath, 62–72. On Polish-Jewish and Polish-Ukrainian relations, see also Hryciuk, *Polacy we Lwowie*, 154–58.
167. AAN, AK-KOL, 203 (MF 2400/5), 3–4: report in AK-KOL "on Jews," June/July 1942.
168. Ibid. AW, sygn. MINF 135, k. 165: report by Marian Hulacki (policeman). Ibid., k. 484–85: report by Jan Bałtro. Ibid., k. 158–60: report by Mieczysław Jasiński (police official).
169. Report on Soviet occupation sent on February 8, 1940, from Rowecki to Sosknowski, in *Armia Krajowa w dokumentach*, vol. 1, 107.
170. *Czerwony Sztandar*, October 20, 1939. *Vilna Ukraïna*, October 18, 1939. See also Hryciuk, *Polacy we Lwowie*, 21.
171. AW sygn. MINF 135, k. 193: report by Alfred Pirszel.
172. Ibid., k. 194–96: report by Bolesław Tober. Ibid., k. 480–82: report by Bronisława Stachowicz. Ibid., k. 424: report by Ernest Bizanz (lieutenant colonel, engineer). Ibid., k. 487–88: Władysław Chrobak (Polish railways). Ibid., k. 180–83: report by Eugeniusz Lipka (policeman).
173. Ibid., k. 510: report by Aleksander Popov (assistant machinist). On the composition of the Soviet militia and how the Polish population viewed the militia, see Gross, *Revolution from Abroad*, 50–53.
174. AAN, AK-KOL, 203 (MF 2400/5), 3–4: report in AK-KOL "On Jews," June/July 1942. AW, sygn. MINF 135, k. 161: report by Krzysztof Izdebski (policeman). Ibid., k. 424: report by Ernest Bizanz (lieutenant colonel and engineer. Ibid., k. 487–88: report by Władysław Chrobak (Polish railways). Ibid., k. 161–62: report by Władysław Duszka (policeman). Ibid., k. 163: report by Stefan Kuszpa (policeman). Ibid., k. 163: report by Bronisława Stachowicz. Ibid., k. 484–85: report by Jan Bałtro. Ibid., k. 489–90: report by Robert Pawelczyk. Ibid., k. 507–508: report by Antoni Twardochleb (retired railway worker). Ibid., k. 439–40: report by Jan Palewicz (major). See also Jones, Żydzi Lwowa w okresie okupacji 1939–1945, 27.
175. AW, sygn. MINF 135, k. 158–60: report by Mieczysław Jasiński (police official). Ibid., k. 434–35: report by Wilhelm Hande. Ibid., k. 441–42: report by Emil Dobrzański. Ibid., k. 492–97: report by Władysław Zawiłło.
176. AW, sygn. MINF 135, k. 158–60: report by Mieczysław Jasinski.
177. Ibid.; ibid., k. 465–66: report by Adam Lipinski.
178. Ibid., k. 454–57: report by Andrzej Mączka.
179. AAN, AK-KOL, 203 (MF 2400/5), 3–4: report in AK-KOL "On Jews," June/July 1942.
180. Ibid., 203 (MF 2400/8), 68–123: report in AK-KOL by "Alfa" on minority questions, n.d. (probably spring 1942). See also AW, sygn. MINF 135, k. 171–72: report by Józef Mroczkowski (policeman). Ibid., k. 440–41: report by Wiktor Adler. Hryciuk, *Polacy we Lwowie*, 157.
181. Ibid.
182. AW, sygn. MINF 135, k. 172–74: report by Bronisław Pawlus (head of a police station). Ibid., k. 193: report by Alfred Pirszel. Ibid., k. 441–42: report by Emil Dobrzański. Ibid., k. 424: report by Dr. Adam Papée. Ibid., k. 428–29: report by Major Zygmunt Dąbrowski. Ibid., k. 492–97: report by Władysław Zawiłło. Ibid., k. 497: report by Bronisław Grajewski. Ibid., k. 454–57: report by Andrzej Mączka. Ibid., k. 161: report by Krzysztof Izdebski (policeman).

183. Ibid., k. 158–60: report by Mieczysław Jasiński. On the elections, see also ibid., k. 161: report by Krzysztof Izdebski (policeman). Ibid., k. 161–62: report by Władysław Duszka (policeman).
184. AR, vol. 3, no. 43, 895. Report by Helena Kagan on her escape to L'viv, 1939 to the end of June 1940, added to the archive by Emanuel Ringelblum, 1941/42, in AR, vol. 3, no. 32, 590–613, here 595. On the perception of ethnic conflicts by Jewish refugees, see Andrzej Żbikowski, "Konflikty narodowościowe na polskich Kresach Wschodnich (1939–1941) w relacjach żydowskich bieżeńców," in *Tygiel narodów*, 409–27.
185. AR, vol. 3, no. 36, 695.
186. Ibid., 688.
187. Ibid., no. 42, 816. Ibid., no. 30, 525–26. Ibid., no. 40, 776.
188. Ibid., no. 40, 776. Ibid., no. 43, 893–94.
189. Ibid., no. 40, 774–75.
190. Ibid., no. 36, 694.
191. Ibid., no. 42, 821–22.
192. Ibid., no. 31, 542.
193. Ibid., no. 43, 896–97.
194. Ibid., no. 31, 549–50.
195. AAN, AK-KOL, 203 (MF 2400/7), 20: report in AK-KOL on the political situation, July 1942. Memorandum "The Ukrainian Problem," December 1943, in Mikołaj Siwicki, *Dzieje konfliktów Polsko-Ukraińskich*, vol. 2, 75.
196. General Rowecki to General Sikorski, Special message 89 "Ukrainian Affairs" between September 1939 and November 1941, November 15, 1941, in *Armia Krajowa w dokumentach 1939–1945*, vol. 2, 137–45. AAN, AK-KOL, 203 (MF 2400/7), 59–60: report in AK-KOL (excerpt), probably from the end of 1941.
197. AR, vol. 3, no. 40, 774–75. Ibid., no. 31, 545–46.
198. Ibid., 542.
199. AAN, AK-KOL, 203 (MF 2400/7), 59–60: report in AK-KOL (excerpt), probably from the end of 1941.
200. AR, vol. 3, no. 30, 520–21. Ibid., no. 43, 895. Ibid., no. 32, 595.
201. Ibid.
202. AZHRL, Materiały S. Kota, sygn. 97, k. 77 (cited after Hryciuk, *Polacy we Lwowie*, 157).
203. Karel Berkhoff and Marco Carynnyk, "The Organization of Ukrainian Nationalists and Its Attitude toward Germans and Jews: Iaroslav Stets'ko's 1941 Zhyttiepys," *Harvard Ukrainian Studies* 23, no. 3/4 (1999): 149–84.
204. A. Diukov, *Vtorosteppenyj vrag: OUN, UPA i reshenie "jevreskogo voprosa"* (Moscow: Regnum, 2008).
205. Paragraph 17 of the resolution. Postanovy II. Velikoho Zboru Orhanizatsii Ukrains'kykh Natsionalistiv, shcho vidbuvsja v kvitni 1941 r, in *OUN v svitli postanov Velykykh Zboriv, konferentsij ta inshykh dokumentiv z borot'by 1929–1955* (place of publication unknown: 1955) (cited after Friedman, *Ukrainian-Jewish Relations*).
206. TsDIAL, f. 406, op. 1, spr. 55, ark. 100–101. Printed in Milena Rudnyts'ka, *Statti, lysty, dokumenty* (L'viv: Misioner, 1999), 704–705: diary entry of Osyp Nazaruk quoting a contribution of Milena Rudnyts'ka to a discussion on Stepan Baran's "What is Happening in Galicia" in Cracow, 1940.
207. John-Paul Himka, "Dimensions of a Triangle: The Polish-Ukrainian-Jewish Relationship," *Polin* 12 (1999): 25–48.

208. AR, vol. 3, no. 31, 545–46. Anonymous report on the situation of the Jewish population in L'viv at the beginning of German occupation (Polish translation from Yiddish), Warsaw 1941/42, in AR, vol. 3, no. 39, 755–70, here 755.
209. Jones, Żydzi Lwowa w okresie okupacji 1939–1945, S. 45.
210. Hryciuk, *Polacy we Lwowie*, 186–91. Hryciuk, "Mordy w więzeniach lwowskich w czerwcu 1941 r.," *Wrocławskie Studia z Historii Najnowszej* 7 (1999): 58–69. See also the documents in Ivan Bilas, *Represyvno-karal'na systema v Ukraïni 1917–1953: Suspil'no politychnyj ta istoriko-pravovyj analiz*, vol. 2 (Kiev: Lybid, 1994), 222–79. Krzysztof Popiński, Aleksandr Kokurin, and Aleksandr Gurianow, *Drogi śmierci: Ewakuacja więzień sowieckich z Kresów Wschodnich II Rzeczypospolitej w czerwcu i lipcu 1941* (Warsaw: Karta, 1995). Krzysztof Popiński, "Ewakuacja więzień sowieckich z Kresów Wschodnich II Rzeczypospolitej w czerwcu i lipcu 1941 roku w świetle relacji świadków," *Wrocławskie Studia Wschodnie* 2 (1998): 133–50.
211. Popiński, "Ewakuacja więzień sowieckich z Kresów Wschodnich II Rzeczypospolitej w czerwcu i lipcu 1941 roku w świetle relacji świadków," 133–34.
212. Ibid. Żygulski, *Jestem z lwowskiego etapu*, 149–50. Jones, Żydzi Lwowa w okresie okupacji 1939–1945, 45. Hryciuk, *Polacy we Lwowie*, 182–84. See also AR, vol. 3, no. 36, 695–96.
213. AR, vol. 3, no. 31, 547. Ibid., no. 43, 896–97.
214. Hryciuk, *Polacy we Lwowie*, 186.
215. AR, vol. 3, no. 31, 547. Ibid., no. 43, 896–97.
216. Ibid., no. 31, 549–50.
217. Report by an anonymous refugee from Warsaw on the situation of the Jewish population under German occupation between July and December 1941, Warsaw, after December 8, 1941, in AR, vol. 3, no. 37, 721–44, here: 721–22. AR, vol. 3, no. 40, 777.
218. Ibid., no. 31, 549–50.
219. Ibid., no. 39, 755.
220. Ibid., 757–59.
221. Ibid., no. 31, 550–51. Hryciuk, *Polacy we Lwowie*, 190–93. Jones, *Żydzi Lwowa w okresie okupacji 1939–1945*, 46–47.
222. AR, vol. 3, no. 39, 755.
223. Ibid., 757–59.
224. AAN, AK-KOL, 203 (MF 2400/7), 20: report in AK-KOL on the political situation, July 1942. Ibid., 203 (MF 2400/7), 59–60: record in AK-KOL, probably from the end of 1941. General Rowecki to General Sikorski, special message 89 "Ukrainian Affairs" between September 1939 and November 1941, November 15, 1941, in *Armia Krajowa w dokumentach 1939–1945*, vol. 2, 137–45.
225. Dotzauer, *Lwowskie wczesne dojrzewanie*, 28.
226. AR, vol. 3, no. 37, 721–22.
227. The expression *Samostijna Ukraïna* means "independent Ukraine"; it was the most common slogan of the Ukrainian national movement.
228. Kosyk, *The Third Reich and Ukraine*, 62–65. Armstrong, *Ukrainian Nationalism*, 55–57.
229. This was a nationalist organization, not to be confused with the Central Committee of the Communist Party of the Ukrainian Socialist Soviet Republic in Kiev. In German, the Cracow organization was called Ukrainischer Hauptausschuß.
230. PA, R-104151: The head of the security service (SD) and of the security police (SiPo) to the Foreign Office, the High Command of the Wehrmacht and the Foreign Office of the National Socialist party, June 21, 1941.

231. Franziska Bruder, *"Den ukrainischen Staat erkämpfen oder sterben!" Die Organisation Ukrainischer Nationalisten (OUN) 1928–1948* (Berlin: Metropol, 2007), 140–145. Kosyk, *The Third Reich and Ukraine*, 94–95. Pohl, *Nationalsozialistische Judenverfolgung in Ostgalizien 1941–1944*, 47, 61.
232. Here I disagree with Dieter Pohl, who wrote that Hans Koch and Theodor Oberländer from the second department of the German Abwehr had supported Stet'sko's plans. Pohl, *Nationalsozialistische Judenverfolgung in Ostgalizien*, 47.
233. Bundesarchiv (BArch), R6, 150, Bl. 4–7: report on a conversation between Undersecretary of State Ernst Kundt and Professor Dr. Hans Koch, July 7, 1941. Pohl, *Nationalsozialistische Judenverfolgung in Ostgalizien*, 48–49. On Stets'ko's perspective, see Jaroslav Stets'ko, *30 chervnja 1941* (Toronto: Liga vyzvolennija Ukraïny, 1967). The proclamation of a Ukrainian state can be found in an English translation in Kosyk, *The Third Reich and Ukraine*, 504–505. See also ibid., 95–100.
234. BArch, R6, 150, Bl. 3–4: report on a conversation between Undersecretary of State Kundt and SS-Obersturmbannführer Beyer, July 8, 1941. Ibid.: report on a conversation between Kundt and the IC officer Major Weiner, July 9, 1941.
235. ŻIH, Teka Lwowska, 229/22: report by Maurycy Allerhand, n.d. See also AR, vol. 3, no. 37, 721–22.
236. AW, II/2514: recollections of Anastasja Klymkowa (1991).
237. AR, vol. 3, no. 31, 551. Ibid., no. 37, 721–22.
238. ŻIH, Teka Lwowska, 229/22: report by Maurycy Allerhand, not dated.
239. Eyewitnesses spoke of up to 15,000 victims. Pohl, *Nationalsozialistische Judenverfolgung in Ostgalizien*, 61. Jones, *Żydzi Lwowa w okresie okupacji 1939–1945*, 48. Filip Friedman, *Zagłada Żydów lwowskich w okresie okupacji niemieckiej*, second ed. (Munich, Wydawnictwo Centralnej Żydowskiej Komisji Historycznej w Polsce, 1947). During the first two weeks of July, between 12,000 and 24,000 Jews were killed in local pogroms in East Galicia. The first estimate is from Dieter Pohl, and the second estimate is from Aharon Weiss. Pohl, *Judenverfolgung in Ostgalizien*, 67. Aharon Weiss, "Jewish-Ukrainian Relations in Western Ukraine during the Holocaust," in *Ukrainian-Jewish Relations in Historical Perspective*, ed. Peter Potichnyj and Howard Aster (Edmonton: Canadian Institute of Ukrainian Studies, 1988), 409–20, here 413.
240. ŻIH, Relacje, 301/230: statement by Jakub Dentel. More gruesome details and examples of how Jews were murdered, beaten, and humiliated in Grzegorz Rossolinski-Liebe, "Der Verlauf und die Täter des Lemberger Pogroms vom Sommer 1941," *Jahrbuch für Antisemitismusforschung*, 22 (2013): 207–43, here 220-236. John-Paul Himka, "The Lviv Pogrom of 1941: The Germans, Ukrainian Nationalists, and the Carnival Crowd," *Canadian Slavonic Papers/revue canadienne des slavistes*, 53 (2011), nos. 2-3-4, 209-243.
241. Telegram from Heydrich to the commanders of the Einsatzgruppen, June 29, 1941, reprinted in *Die Ermordung der europäischen Juden: Eine umfassende Dokumentation des Holocaust 1941–1945*, ed. Peter Longerich (Munich: Institut für Zeitgeschichte, 1989), 118-; Pohl, *Nationalsozialistische Judenverfolgung in Ostgalizien*, 62.
242. AR, vol. 3, no. 31, 551. Ibid., no. 37, 721–22. See also Pohl, *Nationalsozialistische Judenverfolgung in Ostgalizien*, 62. There is no conclusive evidence proving that the two battalions had participated in the murder.
243. AR, vol. 3, no. 31, 551.
244. Ibid., no. 40, 777.
245. Ibid., no. 36, 695–96.
246. AAN, 202, III, 8, p. 45 (cited after Hryciuk, *Polacy we Lwowie*, 204).

247. ŻIH, Teka Lwowska, 229/22: report by Maurycy, not dated. Siehe auch AR, vol. 3, no. 40, 777.
248. AR, vol. 3, no. 40, 777. Ibid., no. 43, 896–97.
249. AR, vol. 3, no. 39, 757–59.
250. Jones, *Żydzi Lwowa w okresie okupacji 1939–1945*, 47–48. ŻIH, Relacje, 301/230: statement by Jakub Dentel.
251. Hannes Heer, "Lemberg 1941: Die Instrumentalisierung der NKVD-Verbrechen für den Judenmord," in *Kriegsverbrechen im 20. Jahrhundert*, ed. Wolfram Wette and Gerd R. Ueberschär (Darmstadt: Primus, 2001), 165–77.
252. Bundesarchiv-Militärarchiv Freiburg (BArch-MA), RH 24-49/8, Bl. 176: entry in the *Diensttagebuch* (service diary) of the 1st Gebirgsjägerdivision (light infantry mountain troops), June 30, 1941.
253. G.P.U. stands for Gosudarstvennoe Politicheskoe Upravlenie (State Political Administration). The G.P.U. was the political police of the People's Commissariat for Internal Affairs (Narodnyj Komissariat Vnutrennykh Del). After 1934 the political police had a different name, but outside the USSR the term G.P.U. was still in use. BArch-MA, RH 28-1/20, Bl. 35: entry in the Diensttagebuch of the 1st Gebirgjägerdivision, July 1, 1941.
254. BArch-MA WF-03/34170: report by the commander of Battalion 800 on the taking of L'viv, July 1, 1941.
255. ŻIH, Teka Lwowska, 229/8: report by Maurycy Allerhand, not dated.
256. ŻIH, Teka Lwowska, 229/25: report by Maurycy Allerhand, not dated. More examples of this attitude of German soldiers and officers in Bogdan Musial, *"Konterrevolutionäre Elemente sind zu erschießen": Die Brutalisierung des deutsch-sowjetischen Krieges im Sommer 1941* (Berlin: Propyläen, 2000), 231–44.
257. Friedman, "Ukrainian-Jewish Relation," 274. Vladimir Melamed, "Organized and Unsolicited Collaboration in the Holocaust: The Multifaceted Ukrainian Context," *East European Jewish Affairs* 37, no. 2 (August 2007): 217–48, here 227.
258. Semchyshyn, *Z knyhy Leva*, 86. Tarnavs'kyj, *Literaturnyj L'viv*, 67.
259. ZIH, Teka Lwowska, 229/22: report by Maurycy Allerhand, not dated. See also AR, vol. 3, no. 40, 777.
260. Metropolit Andrij Sheptyts'kyj to Pope Pius XII on the situation in East Galicia during German occupation, August 29–31, 1942, printed in *Mytropolyt Andrij Sheptyts'kyj, zhyttja i dijal'nist': Dokumenty i materialy 1899–1944*, vol. 2: Tserkva i suspil'ne pytannja, book 2: Lystuvannja (L'viv: Misioner, 1999), 982–86.
261. See also Friedman, "Ukrainian-Jewish Relations," 261. Kai Struve, "Tremors in the Shatterzone of Empires: East Galicia in Summer 1941," in *Shatterzone of Empires: Coexistence and Violence in the German, Habsburg, Russian and Ottoman Borderlands*, ed. Omer Bartov and Eric D. Weitz (Bloomington: Indiana University Press, 2013), 463–84.
262. Friedman, "Ukrainian-Jewish Relations," 275. Andrzej Żbikowski, "Lokalne pogromy Żydów w czerwcu i lipcu 1941 roku na wschodnich rubieżach II Rzeczypospolitej," *Biuletyn Żydowskiego Instytutu Historycznego* 2/3 (1992): 3–18.
263. Pohl, *Nationalsozialistische Judenverfolgung in Ostgalizien*, 52.
264. BArch, R58, 215, Bl. 48–58: event report (Ereignismeldung) USSR no. 34, July 26, 1941. Ibid., 215, Bl. 100–106: event report no. 38, July 30, 1941.
265. Ibid., 215, Bl. 222–27: event report USSR no. 47, August 9, 1941.
266. Ibid., 215, Bl. 190–94: event report USSR no. 44, August 6, 1941. Ibid., 217, Bl. 100–31: event report USSR no. 86, September 17, 1941. Ibid., 216, Bl. 75–78: event report no. 56, August 18, 1941.

267. Ibid., 217: event report USSR no. 86, September 17, 1941.
268. Ibid., 217, Bl. 100–31: event report USSR no. 86, September 17, 1941.
269. Ibid.
270. Ibid., 215, Bl. 156–61: event report USSR no. 43, August 5, 1941. Ibid., 216, Bl. 75–78: event report USSR no. 56, August 18, 1941. Ibid., 216, Bl. 349–57: event report USSR no. 78, September 9, 1941. Ibid., 216., Bl. 209–11: event report USSR no. 66, August 18, 1941. Pohl, *Nationalsozialistische Judenverfolgung in Ostgalizien*, 67–74, 96–138.
271. BArch, R58, 215, Bl. 100–106: event report USSR no. 38, July 30, 1941.
272. Tatiana Berenstein, "Eksterminacja ludności żydowskiej w Dystrykcie Galicja (1941–1943)," *Byuletyn Żydowskiego Instytutu Historycznego* 61 (1967): 3–33, here 5.
273. AR, vol. 3, no. 37, 723–24. "Eksterminacja ludności żydowskiej w Dystrykcie Galicja (1941–1943)," 6. Jones, *Żydzi Lwowa w okresie okupacji 1939–1945*, 52–54.
274. BArch-MA, RH 22–170: decree of the commander of the Rear Area of Army Group South, General Karl von Roques, July 29, 1941.
275. BArch, R6, 150, Bl. 2RS-3: report on a conversation between Undersecretary of State Kundt and SS-Obersturmbannführer Beyer, July 8, 1941. BArch, R58, 215, Bl. 48–58: event report USSR no. 34, July 26, 1941. Ibid., Bl. 7–8: report on a conversation between Undersecretary of State Kundt and Poljans'kyj, July 11, 1941.
276. Pohl, *Nationalsozialistische Judenverfolgung in Ostgalizien*, 45–46.
277. BArch-MA, RH 22–170: special instructions by the Chief of the General Staff von Krosigk on the treatment of the Ukrainian question to the commander of the Rear Army Area 103, July 11, 1941.
278. BArch R6, 150, Bl. 8–10: conversation between Undersecretary of State Kundt with IC officer Major Weiner, July 9, 1941.
279. BArch, R58, 215, Bl. 190–94, 222–27: event reports USSR nos. 44 and 47, August 6 and August 9, 1941. Ibid., 216, Bl. 131–34: event report USSR no. 60, August 22, 1941.
280. Ibid., 215, Bl. 156–61: event report USSR no. 43, May 8, 1941.
281. Ibid., 216, Bl. 75–78: event report USSR no. 56, August 18, 1941.
282. Ibid., 216: event report USSR no. 54, August 16, 1941. Ibid., 216, Bl. 75–78: event report USSR no. 56, August 18, 1941.
283. Ibid., 215, Bl. 48–58: event report USSR no. 34, July 26, 1941. Ibid., 216, Bl. 209–11: event report USSR no. 66, August 28, 1941.
284. BArch-MA, RH 22-5, Dok. 251: Decree no. 3 of the town major (Stadtkommandant) of L'viv, July 14, 1941. On the Ukrainian auxiliary police, see Martin Dean, *Collaboration in the Holocaust: Crimes of the Local Police in Belorussia and Ukraine, 1941–44* (Basingstoke: Macmillan, 2000).
285. Hryciuk, *Polacy we Lwowie*, 218–19. Gabriel N. Finder and Alexander V. Prusin, "Collaboration in East Galicia: The Ukrainian Police and the Holocaust," *East European Jewish Affairs* 34 (2004): no. 2, 95–118.
286. AR, vol. 3, no. 37, 726–34.
287. AR, vol. 3, no. 31, 552.
288. AR, vol. 3, no. 37, 723–24.
289. Tsentral'nyj Derzhavnyj Arkhiv Vyshchykh Orhaniv Vlady ta Upravlinnja Ukraïny (Ukrainian Central State Archive of the Supreme Organs of Power and Administration in Ukraine, TsDAVOVU), f. 3833, op. 1, spr. 126, ark. 49–50: report by the OUN on the situation in L'viv in January and February 1944, March 10, 1944.
290. Diary entry, April 4, 1943, in Arkadij Ljubchenko, *Shchodennyk Arkadija Ljubchenka* (L'viv: M.P. Kots, 1999), 140. See also the diary entry from October 20, 1943, ibid., 179. Friedman, however, believes that the Ukrainian auxiliary police had consisted of the "rubble of Ukrainian society." Friedman, "Ukrainian-Jewish Relations," 282.

291. BArch, R58, 215, Bl. 190–94, 222–27: event report USSR no. 44 and no. 47, August 6 and 9, 1941. Ibid., 216, Bl. 131–34: event report USSR no. 60, August 22, 1941.
292. Ibid., 215, Bl. 100–106: event report USSR no. 38, July 30, 1941.
293. Ibid., 215, Bl. 190–94, 222–27: event report USSR no. 44 and no. 47, August 6 and 9, 1941. Ibid., 216, Bl. 131–34: event report USSR no. 60, August 22, 1941.
294. Ibid., 215, Bl. 17–20: event report USSR no. 32, July 24, 1941.
295. Cited after ibid., 215, Bl. 17–20: event report USSR no. 32, July 24, 1941: protest letters to the German Foreign Office and the Office (*Amt*) Rosenberg.
296. BArch, 43 II, 685, Bl. 7–8: Stets'ko writing on behalf of the Ukrainian government to Adolf Hitler, August 3, 1941.
297. BArch, R58, 215, Bl. 113–15: event report USSR no. 39, July 31, 1941.
298. Ibid., 215, Bl. 100–106: event report USSR no. 38, July 30, 1941.
299. Ibid., 215, Bl. 119–20: event report USSR no. 40, August 1, 1941.
300. The most important departments of the district administration in L'viv were the department of the governor and the departments for internal administration, work, economy, food supplies and agriculture, justice, health, and propaganda. Pohl, *Nationalsozialistische Judenverfolgung in Ostgalizien*, 75–83.
301. BArch, R58, 215, Bl. 259–64: event report USSR no. 50, August 12, 1941.
302. Ibid., 217, Bl. 2–10: event report USSR no. 79, September 10, 1941. Ibid., 217, Bl. 100–31: event report USSR no. 86, September 17, 1941.
303. Ibid., 217, Bl. 138–43: event report USSR no. 87, September 18, 1941.
304. Ibid., 220, Bl. 290–99: event report USSR no. 164, February 4, 1942.
305. Ibid., 217, Bl. 355–59: event report USSR no. 96, September 27, 1941.
306. Armstrong, *Ukrainian Nationalism*, 107–10. Friedman, *Ukrainian-Jewish Relations*, 266–67.
307. The letter was signed by Archbishop Sheptyts'kyj in his role as president of the Ukrainian National Council in L'viv, Professor Mykhajlo Velychkivs'kyj (president of the Ukrainian National Council in Kiev), Andreas (Andrij) Livyts'kyj (the representative of the Ukrainian government-in-exile in Warsaw), General Mykhajlo Omeljanovych-Pavlenko (the chairman of the General Council of Ukrainian combatants in Prague), and Andrij Mel'nyk (the leader of one faction of the Organization of Ukrainian Nationalists, Berlin).
308. BArch, R6, 69, Bl. 139–41: Ukrainian leaders to Hitler, January 14, 1942.
309. Kosyk, *The Third Reich and Ukraine*, 228–30. Hryciuk, *Polacy we Lwowie*, 224–25. Pohl, *Nationalsozialistische Judenverfolgung in Ostgalizien*, 96–101.
310. AAN, AK-KOL, 203 (MF 2400/7), 20: report in AK-KOL on the political situation, July 1942.
311. BArch, R58, 216, Bl. 131–34: event report USSR no. 60, August 22, 1941.
312. Dieter Schenk, *Der Lemberger Professorenmord und der Holocaust in Ostgalizien* (Bonn: Dietz, 2007). Zygmunt Albert, *Kaźń profesorów lwowskich, lipiec 1941* (Wrocław: Wydawnictwo Uniwersytetu Wrocławskiego, 1989). Hryciuk, *Polacy we Lwowie*, 191–93.
313. *Gazeta Lwowska*, December 21, 1942.
314. Hryciuk, *Polacy we Lwowie*, 253–54.
315. AAN, AK-KOL, 203 (MF 2400/5), 120: report by Dawid-Daktyl, February 13, 1943.
316. Hryciuk, *Polacy we Lwowie*, 259–64.
317. AAN, AK-KOL, 203 (MF 2400/7), 15–27: report no. 4, March 20, 1943.
318. Ibid., 203 (MF 2400/3), 91–94: report on the period between May 1 and May 15, 1944. AW, sygn II/1167: recollections of Halina Konopińska.

319. On Ukrainian and Polish cultural life in L'viv, see Luts'kyj and Naumenko, "U roky druhoï svitovoï vijny," 486–88. Hryciuk, *Polacy we Lwowie*, 366–67.
320. BArch, R58, 215, Bl. 113–15: event report USSR no. 39, July 31, 1941. Tatiana Berenstein, "Praca Przymusowa ludności żydowskiej w tzw: Dystrykcie Galicja (1941–1944)," *Biuletyn Żydowskiego Instytutu Historycznego* 69 (1969): 3–45. On the economic dimensions of German occupation policy using the example of Belarus, see Christian Gerlach, *Kalkulierte Morde: Die deutsche Wirtschafts- und Vernichtungspolitik in Weißrußland 1941–1944* (Hamburg: Hamburger Edition, 1999).
321. Hryciuk, *Polacy we Lwowie*, 198–205.
322. BArch, R58, 216, Bl. 11–14: event report USSR no. 52, August 14, 1941.
323. Pohl, *Nationalsozialistische Judenverfolgung in Ostgalizien*, 76–77.
324. Hryciuk, *Polacy we Lwowie*, 216–17.
325. AAN, AK-KOL, 203 (MF 2400/8), 17–23: evaluation of the Ukrainian enemy, November 27, 1942.
326. Ibid., 203 (MF 2400/5), 51–57: report for December 1942.
327. Hryciuk, *Polacy we Lwowie*, 226–27, 326–67.
328. Ibid., 227–29. Hryciuk, "*Kumytet*."
329. BArch, R58, 217, Bl. 445–48: event report USSR no. 99, September 30, 1941.
330. Ibid., 215, Bl. 48–58: event report USSR no. 34, July 26, 1941.
331. Ibid., 216, Bl. 131–34: event report USSR no. 60, August 22, 1941.
332. BArch, R 52/III, 12, Bl. 45–52: protocol of a meeting of the Ukrainian Central Committee (Ukrainischer Hauptausschuß) in Cracow on December 10, 1943.
333. Ibid., Bl. 1–3: memorandum by Kost' Pan'kivs'kyj on the situation in Galicia, probably fall/winter 1943. Ibid., Bl. 4–33: overview of the structure and staff of the Office L'viv of the Ukrainian Central Committee. See also Vasyl Veryha, ed., *The Correspondence of the Ukrainian Central Committee in Cracow with the German Authorities* (Edmonton: Canadian Institute of Ukrainian Studies Press, 2000).
334. BArch, R 52/III, 12, Bl. 34–38: report on the activities of the Department for Schools of the Ukrainian Central Committee for 1943, December 2, 1943.
335. BArch, R58, 215, Bl. 48–58: event report USSR no. 34, July 26, 1941. Ibid., 215, Bl. 100–106: event report USSR no. 38, July 30, 1941.
336. Ibid., 215, Bl. 113–15: event report USSR no. 39, July 31, 1941.
337. Hryciuk, *Polacy we Lwowie*, 198–99.
338. Ibid., 264–66.
339. DALO, f. R-37, op. 3, spr. 28, ark. 32–33: report of the Ukrainian aid committee in L'viv for May 1944, June 9, 1944.
340. BArch, R58, 215, Bl. 259–64: event report USSR no. 50, August 12, 1941.
341. AR, vol. 3, no. 37, 726–34. Ibid., no. 40, 778–79. Ibid., no. 31, 553. ŻIH, Teka Lwowska, 229/7: report by Maurycy Allerhand, not dated. Jones, *Żydzi Lwowa w okresie okupacji 1939–1945*, 50–54. Berenstein, "Eksterminacja ludności żydowskiej w Dystrykcie Galicja (1941–1943)," 7.
342. BArch, R58, 7224, Bl. 96: appeal by the chairman of the Jewish Council, Dr. Parnas, to the Jewish population, July 28, 1941.
343. Hryciuk, *Polacy we Lwowie*, 205.
344. Berenstein, "Eksterminacja ludności żydowskiej w Dystrykcie Galicja (1941–1943)," 20–21.
345. Ibid., 17.
346. Philip Friedman, "The Destruction of the Jews of Lwów, 1941–1944," in *Roads to Extinction: Essays on the Holocaust*, ed. Philip Friedman (New York: Jewish Publication

Society of America, 1980), 244–321, here 251–53. Pohl, *Nationalsozialistische Judenverfolgung in Ostgalizien*, 105–108. On Jewish Councils in general, see Isaiah Trunk, *Judenrat: The Jewish Councils in Eastern Europe under Nazi Occupation* (New York: Macmillan, 1972).
347. Berenstein, "Eksterminacja ludności żydowskiej w Dystrykcie Galicja (1941–1943)," 21–24.
348. AAN, AK, AOL, 203/12 (MF 2400/5): report in AK-KOL, fall 1942.
349. Leon Weliczker Wells, *The Death Brigade* (New York: Holocaust Library, 1978). Joachim Schoenfeld, *Holocaust Memoirs: Jews in the Lwow Ghetto, the Janowski Concentration Camp, and as Deportees in Siberia* (Hoboken, NJ: Ktav Publishing House, 1985). Friedman, "The Destruction of the Jews of Lvov," 306–309. Pohl, *Nationalsozialistische Judenverfolgung in Ostgalizien*, 331–38. Thomas Held, "Vom Pogrom zum Massenmord: Die Vernichtung der jüdischen Bevölkerung Lembergs im Zweiten Weltkrieg," in *Lemberg—Lwów—Lviv: Eine Stadt im Schnittpunkt europäischer Kulturen*, ed. Peter Fässler, Thomas Held, and Dirk Sawitzki (Cologne: Böhlau, 1995), 113–166, here 136–40.
350. Berenstein, "Eksterminacja ludności żydowskiej w Dystrykcie Galicja (1941–1943)," 21–25.
351. Riedl, *We Lwowie*, 27.
352. AW, sygn. II/171: recollections of Janina Kandeler.
353. Metropolit Andrij Sheptyts'kyj to Pope Pius XII on the situation in East Galicia during German occupation, August 29–31, 1942, in *Mytropolyt Andrej Sheptyts'kyj: Zhyttja i Dijal'nist'*, vol. 2: 982–86.
354. Berenstein, "Eksterminacja ludności żydowskiej w Dystrykcie Galicja (1941–1943)," 17–18.
355. Ibid., 19.
356. Ibid., 25–28.
357. AAN, AK-KOL, 203 (MF 2400/5), 120: report by Dawid-Daktyl, February 13, 1943. Ibid., 203 (MF 2400/7), 8–14: report no. 3, February 20, 1943.
358. Ibid., 203 (MF 2400/7), 15–27: report no. 4, March 20, 1943.
359. Ibid., 203 (MF 2400/7), 35–37: report no. 6, June 29, 1943.
360. Berenstein, "Eksterminacja ludności żydowskiej w Dystrykcie Galicja (1941–1943)," 28–30.
361. Pohl, *Nationalsozialistische Judenverfolgung in Ostgalizien*, 263.
362. Ibid., 259. Robert Marshall, *In the Sewers of Lvov: An Heroic Story of Survival from the Holocaust* (London: Collins, 1990), 41–45.
363. BArch-MA, RH 53-23, 42, Bl. 281–97: monthly report by the Oberfeldkommandantur, September 17, 1943.
364. TsDAVOVU, f. 3833, op. 1, spr. 126, ark. 29–36: sociopolitical report on L'viv by OUN(b) for November 1943.
365. According to a report of the OUN, on August 1, 1944, the Soviet authorities in L'viv registered 811 Jews who had survived the war in the city or in neighboring villages: TsDAVO, f. 3833, op. 1, spr. 126, ark. 96–100: report of the OUN from L'viv on the period July 17–August 3, 1944. Pohl quotes a Soviet source, which states that on October 1, 1944, 1,689 Jewish survivors were registered in L'viv. Pohl, *Nationalisozialistische Judenverfolgung in Ostgalizien*, 385–87. Berenstein, "Eksterminacja ludności żydowskiej w Dystrykcie Galicja (1941–1943)," 4. Aharon Weiss, "The Holocaust and the Ukrainian Victims," in *Mosaic of Victims: Non-Jews Persecuted and Murdered by the Nazis*, ed. Michael Berenbaum (New York: New York University Press, 1990), 109–115, here 113.

366. Philip Friedman, "Ukrainian-Jewish Relations during the Nazi Occupation," *YIVO: Annual of Jewish Social Science* 12 (1958/59): 259–96, here 287–90. Hansjakob Stehle, "Der Lemberger Metropolit Šeptyc'kyj und die nationalsozialistische Politik in der Ukraine, *Vierteljahrshefte für Zeitgeschichte* 34 (1986): 407–25, here 419–20. Jones, *Żydzi Lwowa w okresie okupacji 1939–1945*, 206–22. Research on the saving of Jews by Ukrainians tries to correct the stereotype about Ukrainians as "eternal anti-Semites" and helpers of Nazi-Germany's attempt to exterminate the Jewish population. Frank Golczewski, "Die Revision eines Klischees: Die Rettung von verfolgten Juden im Zweiten Weltkrieg durch Ukrainer," in *Solidarität und Hilfe für Juden während der NS-Zeit: Regionalstudien*, vol. 2, ed. Wolfgang Benz (Berlin: Metropol, 1998), 9–82. Shanna Kovba, *Ljudjanist'u bezodni pekla: Povedinka mistsevoho naselennja Skhidnoï Halychyny v roky 'ostatochnoho rozv"jazannja jevrejs'koho pytannja'* (Kiev: Instytut Judaïky), 1998), 93–105.
367. The numbers in the second column are based (until December 1942) on the statistical information of the Jewish Council in L'viv on the number of distributed ration cards. The table is based on data collected by Tatiana Berenstein. Berenstein, "Eksterminacja ludności żydowskiej w Dystrykcie Galicja (1941–1943)," 32. She used the report by the Chief of Police and SS (*Polizei- und SS-Führer*) in the district of Galicia Fritz Katzmann from June 30, 1943, on the "Final Solution of the Jewish Question in the District of Galicia" and the following eyewitness accounts: Friedman, *Zagłada Żydów lwowskich*; Dawid Kahane, *Lvov Ghetto Diary* (Amherst: University of Massachusetts Press, 1990).
368. BArch-MA, RH 53-23, 41, Bl. 300–16: monthly report by Oberfeldkommandantur 365, March 17, 1943.
369. Ibid., Bl. 186–202: monthly report of the Oberfeldkommandantur 365, April 17, 1943.
370. Ibid., Bl. 111–30: monthly report by Oberfeldkommandantur 365, May 18, 1943. Kosyk, *The Third Reich and Ukraine*, 383–86.
371. BArch-MA, RH 53-23, 41, Bl. 111–30: monthly report by Oberfeldkommandantur 365, May 18, 1943.
372. TsDAHOU, f. 1, op. 23, spr. 929, ark. 22–28: S. Volynets on the SS-Division Galicia, *Kalendar'za narod na 1944 god* (L'viv: 1944) (translated from Ukrainian into Russian for the Soviet military counterintelligence agency "Smersh").
373. TsDAHOU, f. 1, op. 23, spr. 929, ark. 22–28: Volynets on the SS-Division Galicia.
374. AAN, AK-KOL, 203 (MF 2400/7), 44–45: report on Ukrainian matters, May 15, 1943.
375. Ibid., 203 (MF 2400/1): report on Ukrainian matters, April 30, 1943.
376. Kosyk, *The Third Reich and Ukraine*, 343–46.
377. BArch-MA, RH 53-23, 42, Bl. 91–104: monthly report by Oberfeldkommandantur 365, July 17, 1943.
378. Andrij Boljanovs'kyj, *Dyvizija 'Halychyna:' Istorija* (L'viv: Instytut Ukraïnoznavstva im. I. Kryp"jakevycha NANU, 2000), 101–104. Kosyk, *Third Reich and Ukraine*, 383–86.
379. AAN, AK-KOL, 203 (MF 2400/5), 51–57: report for December 1942.
380. Ibid., 203 (MF 2400/5), 120: report by Dawid-Daktyl, February 13, 1943. Ibid., 203 (MF 2400/7), 8–14: report no. 3 by AK-KOL, February 20, 1943.
381. Ibid., 203 (MF 2400/7), 35–37: report no. 6 by AK-KOL, June 29, 1943.
382. Hryciuk, *Polacy we Lwowie*, 230–31.
383. Ibid., 232–33.
384. BArch-MA, RH 53-23, 61, Bl. 4–9: unsigned report from Cracow (possibly authored by Theodor Oberländer), mid-1943.

385. BArch-MA, RH 53-23, 61, Bl. 10–15: report by Captain (Hauptmann) Theodor Oberländer, June 22, 1943.
386. AAN, AK-KOL, 203 (MF 2400/7), 8–14: report no. 3, February 20, 1943. Ibid., 203 (MF 2400/7), 15–27: report no. 4, March 20, 1943.
387. Ibid.
388. BArch, R 52/III, 12, Bl. 45–52: protocol of a meeting of the Ukrainian Central Committee (Ukrainischer Hauptausschuß) in Cracow, December 10, 1943.
389. Ibid., Bl. 1–3: memorandum by Kost' Pan'kivs'kyj on the situation in Galicia, probably fall/winter 1943. Ibid., Bl. 4–33: overview of the structure and staff of the Office L'viv of the Ukrainian Central Committee.
390. Ibid., Bl. 53–57: memo of the Ukrainian Central Committee on the report of the Advisory Council of the head of the district of Cracow, December 10, 1943.
391. AAN, 203 (MF 2400/2), 155–77: report in AK-KOL on the period between July 1 and September 1, 1943, December 15, 1943. On the Home Army and other underground organizations in L'viv, see Żygulski, *Jestem z lwowskiego etapu*, 159–65. Jerzy Węgierski, *Komendy lwowskiego obszaru i okręgu Armii Krajowej 1941–1944* (Cracow: Platan, 1997). Grzegorz Mazur and Jerzy Węgierski, *Konspiracja Lwowska 1939–1944*. Tomasz Strzembosz, *Rzeczpospolita podziemna: Społeczeństwo polskie a państwo podziemne 1939–1945* (Warsaw: Krupski i S-ka, 2000).
392. TsDAVOVU, f. 3833, op. 1, spr. 126, ark. 29–36: sociopolitical report on L'viv by OUN(b) for November 1943.
393. Hryciuk, *Polacy we Lwowie*, 255–56.
394. TsDAVOVU, f. 3833, op. 1, spr. 126, ark. 9–10: report by OUN(b) from L'viv district between October 15 and November 15, 1943.
395. TsDAVOVU, f. 3833, op. 1, spr. 126, ark. 29–36: sociopolitical report on L'viv by OUN(b) for November 1943. Hryciuk, *Polacy we Lwowie*, 255–56.
396. Ibid., 237–48.
397. Friedman, "Ukrainian-Jewish Relations during the Nazi Occupation," 271.
398. BArch-MA, RH 53-23, 42, Bl. 160–63: report by a district captain (Kreishauptmann) from the eastern part of Galicia for June and July 1943 (copy, excerpt), August 17, 1943. On the loss of control as a result of attacks by partisans, see BArch-MA, RH 53-23, 41, Bl. 238–41: report by the command of the military district (Wehrkreiskommando) of the Generalgouvernment on the situation in August 1943, September 7, 1943.
399. Ibid., 42, Bl. 281–97: monthly report by Oberfeldkommandantur 365, September 17, 1943. Ibid., 43, Bl. 25–27: report by the command of the military district of the Generalgouvernment, October 13, 1943.
400. Armstrong, *Ukrainian Nationalism*, 158. See also Frank Golczewski, "Die Ukrainer im Zweiten Weltkrieg," in *Geschichte der Ukraine*, ed. Frank Golczewski (Göttingen: Vandenhoeck & Ruprecht, 1993), 241–60. Peter J. Potichnyj and Yevhen Shtendera, eds., *Political Thought of the Ukrainian Underground* (Edmonton: Canadian Institute of Ukrainian Studies Press, 1986).
401. BArch-MA, RH 53-23, 41, Bl. 275–79: report on the situation in a county (*Kreis*) of the District (*Distrikt*) Galicia for October and November 1943 (excerpt).
402. Ibid.
403. Ibid., 41, Bl. 194–218: monthly report by Oberfeldkommandantur 365, November 20, 1943. Ibid., 41, Bl. 260–91: monthly report by Oberfeldkommandantur 365, December 17, 1943. Ibid., 44, Bl. 160–71: monthly report by Oberfeldkommandantur 365, February 20, 1944. Ibid, 44, 252–64: monthly report by Oberfeldkommandantur 365, March 20, 1944. Ibid., 44, Bl. 340–57: monthly report by Oberfeldkommandantur 365, April 19, 1944.

404. AR, vol. 3, no. 37, 726.
405. Ibid., no. 31, 553
406. Ibid., no. 39, 757–59.
407. ŻIH, Teka Lwowska, 229/22: report by Maurycy Allerhand, not dated.
408. AR, vol. 3, no. 37, 726.
409. TsDAVOVU, f. 4620, op. 3, spr. 290, ark. 15–25: Iz stenogrammy vospominanij doktora filosofskykh nauk Fridmana Pilipa Lazarevicha ob unichtozhenii nemetskimi fashistami evrejskogo naselenija vo L'vove, January 22, 1946. AR, vol. 3, no. 43, 896–97.
410. Weliczker Wells, *Janowski Road*, 52.
411. AR, vol. 3, no. 36, 698.
412. Ibid., 203 (MF 2400/5), 1: report on the Jewish topic, July 1942.
413. Ibid., 203 (MF 2400/8), 68–123: report by "Alfa" in AK-KOL on the minority problem, July 4, 1942.
414. Ibid., 203 (MF 2400/7), 20: report in AK-KOL on the political situation, July 1942.
415. Ibid., 203 (MF 2400/5), 12: report in AK-KOL, fall 1942.
416. Ibid., 203 (MF 2400/5), 9: report in AK-KOL on Jewish matters, n.d. (probably 1942/43).
417. Ibid., 203 (MF 2400/5), 51–57: report by AK-KOL for December 1942.
418. Weiss, "Jewish-Ukrainian Relations," 417.
419. Jones, *Żydzi Lwowa w okresie okupacji 1939–1945*, 193–201. Pohl, *Nationalsozialistische Judenverfolgung in Ostgalizien*, 374–77. Golczewski, "Die Revision eines Klischees," 40–43.
420. BArch, R58, 220, Bl. 290–99: event report USSR no. 164, February 4, 1942.
421. Ibid., 216, Bl. 94–97: event report USSR no. 58, August 20, 1941. Ibid., 216, Bl. 131–34: event report USSR no. 60.
422. AAN, AK-KOL, 203 (MF 2400/8), 17–23: evaluation of the Ukrainian enemy, November 27, 1942.
423. Ibid., 203 (MF 2400/7), 59–60: report in AK-KOL (excerpt), probably from the end of 1941.
424. Ibid., 203 (MF 2400/9), 34: report on the Polish cultural vested rights in L'viv, May 1943. Hryciuk, *Polacy we Lwowie*, 154–55.
425. AAN, AK-KOL, 203 (MF 2400/7), 1–7: report no. 2, January 25, 1943. Ibid., 203 (MF 2400/5), 104–11: additional report in AK-KOL for March 10–March 20, 1944.
426. Ibid., 203 (MF 2400/7), 1–7: report no. 2, January 25, 1943. Ibid., 203 (MF 2400/9), 34: report on vested Polish cultural rights in L'viv, May 1943.
427. Ibid., 203 (MF 2400/8), 17–23: evaluation of the Ukrainian enemy, November 27, 1942.
428. The Home Army reported on waves of arrests occurring in November 1942, January 1943, and September 1943. Ibid., 203 (MF 2400/8), 17–23: evaluation of the Ukrainian enemy, November 27, 1942. Ibid., 203 (MF 2400/5), 51–57: report by AK-KOL for December 1942. Ibid., 203 (MF 2400/7), 1–7: report no. 2, January 25, 1943. Ibid., 203 (MF 2400/8), 14–16: report no. 18, September 24, 1943. Memorandum on the "Ukrainian problem," December 1943, in vol. 2, 77.
429. AAN, AK-KOL, 203 (MF 2400/7), 23–25: report on Ukrainian matters, February 15, 1943.
430. Ibid., 203 (MF 2400/7), 21–22: material for a report on Ukrainian matters for January 1943, February 1943.
431. Ibid., 203 (MF 2400/7), 19–22: report until the end of January 1943, February 1943. A similar tendency is displayed in the report on a conversation with a Ukrainian youth

leader: ibid., 203 (MF 2400/7), 35–37. Ibid., 203 (MF 2400/8), 43–53: report on the politicial and military situation in Eastern Little Poland in the light of recent events, beginning of 1944. Ibid., 203 (MF 2400/4), 22–27: draft of an operational plan, October 10, 1944.
432. Kosyk, *The Third Reich and Ukraine*, 259–61. Peter J. Potichnyj, "Ukrainians in World War II: Military Formations: An Overview." http://www.infoukes.com/upa/related/military.html.
433. AAN, AK-KOL, 203 (MF 2400/5), 58–65: report in AK-KOL, end of 1942. Grzegorz Motyka, "Postawy wobec konfliktu polsko-ukraińskiego w latach 1939–1953 w zależności od przynależności etnicznej, państwowej i religijnej," in *Tygiel narodów*, 279–407, here 294–303. AAN, AK-KOL, 203 (MF 2400/7), 35–37: report no. 6, June 29, 1943.
434. Ibid., 203 (MF 2400/7), 38–44: report no. 7, July 23, 1943.
435. Ibid., 203 (MF 2400/8), 63–64: commentary in AK-KOL on a report on the Ukrainian question, beginning of 1944.
436. Ibid., 203 (MF 2400/7), 28–34: report no. 5, May 22, 1943.
437. Ibid., 203 (MF 2400/7), 59–60: report, not dated (probably December 1941). Report no. 22, July 4, 1942, in Siwicki, *Dzieje konfliktów polsko-ukraińskich*, vol. 2, 52.
438. AAN, AK-KOL, 203 (MF 2400/7), 20: report in AK-KOL on the political situation, July 1942. See also the reports for December 1942 (51-7), report no. 2 January 25, 1943 (1-7), report no. 6, June 29, 1943 (35-7). Ibid., 203 (MF 2400/8), 68–123: report by "Alfa" in AK-KOL on the minority problem, July 4, 1942. Memorandum "The Ukrainian Problem," December 1943, in Siwicki, *Dzieje konfliktów polsko-ukraińskich*, vol. 2, 81–82. On the position of Polish political groups, see the report by the officer for information and propaganda of the High Command of the Home Army, May 27, 1943, in Siwicki, *Dzieje konfliktów polsko-ukraińskich*, vol. 2, 233–40. On the more moderate position of the Home Army in Warsaw and the government-in-exile, see Torzecki, *Polacy i Ukraińcy*, 197–200.
439. AAN, AK-KOL, 203 (MF 2400/8), 18–32: project of Lasota, n.d.
440. Ibid., 203 (MF 2400/8), 63–64: commentary to a report on the Ukrainian question, not dated (probably January/February 1944).
441. AAN, AK-KOL, 203 (MF 2400/8), 1–6: report on the Ukrainian situation in February 1943.
442. Ibid., 203 (MF 2400/7), 35–37: report no. 6, June 29, 1943. Ibid., 203 (MF 2400/7), 38–44: report no. 7, July 23, 1943.
443. Ibid., 203 (MF 2400/7), 56–60: report on Ukrainian matters, August 15, 1943.
444. Ibid., 203 (MF 2400/8), 43–53: report on the political and military situation in Eastern Little Poland in light of recent events, beginning in 1944. Ibid., 203 (MF 2400/4), 22–27: draft of an operational plan, October 10, 1944. "In September (1943, CM) 70 Poles were murdered in the vicinity of L'viv, 3 doctors, 5 priests, 15 peasants, 3 workers, 3 civil servants and 17 children." Ibid., 203 (MF 2400/8), 20–26: list of victims of Ukrainian terror, October 1943.
445. Ibid., 203 (MF 2400/8), 14–16: report no. 18, September 24, 1943. Ibid., 203 (MF 2400/8), 17–23: evaluation of the Ukrainian enemy, November 27, 1942.
446. TsDAVOVU, f. 3833, op. 1, spr. 126, ark. 5–7: report by the OUN in the L'viv region on the period between September 15 and October 15, 1943. Motyka, "Postawy wobec konfliktu polsko-ukraińskiego," 336–40.
447. Ibid., ark. 9–10: report by the OUN in the L'viv region on the period between October 15 and November 15, 1943.

448. Ibid., ark. 29–36: sociopolitical report by the OUN on the month of November 1943 in L'viv.
449. AAN, AK-KOL, 203 (MF 2400/8), 63–64: commentary in AK-KOL on a report on the Ukrainian question, beginning of 1944.
450. Ibid., 203 (MF 2400/2), 186: note on Ukrainian matters, March 2, 1944.
451. Ibid., 203 (MF 2400/3), 114–26: surveillance report for March 1–15, 1944. Ibid., 203 (MF 2400/3), 97–100: report for March 15–April 15, 1944. Ibid., 203 (MF 2400/4), 185–90: report for May 15–31, 1944, June 5, 1944.
452. AW, sygn. II/171: recollections of Janina Kandeler.
453. Ibid., 203 (MF 2400/7), 23–25: report on Ukrainian matters, February 15, 1943.
454. TsDAVOVU, f. 3833, op. 1, spr. 126, ark. 49–50: political report by the OUN(b) for January and February 1944.
455. Ibid., ark. 62–64: overview of the sociopolitical situation in L'viv for March 1944.
456. AAN, AK-KOL, 203 (MF 2400/3), 138: report no. 8.
457. Ibid., 203 (MF 2400/9), 16: proclamation of the Armia Krajowa, spring 1944.
458. BArch, R-52/III, 2, Bl. 70–71: an SS-*Obersturmbannführer* acting on behalf of the *Höhere SS- und Polizeiführer im Generalgouvernement* to the head of the administration of the Generalgouvernement, Craushaar, April 12, 1944.
459. TsDAVOVU, f. 3833, op. 1, spr. 126, ark. 62–64: overview of the sociopolitical situation in L'viv for March 1944.
460. AAN, AK-KOL, 203 (MF 2400/7), 19–22: report until the end of January 1943, February 1943. Ibid., 203 (MF 2400/8), 43–53: report on the political and military situation in Eastern Little Poland in light of recent events, beginning of 1944. Ibid., 203 (MF 2400/7), 121–32: draft of an operational plan, June 14, 1943. Ibid., 203 (MF 2400/4), 2–27: draft of an operational plan, January 10, 1944. Ibid., 203 (MF 2400/4), 22–27: draft of an operational plan, October 10, 1944.
461. Ibid., 203 (MF 2400/7), 52–54: report by *Ariel* on training courses July 22, 1943.
462. Ibid., 203 (MF 2400/9), 46–51: plan for securing objects of science, culture, and art in L'viv during the time of the upheaval, spring 1944.
463. Ibid., 203 (MF 2400/4), 384–86: report on the period between June 15 and July 1, 1944.
464. Ibid., 203 (MF 2400/2), 259: operational plan no. 3, August 15, 1943.
465. Ibid., 203 (MF 2400/7), 65–66: report on the planned training for the imminent fight April 1–May 31, 1944, March 21, 1944.
466. BArch, R52 III/I, Bl. 108: Hauptabteilung Innere Verwaltung des Generalgouvernements (v. Craushaar) to Governor Wächter, March 18, 1944.
467. AAN, AK-KOL, 203 (MF 2400/3), 71–72: report on an air raid on L'viv, April 9, 1944. BArch-MA, RH 53-23, 44, Bl. 340–57: monthly report of Oberfeldkommandantur 365, April 19, 1944. TsDAVOVU, f. 3833, op. 1, spr. 126, ark. 70–76: overview by OUN on the political situation in April 1944.
468. Ibid., ark. 70–76: overview of the political situation in April 1944.
469. *Lemberger Zeitung*, May 4, 1944.
470. TsDAVOVU, f. 3833, op. 1, spr. 126, ark. 70–76: overview of the political situation in April 1944.
471. BArch-MA, RH 53-23, 44, Bl. 340–57: monthly report by Oberfeldkommandantur 365, April 19, 1944.
472. *Lemberger Zeitung*, April 24, 1944.
473. Junak-SS in the streets of L'viv, *Lemberger Zeitung*, July 8, 1944.

474. "Für oder gegen Europa—es gibt keinen Kompromiß: Stadthauptmann Dr. Höller zu Lembergs Bevölkerung—Der dritte Jahrestag der Befreiung," *Lemberger Zeitung*, July 9, 1944.
475. Hryciuk, *Polacy we Lwowie*, 246–47.
476. AAN, AK-KOL, 203 (MF 2400/2): report, July 17, 1943.
477. TsDAVOVU, f. 3833, op. 1, spr. 126, ark. 29–36: overview of the sociopolitical situation in L'viv for November 1944.
478. TsDAVOVU, f. 3833, op. 1, spr. 126, ark. 21: extraordinary sociopolitical overview, July 20, 1944.
479. Ibid.
480. TsDAVOVU, f. 3833, op. 1, spr. 126, ark. 96–100: report by the OUN L'viv for the period between July 10 and August 3, 1944.
481. DALO, f. P-3, op. 1, spr. 62, ark. 78–87: Hrushetskyj to Khrushchev, August 3, 1944.
482. Ibid., ark. 20–32: the state attorney of oblast L'viv I. Kornetov to Hrushets'kyj and to the deputy head of the oblast commission for recording and investigating the German-fascist destruction and crimes in oblast L'viv, Kozyrev, September 16, 1944.
483. TsDAVOVU, f. 4620, op. 3, spr. 365, ark. 2–4: chronology of the struggle of the Soviet people against the fascist invaders in L'viv, July 1, 1945. DALO, f. P-221, op. 2, spr. 919, ark. 15: statistics from October 1, 1947.
484. The data was collected by Hryciuk, "Zmiany demograficzne ludności polskiej w latach 1931–1944," 7–76.
485. TsDAVOVU, f. 3833, op. 1, spr. 126, ark. 96–100: report by OUN L'viv on the period from July 10 to August 3, 1944. On the sovietization of L'viv, see Amar, "The Making of Soviet Lviv, 1939–1963."
486. AAN, AK-KOL, 203 (MF 2400/3), 127: report on the activities of AK-KOL L'viv.
487. Motyka, "Postawy wobec konfliktu polsko-ukraińskiego," 305–306. Tomasz Strembosz, *Rzeczpospolita podziemna: Społeczeństwo polskie a państwo podziemne 1939–1945* (Warsaw: Krupski i S-ka, 2000), 276. For an eyewitness account on *Burza*, see Barbara Mękarska-Kozłowska, *Burza nad Lwowem* (London: Polska Fundacja Kulturalna, 1996).
488. TsDAVOVU, f. 3833, op. 1, spr. 126, ark. 96–100: report by the OUN L'viv for the period between July 10 and August 3, 1944.
489. Ibid., ark. 92–95: report by the OUN L'viv on the last events and the situation in L'viv and surrounding areas, August 2, 1944. Ibid., ark. 96–100: report by the OUN L'viv for the period between July 10 and August 3, 1944. According to Mykhajlo Koval', seven hundred Ukrainians have been killed by the Armia Krajowa in L'viv. This figure is probably too high. Mykhajlo Koval', *Ukraïna w Druhij Svitovij i Velykij Vitchyznjanij Vijnach (1939–1945 rr.)* (Kiev: Al'ternatyvy, 1999), 110.
490. DALO, f. 3, op. 1, spr. 63, ark. 69–70 (printed in *Karta*: German edition 2 [2001]: 91). The secretary of the L'viv city committee of the Communist Party (bol'sheviky) of Ukraine Chupis to the responsible organizer of the Central Committee VKP(b) Stepanov, July 28, 1944.
491. DALO, f. P-3, op. 1, spr. 68, ark. 95–100 (printed in *Karta*: German edition 2 [2001]: 72). The head of the NKV of the L'viv region L. Voloshenko to the chairman of the regional party organization Hrushets'kyj, July 29, 1944.
492. TsDAVOVU, f. 3833, op. 1, spr. 126, ark. 92–95: report by the OUN(b) L'viv on the final events and the situation in L'viv and surrounding area, August 2, 1944. Ibid., ark. 96–100: report by the OUN(b) L'viv on the period between July 10 and August 3, 1944.

493. Ibid., ark. 92–95: report by the OUN(b) L'viv on the final events and the situation in L'viv and the surrounding areas, August 2, 1944.
494. Ibid., ark. 96–100: report by the OUN(b) L'viv on the period between July 10 and August 3, 1944.
495. Ibid. Ibid., ark. 92–95: report by the OUN(b) L'viv on the last events and the situation in L'viv and the surrounding areas, August 2, 1944.
496. Ibid., ark. 96–100: report by the OUN(b) L'viv on the period between July 10 and August 3, 1944.
497. Ibid., ark. 92–95: report by the OUN(b) L'viv on the final events and the situation in L'viv and the surrounding areas, August 2, 1944. Ibid., ark. 219–21: report by the OUN(b) on the situation in L'viv, end of August 1944.
498. Ibid., ark. 107–10: report by the OUN(b) (Dmytrenko) on August 1944 in L'viv, August 28, 1944.
499. Ibid., ark. 92–95: report by the OUN(b) L'viv on the final events and the situation in L'viv and the surrounding areas, August 2, 1944.
500. Ibid., ark. 107–10: report by the OUN(b) (Dmytrenko) on August 1944 in L'viv, August 28, 1944.
501. TsDAHOU, f. 1, op. 23, spr. 890, ark. 66–72 (printed in *Kul'turne zhyttja*, 203–11): report on the political mood of the Ukrainian intelligentsia in L'viv during the period of German occupation and the present, authored by the chairman of the party organization of the L'viv region Hrushets'kyj, September 8, 1944. TsDAHOU, f. 1, op. 23, spr. 890, ark. 66–72 (printed in *Kul'turne zhyttja*, vol. 1, 378–401): L. M. Kaganovich on the characteristics of the Ukrainian intelligentsia in L'viv, April 5, 1947.
502. TsDAHOU, f. 1, op. 23, spr. 1674, ark. 2–11 (printed in Serhijchuk, *Desjat' buremnych lit*, 195–201): decree by the Central Committee of the Communist Party (Bol'shevik) of Ukraine, CC KP(b)U, N. S. Khrushchev, January 10, 1945. TsDAHOU, f. 1, op. 16, spr. 32, ark. 24–27 (printed in Serhijchuk, *Desjat' buremnych lit*, 572–74): decree by the Politburo of the CC KP(b)U on strengthening the struggle against the Ukrainian-nationalist underground in the western regions of the Ukrainian Socialist Soviet Republic (UkrSSR), April 5, 1947.
503. TsDAHOU, f. 1, op. 23, spr. 1670, ark. 1–7 (printed in Serhijchuk, *Desjat' buremnych lit*, 295–98): transcript of a speech by N. S. Chrushchev at this meeting, May 15, 1945.
504. TsDAHOU, f. 1, op. 16, spr. 29, ark. 138–54 (printed in Serhijchuk, *Desjat' buremnych lit*, 238–47): decree by CC KP(b)U, February 26, 1945.
505. TsDAHOU, f. 1, op. 23, spr. 703, ark. 30–36 (printed in Serhijchuk, *Desjat' buremnych lit*, 91–94): for example, Khrushchev to Stalin, July 28, 1944. See also TsDAHOU, f. 1, op. 23, spr. 892, ark. 18–33 (printed in Serhijchuk, *Desjat' buremnych lit*, 65–74): report by the regional party secretary in Rivno for Khrushchev, May 31, 1944.
506. DALO, f. P-3, op. 1, spr. 63, ark. 14–16 (printed in *Kul'turne zhyttja*, 197–98): Litvin, Hrushets'kyj, and Bazhan to Khrushchev, August 1944. TsDAHOU, f. 1, op. 23, spr. 790, ark 137–39 (printed in Serhijchuk, *Desjat' buremnych lit*, 168–69): Khrushchev to Stalin, November 29, 1944.
507. On "ethnic cleansing" in the Soviet Union, see Peter Holquist, "'Conduct Merciless Mass Terror': Decossackization on the Don, 1919," *Cahiers du Monde Russe* 38 (January–June 1997): 127–62. Terry Martin, "The Origins of Soviet Ethnic Cleansing," *The Journal of Modern History* 70 (December 1998), 813–61. On Poland, see Timothy Snyder, "'To Resolve the Ukrainian Problem Once and for All': The Ethnic Cleansing of Ukrainians in Poland 1943–1947," *Journal of Cold War Studies* 1 (Spring 1999): 86–120. On "ethnic cleansing" in a European comparison, see Norman M. Naimark,

Fires of Hatred: Ethnic Cleansing in Twentieth-Century Europe (Cambridge, MA: Harvard University Press, 2001).
508. Edward Jaworski, *Lwów: Losy mieszkańców i żołnierzy Armii Krajowej w latach 1939–1956* (Pruszków: Ajaks, 1999), 140–51.
509. Grzegorz Hryciuk, "Nastroje i stosunek ludności polskiej tzw: Ukrainy zachodniej do przesiedleń w latach 1944–1945 w świetle sprawozdań radzieckich," in *Polska i Ukraina po II: wojnie światowej* (Rzeszów: Wydawnictwo Wyższej Szkoły Pedagogicznej, 1998), 209–22.
510. The proposal came from the secretary for propaganda of the regional party committee in L'viv, June 1947: DALO, f. P-3, op. 2, spr. 181, ark. 67 (excerpt printed in *Kul'turne zhyttja*, 412).
511. According to an internal report of the Soviet Ministry of the Interior (in March 1946 the People's Commissariats became Ministries) in May 1946, there were only 101 officers of the security services with only a few thousand troops in six of the seven western Ukrainian regions. About 5.3 million people lived in this territory. Gosudarstvennyj Arkhiv Rossijskoj Federatsii (GARF), f. 9478, op. 1s, d. 527, ll. 109–17 (cited after Jeffrey Burds, "AGENTURA: Soviet Informants' Network of the Ukrainian Underground in Galicia, 1944–1948," *East European Politics and Societies* 11, no. 1 [Winter 1997]: 89–130, here 113): V. S. Rjasnoj and Leont'ev to the Soviet minister of the interior, May 1946.
512. DALO, f. P-3, op. 1, spr. 62, ark. 1–13: Hrushets'kyj to Khrushchev, July 17, 1944.
513. TsDAHOU, f. 1, op. 23, spr. 362, ark. 16 (printed in Serhijchuk, *Desjat' buremnych lit*, 16–17): proclamation of the party leadership and the government of the UKrSSR to the population in the temporary occupied regions of Ukraine, January 12, 1944.
514. TsDAVOVU, f. 3967, op. 1, spr. 31, ark. 1 (printed in Serhijchuk, *Desjat' buremnych lit*, 40): proclamation of the OUN, March 30, 1944.
515. TsDAHOU, f. 1, op. 23, spr. 703, ark. 1–19 (printed in Serhijchuk, *Desjat' buremnych lit*, 42–52): Khrushchev to Stalin on the situation in the regions of Rovno and Volhynia, March 1944.
516. TsDAHOU, f. 1, op. 23, spr. 1716, ark. 7–17 (printed in Serhijchuk, *Desjat' buremnych lit*, 349–60): instruction of the leadership of the OUN to local leaders, November 27, 1945. TsDAHOU, f. 1, op. 23, spr. 1716, ark 4 (printed in Serhijchuk, *Desjat' buremnych lit*, 256–58): communiqé of the UPA for all directors, managers, and teachers, 1945.
517. Rubl'jov/Cherchenko, *Stalinshchyna j dolja zakhidnoukraïns'koï intelihenciï*, 211–12.
518. Burds, "AGENTURA," 107.
519. Ibid., 100.
520. Ibid., 109.
521. Koval', *Ukraïna w Druhij Svitovij i Velykij Vitchyznjanij Vijnach*, 46–47. Burds, "AGENTURA," 110.
522. L. P. Berija mentioned these numbers in a report for Stalin, November 22, 1945. GARF, f. R-9401, op. 2, d. 102, ll. 1–5 (cited after Burds, "AGENTURA," 97).
523. TsDAHOU, f. 1, op. 23, spr. 1700, ark. 69–78 (printed in Serhijchuk, *Desjat' buremnych lit*, 188–94): report by the secretary of the regional party committee in L'viv for Khrushchev, January 5, 1945.
524. Burds, "AGENTURA," 111.
525. TsDAHOU, f. 1, op. 23, spr. 703, ark. 1–19 (printed in Serhijchuk, *Desjat' buremnych lit*, 42–52): Khrushchev to Stalin on the situation in the regions of Rovno and Volhynia, March 1944.

526. TsDAHOU, f. 1, op. 23, spr. 2977, ark. 97–103 (printed in Serhijchuk, *Desjat' buremnych lit*, 518–523): report by the secretary of the regional party committee in Drohobych for Khrushchev, September 13, 1946.
527. TsDAHOU, f. 1, op. 75, spr. 75, ark. 147–68 (printed in Serhijchuk, *Desjat' buremnych lit*, 575–87): protocol of a meeting of the regional party secretaries and the heads of the regional administration of the Ministry of State Security (MGB) with Kaganovich and Khrushchev in L'viv, April 23, 1947.
528. TsDAHOU, f. 1, op. 23, spr. 1362, ark. 36–37 (printed in Serhijchuk, *Desjat' buremnych lit*, 164–66): decree of the regional party committee in Ternopil, November 23, 1944. More examples for "violations of Soviet legality" in TsDAHOU, f. 1, op. 16, spr. 29, ark. 192–96 (printed in Serhijchuk, *Desjat' buremnych lit*, 234–38: report by the state attorney of the UkrSSR for Khrushchev, February 24, 1945.
529. TsDAHOU, f. 1, op. 23, spr. 1713, ark. 3–12 (printed in Serhijchuk, *Desjat' buremnych lit*, 266–79): V. P. Kuz'min (Orlyk) to the secretary of the regional party committee in Stanyslaviv, M. Slon', April 14, 1945.
530. TsDAHOU, f. 1, op. 23, spr. 703, ark. 1–19 (printed in Serhijchuk, *Desjat' buremnych lit*, 42–52): Khrushchev to Stalin on the situation in the regions of Rovno and Volhynia, March 1944.
531. TsDAHOU, f. 1, op. 23, spr. 1695, ark. 2 (printed in Serhijchuk, *Desjat' buremnych lit*, 194–95): information of the head of the department for organization and instruction of the regional party committee in Drohobych for the CC CP(b)U, January 11, 1945.
532. Burds, "AGENTURA," 98.
533. TsDAHOU, f. 1, op. 23, spr. 919, ark. 96–106 (printed in Serhijchuk, *Desjat' buremnych lit*, 156–63): information of the head of the department for organization of the regional party committee in L'viv, I. Bogorodchenko, for Zlenko from CC CP(b)U, November 9, 1944.
534. TsDAHOU, f. 1, op. 23, spr. 2975, ark. 62–66 (printed in Serhijchuk, *Desjat' buremnych lit*, 416–19): information on an operation against the Ukrainian underground in the region of Drohobych, January 25, 1946.
535. TsDAHOU, f. 1, op. 23, spr. 2977, ark. 97–103 (printed in Serhijchuk, *Desjat' buremnych lit*, 518–23): report by the secretary of the regional party committee in Drohobych for Khrushchev, September 13, 1946.
536. Burds, "AGENTURA," 98.
537. TsDAHOU, f. 1, op. 23, spr. 1716, ark. 7–17 (printed in Serhijchuk, *Desjat' buremnych lit*, 349–60): instruction by the leadership of the OUN to local leaders, November 27, 1945. See also Burds, "AGENTURA," 101.
538. TsDAHOU, f. 1, op. 23, spr. 1716, ark. 7–17 (printed in Serhijchuk, *Desjat' buremnych lit*, 349–60): instruction by the leadership of the OUN to local leaders, November 27, 1945.
539. TsDAVOVU, f. 3967, op. 1, spr. 31, ark. 1 (printed in Serhijchuk, *Desjat' buremnych lit*, 40): proclamation of the OUN, March 30, 1944.
540. TsDAVOVU, f. 3833, op. 1, spr. 188, ark. 42 (printed in Serhijchuk, *Desjat' buremnych lit*, 99–100): report by the OUN on the activities of the NKVD in the Ternopil region, August 5, 1944.
541. TsDAHOU, f. 1, op. 23, spr. 1362, ark. 39–40 (printed in Serhijchuk, *Desjat' buremnych lit*, 170–71): report by the state attorney of the UkrSSR S. Shugurov to the secretary of the CC CP(b)U, D. Korotchenko, December 5, 1944.
542. TsDAVOU, f. 3833, op. 1, spr. 188, ark. 44: information by the OUN(b) from the Ternopol region, August 14, 1944.

543. Grzegorz Motyka and Rafał Wnuk, *Pany i rezuny: Współpraca AK-WiN i UPA* (Warsaw: Volumen, 1997). TsDAHOU, f. 1, op. 23, spr. 929, ark. 101–11: Hrushets'kyj to Khrushchev, December 14, 1944.
544. Burds, "AGENTURA," 102–27.
545. This is the opinion of Burds, "AGENTURA," 116.
546. Serhy Yekelchyk, "Stalinist Patriotism as Imperial Discourse: Reconciling the Ukrainian and Russian 'Heroic Pasts,' 1939–1945," *Kritika* 3 (Winter 2000): 51–80.
547. TsDAHOU, f. 1, op. 23, spr. 1691, ark. 197–203 (printed in Serhijchuk, *Desjat' buremnych lit*, 279–86): information on the head of the department for organization of the regional party committee in L'viv, J. Bohorodchenko, for Zlenko, CC CP(b)U, April 21, 1945.
548. GARF, f. R-6991, op. 1, d. 33, l. 13–19: the plenipotentiary of the Council for Affairs of the Orthodox Church at the Council of the People's Commissars of the UkrSSR P. Khodchenko to the chairman of the Council for the Affairs of the Russian Orthodox Church at the Council of the People's Commissars of the USSR, R. G. Karpov, June 11, 1945.
549. GARF, f. R-6991, op. 1, d. 33, l. 97–101: Serhij S. Khruts'kyj to Khodchenko, n.d. (probably September 1945).
550. GARF f. R-6991, op. 1, d. 32, l. 167: Reshenie Soboru Greko-Katolicheskoj Uniatskoj Tserkvi v L'vove, March 8–10, 1946 (translation from Ukrainian to Russian).
551. TsDAHOU, f. 1, op. 24, spr. 40–81, ark. 26–27 (printed in Serhijchuk, *Desjat' buremnych lit*, 528–29): report by the Ministry for State Security (MGB) from the L'viv region, September 26, 1946.
552. TsDAHOU, f. 1, op. 23, spr. 1605, ark. 73–80 (printed in *Kul'turne zhyttja*, 262–67): information on the People's Commissariat for State Security (NKGB) of the UkrSSR on the reaction of the population in West Ukraine to the article "With Cross or with Sword" and the arrest of Greek Catholic priests, April 26, 1945. TsDAHOU, f. 1, op. 23, spr. 1605, ark. 33–43 (printed in *Kul'turne zhyttja*, 267–276): report by the NKGB on the mood of the population, April 1945.
553. TsDAHOU, f. 1, op. 23, spr. 1641, ark. 9–14 (printed in *Kult'turne zhyttja*, 286–90): Hrushets'kyj to Khrushchev with a report on the mood in L'viv, June 7, 1945. TsDAHOU, f. 1, op. 23, spr. 1605, ark. 33–43 (printed in *Kul'turne zhyttja*, 267–76): report by the NKGB on the mood of the population, April 1945.
554. TsDAHOU, f. 1, op. 23, spr. 1639, ark. 103–13 (printed in *Kul'turne zhyttja*, 285–92): report by Hrushets'kyj for Khrushchev on the preparation for the unification of Uniate (Greek Catholic) and Orthodox Church, September 5, 1945.
555. GARF, f. R-6991, op. 1, d. 532, l. 3–14: report by the plenipotentiary for the Orthodox Church in the L'viv region, Vyshnevskij, for Karpov and Khodchenko, March 2, 1949.
556. TsDAHOU, f. 1, op. 23, spr. 1716, ark. 7–17 (printed in Serhijchuk, *Desjat' buremnych lit*, S. 349–60): instructions of the OUN leadership to local leaders, November 27, 1945.
557. TsDAHOU, f. 1, op. 23, spr. 1691, ark. 91–100: Hrushets'kyj and others to Khrushchev, March 5, 1945.
558. The figures were 15,120 to 1,832 (12.1 percent). *Istorija Ukraïny* (L'viv: Svit 1996), 330 (cited after Ivan Pater, "Povojennyj L'viv," in *L'viv: Istorychni Narysy*, 506–519, here 510).
559. Rubl'jov and Cherchenko, *Stalinshchyna j dolja zakhidnoukraïns'koï intelihenciï*, 213.
560. DALO, f. P-3, op. 2, spr. 181, ark. 33–35 (printed in *Kul'turne zhyttja*, 438–42): information on the regional party committee in L'viv for Kaganovich, August 18, 1947.

561. In April 1945, out of a total of 126 professors, 68 were Poles, 41 Ukrainians, and 17 Russians. Forty-three had arrived from the "old" Soviet Union, and only 15 came from western Ukraine. There were more western Ukrainians below the level of professor. There were even fewer Ukrainian professors at the Technical University (14 of 78). DALO, f. P-3, op. 1, spr. 311, ark. 104–105 (printed in *Kul'turne zhyttja*, 257–58): report by the cultural sector of the regional party committee in L'viv, n.d. (after April 1, 1945).
562. Yekelchyk, "Stalinist Patriotism as Imperial Discourse," 79–80.
563. TsDAHOU, f. 1, op. 23, spr. 4558, ark. 1–34 (printed in *Kul'turne zhyttja*, 378–401): report by the regional party committee in L'viv on the characteristics of the Ukrainian intelligentsia in L'viv for Kaganovich, March 1947.
564. Rubl'jov and Cherchenko, *Stalinshchyna j dolja zakhidnoukraïns'koï inteligentsiï*, 215–22.
565. RGASPI, f. 17, op. 125, spr. 405, ark. 38–39 (printed in *Kul'turne zhyttja*, 340–41): report by the commission of the department for Agitprop CC VKP(b) on the state of ideological work in Ukraine for the head of the Agitprop department CC VKP(b), G. F. Aleksandrov, July 1, 1946.
566. Rubl'jov and Cherchenko, *Stalinshchyna j dolja zakhidnoukraïns'koï inteligentsiï*, 218–19.
567. TsDAHOU, f. 1, op. 23, spr. 2843, ark. 17–22 (printed in *Kul'turne zhyttja*, 348–52): information of the regional party committee in L'viv on the transfer of the humanities' institutes of the Academy of Science to Kiev and Hrushevs'kyj's criticism, prepared for Khrushchev, September 27, 1946. TsDAVOU, f. 2, op. 7, spr. 3934, ark. 143 (printed in *Kul'turne zhyttja*, 357): decree of the Council of Ministers of the UkrSSR, October 28, 1946.
568. Rubl'jov and Cherchenko, *Stalinshchyna j dolja zakhidnoukraïns'koï inteligentsiï*, 220–21.
569. Ibid., 223–34. DALO, f. P-3, op. 2, spr. 262, ark. 26, 33–34 (printed in *Kul'turne zhyttja*, 408–10): report by the regional party committee L'viv on the work of the State Conservatory in the 1946/47 season (excerpt), n.d. (after June 20, 1947).
570. DALO, f. P-4, op. 1, spr. 155, ark. 34, 81–82: from the stenogram of a meeting of the intelligentsia of L'viv, July 24, 1947.
571. TsDAHOU, f. 1, op. 23, spr. 4559, ark. 1–4 (printed in *Kul'turne zhyttja*, 423–26): information of the regional party committee for the CC CP(b)U on the reaction of the intelligentsia in L'viv to the presentation of Manuil'skij on "Against the Ukrainian Bourgeois Nationalism," July 30, 1947.
572. See the documents in *Kul'turne zhyttja*, 427–47.
573. TsDAHOU, f. 1, op. 23, spr.1 4558, ark. 44–48, 52 (printed in *Kul'turne zhyttja*, 468–72): Hrushets'kyj to Kaganovich: "Information on the Political Mood of the Working Population in L'viv Region," October 17, 1947.
574. Ibid.
575. TsDAHOU, f. 1, op. 70, spr. 1096, ark. 34–35 (printed in *Kul'turne zhyttja*, 404–405): report by the regional party committee in L'viv for the department for schools of the CC CP(b)U, May 30, 1947. Rubl'jov and Cherchenko, *Stalinshczyna*, 218–35.
576. TsDAHOU, f. 1, op. 23, spr. 5686, ark. 125–29: Iryna Vil'de to Stalin, April 10, 1949.
577. On the view of Khmel'nyts'kyj in today's Ukraine, see Frank E. Sysyn, "Bohdan Chmel'nyc'kyjs Image in Ukrainian Historiography since Independence," Österreichische Osthefte 42, no 3/4 (2000): 179–88.
578. TsDAHOU, f. 1, op. 23, spr. 5686, ark. 125–29: Iryna Vil'de to Stalin, April, 10, 1949.

579. Grzegorz Hryciuk, "Działalność OUN i UPA w latach czterdziestych i pięćdziesiątych w najnowszych publikacjach na Ukrainie," *Studia z dziejów Europy Wschodniej* 1 (2002), 181–99. *Ukraïns'ka Povstans'ka Armija i natsionalno-vyzvolna borot'ba v Ukraïni u 1940-1950 r.: Materialy Vseukraïns'koï naukovoï konferentsiï 25-26 serpnia 1992 r.* (Kiev: Instytut Istoriï Ukraïny Akademiï Nauk Ukraïny, 1992).

CHAPTER 6

Conclusion

When I traveled to L'viv for the first time in November 1998, I met two historians from Israel who were also working in the archives. They told me they had been appalled by a banner mounted on the town hall bearing the words "350 Years' Liberation of L'viv by Bohdan Khmel'nyts'kyj."[1] In Jewish history, Khmel'nyts'kyj is the greatest persecutor of Jews in the early modern era. In the Polish view of history, he stands for the "bloodthirsty ferocity and savagery" of the Cossacks, whose rebellion brought the aristocratic republic to the brink of destruction. In Ukrainian tradition, however, the hetman is a war hero, a statesman, and a fighter for Ukrainian independence. This is only one of many incompatible views of history for the period in which Poles, Ukrainians, and Jews lived together in East Galicia.

But in November 1998, the Khmel'nyts'kyj anniversary was of only secondary importance. A quite different event was being celebrated: the anniversary of the proclamation of the West Ukrainian People's Republic and the Ukrainian seizure of power in L'viv on November 1, 1918. The eightieth anniversary of the "November deed" (*Lystopadovyj chyn*) was extravagantly commemorated. Even the president of Ukraine, Leonid Kuchma, traveled to L'viv to participate in the celebrations. In the Ukrainian view of history, both events serve as proof that the Ukrainians have been fighting for their independence since hundreds of years and that they never renounced their claim to L'viv. The Orthodox Cossacks under Hetman Khmel'nyts'kyj, the Ukrainophile activists around 1900, the soldiers of the Ukrainian Galician Army, and the fighters of the Ukrainian Insurgent Army (UPA) and SS-Division Galicia are all part of this line of tradition. There is now a huge memorial to Stepan Bandera, completed in 2007 and sporting a more than life-sized statue. In the Ukrainian memorial complex in Lychakivs'kyj Cemetery "graves of honor" have been prepared for former soldiers of the Ukrainian SS-Division.[2]

In the middle of the nineteenth century, it was not yet clear whether Ukrainian nation building would be successful. Who would win the battle for the hearts of the peasantry? Should the Greek Catholic Ukrainian-speaking peasants be absorbed by the Russian nation or by the Polish nation? Should they form their own Ruthenian nation, or did they form a Ukrainian nation together with the Orthodox Ukrainian-speaking population in the Russian Empire? Only after the turn of the century did it become apparent that the Ukrainian option would prevail. The success of Ukrainian "organic work" was evidenced by the close network of national education societies and cooperatives. Ukrainian nation building accelerated in competition with the Polish national movement and had caught up with it by the start of World War I. In 1914 national mobilization among West Ukrainian peasants was stronger than among the Polish peasants living in West Galicia. In contrast, the centuries-old suppression of the "Ukrainian idea" in Russian East Ukraine and the lack of a Ukrainian-language education system and Ukrainian-language publishing stood in the way of a "nationalization of the masses."

Among the Jewish population, the perception of Jews as a separate nation in their own right also became more widespread. The Zionist movement grew, but it did not take hold among the majority of Orthodox Jews who preferred to remain in their religious environment. Assimilation to the Polish nation had many supporters among the Jewish elites but enjoyed no general support among the Galician Jewry.

World War I boosted nationalization. The tensions between the three groups increased, but conflicts were not (yet) settled by violence. The collapse of the Russian Empire in 1917 opened up the prospect of achieving a state of their own to both the Poles and the Ukrainians. Four years later, after the experiences of a world war and countless instances of violence, the two groups were prepared, despite their multifold familial ties and despite the centuries of coexistence, to take up arms and fight for the incorporation of the region into a Polish or Ukrainian state. Previously blurred boundaries were now sharply delineated. The Polish–Ukrainian war forced people to opt for one side and choose their nation. The Jewish population was caught between the two camps. Anti-Semitism had increased in Christian society during the war. Jews were held collectively liable for the high prices, the prevailing want and misery. Jewish neutrality in the Polish–Ukrainian conflict was interpreted by Polish society as a betrayal of Poland.

November 1918 is the key to understanding the conflicts in L'viv and East Galicia in the interwar period. The Polish–Ukrainian war brought matters to a temporary halt and created new conditions that strongly influenced the way conflicts would be settled in future. Certain historical options—for example, those committed to some form of accommodation and reconciliation—became unlikely; others—for example, the forcible resolution of conflicts—became probable. For the Jewish population, November 1918 was indissolubly linked to the memory of a pogrom that was not amenable to any form of positive interpretation. The Zionist movement enjoyed a strong rise in popularity; at the same time, anti-Semitism in the Polish population increased. It was difficult for Jewish citizens of L'viv to participate in the November celebrations. In a key area—the Obrona Lwowa—they were excluded from the Polish community of memory. The Ukrainians created their own opposing community of memory. The memorial practices of Polish and Ukrainian society passed on the experiences of November 1918 to the following generations. The young generation of Ukrainian nationalists rejected the democratic ideas of the older generation of Ukrainian politicians and drew its own conclusions from the defeat. Integral nationalism became the driving force behind the ideology of the Organization of Ukrainian Nationalists (OUN).

The Russian occupation in World War I hit the Ukrainian national movement hard. Ukrainian nationalism was suppressed, and Ukrainians were claimed for the Russian people as "Little Russians." In contrast, the Soviet Union initially followed a more flexible and, ultimately, more successful nationalities policy. During the 1920s, the Soviet Union supported the titular nation in the Ukrainian Socialist Soviet Republic and allowed Ukrainian Bolsheviks considerable leeway during the period of "nativization" (*korenizatsija*) of Ukrainian culture. But the appeal of the Soviet Ukrainian state for western Ukrainians disappeared with the famine of 1932–1934 in which up to five million Ukrainian peasants perished. Following these experiences, western Ukrainian elites fiercely opposed Soviet rule. This did not change even after the invasion of the Soviet Army in September 1939.

Neither Poles nor Ukrainians could be initially sure which occupation would offer them the greater advantages. They faced a choice between two evils. Their behavior was determined by the expected prospects for their own nation, their own group, or themselves. The alternatives open to the Jews, however, were hugely unequal. Although the Nazis' intention to completely annihilate all Jews was not generally known, Nazi anti-Semitism had already shown its murderous face. Fear of the Germans meant that the majority of Jews tended to favor the Soviet Union. The Soviet Union granted the Jewish population equal rights and open anti-Semitism was not tolerated. Jews were not treated differently from their Polish and Ukrainian neighbors. The new rulers opposed all religions equally, arrested and deported members of all prewar elites and nationalized all businesses. After these initial experiences, tens of thousands of Jews wanted to flee the Soviet occupied territories and return to German-occupied Poland. But the Soviet Union was still the only power that could prevent Galician Jews from falling into German hands. A paradoxical situation was created in which deportation offered persons an incomparably greater chance of survival than coming under German rule.

But although western Ukrainians were members of the titular nation of the Ukrainian Socialist Soviet Republic and were granted privileges in terms of schools, culture, and administration, Ukrainization was not the same thing as national self-determination. Leading Ukrainian politicians were persecuted, national organizations were smashed, and the forcible collectivization of agriculture continued. Ukrainian nationalists did not give up their goal of an independent nation-state and were not prepared to accept Soviet tutelage. As it was not possible to achieve the goal of an independent state in 1941 by their own efforts, Ukrainians pinned their hopes on Nazi Germany.

With the exception of a few scattered communists, the Polish population did not have positive expectations of either occupying power. Poles were hit hardest by Sovietization and lost their dominant position. The Soviets did not shrink from committing mass murder. Twenty-two thousand Polish officers, politicians and intellectuals were shot; more than one hundred thousand Poles were arrested or deported to the east. Even the change in Soviet policy in the spring of 1941 could not alter the antipathy of the Polish population toward the Soviet Union. The closures of numerous Polish schools, the expropriations, and the many waves of arrests and deportations ensured that the Soviet charm offensive largely fell flat, even though some leftist Polish intellectuals allied themselves with the Soviet Union.

Laying the crimes committed by the Soviet regime at the door of the Jews was one way of justifying anti-Semitism. In the absence of the perpetrators, the NKVD units, or other Soviet cadres, the local populations followed an age-old tradition. Long-established prejudices against Jews, the stereotype of "Jewish bolshevism," German anti-Semitic propaganda, current frustrations, rapacity, and terrible hatred all merged together.[3] The pogroms carried out in the first days of July 1941 followed historic patterns but the attitude of the German occupiers meant that these took on a new quality. The new—German—authorities wanted pogroms and incited the population to carry them out. Prevailing on local populations to become complicit in the mass murder of Jews was part of the Nazi policy of extermination.

The Sovietization of Western Ukraine after 1944 was a fast-play repeat of the building of socialism previously carried out in the Soviet Union. The resettlement of the Polish population followed the tradition of "ethnic cleansing" in the 1930s. The Soviet Union did not even attempt to incorporate the Polish minority into the new society. Nevertheless, Soviet actions toward the Polish population were motivated by tactical and pragmatic considerations rather than ideology. The resettlement was part of the measures taken to pacify the newly acquired western territories. It destroyed the basis for the Polish–Ukrainian conflict. The Soviet leadership nursed a deep distrust of the Polish population. This distrust had its roots in the Polish–Soviet war of 1920 when the overwhelming majority of Polish workers supported the bourgeois Polish state and not proletarian Russia. In 1944/1945 Soviet agents reported that the Polish population was uniformly nationalist.

It is difficult to link the conflicts of memory in the interwar period to the memory of the terror, genocide, flight, and forced migration. As a starting point let me briefly mention another personal experience. At the end of June 2001, there was much excitement in L'viv. A large crowd had gathered in front of the new Shevchenko monument on Freedom Prospect (its name in Polish times was Wały Hetmańskie; under German occupation, it was called Adolf-Hitler-Ring; under Soviet rule, it was known as Lenin Prospect) to commemorate June 30, 1941. The first thought of someone who knows something of L'viv's history in World War II is of the German invasion, which occurred on the same day, or the start of the pogrom, which cost the lives of between four and seven thousand Jews over a period of three days. But the Ukrainians who had gathered in the city center were in a festive mood. They were celebrating the sixtieth anniversary of the formation of the Ukrainian government that had been set up in L'viv on that day.

When the interethnic relations in the World War II are discussed today, current interpretations diverge as widely from one another as the interpretations of November 1918 did in the interwar period. This applies equally to contemporary eyewitnesses and survivors of the war and to historians. Ukrainian authors prefer to evade questions about the participation of Ukrainians in pogroms and the role of the Ukrainian auxiliary police or point to the alleged collaboration of the Jewish population with the Soviet authorities. Jewish authors of memoirs strongly condemn Poles and Ukrainians and accuse them of not having offered any assistance or even of having participated in the genocide. Holocaust survivor and historian Philip Friedman wrote in 1959 of the "wide gulf separating the Jewish and Ukrainian interpretations."[4] The same applies to Jewish–Polish and Polish–Ukrainian relations during the war.[5]

Ukrainians and Poles suffered much. Millions were murdered, tortured, or deported; nevertheless, they did not face the threat of total annihilation. Almost the entire Jewish population was murdered; for every one of them, it was an issue of sheer survival. Ukrainians and Poles were also fighting for their lives, but they also fought for territories, political programs, and self-determination. These differing experiences had an effect on the respective memories. This is what makes it so difficult for Poles, Ukrainians, and Jews to understand how the "others" experienced the war and remembered it.

This is where *Erfahrungsgeschichte*—experiential history—offers a solution. The experiences of Poles, Jews, and Ukrainians under different rulers, with occupation regimes, and with one another contradict each other. It is therefore important to take these experiences seriously and to avoid creating a hierarchy of experiences based on the degree to which they conform to a reconstructed reality. As communicated experiences, they have gone through a complex process of interpretation. *Erfahrungsgeschichte* does not censure experiences as expressions of false consciousness; instead, it assumes that they corresponded to the interpretations of reality of the respective authors and were therefore relevant for their behavior and actions. An experiential historical approach could potentially have the ability to break the deadlock of petrified historiography.

The Polish experience was shaped by the devastating attacks of Ukrainian partisans on Polish villages and finally by the loss of their homeland. The West Ukrainian experience was closely linked to the fight against the Poles for East Galicia, the ethnic cleansing of Ukrainians in Poland, the failure to build a nation in the postwar period, the terrible Soviet repression after 1944, and the bloody and exhausting guerrilla war against Sovietization. In Ukrainian–Polish relations, crimes stand against crimes. The task here for each side is to accept the suffering of the "other" side and condemn the crimes committed by the "own" side.

This is difficult enough in itself, but with regard to Jews, there is an asymmetric relationship. First, there are virtually no Galician Jews left in western Ukraine or Poland. Second, it is difficult to accept that the dimension of victimhood is extremely unequal. This was already a problem during the war and has remained a problem to the present day.

Notes

1. The text on the banner was not quite correct. Khmel'nyts'kyj never conquered L'viv.
2. Christoph Mick, "Kriegserfahrungen und die Konstruktion von Kontinuität: Schlachten und Kriege im ukrainischen und polnischen kollektiven Gedächtnis 1900–1930," in *Gründungsmythen—Genealogien—Memorialzeichen: Beiträge zur institutionellen Konstruktion von Kontinuität*, ed. Gert Melville and Karl-Siegbert Rehberg (Cologne: Böhlau, 2004), 109–32.
3. See also Aharon Weiss, "Jewish-Ukrainian Relations during the Holocaust," 409–20, here 413.
4. Friedman, "Ukrainian-Jewish Relations," 295–96.
5. Piotr Wróbel, "Double Memory: Poles and Jews after the Holocaust," *East European Politics and Societies* 11, no. 3 (Fall 1997): 560–74.

Appendix

Maps

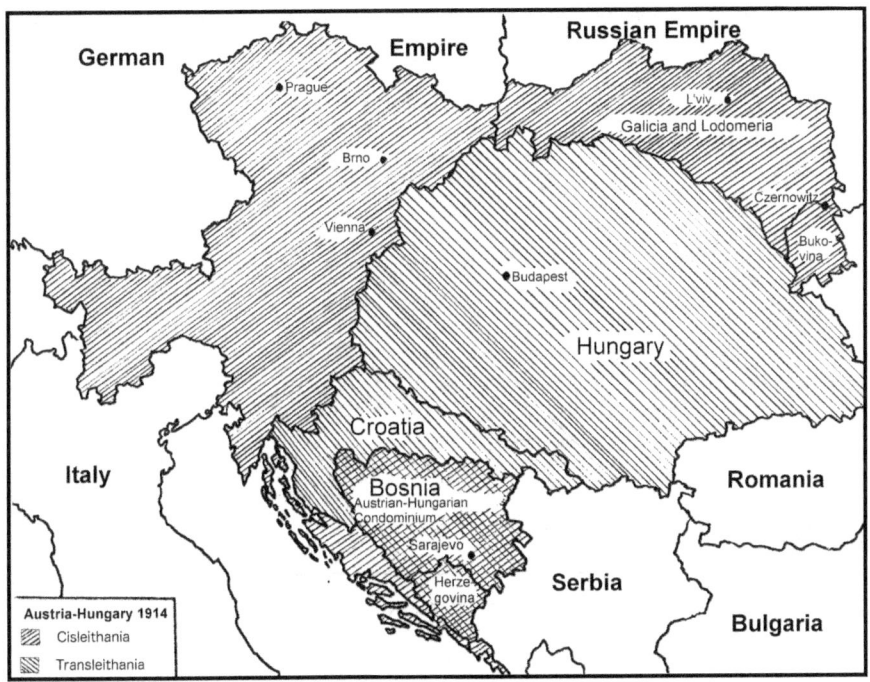

Map 1. Austria-Hungary, 1914.

Map 2. Interwar Poland, 1919-1939.

Appendix ♦ 381

- - - - German-Soviet demarcation line after the Molotov-Ribbentrop Pact, 23 August 1939.

Map 3. Poland after the Molotov-Ribbentrop Pact.

Map 4. German occupation.

Acronyms

AAN	Archiwum Akt Nowych [Archive of New Documents]
AK	Armia Krajowa [Home Army]
AOK	Armeeoberkommando [Army High Command]
ark.	Arkush [page]
AVA	Allgemeines Verwaltungsarchiv [General Archive of the Administration], Vienna
AVPRI	Arkhiv Vneshnej Politiki Rossijskoj Imperii [Archive of Foreign Policy of the Russian Empire]
AW	Archiwum Wschodni Ośrodku Karta [East Archive of the Centre "Karta"]
BArch	Bundesarchiv [Federal Archive], Berlin
BArch-MA	Bundesarchiv-Militärarchiv [Federal Archive/Military Archive], Freiburg
BBWR	Bezpartyjny Block Współpracy z Rządem [Nonparty Block for Cooperation with the Government]
Bund	Allgemeiner Jüdischer Arbeiterbund [General Jewish Labor Bund of Lithuania, Poland, and Russia]
COL	Cmentarz Obrońców Lwowa [Cemetery of the Defenders of Lwów]
d.	Delo [file]
DALO	Derzhavnyj Arkhiv L'vivs'koï Oblasti [State Archive of the L'viv region]
Endecja	Polish National Democratic Party
GARF	Gosudarstvennyj Arkhiv Rossijskoj Federatsii [State Archive of the Russian Federation]
Gestapo	Geheime Staatspolizei [Secret State Police]
GC	Greek Catholic

HHStA	Haus-, Hof- und Staatsarchiv Wien [Austrian Imperial Archive]
k. u. k.	Kaiserlich und königlich [imperial and royal]
KOL	Komenda Obszara Lwowa [Regional command of the Polish Home Army of L'viv]
KP(b)U	Kommunisticheskaja Partija [bol'sheviki] Ukraïny [Communist Party (Bolsheviks) of Ukraine]
l.	List [page]
MdI	Ministerium des Innern [Ministry of the Interior]
MGB	Ministerstvo Gosudarstvennoj Bezopasnosti [Ministry of State Security]
MVD	Ministerstvo Vnutrennykh Del' [Ministry of Internal Affairs]
NKGB	Narodnyj Komissariat Gosudarstvennoj Bezopasnosti [People's Commissariate for State Security]
NKVD	Narodnyj Komissariat Vnutrennykh Del' [People's Commissariate for Domestic Affairs]
NS	Nationalsozialismus [National Socialism]
OUN	Orhanizatsija Ukraïns'kykh Natsionalistiv [Organization of Ukrainian Nationalists]
OUN-B	OUN-Bandera
OUN-M	OUN-Mel'nyk
OZN	Obóz Zjednoczenia Narodowego [Camp of National Unification]
PA	Politisches Archiv des Auswärtigen Amtes in Berlin [Political Archive of the Foreign Office in Berlin]
PKN	Polskie Kadry Wojskowe [Polish Military Cadres]
POW	Polska Organizacja Wojskowa [Polish Military Organization]
PPS	Polska Partia Socjalistyczna [Polish Socialist Party]
PPSD	Polska Partia Socjalno-Demokratyczna Galicji i Śląska [Polish Social Democratic Party of Galicia and Silesia]
PSL	Polskie Stronnictwo Ludowe [Polish People's Party]
RC	Roman Catholic
Rel.	Relacja [Record]
RGIA	Rossijskij Gosudarstvennyj Istoricheskij Arkhiv [Russian Historical State Archive]

RGVA	Rossijskij Gosudarstvennyj Voennyj Arkhiv [Russian Military State Archive]
RGVIA	Rossijskij Gosudarstvennyj Voenno-Istoricheskij Arkhiv [Russian Military Historical State Archive]
Ring	Archiwum Ringelbluma [Ringelblum Archive]
ROC	Russian Orthodox Church
S.	Storinka [page]
SD	Sicherheits-Dienst [Security Service]
SDKPiL	Socjaldemokracja Królestwa Polskiego i Litwy [Social Democracy of the Kingdom of Poland and Lithuania]
spr.	Sprawa [file]
SS	Schutzstaffel [Protection squadron]
TBHOL	Towarzystwo Badania Historii Obrony Lwowa i województw południowo-wschodnich [Society for the Study of the History of the Defense of Lwów and the Southeastern Voivodeships]
TsDAHOU	Tsentral'nyj Derzhavnyj Arkhiv Hromads'kykh Orhaniv Vladi i Upravlenn'ja Ukraïny [Central State Archive for Public Organisations of Ukraine]
TsDAVOVU	Tsentral'nyj Derzhavnyj Arkhiv Vyshchych Orhaniv Vlady ta Upravlinnja Ukraïny [Central State Archive of the Highest Organs of Power and Administration of Ukraine]
TsDIAK	Tsentral'nyj Derzhavnyj Istorychnyj Arkhiv Ukraïny, m. Kyïv [Central Historical State Archiv of Ukraine, Kiev]
TsDIAL	Tsentral'nyj Derzhavnyj Istorychnyj Arkhiv Ukraïny, m. L'viv [Central Historical State Archive of Ukraine, L'viv]
TsK KP(b)U	Tsentral'nyj Komitet Kommunisticheskoj Partii (bol'sheviki) Ukrainy [Central Committee of the Communist Party (bol'sheviki) of Ukraine]
UHA	Ukraïns'ka Halyts'ka Armija [Ukrainian Galician Army]
UkrSSR	Ukrains'kaja Sovetskaja Sotsialisticheskaja Respublika [Ukrainian Soviet Socialist Republic]
UNDO	Ukraïns'ke Natsional'no-Demokratychna Ob"ednannja [Ukrainian National Democratic Union]
UNR	Ukraïns'ka Narodna Respublika [Ukrainian People's Republic]

UPA	Ukraïns'ka Povstans'ka Armija [Ukrainian Insurgent Army]
USSR	Union of Socialist Soviet Republics
UTsK	Ukraïns'kyj Tsentral'nyj Komitet, in German: Ukrainischer Hauptausschuss [Ukrainian Central Committee]
ŻIH	Żydowski Instytut Historyczny [Jewish Historical Institute]
ZOUNR	Zakhidniï Oblast' Ukraïns'ka Narodna Respublika [Western Region of the Ukrainian People's Republic]
ZUNR	Zakhidno-Ukraïns'ka Narodna Respublika [West Ukrainian People's Republic]
ZZZ	Związek Związków Zawodowych [Union of Trade Unions]

Bibliography

Archives

Ukraine

Tsentral'nyj Derzhavnyj Istorychnyj Arkhiv Ukraïny, m. L'viv (TsDIAL)
Central Historical State Archive of Ukraine in L'viv

f. 79	Rutovs'kyj Tadej (Rutowski, Tadeusz)
f. 146	Halyts'ke namisnytstvo (K.u.k Statthalterei in Galizien)
f. 178	Krajova shkil'na rada, m. L'viv
	(C. K. Rada szkolna krajowa we Lwowie)
f. 201	Greko-Katolyts'ka mytropolycha konystorija, m. L'viv
f. 205	Prokuratura apeljacijnoho sudu, m. L'viv
	(Prokuratura sądu apelacyjnego we Lwowie)
f. 309	Naukove tovarystvo im. Shevchenka, m. L'viv
f. 355	Zakhidno-ukraïns'ke tovarystvo Ligy Natsij, m. Viden'
f. 359	Nazaruk, Osyp
f. 368	Tomashivs'kyj Stepan
f. 391	Zahal'noukraïns'ka kul'turna rada, m. Viden'
f. 408	Greko-katolyts'kyj mytropolychyj ordinariat, m. L'viv
f. 462	Ukraïns'kyj horozhans'kyj komitet, m. L'viv
f. 485	Tovarystvo vchyteliv vyshchych ta serednich shkil L'vivs'koho shkil'noho okruhu (Zarząd okręgu Lwowskiego Towarzystwa Nauczycieli Szkół Średnich i Wyższych)
f. 493	Ministerstvo vnutrishnikh sprav, m. Varshava (Ministerstwo spraw wewnętrznych w Warszawie)

f. 505 Komitet dopomohy jevrejs'komu naselennju, m. L'viv
(Żydowski komitet ratunkowy we Lwowie)
f. 581 Kolektsija dokumentiv pro dijal'nist' urjadiv ta armij Ukraïns'koï Narodnoï Respubliky ta Zakhidno-Ukraïns'koï Narodnoï Respubliky
f. 694 Kolektsija dokumentiv do istoriï perebuvannja rosijs'kych vijs'k na terytoriï Halychyny v period Peršhoï svitovoï vijny
f. 701 Jevrejs'ka relihijna hromada, m. L'viv (Israelitische Cultus-Gemeinde in Lemberg)
f. 717 Koło Polskie, m. Wiedeń
f. 837 Svezhavs'kyj Adam-Julian (Swieżawski, Adam-Juliusz)
f. 841 Ob"jednannja pol's'kykh zhinochykh khrystyjans'kykh tovarystv, m. L'viv (Zjednoczenie polskich czreścijańskich towarzystw kobiecych we Lwowie)
f. 859 Narodni Zbory Zakhidnoï Ukraïny, m. L'viv

Derzhavnyj Arkhiv L'vivs'koï Oblasti (DALO)

State Archive of L'viv region

f. 1 Administration of the voivodeship, L'viv
f. 2 City administration, L'viv
f. 3 City administration, L'viv
f. 27 Polytechnical University
f. 110 Police Directorate L'viv, 1928–1939
f. 257 Towarzystwo Badania Historii Obrony Lwowa i województw południowo-wschodnich (Society for the Study of the History of the Defense of Lwów and the Southeastern Voivodeships)
f. 269 Stadthauptmann Lemberg (City captain, L'viv)
f. 271 Police directorate, L'viv, 1918–1928
f. 350 Police directorate, L'viv, until 1918
f. P-3 Committee of L'viv Region of the Communist Party (bolsheviki) of Ukraine
f. P-221 Regional Soviet (council), L'viv
f. R-6 City Soviet (council), L'viv
f. R-16 Commissariates (commissioner's offices) of the Ukrainian police, L'viv
f. R-24 Kreishauptmann Lemberg-Land (District captain, L'viv region)
f. R-30 Stadtkommandantur Lemberg (Office of the town major, L'viv)
f. R-35 Amt des Distrikts Galizien (Office of the District of Galicia)
f. R-37 Stadthaupmann Lemberg (City captain, L'viv)

Also used: f. 30, f. 121, f. 126sc, f. R-121

Biblioteka Stefanyka

Stefanyk Library (previously: Ossolineum)

f. 102   Savchenko

Tsentral'nyj Derzhavnyj Istorychnyj Arkhiv Ukraïny, m. Kyïv (CDIAK)

Central Historical State Archive of Ukraine in Kiev

f. 361   Kantseljarija Voennogo General-Gubernatora Galicii

Tsentral'nyj Derzhavnyj Arkhiv Vyshchykh Orhaniv Vlady ta Upravlinnja Ukraïny (TsDAVOVU)

Central State Archive of the Highest Organs of Power and Administration of Ukraine in Kiev

f. 3833   Regional leader of the OUN in Western Ukrainian territories
f. 3967   Office of Reichsleiter Rosenberg
f. 4620   Collection Great Patriotic War

Tsentral'nyj Derzhavnyj Arkhiv Hromads'kykh Ob"jednan' Ukraïny (TsDAHOU)

Central State Archive for Public Organizations of Ukraine

f. 1   Tsentral'nyj Komitet KP Ukrainy: Osobyj sektor i organizatsionno-instruktorskij otdel

Poland

Archiwum Akt Nowych (AAN)

Archive of New Documents in Warsaw

Ambasada Rzeczypospolitej Polski w Londynie

111   Government of the Generalgouvernement
203   Armia Krajowa: Komenda Obszara Lwowa
540/1   Stadthauptmann (city captain), Lemberg
689   Amt des Distrikts Galizien (Office of the District of Galicia)

Archiwum Wschodni Ośrodku Karta (AW)

Eastern Archive of the centre Karta in Warsaw

sygn. MINF 135 Lwów Relacje
sygn. II Pamiętniki

Żydowski Instytut Historyczny (ŻIH)

Jewish Historical Institute in Warsaw

Archiwum Ringelbluma (Ring)

229 Teka Lwowska
301 Relacje woj. Lwowskie
302 Pamiętniki

Russia

Gosudarstvennyj Arkhiv Rossijskoj Federatsii (GARF)

State Archive of the Russian Federation in Moscow

f. R-6991   Sovet po delam religii pri Sovet Ministrov SSSR

Rossijskij Gosudarstvennyj Voenno-Istoricheskij Archiv (RGVIA)

Russian Military Historical State Archive in Moscow

f. 2005 Voenno-politicheskoe i grazhdanskoe upravlenie pri Verkhovnoj glavnokomandujushchem 1914–1918
f. 2067 Shtab glavnokomandujushchego armijami jugozapadnogo fronta

Rossijskij Gosudarstvennyj Voennyj Arkhiv/Osobyj Archiv (RGVA)

Russian Military State Archive/Special Archive in Moscow

f. 462   Ekspozitura Nr. 5, II. Otdel General'nogo shtaba g. L'vov (Ekspozytura N 5 Oddziały II. Sztabu Generalnego Lwów)
f. 483   Politicheskie organizatsii Pol'shi perioda I mirovoj vojny (1914–1918)
f. 1447 Nemetsko-fashistskie administrativnye i sudebnye organy na vremenno okkupirovannykh territorijakh

Austria

Haus-, Hof- und Staatsarchiv Wien (HHStA)

P.A.I., 931   K. u. k. Ministerium des Äußeren

Allgemeines Verwaltungsarchiv Wien (AVA)

MdI, Präsidiale Allgemeine Abteilung

Germany

Bundesarchiv Berlin (BArch)

Federal Archive in Berlin

NS-43	Außenpolitisches Amt der NSDAP
R-6	Reichsministerium für die besetzten Ostgebiete
R-43 II	Reichskanzlei
R-49	Reichskommissar für die Festigung des deutschen Volkstums
R-52	Regierung des Generalgouvernements
R-58	Reichssicherheitshauptamt
R-59	Volksdeutsche Mittelstelle
R-70 PL	Polizeidienststellen in Polen

Politisches Archiv des Auswärtigen Amtes in Berlin (PA)

Political Archive of the Foreign Office in Berlin

Konsulat Lemberg

Briefwechsel Konsulat Auswärtiges Amt

Bundesarchiv-Militärarchiv Freiburg (BArch-MA)

Federal Archive/Military Archive in Freiburg

RH 24	Generalkommandos der Armeekorps
WF-03	
RH 22	Befehlshaber des rückwärtigen Heeresgebietes Süd
RH 28	Gebirgsdivisionen
RH 53-23	Wehrkreis Generalgouvernement

Newspapers and Journals

Chwila
Czerwony Sztandar
Dilo
Dziennik Ludowy
Dziennik Lwowski
Gazeta Lwowska
Gazeta Poranna
Gazeta Wieczorna
Gazetka Żółnierska
Głos Narodu
Jüdische Volksstimme
Jüdisches Kriegsarchiv
Kurier Lwowski
Kurier Warszawski
Lemberger Zeitung
Litopys Chervonoï Kalyny
Neue Lemberger Zeitung
Novoe Vremja
Novyj Chas
Nowy Dziennik
Pobudka
Prikarpatskaja Rus'
Ruthenische Revue
Słowo Narodowe
Słowo Polskie
Ukrainische Korrespondenz
Ukrainische Rundschau
Ukraïns'ke Slovo
Vil'na Ukraïna
Vpered
Wiek Nowy

Printed Sources

Czarnocka, Halina, Józef Garliński, and Józef Żmigrodzki eds. *Armia Krajowa w dokumentach: 1939–1945*. Vol. 1: *September 1939–April 1941*. London: Księgarnia SPK, 1970.

Deportatsiï: Zakhidni zemli Ukraïny kintsja 30-kh: pochatku 50-kh rokiv. Dokumenty, spohady. Vol. 1: *1939–1945*, vol 2: *1946–1947*. L'viv: Natsional'na

Akademia Nauk Ukraïny, Instytut Ukraïnoznavstva im. I. Kryp'jakevycha, 1996, 1998.
Grynberg, Michał, and Maria Kotowska, eds. *Życie i zagłada Żydów polskich 1939–1945: Relacje świadków*. Warsaw: Oficyna Naukowa, 2003.
Hornykiewicz, Theophil, ed. *Ereignisse in der Ukraine 1914–1922, deren Bedeutung und historische Hintergründe*. Philadelphia: W. K. Lypynsky East European Research Institute, 1966.
Hunczak, Taras, and Roman Sol'chanyk, eds. *Ukraïns'ka suspil'no-politychna dumka v 20 stolitti: dokumenty i materialy*. New York: Suchasnist', 1983.
Jedlins'ka, Uljana Ja, ed. *Istorija L'vova v dokumentakh i materialakh*. Kiev: Naukova Dumka, 1986.
Kravchuk, Andrij, ed. *Mytropolyt Andrij Sheptyts'kyj: Zhyttja i Dijal'nist': Dokumenty i Materialy 1899–1944*. Vol. 2: *Tserkva i suspil'ne pytannja*. Knyha 2: *Lystuvannja*. L'viv: Misioner, 1999.
Kul'turne zhyttja v Ukraïni: Zakhidni Zemli. Vol. 1: *1939–1953*. Kiev: Naukova Dumka, 1995.
Leinwand, Artur, ed. *Dokumenty Obrony Lwowa 1939*. Warsaw: Instytut Lwowski, 1997.
Lindheim, Ralph, and George S. N. Luckyj, eds. *Towards an Intellectual History of Ukraine: An Anthology of Ukrainian Thought from 1710 to 1995*. Toronto: University of Toronto Press, 1995.
Litopys' Ukraïns'koï povstans'koï armiï. Toronto: Vydavnytstvo Litopys UPA, 1977–2008.
Obrona Lwowa: Źródła do dziejów walk o Lwów i województwa południowo-wschodnie 1918–1920. Vols 1–2: *Relacje Uczestników*. L'viv: Publisher unknown, 1933, 1936 (reprint: Warsaw: Volumen, 1991, 1993); Vol. 3: *Organizacja listopadowej obrony Lwowa, ewidencja uczestników walk, lista strat*. L'viv: Publisher unknown, 1938 (reprint: Warsaw, Volumen, 1994).
Postanovy II. Velikoho zboru Orhanizatsii Ukrains'kykh Natsionalistiv, shcho vidbuvsja v kvitni 1941 r; OUN v svitli postanov Velykykh Zboriv, Konferentsij ta inshych dokumentiv z borot'by 1929–1955. Publisher unknown, 1955.
Potichnyj, Peter J., and Yevhen Shtendera, eds. *Political Thought of the Ukrainian Underground*. Edmonton: Canadian Institute of Ukrainian Studies Press, 1986.
Rudnyts'ka, Milena. *Statti, lysty, dokumenty*. L'viv: Misioner, 1999.
Sabelanka, Ewa, and K. Kozniewski, eds. *7599 dni Drugiej Rzeczpospolitej: Antologia reportażu 1919–1939*. Warsaw: Iskry, 1983.
Siwicki, Mikołaj. *Dzieje konfliktów polsko-ukraińskich*. 3 vols. Warsaw: Tyrsa, 1992.
Stenograficzne sprawozdania Sejmu Krajowego. L'viv: Sejm Krajowy Królestwa Galicyi i Lodomeryi wraz z Wielkiem Księstwem Krakowskiem, 1890.

The Correspondence of the Ukrainian Central Committee in Cracow and Lviv with the German Authorities. Edmonton: Canadian Institute of Ukrainian Studies Press, 2000.

Wiadomości statystyczne o mieście Lwowie. Vol. 15: *1912–1922*. L'viv: Gmina Królewskiego Stołecznego miasta Lwowa, 1926.

Wółczański, Józef, ed. *Nieznana korespondencja arcybiskupów metropolitów lwowskich Józefa Bilczewskiego z Andrzejem Szeptyckim w czasie wojny polsko-ukraińskiej 1918–1919.* L'viv: Wydawnictwo Bł. Jakuba Strzemię Archidiecezji Lwowskiej Ob. Łac, 1997.

Żbikowski, Andrzej, ed. *Archiwum Ringelbluma: Konspiracyjne Archiwum Getta Warszawy.* Vol. 3: *Relacje z Kresów.* Warsaw: ANTA, 2000.

Printed Memoirs and Diaries (Published after 1945)

Ansky, Salomon. *The Enemy at his Pleasure: A Journey through the Jewish Pale of Settlement during World War I.* New York: Metropolitan Books, 2002.

Berezowski, Jerzy. *Ten stary Lwów.* Warsaw: Publisher unknown, 1995.

Bilostots'kyj, Tymish. *Spohady.* Nakladom Bratstva kol: Vojakiv 1-oï UD UNA, 2000.

Chajes, Viktor. *Semper Fidelis: Pamiętnik Polaka wyznania mojżeszowego z lat 1926–1939.* Cracow: Księgarnia Akademicka, 1997.

Dabulewicz-Rutkowska, Jadwiga. *Miejsce na Ziemi: Lwów 1941–1942.* Second edition. Wrocław: Atla 2, 2000.

———. *Poezja, proza i dramat: Pamiętnik nastolatki, Lwów 1939–1941.* Wrocław: W Kolorach Tęczy, 1998.

Dotzauer, Adam. *Lwowskie wczesne dojrzewanie.* Wrocław: Sudety, 2000.

Drix, Samuel. *Witness to Annihilation: Surving the Holocaust: A Memoir.* Washington: Brassey's, 1994.

Evlogij (Georgievskij) Mitropolit. *Put' mojej zhizni: Vospominanija Mitropolita Evlogija (Georgievskogo), islozhennye po ego rasskazam T. Manukhinoj.* Moscow: Moskovskij Rabochij, 1994, first published in Paris: 1947.

Fishman, Lala, and Steven Weingartner. *Lala's Story: A Memoir of the Holocaust.* Evanston, IL: Northwestern University Press, 1997.

Grząska, Oktawia. *Byłam więźniarką.* Warsaw: Muzeum Niepodległości, 1999.

Janicki, Jerzy. *A do Lwowa daleko aż starch.* Warsaw: BGW, 1996.

Kahane, David. *Lvov Ghetto Diary.* Amherst: University of Massachusetts Press, 1990.

Komar, Ljuba. *Proces 59-ty.* L'viv: Naukove Tovarysto im. Shevchenka, 1997.

Krysiak, Franciszek Salezy. *Z dni grozy we Lwowie (1–22 listopada 1918).* Cracow: G. Gebethner, 1919 (reprinted: Rzeszów: Rybnik, 2003).

Lanckorońska, Karolina. *Those Who Trespass against Us: One Woman's War against the Nazis.* Translated by Noel Clark. London: Pimlico, 2005.

Levyts'kyj, Kost'. *Istorija politichnoï dumky halyts'kykh ukraïntsiv, 1848–1914.* 2 vols. L'viv: Author, 1926.

Ljubchenko, Arkadij. *Shchodennyk Arkadija Ljubchenka.* L'viv: P. M. Kots', 1999.

Maschler, Ilana. *Moskauer Zeit.* Göttingen: Steidl, 1995.

Mękarska-Kozłowska, Barbara. *Burza nad Lwowem.* London: Polska Fundacja Kulturalna, 1996.

Michotek, Jerzy. *Tylko we Lwowie.* Warsaw: Omnipress, 1990.

Morgenbesser, Aleksander. *Wspomnienia z lwowskiego więzienia.* Warsaw: Semper, 1993.

Nazaruk, Osyp. *Zi L'vova do Varshavy, 2-13 zhovtnja 1939 roku.* L'viv: Naukove Tovarystvo imeni Shevchenka, 1995.

Nieznana korespondencja arcybiskupów metropolitów Lwowskich Józefa Bilczewskiego z Andrzejem Szeptyckim w czasie wojny Polsko-Ukraińskiej 1918–1919. L'viv: Wydawn. B·l. Jakuba Strzemię Archidiecezji Lwowskiej Ob. ·Łac, 1997.

Obercowa, Maria, *Z wycieczką do Lwowa? Z wycieczką do mego domu?* Cracow: Herbert Oleschko, 1996.

Olijnyk, Pavlo. *Zoshyty.* Kiev: Instytut Ukraïns'koï arkheografiï na dzhereloznavstva im. M.S. Hrushevs'koho NAN Ukraïny, 1995.

Opałek, Mieczysław. *O Lwowie i mojej młodości: Kartki z pamiętnika 1881–1901.* Wrocław: Zakład Narodowy im. Ossolińskich, 1987.

Riedl, Tadeusz. *We Lwowie: Relacje.* Wrocław: Sudety, 1996.

Semchyshyn, Myroslav. *Z knyhy Leva: Ukraïns'kyj L'viv dvadtsjatykh-sorokovykh rokiv.* L'viv: Naukove Tovarystvo im. Shevchenka, 1998.

Sonevyts'kyj, Mykhajlo. *Spohady staroho pedahoha.* L'viv: Ridna Shkola, 2001.

Stets'ko, Jaroslav. *30 chervnja 1941.* Toronto: Liha vyzvolennija Ukraïny, 1967.

Tarnavs'kyj, Ostap. *Literaturnyj L'viv 1939–1944: Spomyny.* L'viv: Prosvita, 1995.

Tyrowicz, Marian. *Wspomnienia o życiu kulturalnym i obyczajowym Lwowa 1918–1939.* Wrocław: Zakład Narodowy im. Ossolińskich, 1991.

Wasylewski, Stanisław. *Bardzo przyjemne miasto.* Katowice: Śląsk, 1990.

Weliczker Wells, Leon. *The Janowska Road.* London: Jonathan Cape, 1966. Also published as *The Death Brigade.* New York: The United States Holocaust Memorial Museum, 1978.

Wigierski, Mirosław. *Ze Lwowa na Kołymę.* Wrocław: Nortom, 1998.

Wittlin, Józef. *Mein Lemberg.* Frankfurt/Main: Suhrkamp, 1994.

Żygulski, Kazimierz. *Jestem z lwowskiego etapu.* Warsaw: PAX, 1994.

Contemporary Literature

Al'manakh Chervona Kalyna. L'viv: Chervona Kalyna, 1934.

Bachyns'kyj, Julijan. *Ukraïna Irredenta*. L'viv: Universal'naja Biblioteka, 1895.

Bałaban, Majer. *Dzieje żydów w Galicyi i w Rzeczypospolitej Krakowskiej 1772–1968*. L'viv: Księgarnia Polska B. Połonieckiego, 1916.

———. *Historia i literatura żydowska ze szczególnem uwzględnieniem historii żydów w Polsce*. 3 vols. L'viv: Wydawnictwo Zakładu Narodowego im. Ossolińskich, 1925.

Bartoszewicz, Kazimierz. *Dzieje Galicyi: Jej stan przed wojną i "wyodrębnienie."* Warsaw: Gebethner i Wolff, 1917.

Beck, Adolf. *Uniwersytet Jana Kazimierza we Lwowie podczas inwazji rosyjskiej w roku 1914–15*. L'viv: Uniwersytet Jana Kazimierza we Lwowie, 1935.

Bendow, Josef. *Der Lemberger Judenpogrom*. Vienna: Hickl, 1919.

Białynia-Chołodecki, Józef. "Boje o Lwów," in *W obronie Lwowa i kresów wschodnich*, 27-48. L'viv: Nakładem Straży Mogił Polskich Bohaterów, 1926.

———. *Lwów w czasie okupacji rosyjskiej*. L'viv: Wschód, 1930.

———. "Obrona Lwowa przeciw najazdowi bolszewików w r. 1920." In *W dziesiątą rocznicę bitwy pod Zadwórzem*. L'viv: We Lwowie, 1920.

———. *Wojenny posiew Anioła śmierci i kult pamięci poległych*. L'viv: Nakł. Polskiego Towarzystwa Opieki nad Grobami Bohaterów, 1926.

———. *Wspomnienia z lat niedoli i niewoli 1914–1918*. L'viv: Author, 1919.

Bohdan, Janusz. *293 dni rządów rosyjskich we Lwowie (3.IX.1914–22.VI.1915)*. L'viv: Księgarnia Polska, 1915.

Chlamtacz, Marceli. *Lembergs politische Physiognomie während der russischen Invasion, 3.9.1914–22.6.1915: Erinnerungen und Betrachtungen*. Vienna: R. Lechner und Sohn, 1916.

———. "Relacja o obronie Lwowa w listopadzie 1918 r.," in *Obrona Lwowa*, vol. 2, 113-120.

———. "Wyjaśnienie i sprostowanie w związku na marginesie relacji Prof. Dr. Antoniego Jakubskiego pt. 'Walki listopadowe we Lwowie w świetle krytyki,'" in *Obrona Lwowa*, vol. 2, 763–79.

Czołowski, Aleksander. *Pogląd na organizację i działalność dawnych władz miasta Lwowa do 1848 r.* L'viv: Gmina Królestwa Stołecznego Miasta Lwowa, 1896.

Dontsov, Dmytro. *Natsionalizm*. (London: Ukraïns'ka vydavnycha spilka, 1966 [first published in Zhovkva in 1926].

"Drugi powszechny spis ludności z dnia 9 XII 1931 r.: Mieszkania i gospodarstwa domowe, ludność, stosunki zawodowe." In *Statystyka Polski*, seria C, zeszyt 62. Warsaw: Główny Urząd Statystyczny, 1937.

Evlogij, arkhiepiskop Volynskij. *Obrashchenie k galitsko-russkomu narodu i dukhovenstvu.* Publisher unknown, 1914.

Feldman, Wilhelm. *Stronnictwa i programy polityczne w Galicyi 1846–1906.* 2 vols. Cracow: Książka, 1907.

Gember, Maria von. "Die Russen in Lemberg." In *An den Grenzen Rußlands: Elf Abhandlungen aus der Sammlung "Der Weltkrieg,"* edited by the Sekretariat sozialer Studentenarbeit, 153-68. Mönchengladbach: Volksvereinsverlag, 1916,

Hoszowski, Stanislaw. *Ekonomiczny rozwój Lwowa 1772–1914.* L'viv: Izba Przemysłowo-Handlowa, 1935.

Insler, Abram. *Dokumenty fałszu.* L'viv: I. Jaeger, 1933.

Jakubski, Antoni. "Walki listopadowe we Lwowie w świetle krytyk," in *Obrona Lwowa,* vol. 1, 99-240.

Klink, Józef. "W przededniu listopadowej obrony Lwowy," in *Obrona Lwowa,* vol. 2, 636-652.

Kuz'ma, Oleksa. *Lystopadovi dni 1918 r.* L'viv: Chervona Kalyna, 1931.

Levyts'kyj, Kost'. *Istorija politichnoï dumky halyts'kykh ukraïntsiv 1848–1914.* 2 vols. L'viv: 1926.

———. *Velykyj zryv.* L'viv: Samoosvita, 1931.

Lozhyns'ky, Mychajlo. *Halychyna w rokach 1918–1920.* Vienna: Institut Sociologique Ukrainien, 1922.

Lewartowska, Zofja. *Lwów chlubą narodu: Dramat w 4 aktach na tle obrony Lwowa w roku 1918.* L'viv: Małopolska Straż Obywatelska, 1928.

Lewicki, Witold. *Zagadnienie gospodarcze Galicyi.* L'viv: Księgarnia Polska Bernarda Połonieckiego, 1914.

Mączyński, Czesław. *Boje lwowskie.* 2 vols. Warsaw: Spółka wyd. Rzeczpospolita, 1921.

Materiały do bibliografii Historii Obrony Lwowa i województw południowowschodnich. L'viv: Towarzystwo Badań Historji Obrony Lwowa i Województw Południowo-Wschodnich, 1935.

Na vichny pamjat' herojam. L'viv: 1921.

Paliïv, Dmytro. *Lystopadova revoljutsija: Z moïch spomyniv.* L'viv: Novyj Chas, 1929.

Papée, Fryderyk. *Historia Miasta Lwowa w zarysie.* Second edition. L'viv: Ksiąznica Polska, 1924.

Rocznik statystyki RP. Warsaw: Nakładem Głównego Urzędu Statystycznego, 1926.

Rocznik Towarzystwa Badania Historii Obrony Lwowa. L'viv: Towarzystwo Badania Historii Obrony Lwowa i Województw Południowo-Wschodnich, 1936, 1937.

Roth, Joseph. "Lemberg: Die Stadt," *Frankfurter Zeitung*, November 1911, 1924 (printed in Joseph Roth, *Werke*, vol. 2 [Cologne: Kiepenheuer & Witsch, 1990], 285-289.

Roja, Bolesław. *Legendy i fakty*. Warsaw: Nakł. Księg. F. Hoesicka, 1931.

Rossowski, Stanisław. *Lwów podczas inwazyi*. L'viv: H. Altenberg et al., 1916.

Sahajdachnyj, Petro. "Jednist' dumky i chynu," in *Istorychnyj kalendar-al'manach 'Chervonoï Kalyna 1938 rik*, 3-9. L'viv: Chervona Kalyna, 1937.

Schnür-Pepłowski, Stanisław. *Obrazy z przeszłości Galicji i Krakowa*. Vol. 1: *Lwów i lowowianie*. L'viv: Księgarnia Gubrynowicza i Schmidta, 1896.

Shchurat, Vasyl'. "Dlja tykh, shcho vstanut. . . ,'" in *Na vichny pamjat' herojam*. L'viv: unknown publisher, 1921.

Skoczek, J. *Dotychczasowy stan badań nad historią Lwowa*. L'viv: Nakładem Księgarni Gubrynowicza i Syna, 1925.

Służba ojczyźnie: Wspomnienia uczestniczek walk o niepodległość 1915–1918. Edited by Maria Rychterówna. Warsaw: Główna księgarnia wojskowa, 1929.

Swistun, Filipp. *Prikarpatskaja Rus' pod władeniem Austrii*, 2 vols. L'viv: unknown publisher, 1896–1897 (reprint: Trumbull, Hardy, 1970).

Vityk, Semen. *Precz z Rusinami! Za San z Polakami!* L'viv: Author, 1903.

W obronie Lwowa i kresów wschodnich. L'viv: Straż Mogił Polskich Bohaterów, 1926.

Wąsowicz, Jerzy. *Listopad 1.–21.XI.1918 we Lwowie*. L'viv: Zakład narod. im. Ossolińskich. 1919.

Wawrzkowicz, Eugeniusz, and Józef Klink. *Walczący Lwów w listopadzie 1918*. L'viv: Książnica-Atlas, 1939.

Wiadomości statystyczne o mieście Lwowie. Vol. 14: *1910–1911*. Opracowane przez Miejskie Biuro Statystyczne. L'viv: Nakladem gminy krol. stol. M. Lwowa, 1914.

Wiadomości statystyczne o mieście Lwowie. Vol. 15: *1912–1922*. Opracowane przez Miejskie Biuro Statystyczne. L'viv: Gmina Lwowa, 1926.

Wiadomości statystyczne o mieście Lwowie. Vol. 16: *1923–1925*. Opracowane przez Miejskie Biuro Statystyczne. L'viv: Gmina Lwowa, 1928.

Wierna służba: Wspomnienia uczestniczek walk o niepodległość. Edited by Aleksandra Piłsudska et al. Warsaw: Główna Księgarnia Wojskowa, 1927.

Zieliński, Zygmunt. *Lwów po inwazyi rosyjskiej, Wrzesień-Grudzień 1914*. Vienna, Z. Machnowski, 1914.

Secondary Literature

Ackermann, Volker. "'Ceux qui sont pieusement morts pour la France . . .' Die Identität des Unbekannten Soldaten." In *Der politische Totenkult: Kriegerden-*

kmäler in der Moderne, edited by Reinhart Koselleck und Michael Jeismann, 281–314. Munich: Fink, 1993.

Albert, Zygmunt. *Kaźń profesorów lwowskich, lipiec 1941*. Wrocław: Wydawnictwo Uniwersytetu Wrocławskiego, 1989.

Amar, Tarik. "The Making of Soviet Lviv, 1939–1963." Dissertation, Princeton University, 2006.

Anderson, Benedict. *Imagined Communities: Reflections on the Origin and Spread of Nationalism*. London: Verso, revised edition, 1991.

Arkusha, Olena. *Halits'kyj Sejm. Vyborchi kampaniï 1889 i 1895 rr*. L'viv: Natsional'na Akademija Nauk Ukraïny, Instytut Ukraïnoznavstva im. I. Kryp"jakevycha, 1996.

———. "Pol's'ki politychni seredobyshcha L'vova ta Krakova na zlami XIX–XX stolit': sproba poruvnjannja." In *L'viv: Misto—suspil'stvo—kul'tura*, vol. 3, edited by Mar'jan Mudryj, 362–77. L'viv: L'vivs'kyj Derzhavnyj Universytet imeni Ivana Franka, 1999.

Armstrong, John A. *Ukrainian Nationalism*. Second edition. Littleton, CO: Ukrainian Academic Press, 1980.

Asche, Matthias, and Anton Schindling, eds. *Das Strafgericht Gottes: Kriegserfahrungen und Religion im Heiligen Römischen Reich Deutscher Nation im Zeitalter des Dreißigjährigen Krieges*. Münster: Aschendorffsche Verlagsbuchhandlung, 2001.

Bachmann, Klaus. *Ein Herd der Feindschaft gegen Russland: Galizien als Krisenherd in den Beziehungen der Donaumonarchie mit Russland (1907–1914)*. Vienna: Oldenbourg, 2001.

Bailly, Rosa. *A City Fights for Freedom: The Rising of Lwów in 1918–1919*. London: Publishing Committee Leopolis, 1956.

Bakhturina, Aleksandra Ju. *Politika Rossijskoj Imperii v Vostochnoj Galitsii v gody Pervoj Mirovoj Vojny*. Moscow: Assotsiatsija Issledovatelej Rossijskogo Obshchestva 20 veka, 2000.

Bartal, Israel, and Antoni Polonsky, eds. *Focusing on Galicia: Jews, Poles, and Ukrainians, 1772–1918*. London: Littman Library of Jewish Civilization, 1999.

Barth, Fredric. Introduction to *Ethnic Groups and Boundaries: The Social Organization of Culture Difference*. Edited by Fredric Barth. London: Little Brown, 1969.

Baumgart, Werner. *Deutsche Ostpolitik 1918: Von Brest-Litowsk bis zum Ende des Ersten Weltkrieges*. Vienna, Munich: Oldenbourg, 1966.

Becker, Annette. "From Death to Memory: The National Ossuaries in France after the Great War." *History and Memory* 5 (1993): 32–49.

———. *La guerre et la foi: De la mort à la mémoire, 1914–1930*. Paris: A. Folin, 1994.

Becoming National: A Reader. Edited by Geoff Eley and Ronald G. Suny. New York: Oxford University Press, 1996.

Behrenbeck, Sabine. *Der Kult um die toten Helden: Nationalsozialistische Mythen, Riten und Symbole*. Vierow: SH Verlag, 1996.

Benecke, Werner. *Die Ostgebiete der Zweiten Polnischen Republik: Staatsmacht und öffentliche Ordnung in einer Minderheitenregion 1918–1939*. Cologne: Böhlau, 1999.

Berenstein, Tatiana. "Eksterminacja ludności żydowskiej w Dystrykcie Galicja (1941–1943)." *Byuletyn Żydowskiego Instytutu Historycznego* 61 (1967): 3–33.

———. "Praca Przymusowa ludności żydowskiej w tzw: Dystrykcie Galicja (1941–1944)." *Biuletyn Żydowskiego Instytutu Historycznego* 69 (1969): 3–45.

Berger, Peter, and Thomas Luckmann. *Die gesellschaftliche Konstruktion der Wirklichkeit: Eine Theorie der Wissenssoziologie*. Frankfurt/Main: Fischer, 1980.

———. *The Social Construction of Reality: A Treatise in the Sociology of Knowledge*. Garden City, NY: Anchor Books, 1966.

Bergmann, Olaf. *Narodowa Demokracja wobec problematyki żydowskiej w latach 1918–1929*. Poznań: Wydawnictwo Poznańskie, 1998.

Berkhoff, Karel C. "Ukraine under Nazi Rule (1941–1944): Sources and Finding Aids." *Jahrbücher für Geschichte Osteuropas* 45 (1997): part 1: 85–103; part 2: 273–309.

Berkhoff, Karel, and Marco Carynnyk. "The Organization of Ukrainian Nationalists and Its Attitude toward Germans and Jews: Iaroslav Stets'ko's 1941 Zhyttiepys." *Harvard Ukrainian Studies* 23, no. 3/4 (1999): 149–84.

Beyrau, Dietrich. "Antisemitismus und Judentum in Polen, 1918–1939." *Geschichte und Gesellschaft* 8 (1982): 205–32.

Bieberstein, Christoph Freiherr Marschall von. *Freiheit in der Unfreiheit: Die nationale Autonomie der Polen in Galizien nach dem österreichisch-ungarischen Ausgleich von 1867: Ein konservativer Aufbruch im mitteleuropäischen Vergleich*. Wiesbaden: Harrassowitz, 1993.

Bihl, Wolfdieter. "Aufgegangen in Großreichen: Die Ukraine als österreichische und russische Provinz." In *Geschichte der Ukraine*, edited by Frank Golczewski, 127–57. Göttingen: Vandenhoeck and Ruprecht, 1993.

———. "Die Ruthenen." In *Die Habsburger Monarchie*, vol. 3: *Die Völker des Reiches*, edited by Adam Wandruszka and Peter Urbanitsch, 555–84. Vienna: Verlag der Österreichischen Akademie der Wissenschaften, 1980.

———. *Österreich-Ungarn und die Friedensschlüsse von Brest-Litovsk*. Vienna: Böhlau, 1970.

Bilas, Ivan. *Represyvno-karal'na systema v Ukraïni 1917–1953: Suspil'no politychnyj ta istoriko-pravovyj analiz.* Vol. 2. Kiev: Lybid, 1994.

Bilinsky, Yaroslav. "The Incorporation of Western Ukraine and Its Impact on Politics and Society in Soviet Ukraine." In *The Influence of East Europe and the Soviet West on the USSR*, edited by Roman Szporluk, 180–228. New York: Praeger, 1975.

Binder, Harald. "Die Wahlreform von 1907 und der polnisch-ruthenische Konflikt in Ostgalizien." Österreichische Osthefte 38 (1996): 293–320.

———. *Galizien in Wien: Parteien, Fraktionen und Abgeordnete im Übergang zur Massenpolitik.* Vienna: Verlag der Österreichischen Akademie der Wissenschaften, 2005.

Bizeul, Yves. "Theorien der politischen Mythen und Rituale." In *Politische Mythen und Rituale in Deutschland, Frankreich und Polen*, edited by Yves Bizeul, 15–39. Berlin: Duncker & Humblot, 2000.

Blöchl, Andrea. "Die Kaisergedenktage." In *Der Kampf um das Gedächtnis. Öffentliche Gedenktage in Mitteleuropa*, edited by Emil Brix and Hannes Stekl, 117–44. Vienna: Böhlau, 1997.

Bobrzyński, Michał. *Z moich pamiętników.* Wrocław: Wydawnictwo Zakładu Narodowego im. Osslińskich, 1957.

Bociurkiw, Bohdan R. *The Ukrainian Greek Catholic Church and the Soviet State (1939–1950).* Edmonton: Canadian Institute of Ukrainian Studies Press, 1996.

Bodnar, John. *Remaking America: Public Memory, Commemoration, and Patriotism in the Twentieth Century.* Princeton, NJ: Princeton University Press, 1992.

Boeckh, Katrin. "Kontinuität und Ende der sowjetischen Herrschaft—die Ukrainische Sozialistische Sowjetrepublik 1945–1991." In *Ukraine: Geographie—Ethnische Struktur—Geschichte—Sprache und Literatur—Kultur—Politik—Bildung—Wirtschaft—Recht*, edited by Peter Jordan et al., 363-88. Vienna: Österreichisches Ost- und Südosteuropa-Institut, 2000.

Boljanovs'kyj, Andrij. *Dyvizija 'Halychyna:' Istorija.* L'viv: Instytut Ukraaïnoznavstva im. I. Kryp"jakevycha NANU, 2000.

Bonusiak, Andrzej. *Lwów w latach 1918–1939.* Rzeszów: Wydawnictwo Naukowe Wyższej Szkoły Pedagogicznej w Rzeszowie, 2000.

———. "'Niedemokratyczna demokracja': Rzecz o Lwowie w latach 1918–1934." In *Lwów: Miasto—społeczeństwo—kultura*, vol. 2, 215–34.

Bonusiak, Włodzimierz. "Powstanie i działalność władz okupacyjnych we Lwowie w okresie IX 1939–VI 1941." In *Lwów: Miasto—społeczeństwo—kultura*, vol. 2, 307–18.

———. "Sowietyzacja gospodarki Lwowa (IX 1939–VI 1941)." In *L'viv: Misto—suspil'stvo—kul'tura*, 462–68.

Borodziej, Włodzimierz. *Terror i polityka: Policja niemiecka a polski ruch oporu w Generalgouvernement 1939–1944*. Warsaw: Instytut Wydawniczy Pax, 1985.

Brix, Emil, and Hannes Stekl, eds. *Der Kampf um das Gedächtnis: Öffentliche Gedenktage in Mitteleuropa*. Vienna: Böhlau, 1997.

Bronsztejn, Szyja. "Polish-Jewish Relations as Reflected in Memoirs of the Interwar Period." *Polin* 8 (1994): 66–88.

Broszat, Martin. *Nationalsozialistische Polenpolitik*. Second edition. Frankfurt: Deutsche Verlags-Anstalt, 1965.

Bruder, Franziska. *"Den ukrainischen Staat erkämpfen oder sterben!" Die Organisation Ukrainischer Nationalisten (OUN) 1928–1948*. Berlin: Metropol, 2007.

Burds, Jeffrey. "AGENTURA: Soviet Informants' Network and the Ukrainian Underground in Galicia, 1944–1948." *East European Politics and Societies* 11, no. 1 (Winter 1997): 89–130.

Buschmann, Nikolaus, and Aribert Reimann. "Die Konstruktion historischer Erfahrung: Neue Wege zu einer Erfahrungsgeschichte des Krieges." In *Die Erfahrung des Krieges*, 261–71.

Buschmann, Nikolaus, and Horst Carl. *Die Erfahrung des Krieges: Erfahrungsgeschichtliche Perspektiven von der französischen Revolution bis zum Zweiten Weltkrieg*. Paderborn: Ferdinand Schöningh, 2001.

———. "Zugänge zur Erfahrungsgeschichte des Krieges: Forschung, Theorie, Fragestellung." In *Die Erfahrung des Krieges*, 11–26.

Buszko, Józef. "Die Stellung der Polen und Ukrainer zur jüdischen Frage im autonomen Galizien." *Österreichische Osthefte* 38, no. 3 (1996): 275–91.

———. *Dzieje ruchu robotniczego v Galicji Zachodniej, 1848–1918*. Cracow: Wydawnictwo Literackie, 1978.

———. *Polacy w Parlamencie Wiedeńskim 1848–1918*. Warsaw: Wydawnictwo Sejmowe, 1996.

———. *Sejmowa reforma wyborcze w Galicji 1905–1914*. Warsaw: Państwowe Wydawnictwo Naukowe, 1957.

———. "Zur politischen Krise von 1908: Slawen der Donaumonarchie. Das tragische Ende des Grafen Andrzej Potocki als Statthalter von Galizien." *Österreichische Osthefte* 11 (1968): 321–28.

Chonigsman, Jakov S. *Juden in der Westukraine: Jüdisches Leben und Leiden in Ostgalizien, Wolhynien, der Bukowina und Transkarpatien 1933–1945*. Translated by Juri Schatton. Konstanz: Hartung-Gorre, 2001.

———. *Katastrofa evrejstva Zapadnoj Ukrainy*. L'viv: Publisher unknown, 1998.

Chrobaczyński, Jacek. *Pracy oświatowa w Krakowie 1939–1945*. Cracow: Wyższa Szkoła Pedagogiczna w Krakowie, 1986.

Cieślikowa, Agnieszka. *Prasa okupanowego Lwowa*. Warsaw: Neriton, 1997.

Czubiński, Antoni. "Problem obszaru i granic odrodzonego państwa polskiego." In *Polska i kraje Europy Środkowo-Wschodniej XIX-XX w*. Warsaw: Instytut Historii PAN, 1995.

Dąbkowski, Tadeusz. *Ukraiński ruch narodowy w Galicji Wschodniej: 1912–1923*. Warsaw: Instytut Krajów Socjalistychnych PAN, 1985.

Dashkevych, Jaroslav R. "Vzajemovidnosyny mizh ukraïns'kym ta jevrejs'kym naselennjam u Skhidnyj Halychyni (kinets XIX–pochatok XX st.)." *Ukraïns'kyj Istorychnyj Zhurnal* 10 (1990): 70–86.

Davies, Norman. *God's Playground: A History of Poland*. Vol. 2. Rev. second ed. (New York: Columbia University Press, 2005).

———. *Heart of Europe: A Short History of Poland*. Oxford: Clarendon Press, 1984.

Dean, Martin. *Collaboration in the Holocaust: Crimes of the Local Police in Belorussia and Ukraine, 1941–44*. Basingstoke: Macmillan, 2000.

Djadjuk, Myroslava. *Polityzatsija Ukraïns'koho zhinochoho rukhu w Halychyni: 1921–1939 rr. Avtoreferat dysertatsiï na zdobuttja naukovoho stupenja kandydata istorychnykh nauk*. L'viv, unpublished manuscript, 2002.

———. *Ukraïns'kyj zhinochyj rukh u mizhvojennij Halychyni: mizh hendernoju identychnistju ta natsional'noju zaanhazhovanistju*. L'viv: Astroljabija, 2011.

Djukov, A. *Vtorosteppenyj vrag: OUN, UPA i reshenie "jevreskogo voprosa."* Moscow: Regnum, 2008.

Döblin, Alfred. *Reise in Polen 1924*. Second edition. Munich: dtv, 1993.

Dörner, Andreas. *Politischer Mythos und symbolische Politik. Der Hermannsmythos: Zur Entstehung des Nationalbewusstseins der Deutschen*. Reinbek: Rowohlt, 1996.

Encyklopedia Historii Drugiej Rzeczypospolitej. Warsaw: Bellona, 1999.

Encyklopedija Ukraïnoznavstva. 8 vols. L'viv: Vydawnictwo Molode Zhyttja, 1993 (first edition: Paris: Shevchenko Scientific Society, 1962).

Everett, Leila P. "The Rise of Jewish National Politics in Galicia, 1905–1907." In *Nationbuilding and the Politics of Nationalism: Essays on Austrian Galicia*, edited by Andrei S. Markovits and Frank E. Sysyn, 149–77. Cambridge, MA: Harvard University Press, 1982.

Fäßler, Peter, Thomas Held, and Dirk Sawitzki. *Lemberg—Lwów—Lviv: eine Stadt im Schnittpunkt europäischer Kulturen*. Cologne: Böhlau, 1993.

Feuerman, Elesar J. "Moi Lwowscy profesorowie." *Zeszyty Historyczne* 117 (1996): 55–72.

Figes, Orlando. *A People's Tragedy: The Russian Revolution, 1891–1924*. London: Jonathan Cape, 1996.

Figura, Marek. *Konflikt polsko-ukraiński w prasie Polski Zachodniej w latach 1918–1923*. Poznań: Wydawnictwo Poznańskie, 2001.

Fihol', D. I. "Do istoriï pobutu robitnykiv L'vova v kintsi XIX—na pochatku XX st." In *Materialy z etnografiï ta mystetstvoznavstva*, 13–18. Kiev: Vyd. Akademiï nauk Ukraïn'skoï RSR, 1959.

Finder, Gabriel N., and Alexander V. Prusin. "Collaboration in Eastern Galicia: The Ukrainian Police and the Holocaust." *East European Jewish Affairs* 34, no. 2 (2004): 95–118.

Foucault, Michel. *Language, Counter-Memory, Practice*. Ithaca, NY: Cornell University Press, 1977.

Friedman, Philip. "The Destruction of the Jews of Lwów, 1941–1944." In *Roads to Extinction: Essays on the Holocaust*, edited by Philip Friedman, 244–321. New York: Jewish Publication Society of America, 1980.

———. "Ukrainian-Jewish Relations during the Nazi Occupation." *YIVO: Annual of Jewish Social Science* 12 (1959): 259–96.

———. *Zagłada Żydów lwowskich w okresie okupacji niemieckiej*. Second edition. Munich: Wydawnictwo Centralnej Żydowskiej Komisji Historycznej w Polsce ,1947.

Fussell, Paul. *The Great War and Modern Memory*. London: Oxford University Press, 1975.

Gaisbauer, Adolf. *Davidstern und Doppeladler: Zionismus und jüdischer Nationalismus in Österreich*. Vienna: Böhlau, 1988.

Gałązka, Wanda. "Stan i perspektywy śledztw w sprawach dotyczących zbrodni nacjonalistów ukraińskich." In *Polska i Ukraina po II. wojnie światowej*, edited by Włodzimierz Bonusiak, 345–52. Rzeszów: Wydawnictwo Wyższej Szkoły Pedagogicznej w Rzeszowie, 1998.

Galicja i jej dziedzictwo. Rzeszów: Wydawnictwo Wyższej Szkoły Pedagogicznej w Rzeszowie, 1994–2013.

Ganelin, R. "Evrejskij vopros vo vnutrennej politike Rossii v 1915 godu," *Vestnik evrejskogo universiteta v Moskve* 1, no. 14 (1997): 41–65.

Gerlach, Christian. *Kalkulierte Morde: Die deutsche Wirtschafts- und Vernichtungspolitik in Weißrußland 1941–1944*. Hamburg: Hamburger Edition, 1999.

Gilley, Christopher. "A Simple Question of 'Pragmatism'? Sovietophilism in the West Ukrainian Emigration in the 1920s." KICES Working Papers, no. 4, March 2006.

Gillis, John R. "Remembering Memory: A Challenge for Public Historians in a Post-National Era." *The Public Historian* 14 (1992): 91–101.

Golczewski, Frank. *Deutsche und Ukrainer 1914–1939*. Paderborn: Schöningh, 2010.

———. "Die Revision eines Klischees. Die Rettung von verfolgten Juden im Zweiten Weltkrieg durch Ukrainer." In *Solidarität und Hilfe für Juden während der NS-Zeit*, vol. 2, edited by Wolfgang Benz et al., 9–82. Berlin: Metropol, 1998.

———. "Die Ukrainer im Zweiten Weltkrieg." In *Geschichte der Ukraine*, 241–60.

———, ed. *Geschichte der Ukraine*. Göttingen: Vandenhoeck & Ruprecht, 1993.

———. *Polnisch-jüdische Beziehungen 1881–1922: Eine Studie zur Geschichte des Antisemitismus in Osteuropa*. Wiesbaden: Steiner, 1981.

———. "Ukrainische Reaktionen auf die deutsche Besetzung 1939/41." In *Anpassung—Kollaboration—Widerstand: Kollektive Reaktionen auf die Okkupation*, edited by Wolfgang Benz et al., 199–211. Berlin: Metropol, 1996.

Grebing, Helga. "Österreich-Ungarn und die 'Ukrainische Aktion,' 1914–1918." *Jahrbücher für Geschichte Osteuropas* 7 (1959): 270–96.

Grodziski, Stanisław. "Nationalfeiertage und öffentliche Gedenktage Polens im 19. und 20. Jahrhundert." In *Der Kampf um das Gedächtnis: Öffentliche Gedenktage in Mitteleuropa*, edited by Emil Brix and Hannes Stekl, 205–15. Vienna: Böhlau, 1997.

Gross, Jan. *Polish Society under German Occupation: The Generalgouvernement 1939–1944*. Princeton, NJ: Princeton University Press, 1979.

———. *Revolution from Abroad: The Soviet Conquest of Poland's Western Ukraine and Western Belorussia*. Expanded Edition. Princeton, NJ: Princeton University Press, 2002.

Gruchała, Jan. *Rząd austriacki i polskie stronnictwa polityczne w Galicij wobec kwestii ukraińskiej 1890–1914*. Katowice: Uniwersytet Śląski, 1988.

Grudzinska-Gros, Irena, and Jan Gross, eds. *War through Children's Eyes: The Soviet Occupation of Poland and the Deportations 1939–1941*. Stanford: Hoover Institution Press, 1981.

Grzelak, Czesław K. *Kresy w czerwieni: Agresja Związku Sowieckiego na polskę w 1939 roku*. Warsaw: Neriton, 1998.

Hagen, Mark von. *War in a European Borderland: Occupations and Occupation Plans in Galicia and Ukraine, 1914–1918*. Seattle: University of Washington Press, 2007.

Hagen, William H. "The Moral Economy of Ethnic Violence: The Pogrom in Lwow, November 1918." *Geschichte und Gesellschaft* 31 (2005): 203–26.

Halbwachs, Maurice. *Das Gedächtnis und seine sozialen Bedingungen*. Berlin: Luchterhand, 1966.

———. *Das kollektive Gedächtnis*. Frankfurt: F. Enke, 1985 (French original edition: *La mémoire collective*. Paris: Presses universitaires de France, 1950).

Hampel, Józef. "Lwowskie środowiska ukraińskie wobec narodzin ruchu ludowego w Galicji." In *Lwów: Miasto—społeczeństwo—kultura*, vol. 1, 110–18.

Heer, Hannes. "Lemberg 1941: Die Instrumentalisierung der NKVD-Verbrechen für den Judenmord." In *Kriegsverbrechen im 20. Jahrhundert*, edited by Wolfram Wette and Gerd R. Ueberschär, 165–77. Darmstadt: Primus, 2001.

Hein, Heidi. "Die Entwicklung der Lemberger Selbstverwaltung im Rahmen der habsburgischen Gemeindeordnung von der Revolution 1848 bis zur Verabschiedung des Statuts 1870." In *Stadtleben und Nationalität: ausgewählte Beiträge zur Stadtgeschichtsforschung in Ostmitteleuropa im 19. und 20. Jahrhundert*, edited by Markus Krzoska and Isabell Röskau-Rydel, 83–106. Munich: Martin Meidenbauer, 2006.

Held, Thomas. "Vom Pogrom zum Massenmord: Die Vernichtung der jüdischen Bevölkerung Lembergs im Zweiten Weltkrieg." In *Lemberg—Lwów—Lviv*, 113–66.

Heller, Celia S. *On the Edge of Destruction: Jews of Poland between the Two World Wars*. New York: Columbia University Press, 1977.

Hettling, Manfred. "Erlebnisraum und Ritual. Die Geschichte des 18. März 1848 im Jahrhundert bis 1948." *Historische Anthropologie* 5 (1997): 417–34.

Hiller, Marlene, ed. *Städte im Zweiten Weltkrieg: ein internationaler Vergleich*. Essen: Klartext, 1991.

Himka, John-Paul. "Construction of Nationality in Galician Rus': Icarian Flights in Almost all Directions," in *Intellectuals and the Articulation of the Nation*, edited by Michael D. Kennedy and Ronald G. Suny, 109-64. Ann Arbor: University of Michigan Press, 1999.

———. "Dimensions of a Triangle: The Polish-Ukrainian-Jewish Relationship." *Polin* 12 (1999): 25–48.

———. *Galician Villagers and the Ukrainian National Movement in the Nineteenth Century*. Houndmills: Palgrave Macmillan, 1988.

———. "German Culture and the National Awakening in Western Ukraine before the Revolution of 1848." In *German-Ukrainian Relations in Historical Perspective*, edited by John-Paul Himka and Hans-Joachim Torke, 29–44. Edmonton: Canadian Institute of Ukrainian Studies Press, 1994.

———. "The Greek Catholic Church and Nation-Building in Galicia, 1772–1918." *Harvard Ukrainian Studies* 8 (December 1984): 426–52.

———. "Hope in the Tsar: Displaced Naive Monarchism among the Ukrainians of the Habsburg Empire." *Russian History/Histoire Russe* 7 (1980): 125–38.

———. "The Lviv Pogrom of 1941: The Germans, Ukrainian Nationalists, and the Carnival Crowd." *Canadian Slavonic Papers* 53, no. 2–4 (2011): 209–43.

———. "Priests and Peasants: The Greek Catholic Pastor and the Ukrainian National Movement in Austria, 1867–1900." *Canadian Slavonic Papers* 21 (1979): 1–14.

———. *Socialism in Galicia: The Emergence of Polish Social Democracy and Ukrainian Radicalism (1860–1890)*. Cambridge, MA: Harvard University Press, 1978.

———. "The Transformation and Formation of Social Strata and their Place in the Ukrainian National Movement in Nineteenth-Century Galicia." *Journal of Ukrainian Studies* 23 (Winter 1993): 3–22.

———. "Ukrainian-Jewish Antagonism in the Galician Countryside during the Late Nineteenth Century." In *Ukrainian-Jewish Relations in Historical Perspective*, edited by Peter Potichnyj and Howard Aster, 121–39. Edmonton Canadian Institute of Ukrainian Studies, University of Alberta, 1988.

———. "War Criminality: A Blank Spot in the Collective Memory of the Ukrainian Diaspora." *Spaces of Identity* 5, no 1 (2005): 9–24.

———. "Young Radicals and Independent Statehood: The Idea of a Ukrainian Nation-State, 1890–1895." *Slavic Review* 41 (1982): 219–35.

Hirsch, Francine. "Race without the Practice of Racial Politics." *Slavic Review* 61 (2002): 30–43.

Hirschhausen, Ulrike von, and Jörn Leonhard. "Europäische Nationalismen im West-Ost-Vergleich: Von der Typologie zur Differenzbestimmung." In *Nationalismen in Europa: West- und Osteuropa im Vergleich*, edited by Ulrike von Hirschhausen and Jörn Leonhard, 1–45. Göttingen: Wallstein, 2001.

Hobsbawm, Eric J., and Terence Ranger, eds. *The Invention of Tradition*. Cambridge: Cambridge University Press, 1983.

Hoffmann-Curtius, Kathrin. "Opfermodelle am Altar des Vaterlandes seit der Französischen Revolution." In *Schrift der Flammen: Opfermythen und Weiblichkeitsentwürfe im 20. Jahrhundert*, edited by Gudrun Kohn-Waechter, 57–92. Berlin: Orlanda Frauenverlag, 1991.

Holquist, Peter. "'Conduct Merciless Mass Terror': Decossackization on the Don, 1919." *Cahiers du Monde Russe* 38 (January–June 1997): 127–62.

Holzer, Jerzy. "'Vom Orient die Fantasie, und in der Brust der Slawen Feuer...' Jüdisches Leben und Akkulturation im Lemberg des 19. und 20. Jahrhundert." In *Lemberg—Lwów—Lviv*, 75–91.

———. "Zur Frage der Akkulturation der Juden in Galizien im 19. und 20. Jahrhundert." *Jahrbücher für Geschichte Osteuropas* 37 (1989): 217–27.

Horak, Stephan M. *The First Treaty of World War I: Ukraine's Treaty with the Central Powers of February 9, 1918*. New York: Columbia University Press, 1988.

Hoshko, Tetjana. "Doslidzhennja istoriï mis'koho samovrjaduvannja XIV-XVII st. Pol's'kymy istorykamy L'vova (Pochatok XX st.)." In *L'viv: Misto—suspil'stvo—kul'tura*, vol. 3, 462–68.

Hroch, Miroslav. "From National Movement to the Fully-Formed Nation: The Nation-Building Process in Europe." In *Becoming National*, 59–77.

———. "Zionism as a European National Movement." *Jewish Studies* 38 (1998): 73–81.

Hryciuk, Grzegorz. "Działalność OUN i UPA w latach czterdziestych i pięćdziesiątych w najnowszych publikacjach na Ukrainie." *Studia z dziejów Europy Wschodniej* 1 (2002), 181–99.

———. *"Gazeta Lwowska," 1941–1944.* Second revised edition. Wrocław: Wydawnictwo Uniwersytetu Wrocławskiego, 1996.

———. *"Kumytet:" Polski Komitet Opiekuńczy Lwów Miasto w latach 1941–1944.* Toruń: Adam Marszałek, 2000.

———. "Mordy w więzieniach lwowskich w czerwcu 1941 r." *Wrocławskie Studia z Historii Najnowszej* 7 (1994): 58–69.

———. "Nastroje i stosunek ludności polskiej tzw: Ukrainy zachodniej do przesiedleń w latach 1944–1945 w świetle sprawozdań radzieckich." In *Polska i Ukraina po II: wojnie światowej*, edited by Włodzimierz Bonusiak, 209–22. Rzeszów: Wydawnictwo Wyższej Szkoły Pedagogicznej, 1998.

———. "'Nowy Kurs?' Ewolucja polityki radzieckiej wobec Polaków we Lwowie (Czerwiec 1940–Czerwiec 1941)." *Wrocławskie Studia z Historii Najnowszej* 6 (1998): 47–66.

———. *Polacy we Lwowie 1939–1944: Życie codzienne.* Warsaw: Książka i Wiedza, 2000.

———. "Polityka radziecka wobec ludności polskiej na Wołyniu i w Galicji Wschodniej w latach 1944–1946." *Studia z dziejów Europy Wschodniej* 1 (2002): 92–120.

———. "Prasa ukraińska i ukraińskojęzyczna w Galicji Wschodniej w latach 1939–1944." *Dzieje Najnowsze* 27 (1997): 47–66.

———. "Zmiany demograficzne ludności polskiej we Lwowie w latach 1931–1944." In *Wschodnie losy Polaków*, edited by Stanisław Ciesielski, 7–76. Wrocław: Instytut Historyczny Uniwersytetu Wrocławskiego, 1991.

Hryciuk, Grzegorz, and Jarosław Stoćky. *Studia nad demografią historyczną i sytuacją religijną Ukrainy.* Lublin: Instytut Europy Środkowo-Wschodniej, 2000.

Hryniuk, Stella. "Polish Lords and Ukrainian Peasants: Conflict, Deference, and Accomodation in Eastern Galicia in the Late Nineteenth Century." *Austrian History Yearbook* 24 (1993): 119–32.

Hrytsak, Jaroslav. *Narys Istoriï Ukraïny: Formuvannja modernoï ukraïns'koï natsiï XIX–XX stolittja.* Kiev: Heneza, 1996.

Hrycak [Hrytsak], Jaroslav. *Historia Ukrainy 1772–1999.* Lublin: Instytut Europy Środkowo Wschodniej, 2000.

Hübner-Wojciechowska, Joanna. *Grób Nieznanego Żołnierza.* Warsaw: Państwowe Wydawnictwo Naukowe, 1991.

Inglis, Ken S. "Entombing Unknown Soldiers: From London and Paris to Baghdad." *History and Memory* 5 (1993): 7–31.

Inglot, Mieczysław. "Obraz ojczyzny w liryce polskiej okupowanego Lwowa lat 1939–1945." In *Europa nie prowincjonalna: Przemiany na ziemiach wschodnich dawnej Rzeczypospolitej (Białoruś, Litwa, Łotwa, Ukraina, wschodnie pogranicze III Rzeczypospolitej Polskiej) w latach 1772–1999*, edited by Krzysztow Jasiewicz, 168–80. Warsaw: Rytm, 1999.

Isaevych, V. A., et al., eds. *L'viv: Istorychni narysy*. L'viv: Instytut Ukraïnoznavstva im. I. Kryp"jakevycha NAN Ukraïny, 1996.

Istorija gorodov i sel Ukrainskoj SSR: L'vovskaja oblast'. Kiev: Ukr. Sov. Entsiklopedija, 1978.

Istorija L'vova: Korotkyj narys. L'viv: Vydavnytstvo L'vivskoho Universytetu, 1956.

Jabłonowski, Marek. *Polityczne aspekty ruchu byłych wojskowych we Polsce 1918–1939*. Warsaw: Centralny Ośrodek Metodyczny Studiów Nauk Politycznych, 1989.

Jacobmeyer, Wolfgang. *Heimat und Exil: Die Anfänge der polnischen Untergrundbewegung im Zweiten Weltkrieg*. Hamburg: Leibniz-Verlag, 1973.

Jagóra, Maciej L. "Walki o Lwów w listopadzie i grudniu 1918 roku." *Dzieje Najnowsze* 25, no. 3 (1993): 83–96.

Jakubowska, Urszula. *Lwów na przełomie XIX i XX wieku: przegląd środowisk prawotwórczych*. Warsaw: Instytut Badań Literackich PAN, 1991.

———. "Życie polityczne we Lwowie na przełomie XIX i XX wieku." In *Galicja i jej dziedzictwo*. Vol. 1: *Historia i Polityka*, 83–97.

Jarosh, B. O. *Totalitarnyj rezhym na zakhidnoukraïns'kykh zemljach: 30-50-ti roky XX stolittja*. Luts'k: Nadstyr'ja, 1995.

Jasiewicz, Krzysztof, ed. *Tygiel narodów: Stosunki społeczne i etniczne na dawnych ziemiach wschodnich Rzeczypospolitej 1939–1953*. Warsaw: Rytm, 2002.

Jaworski, Edward. *Lwów: Losy mieszkańców i żołnierzy Armii Krajowej w latach 1939–1956*. Pruszków: Ajaks, 1999.

Jeismann, Michael. *Das Vaterland der Feinde: Studien zum nationalen Feindbegriff und Selbstverständnis in Deutschland und Frankreich 1792–1918*. Stuttgart: Klett-Cotta, 1992.

Jobst, Kerstin S. *Der Mythos des Miteinander: Galizien in Literatur und Geschichte*. Hamburg: Deutsche Gesellschaft für Osteuropakunde, Zweigstelle Hamburg, 1998.

———. *Zwischen Nationalismus und Internationalismus: Die polnische und ukrainische Sozialdemokratie in Galizien von 1890 bis 1914. Ein Beitrag zur Nationalitätenfrage im Habsburgerreich*. Hamburg: Dölling und Gallitz, 1996.

Jones, Eliyahu. *Żydzi Lwowa w okresie okupacji 1939–1945*. Łódź: Oficyna Bibliofilów, 1999.

Jordan, Peter, et al., eds. *Ukraine: Geographie—Ethnische Struktur—Geschichte—Sprache und Literatur—Kultur—Politik—Bildung—Wirtschaft—Recht*. Vienna: Österreichisches Ost- und Südosteuropa-Institut, 2000.

Kachmar, Volodymyr. "Pytannja pro stvorennja ukraïns'koho universytetu u L'vovi v avstrijs'komu parlamenti na pochatku XX st." In *L'viv: Misto—suspil'stvo—kul'tura*, vol. 3, 421–30.

Kamenetsky, Ihor. *Hitler's Occupation of Ukraine 1941–1944: A Study of Totalitarian Imperialism*. Milwaukee: Marquette University Press, 1956.

Kappeler, Andreas. "Die Ukraine in der deutschsprachigen Historiographie." Österreichische Osthefte 42, no. 3/4 (2000): 161–77.

———. *Kleine Geschichte der Ukraine*. Munich: Beck, 1994.

Kapralska, Łucja. *Pluralizm kulturowy i etniczny a odrębność regionalna Kresów południowo-wschodnich w latach 1918–1939*. Cracow: Nomos, 2000.

Karpus, Zbigniew, Waldemar Rezmer, and Emilian Wiszka, eds. *Polska i Ukraina: Sojusz 1920 roku i jego następstwa*. Toruń: Wydawnictwo Uniwersytetu Mikołaja Kopernika, 1997.

Kaschuba, Wolfgang. "Ritual und Fest: Das Volk auf der Straße." In *Dynamik der Tradition: Studien zur historischen Kulturforschung 4*, edited by Richard van Dülmen, 204–67. Frankfurt/Main: Fischer, 1992.

Kersten, Krystyna. "The Polish-Ukrainian Conflict under Communist Rule." *Acta Poloniae Historica* 73 (1996): 135–51.

Kiryk, Feliks, ed. *Żydzi w Małopolsce: Studia z dziejów osadnictwa i życia społecznego*. Przemyśl: Południowo-Wschodni Instytut Naukowy w Przemyślu, 1991.

Kiselychnyk, Vasyl'. "Rozrobka i nadannja L'vovu u 1870 r. statutu na mis'ke samovrjaduvannja." In *Lwów: Miasto—społeczeństwo—kultura*, vol. 2, 125–31.

Kleßmann, Christoph. *Die Selbstbehauptung einer Nation: NS-Kulturpolitik und polnische Widerstandsbewegung im Generalgouvernement 1939–1945*. Düsseldorf: Bertelsmann-Universitätsverlag, 1971.

Klimecki, Michał. "Das Ende der österreichischen Souveränität in Galizien im Oktober–November 1918." In *Między Wiedniem a Lwowem: Zwischen Wien und Lemberg. Die Vorträge der polnisch-österreichischen Tagung zum 80. Jahrestag des Ausbruchs des Ersten Weltkriegs, Warschau, den 17. November 1994*, ed. Andrzej Rzepniewski, 163–70. Warsaw: Austriacki Instytut Kultury we Warszawie, Wojskowy Instytut Historyczny, 1996.

———. *Lwów 1918–1919*. Warsaw: Bellona, 1998.

———. *Polsko-ukraińska wojna o Lwów i Galicję Wschodnią 1918–1919*. Warsaw: Volumen, 2000.

Klimecki, Michał, and Gerard Położyński. *Czas próby: Wojna polsko-sowiecka 1919–1920 r*. Warsaw: Vipart, 2000.

Komar, Ljuba. *Proces 59-ty*. L'viv: Naukove Tovarystvo im. Shevchenka, 1997.
Korboński, Stefan. *The Polish Underground State: A Guide to the Underground 1939–1945*. New York: Columbia University Press, 1978.
Korzec, Paweł. "Das Abkommen zwischen der Regierung Grabski und der jüdischen Parlamentsvertretung." *Jahrbücher für Geschichte Osteuropas* 20 (1972): 331–66.
———. "The Steiger Affair." *Soviet Jewish Affairs* 3, no. 2 (1973): 38–57.
Koselleck, Reinhart. "Der Einfluß der beiden Weltkriege auf das soziale Bewußtsein." In *Der Krieg des kleinen Mannes: Eine Militärgeschichte von unten*, second edition, edited by Wolfram Wette, 324–43. Munich: Piper, 1995.
———. "Einleitung." In *Der politische Totenkult: Kriegerdenkmäler in der Moderne*, edited by Reinhart Koselleck and Michael Jeismann, 9-20. Munich: Fink, 1993.
———. "'Erfahrungsraum' und 'Erwartungshorizont'—zwei historische Kategorien." In *Vergangene Zukunft: Zur Semantik geschichtlicher Zeiten*, edited by Reinhart Kosellek, 349–72. Frankfurt am Main: Suhrkamp, 1989.
———. "Erfahrungswandel und Methodenwechsel: Eine historisch-anthropologische Skizze." In *Historische Methode*, edited by Christian Meier and Jörn Rüsen, 13–61. Munich: dtv, 1988.
Koselleck, Reinhart, Wolfgang J. Mommsen, and Jörn Rüsen. *Objektivität und Parteilichkeit in der Geschichtswissenschaft*. Munich: dtv, 1982.
Kosyk, Wolodymyr. *The Third Reich and the Ukraine*. New York: Peter Lang, 1993.
Koval', M. S. *Ukraïna u Druhij Svitovij i Velykij Vitchyznjanij vijnach, 1939–1945 gg. Sproba suchasnoho kontseptual'noho bachennja*. Kiev: Al'ternatyvy, 1994.
Kovba, Zhanna. *Ljudjanist' u bezodni pekla: Povedinka mistsevoho naselennja Skhidnoï Halychyny v roky "ostatochnoho rozv"jazannja jevrejs'koho pytannja"* Kiev: Instytut Judaïky, 1998.
Kozik, Jan. *Ukraiński ruch narodowy w Galicji w latach 1830–1848*. Cracow: Wydawnictwo Literackie, 1973.
Kozłowski, Maciej. *Między Sanem a Zbruczem: Walki o Lwów i Galicję Wschodnią 1918–1919*. Cracow: Znak, 1990.
———. *Zapomniana wojna: Walki o Lwów i Galicję Wschodnią 1918–1919*. Second edition. Bydgoszcz: Instytut Wydawniczy Świadectwo, 1999.
Kramarz, Henryka. *Samorząd Lwowa w czasie pierwszej wojny światowej i jego rola w życiu miasta*. Cracow: Wydawnictwo Naukowe WSP, 1994.
———. "Ze sceny walk polsko-ukraińskich o Lwów." In *Galicja i jej dziedzictwo*. Vol. 1: *Historia i polityka*, edited by Kazimierz Karolczak, 99–115. Rzeszów: Wydawnictwo Wyższej Szkoły Pedagogicznej w Rzeszowie, 1994.

Krasuski, Jósef. *Tajne szkolnictwo Polskie w okresie okupacji hitlerowskiej 1939–1945*. Warsaw: Państwowe Wydawnictwo Naukowe, 1971.

Krezub, Antin. *Narys istoriji ukraïns'ko-pol'skoï vijny 1918–1919*. New York: Oko, 1966.

Kul'chyts'kyj, S. V. *Orhanizatsija Ukraïns'kykh Natsionalistiv i Ukraïns'ka Povstans'ka Armija*. Kiev: Nauk. Dumka, 2005.

Kurek, Ewa. *Polish-Jewish Relations 1939–1945: Beyond the Limits of Solidarity*. Bloomington, IN: iUniverse, 2012.

Kutschabsky, W. [Vasyl' Kuchabs'kyj.]. *Die Westukraine im Kampfe mit Polen und dem Bolschewismus in den Jahren 1918–1923*. Berlin: Junker and Dünnhaupt, 1934.

Lambert, Dean Warren. *The Deterioration of the Imperial Russian Army in the First World War, August 1914–March 1917*. Dissertation, University of Kentucky, 1975.

Landau, Zbigniew, and Jerzy Tomaszewski. *Robotnicy przemysłowi w Polsce 1918–1939*. Warsaw: Książka i Wiedza, 1971.

Landwehr, Achim. *Geschichte des Sagbaren: Einführung in die Historische Diskursanalyse*. Tübingen: Edition diskord, 2001.

Langewiesche, Dieter. "'Nation,' 'Nationalismus,' 'Nationalstaat' in der europäischen Geschichte seit dem Mittelalter—Versuch einer Bilanz." In *Nation, Nationalismus, Nationalstaat in Deutschland und Europa*, 14–34.

———. *Nation, Nationalismus, Nationalstaat in Deutschland und Europa*. Munich: C. H. Beck, 2000.

———. "Nationalismus im 19. und 20. Jahrhundert: zwischen Partizpation und Aggression." In *Nation, Nationalismus, Nationalstaat in Deutschland und Europa*, 35–54.

Latzel, Klaus. *Deutsche Soldaten—nationalsozialistischer Krieg? Kriegserlebnis—Kriegserfahrung 1939–1945*. Paderborn: Schöningh, 1998.

———. "Vom Kriegserlebnis zur Kriegserfahrung: Theoretische und methodische Überlegungen zur erfahrungsgeschichtlichen Untersuchung von Feldpostbriefen." *Militärgeschichtliche Mitteilungen* 56 (1997): 1–30.

Leinwand, Artur. "Obrona Lwowa w 1920 roku." In *Rocznik Lwowski*, 30–31. Warsaw: Instytut Lwowski, 1991.

Lemberg, Eugen. *Nationalismus*. 2 vols. Reinbek: Rowohlt, 1964.

Lemberg, Hans. "Das Konzept der ethnischen Säuberungen im 20. Jahrhundert." In *Lager, Zwangsarbeit, Vertreibung und Deportation: Dimensionen der Massenverbrechen in der Sowjetunion und in Deutschland 1933 bis 1945*, edited by Dittmar Dahlmann and Gerhard Hirschfeld, 485–91. Essen: Klartext, 1999.

Lesser, Gabriele. *Leben als ob: Die Untergrunduniversität Krakau im Zweiten Weltkrieg*. Freiburg: Treffpunkt, 1988.

Lewandowska, Wanda. *Życie codzienne Wilna w latach II wojny światowej*. Warsaw: Neriton, 1997.
Lichtblau, Albert, and Michael John. *Jewries in Galicia and Bukovina, in Lemberg and Czernowitz*. http://czernowitz.org/Lichtblau/lichtblau.html.
Lichten, Józef. "O Asymilacji Żydów w Polsce od wybuchu pierwszej wojny światowej do końca drugiej wojny (1914–1945)." *Zeszyty Historyczne* 42 (1977): 96–134.
Lohr, Eric. "The Russian Army and the Jews: Mass Deportations, Hostages and Violence." *Russian Review* 60 (2001): 404–19.
Longerich, Peter, ed. *Die Ermordung der europäischen Juden: Eine umfassende Dokumentation des Holocaust 1941-1945*. Munich: Institut für Zeitgeschichte, 1989.
Luckmann, Thomas. "Lebensweltliche Zeitkategorien, Zeitstrukturen des Alltags und der Ort des 'historischen Bewußtseins.'" In *Wissen und Gesellschaft: Ausgewählte Aufsätze 1981–2002*, edited by Thomas Luckmann, 56–66. Konstanz: UVK Verlagsgesellschaft, 2002.
Lukas, Richard C. *The Forgotten Holocaust: The Poles under German Occupation 1939–1944*. The University Press of Kentucky, 1986.
Łukomski, Grzegorz, Czesław Partacz, and Bogusław Polak. *Wojna Polsko-Ukraińska 1918–1919*. Koszalin: Wydawnictwo Uczelniane Wyższej Szkoły Inżynierskiej w Koszalinie, 1994.
Luts'kyj, Oleksandr. "Intelihentsija L'vova (veresen' 1939–cherven' 1941 rr.)." In *L'viv: Misto—suspil'stvo—kul'tura*, vol. 3, 574–91.
Luts'kyj, Oleksandr, and Kim Naumenko. "U roky Druhoï Svitovoï vijny." In *L'viv: Istorychni narysy*, 435–506.
Lytvyn, Mykola. "Stolytsa Zakhidno-Ukraïns'koï Narodnoï Respubliky." In *L'viv: Istorychni narysy*, 330–56.
———. "Ukraïns'ko-pol's'ka borot'ba za L'viv: vijs'kovo-politychnyj aspekt (Lystopad 1918–sichen' 1919 rr.)." In *L'viv: Misto—suspil'stvo—kul'tura*, vol. 3, 462–68.
Lytvyn, Mykola, and Klim Naumenko. *Istorija ZUNR*. L'viv: OLIR, 1995.
Maciak, Dariusz. *Próba porozumienia polsko-ukraińskiego w Galicji w latach 1888–1895*. Warsaw: Wydawnictwo Uniwersytetu Warszawskiego, 2006.
Madajczyk, Czesław. *Faszyzm i okupacje 1938–1945: Wykonywanie okupacji przez państwa Osi w Europie*. 2 vols. Poznań: Wydawnictwo Poznańskie, 1983–1984 (abridged and revised German version: *Die Okkupationspolitik Nazideutschlands in Polen 1939–1945*. Cologne: Pahl-Rugenstein, 1988).
Madurowicz-Urbańska, Helena. "Lemberg—Hauptstadt Galiziens: Forschungsstand zur demographischen, wirtschaftlichen und zivilisatorischen Entwicklung der Stadt in der Zeit der Autonomie Galiziens aus der Sicht der polnischen

Historiographie." Österreich—*Polen: 1000 Jahre Beziehungen. Studia Austro-Polonica* 5 (1996): 185–92.

Makarchuk, Stepan A. "Hromads'ko-politychnyj tsentr Zakhidnoukraïns'koho kraju." In *L'viv: Istorychni narysy*, 267–90.

———. "Lwów w warunkach rosyjskiej okupacji 1914–1915." In *Lwów: Miasto—społeczeństwo—kultura*, vol. 1, 131–37.

———. "Naselennja 'Stolytsi' u druhij polovyni XIX pershij tretyni XX st." In *L'viv: Istorychni narysy*, 207–24.

———. *Ukraïns'ka Respublika Halychan.* L'viv: Svit, 1997.

Mark, Rudolf A. *Galizien unter österreichischer Herrschaft: Verwaltung—Kirche—Bevölkerung.* Marburg: Herder-Institut, 1994.

———. "'Polnische Bastion und ukrainisches Piemont:' Lemberg 1772–1921." In *Lemberg—Lwów—Lviv*, 46–74.

———. *Symon Petljura und die UNR: Vom Sturz des Hetman Skoropads'kyj bis zum Exil in Polen.* Wiesbaden: Harrassowitz, 1988.

Markovits, Andrei S., and Frank E. Sysyn, eds. *Nationbuilding and the Politics of Nationalism. Essays on Austrian Galicia.* Cambridge, MA: Harvard University Press, 1982.

Marples, David R. *Heroes and Villains: Creating National History in Contemporary Ukraine.* Budapest: Central European University Press, 2007.

———. *Stalinism in Ukraine in the 1940s.* London: St. Martin's Press, 1992.

Marshall, Robert. *In the Sewers of Lvov: The Last Sanctuary from the Holocaust.* London: Collins, 1990.

Marszałek, Agnieszka. *Lwowskie przedsiębiorstwa teatralne lat 1872–1886.* Cracow: Towarzystwo Naukowe 'Societas Vistulana,' 1999.

Martin, Terry. *The Affirmative Action Empire: Nations and Nationalism in the Soviet Union, 1923–1939.* Ithaca, NY: Cornell University Press, 2001.

———. "The Origins of Soviet Ethnic Cleansing." *The Journal of Modern History* 70 (December 1998): 813–61.

Mazur, Grzegorz. *Życie polityczne polskiego Lwowa 1918–1939.* Cracow: Księgarnia Akademicka, 2007.

Mazur, Grzegorz, and Jerzy Węgierski. *Konspiracja Lwowska 1939–1944: Słownik Biograficzny.* Katowice: Wydawnictwo Unia, 1997.

Mazur, Orest, and Ivan Pater. "L'viv u roky pershoï svitovoï vijny." In *L'viv: Istorychni narysy*, 304–24.

Mędrzecki, Włodzimierz. "Ukraińska Reprezentacja Parlamentarna w Drugiej Rzeczypospolitej." *Warszawskie Zeszyty Ukrainoznawcze* 3 (1994): 220–34.

Melamed, Vladimir. *Evrei vo L'vove (XII–pervaja polovina XX veka): Sobytija, obshchestvo, ljudi.* L'viv: Tekop, 1994.

———. "Organized and Unsolicited Collaboration in the Holocaust: The Multifaceted Ukrainian Context." *East European Jewish Affairs* 37, no. 2 (August 2007): 217–48.

Mendelsohn, Ezra. "Jewish Assimilation in L'viv: The Case of Wilhelm Feldmann." In *Nationbuilding and the Politics of Nationalism*, 94–110.

———. "Jewish Politics in Interwar Poland: An Overview." In *The Jews of Poland between Two World Wars*, edited by Yisrael Gutman, Ezra Mendelsohn, Jehuda Reinharz, and Chone Shemruk, 9–19. Hanover: Brandeis University Press, 1989.

———. *Zionism in Poland: The Formative Years, 1915–1926*. New Haven, CT: Yale University Press, 1981.

Mergel, Thomas, and Thomas Welskopp, eds. *Geschichte zwischen Kultur und Gesellschaft: Beiträge zur Theoriedebatte*. Munich: Beck, 1997.

Mick, Christoph. "Der Kult um den 'Unbekannten Soldaten' im Polen der Zwischenkriegszeit." In *Nationalisierung der Religion und Sakralisierung der Religion im östlichen Europa*, edited by Martin Schulze-Wessel, 181–200. Stuttgart: Steiner Verlag, 2006.

———. "Die Ethnisierung des Stalinismus: Zur Wirksamkeit ethnischer Kategorien bei der Sowjetisierung der Westukraine 1944-1948," in *Moderne Zeiten? Krieg, Revolution und Gewalt im 20. Jahrhundert,* edited by Jörg Baberowski, 145-173. Göttingen: Vandenhoeck & Ruprecht, 2006.

———. "Incompatible experiences: Poles, Ukrainians and Jews under Soviet and German Occupation," *Journal of Contemporary History* 46, no. 2 (2011), 336-363.

———. "Kollektive Gewalt in Lemberg, 1918-1939." In *Kollektive Gewalt in der Stadt: Eujropa 1890-1939,* edited by Friedrich Lenger, 149-167. Munich: Oldenbourg, 2013.

———. "Kriegserfahrungen und die Konstruktion von Kontinuität: Schlachten und Kriege im ukrainischen und polnischen kollektiven Gedächtnis 1900–1930." In *Gründungsmythen—Genealogien—Memorialzeichen: Beiträge zur institutionellen Konstruktion von Kontinuität*, edited by Gert Melville and Karl-Siegbert Rehberg, 109–32. Cologne: Böhlau.

———. "Lviv under Soviet Rule, 1939-1941." In *Stalin and Europe: Imitation and Domination, 1928-1953*, edited by Timothy Snyder and Ray Brandon, 138-162. Oxford: Oxford University Press, 2014.

———. "Nationale Festkultur in Lemberg vor dem Ersten Weltkrieg." In *Identitätenwandel und nationale Mobilisierung in Regionen ethnischer Diversität: Ein regionaler Vergleich zwischen Westpreußen und Galizien am Ende des 19. und Anfang des 20. Jahrhunderts*, edited by Michael G. Müller and Ralph Schattkowsky, 113–32. Marburg: Herder-Institut, 2004.

———. "Nationalisierung in einer multiethnischen Stadt: Interethnische Konflikte in Lemberg 1890–1920." *Archiv für Sozialgeschichte* 40 (2000): 113–46.

———. "Nationalismus und Modernisierung in Lemberg." In *Städte im östlichen Europa: zur Problematik von Modernisierung und Raum vom Spätmittelalter bis zum 20. Jahrhundert,* edited by Carsten Goehrke and Bianka Pietrow-Ennker, 171–213. Zurich: Chronos, 2006.

———. "'Only the Jews do not waver...' Lviv under Soviet Occupation," in *Shared History – Divided Memory: Jews and Others in Soviet Occupied Poland, 1939-1941,* edited by Elazar Barkan, Elizabeth A. Cole, and Kai Struve, 245-262. Leipzig: Leipziger Universitätsverlag, 2007.

———. "War and Conflicting Memories – Poles, Ukrainians and Jews in Lvov 1914–1939 " *Simon Dubnow Institute Yearbook,* 4 (2005), pp. 257-278.

Miller, Alexei. *The Ukrainian Question: The Russian Empire and Nationalism in the Nineteenth Century.* Budapest: Central European University Press, 2003.

Misiło, Eugeniusz, ed. *Repatriacja czy deportacja: przesiedlenie Ukraińców z Polski do USRR 1944–1946.* 2 vols. Warsaw: Archiwum Ukraińskie, 1996, 1999.

Moser, Michael. "Die Entwicklung der ukrainischen Schriftsprache." *Österreichische Osthefte* 42, no. 3/4 (2000): 483–496.

Mosse, George L. *Die Nationalisierung der Massen: Politische Symbolik und Massenbewegungen in Deutschland von den Napoloeonischen Kriegen Befreiungskriegen bis zum Dritten Reich.* Frankfurt/Main: Ullstein, 1976.

———. *Fallen Soldiers: Reshaping the Memory of the World Wars.* New York: Oxford University Press, 1990.

Motyka, Grzegorz. "Między porozumieniem a zbrodnią: II. wojna światowa oraz jej skutki w stosunkach polsko-ukraińskich." In *Tematy polsko-ukraińskie,* edited by Robert Traba, 93–102. Olsztyn: Wspólnota Kulturowa Borussia, 2001.

———. "Postawy wobec konfliktu polsko-ukraińskiego w latach 1939–1953 w zależności od przynależności etnicznej, państwowej i religijnej." In *Tygiel narodów,* 279–407.

———. *Tak było w Bieszczadach.* Warsaw: Volumen, 1999.

———. *Ukraińska partyzantka 1942–1960: działalność Organizacji Ukraińskich Nacjonalistów i Ukraińskiej Powstańczej Armii.* Warsaw: RYTM, 2006.

Motyka, Grzegorz, and Rafał Wnuk. *Pany i rezuny: Współpraca AK-WiN i UPA.* Warsaw: Volumen, 1997.

Motyl, Alexander J. *The Turn to the Right: The Ideological Origins and Development of Ukrainian Nationalism 1919–1929.* New York: Columbia University Press, 1980.

Mroczka, Ludwik. "Przyczynek do kwestii żydowskiej w Galicji u progu Drugiej Rzeczypospolitej." In *Żydzi w Małopolsce,* 297–308.

———. *Spór o Galicję Wschodnią 1914–1923*. Cracow: Wydawnictwo Naukowe WSP, 1998.

Mudryj, Mar'jan. "Halyts'ki Namisnyky v systemi Ukraïns'ko-pol's'kych vzajemyn (1849–1914)." *Visnyk L'vivs'koho Universytetu: Serija Istorychna* 33 (1999): 91–101.

———, ed. *L'viv: Misto—suspil'stvo—kul'tura*, vol. 3. L'viv: L'vivs'kyj Derzhavnyj Universytet imeni Ivana Franka, 1999.

———. "Ukraïns'ki narodni vicha u L'vovi 1880 i 1883 rokiv (misto na shljachu do masovo polityky). In *L'viv. Misto—suspil'stvo—kul'tura*, vol. 3, 333–47.

Mudryj, Vasyl'. *Zmahannja za ukraïns'ki universytety v Halychyni*. L'viv: Naukove tovarystvo imeni Shevchenka, 1999.

Müller, Sepp. *Von der Ansiedlung bis zur Umsiedlung: Das Deutschtum Galiziens, insbesondere Lembergs, 1772–1940*. Marburg: Johann Gottfried Herder-Institut, 1961.

Münch, Paul. "Fêtes pour le peuple, rien par le people: 'Öffentliche' Feste im Programm der Aufklärung." In *Öffentliche Festkultur*, edited by Dieter Düding et al., 25–45. Reinbek: Rowohlt, 1988.

Münkler, Herfried. "Siegfrieden." In *Siegfrieden: Politik mit einem deutschen Mythos*, edited by Herfried Münkler and Wolfgang Storch, 49–142. Berlin: Rotbuch-Verlag, 1988.

Musial, Bogdan. *"Konterrevolutionäre Elemente sind zu erschießen": Die Brutalisierung des deutsch-sowjetischen Krieges im Sommer 1941*. Munich: Propyläen, 2000.

Muszynka, Mykoła. "Towarzystwo Naukowe im. Szewczenki i jego rola w narodowym odrodzeniu Ukraińców na terenie Galicji." In *Galicja i jej dziedzictwo*. Vol. 3: *Nauka i oświata*, edited by Andrzej Meissner and Jerzy Wyrozumski, 69–78. Rzeszów: Wydawnictwo Wyższej Szkoły Pedagogicznej w Rzeszowie, 1995.

Mychal's'kyj, Jurij. "Pol's'ki demokraty ta Ukraïns'ke pytannja v Halychyni naprykintsi XIX–na pochatku XX stolittja do 1914 roku." *Visnyk L'vivs'koho Universytetu*: Serija Istorychna 33 (1998): 122–30.

———. *Pol's'ka suspil'nist' ta ukrains'ka pytannja v Halychyni v period sejmovych vyboriv 1908 r.* L'viv: Kamenjar, 1997.

Naimark, Norman M. *Fires of Hatred: Ethnic Cleansing in Twentieth-Century Europe*. Cambridge, MA: Harvard University Press, 2001.

Najdus, Walentyna. "Kształtowanie się nowoczesnych więzów społeczno-organizacyjnych ludności ukraińskiej Galicji Wschodniej w dobie konstytucyjnej." In *Lwów: Miasto—społeczeństwo—kultura*, vol. 2, 137–81.

———. *Rozwój ruchu strajkowego w Galicji w latach 1900–1914*. Warsaw: Publisher unknown, 1972.

Nicieja, Stanisław Sławomir. "Lwów—fenomen wielu kultur i narodów." *Przegląd Wschodni* 3 (1994): 717–32.

———. *Łyczaków: Dzielnica za Styksem*. Wrocław: Zakład Narodowy im. Ossolińskich, 1998.

Niethammer, Lutz. *Kollektive Identität: Heimliche Quellen einer unheimlichen Konjunktur*. Reinbek: Rowohlt, 2000.

Nietzsche, Friedrich. *Vom Nutzen und Nachteil der Historie für das Leben*. Munich: dtv, 1996.

Nora, Pierre. *Zwischen Geschichte und Gedächtnis*. Frankfurt/Main: Fischer Taschenbuch, 1998.

———. "Between Memory and History: Les Lieux de Mémoire," *Representations* 26 (1989): 7–24.

Pacholkiv, Svjatoslav. *Emanzipation durch Bildung: Entwicklung und gesellschaftliche Rolle der ukrainischen Intelligenz im habsburgischen Galizien (1890–1914)*. Vienna: Verlag für Geschichte und Politik, 2002.

Papierzyńska-Turek, Mirosława. *Sprawa ukraińska w Drugiej Rzeczypospolitej 1922–1926*. Cracow: Wydawnictwo Literackie, 1979.

Partacz, Czesław. *Od Badeniego do Potockiego: Stosunki Polsko-Ukraińskie w Galicji w latach 1888–1908*. Toruń: Wydawnictwo Adam Marszałek, 1996.

———. "Przyczyny i przebieg konfliktu Ukraińsko-Polskiego." *Przegląd Wschodni* 2 (1992/93): 841–49.

Pater, Ivan. "Naddniprjan'ska politychna emigratsija u L'vovi, pochatku XX stolittja." In *L'viv: Istorychni narysy*, 291–303.

———. "Povojennyj L'viv." In *L'viv: Istorychni narysy*, 506–19.

———. "Sojuz Vyzvolennja Ukraïny: zasnuvannja, politychna platforma ta orijentatsija." *Visnyk L'vivs'koho Universytetu: Serija Istorychna* 34 (1999): 331–39.

Pavlyshyn, Oleh Josyf. *Formuvannja ta dijal'nist' predstavnyts'kych orhaniv vlady ZUNR-ZOUNR (zhovten' 1918–cherven' 1919 rr.): Avtoreferat dissertatsiï na zdobuttja naukovoho stupenja kandydata istorychnych nauk*. L'viv: L'viv University, 2001.

Pawluczuk, Zdzisław. "Ukraińska Spółdzielczość w Polsce do 1939 roku." *Przegląd Wschodni* 2 (1992/93): 863–72.

Pelenski, Jaroslav. *Soviet Ukrainian Historiography after World War II: Jahrbücher für Geschichte Osteuropas* 12 (1964): 375–418.

Podhorodecki, Leszek. *Dzieje Lwowa*. Warsaw: Volumen, 1993.

Podraza. Antoni. , "Problem pograniczy w Europie Środkowo-Wschodniej (na przykładzie pogranicza polsko-ukraińskiego)," in *Prace Komisji Środkowoeuropejskiej Polskiej Akademii Umiejętności*, vol. 4 (Cracow: Polska Akademia Umiejętności, 1996), 106.

Pogonowski, Iwo Cyprian. *Jews in Poland: A Documentary History: The Rise of Jews as a Nation from Congressus Judaicus in Poland to the Knesset in Israel.* New York: Hippocrene Books, 1993.

Pohl, Dieter. "Die Ukraine im Zweiten Weltkrieg." *Österreichische Osthefte* 42, no. 3/4 (2000): 339–62.

———. *Nationalsozialistische Judenverfolgung in Ostgalizien 1941–1944: Organisation und Durchführung eines staatlichen Massenverbrechens.* Second edition. Munich: Oldenbourg, 1997.

Pollack, Martin. *Nach Galizien: Von Chassiden, Huzulen, Polen und Ruthenen.* Third edition. Vienna: Christian Brandstätter, 1994.

Polonsky, Antony. "A Failed Pogrom: The Demonstrations in Lwów, June 1929." In *The Jews of Poland between Two World Wars,* edited by Yisrael Gutmann, Ezra Mendelsohn, Jehuda Reinharz, and Chone Shemruk, 109–25. Hanover: Brandeis University Press, 1989.

———, ed. *Jews in Independent Poland 1918–1939.* London: The Littman Library of Jewish Civilization, 1994.

———. *Politics in Independent Poland, 1921–1939.* Oxford: Clarendon Press, 1972.

———. *The Jews in Poland and Russia,* vol. 3: 1914–2008. New York: Littmann Library, 2012.

Popiński, Krzysztof. "Ewakuacja więzień sowieckich z Kresów Wschodnich II Rzeczypospolitej w czerwcu i lipcu 1941 roku w świetle relacji świadków." *Wrocławskie Studia Wschodnie* 2 (1998): 133–50.

Popiński, Krzysztof, Aleksandr Kokurin, and Aleksandr Gurjanov. *Drogi śmierci: Ewakuacja więzień sowieckich z Kresów Wschodnich II Rzeczypospolitej w czerwcu i lipcu 1941.* Warsaw: Karta, 1995.

Potichnyj, Peter J. "Ukrainians in World War II Military Formations: An Overview." http://www.infoukes.com/upa/related/military.html.

Potichnyj, Peter J., and Howard Aster, eds. *Ukrainian-Jewish Relations in Historical Perspective.* Edmonton: Canadian Institute of Ukrainian Studies, 1988.

Prus, Edward. *Holocaust po Banderowsku.* Wrocław: Nortom, 1995.

Prusin, Alexander Victor. *Nationalizing a Borderland: War, Ethnicity, and Anti-Jewish Violence in East Galicia, 1914–1920.* Tuscaloosa: University of Alabama Press, 2005.

Prutsch, Ursula, and Klaus Zeyringer, eds. *Leopold von Andrian (1875–1951): Korrespondenzen, Notizen, Essays, Berichte.* Vienna: Böhlau, 2003.

Rabinowicz, Harry M. *The Legacy of Polish Jewry: A History of Polish Jews in the Inter-War Years, 1919–1939.* New York: T. Yoseloff, 1965.

Rader, Olaf B. "Der entführte Alexander: Über die Rolle von Leichen und Gräbern bei der Herrschaftslegitimation." *Zeitschrift für Geschichtswissenschaft* 45 (1997): 1061–85.

Röskau-Rydel, Isabel. *Deutsche Geschichte im Osten Europas: Galizien, Bukowina, Moldau.* Munich: Siedler, 2002.

———. *Kultur an der Peripherie des Habsburger Reiches: die Geschichte des Bildungswesens und der kulturellen Einrichtungen in Lemberg von 1772 bis 1848.* Wiesbaden: Harrassowitz, 1993.

Rossolinski-Liebe, Grzegorz. *Stepan Bandera: The Life and Afterlife of a Ukrainian Fascist: Fascism, Genocide and Cult.* Stuttgart: ibidem, 2014.

———. "Der Verlauf und die Täter des Lemberger Pogroms vom Sommer 1941," *Jahrbuch für Antisemitismusforschung*, 22 (2013): 207–43.

Rubl'jov, O. S., and Ju. A. Cherchenko. *Stalinshchyna i dolja zakhidnoukraïns'koï intelihentsiï.* Kiev: Naukova Dumka, 1994.

Rudling, Per Anders. "Historical Representations of the Wartime Accounts of the Activities of the OUN-UPA (Organization of Ukrainian Nationalists/Ukrainian Insurgent Army)." *East European Jewish Affairs* 36, no. 2 (2006): 163–89.

Rudnyts'ka, Milena. *Zakhidnja Ukraïna pid Bol'shevykami.* New York: Naukove tovarystvo imeni Shevchenka v Amerytsi, 1958.

Rutkowska, Ewa. *Wyznania i narodowości we Lwowie w latach 1857–1939 na tle ogólnej struktury demograficznej miasta.* Unpublished master's thesis, Uniwersytet Jagielloński, Cracow, 1993.

Sandkühler, Thomas. *"Endlösung" in Galizien: Der Judenmord in Ostpolen und die Rettungsinitiativen von Berthold Beitz 1941–1944.* Bonn: Dietz, 1996.

Sarasin, Philipp. *Geschichtswissenschaft und Diskursanalyse.* Frankfurt/Main: Suhrkamp, 2003.

Schall, Jakób. *Żydostwo Galicyjskie w czasie inwazji rosyjskiej (w latach 1914–1916).* L'viv: I. Madfes, 1936.

Schellack, Fritz. "Sedan- und Kaisergeburtstagsfeste." In *Öffentliche Festkultur*, edited by Dieter Düding et al., 278–97. Reinbek: Rowohlt, 1988.

Schenk, Dieter. *Der Lemberger Professorenmord und der Holocaust in Ostgalizien.* Bonn: Dietz, 2007.

Schivelbusch, Wolfgang. *Die Kultur der Niederlage: Der amerikanische Süden 1865—Frankreich 1871—Deutschland 1918.* Second edition. Berlin: A. Fest Verlag, 2001.

Schneider, Ute. *Politische Festkultur im 19. Jahrhundert: die Rheinprovinz von der französischen Zeit bis zum Ende des Ersten Weltkriegs (1806–1918).* Essen: Klartext, 1995.

Schoenfeld, Joachim. *Holocaust Memoirs: Jews in the Lwow Ghetto, the Janowski Concentration Camp, and as Deportees in Sibiria.* Hoboken, NJ: Ktav Publishing House, 1985.

Schreiner, Klaus H. "Tote—Helden—Ahnen: Die rituelle Konstruktion der Nation." *Historische Anthropologie* 9 (2001): 54-77.

Serczyk, Władysław A. "Die sowjetische und die 'polnische' Ukraine zwischen den Weltkriegen." In *Geschichte der Ukraine*, 202–23.

Shankovs'kyj, Lev. *Ukraïns'ka Halyts'ka Armija*. Second edition. L'viv: Naukove Tovarystvo imeni Shevchenka, 1999 (first edition: Winnipeg: 1974).

Sherman, Daniel J. "Bodies and Names: The Emergence of Commemoration in Interwar France." *American Historical Review* 103 (1998): 443–66.

Shvahuljak, Mykhajlo: "L'viv: vid stolytsi zakhidno-ukraïns'koï derzhavy do politychnoho tsentru Ukraïntsiv Halychyny (1918–1939 rr.)." In *L'viv: Misto—suspil'stvo—kul'tura*, vol. 3, 469–92.

———. "Shtrykhy do politychnoho portreta L'vova (druha polovyna XIX–pochatok XX st.)." In *Lwów: Miasto—społeczeństwo—kultura*, vol. 2, 183–194.

Siudut, Grzegorz. "Warunki kształcenia inteligencji w lwowskich gimnazjach państwowych w dobie autonomii 1867–1914." In *Lwów: Miasto—społeczeństwo—kultura*, vol. 1, 78–89.

Skrzypek, Józef. "Ukraińcy w Austrii podczas wielkiej wojny i geneza zamachu na Lwów." *Niepodległość* 20, no. 53 (1939): 349–87.

Slapnicka, Helmut. "Gemeindeautonomie in der Donaumonarchie und in den Nachfolgestaaten." *Österreichische Osthefte* 34, no. 1 (1992): 72–89.

Smith, Anthony D. *National Identity*. Reno: University of Nevada Press, 1991.

———. *Nationalism and Modernism: A Critical Survey of Recent Theories of Nations and Nationalism*. London: Routledge, 1998.

———. "The Origins of Nations." In *Becoming National*, 106–30.

Snopko, Jan. *Polskie towarzystwo gimnastyczne "Sokół" w Galicji 1867–1914*. Białystok: Wydawnictwo Uniwersytetu w Białymstoku, 1997.

Snyder, Timothy. *Bloodlands: Europe between Hitler and Stalin*. New York: Basic Books, 2010.

———. *Sketches from a Secret War: A Polish Artist's Mission to Liberate Ukraine*. New Haven, CT: Yale University Press, 2007.

———. *The Red Prince: The Secret Lives of a Habsburg Archduke*. London: Bodley Head, 2008.

———. "'To Resolve the Ukrainian Problem Once and for All': The Ethnic Cleansing of Ukrainians in Poland 1943–1947." *Journal of Cold War Studies* 1 (Spring 1999): 86–120.

Stachiw, Matthew, and Jaroslaw Sztendera. *Western Ukraine at the Turning Point of Europe's History 1918–1923*. New York: The Ukrainian Scientific Historical Library, 1969.

Steffen, Katrin. "Jüdische Identität in Polen zwischen den Weltkriegen: Studien zur polnischsprachigen jüdischen Presse." In *Nationalismus und nationale Identität in Ostmitteleuropa im 19. und 20. Jahrhundert*, edited by Bernard Linek and Kai Struve, 113–34. Marburg: Herder Institut, 2000.

———. *Jüdische Polonität: Ethnizität und Nation im Spiegel der polnischsprachigen jüdischen Presse, 1918–1939*. Vandenhoeck & Ruprecht, 2004.

Stegmann, Natali. "'Wie die Soldaten im Feld': Der widersprüchliche Kampf polnischer Frauen für 'Vaterland' und Frauenrechte im Ersten Weltkrieg." In *Geschlecht und Nationalismus in Mittel- und Osteuropa 1848–1918*, edited by Sophia Kemlein, 167–216. Osnabrück: Fibre, 2000.

Stehle, Hansjakob. "Der Lemberger Metropolit Šeptyc'kyj und die nationalsozialistische Politik in der Ukraine." *Vierteljahrshefte für Zeitgeschichte* 34 (1986): 407–25.

Stępień, Stanisław. "Wysiłki Polaków i Ukraińców na rzecz wzajemnego porozumienia w latach 1918–1939." *Warszawskie Zeszyty Ukrainoznawcze* 2 (1994): 96–105.

Stourzh, Georg. "Die Gleichberechtigung der Volksstämme als Verfassungsprinzip 1848–1867." In *Die Habsburgermonarchie 1848–1918*. Vol. 3, part 2: *Die Völker des Reiches*, edited by Adam Wandruszka and Peter Urbanitsch, 975–1206. Vienna: Österreichische Akademie der Wissenschaften, 1980.

Strembosz, Tomasz. *Rzeczpospolita podziemna: Społeczeństwo polskie a państwo podziemne 1939–1945*. Warsaw: Krupski i S-ka, 2000.

Struve, Kai. *Bauern und Nation in Galizien: Über Zugehörigkeit und soziale Emanzipation im 19. Jahrhundert*. Göttingen: Vandenhoeck & Ruprecht, 2005.

———. "Bauern und Nation in Ostmitteleuropa: Soziale Emanzipation und nationale Identität der galizischen Bauern im 19. Jahrhundert." In *Nationalismen in Europa: West- und Osteuropa im Vergleich*, edited by Ulrike von Hirschhausen and Jörn Leonhard, 347–71. Göttingen: Wallstein, 2001.

———. "Tremors in the Shatterzone of Empires: East Galicia in Summer 1941," in *Shatterzone of Empires: Coexistence and Violence in the German, Habsburg, Russian and Ottoman Borderlands*, edited by Omer Bartov and Eric D. Weitz, 463-84. Bloomington: Indiana University Press, 2013.

Subtelny, Orest. *Ukraine: A History*. Third edition. Toronto: University of Toronto Press, 2000.

Sudoł, Adam. *Początki sowietyzacji kresów wschodnich: Jesień 1939 roku*. Bydgoszcz: Wyższa Szkoła Pedagogiczna w Bydgoszczy, 1997.

Sukhyj, Oleksij. *Halychyna: mizh skhodom i zakhodom: Narysy istoriï XIX–pochatku XX st.* L'viv: L'vivsk'kyj Derzhavnyj Universytet, 1997.

Sword, Keith. *Deportation and Exile: Poles in the Soviet Union, 1939–48*. New revised edition. Houndsmills: Macmillan, 1996.

Sycz, Mirosław. *Spółdzielczość ukraińska w Galicji w okresie II wojny światowej*. Warsaw: Pracownia Wydawnicza, 1997.

Sysyn, Frank E. "Bohdan Chmel'nyc'kyjs Image in Ukrainian Historiography since Independence." *Österreichische Osthefte* 42, no. 3/4 (2000): 179–88.

Szarota, Tomasz. *Warschau unter dem Hakenkreuz: Leben und Alltag im besetzten Warschau 1.10.1939 bis 31.7.1944*. Paderborn: Schöningh, 1985.

Szczepański, Janusz. *Społeczeństwo Polski w walce z najazdem bolszewickim 1920 roku*. Warszawa: Pułtusk, 2000.

Szydłowska, Mariola. *Cenzura teatralna w Galicji w dobie autonomicznej 1860–1918*. Cracow: Universitas, 1995.

Tomasz, Strzembosz. *Rzeczpospolita podziemna: Społeczeństwo polskie a państwo podziemne 1939–1945*. Warsaw: Krupski I S-ka, 2000.

Tomaszewski, Jerzy. "Lwów, 22 listopada 1918." *Przegląd Historyczny* 75 (1984): 279–85.

———. *Rzeczpospolita wielu narodów*. Warsaw: Czytelnik, 1985.

Tomaszewski, Leszek. "Lwów—Listopad 1918: Niezwykłe losy pewnego dokumenty (Listy do Redakcji). *Dzieje Najnowsze* 25, no. 4 (1993): 163–73.

Torzecki, Ryszard. *Kwestia ukraińska w Polsce w latach 1923–1929*. Cracow: Wydawnictwo Literackie, 1989.

———. *Polacy i Ukraińcy: Sprawa ukraińska w czasie II wojny światowej na terenie II Rzeczypospolitej*. Warsaw: Wydawnictwo Naukowe PWN, 1993.

Trunk, Isaiah. *Judenrat: The Jewish Councils in Eastern Europe under Nazi Occupation*. New York: Macmillan, 1972.

Tyshchyk, B., and O. Vivcharenko. *Zakhidnoukraïns'ka Narodna Respublika 1918–1923 rr. (do 75-richja utvorennja i dijal'nosti)*. Kolomyja: Svit, 1993.

Ukraïns'ka Povstans'ka Armija i natsional'no-vyzvol'na borot'ba v Ukraïni u 1940–1950 r.: Materialy Vseukraïns'koï naukovoï konferentsiï 25-26 serpnia 1992 r. Kiev: Instytut Istoriï Ukraïny Akademiï Nauk Ukraïny, 1992.

Veryha, Vasyl'. *Vyzvol'ni zmahannja v Ukraïni 1914–1923 rr*. 2 vols. L'viv: Misioner, 1998.

Volyn' 1943: Borot'ba za zemlju. L'viv: Redaktsija zhurnalu "Ï", 2003.

Vulpius, Ricarda. *Nationalisierung der Religion: Russifizierungspolitik und ukrainische Nationsbildung 1860–1920*. Wiesbaden: Harrassowitz, 2005.

Węgierski, Jerzy. *Komendy lwowskiego obszaru i okręgu Armii Krajowej 1941–1944*. Cracow: Platan, 1997.

———. *Lwów pod okupacją sowiecką 1939–1941*. Warsaw: Editions Spotkania, 1991.

Wehrhahn, Torsten. *Die Westukrainische Volksrepublik: Zu den polnisch-ukrainischen Beziehungen und dem Problem der ukrainischen Staatlichkeit in den Jahren 1918 bis 1923*. Berlin: Weißensee Verlag, 2004.

Weiner, Amir. *Making Sense of War: The Second World War and the Fate of the Bolshevik Revolution*. Princeton, NJ: Princeton University Press, 2001.

Weiss, Aharon. "The Holocaust and the Ukrainian Victims." In *Mosaic of Victims: Non-Jews Persecuted and Murdered by the Nazis*, edited by Michael Berenbaum, 109–15. New York: New York University Press, 1990.

———. "Jewish-Ukrainian Relations in Western Ukraine during the Holocaust." In *Ukrainian-Jewish Relations in Historical Perspective*, 409–20.
Wendland, Anna Veronika. *Die Russophilen in Galizien: Ukrainische Konservative zwischen Österreich und Russland 1848–1915*. Vienna: Verlag der Österreichischen Akademie der Wissenschaften, 2001.
———. "Galizien: Westen des Ostens, Osten des Westens: Annäherung an eine ukrainische Grenzlandschaft." Österreichische Osthefte 42, no. 3/4 (2000): 389–421.
Wereszycki, Henryk. *Historia polityczna Polski 1864–1918*. Wrocław: Wiedza, 1990.
———. *Pod berłem Habsburgów: Zagadnienia narodowościowe*. Cracow: Wydawnictwo Literackie, 1975.
Wierzbieniec, Wacław. "Związek Żydów Uczestników Walk o Niepodległość Polski we Lwowie (1932–1939)." In *Lwów: Miasto—społeczeństwo—kultura*, vol. 2, 281–305.
Winnicka, H. "Lwowskie środowisko historyczne 1918–1939." In Środowiska historyczne II Rzeczypospolitej. Part. 5, edited by Jerzy Maternicki, 121–37. Warsaw: Centralny Ośrodek Metodyczny Studiów Nauk Politycznych, 1990.
Winter, Jay. *Sites of Memory, Sites of Mourning: The Great War in European Cultural History*. Cambridge: Cambridge University Press, 1995.
Winter, Jay, and Jean-Louis Robert, eds. *Capital Cities at War: Paris, London, Berlin 1914–1919*. Cambridge: Cambridge University Press, 1997.
Witz-Margulies, Bronisława. "Jan Kazimierz University 1936–1939: A Memoir." *Polin* 14 (2001): 223–36.
Wnuk, Rafał. "Polska konspiracja antysowiecka na Kresach Wschodnich II RP w latach 1939–1941 i 1944–1952. In *Tygiel narodów*, 157–249.
Wróbel, Piotr. "Double Memory: Poles and Jews after the Holocaust." *East European Politics and Societies* 11, no. 3 (Fall 1997): 560–574.
———. "The Jews of Galicia under Austrian-Polish Rule 1869–1918." *Austrian History Yearbook* 15 (1994): 97–138.
Yekelchyk, Serhy. "How the 'Iron Minister' Kaganovich Failed to Discipline Ukrainian Historians: A Stalinist Ideological Campaign Reconsidered." *Nationalities Papers* 27 (1994): 579–604.
———. "Stalinist Patriotism as Imperial Discourse: Reconciling the Ukrainian and Russian 'Heroic Pasts,' 1939–1945." *Kritika* 3 (Winter 2000): 51–80.
Young, James E. "Zwischen Geschichte und Erinnerung." In *Das soziale Gedächtnis: Geschichte—Erinnerung—Tradierung*, edited by Harald Welzer, 41–62. Hamburg: Hamburger Edition, 2001.
Zabrowarny, Stefan. "Instytucjonalny rozwój ukraińskiego ruchu narodowego we Galicji w latach 1864–1914." *Warszawskie Zeszyty Ukrainoznawcze* 2 (1994): 69–81.

Żaliński, Henryk W., and Kazimierz Karolczak *Lwów: Miasto—społeczeństwo—kultura*. Vol. 1. Cracow: Wydawnictwo Naukowe Wyższej Szkoły Pedagogicznej, 1995.

———. *Lwów: Miasto—społeczeństwo—kultura*. Vol. 2. Cracow: Wydawnictwo Naukowe Wyższej Szkoły Pedagogicznej, 1998.

———. *Lwów: Miasto—społeczeństwo—kultura*. Vols. 4–5. Cracow: Wydawnictwo Naukowe Uniwersytetu Pedagogicznego, 2002, 2005.

Żbikowski, Andrzej. "Jewish Reaction to the Soviet Arrival in the Kresy in September 1939." *Polin* 13 (2000): 62–72.

———. "Konflikty narodowościowe na polskich Kresach Wschodnich (1939–1941) w relacjach żydowskich bieżeńców." In *Tygiel narodów*, 409–427.

———. "Lokalne pogromy Żydów w czerwcu i lipcu 1941 roku na wschodnich rubieżach II Rzeczypospolitej." *Biuletyn Żydowskiego Instytutu Historycznego* 2/3 (1992): 3–18.

Zielecki, Alojzy. "Żydzi w polskim ruchu niepodległościowym w Galicji przed Pierwszą Wojną Światową i w czasie jej trwania." In *Żydzi w Małopolsce*, 273–88.

Żurawski vel Grajewski, Przemysław Piotr. *Sprawa Ukraińska na konferencji pokojowej w Paryżu w roku 1919*. Warsaw: Semper, 1995.

Zyblikiewicz, Lidia. *Małżeństwa we Lwowie w latach 1857–1939*. Unpublished anuscript, University of Cracow.

Żyndul, Jolanda. *Zajścia antyżydowskie w Polsce w latach 1935–1937*. Warsaw: Fundacja im. K. Kelles-Krauza, 1994.

Index

Agid, Moses	Inhabitant of L'viv	161
Agid, Stella	Teacher in L'viv	161
Ahne, Theodor	Police agent	67, 75
Allenstein (Olsztyn)		187
Allerhand, Jonatan (Joachim) (1897–1970)	Lawyer, son of Maurycy Allerhand	291–92
Allerhand, Maurycy (1868–1942)	Professor of law and chairman of the Jewish Religious Community in L'viv (1929–?)	290–92, 305, 316
Andrian zu Werburg, Leopold von (1875–1951)	Austrian diplomat	20, 56, 60, 64–66, 74
Askenaze, Tobiasz (1863–1920)	Chairman of the L'viv Bar Association, vice-mayor of L'viv	74, 169–72, 174, 231
Bachyns'kyj, Lev (1872–1930)	Chairman of the Ukrainian Radical Party	78
Bach-Zelewski, Erich von dem (1899–1972)	SS-Obergruppenführer	314
Badeni, Kazimierz (1846–1909)	Count, governor of Galicia (October 1888 – September 1895) and Austrian minister-president	31
Bakhturina, Aleksandra Ju.	Historian	3
Bandera, Stepan (1909–1959)	Leader of the OUN-Bandera	217, 247, 289–90, 296–99, 302, 311, 315, 318–19, 373
Bandurski, Władysław (1865–1932)	Roman Catholic suffragan bishop	109
Baran, Stepan (1879–1953)	Ukrainian lawyer and politician (UNDO)	144
Bartel, Kazimierz (1882–1941)	Professor of mathematics, rector of L'viv Technical University, Polish minister-president (1926–1930)	280, 300

Barthélemy, Marie Joseph (1867–1951)	French general	170–71, 182
Barvins'kyj, Vasyl' (1888–1963)	Ukrainian composer	341
Bazili, Nikolaj A. (1883–1963)	Russian chamberlain	28, 31, 42, 59
Beck, Adolf (1863–1942)	Physiologist, rector of L'viv University	33, 57, 306
Bełżec		304–06, 309, 317
Berdyczów (Berdychiv)		181
Berger, Peter	Sociologist	2
Bernstein, Izak	Inhabitant of Nadwórna	25
Biała (Bielitz)		69, 98
Białynia-Chołodecki, Józef (1852–1934)	Historian from L'viv	98
Bieliński, Zdzisław (1908–1945)	Doctor and lecturer of physiology	245
Bielski, Wacław	Polish lieutenant-colonel	172
Bilak, Stepan (1890–1950)	Ukrainian national democratic deputy to the Sejm	311, 323–24
Bilczewski, Józef (1860–1923)	Roman Catholic archbishop of L'viv	29, 31, 55, 65, 68, 81, 84, 149, 162–63, 176
Bilets'kyj, Andrij (1847–1927)	Vicar general of the Greek Catholic Church	53–54, 81
Biliński, Leon (1846–1923)	Austrian-Hungarian minister of finance, chairman of the Polish club in the Austrian House of Deputies	74
Bisanz, Alfred (1890–1951)	Advisor for Ukrainian affairs of the governor of the Distrikt Galizien	310
Bitschan, Jurek (1904–1918)	Youngest "defender of Lwów"	222, 224, 236
Bobrinskij, Georgij A. (1863–1928)	Military governor-general of Galicia during Russian occupation, 1914/15	25–29, 31–34, 37, 39–43, 49–50, 52–55, 57, 62
Bobrzyński, Michał (1849–1935)	Governor of Galicia (May 1908 – April 1913)	10, 18
Bodenstein, Mechel	Inhabitant of Rymanów	72
Böhm-Ermoli, Eduard Freiherr von (1856–1941)	Austrian field marshall	77
Bohorodczany (Bohorodchany)		53
Bohun, Ivan (ca. 1618–1664)	Cossack colonel	269
Borejsza, Jerzy (1905–1952)	Polish author	279

Borysław (Boryslav)		72, 82, 102, 177
Boy-Żeleński, Tadeusz (1874–1941)	Polish author and literary critic	279–80
Brandl, Josef (1901–?)	Head of the administration of the District of Galicia (Distrikt Galizien) under German occupation	323
Braude, Leib	Rabbi in L'viv	40, 81, 169
Brest-Litovsk (Brest-Litowsk)		85, 87–88, 95, 100–01, 103–04, 109–10
Brody		25, 56–57, 180, 325
Brusilov, Aleksej A. (1853–1926)	Russian general	19
Buber, Rafał (1866–1931)	Member of L'viv City Council	166–67
Buczacz (Buchach)		25, 190, 293
Bukovina		10, 85, 88, 96, 102, 108, 139–40, 144, 146, 154, 177–78
Bulanda, Edmund (1882–1951)	Archeologist and rector of L'viv University (1938/39)	244
Bürger, Izaak	Lawyer in L'viv	234
Canaris, Wilhelm (1887–1945)	Admiral and head of the German military security service (Abwehr)	248
Carpathians (Karpathen)		7, 17, 55
Chajes, Wiktor (1875–1940)	Banker and vice-mayor of L'viv (1930–1939)	169, 174, 219, 233–34, 243, 264
Charles I (1887–1922)	Emperor of Austria and King of Hungary	79, 86, 94–95, 108, 139
Charles XII (1682–1718)	King of Sweden	36, 342
Chełm, Cholm region		48, 76, 79, 88, 95–96, 105, 218, 273, 290
Chikhachev, Dmitrij N. (1876–1909)	Deputy to the Russian State Duma	33
Chlamtacz, Marceli (1865–1947)	Professor of law at L'viv university, vice-mayor of L'viv (1918–1927)	23, 31, 69, 141, 311, 324
Chołojów		180
Colard, Hermann von (1857–1916)	Austrian general and governor of Galicia (August 1915 – April 1916)	66–67, 72

Cracow		18, 28, 74, 77, 80, 82, 86–87, 89–90, 98, 104, 138, 143, 148, 150, 160, 177, 187, 213, 215, 289, 298, 301, 312
Curzon, Georg (1859–1925)	British foreign minister	187, 193
Czernin, Ottokar (1872–1932)	Foreign minister of Austria-Hungary	88, 90
Czernowitz (Chernivtsi)		28, 43–44, 57, 62, 76, 108
Czortków		190
Daszyński, Ignacy (1866–1936)	Chairman of the Polish Galician Social Democratic Party	138, 187
Dębice		25
Delatyn, Deljatyn		25
Dentel, Jakub	Inhabitant of L'viv, survived the Holocaust	291
Detsykevych, Volodymyr (1865–1946)	Vice-governor of Galicia in 1918	146
Diamand, Herman (1860–1931)	Galician social democrat	74, 82
Diamand, Jakób	Vice-chairman of the Jewish Religious Community in L'viv	39–40
Diller, Erich von (1859–1926)	Governor of Galicia (April 1916 – March 1917)	76
Djatlov, M. D.	Head of the NKVD of L'viv region	265
Dmowski, Roman (1864–1939)	Chairman of the Polish National-Democratic Party	18, 182, 187
Dobromil (Dobromił)		44, 92
Dolina		72, 184
Dontsov, Dmytro (1883–1973)	Ukrainian political thinker	217, 230
Drohobycz (Drohobych)		72, 94, 184, 307
Dubkovcy (Dubkivtsy, Dubivtsy)		34
Dudykevych, Volodymyr F. (1861–1922)	Leader of the Galician Russophiles	46
Dymowicz, Włodzimierz (?)	Member of the High Court in Warsaw	172
Dziędzielewicz. Józef (?)	Roman Catholic priest	83
East Prussia		47, 55

Eremenko, Fjodor I.	Chairman of L'viv city soviet (council) (1939–1941)	264, 277
Ernst zu Eickern, Wilhelm (1896–1955)	German officer	290
Evlogij (Georgievskij, V. S., 1868–1946)	Russian Orthodox archbishop of Galicia	47–50, 52–55
Fedak, Stepan (1861–1937)	Ukrainian lawyer and politician, father of Stepan Fedak jr.	81, 152
Fedak, Stepan (1901–1945)	Ukrainian nationalist (tried to kill Piłsudski and the voivode of L'viv, Grabowski in 1921)	214
Feinberg (Fejnberg), David (1860–1916)	Member of the central committee of the Jewish Colonisation Society in St. Petersburg	39
Feldstein (Felsztyn), Herman (ca. 1863–1935)	Engineer in L'viv	75
Feldstein (Felsztyn), Roman (1901–1919)	"Defender of Lwów"	224
Feldstein (Felsztyn, Tadeusz (1894–1963)	"Defender of Lwów"	233
Finsterbusch, Leon (?)	Merchant from Sambor	73
Fischer, Eduard von (1862–1935)	Major general of the k.u.k. gendarmerie	102, 104, 106, 109–10
Fishman, Lala (1922–2011)	Inhabitant of L'viv and Holocaust survivor	
Foucault, Michel (1926–1984)	French philosopher	237
Franko, Ivan (1856–1916)	Ukrainian author and politician	266, 269
Franz Josef I. (1830–1916)	Emperor of Austria and King of Hungary	29–30
Friedman, Philip (Filip) (1901–1960)	Historian and Holocaust survivor	316, 377
Friedrich of Austria (1856–1936)	Archduke, commander-in-chief of the k. u. k. Army	21
Gałecki. Kazimierz (1863–1941)	Delegate of the Polish government of Eastern Lesser Poland	189
Gdynia		213
Gember, Maria von	Inhabitant of L'viv	20, 30, 38, 59, 62
Giesl Freiherr von Gieslingen, Wladimir (1860–1936)	Liaison officer of the k. u. k. Foreign Ministry to the Army Headquarters	20
Głąbiński, Stanisław (1862–1941)	Professor of Law at L'viv University, Polish national democratic politician	89, 138, 270

Glanz, Jakób	Head of the Jewish Religious Community in Przemyśl	74
Glazewski, (?)	District commissioner in Dolina	72
Gorbatjuk, Volodymyr T.	Ukrainian historian, dean of the Faculty of History, L'viv university	
Goremykin, Ivan L. (1837–1917)	Russian minister-president	42, 45
Gorlice		57
Grabowski, Kazimierz (1866–1932)	Austrian government commissioner for L'viv (1915–1916), Voivode of L'viv region (1921–1924)	69, 77, 214–15
Grabski, Stanisław (1871–1949)	Professor of economy at L'viv University, Polish national democratic politician and minister of education	28, 31–32, 65, 215, 270
Grekov, Oleksander (1875–1958)	Commander-in-chief of the Ukrainian-Galician Army since May 1919	183
Gródek-Jagielloński (Gródek, Horodok)		94, 167
Grünbaum, Izaak (1879–1970)	Zionist politician	218
Grunwald		282
Grzimek (or Grzymek), Josef (1905–1950)	SS-Unterscharführer, commander of "Judenlager Lemberg"	306
Grzybów		169
Guttmann, Samuel	Rabbi of the progressive Jewish community in L'viv	81, 169, 174
Haller, Józef (1873–1960)	Commander of the II Brigade of the Polish Legions, commander of Haller's Army of Polish prisoners of war in France	167, 182, 191
Halych (Halicz)		47
Hankevych, Lev (1883–1962)	Ukrainian social democrat	149, 166
Hankevych, Mykola (1867–1931)	Ukrainian social democrat	44, 162–63
Hauser, Bernard	Rabbi in L'viv	19, 40
Heczko, Alma	Inhabitant of L'viv	236, 272
Heinze, Eduard (1863–?)	German consul in L'viv	59, 81, 144, 155, 162
Herschtal, Samuel	Jewish social democrat	233

Heydrich, Reinhard (1904–1942)	Head of the security service (SD) and of the security police (SiPo) and head of the Reich Main Security Office (Reichssicherheitshauptamt)	291, 293–94
Himka, John-Paul	Historian	8
Hintz, L.	Rittmeister of k. u. k. gendarmerie	95–96, 105, 108
Hitler, Adolf (1889–1945)	National socialist politician and dictator of Germany	245, 247–48, 269, 297, 299–300, 310, 323–24, 328
Hollender, Tadeusz (1910–1943)	Author	279
Höller, Egon (1907–?)	Stadthauptmann (city captain) of L'viv (1942–1944)	301, 323
Hołówko, Tadeusz 1889–1931)	Polish politician	217
Hrubieszów (Hrubeshiv)		79
Hrushets'kyj, Ivan S. (1904–1982)	Secretary of the Communist Party of L'viv region (1944–1951, 1961/62)	332, 340–41
Hrushevs'kyj, Mychajlo (1866–1934)	Professor of history at L'viv University, chairman of the Central Rada (council) of the Ukrainian People's Republic	85, 267, 340–41
Hryciuk, Grzegorz	Historian	3, 271–73, 288,
Hryshchuk, Leonid S. (1906–1960)	First Secretary of the Communist Party of L'viv city and region (1939–1941)	264
Husiatyn (Husjatyn)		25
Huyn, Karl von (1857–1938)	Last Austrian governor of Galicia (July 1917–November 1918)	69, 88, 90, 92–93, 104, 107, 139, 142–44, 146
Il'nyts'kyj, Roman	Member of OUN-Bandera	298
Indruch, Rudolf (1892–1927)	Architect of the "Cemetery of the Defenders of Lwów"	235
Irzyk, Franciszek	Vice-mayor of L'viv	264
Janushkevich, Nikolaj N. (1868–1918)	Chief of the General Staff of the Russian Army	25–26, 28, 32–33, 42–43, 47–49
Janusz, Bohdan (1888–1930)	Historian from L'viv	26, 35, 41–42, 61
Jarosław (Jaroslau)		94
Jasiński, Mieczysław	Polish policeman	284
Jasna Góra		220
Jaworów		190

Jędrzejewicz, Janusz (1885–1951)	Polish minister-president (1933–1934)	217
Józewski, Henryk (1892–1981)	Voivode of Wolhynia	216
Jóźwiak, Wanda	Inhabitant of L'viv	261, 282
Kalytovs'kyj, Je.	Diarist from Stryj	61
Kam'janets'-Podil's'k (Kamieniec-Podolski)		183
Kamionka-Strumilowa (Kamionka-Bużanska, Kamjanka-Buz'ka)		64
Katyn, Katyškov, Leonidnar M.h von demrianhen Partei der Sowjetunion und st)rń		270, 279
Katzmann, Friedrich (1906–1957)	SS-Gruppenführer, Head of SS and police (SS- und Polizeiführer) of the Distric of Galicia (Distrikt Galizien)	298, 306–07
Kazakhstan		271, 280
Keller, Leib	Inhabitant of Rymanów	72
Khmel'nyts'kyj, Bohdan (ca. 1596–1657)	Cossack hetman	175, 223, 227, 342, 373
Khomyshyn, Hryrorij (1867–1947)	Greek Catholic bishop of Stanyslaviv, Stanislau, Stanisławów	67
Khrushchev, Nikita S. (ukr.: Mykyta S. Khrushchov) (1894–1971)	First secretary of the central committee of the Communist Party of the Ukrainian SSR	265, 278, 333
Kiev, Kyiv, Kyïv		4, 50, 57, 95, 98, 178, 188, 263, 274, 299, 330, 334, 338–41
Klof, Michał	Polish police corporal	261
Klymkova, Anastasja	Inhabitant of L'viv	291
Koch, Hans (1894–1959)	Officer of the German military security service "Abwehr"	290
Koerber, Ernest von (1850–1919)	Austrian minister-president	78
Kolomea (Kołomyja, Kolomyja)		25, 182
Konovalets, Jevhen (1891–1938)	Leader of the Organization of Ukrainian Nationalists (1929–1938)	217, 246–47
Korduba, Myron (1867–1947)	Ukrainian historian	340
Kornijchuk, Oleksander (1905–1972)	Ukrainian author	266

Korytowski, Witold (1850–1923)	Governor of Galicia (May 1913 – August 1915)	19–20, 69, 79
Kościuszko, Tadeusz (1746–1817)	Polish general and leader of the 1794 uprising	77, 83–84, 268
Koselleck, Reinhart	Historian	2
Koss	Public prosecutor	172
Kossak, Hryhorij (1882–1932)	Colonel of the Ukrainian riflemen	155
Kossak, Wojciech (1857–1942)	Polish painter	221
Kostel'nyk, Havryïl (1886–1948)	Greek Catholic priest	337–38
Kovpak, Sidor (Sydir) A. (1887–1967)	Soviet general and commander of partisan units	314
Kozłowski, Leon (1892–1944)	Archeologist and Polish minister-president 1934/35	270
Kramarz, Henryka	Historian	3
Krosigk, Ernst-Anton von (1898–1945)	German general	295
Kryp"jakevych, Ivan (1886–1967)	Ukrainian historian	338, 340–41
Kubijovych, Volodymyr (1900–1985)	Geograph and chairman of the Ukrainian Central Committee (under Nazi occupation)	289, 310
Kuchma, Leonid (b. 1938)	President of Ukraine (1994–2005)	373
Kühlmann, Richard von (1873–1948)	State secretary in the German Foreign Office (1917/18)	88
Kujath, Hans (1907–1963?)	SS-Hauptsturmführer, city captain of L'viv in 1941/42	298, 301
Kulczyński, Stanisław (1895–1975)	Botanist and rector of L'viv university (1936–1938)	244
Kursk		51
Kuz'ma, Oleksa	Eyewitness of the "Defense of Lwów"	145, 155
Lanckorońska, Karolina (1898–2002)	Polish art historian and countess	266, 274, 276, 279
Łancut		108
Landesberg, Markus (?–1939)	Student of the Polytechnical University in L'viv	245
Langner, Władysław (1896–1972)	Polish general, commander of Polish troops in L'viv	260
Lasch, Karl (1904–1942)	Governor of District Galicia in 1941/42	298, 301

Lashenko, V. Sh.	Head of the NKVD of L'viv region	265
Lec, Stanisław Jerzy (1909–1966)	Polish author	279
Lenin, Vladimir Il'ich (1870–1924)	Chairman of the Council of People's Commissars of the Russian Federative Socialist Soviet Republic	188, 263, 265, 269, 275, 342, 377
Lerner, Jakob	Inhabitant of Rymanów	72
Levyts'kyj, Jaroslav (1878–1961)	Greek Catholic Priest	21, 35, 42, 46, 56, 58, 63, 70
Levyts'kyj, Jevhen (1870–1925)	Ukrainian national democratic politician	85
Levyts'kyj, Kost' (1859–1941)	Chairman of the Ukrainian National Democratic Party	63, 75, 78–81, 84, 93–95, 110, 140, 142, 145, 148–50, 270, 278
Levyts'kyj, Kyryl	Greek Catholic priest	45, 59
Lewartowska, Zofja	Polish author	222–23
Lewin, Aron (1879–1941)	Chief rabbi in Rzeszów	73
Leżajsk		108
Liff, Aron	Inhabitant of Rymanów	72
Liff, Nathan	Inhabitant of Rymanów	72
Ljubchenko, Arkadij (1899–1945)	Ukrainian author	
Łódź		218
Losacker, Ludwig (1906–1991)	SS-Obersturmbannführer	298
Lublin		79, 88, 103, 240, 331
Luckmann, Thomas	Sociologist	2
Łuczycki, Zdsisław	Roman Catholic priest	103
Lysnych		308
Makarejko	Head of L'viv economic administration during Soviet occupation	277
Maklakov, Nikolaj A. (1871–1918)	Minister of the interior of the Russian Empire	47
Malyts'ka, Konstantina (1872–1947)	Ukrainian author and teacher	56, 58, 61
Manuil'skij, Dmitrij Z. (Dmytro Z. Manuïl's'kyj, 1883–1959)	Soviet politician	341

Marienwerder		187
Maschler, Ilana (1912–2003)	Inhabitant of L'viv and Holocaust survivor	273
Mazepa, Ivan (1639–1709)	Cossack hetman in left-bank Ukraine	36, 342
Meisel, Adolf	Butcher in L'viv	160
Mel'nyk (Melnyk), Andrij (1890–1964)	Leader of the Organisation of Ukrainian Nationalists (Melnyk-faction)	247, 289, 298–99, 302
Melen', Teofil' (1879–1915)	Ukrainian social democrat	41
Merkulov, Vsevolod (1895–1953)	Deputy people's commissar of the NKVD	265
Mickiewicz, Adam (1798–1955)	Polish poet	77, 86–87, 90, 92, 138, 142, 185, 240, 246–47, 266, 268, 280–81
Mikhail Aleksandrovich Romanov (1878–1918)	Russian grand-duke, commander of the "Wild Division"	30
Minsk		187
Moscow		4, 44, 263, 274–75, 280, 286, 330, 334, 338, 339
Mroczkowski, Józef	Polish policeman	261
Nadwórna (Nadvirna)		25
Nadziakiewicz, Marceli	Mayor of Rymanów	72
Nazaruk, Osyp (1883–1940)	Ukrainian politican, lawyer and journalist	278
Neumann, Józef (1857–1932)	Mayor of L'viv (1911–1914, 1919–1927)	19, 28, 232
Neu-Sandez (Nowy Sącz)		92
Nieborski, Antoś	"Defender of Lwów"	222
Niemiec, Jan	Teacher and author	222
Niezabitowski, Stanisław (1860–1941)	Lord Marshall (Landesmarschall) of the Galician diet	86, 148–50
Nikolaj II. Romanov (1868–1918)	Emperor of Russia	29, 48–49, 55
Nikolaj Nikolaevich Romanov (1856–1929)	Grand-Duke, Commander-in-Chief of the Russian Army	28, 43, 48,
Nimchuk, Ivan (1891–1956)	Editor-in-chief of the Ukrainian daily *Dilo*	238–39
Nowy Targ		92

Oberländer, Theodor (1905–1998)	Expert for Ukraine of the High Command of the German Army (Wehrmacht)	311
Olfer'ev, Vasilij V.	Russian diplomat	61
Omeljanovych-Pavlenko, Mychajlo (1878–1952)	Commander-in-chief of the Ukrainian Galician Army	179
Ortwin, Ostap (1876–1942)	Polish journalist and literary critic	279
Ostashkov		270
Ostrowski, Adam (1911–1977)	Delegate of the Polish government-in-exile (London) in L'viv	331
Ostrowski, Stanisław (1892–1982)	Mayor of L'viv (1936–1939)	247, 264
Paderewski, Ignacy Jan (1866–1941)	Pianist and Polish minister-president (prime minister) in 1919	168, 171–72, 182
Palestine		328
Paliïv, Dmytro (1896–1944)	Ukrainian nationalist and Hauptsturmführer of the SS-Division Galicia (Galizien)	144, 230, 247
Pan'kivs'kyj, Konstantin or Kost' (Pankovskyj) (1897–1973)	Head of the L'viv representation of the Ukrainian Main Council, Son of Kost' Pan'kivs'kyj	302, 310, 312
Paris		57, 182, 187, 333
Parnas, Emil	Acting chairman of the Jewish Religious Community in L'viv	74, 189
Pasternak, Leon (1910–1969)	Polish author	279
Pavlyk, Mykhajlo (1853–1915)	Ukrainian politician and author	46
Pavlyshyn, Oleh	Historian	177
Petljura, Symon (1879–1926)	Leader of the Directorate (head of government) of the Ukrainian People's Republic (1918–1921)	178, 183, 188–93, 292, 294, 309
Petrushevych, Jevhen (1863–1940)	President of the West Ukrainian People's Republic	78–79, 85, 96, 110, 140–41, 178, 183
Pieracki, Bronisław (1895–1934)	Polish minister of the interior	217, 300
Pieracki, Jan (1872–1940)	National democratic councilor of L'viv city council and member of the Polish parliament	233
Piłsudski, Józef (1867–1935)	Polish politician and head of state	90–91, 101, 144, 162, 168, 171–72, 187–88, 193, 214–16, 218, 226, 243

Piniński, Leon Graf (1857–1938)	Governor of Galicia (March 1898 – June 1903)	31, 86
Pius XII (1876–1958)	Pope	293, 306
Podlasie		88, 96, 209, 218, 314
Podzamcze		144
Poljans'kyj, Jurij I. (1892–1975)	Geograph, acting mayor of L'viv (1941–1944)	295
Poltava		299
Pommerenke, Karl	SS Rottenführer	314
Popiński, Krzystof	Historian	288
Posen/Poznań		32, 47, 82, 167, 176, 187, 191
Potocki, Andrzej (1861–1908)	Count, governor of Galicia (June 1903 – April 1908)	9–10
Prague		143, 247
Proweller, Samuel (?–1939)	Student of the Polytechnical University in L'viv	245
Prystor, Aleksander (1874–1941)	Polish minister-president (1931–1933)	270
Przemyśl		20, 28–29, 42, 44, 55, 57, 61, 63, 72, 74–76, 91–95, 101–02, 104–05, 107, 177
Putrament, Jerzy (1910–1986)	Polish author	279
Racławice		77
Racziewicz, Władysław (1885–1947)	President of the Polish government-in-exile	282
Radom		298, 301
Radymno		92
Radziechów (Radekhiv)		180
Rakovs'kyj, Christian (1873–1941)	Bulgarian socialist, Soviet politician, head of the second Soviet Ukrainian government	189
Rarańcza		88
Rawa-Ruska (Rava-Rus'ka)		64, 92, 101–02
Rawicz, Salomon	Inhabitant of L'viv	161
Reich, Leon (1879–1929)	Zionist politician	218
Reinlender, Józef (?–1941)	Head of Police (Polizeidirektor) in L'viv	73, 77, 81, 89, 102–03, 105, 144, 189

Rhineland		245
Riedl, Tadeusz (b. 1933)	Inhabitant of L'viv	270
Riga		193
Riml von Altrosenburg, Franz (1867–	Austrian major general	63, 65, 70, 77
Rinaldini, Rinaldo	Italian robber captain in the novel 'Rinaldo Rinaldini – Räuberhauptmann" by Christian August Vulpius (1799)	176
Rohatyn		25
Romanchuk, Julijan (1842–1932)	Chairman of the Ukrainian National Council	78
Roques, Karl von (1880–1949)	German general and commander of the rear area of Army Group South	295, 298
Różycki, Stanisław	Jewish refugee from L'viv	279, 284–85, 288, 291
Rücker, Jakob	Inhabitant of Rymanów	72
Rudki		189
Rudnyts'ka, Milena (1892–1976)	Ukrainian feminist	286
Rudnyts'kyj, Mychajlo (1889–1975)	Ukrainian author and scientist	341
Russocki, Zygmunt Maria (1897–1952)	Count, diarist	22, 26
Rutowski, Tadeusz (1852–1918)	Vice-mayor and mayor of L'viv during the First World War	25, 28–29, 31, 33–34, 36–37, 57, 80–84, 86, 89
Sabler, Vladimir K. (1847–1923)	Ober-procurator of the Holy Synod	47
Sambor (Sambir)		44, 73, 181, 184, 325
Sanok		73
Schaff, Szymon (ca. 1838–1917)	Chairman of the Jewish Religious Community in L'viv	74
Schall, Jakób (1890–1941)	Educator and historian	41, 63
Schleicher, Filip (1870–1932)	Vice-mayor of L'viv during the First World War	28, 39–40, 57, 73, 98–100, 149–50
Schöngarth, Karl Eberhard (1903–1946)	SS Brigadeführer and brigadier general of the police	300
Schorr, Mojżesz (1874–1941)	Historian	169
Schreiber, Dawid (1871–1941)	Zionist politician	232–33

Schreiber, Israel	Inhabitant of Rymanów	72
Seelos, Gebhard (1901–1984)	German consul in L'viv	248
Seidler, Ernst Freiherr von Feuchtenegg (1862–1931)	Austrian minister-president	85, 100
Semchyshyn, Myroslav	Ukrainian literary scholar	269, 286, 293
Serhijenko, V. T.	Major und head of the NKVD of L'viv region	165
Serov, Ivan A. (1905–1990)	Deputy People's Commissar of the NKVD	265
Shchurat, Vasyl' (1871–1948)	Literary scholar and rector of the secret Ukrainian University in L'viv	238
Sheptyts'kyj, Andrij (1865–1944)	Count, Greek Catholic archbishop of L'viv	8, 18, 26, 46, 51, 58, 67, 81, 85, 139, 146, 148, 176, 189, 247, 273, 293, 297, 302, 306, 308, 318, 337, 341
Sheremetev, Sergej (1880–1968)	Colonel, Russian military governor of L'viv in 1914	26–27
Shevchenko, Taras (1814–1861)	Ukrainian poet	94, 152, 241, 267, 303, 312, 377
Siberia		37, 258, 271, 333
Sichyns'kyj, Myroslav (1887–1968)	Ukrainian student, assassin of Governor Potocki in 1908	9
Sienkiewicz, Henryk (1846–1916)	Polish author	220, 282
Sikorski, Władysław (1881–1943)	Polish minister of war, minister-president of the Polish government-in-exile	167, 171, 236, 282, 324
Silbermann, Markus Leib	Inhabitant of Rymanów	72
Silesia		47, 154, 187, 245
Simon, Binem	Inhabitant of Rymanów	72
Skarbek, Aleksander (1874–1921)	Count, Polish national democratic politician and estate owner	86
Skarbek, Stanisław (1780–1848)	Count, estate owner and benefactor	244
Skole		92
Skoropads'kyj, Pavlo (1873–1945)	Hetman of the Ukrainian state	95, 109, 248
Slipyj, Josyf (1892–1984)	Greek Catholic archbishop	337
Śniatyn (Snjatyn)		44, 95
Sokal (Sokal')		19, 44, 184, 186

Sokolniki		167
Sokołowski, Jan	Polish resistance fighter	281
Sołotwino (Solotvyno)		25
Sopuch, Stanisław (1869–1941)	Jesuit priest	55
Sosnkowski, Kazimierz (1885–1969)	Polish general and minister for military affairs	191
St. Petersburg, Petrograd, Leningrad		29–31, 39, 41, 54, 339
Stachowicz, Bronisława	Teacher for Polish Military Training for Women	261
Stahl, Leonard (1866–1929)	Vice-mayor of L'viv	28, 57, 150, 170
Stalin, Iosif V. (1879–1953)	Soviet dictator and general secretary of the Communist Party of the Soviet Union	263, 265, 170, 275, 280, 329, 331, 341–43
Stalingrad		308, 311
Stanislau (Stanisławów, Stanyslaviv)		24, 43, 65, 67, 178, 182–83, 209–10
Starzyński, Stanisław (1853–1935)	Rector of L'viv University	33
Stepaniv, Olena (1892–1963)	Ukrainian author and political activist	341
Stesłowicz, Władysław (1867–1940)	Polish politician, government commissioner of L'viv in 1918/19	83, 149–50, 162
Stets'ko, Jaroslav (1912–1986)	Member of the OUN(b)	290, 297–98
Stots'kyj, Jaroslav	Historian	271
Stryj		43, 61
Sudetenland		245
Suzdal'		51
Szeptycki, Stanisław Graf (1867–1950)	Polish general, brother of Archbishop Andrij Sheptyts'kyj	88
Tannenberg		55
Tarnavs'kyj, Ostap (1917–1992)	Ukrainian literary critic and author	
Tarnopol (Ternopil, Ternopil')		28, 42, 171, 182, 188, 192, 209–10, 334
Tarnów		25, 57, 73
Teodorowicz, Józef (1864–1938)	Armenian Catholic archbishop of L'viv	31, 65, 68

Index ♦ 443

Terovskij, A.	Russian critic of Russian occupation policy in Galicia	62
Teschen (Cieszyn)		187, 245
Thullie, Maksymilian (1853–1939)	Rector of L'viv Polytechnical University and politician	162
Tilles, Samuel (1862–1937)	Chairman of the Jewish Religious Community in Cracow	74
Tłuste		25
Tokarzewski-Karaszewicz, Michał (1893–1964)	Polish general	281
Tomaszów		79
Tsehel's'kyj, Longin (1865–1950)	Ukrainian national democratic politician	79, 94, 150
Tukhachevskij, Michail N. (1893–1937)	Soviet general	188, 193
Twardowski, Bolesław (1864–1944)	Roman Catholic archbishop of L'viv	321
Twardowski, Kazimierz (1866–1938)	Philosopher and rector of L'viv University	77
Ukraïnka, Lesja (Larysa Petrivna Kosach-Kvitka, 1871–1913)	Ukrainian poet	269
Vasyl'ko, Mykola Ritter (1868–1924)	Ukrainian estate owner and member of the Austrian parliament (Reichsrat)	85, 88, 176
Vergun, Dmitrij N. (1871–1951)	Russian journalist	30
Vienna, Wien		4–6, 9–10, 18–19, 21–23, 64, 70–71, 78–80, 92, 96, 100–02, 109, 140, 143, 172, 215, 217, 230
Vil'de, Iryna (1907–1982)	Ukrainian author	341–42
Vilnius (Wilna)		82, 187
Vitovs'kyj, Dmytro (1877–1919)	Commander-in-chief of the Ukrainian Galician Army in November 1918	110
Vityk, Semen (1876–1937)	Ukrainian social democrat	78, 140, 142, 183
Vlasov, Andrej (1901–1946)	Soviet general, taken prisoner-of-war by the German Wehrmacht, since Autumn 1944 commander of the anti-Soviet Russian Liberation Army	310

Volhynia		48, 88, 175, 179, 209, 215–16, 271, 273, 312, 314–15, 319, 322
Voznjak, Mychajlo (1881–1954)	Ukrainian literary scholar	269, 341
Vynnychenko, Volodymyr (1880–1951)	Head of the government of the Ukrainian People's Republic	178
Wächter, Otto (1901–1949)	SS-Brigadeführer, governor of District Galicia (Distrikt Galizien of the Generalgouvernement), 1942–1944	301, 310, 323–24
Warsaw		2, 4, 17, 32–33, 57, 81–82, 86, 88, 138, 142, 153, 164–65, 172, 181, 184, 187, 193, 213, 218, 236, 247, 281, 317, 319
Wasilewska, Wanda (1905–1964)	Polish author	279–81
Wasser, Ozyasz (Ozjasz)	Acting chairman of the Jewish Religious Community in L'viv	78, 81, 169
Wehrhahn, Torsten	Historian	3
Weiss, Aharon	Historian	308
Weliczker-Wells, Leon (1925–2009)	Inhabitant of L'viv and Holocaust survivor	273, 276, 316

Weryński, Jan	Vice-mayor of L'viv	264
Wilhelm von Habsburg (Vasyl' Vyshyvanyj) (1895–1948)	Archduke and commander of the Ukrainian Sich riflemen	110, 146, 179
Winniki (Vynnyky)		76
Witos, Wincenty (1874–1945)	Polish politician, chairman of the Polish People's Party and minister-president of Poland	143, 216
Witz-Margulies, Bronsisława	Student of L'viv University	244
Zadwórze		193
Zajączkowski, Bolesław (1891–1920)	Commander of a Polish volunteer battalion in the war against Soviet Russia	193
Zatons'kyj, Volodymyr (1888–1938)	Soviet Ukrainian politician	188
Zawiłło, Władysław	Polish railroad worker	261
Zbaraż		220
Żegota-Januszaitis, Marian (1889–1973)	Polish general	281
Zellermayer, Karol (?–1938)	Student of L'viv University	245
Zhdanov, Andrej (1896–1948)	Soviet politician	339
Złoczów (Zolochiv)		64, 182
Żółkiew (Zhovkva)		64, 73, 94, 313
Zorn, Mechl	Inhabitant of L'viv	159–60
Żydaczów (Zhydachiv)		72

www.ingramcontent.com/pod-product-compliance
Lightning Source LLC
Chambersburg PA
CBHW071434300426
44114CB00013B/1425